The **Rough Guide** to

Languedoc and Roussillon

written and researched by

Brian Catlos

ROUGH
GUIDES

www.roughguides.com

Contents

**The Land of the
Cathars** colour section
following p.112

Food and wine
colour section
following p.208

◄◄ *Gardian* and his horse, Petite Camargue ◄ Carcassonne

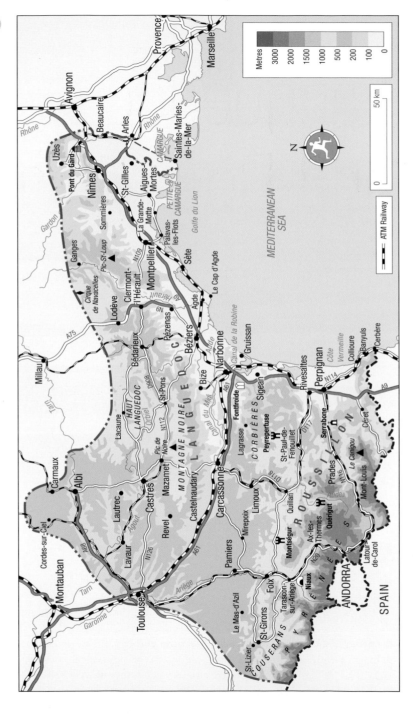

Introduction to

Languedoc and Roussillon

The Languedoc and Roussillon region is one of France's best-kept secrets. While Provence and the Côte d'Azur just across the Rhône have been living it up, attracting movie stars and the masses, its less pretentious neighbour has remained in comfortable obscurity. And so much the better for those in the know. Dramatically varied landscapes, two distinct, proud cultures (Occitan and Catalan), a tradition of heresy and steadfast rebellion and age-old customs all combine to make this a great region unmatched in its romantic associations, at once epitomizing and defying everything that is France. Now shaking off centuries of sleepy neglect, Languedoc and Roussillon are emerging as one of the most enticing parts of the country, with remote villages and little-travelled byways affording a window onto a vanishing European rural culture, as well as beaches and cities offering a thrilling diversity of activity.

The boundaries of **Languedoc** have never been easy to fix. In its broadest – and original – sense, Languedoc includes the lands where the Occitan language (the *langue d'Oc*) was spoken in the Middle Ages, an area stretching along the north towards Savoy, through the Massif Central and west along the Atlantic coast, taking in even Bordeaux. Nowadays, for administrative purposes, it has been lumped in together with its neighbour as the modern *région* of Languedoc-Roussillon, and trimmed down to the strip of coast running from Montpellier west to the border of Spain, including the inland region jutting north of Nîmes. But this

Fact file

- The area covered by this guide includes most of the modern *région* of Languedoc-Roussillon and some of the most populated parts of the Midi-Pyrénées. The population of this area is approximately 3,400,000, concentrated in a handful of urban centres, including Toulouse, Montpellier, Nîmes and Perpignan. Mid-sized towns include Albi, Béziers, Narbonne, Sète and Carcassonne. Away from the coast, the broad plains of the Lauragais are lightly populated, and many areas of the hilly uplands are all but deserted.

- Languedoc's terrain is highly varied. Although rocky in the shadow of the Pyrenees, the windswept coast is generally a flat and sandy expanse, punctuated by salty inlets. Scrubby *garrigues*, rocky hills, rise out of the sun-baked littoral plain, providing shelter for vineyards. Further from the sea, the highlands of Haut Languedoc and the cordillera of the Pyrenees are covered by cooler and damper forests, and mark the transition from the Mediterranean to the Atlantic climate zone. On their far side, broad expanses of grain-lands are cut across by the occasional river-valley or ridge.

- Gone are the glory days of woad and silk; today, aside from the industry of Toulouse – and on a smaller scale, that of Carcassonne, Perpignan, Sète and Montpellier – the region's economy depends for the most part on wine and, increasingly, tourism. On the coast, mollusc farming supplements the still functioning but declining fishing industry.

latter, narrow definition of Languedoc is as inappropriate as the traditional one is vague. In defining Languedoc in this guide we've avoided artificial boundaries in favour of cultural and historical cohesion and the logistics of travel, so that the region butts up to neighbouring Provence at the Rhône, and stretches west and inland to include the medieval capital of Toulouse, as well as the lands of Foix and Albi. **Roussillon**, Languedoc's accidental partner, squashed in between the eastern Pyrenees and the Corbières hills, is also characterized by a particular linguistic heritage, derived in this case from a long history as part of the Catalan confederacy centred in Barcelona. Both regimes have distinct cultures but, in addition to their border, share a common history of occupation and of resistance and eventual submission to the modern France of Paris and the North.

▼ Market, Uzès

Where to go

With the tremendous range of sights and activities on offer in Languedoc and Roussillon, where you go will be determined by your interests and inclinations. **Toulouse** is the region's largest city and its most important cultural hub. Here you'll find a thriving nightlife and a collection of world-class museums and monuments, including the Les Abattoirs contemporary art museum and the basilica of St-Sernin. North of the city, the famous vineyards of **Gaillac** stretch up towards **Albi**, home to the Toulouse-Lautrec museum and an obligatory stop for anyone interested in modern painting. Nearby, the hills and forests of the **Parc du Haut Languedoc**, once the refuge of Protestant Huguenots, are now presided over by the herds of Lacaune ewes which give Roquefort cheese its famous flavour. To the south, the Ariège river, excellent for rafting in the summer, can be followed up into the Pyrenees. Here, south of medieval **Foix**, you'll find some of Europe's oldest and most enigmatic prehistoric caves. The mountains themselves have trails and pistes which make for spectacular hiking or skiing, depending on the season.

The **Canal du Midi**, a placid tree-lined waterway and the largest UNESCO World Heritage site on earth, leads east from Toulouse towards the Mediterranean, passing beneath the walls of **Carcassonne**, the greatest of the heretic fortresses and France's most recognizable medieval monument. Southeast of here, at the upper end of the Aude valley, **Montségur** lies deep in Cathar country, its stunning array of castle ruins romantically perched on isolated cliff-tops.

Nothing could contrast with this more than the **Petite Camargue**, the swampy delta of the Rhône, which forms Languedoc's northern frontier – home to the bull ranches which fuel the region's passion for the *corrida* (bullfights). The beauty of the sun-baked *garrigues* just inland was well known to the Romans, whose monuments in and around **Nîmes**, including the famous **Pont du Gard** aqueduct, bear witness to the area's ancient glory. From here, you can either follow the path of the Roman super-highway, the **Via Domitia**, or the medieval Santiago de Compostela pilgrim route past a series of atmospheric fortress-towns, such as **Aigues-Mortes** and **Sommières**, or you can dip down to the coast, a long swathe of sandy beach broken only by the salty inlets that are home to shellfish and windsurfers. Just south, **Montpellier** is a thriving multicultural city, close to the sea and with a lively street-life sustained by the student population of its famous university, which has been turning out graduates for eight hundred years. From here, the Hérault valley provides access to a rocky hinterland where you can visit the ancient monastery of **St-Guilhem-le-Désert** or hike through the spectacular **Cirque de Navacelles**.

At **Pézenas**, a town whose cobbled streets are girded by seventeenth-century palaces, the Languedocian plain opens out. Medieval **Béziers** and Roman **Narbonne** preside over an expanse of archetypal Midi landscape. Blue skies are set off against the red soil and the iridescent green of seemingly endless vineyards. Only the ports, **Agde** and **Sète**, justly famed for their seafood and maritime traditions, manage to shake off the pleasant torpor of the plains.

Further south, Roussillon (French Catalonia), snuggles in the foothills of the Pyrenees, a region whose vivid contrasts have inspired artists including the Fauvists and Picasso. The capital, **Perpignan**, makes an ideal jumping-off point for visiting the rocky coves of the Côte Vermeille, or ascending the river valleys into the heart of the *département*. On the coast, **Collioure** and **Banyuls** are beautifully set beach towns, immune from the crass commercialism which characterizes the worst of the coastal resorts. Inland, the narrow-gauge **Train Jaune** winds upwards past **Le Canigou**, the mountain-symbol of the Catalan people, and the evocative old garrison towns of **Villefranche** and **Mont-Louis**, while the festivals at **Prades** and **Céret** make a great introduction to the lively Catalan folk traditions.

When to go

Whenever you visit, Languedoc and Roussillon offer a rich range of sights and activities to enjoy. The **summer season**, the time when most people come, has many advantages but also some short-comings. In July and August you can count on long **museum and monument hours**, as well as the widest selection of hotels and restaurants, many of which

▲ Street party, Sète

Cathars

It's hard to imagine a more romantic episode of the Middle Ages. A peaceful people, living in a land of troubadours and poets, following the religion of their choosing, are declared **heretics** by a grasping and imperious papacy. This unleashes a series of brutal and drawn-out military campaigns, sanctified as **Crusades**, but in fact wars of aggressive colonialism waged by northern French nobles and churchmen on the unsuspecting locals. It's a story of knights and lords, martyrdoms, **Inquisition**, lost treasures, a proud but beleaguered nation and **castles** perched on rocky spurs, ending in the destruction of the **Cathar** faith, the suppression of Occitan culture and the subjugation of the people of Languedoc. The truth was far more complex than this popular and exaggerated Sir Walter Scott-ish version of events, but the story of the Cathars is a fascinating and exciting introduction to the region's history, long buried by the modern French state. For the full story, see *The Land of the Cathars* colour section and Contexts, p.332.

are seasonal. The weather is generally **warm** and **sunny** enough that you can swim throughout the region, be it in the Mediterranean or in the nearest lake or river. Many of the region's village **festivals** take place in the summer, along with an array of special concert series. On the other hand, queues lengthen along with the opening hours. In the summer months competition for accommodation is often fierce; you'll be forced to book ahead for hotels, particularly on the coast, and this can detract from the spontaneous aspect of your travels. Traffic is also increasingly problematic in summer; the coastal highways and byways are chock-a-block with frenzied drivers rushing to get either to the beach or back home. If you're thinking of a cycling holiday, you'll probably want to confine yourself to the quieter (and hillier) upland roads.

On the other hand, the long **off-season**, from November through to Easter, sees many services shut down and museum and monument hours reduced. Many of the villages, along with a lot of hotels and restaurants, all but shut down, with the exception of the Pyrenean **ski resorts** which, of course, are at their busiest. The weather is unreliable; it is frequently cold and grey, and a light layer of snow makes the Cathar ruins more **romantic** but less comfortable to explore. This is, however, arguably the best time to visit urban centres like Toulouse and Montpellier; with their student populations in residence, these cities spring to life. Not only do theatre and opera seasons get under way, but the **bars** and **clubs** pack out with throngs of young folk. Christmas and Lent breathe additional life into the countryside with an array of colourful and unique festivities.

Canal du Midi

In the 1660s a local tax-collector, **Paul Riquet**, dreamed of bringing prosperity back to Languedoc by building a **canal** to link it to the Mediterranean and the Atlantic. This mammoth undertaking was the most ambitious and complex civic engineering project since the time of the Romans. Although it bankrupted the visionary Riquet, who did not live to see its inauguration, by 1856 the canal was carrying one million passengers and more than 100,000 tonnes of freight per year. Struck down into sudden obsolescence by the invention of the steam engine, the canal system languished in over a century of disrepair, before being resurrected in the last few decades as a tourist attraction. The quintessential Languedoc experience is to **boat**, **walk** or **cycle** along Riquet's canal, travelling at an easy pace, the tree-lined hedges providing shelter from the same sun which coaxes up the region's famous grapes.

The best time to go is probably during the **shoulder seasons**, May and June, and in September, which offer a good balance between tranquillity and action. In early June you can visit a town like Cordes and find it quiet and not yet overrun. The cities will be winding down their university seasons and the cultural programmes are preparing their finales. With a bit of luck, you'll get good weather, although you may find swimming only suits the brave. The **grape harvest** and **bull-fighting** festivals are in full swing, and you'll avoid the worst of the high-season traffic. You'll also more or less have your pick of the hotels and restaurants and will generally still be charged low-season prices.

Average temperatures and rainfall

	Jan	Apr	Jul	Oct
Toulouse				
rainfall mm/in	50/2	60/2.4	38/1.5	58/2.3
average high temp °C/F	7/45	17/63	27/81	17/63
average low temp °C/F	3/38	6/43	15/59	9/48
Montpellier				
rainfall mm/in	50/2	60/2.4	38/1.5	58/2.3
average high temp °C/F	10/50	17/63	28/82	19/66
average low temp °C/F	2/36	6/43	16/60	9/48
Foix				
rainfall mm/in	68/2.7	54/2.1	22/0.9	61/2.4
average high temp °C/F	10/50	17/63	27/81	19/66
average low temp °C/F	2/36	9/48	17/63	10/50
Perpignan				
rainfall mm/in	50/2	56/2.2	18/0.7	89/3.6
average high temp °C/F	12/54	17/63	28/82	20/68
average low temp °C/F	4/40	9/48	19/66	12/54

15

things not to miss

It's not possible to see everything that Languedoc and Roussillon have to offer in one trip – and we don't suggest you try. What follows, in no particular order, is a selective and subjective taste of the region's highlights: outstanding natural features, spectacular cities, history, culture and beautiful architecture. They're arranged in five colour-coded categories to help you find the very best things to see, do and experience. All entries have a page reference to take you straight into the Guide, where you can find out more.

01 **Cordes-sur-Ciel** Page **150** • Cruise the boutiques or enjoy the evocative atmosphere in this hill-top Cathar town.

02 Collioure Page **320** • Roussillon at its most Catalan: a colourful, picturesque beach town presided over by a medieval castle.

03 Seafood See *Food and wine* colour **section** • Whether cultivated in the Bassin de Thau or fished from the sea, the area's seafood is a must.

04 Swimming at the Pont du Gard Page **196** • Take a dip under the lofty arches of this extraordinary Roman aqueduct.

05 Toulouse-Lautrec Page **144** • This Languedoc native revolutionized nineteenth-century art; enjoy the largest collection of his work and visit his childhood estate.

06 **Train Jaune** Page **307** • Twisting up into the high valleys of the Pyrenees, this revived narrow-gauge line is a thrilling excursion in itself and perfect for hikers.

07 **Le Canigou** Page **304** • Bonfires and a torch-lit pilgrimage illuminate Catalonia's sacred mountain in mid-summer.

08 **Tauromachie** Page **209** • Get swept up in the excitement and drama of the "art of the bull".

09 **Water-jousting** Page **233** • Originating centuries ago in Sète, this sport is now a passionate fixture of Languedoc traditional culture.

10 **Montségur** Page **112** • The romantic and mysterious last redoubt of the Cathars is wonderfully atmospheric.

11 **Petite Camargue** Page **205** • Admire the horsemanship of the *gardians* of Durrelll's "Little Argentina".

12 Beaches Page **210** • From naked hedonism to romantic solitude, Languedoc's Mediterranean beaches, such as Le Grau-du-Roi, offer it all.

13 La Grotte de Niaux Page **129** • The finest of the Pyrenean caves, the remote Grotte de Niaux is known for its enigmatic prehistoric paintings.

14 Transhumance Page **126** • The ancient tradition of transhumance sees thousands of sheep driven up the valleys of the Couserans – see it happen in June at Seix.

15 Carcassonne Page **96** • France's most famous and evocative medieval citadel is a must-see while in Languedoc.

Basics

Basics

Getting there

Languedoc and Roussillon's major transport hub is Toulouse, home to the region's largest international airport and served by trains from England (via Paris or Lille) and Spain.

In general, the quickest and most cost-effective way of reaching Languedoc and Roussillon **from Britain** is by air, though from the southeast of England it's worth considering the Eurostar, which links with fast and efficient TGV services south from Lille and Paris.

From North America there are direct flights from over thirty major cities to Paris, from where you can either take an internal flight or transfer to France's excellent train network. Many people heading for France **from Australia and New Zealand** travel via London, although there are scheduled flights to Paris from Sydney, Melbourne, Brisbane, Cairns, Perth and Auckland.

Airfares always depend on the **season**, with the highest being around mid-June to mid-September, when the weather is best; fares drop during the "shoulder" seasons – Easter to mid-June and mid-September through October – and you'll get the best prices during the low season, November to Easter (excluding Christmas and New Year). Note also that flying on weekends ordinarily adds to the round-trip fare; price ranges quoted below assume **midweek travel**.

Flights from the UK and Ireland

Flying is the quickest way of getting to Languedoc and Roussillon, with journey times from London to Toulouse of less than two hours. You can also get direct budget flights there from a variety of British regional airports.

Several **low-cost airlines** – Ryanair, bmibaby, Flybe and easyJet – offer scheduled flights into the region, or to hubs within easy striking distance of it. **Ryanair** flies from various airports in Ireland and Great Britain to Béziers, Carcassonne, Montpellier, Nîmes, and Perpignan, as well as nearby Biarritz, Bordeaux and Marseille. **EasyJet** flies daily to Montpellier and Toulouse, while **bmibaby** flies to Perpignan and Toulouse. Both easyJet and Ryanair also have regular services from many British regional airports to **Girona** airport in Catalonia, just 60km from the border of Roussillon. Return fares on all the budget airlines start at around £30, but generally range from £60–150 for Carcassonne, and £45–125 for other destinations.

British Airways flies twice daily from Heathrow to Toulouse (about £160 return), and Aer Lingus has flights from Dublin to Toulouse from May to October (about €160 return), but there are no direct flights to the region on Air France from either the UK or Ireland. All three airlines also have frequent daily flights from London, Dublin and many British and Irish regional airports to Paris, from where travellers can continue overland (see p.21).

Flights from the US and Canada

To get to Languedoc and Roussillon from North America, you can either fly to London

---

Travelling with pets from the UK

If you wish to take your dog (or cat) to France, the **Pet Travel Scheme (PETS)** enables you to avoid putting it in quarantine when re-entering the UK as long as certain conditions are met. Current regulations are available on the Department for Environment, Food and Rural Affairs (DEFRA) website ⓦ www.defra.gov.uk or through the PETS Helpline (☎0870/241 1710).

and hook up with a **budget airline** (see p.19), or, better, fly to Paris and continue overland, by renting a car or using France's excellent **rail** system (see p.24).

Transatlantic fares to Paris **from the US** are very reasonable, thanks to intense competition. A typical return fare for a midweek flight costs around $950 from Houston, $850 from Los Angeles and $750 from New York. **From Canada**, prices to Paris are in the region of Can$850 from Montréal and Toronto, and Can$1200 from Vancouver, but fares can almost double in high season. For contact details of airlines that fly from the US and Canada to Paris and London, see p.23.

Flights from Australia, New Zealand and South Africa

From Australia, New Zealand and South Africa, the best way to reach Languedoc and Roussillon is to fly to Paris then continue overland by train (see p.21). However, you can find a wider range of options by flying to another European capital – usually London – and picking up a budget flight there (see p.19).

Airfares **from east-coast gateways** to Paris tend not to vary in price from carrier to carrier, with regular tourist-class fares starting at around Aus$2000 in low season, or Aus$2500 in high season. **From Perth and Darwin** flights cost around Aus$100–300 less via Asia, and Aus$400 more via the US. **From New Zealand**, fares from Auckland start at around NZ$2000 in low season, up to NZ$3000 in peak season.

From South Africa, Air France flies direct from Johannesburg to Paris from around 6140ZAR return. BA, flying via London, comes in slightly more expensive, at around 10,000ZAR from Cape Town and 8600ZAR from Johannesburg. Flight times are around

---

Six steps to a better kind of travel

At Rough Guides we are passionately committed to travel. We feel strongly that only through travelling do we truly come to understand the world we live in and the people we share it with – plus tourism has brought a great deal of **benefit** to developing economies around the world over the last few decades. But the extraordinary growth in tourism has also damaged some places irreparably, and of course **climate change** is exacerbated by most forms of transport, especially flying. This means that now more than ever it's important to **travel thoughtfully** and **responsibly**, with respect for the cultures you're visiting – not only to derive the most benefit from your trip but also to preserve the best bits of the planet for everyone to enjoy. At Rough Guides we feel there are six main areas in which you can make a difference:

- Consider what you're contributing to the **local economy**, and how much the services you use do the same, whether it's through employing local workers and guides or sourcing locally grown produce and local services.
- Consider the **environment** on holiday as well as at home. Water is scarce in many developing destinations, and the biodiversity of local flora and fauna can be adversely affected by tourism. Try to patronize businesses that take account of this.
- Travel with a purpose, not just to tick off experiences. Consider **spending longer** in a place, and getting to know it and its people.
- Give thought to how often you **fly**. Try to avoid short hops by air and more harmful night flights.
- Consider **alternatives to flying**, travelling instead by bus, train, boat and even by bike or on foot where possible.
- Make your trips **"climate neutral"** via a reputable carbon offset scheme. All Rough Guide flights are offset, and every year we donate money to a variety of charities devoted to combating the effects of climate change.

ten hours from Johannesburg to Paris, and fourteen hours from Cape Town including a stopover.

Trains

The quickest way to get to Languedoc and Roussillon by train from the UK is on the **Eurostar** from London or Ashford in Kent through the Channel Tunnel to Paris or Lille and then changing onto a fast TGV train to Toulouse (9–10hr), Perpignan (9hr), Montpellier (7–8hr) or Nîmes (7hr) – note that these times are for the total journey, starting in London. The cheapest return ticket to Paris is currently £49, but Eurostar can also book the TGV leg: return fares from London to all four destinations above start at around £120, though these are non-flexible. Note that Inter-Rail passes (see below) give discounts on the Eurostar service.

Travelling by **regular train and ferry** or hovercraft via Calais, Boulogne or Dieppe, then making onward connections to Languedoc and Roussillon by train can work out slightly cheaper than using the Channel Tunnel, but it takes considerably longer, and is generally less convenient.

Rail passes

There's a huge array of **rail passes** available, which may be worth considering if you're visiting Languedoc and Roussillon as part of a longer pan-European journey. For details of local SNCF rail passes valid for journeys within France, see "Getting around", p.24.

Inter-Rail pass

Inter-Rail passes are only available to European residents, and you will be asked to provide proof of residency before being allowed to purchase one. They come in over-26 and (cheaper) under-26 versions, and cover 28 European countries (including Turkey and Morocco) grouped together in zones. The Zone E Pass includes France, Belgium, the Netherlands and Luxembourg. The passes are available for sixteen days (one zone only), 22 days, or one month and you can purchase up to three zones or a global pass covering all zones. Inter-Rail passes do not include travel between Britain and the continent, although pass holders are eligible for discounts on rail travel in Britain and Northern Ireland, including Eurostar, and cross-Channel ferries, plus discounts on other shipping services around the Mediterranean, Scandinavia and the Balearics.

Euro Domino pass

The **Euro Domino pass** is only available to European residents. Individual country passes provide unlimited travel in 28 European and North African countries. The passes are available for between three and eight days' travel within a one-month period; prices vary depending on the country, but include most high-speed train supplements. You can buy as many separate country passes as you want. There is a discounted youth price for those under 26, and a half-price child (age 4–11) fare.

Eurailpasses

The **Eurailpass**, which must be purchased before arrival in Europe (and cannot be purchased by European residents), allows unlimited free first-class train travel in France and seventeen other countries, and is available in increments of fifteen days, 21 days, one month, two months and three months. If you're under 26, you can save money with a **Eurailpass Youth**, which is valid for second-class travel or, if you're travelling with one to five other companions, a joint **Eurailpass Saver**, both of which are available in the same increments as the Eurailpass. You stand a better chance of getting your money's worth out of a **Eurailpass Flexi**, which is good for ten or fifteen days' first-class travel within a two-month period. This, too, comes in under-26/second-class (**Eurailpass Youth Flexi**) and group (**Eurailpass Saver Flexi**) versions.

In addition, a scaled-down version of the Eurailpass Flexi, the **Eurail Selectpass**, is available, which allows travel in your choice of three, four or five of the seventeen countries Eurail covers (they must be adjoining, by either rail or ship) for any five days, six days, eight days, ten days or fifteen days (five-country option only) within a two-month period. In this plan, Belgium, the Netherlands and Luxembourg are taken as one "country". Like the Eurailpass, the Selectpass is also available in first-class, second-class youth, or first-class saver options.

Details of prices for all these passes can be found on the Eurail website (Ⓦwww .eurail.com).

By car and ferry

It's a good nine hours' drive south from Calais on the north coast of France to Toulouse, but if you do want **to drive**, the quickest way across the Channel is via the Channel Tunnel (35 minutes), on **Eurotunnel**'s (Ⓦwww.eurotunnel.com) daily shuttles. Due to the frequency of the service, you don't have to buy a ticket in advance (though it is advisable in mid-summer and during other school holidays), but you must arrive at least thirty minutes before departure; the target loading time is just ten minutes.

Fares are calculated per car, regardless of the number of passengers, and rates depend on the time of year, time of day and length of stay (the cheapest ticket is for a day-trip, followed by a five-day return); it's cheaper to travel between 10pm and 6am, while the highest fares are reserved for weekend departures and returns in July and August. A two-week fixed-date return trip can cost as little as £110, even in peak

periods, but you should book far ahead to get this fare.

Alternatively, you can get to France by **ferry** from various ports along England's south coast to the north coast of France. If you're coming from the north of England or Scotland, consider an overnight ferry to Zeebrugge (Belgium), either from Hull or from Rosyth. From Ireland you can take a ferry direct from Rosslare (near Wexford) to either Cherbourg or Roscoff.

Ferry **prices** are seasonal and, for motorists, depend on the size of your vehicle. The popular Dover–Calais route costs from £120 one-way for a car and two adults. Note that return prices are substantially cheaper than one-way fares, but generally need to be booked in advance – details of routes and companies are listed below. You can either contact the companies direct to reserve space in advance – essential in peak season if you're intending to drive – or any travel agent in the UK or France will do it for you. All ferry companies also offer foot passenger fares from £20 one-way; accompanying bicycles can usually be carried free, at least in the low season, and for a charge of around £5 one-way in mid- and high seasons. The ferry companies also often offer **special deals** on

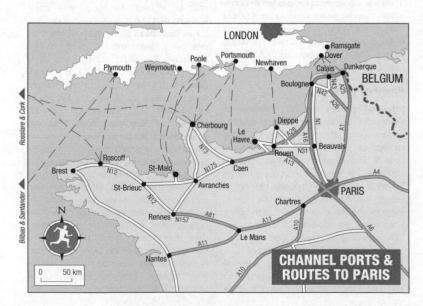

CHANNEL PORTS & ROUTES TO PARIS

three-, five- and ten-day returns, or discounts for regular users who own a property abroad, while the tour operator Eurodrive (☎020/8324 4009, 🌐www .eurodrive.co.uk) can also arrange discounts on car-ferry crossings.

The cheapest way of getting to France **from Ireland** – though far from the quickest – is by ferry from Cork or Rosslare outside Wexford to Cherbourg or Roscoff, in Brittany, and then continuing overland.

If you don't want to drive far when you've reached France, you can take advantage of SNCF's **motorail**, which you can book through Rail Europe (see below), putting your car on the train in either Calais or Paris for Narbonne or Toulouse. This is a relatively expensive option though: for four people travelling from Calais to Toulouse, for example, the regular one-way price ranges from £289, dependent on the time of year.

Buses

Eurolines run regular bus-ferry services from London Victoria to over sixty French cities. Prices are much lower than for the same journey by train, with adult return fares of around £60 to Toulouse (£35 if booked 30 days in advance); the journey time is roughly nineteen hours. Regional return fares from the rest of England and from Wales are available, as are student and youth discounts. **Tickets** can be bought directly from the company, from National Express agents and from most high-street travel agents.

Agents, airlines and specialist operators

Many airlines and discount travel websites offer you the opportunity to book your tickets **online**, cutting out the costs of agents and middlemen. Good deals can often be found through discount or auction sites, as well as through the **airlines'** own websites. There are also many tour operators offering **specialist tours** of Languedoc and Roussillon, such as walking, biking and boating.

Airlines

Aer Lingus 🌐 www.aerlingus.com.
Air France 🌐 www.airfrance.com.
bmi 🌐 www.flybmi.com.
bmibaby 🌐 www.bmibaby.com.

British Airways 🌐 www.ba.com.
easyJet 🌐 www.easyjet.com.
Flybe 🌐 www.flybe.com.
Ryanair 🌐 www.ryanair.com.

Specialist tour operators

Abercrombie & Kent 🌐 www.abercrombiekent .com. Upmarket biking and walking tours. Several trips in the region, including Canal du Midi and Camargue.
Adventure Center 🌐 www.adventurecenter.com. Hiking and "soft adventure" specialists, with a Canal du Midi trip.
Baronnie de Bourgade 🌐 www.baronnie-de -bourgade.com. This Béziers outfit offers week-long tours that combine regional highlights with wine tasting.
BKTours 🌐 www.bkwine.com. Swedish-based company which runs Languedoc wine tours around Nîmes.
Caprice Tours 🌐 www.caprice-tours.com. Cultural and linguistic tours.
Château de Quarante 🌐 chateaudequarante.com. Upmarket, gourmet living in a private castle by night, chauffeur-driven custom tours by day.
Discover France 🌐 www.discoverfrance.com. Bike and hiking tours in Languedoc.
Explore Holidays 🌐 www.exploreholidays.com.au. Accommodation, boat rental and package tours.
French Cycling Holidays 🌐 www.frenchcycling holidays.com. Cycling specialists who run both leisure and sport cycling tours in Languedoc and Roussillon.
French Travel Connection 🌐 www.frenchtravel .com.au. Everything to do with travel to and around France.
Languedoc Nature 🌐 www.languedoc-nature .com. Organizes a range of tours based on outdoor activities, history and gastronomy.
Passport Travel 🌐 www.travelcentre.com.au. Small-group walking and cycling holidays.
Tastes of Languedoc 🌐 www.tastesoflanguedoc .com. Organizes custom wine tours in Languedoc and Roussillon.

Rail contacts

European Rail UK ☎ 020/7619 1083, 🌐 www .europeanrail.com.
Europrail International Canada ☎ 1-888/667- 9734, 🌐 www.europrail.net.
Eurostar UK ☎ 0870/518 6186, 🌐 www.eurostar .com.
Rail Europe US ☎ 1-888/382-7245, Canada ☎ 1-800/361-7245, UK ☎ 0844/848 4064, Australia ☎ 03/9642 8644, South Africa ☎ 11/628 2319, 🌐 www.raileurope.com. This is the SNCF's overseas agent; you can contact them for enquiries or bookings.

Bus contacts

Busabout UK ☎ 020/7950 1661, ⓦ www
.busabout.com.
Eurolines UK ☎ 0870/5 808080, Republic of
Ireland ☎ 01/836 6111; ⓦ www.nationalexpress
.com/eurolines.

Ferry contacts

Brittany Ferries UK ☎ 0871/244 0744, ⓦ www
.brittanyferries.co.uk. Poole to Cherbourg; Portsmouth
to Caen, Cherbourg and St-Malo; Plymouth to Roscoff
and Santander; Cork to Roscoff (March–Oct only).
Condor Ferries UK ☎ 0870/243 5140, ⓦ www
.condorferries.co.uk. Portsmouth to Cherbourg
(May–Sept); Poole to St-Malo (May–Sept); and
Weymouth to St-Malo via the Channel Islands.
Irish Ferries Republic of Ireland ☎ 0818/300 400,
UK ☎ 0870/517 1717, ⓦ www.irishferries.com.
Rosslare to Cherbourg and Roscoff (March–Sept).

Norfolkline UK ☎ 0844/847 5042, ⓦ www
.norfolkline.com. Dover to Dunkerque.
P&O Ferries UK ☎ 0871/664 5645, ⓦ www
.poferries.com. Dover to Calais; Portsmouth to Bilbao;
and Hull to Zeebrugge.
Sea France UK ☎ 0871/222 2500, ⓦ www
.seafrance.com. Dover to Calais.
SpeedFerries UK ☎ 0870/220 0570, ⓦ www
.speedferries.com. Dover to Boulogne.
Superfast Ferries UK ☎ 0844/576 5503, ⓦ www
.superfast.com. Rosyth near Edinburgh to Zeebrugge
(Belgium).
Transmanche Ferries UK ☎ 0800/917 1201,
ⓦ www.transmancheferries.com. Newhaven to
Dieppe.

Channel Tunnel

Eurotunnel UK ☎ 0870/535 3535, ⓦ www
.eurotunnel.com.

Getting around

France has the most extensive train network in western Europe, and rail is the
best way of travelling between almost all the major towns within Languedoc and
Roussillon. The nationally owned French train company, the SNCF (Société
Nationale des Chemins de Fer), runs fast, modern trains. In rural areas where
branch lines have been closed, routes (such as Castres–Montpellier) are covered
by buses operated solely by SNCF or in partnership with independent companies.
It's an integrated service, with buses timetabled to meet trains and the same
ticket covering both.

The private **bus** services that supplement
the SNCF services are confusing and
uncoordinated. Some areas, such as the
coast or around larger centres like Toulouse,
Albi and Castres, are quite well served, while
the service in less populated regions, like the
Corbières and parts of the Pyrenees and
Haut Languedoc, is barely existent – often
designed to carry the inhabitants of hamlets
to and from weekly markets, and thus not
very useful for tourists. Weekends and
holidays frequently have no service.

The SNCF has pioneered one of the most
efficient, comfortable and user-friendly

railway systems in the world. Its staff are,
with few exceptions, courteous and helpful,
and its trains – for the most part, fast, clean
and frequent – continue, in spite of the
closure of some rural lines, to cover much of
Languedoc and Roussillon; a main rail
corridor runs from Toulouse to Narbonne,
where it joins the coastal line, linking Cerbère
on the Spanish border and Beaucaire
(Tarascon) at the Rhône, while spur lines run
up major river valleys – including the Tarn,
Ariège and Conflent. For **national train
information**, phone ☎ 08.36.35.35.35 from
within France (€0.34 per minute) or check

@ www.voyages-sncf.com. Alternatively, for advance information before you travel to France, contact Rail Europe (see p.23), the SNCF's overseas arm.

Pride and joy of the system are the high-speed **TGVs** (*trains à grande vitesse*), capable of 300kmph, and their offspring Eurostar. There are several stations connected to the TGV in Languedoc and Roussillon, among them Nîmes (journey time from Paris 4hr), Montpellier (4hr 30min), Narbonne (5hr), Béziers (4hr 45min), Perpignan (6hr) and Toulouse (4hr 30min). The only difference between TGV and other train fares is that you pay a compulsory reservation charge (from €3), plus a supplement on certain peak-hour trains. Check the SNCF **website**, however, for a whole range of last-minute **special deals** and **upgrades**.

In person, it is easiest to use the counter service for **buying tickets**, though the touch-screen computerized system available in most stations can be read in English and is a good way to check fares and times – if need be, you can always press the red *annuler* button to cancel the transaction before committing yourself. All tickets – but not passes (see below) – must be **validated** in the orange machines at station platform entrances, and it is an offence not to follow the instruction *Compostez votre billet* ("Validate your ticket"). Train journeys may be broken any time, anywhere, for as long as the ticket is valid (usually two months), but after a break of 24 hours you must validate your ticket again when you resume your journey.

After a spate of terrorist bombings in the late 1990s, most train stations closed their **luggage lockers** (*consignes automatiques*); these days a few have reopened, and larger stations have a staffed luggage check-in, usually with limited hours (*consignes* are noted in the Guide).

Regional rail **maps** and complete **timeta-bles** are sold in tobacconist shops (*tabacs*). Leaflet timetables for particular lines are available free at stations. *Autocar* or a bullet symbol at the top of a column means it's an SNCF bus service, on which rail tickets and passes are valid.

Aside from the regular lines there are a number of tourist-oriented railways, including the spectacular **Train Jaune** (see p.307) which winds its way up through the Pyrenees, and the *Train du Pays Cathare et du Fenouillèdes* which runs up into the Cathar heartland (see p.300).

French rail discounts and passes

SNCF offers a whole range of **discounted fares** within France on standard rail prices on *période bleue* (blue period) and *période blanche* (white period) days. A leaflet showing the blue, white (smaller discount) and red (peak) periods is given out at stations. In addition, any two people travelling together (*à deux*), or a small group of up to five people, are entitled to a 25 percent discount on return tickets on TGVs, subject to availability, or on other trains if they start their journey on a blue period day; the same reduction applies to a group of up to four people travelling with a child under 12, to under-26-year-olds, over-60s, and for anyone who books a return journey of at least 200km in distance, including a Saturday night away (this latter is called the *séjour*).

Finally, a range of train passes that give discounts (valid for a year) can be purchased from main stations and most travel agents in France. Over-60s can buy the **Carte Senior** for €56, which offers up to fifty percent off tickets on TGVs, or other journeys starting in blue periods, a 25 percent reduction on white period journeys, as well as a thirty percent reduction on international journeys involving most countries in western and central Europe. The same reductions are available for under-26s with a **Carte 12–25** pass, which costs €49. Under-12s can obtain the same advantages for themselves and up to four travelling companions of any age by purchasing the **Enfant+ Carte** (€70). Those aged between 26 and 59 years can purchase a **Carte Escapades** (€85), but this only entitles the holder to a 40 percent reduction on normal, white-period fares. For details of pan-European rail passes, see "Getting there", p.21.

By bus

The most convenient **bus services** are those run as extensions of rail links by SNCF, which always run to and from the SNCF station and access areas formerly served by rail. In addition to SNCF buses, private, municipal and *départemental* buses can be useful for mid- to long-distance journeys. The most frustrating thing about them is the multiplicity of services and the difficulty in obtaining departure information other than at bus stops and stations. In Toulouse, city buses can be used to access outlying villages, and in Montpellier the network goes as far out as the coast. Some *départements*, like the Hérault and the Tarn, have rural bus networks; their roadside stops usually have a copy of the schedule attached to the sign or shelter. Private operators cover much of rural Languedoc and Roussillon too – unfortunately, their routes miss some of the more interesting and less-inhabited areas, and the **timetable** is constructed to suit working, market and school hours – all often dauntingly early. All buses are, generally speaking, cheaper and slower than trains.

Larger towns usually have a **gare routière** (bus station), often next to the gare SNCF. However, the private bus companies don't always work together and you'll frequently find them leaving from an array of different points (the local tourist office will usually help locate them).

By car

Driving in Languedoc and Roussillon can be a real pleasure, and gives you the freedom to explore parts of the region that would otherwise remain inaccessible, in particular the sparsely populated upland of Haut Languedoc, the Hérault and the Pyrenees. **Autoroutes** in the region run through the same corridors as the main rail lines, connecting Toulouse and Narbonne, and from here, running north and south along the Mediterranean coast. If you are in a hurry, it is well worth paying the toll (see below) for their use, as the free national routes, which also follow this corridor, tend to be heavily travelled by both local drivers and long-distance truckers. By *autoroute*, in good traffic conditions, you can reach Nîmes from Toulouse in two to three hours. Away from the main arteries, the older main roads or *routes nationales* (marked N9 or RN230, for example, on signs and maps) are generally

uncongested and, passing through the centres of the towns along the way, make for a more scenic, if slower, drive than the *autoroutes*. Smaller **routes** *départementales* (marked D) should not be shunned. Although they are occasionally in relatively poor condition, you can often travel for kilometres across country, seeing few other cars, on broad and well-maintained roads.

The most challenging part of driving in Languedoc and Roussillon is likely to be entering large cities for the first time: as a general rule of thumb you can usually reach the centre by following signs for the tourist office. That said, **parking** is likely to be problematic, so you may instead want to follow signs for the gare SNCF, which will have some pay parking and most likely be within walking distance of the centre. Most cities also have sufficient underground parking **garages** (typical clearance 1.70–2m), where you may pay up to €30 overnight. Outside of the city cores, street parking is usually free, although it may mean spending a considerable time hunting around. Many hotels have garages for which they typically charge €5 and up per night.

Of course, there are times when it is wiser not to drive: **congestion** is a major problem on the *Autoroute Méditerranéenne* in summer, particularly on the first and last few days of July and August, and the same goes for roads of all categories along the coast on summer weekends, when the going is frustratingly slow. The high cost of **petrol** (*essence*) can also be a discouraging factor: prices at the time of writing were around €1.25 a litre for four-star unleaded (*super sans plomb*) and around €1.12 a litre for diesel (*gasoil*). There are 3.8 litres to the US gallon. The cheapest petrol or diesel fuel can usually be found at out-of-town superstores or *hypermarchés*, though note that many of these are automated and do not recognize most non-French credit cards.

In addition, you have to pay a **toll** (*péage*) on most *autoroutes*. Rates vary, but to give you an idea, travelling only by motorway the 1039km from Calais to Montpellier would cost you around €59.60 for a car without trailer, plus €62.34 in fuel (based on a mid-sized car), and take approximately ten hours. All the major car manufacturers have **garages** and

service stations in Languedoc and Roussillon, which can help if you run into mechanical difficulties. You can find them in the Yellow Pages (Ⓦwww.pagesjaunes.fr) under *"Garages d'automobiles"*. For break-downs, look under *"Dépannages"*. If you have an accident or break-in, you should report it to the local police (and keep a copy) in order to make an insurance claim. Many car insurance policies cover your car in Europe, but you're advised to take out extra cover for motor assistance in case your car breaks down, costing around £50 for seven days. Check with your local automobile association before leaving home.

Traffic information and route planning

For up-to-the-minute **traffic information** regarding traffic jams and road works on *autoroutes* throughout France, ring Ⓣ08.92.68.10.77 (€0.34/min; French only) or consult the bilingual website Ⓦwww.autoroutes.fr. Traffic information for other roads can be obtained from the *Bison Futé* recorded information service (Ⓣ08.26.02.20.22; €0.15/min; French only) or its website Ⓦwww.bison-fute.equipement.gouv.fr.

For **route planning**, Ⓦwww.viamichelin.com can provide you with point-to-point driving directions for itineraries throughout France.

Rules of the road

British, Irish, Australian, Canadian, New Zealand and US **driving licences** are valid in France, though an International Driver's Licence makes life easier if you get a police officer unwilling to peruse a document in English. If the vehicle is rented, its registration document (*carte grise*) and the insurance papers must be carried. GB stickers must, by law, be displayed, and a Green Card proving your liability insurance coverage, though not a legal requirement, might save some hassle. If your car is right-hand drive, you must have your headlight dip adjusted to the right before you go – it's a legal requirement – and as a courtesy change or paint them to yellow or stick on black glare deflectors. Remember also that you have to be 18 years of age to drive in France, regardless of whether you hold a licence in your own country.

The law of *priorité à droite* – **giving way** to traffic coming from your right, even when it is coming from a minor road – is being phased out as it is a major cause of accidents. It still applies in built-up areas, so you have to be vigilant in towns, keeping a lookout for signs along the roadside with the yellow diamond on a white background that gives you right of way – until you see the same sign with an oblique black slash, which indicates vehicles emerging from the right have right of way. At roundabouts the *priorité à droite* law no longer applies. *Stop* signs mean stop completely; *Cédez le passage* means "Give way". Other signs warning of potential dangers are *déviation* (diversion), *gravillons* (loose chippings), *nids de poules* (potholes) and *chaussée déformée* (uneven surface).

Speed limits in France are: 130kmph (80mph) on *autoroutes*; 110kph (68mph) on dual carriageways; 90kmph (56mph) on other roads; and 50kmph (31mph) in towns. The town limit is constant, but in wet weather, and for drivers with less than two years' experi-ence, the three road limits are 110kmph (68mph), 100kmph (62mph) and 80kmph (50mph) respectively. The standard **fine** for exceeding the speed limit by 20kmph (12mph), for example, is €90; above 40kmph (25mph) you will not only be fined but will also have to go to court. The legal blood **alcohol limit** while driving is 0.05 percent alcohol (lower than in the UK and North America), and random breath tests are common: if you are caught over the limit, your driving privi-leges may be immediately suspended.

Car rental

Car rental in France costs upwards of €275 a week (from around €70 a day), but can be cheaper if arranged before you leave home. You'll find the big firms – Hertz, Avis, Europcar and Budget – at airports and in most big cities, with addresses detailed throughout the Guide. Rental from airports normally includes a surcharge. Local firms can be cheaper but you need to check the small print and be sure of where the car can be returned to. It's normal to pay an indemnity of €150–300 against any damage to the car – they will take your credit card number rather than cash. You should return the car with a full tank of fuel. The cost of car rental includes the basic legally necessary car insurance.

North Americans and Australians in particular should be forewarned that it is very difficult to arrange the hire of a car with **automatic** transmission; if you can't drive a manual you should try to book an automatic well in advance, possibly before you leave home, and be prepared to pay a much higher price for it.

Most rental companies will only deal with people over 25 unless an extra insurance premium, typically around €20–25 per day, is paid (but you still must be over 21 and have driven for at least one year). OTU Voyage (℡01.55.82.32.32, ⓦwww.otu.fr), the student travel agency, can arrange car rental for young drivers.

Car rental agencies

Avis ⓦwww.avis.com.
Budget ⓦwww.budget.com.
Europcar ⓦwww.europcar.com.
Europe by Car ⓦwww.europebycar.com.
Hertz ⓦwww.hertz.com.
Holiday Autos ⓦwww.holidayautos.co.uk.
National ⓦwww.nationalcar.com.
SIXT ⓦwww.sixt.com.
Thrifty ⓦwww.thrifty.com.

Moped and motorbike rental

Mopeds and scooters are relatively easy to find; outside the mountainous areas everyone from young kids to grandmas seems to ride them, and although they're not built for any kind of long-distance travel, they're ideal for shooting around town and nearby. Places that rent out bicycles will often also rent out mopeds; you can expect to pay €40 a day for a 50cc Suzuki. No licence is needed for 50cc and under bikes, but for anything larger you'll need a valid **motorbike** licence. Rental prices are around €55 a day for a 125cc motorbike; also expect to leave a hefty deposit by cash or credit card – €1000 is not unusual – which you may lose in the event of damage or theft. Crash helmets are now compulsory on all mopeds and motorbikes.

Hitching

If you're intent on **hitching**, you'll have to rely almost exclusively on car drivers, as lorries very rarely give lifts. Even so, it won't be easy. Looking as clean and respectable as possible makes a big difference, and hitching the less frequented D roads is much quicker. In mountain areas a rucksack and hiking gear will help procure a lift from fellow hikers.

Autoroutes are a special case. Hitching on the *autoroute* itself is strictly illegal, but you can make excellent time going from one service station to another and, if you get stuck, at least there's food, drink, shelter and washing facilities at most service stations. It helps to have the *Guide des Autoroutes*, published by Michelin, which shows all the rest stops, service stations, tollbooths (*péages*), exits and so on. Remember to get out at the service station before your driver leaves the *autoroute*. The tollbooths are a second best (and legal) option; ordinary approach roads tend to be difficult and can easily lead to a fine.

For long-distance rides, or for greater security, you might consider using the national **hitching organization**, Allostop (℡01.53.20.42.42, ⓦwww.allostop.net); reservations are normally made through the Paris number, but there is also a local branch in Montpellier. Similar net-based services include Covoiture (ⓦwww.covoiturage.com) and Gnafou (ⓦwww.gnafou.net). Generally the cost of using these services amounts to 20–40 percent of the price of normal public transport.

Taxis

Unlike in much of the world, taxis are not generally hailed on the street but rather at established taxi stands or booked by phone. If your French is not strong, your hotel or restaurant staff should assist if you need to call one.

All taxis are metered and function on the basis of mileage/time elapsed and time of day. Prices vary by *département*. In Languedoc-Roussillon the meter should start at between €1.80 and 2.50, while the distance charge varies from €0.72 to 2.80 per km and the hourly rate €17–21 per hour. There may be extra charges for luggage, airport service, waiting time and so on. For precise tariffs by region, see ⓦwww.taxis-de-france.com /professionnel/tarifstaxis.htm.

Cycling

Bicycles (*vélos*) have high status in France, and the French respect cyclists – both as traffic and, when you stop off at a restaurant or hotel, as customers. In addition, municipalities like Toulouse and Montpellier, and their respective *départements* – Haute Garonne and Hérault – are actively promoting cycling, not only with city paths, but with comprehensive networks linking rural areas (frequently utilizing disused roadways and rail rights of way). These days more and more cyclists are using **mountain bikes**, which the French call VTTs (*vélos tout terrain*), even for touring holidays, although it's much less effort, and much quicker, to cycle long distances and carry luggage on a traditionally styled touring or racing bike. Your primary concern using bicycle transport in this region will likely be the **traffic**, which on the narrow two-lane *routes nationales* is frequently heavy and extremely fast.

Dedicated and experienced cyclists may want to tackle all or part of the ten-day *Raid Pyrénéen*, a mountainous 879km route from Cerbère on the Med to Hendaye on the Atlantic. For more information or to get official recognition for having completed the *Raid*, contact Cyclo Club Béarnais (59 av L-Sallenave, 64000 Pau; ☎05.59.84.32.64 Fri only 6–7.30pm). The Fédération Française de Cyclotourisme (⊛www.ffct.org) is a further useful source of **information** on all things to do with cycling in France.

Most large towns have well-stocked retail and **repair shops**, where parts are normally cheaper than in Britain or the US. However, if you're using a foreign-made bike which doesn't have standard metric wheels, it's a good idea to carry spare tyres. Inner tubes are not a problem, as they adapt to either size, though make sure you get the right valves.

The **train** network runs various schemes for cyclists, all of them covered by the free leaflet *Guide du Train et du Vélo*, available from most stations. Trains marked with a bicycle in the timetable allow you to take a bike as free accompanied luggage. Otherwise, you have to send your bike parcelled up as registered luggage for a fee of €25. Although it may well arrive in less time, the SNCF won't guarantee delivery in under five days, and you do hear stories of bicycles disappearing altogether.

Ferries either take bikes for free or charge a maximum of £5 one-way. British Airways and Air France both take bikes free of charge – you may have to box them though, and you should contact the airlines first. **Eurostar** allows you to take your bicycle as part of your baggage allowance provided it is dismantled and stored in a special bike bag, and the dimensions don't exceed 120cm by 90cm. Otherwise it needs to be sent on unaccompanied, with a guaranteed arrival of 24 hours – you can register it up to ten days in advance; book through Esprit Europe (☎08705/850 850, ⊛www.espriteurope.co.uk); the fee is £20 one-way.

Bikes – usually mountain bikes – are often available to **rent** from campsites, hostels and *gîtes d'étapes*, as well as from specialist cycle shops and some tourist offices for around €15–20 per day. The bikes are often not insured, however, and you will be presented with the bill for their replacement if they're stolen or damaged. Check whether your travel insurance policy covers you for this if you intend to rent a bike.

As for **maps**, a minimum requirement is the IGN 1:100,000 series (see p.49) – the smallest scale that carries contours. The

Municipal bike networks

Toulouse and Montpellier both have **municipal bike networks**, designed for short-term hops within the city. Once you have subscribed (see the individual city listings) you pick up and drop off bikes at automated stations which are peppered throughout each city. Charges are minimal, although there may be fines for overuse. If you are considering using these bike systems, sign up ahead of time by internet; typically you need to register a credit card to cover the fees.

UK's national cyclists' association, the CTC (℡0870/873 0060, ⓦwww.ctc.org.uk), can suggest routes and supply advice for members, as well as running a particularly good insurance scheme. Companies offering specialist **bike touring holidays** are listed on p.23. Useful **vocabulary** for cyclists is given on p.364.

Walking

Long-distance **walkers** are well served in Languedoc and Roussillon by an extensive network of marked footpaths, including long-distance routes, known as *sentiers de grande randonnée* or, more commonly, **GRs** (see also p.42). They're fully signposted and equipped with campsites and rest huts along the way. Some of the main routes in the region are the **GR10**, which runs the length of the Pyrenees, the **GRs 7** and **36**, which wind their way down from Haut Languedoc through the Corbières, and **GR653** which follows the medieval Arles–Jaca pilgrimage route (*le chemin de St-Jacques*) to Santiago in Spain. Other routes are composites, like the "**Sentier Cathar**", which utilizes various GRs and ARs (local paths) to link Cathar sites between Perpignan and Foix.

Each path is described in a *Topoguide* (available in Britain from Stanfords; ⓦwww.standords.co.uk) which gives a detailed account of the route (in French), including maps, campsites, refuge huts and sources of provisions. *Topoguides* are produced by the principal French walkers' organization, the Fédération Française de la Randonnée Pédestre (℡01.44.89.93.93, ⓦwww.ffrp.asso.fr), and are widely available in bookshops and *tabacs*. In addition, many tourist offices can provide **guides** to their local footpaths, especially in popular hiking areas, where they often share premises with professional mountain guides and hike leaders. The latter organize climbing and walking expeditions for all levels of experience.

The main **climbing** organization is the Club Alpin Français (℡01.53.72.87.00, ⓦwww.ffcam.fr); most major towns in the region have a branch office, the most useful being the CAF de Toulouse, 3 rue de l'Orient, 31000 Toulouse (Mon 2–5pm, Tues–Fri 9am–noon & 2–7pm; ℡05.61.63.74.42, ⓦperso.orange.fr/clubalpintoulouse).

Inland waterways

Languedoc is home to one of France's most famous inland waterways, the **Canal du Midi**, which leads from Toulouse (where it hooks up with the River Garonne) to Agde and Sète, passing Carcassonne and Béziers en route. A spur, the **Canal de la Robine**, passes Narbonne before reaching the sea at Gruissan and Port-Nouvelle. From Sète, you can enter the **Canal du Rhône à Sète**, which heads east, passing St-Gilles and Beaucaire, until it reaches the Rhône. Subsidiary canals branch out through the flatlands of the Petite Camargue, and penetrate the extensive Rhône delta. For information on maximum dimensions, documentation, regulations and so forth, ask at a French Government Tourist Office for their booklet *Boating on the Waterways*, or contact Voies Navigables de France, 175 rue Ludovic Boutleux, 62408 Bethune (℡03.21.63.24.24, ⓦwww.vnf.fr), which has information on boating in Languedoc and Roussillon, and lists of French firms that rent out boats. In addition, you'll find detailed information in this guide on the Canal du Midi on p.90 and p.268.

Accommodation

Outside of summer, you can turn up in any town in Languedoc and Roussillon and find a room, or a place in a campsite. Booking a couple of nights in advance can be reassuring, however, and in high season it is often indispensible. The "Language" section at the back of the Guide (see p.353) should help you make a reservation, though many hoteliers and campsite managers – and almost all hostel managers – speak some English. In most towns you'll be able to get a double room for around €40–60, or a single for €35–50; as a general rule the areas around train stations have the highest density of cheap hotels. Note that many municipalities charge a hotel tax, calculated on top of the posted rate, ranging from €0.20 to €3 per night.

Some tourist offices offer a **booking service** but they cannot guarantee rooms at a particular price. All tourist offices can provide lists of hotels, hostels or organizations such as CROUS (see p.33) as well as details of campsites and bed-and-breakfasts. With **campsites**, you can be more relaxed about finding an empty space, unless you're touring with a caravan or camper van or looking for a place on the Mediterranean coast or upper Ariège valley.

Hotels

Most French **hotels** are **graded** from zero to five stars, but price is often a better guide to quality. In the cheapest hotels rooms usually have a sink (*lavabo*) in one corner, sometimes with a toilet (*WC*) behind a screen as well; bathrooms and showers (*douches*) are almost invariably found on the landing – referred to as *douche et WC dans le palier*. As you climb up the price scale amenities such as *en-suite* bathroom, television, internet connection, cable TV and so on, appear.

Breakfast is not normally included and can add €8–12 per person to a bill – though there is no obligation to take it and you will nearly always do better at a café. The cost of eating **dinner** in a hotel's restaurant can be a more important factor to bear in mind when picking a place to stay. Officially, it is illegal for hotels to insist on your taking meals, but they often do in places heavily dependent on seasonal tourism. However, this is not always such a bad thing, and you can sometimes get a real bargain. **Single rooms** are only marginally cheaper than doubles, so sharing always slashes costs. Most hotels willingly provide rooms with **extra beds**, for three or more people, at good discounts.

Note that many family-run hotels are closed every year for two or three weeks sometime between May and September – where possible we've detailed this in the text. In addition, some hotels in smaller towns and villages close for one or two nights a week, usually Sunday or Monday – if in doubt, ring first to check.

Accommodation price codes

All the hotels and guesthouses listed in this book have been price-coded according to the following scale. The prices quoted are for the **cheapest available double room** in high season.

❶ €30 and under	❹ €56–70	❼ €101–125
❷ €31–40	❺ €71–85	❽ €126–150
❸ €41–55	❻ €86–100	❾ €151 and over

A very useful option, especially if it's late at night, are the **motel chains**. In contrast to the downtown hotels which often offer doubtful value (worn-out mattresses, dust, noise, etc) you can count on a decent and reliable standard in the chains even if they are without much charm.

Among the cheapest is the one-star **Formule 1** chain (☏08.92.68.56.85, ⓦwww .hotelformule1.com), well signposted on the outskirts of most big towns. They are characterless, but provide rooms for up to three people from €29. With a Visa, Master-Card, EuroCard or American Express credit card, you can let yourself into a room at any hour of the day or night. Other budget chains include **B&B** (☏08.92.78.29.29, ⓦwww.hotel-bb.com) and the slightly more comfortable **Première Classe** (☏08.25.00.30.03, ⓦwww.premiereclasse .fr) and **Etap Hôtel** (☏08.92.68.89.00, ⓦwww.etaphotel.com). More upmarket but still affordable chains include **Ibis** (☏08.92.68.66.86, ⓦwww.ibishotel.com) and **Campanile** (☏01.64.62.46.00, ⓦwww .campanile.fr), where en-suite rooms with satellite TV and direct-dial phones cost from around €50–60. Aside from the chains, there are a number of **hotel federations** in France. The biggest of these is **Logis de France** (☏01.45.84.83.84, ⓦwww.logis -de-france.fr), an association of over three thousand hotels nationwide. Other good resources include ⓦwww.resinfrance.fr, an official central reservation service, or ⓦwww .francehotelreservation.com.

Several cities in Languedoc and Roussillon participate in the "**Bon Weekend en Ville**" programme, whereby you book through the local tourist office and get two nights for the price of one (Oct–May only) at participating hotels, as well as an array of discount coupons and special deals. Participating towns include Albi, Carcassonne, Nîmes and Toulouse, but the list is growing, so it's worth enquiring about when you are making arrangements to stay in larger towns. If you are planning your trip in advance, contact local tourist offices before arrival; there are very often special accommodation deals on offer, especially outside high season.

Bed-and-breakfast accommodation

An excellent alternative to hotels are **chambres d'hôtes** (B&Bs) which are found in towns, villages and the countryside, and **fermes auberges** (farm B&Bs). The cost is usually around that of a two-star hotel, but they are an excellent option for getting to know locals and French travellers. It should be noted that *chambres d'hôtes* vary tremendously in style, amenities and price, ranging from rooms in rather non descript townhouses to rural cottages to full-blown castles. The key is to research well ahead of time and reserve in advance during high season. Most of these establishments can provide an evening meal. These are called *table d'hôtes* (although some places which provide meals do not have rooms). Meals must be booked a day in advance, and are usually in the €15–25 range. For this price you will be treated to excellent home cooking, featuring market-fresh ingredients; sometimes you will eat with the family and almost always with fellow tourists (usually French). Local tourist offices usually provide comprehensive listings on their websites.

Gîtes de France (☏01.49.70.75.75, ⓦwww.gites-de-france.fr) is a government-funded agency which promotes and manages a range of bed-and-breakfast and self-catering accommodation in France, the latter usually consisting of a self-contained country cottage, known as a *gîte rural* or *gîte de séjour*. Further details can be found in their two national guides – *Chambres et Tables d'Hôtes* and *Chambres d'Hôtes de Prestige et Gîtes de Charme* – which are also sometimes on sale in bookshops and tourist offices. The national guides, however, are not exhaustive; complete listings (with photos) are available in the guides distributed by depart-mental Gîtes de France offices – you can either contact the main office for a complete list, or pick up copies from local and depart-mental tourist offices. If you're planning from home, the simplest way to make reservations is through their website. For rural bed-and-breakfast and dining accommodation contact Bienvenue à la Ferme (☏01.53.57.11.44, ⓦwww.bienvenue-a-la-ferme.com), which also publishes regional and departmental guides, and also lists farms which sell fresh produce.

Renting a house

If you are planning to stay a week or more in any one place it might be worth considering **renting a house**, and there are many websites for agencies or for booking directly with owners (see below). If you're looking to save money, house-swapping is also an option. Otherwise, economical longer-term, self-catering options include the *gîtes ruraux* (rural homes renting for €300 and up per week, administered by Gîtes de France) and the *Clévacances* programme, which has mainly town properties for rent. Contact the Fédération Nationale des Locations de France Clévacances (☎05.61.13.55.66, ⓦwww.clevacances.fr). Alternatively check local tourist office listings for *appartements* or *meublés*.

Hostels

At between €16 and €22 per night for a dormitory bed, and generally with breakfast thrown in, **hostels** – *auberges de jeunesse* – are invaluable for single travellers on a budget. For hostels, **per-person prices** of dorm beds are given throughout the Guide. Many modern hostels now also offer rooms for couples, with en-suite showers, but they don't necessarily work out cheaper than hotels – particularly if you've had to pay a bus fare out to the edge of town to reach them. However, many hostels are beautifully sited, and they allow you to cut costs by preparing your own food in their kitchens, or eating in their cheap canteens.

There are three rival French **hostelling associations**: the main two are the Fédération Unie des Auberges de Jeunesse (FUAJ;

Holiday rental websites

ⓦwww.brittany-ferries.co.uk
ⓦwww.cheznous.com
ⓦwww.gites-de-france.fr
ⓦwww.holidayfrancedirect.co.uk
ⓦwww.holiday-rentals.co.uk
ⓦwww.homelidays.co.uk

☎01.44.89.87.27, ⓦwww.fuaj.org), which has its hostels detailed in the *International Handbook*, and the Ligue Française pour les Auberges de Jeunesse (LFAJ; ☎01.45.48.69.84, ⓦwww.auberges-de-jeunesse.com). Normally, to stay at FUAJ or LFAJ hostels, you must be a member of Hostelling International (HI) or the International Youth Hostel Federation (IYHF). If you don't join up before you leave home, you can purchase a **membership card** on arrival in the French hostel for €15.25 (€10.70 for under-26s). The third hostelling organization is the Union des Centres de Rencontres Internationales de France (☎01.40.26.57.64, ⓔinfo@ucrif.asso.fr), with sixty hostels in France; membership is not required.

At the height of summer (usually July and Aug only), there's also the possibility of staying in **student accommodation** in university towns and cities. The main organization to contact for this is CROUS (☎01.40.51.55.55, ⓦwww.crous-paris.fr). Prices are similar to the official hostels, from around €14 per person, and you don't need membership.

Camping

Practically every village and town in France has at least one **campsite** to cater for the thousands of people who spend their holiday under canvas – camping is a very big deal in France. The cheapest – at around €6–10 per person per night – is usually the *camping municipal*, run by the local municipality. In season or whenever they're officially open, they are always clean and have plenty of hot water; often they are situated in prime local positions. Out of season, those that stay open often don't bother to collect the overnight charge. Even if camping isn't your thing, keep in mind that many sites rent mobile homes and bungalows, providing an affordable, self-catering option and a good fall-back when local hotels are full up.

If you're planning to do a lot of camping, an **international camping carnet** is a good investment. The carnet serves as useful identification, covers you for third-party insurance when camping and gives ten-percent reductions at campsites listed in the CCI information booklet that comes with your carnet. It is available in the UK from the AA, the RAC or the Carefree Travel Service (℡0247/642 2024, ⓦwww.campingandcaravanningclub .co.uk), who also book inspected camping sites in Europe and arrange ferry crossings; in the US or Canada, contact Family Campers and RVers (℡1-800/245-9755, ⓦwww.fcrv .org).

On the coast around the beach towns, there are **superior categories** of campsite where you'll pay prices similar to those of a hotel for the facilities – bars, restaurants and sometimes swimming pools. These have rather more permanent status than the *campings municipaux*, with people often spending a whole holiday in the one base. If you plan to do the same, and particularly if you have a caravan, camper or a big tent, it's wise to book ahead – reckon on paying at least €8 a head with a tent or a camper van. Inland, *camping à la ferme* – on somebody's farm – is another possibility (generally without facilities). Lists of sites are detailed in the Tourist Board's *Accueil à la Campagne* booklet.

A number of companies in the UK also specialize in **camping holidays** with well-equipped tents provided: try Canvas Holidays (℡0870/192 1154, ⓦwww.canvas .co.uk) or Eurocamp (℡0870/9019 410, ⓦwww.eurocamp.co.uk). Twelve nights' camping at Argelès, near Perpignan, with Canvas, for example, costs about £900 in high season for two adults and up to four children, including Channel ferry.

Lastly, a word of caution: never **camp rough** (*camping sauvage*, as the French call it) on anyone's land without first asking permission, as you may well have to deal with an irate farmer and his dogs. On the other hand, a politely phrased request for permission will as often as not get positive results. Camping on public land is not officially permitted, but is widely practised by the French, and if you are discreet you will likely not meet with problems. On beaches, it's best to camp out only where other people are doing so.

Food and drink

Languedoc-Roussillon – a traditionally poor and marginalized region – isn't known for the elaborate haute cuisine which typifies French cookery in the popular imagination. The food of this overwhelmingly rural region tends to be simple, with small family restaurants serving classic peasant (terroir) dishes based on local produce for under €20 a head. As you cross the region, however, you'll find that the huge diversity of the landscape has contributed to a correspondingly wide range in local specialities – immediately obvious when you visit town and village produce markets – and in all but the most out-of-the-way hamlet you'll be able to find a more adventurous (and expensive) gastronomique restaurant. Due to its relative isolation Languedoc-Roussillon has also fared better than many regions in escaping the processed, boil-in-the-bag and ready-to-microwave productions – known in France as mal-bouffe ("bad grub") – of the global food industry. For regional specialities, see the *Food and wine* colour section.

In the rarefied world of **haute cuisine**, where the top chefs are national celebrities, a battle is currently raging between traditionalists, determined to preserve the purity of French cuisine, and those who experiment with different flavours from around the world to create novel combinations. At this level, French food is still brilliant – in both camps – and the good news is that prices are continuing to come down. Many gourmet palaces offer weekday lunch-time menus where you can sample culinary genius for around €50.

Languedoc and Roussillon are also great places for **foreign cuisine**, in particular North African, Caribbean (known as *Antillais*) and Asiatic. Moroccan, Thai or Vietnamese restaurants are not necessarily cheap options but they are usually good value for money. Chinese restaurants tend, on the other hand, to be inexpensive but disappointing.

On the whole, **vegetarians** can expect a somewhat lean time in Languedoc and Roussillon; *cuisine rurale* is relentlessly meat-based, and in some traditional farming villages even understanding the concept of vegetarianism can be a stretch. A few cities have specifically vegetarian restaurants (detailed in the text), but elsewhere you'll have to rely on crêperies and pizzerias, or hope you find a sympathetic restaurant willing to replace a meat dish on the *menu fixe* with an omelette. Remember the phrase "*Je suis végétarien(ne)*; *il y a quelques plats sans viande?*" (I'm a vegetarian; are there any non-meat dishes?). **Vegans**, however, should probably forget all about eating in French restaurants and stick to self-catering.

For a **food glossary**, see pp.365–372.

Breakfast and snacks

A croissant, *pain au chocolat*, or a sandwich in a bar or café, with hot chocolate or coffee, is generally the best **breakfast** you'll get – at a fraction of the cost charged by most hotels. (The days when hotels gave you mounds of croissants or brioches for breakfast seem to be long gone; now it's virtually always bread, jam and a jug of coffee or tea for about €5.) Croissants and sometimes hard-boiled eggs are displayed on bar counters until around 9.30 or 10am. If you stand – cheaper than sitting down – you just help yourself to these with your coffee, the waiter keeps an eye on how many you've eaten and bills you accordingly.

At **lunch time**, and sometimes in the evening, you may find cafés offering a *plat du jour* (chef's daily special) at between €9 and €14, or *formules*, a limited or no-choice menu. *Croques-monsieur* or *croques-madame* (variations on the toasted-cheese sandwich) are sold at cafés, brasseries and many street stands, along with *frites* (potato fries), crêpes, *galettes* (wholewheat pancakes), *gauffres* (waffles), *glaces* (ice creams) and all kinds of fresh-filled baguettes (these very filling sandwiches usually cost €3–5 to take away). For variety, there are Tunisian snacks like *brik à l'œuf* (a fried pastry with an egg inside), *merguez* (spicy North African sausage), Greek *souvlaki* (kebabs) and Middle Eastern falafel (deep-fried chickpea balls in flat bread with salad). Wine bars are good for regional sausages and cheese, usually served with brown bread (*pain de campagne*).

Crêpes, or pancakes with fillings, served up at ubiquitous crêperies, are popular lunch-time food. The savoury buckwheat variety (*galettes*) provide the main course; the sweet white-flour ones are dessert. They taste nice enough, but are usually poor value in comparison with a restaurant meal; you need at least three, normally at over €5 each, to feel full. **Pizzerias**, usually *au feu de bois* (wood-fire-baked), are also very common. They are somewhat better value than crêperies, but quality and quantity vary greatly – look before you leap into the nearest empty seats.

Gallic culture is incredibly **picnic**-tolerant, and there's no problem in pulling off the road and spreading your blanket wherever you are. It's a very economical and pleasant way of dining, with the local outdoor market or supermarket able to provide everything you need from tomatoes and avocados to cheese and pâté. Cooked meat, prepared snacks, ready-made dishes and assorted salads can be bought at *charcuteries* (delicatessens), which you'll find everywhere – even in small villages, though the same things are cheaper at supermarket counters. You purchase by weight, or you can ask for *une tranche* (a slice), *une barquette* (a carton) or *une part* (a portion).

Salons de thé, which open from mid-morning to late evening, serve brunches, salads, quiches and so on, as well as gateaux, ice cream and a wide selection of teas. They tend to be a good deal pricier than cafés or brasseries – you're paying for the posh surroundings – and generally have a more female ambience and clientele. For cakes and pastries to take away, you'll find impressive arrays at every *boulangerie-pâtisserie*.

Meals

There's no difference between **restaurants** (or *auberges* or *relais* as they sometimes call themselves) and **brasseries** in terms of quality or price range. The distinction is that brasseries, which resemble cafés, serve quicker meals at most hours of the day, while restaurants tend to stick to the traditional meal times of noon to 2pm, and 7pm to 9.30pm or 10.30pm. After 9pm or so, restaurants often serve only à la carte meals (single dishes chosen from the menu) – invariably more expensive than eating the set *menu fixe*. In touristy areas in high season, and for all the more upmarket places, it's wise to make reservations – easily done on the same day. In small towns it may be impossible to get anything other than a bar sandwich after 10pm or even earlier; in major cities, town-centre brasseries will serve until 11pm or midnight and one or two may stay open all night.

When hunting for places to eat, avoid those that are half-empty at peak time, use your nose and regard long menus with suspicion. Don't forget that **hotel restaurants** are open to non-residents, and are often very good value. In many small towns and villages, you'll find the only restaurants are in hotels. Since restaurants change hands frequently and have their ups and downs, it's also worth asking locals for recommendations. This is the conversational equivalent of commenting on the weather in Britain and will usually elicit strong views and sound advice.

Prices, and what you get for them, are posted outside. Normally there's a choice between one or more *menus fixes*, where the number of courses has already been determined and the choice is limited, and choosing individually from the *carte* (menu). **Menus fixes** are normally the cheapest option. At the bottom end of the price range, they revolve around standard dishes such as steak and chips (steak frites), chicken and chips (*poulet frites*) and various concoctions involving innards. But further up the scale they can be much the best-value way of sampling regional specialities, sometimes running to five or more courses. If you're simply not that hungry, just go for the *plat du jour*.

Going **à la carte** offers greater choice and,

in the better restaurants, unlimited access to the chef's specialities – though you'll pay for the privilege. A simple and perfectly legitimate tactic is to have just one course instead of the expected three or four. You can share dishes or go for several starters – a useful strategy for vegetarians. There's no minimum charge.

In the French **sequence of courses**, any salad (sometimes vegetables, too) comes separate from the main dish, and cheese precedes a dessert. You will be offered coffee, which is always extra, to finish off the meal.

Wine (*vin*) or a **drink** (*boisson*) is occasionally included (*compris*) in the cost of a *menu fixe*. When ordering house wine, the cheapest option, ask for *un quart* (0.25 litre), *un demi-litre* (0.5 litre) or *une carafe* (1 litre). If you're worried about the cost ask for *vin ordinaire* or the *vin de table*. In the Guide the lowest price menu or the range of menus is given; where average à la carte prices are given it assumes you'll have three courses and half a bottle of wine.

The French are much better disposed towards **children** in restaurants than other nationalities, not simply by offering reduced-price children's menus but in creating an atmosphere – even in otherwise fairly snooty establishments – that positively welcomes kids; some even have in-house games and toys for them to occupy themselves with. It is regarded as self-evident that large family groups should be able to eat out together.

A rather murkier area is that of **dogs** in the dining room; it can be quite a shock in a provincial hotel to realize that the majority of your fellow diners are attempting to keep dogs concealed beneath their tables.

Drink

Wherever you can eat you can invariably drink, and vice versa. **Drinking** is done at a leisurely pace whether it's a prelude to food (*apéritif*), a sequel (*digestif*), or the accompaniment, and cafés are the standard places to do it. Every bar or café has to display its full price list, usually without the fifteen-percent service charge added, with the cheapest drinks at the bar (*au comptoir*), and progressively increasing prices for sitting at a table inside (*la salle*), or outside (*la terrasse*). If you

are sitting outside, particularly in a touristy area, unpleasantness can be avoided by checking the price with the waiter when you put in your order. You pay when you leave, and it's perfectly acceptable to sit for hours over just one cup of coffee.

Wine (*vin*) is drunk at just about every meal or social occasion, be it red (*rouge*), white (*blanc*) or rosé. *Vin de table* or *vin ordinaire* – table wine – is generally drinkable and always cheap, although it may be disguised and priced up as the house wine, or *cuvée*. The price of AOC (*appellation d'origine contrôlée*) wines can vary from €1.80 to around €15 a bottle, and that's the vineyard price. You can buy a very decent bottle of wine for €3 to €5, and €10 and over will buy you something really nice. By the time restaurants have added their considerable mark-up, however, wine can constitute an alarming proportion of the bill.

The basic **wine terms** are: *brut*, very dry; *sec*, dry; *demi-sec*, sweet; *doux*, very sweet; *mousseux*, sparkling; *méthode champenoise*, mature and sparkling. A glass of wine is simply *un rouge*, *un rosé* or *un blanc*. You may have the choice of *un ballon* (round glass) or a smaller glass (*un verre*). *Un pichet* (a pitcher) is normally a quarter-litre. A glass of wine in a bar will cost around €3.

The best way to **buy bottles** of wine is directly from the producers (*vignerons*), either at vineyards, at Maisons or Syndicats du Vin (representing a group of wine-producers), or at Coopératifs Vinicoles (wine-producer co-ops). At all these places you can sample the wines first. It's best to make clear at the start how much you want to buy (if it's only one or two bottles) and you will not be popular if you drink several glasses and then leave without making a purchase. The most economical option is to buy *en vrac*, which you can also do at some wine shops (*caves*), taking an easily obtainable plastic five- or ten-litre container (usually sold on the premises) and getting it filled straight from the barrel. In cities, supermarkets are the best places to buy your wine, and their prices often beat those of the *vignerons*.

In Languedoc and Roussillon, some good **regional wines** can be found in the *vins de pays* category (also known as *vins d'Oc* in these parts). Quality wines are denoted by the *appellation d'origine contrôlée* (AOC), which strictly controls quality and the amount of wine that a particular area may produce. Within each appellation there is enormous diversity generated by the different types of soil, the lie of the land, the type of grape grown – there are over forty varieties grown in Languedoc and Roussillon – the ability of the wine to age and the individual skills of the wine-grower. For more details on local wines, see the *Food and wine* colour section.

Familiar light Belgian and German brands, plus French brands from Alsace, account for most of the **beer** you'll find. Draught beer (*à la pression*) – usually Kronenbourg – is the cheapest drink you can have next to coffee and wine; ask for *une pression* or *un demi* (0.33 litre). A *demi* costs around €3. For a wider choice of draught and bottled beer you need to go to the special beer-drinking establishments or English-style pubs found in most city centres and resorts. A small bottle at one of these places will cost at least twice as much as a *demi* in a café. In supermarkets, however, bottled or canned beer is exceptionally cheap.

Strong alcohol is consumed from as early as 5am as a pre-work fortifier, and then at any time through the day according to circumstance, though the national reputation for drunkenness has lost much of its truth. Brandies and the dozens of *eaux de vie* (spirits) and liqueurs are always available. *Pastis* – the generic name of aniseed drinks such as Pernod or Ricard and a favourite throughout Languedoc – is served diluted with water and ice (*glaçons*). It's very refreshing and not expensive. Mixed with *crème de menthe* it's known as a *perroquet*. Among less familiar names, try Poire William (pear brandy), or Marc (a spirit distilled from grape pulp). Measures are generous, but they don't come cheap: the same applies to imported spirits like whisky (*Scotch*). Two drinks designed to stimulate the appetite – *un apéritif* – are Pineau (cognac and grape juice) and Kir (white wine with a dash of Cassis – blackcurrant liquor – or with champagne instead of wine for a Kir Royal). **Cocktails** are served at most late-night bars, discos and music places, as well as at upmarket hotel bars and at every seaside promenade café; they usually cost at least €7.

On the **soft drink** front, you can buy cartons of unsweetened fruit juice in supermarkets, although in the cafés the bottled (sweetened) nectars such as apricot (*jus d'abricot*) and blackcurrant (*cassis*) still hold sway. You can also get fresh orange or lemon juice (*orange/citron pressé*), at a price. A *citron pressé* is a refreshing choice for the extremely thirsty on a hot day – the lemon juice is served in the bottom of a long ice-filled glass, with a jug of water and a sugar bowl to sweeten it to your taste. Other drinks to try are syrups (*sirops*) of mint, grenadine or other flavours mixed with water. The standard fizzy drinks of lemonade (*limonade*), Coke (*coca*) and so forth are all available. Bottles of **mineral water** (*eau minérale*) and spring water (*eau de source*) – either sparkling (*gazeuse*) or still (*eau plate*) – abound, from the big brand names to more obscure spa product. But there's nothing wrong with the tap water (*l'eau du robinet* or *une carafe d'eau*), which will always be brought free to your table if you ask for it.

Coffee is invariably espresso – small, black and very strong. *Un café* or *un express* is the regular; *un crème* is with milk; *un grand café* or *un grand crème* are large cups. In the morning you could also ask for *un café au lait* – espresso in a large cup or bowl filled up with hot milk. *Un déca* is decaffeinated, now widely available. Ordinary **tea** (*thé*) is Lipton's nine times out of ten, and is normally served black, and you can usually have a slice of lemon (*citron*) with it if you want; to have milk with it, ask for *un peu de lait frais* (some fresh milk). *Chocolat chaud* – **hot chocolate** – unlike tea, lives up to the high standards of French food and drink and can be had in any café. After eating, **herb teas** (*infusions* or *tisanes*), served in every *salon de thé*, can be soothing. The more common ones are *verveine* (verbena), *tilleul* (lime blossom), *menthe* (mint) and *camomille* (camomile).

Tipping

With the general exception of the most expensive places, bars and restaurants in France calculate the service charge, or tip, and factor it into your bill. When you see "service compris" or "s.c." on a menu, you will be expected only to leave small change as a sign of gratitude – perhaps €0.20 for a drink or up to €2.50 for a meal. When you see "service non compris", "s.n.c." or "servis en sus" you should be prepared to leave a gratuity of fifteen percent for standard-quality service. It's worth remembering that tipping less may penalize a waiter who will share out tips with kitchen staff based on the total he or she has billed.

The media

English-language newspapers, such as The Times, the Washington Post, New York Times and the International Herald Tribune, are on sale the day of publication in some of the region's larger cities, including Toulouse, Montpellier and Nîmes, and the day after publication at many resorts. Of the French daily papers, Le Monde is the most intellectual; it is widely respected, but somewhat austere, while Libération, founded by Jean-Paul Sartre in the 1960s, is moderately left-wing, independent and more colloquial, with good, if choosy, coverage. Rigorous left-wing criticism of the French government comes from L'Humanité, the Communist Party paper. The other nationals are all firmly right-wing, with Le Figaro being the most respected. The top-selling national is L'Équipe, which is dedicated to sports, while Paris-Turf focuses on horse-racing. Languedoc-Roussillon's regional daily paper is the Midi-Libre: for visitors, it's mainly of interest for its listings, although it does have good local travel features.

Newspapers and magazines

Weeklies, along the lines of Newsweek/Time, include the wide-ranging and socialist-leaning Le Nouvel Observateur, its right-wing counterpoint L'Express, the boringly centrist L'Événement du Jeudi and the newcomer with a bite, Marianne. The best investigative journalism is to be found in the weekly satirical paper Le Canard Enchaîné, while Charlie Hebdo is a sort of Private Eye equivalent. There is also Paris-Match for gossip about stars and royal families. **Monthlies** include the young, trendy and cheap Nova, which has excellent listings of cultural events, and Actuel, which is good for current events. There are, of course, the French versions of Vogue, Elle (weekly) and Marie-Claire, and the relentlessly urban Biba, for women's fashion and lifestyle.

Moral **censorship** of the press is rare. On the news stands you'll find pornography of every shade, as well as covers featuring drugs, sex, blasphemy and bizarre forms of grossness alongside knitting patterns and DIY. You'll also find French **comics** (bandes dessinées), which often indulge such adult interests: wildly and wonderfully illustrated, they are considered to be quite an art form and whole museums are devoted to them.

Some of the huge numbers of homeless people in France (les sans-abri) make a bit of money by selling magazines on the streets which combine culture, humour and self-help with social and political issues. Costing €1.50, the best known of these is L'Itinerant.

Television and radio

French TV has six channels: three public (France 2, France 3 and Arte/France 5); one subscription (Canal Plus – with some unencrypted programmes); and two commercial open broadcasts (TF1 and M6).

Of these, **TF1** and **France 2** are the most popular channels, showing a broad mix of programmes. **Arte/France 5** (also known as La Cinquième) is a joint Franco-German cultural venture that transmits simultaneously in French and German: offerings include highbrow programmes, daily documentaries, art criticism, serious French and German movies and complete operas. During the day (7am–7pm), France 5 uses the frequency to broadcast educational programmes. **Canal Plus** is the main movie channel, with repeats of foreign films usually shown at least once in the original language. **France 3** is strong on regional news and more heavyweight movies, including a fair number of undubbed foreign films, while **M6** shows a lot of US imports and programmes aimed at a younger market. The main French **news broadcasts** are at 8pm on France 2 and TF1. In addition there are any number of **cable** and satellite channels, including CNN, BBC World and BBC Prime, Eurosport, MTV, Planète, which specializes in documentaries, Ciné Première, and Canal Jimmy (*Friends* and the like in French). The main French-run **music channel** is MCM.

If you've got a **radio**, you can tune in to English-language news on the BBC World Service (ⓦ www.bbc.co.uk/worldservice) on 648kHz AM or 198kHz long wave from midnight to 5am (and Radio 4 during the day). The Voice of America (ⓦ www.voa.gov) transmits on 90.5, 98.8 and 102.4 FM. For radio **news in French**, there's the state-run France Inter (87.8 FM), Europe 1 (104.7 FM) and round-the-clock news on France Infos (105.5 FM).

Festivals

It's hard to beat the experience of arriving in a small French village, expecting no more than a bed for the night, to discover the streets decked out with flags and streamers, a band playing in the square and the entire population out celebrating the feast of their patron saint. Apart from Bastille Day (July 14) and the Assumption of the Virgin Mary (August 15), there are many traditional folk festivals thriving in Languedoc and Roussillon. Moreover, local and municipal governments have invested heavily in summer *fêtes* and free concert series, designed to bring visitors into the region's villages.

Celebrations of local patron saints are concentrated in summer months and are the occasion for fireworks, dancing and *pétanque* competitions. These are particularly colourful in the fishing ports of the Languedoc coast, where saints' effigies are paraded down to the sea and events include **water-borne jousting** competitions. In wine country, there are inevitably festivals coinciding with the grape harvest, and in other regions with that of the dominant local product. Throughout the Languedocian plain – notably east from Béziers and in certain towns of the Pyrenees –

tauromachie (see p.209), which involves Spanish-style *corridas* (**bullfights**) or indigenous *courses camarguaises*, occurs regularly throughout the summer, and at other big holidays, such as Pentecost and the pre-Lenten carnival. The **concert and theatre** season is typically from October to May, although there are also major arts festivals in summer. The most important and interesting regional festivals are outlined at the beginning of each chapter of the Guide, but it is worth consulting departmental tourist boards (see p.53) for specific and local events.

Sports and outdoor pursuits

Languedoc and Roussillon offer a wide range of sports, both to watch and take part in. As well as seeing local teams play big-league sports such as football, regionally popular games like rugby are also worth seeking out. In addition, you can partake in a variety of outdoor activities, including hiking, cycling and skiing, and water-borne diversions such as rafting and sailing.

As well as rugby, the outdoor spectacle of **bullfighting**, or more properly, *tauromachie*, is incredibly popular across the region, both in Spanish and indigenous styles. **Water-jousting** (see box, p.233), a coastal tradition which pits boat-borne jousting teams against each other in an effort to unseat their opponents, has its home in Sète, but is practised along the length of the coast. **Pétanque**, or *boules*, is a game you'll see played in towns and villages throughout the region, and which you can play yourself if you purchase a set (available at sports shops and large department stores).

Football and rugby

Languedoc and Roussillon are not the best places in France for **football**, and the only city in the region with a team in the First Division (*Ligue 1*) is Toulouse, whose club tends to hover around the lower regions of the league. Montpellier are currently languishing in the second division, a far cry from their finest moment when they won the French Cup in 1990.

Rugby is the field game of choice in the region, and virtually every town of any size boasts a team. Top teams in the region include Toulouse, Narbonne, Perpignan, Nîmes and Castres, who have traditionally provided the core of the French national side. Rugby originated in 1832, in England, and although it arrived in France not long after, it only really caught on in the Occitan south – perhaps as an unconscious means of marking a difference from the northern French. Post-game camaraderie is a big part of the whole experience, and you'll find yourself caught up in the cheerful spirit of things whether you see a major team like Stade Toulousain in action, or a small-town

match with teams of the level of Albi or Pamiers.

Tauromachie

Bulls have been raised in eastern Languedoc since time immemorial, and in the last centuries **tauromachie** – "the art of the bull" (see box, p.209) – has come to play an important role in the culture of the whole region. While the people of the Petite Camargue ranchlands see it as a measure of virility, Occitan patriots are attracted to it as a custom which has no equivalent in the north of France. To capture the authentic feel of southern French *tauromachie* try to see a *corrida* in the amphitheatre at Nîmes (see p.187) or one of the *courses camarguaises* that take place in the Petite Camargue from March to September (see Chapter 4).

Pétanque

Once the preserve of sweatered old men in berets, **pétanque**, or *boules*, has recently seen a surge in popularity and a broadening of appeal to include more young people and women. The game is similar to English bowls. Two equally numbered teams (from one to three persons) find a space of hard, compact ground and throw a *cochonnet* (jack) a few metres (technically six to ten). A small circle is then marked on the ground to show the limit of the area in which the throwers must stand (hence *pétanque* from the Provençal "pieds tanqués" or "feet together"). They then proceed in turns to launch a total of three balls (two in a six-person match), each with the object of having their metal *boules* closest to the *cochonnet* at the end of the exchange. A point is gained for each ball that is closer than the nearest ball of the opposing team.

The jack is then thrown again and play continues until one side scores thirteen. *Pétanque* matches invariably draw a crowd of onlookers, and you will not be considered rude if you stop to observe. The best times to watch are during village *fêtes*, which invariably include a tournament, drawing out the best players in the village.

Hiking, biking and riding

Walking is undoubtedly the way to get the most out of a visit to the region. Well-marked and maintained **GR paths**, signposted with their distinctive yellow and red bars, span the region, punctuated by *gîtes*, refuges and campsites along the way. The highest concentration of paths (and the best hiking scenery) is found in the Pyrenees and its foothills, where you will find an extensive network of yellow- and- red-marked GRP (*grandes randonnées du pays*) paths as well as HRP (*haute route des Pyrénées*) routes. In addition, local AR footpaths abound, and in virtually every village you'll find an information board with a map outlining local itineraries of varying length and difficulty. Even if you're spending only a few hours in a village, it's worth enquiring at the tourist office, which will almost certainly have a pamphlet outlining local walks.

Recently a series of excellent *Topoguides* has been published for each *région* and *département*, by the Fédération Française de la Randonnée Pédestre (☎01.44.89.93.90, ⓦwww.ffrp.asso.fr). Regional guides detail eighty walks and VTT (mountain bike) routes (€13.95) and departmental guides have forty (€11.95); the series is widely available in bookshops. Most tourist offices also give away free or cheap (under €5) guides to local walks and bike trails. If you're travelling with children or are looking for less challenging routes, try the FFRP's *Les Sentiers d'Emilie*, which details thirty easy walks in the Pyrénées-Orientales. All these guides are in French, but even non-French-speakers will be able to use them with the help of a pocket dictionary. For mountain refuges, the Club Alpin Français (ⓦwww.ffcam.fr) has online information and publishes an annual guide.

Biking is the next best option, and the cities of the south have been remarkably quick to adapt to two-wheeled transport, particularly Toulouse and Montpellier. Around Montpellier, Agde and Narbonne, extensive networks of **bike paths**, often using decommissioned roads, link the coastal villages and the cities. In the countryside disused rail lines, such as the Gijou Valley Trail (see p.166), have been set up as bicycle (VTT) routes, and canal towpaths make it possible to cross the region with ease. Traffic off the main roads is surprisingly light, but be warned that some of the narrow *routes nationales* often see heavy, fast traffic.

That said, with the exception of the coastal plain you may find the biggest challenge to be the hilliness of the terrain. For recreational riding, as opposed to transportational riding, several of the ski resorts in the Ariège and in Roussillon open their pistes in summer to mountain bikers (check the web pages of the resorts in the chapters).

While **horseriding** is not practical as a means of transport, it is an excellent way of enjoying the countryside. Practically every town and many farms have equestrian centres where you can ride unaccompanied or with a guide on local trails. In the Pyrenees **mules** provide a more practical alternative. Local tourist offices can give you information on riding centres or you can contact the regional equestrian tourism organization ATECREL, 14 rue des Logis, 34140 Loupian (☎04.67.43.82.50), or the Fédération Française d'Équitation (DNTE), 30 av d'Iéna, 75116 Paris (☎01.53.67.44.44, ⓦwww.ffe .com). For mule-trekking, contact the Fédération Nationale Ânes et Randonnées, Broissieux, 73340 Bellecombe-en-Bauges (☎04.79.63.84.01, ⓦwww.ane-et-rando.com).

Skiing, rafting and watersports

There are a number of **ski stations** in the eastern Pyrenees, and although they cannot offer anything to compare with the great resorts of the French Alps, you will be able to find some decent downhill skiing between November and April. Cross-country skiing, or *ski de fond*, is also a possibility, and the broad massifs of the Cerdagne and Ariège are particularly well suited to it. The relatively low altitude of some resorts is partially offset by the extensive use of snow-making machines. The most important and better-known resorts, among them Font-Romeu, Formiguères and Porté-Puymorens, are detailed in the Guide, and the Ariège and Pyrénées-Orientales tourist offices (see p.53) also have information, with the CDT Ariège website (Ⓦwww .ariegepyrenees.com) often offering accommodation and lift-ticket deals. Alternatively, for winter sports (including snowshoeing) contact the Pyrénées Club de France, 8 rue de la Colombette, 3100 Toulouse (Ⓣ05.62.73.56.35, Ⓦwww.pyrenees-club .asso.fr).

While you are exploring the hilly uplands of the Languedoc and Roussillon, you ought to sample also the thrill of **rafting** down one of the region's many dramatic rivers. This sport has exploded in recent years, and you will scarcely pass a gorge which is not capped by a rafting outfit at its upper end. The biggest concentration is in the upper Hérault, south of Ganges, but good opportunities can be found on the Orbiel, west of

Lamalou, and on the Ariège around Tarascon. More placid paddling can be done by **canoe**, notably on the calmer stretches of water of the Aude and Gardon, and at the Pont du Gard. **Pot-holing** and **climbing** are also popular throughout Languedoc and Roussillon – tourist offices can hook you up with local guides and operators.

Most of the region's seaside towns are fully developed resorts, and have facilities for the whole gamut of **watersports**: in summer months you'll find everything from jet skis and sailboards to houseboats and yachts for rent. If you are specifically looking for beachside activities, Le-Grau-du-Roi has the best range of facilities, with La Grande-Motte a close second. There are a number of scuba-diving clubs in the beach towns of Roussillon, such as Cap d'Agde, Banyuls, Argelès-Plage, Sète and Port-Camargue, which arrange outings and run certified basic diving courses.

Shopping

It'll be hard not to be tempted to bring home a piece of Languedoc and Roussillon, particularly food and drink – wine, olive oil, cheese, sausage, and so on. One thing to check is your home country's rules regarding importation, both in terms of quantity and types of foods allowed. Generally fresh meat, cheese and produce are a no-no, unless they are vacuum-sealed. Another excellent thing to shop for is antiques; see the box on p.239 for suggestions on shopping.

In general, the French country market experience is not to be missed. Villages typically hold a farmer's market weekly, larger towns twice weekly. Here you'll find fresh produce, baked goods, regional cheeses, sausages and meats, and a selection of ready-to-eat foods such as roast chicken, which makes putting together a picnic a pleasure. But even if you aren't buying, the ambience of these markets is something to be savoured – a vestige of "authenticity" which so many

visitors seek out, but which is increasingly elusive in our mass-marketed and pre-packaged world.

For ordinary items such as **clothing** and accessories prices are likely to be less expensive than the UK but more than in North America, perhaps with the exception of the major sale (*soldes*) periods – mid- to late summer and early January. On the other hand, selection may be better, and many designs will be distinctively French.

Travelling with children

Children are generally welcome everywhere in France, including in most bars and restaurants. Especially in seaside towns, many restaurants have children's menus (*menu enfant*), while some will provide smaller portions of adult dishes on request. Most hotels charge by the room, with a small supplement for an additional bed or cot, while family-run places will usually babysit or offer a listening service while you eat or go out.

Under-4s travel free on SNCF **trains and buses**, while 4–11s pay half-fare (see p.25 for other reductions). In most **museums**, children under 4 are free, with discounts of 50 percent or more for under-18s, while entry to many monuments is free for under-12s.

If you're travelling with a baby, be aware that most French **baby foods** have added sugar and salt, and the milk powders may be richer than your baby is accustomed to – soy-based milk is only available at pharmacies, and is very expensive. Disposable **nappies/diapers** (*couches à jeter*) are available everywhere. Breast-feeding in public will generally raise few eyebrows, if done discreetly.

Most local tourist offices have details of specific **activities** for children – in particular, many resorts supervise "clubs" for children on the beach. Most **parks** have a children's play area; unfortunately the majority of parks are gravelled rather than grassed and when there are lawns they are often out of bounds (*pelouse interdite*). Something to be aware of is the difficulty of negotiating a child's **buggy** over the large cobbles that cover many of the older streets in town centres; if you don't have one already, consider purchasing a backpack-style carrier, which can be useful not only on trails, but also in towns.

 # Travel essentials

Costs

Because of the relatively low cost of accommodation and eating out, Languedoc and Roussillon are not expensive by northern European standards. For a reasonably comfortable existence, including a hotel room for two, a light restaurant lunch and a proper restaurant dinner plus moving around, café stops and museum visits, allow around €100 a day per person. But by counting the pennies, staying at cheap hostels (around €18 for bed and breakfast) or camping (from €9), and being strong-willed about extra cups of coffee and

doses of culture, you could manage on €50 a day, including a cheap restaurant meal.

For two or more people, **hotel accommodation** is nearly always cheaper and better value than hostels, though hotel rates rise throughout the region in July and August, most dramatically in coastal resorts, and major tourist towns like Carcassonne. Many **restaurants** offer reasonable three- or four-course menus for between €12 and €25, though the lunch-time or *midi* menu is nearly always cheaper. **Wine** and **beer** are both very cheap in supermarkets, while buying wine from the barrel at village co-op cellars is even better value for money. The mark-up on wine in restaurants is high, though house wine in cheaper establishments is still very good value. **Drinks** in cafés and bars are what really make a hole in your pocket – remember that it's cheaper to drink at the bar than at a table. Also, given that a small bottle of water typically costs somewhere between €2.50 and €4, you can save considerably by ordering tap water – *une carafe d'eau* – which is always free.

French **trains** are good value, with many discounts available (see p.25 for details), though **buses** remain marginally cheaper. Admission to **museums and monuments** can be pricey, though reduced admission is often available for those over 60 and under 18 (for which you'll need your passport as proof of age) and for students under 26. Many museums and monuments are free for children (the age bar for which may range from 12 to 18), and nearly always for kids under 4. Several towns operate a discount pass for their museums and monuments, which can be good value if you plan to visit a few.

Youth and student ID cards can soon pay for themselves in savings: full-time students are eligible for the International Student ID Card (ISIC; Ⓦwww.isiccard.com, or Ⓦwww.isic.org in the US and Canada), which entitles the bearer to reduced air, rail and bus fares and discounts at museums, theatres and other attractions. Those under 26 can buy the **International Youth Travel Card**, which carries the same benefits. Under-26s can also get a **youth card**, or *Carte Jeune*, available in France from main tourist offices for under €20 (valid for a year), which entitles you to reductions on museums, sights and other services in France. A university photo ID might also open some doors, though it's not as easily recognizable as an ISIC card.

Crime and personal safety

Petty theft is endemic in all the major cities and along the coast. Drivers, particularly with foreign number plates or in rental cars with Parisian registration, face a high risk of break-ins. Vehicles are rarely stolen, but car radios and luggage make tempting targets.

If you need to **report a theft**, go to the *commissariat de police* (addresses are given in the Guide for the major cities), where they will fill out a *constat de vol*: you'll need to show your passport, and vehicle documents if relevant. If you have an **accident** while driving, you have to fill in and sign a *constat à l'amiable* (jointly agreed statement); car insurers are supposed to give you this with the policy, though in practice few seem to have heard of it. For **non-criminal driving offences** such as speeding, the police can impose an on-the-spot fine.

The two main types of **police** that you are likely to come into contact with are the *Police Nationale*, who patrol cities and larger towns, and the *Gendarmerie Nationale*, who patrol the highways and rural areas. Some large cities also have a municipal force, which often has jurisdiction only over traffic. In the Pyrenees, you may also come across specialized mountaineering sections of the police, who provide rescue services and guidance, and are unfailingly helpful, friendly and approachable. In case of trouble or loss head for the nearest police station and they will direct you to the proper authorities.

Travellers of non-European origin, particularly those of African or Middle Eastern extraction, may encounter **racism**, such as hotels claiming to be booked up, police demanding to see papers and abuse. If you suffer a racial assault, you're likely to get a much more sympathetic hearing from your consulate than from the police. There are many anti-racism organizations which will offer support (though they may not have English-speakers): Mouvement Contre le Racisme et pour l'Amitié entre les Peuples (MRAP; Ⓦwww.mrap.asso.fr) and SOS Racism have offices in most big cities.

Emergency numbers

All these numbers are free.
Fire brigade (pompiers) ☎18
Medical emergencies ☎15
Police ☎17
Rape crisis (SOS Viol) ☎08.00.05.95.95

Electricity

This is almost always 220V, using plugs with two round pins. If you haven't bought the appropriate transformer with you, you can buy one for around €10 from the electrical section of a department store. Before you plug in, check that the transformer is of sufficient voltage and amperage for the appliance you plan on plugging in.

Entry requirements

Citizens of EU (European Union) countries can enter and travel freely within France with just a passport. Citizens of Australia, Canada, the United States and New Zealand, among other countries, can enter France and stay for up to ninety days without needing a visa. However, the situation can change and it is advisable to check with the French embassy or consulate in your own country before departure.

EU citizens (or other non-visa citizens) who stay longer than three months are officially supposed to apply for a *carte de séjour*, for which you'll have to show proof of income at least equal to the minimum wage (around €1250 a month). However, EU passports are rarely stamped, so there is no evidence of how long you've been in the country. If your passport does get stamped, you can cross the border – to Spain, for example – and re-enter for another ninety days legitimately.

French embassies and consulates overseas

Australia Canberra ☎02/6216 0100; Sydney ☎02/9261 5779, ⓦwww.ambafrance-au.org.
Britain London ☎020/7073 1200, ⓦwww.ambafrance-uk.org; Edinburgh ☎0131/220 6324, ⓦwww.consulfrance-edimbourg.org.
Canada Montréal ☎514/878-4385, ⓦwww.consulfrance-montreal.org; Québec ☎418/694-2294, ⓦwww.consulfrance-quebec.org; Toronto ☎416/925-8041, ⓦwww.consulfrance-toronto.org; Vancouver ☎604/681-4345, ⓦwww.consulfrance-vancouver.org.
Ireland Dublin ☎01/260 1666, ⓦwww.ambafrance-ie.org.
New Zealand Wellington ☎04/384 2555, ⓦwww.ambafrance-nz.org.
South Africa Johannesburg ☎11/778 5600, ⓦwww.consulfrance-jhb.org; Le Cap ☎21/423 1575, ⓦwww.consulfrance-lecap.org.
USA Atlanta ☎404/495-1660, ⓦwww.consulfrance-atlanta.org; Boston ☎617/542-7735, ⓦwww.consulfrance-boston.org; Chicago ☎312/787-5359, ⓦwww.consulfrance-chicago.org; Houston ☎713/572-2799, ⓦwww.consulfrance-houston.org; Los Angeles ☎310/235-3200, ⓦwww.consulfrance-losangeles.org; Miami ☎305/372-9798, ⓦwww.consulfrance-miami.org; New Orleans

☎504/523-5772, ⓦwww.consulfrance-nouvelleorleans.org; New York ☎212/606-3600, ⓦwww.consulfrance-newyork.org; San Francisco ☎415/616-4910, ⓦwww.consulfrance-sanfrancisco.org; Washington ☎202/944-6200, ⓦwww.ambafrance-us.org.

Foreign embassies in France

Australia 4 rue Jean Rey, Paris ☎01.40.59.33.00, ⓦwww.austgov.fr.
Britain 35 rue du Faubourg St Honoré, Paris ☎01.44.51.31.00, ⓦwww.ukinfrance.fco.gov.uk.
Canada 35 av Montaigne, Paris ☎01.44.43.29.00, ⓦwww.amb-canada.fr.
Ireland 12 av Foch, Paris ☎ 01.44.17.67.00, ⓦwww.embassyofireland.fr.
New Zealand 7 rue Léonardo de Vinci, Paris ☎01.45.01.43.43, ⓦwww.nzembassy.com.
USA 2 av Gabriel, Paris ☎01.43.12.22.22, ⓦwww.amb-usa.fr.

Foreign consulates in Languedoc

Britain, Honorary Consulate 64 rue Alcyone, Nîmes (M. Norman Paget, Honorary Consul; by appointment only, ☎04.67.15.34.04).
Canada 10 rue Jules de Resseguier, Toulouse (☎05.61.52.19.06, ⓔconsulat.canada-toulouse@amb-canada.fr).
USA 25 allées Jean-Jaurès, Toulouse (☎05.34.41.36.50, ⓦwww.amb-usa.fr).

Gay and lesbian travellers

France is more liberal on **homosexuality** than most other European countries, with the legal **age of consent** being 16. In Languedoc, gay communities thrive in larger centres, such as Toulouse and Montpellier, and some beach towns, like Palavas, though lesbian life is rather less upfront.

In general, the French consider sexuality to be a private matter and homophobic assaults are very rare. On the whole, gays tend to be discreet outside specific gay venues, parades and certain coastal resorts. **Toulouse** has a reputation for being a city with a vibrant gay and lesbian culture, although there is no notable gay "ghetto" as such. **Montpellier**, traditionally politically left-wing and socially liberal, officially embraces gay culture, supporting many events in the city.

Contacts for gay and lesbian travellers

ARCL ☎01.46.28.54.94, ✉archives.lesbiennes @orange.fr. ARCL publishes a biannual directory of lesbian, gay and feminist contacts in France, *L'Annuaire*, and organizes frequent events.

Centre Gai et Lesbienne Toulouse 4 rue de Belfort ☎05.61.62.30.62. Open Mon–Fri 5–8pm, Sat 3–8pm for information and advice, and also hosts a Sunday afternoon (3 –7pm) social event, Café Positif, which is great for meeting people. It is associated with Arc-en-Ciel Toulouse, a local activist and community service; see ⊛www.aectoulouse.fr.

Dykeplanet ⊛www.dykeplanet.com. Sells *Le dykeGuide*, a guidebook listing lesbian-friendly places across France. Published annually, in French only: also available from FNAC and other bookstores.

Fréquence Gaie (FG) 98.2 FM. 24hr gay and lesbian radio station with music, news, chat, information on groups and events, etc.

Minitel 36.15 GAY is the Minitel number to dial for information on groups, contacts, messages, and so forth.

Guide Gai Pied The most comprehensive gay guide to France, published annually. Its website ⊛www .gaipied.fr has a good selection of lesbian and gay contacts.

Lesbia The most widely available lesbian publication, available from most newsagents. Each monthly issue features a wide range of articles, listings, reviews, lonely hearts and contacts.

Têtu ⊛www.tetu.com. Highly rated French gay/ lesbian magazine with events listings and contact addresses; you can buy it in bookshops or through their website, which is also an excellent source of information.

Health

With its gentle climate, easy pace of life and world-beating **healthcare system**, France is one of the world's healthiest destinations. All **tap water** is safe to drink (except from taps labelled *"eau non potable"*) and there are no nasty local maladies. No visitor requires any vaccinations. Languedoc and Roussillon will present you with few specific health risks, other than mosquito bites (especially on the coast and in the Camargue) or sunburn.

For minor ailments, your immediate recourse should be to a **pharmacy**, marked by a flashing neon green cross. *Pharmacies* tend to be expensive, but well stocked and extremely efficient, and the pharmacist is well qualified to dispense advice as well as remedies. Opening hours are normally the same as shops (roughly 8/9am–noon & 2/3–6pm). Cities maintain a *pharmacie de garde* that stays open 24 hours according to a rota; addresses and hours are displayed in all pharmacy windows.

For more **serious complaints**, pharmacists, tourist offices or police stations can direct you to a **doctor**, or you can always find one yourself by looking under *"Médecins général-istes"* in the *Yellow Pages* (*Pages Jaunes*). Many speak reasonably good English. Consultation fees, which you have to pay upfront, are €20 for a government-registered doctor (*un médecin conventionné*) – though fees are sometimes waived on an informal basis, partly to avoid paperwork. Non-registered doctors (*médecins non-conventionnés*), however, particularly specialists, may charge considerably more.

In serious **emergencies** you should take yourself off to the nearest *Centre Hospitalier* (hospital), or call an **ambulance** (SAMU) on ☎15. In an accident or injury situation, the **fire service** (*les pompiers*) is usually fastest, and firemen and women are trained in first aid: call ☎18. Hospital phone numbers are given in "Listings" at the end of the main city accounts in the Guide.

EU citizens are entitled to a refund (usually around seventy percent) of the standard fees of registered doctors and dentists. To apply for this refund, British citizens technically need a **European Health Insurance Card** (EHIC), available from post offices, which has replaced the old form E111. In practice, the card exists mainly to smooth the refund process rather than to guarantee it. If you don't have a card and need one, you can always apply for a "provisional replacement certificate". **Non-EU visitors**, including North Americans, should be sure to have their own adequate medical-insurance cover.

French doctors are enthusiastic issuers of prescriptions (*ordonnances*), which can add considerably to the final cost of treatment. You will be given a **Statement of Treatment** (*feuille de soins*) with little stickers (*vignettes*) for each medicine prescribed, which you can use for insurance claims or – in the case of EU citizens – to be reimbursed on your return home under the terms of your EHIC (usually between 35 and 65 percent of the cost of prescription drugs and remedies).

Similarly, if you're **treated at a hospital**, you'll have to pay upfront for out-patient treatment and then claim a refund later. If you are hospitalized, in-patients who are EU citizens can proffer their European Health Insurance Card to get 75 percent refunds on bills. The other 25 percent, and a daily hospital charge (*forfait journalier*), however, are non-refundable.

Insurance

Even though EU healthcare privileges apply in France, you'd do well to take out an **insurance policy** before travelling to cover against theft, loss and illness or injury. Most insurance companies charge an extra premium to include so-called **dangerous sports**, so if you plan to do any skiing, whitewater rafting, rock climbing or pot-holing, make you sure you are covered.

If you need to make a claim on your insurance policy, you should keep **receipts** for medicines and medical treatment, and in the event you have anything stolen, you must obtain an **official statement from the police** (called a *constat de vol*).

Internet

Practically every reasonable-sized town in Languedoc and Roussillon has a **cybercafé** or internet connection point of some sort, costing from €3 to €8 per hour. In less populated areas, many post offices now have public internet terminals, which are operated with a pre-paid card, though they are rather expensive at €7 for the first hour. In addition, France Télécom has street-side internet kiosks in major cities. **Email** is the cheapest and easiest way of staying in touch with home while in France, and it's easy to open a free email account with Hotmail (ⓦwww.hotmail.com), Yahoo (ⓦwww.yahoo.com) or Google (ⓦwww.google.com).

Laundry

Laundries are common in French towns: some are listed in the "Listings" section of the Guide, otherwise look in the phone book under "*Laveries Automatiques*". They are often unattended, so come pre-armed with small change. Machines are normally graded into 5kg, 8kg or 10kg wash sizes, and the smallest costs around €2.50 for a load, though some laundries only have bigger machines and charge around €4. If you're doing your own washing in hotels, keep quantities small as most forbid doing any laundry in your room.

Living and working in France

Unemployment in France is very high, and particularly so in traditionally depressed Languedoc and Roussillon, where it hovers around 23 percent. In the cities, bar work, club work, freelance translating, teaching English, software fixing, data processing and typing, or working as an au pair are some of the most likely employment options, while in the countryside, it comes down to seasonal fruit- or grape-picking (*vendange*), teaching English, busking or DIY odd-jobbing. Obviously, the better your French, the better your chances are of finding work.

An offbeat possibility if you want to discover rural life is being a **working guest** on an organic farm, for anything from a week to a

---

Rough Guides travel insurance

Rough Guides has teamed up with WorldNomads.com to offer great **travel insurance** deals. Policies are available to residents of over 150 countries, with cover for a wide range of **adventure sports**, 24hr emergency assistance, high levels of medical and evacuation cover and a stream of **travel safety information**. Roughguides.com users can take advantage of their policies online 24/7, from anywhere in the world – even if you're already travelling. And since plans often change when you're on the road, you can extend your policy and even claim online. Roughguides.com users who buy travel insurance with WorldNomads.com can also leave a positive footprint and donate to a community development project. For more information go to ⓦ**www.roughguides.com/shop**.

couple of months. The work may involve cheese making, market gardening, beekeeping, wine producing and building. For details of the scheme and a list of French addresses contact Willing Workers on Organic Farms (WWOOF) at ⓦ www.wwoof.org.

Finally, if the region's splendid climate and laidback Mediterranean atmosphere tempt you to **buy a property or relocate**, you'll find a thriving expat community on hand to provide information and advice, with plenty of local businesses, services and cultural activities catering to English speakers. As a starting point, see the *Languedoc Sun* (ⓦ www.languedocsun.com), a free bi monthly newsletter, and the websites ⓦ www. frenchentree.com and ⓦ www.french -property.com.

Mail

French **post offices** (*bureaux de poste* or *PTTs*) – look for bright yellow *La Poste* signs – are generally open Monday to Friday 9am–7pm and Saturday 9am–noon. In smaller towns and villages, however, offices may close earlier and for lunch. The cost of posting standard **letters** (20g or less) and postcards is €0.56 within France, €0.70 to EU countries, and €0.85 to North America, Australia and New Zealand. **Stamps** (*timbres*) can also be bought from *tabacs*, often with less queuing. To post your letter on the street, look for the bright yellow postboxes.

Inside many post offices you will find a row of yellow *guichets automatiques* – automatic ticket machines – with instructions in English, where you can weigh packages and buy the appropriate stamps; sticky labels and tape are also dispensed. If you're sending parcels abroad, you can check prices on the *guichet* or in various leaflets: small post offices don't often send foreign mail and may need reminding, for example, of the reductions for printed papers and books. See ⓦ www.laposte.fr for details on rates and services.

You can receive mail at the central post offices of most towns. It should be addressed (preferably with the surname first and in capitals) "**Poste Restante**, Poste Centrale", followed by the name of the town and its postcode. To collect your mail you need a passport or other ID and there may

be a charge of a couple of euros. You should ask for all your names to be checked, as filing systems are not brilliant.

You can also use Minitel (see below) at post offices, as well as change money, make photocopies, send faxes and make phone calls.

Maps

The best up-to-date **road maps** are the 1:100,000 maps of France produced by Michelin (ⓦ www.viamichelin.fr) or the Institut Géographique National (IGN; ⓦ www.ign.fr). Both companies also issue good **regional maps** either as individual sheets or in one large spiral-bound "*atlas routier*"; Michelin's version is available in English as the *France Tourist & Motoring Atlas* (£13.99). Rough Guides also produces maps to France, and the Pyrenees.

If **walking or cycling**, it's worth investing in the more detailed IGN maps (see above). Their *Carte de Randonnée* series (1:25,000) is specifically designed for walkers, while the *Carte de Promenade* (1:100,000) is good for cyclists. For further details of walking guides, also see "biking and riding" on p.42.

Minitel

Some French phone subscribers still have the now-primitive **Minitel** telnet system which France pioneered. A sort of early email/internet system, which allows access through the phone lines to directories, databases, chat lines and so on, it is still available in post offices, though it's gradually being displaced by the internet. Most organizations, from sports federations to government institutions to gay groups, have a Minitel code consisting of numbers and letters, which you can call up for information, to leave messages and make reservations. You dial the number on the phone, wait for a fax-type tone, then type the letters on the keyboard, and finally press *Connexion Fin* (the same key ends the connection). If you're at all computer-literate and can understand basic keyboard terms in French (*retour* – return, *envoi* – enter, etc), you shouldn't find them hard to use. Be warned that most services cost more than phone rates. Directory enquiries (☎12) are free.

49

Money

The French **currency** is the **euro** (*eh-oo-ro*; €), with bank notes in denominations of 5, 10, 20, 50, 100, 200 and 500 euros, as well as coins of 1, 2, 5, 10, 20 and 50 cents and 1 and 2 euros. Current **exchange rates** are: €1.01 to the pound sterling (€1=£0.91), €0.67 to the US dollar (€1=$1.49), €0.65 to the Canadian dollar (€1=$1.54), €0.62 to the Australian dollar (€1=$1.62), and €0.50 to the New Zealand dollar (€1=$2).

By far the easiest way to access money in France is to use your credit or debit card to withdraw cash from an **ATM** (known as a *distributeur* or *point argent*); most machines give instructions in a variety of European languages. Note that there is often a transaction fee, so it's more efficient to take out a sizeable sum each time rather than making lots of small withdrawals.

Credit and debit cards are also widely accepted in shops, hotels and restaurants, although some smaller establishments don't accept them or levy a minimum purchase. Visa – called Carte Bleue in France – is almost universally recognized, followed by MasterCard (also known as EuroCard). American Express is less widely accepted. Note that most French transactions require a PIN number: if your card is not a chip and PIN, explain that yours is a *carte à piste* and not a *carte à puce*.

If you prefer to take **traveller's cheques**, the most widely recognized brands are Visa, Thomas Cook and American Express, which most banks will change. American Express traveller's cheques can also be cashed at post offices. **Euro traveller's cheques** can be used as cash in some shops, hotels and restaurants, and you should get the face value of the cheques when you change them, so commission is only paid on purchase. Banks being banks, however, this is not always the case.

Rates and commission vary from bank to bank, so it's worth shopping around; the usual rate is a 1–2 percent commission on traveller's cheques and a flat rate charge on cash. Be wary of banks claiming to charge no commission – they merely adjust the exchange rate to their own advantage to compensate. Standard **banking hours** are Monday to Friday 9am to 4pm or 5pm.

Some close at midday (noon/12.30pm–2/2.30pm); some are open on Saturday 9am to noon. All are closed on Sunday and public holidays. They will have a notice on the door if they do currency exchange. **Money exchange counters** (*bureaux de change*) open longer hours than the banks: you'll find them at all the airports in the region and at the train stations in Toulouse and Montpellier, with usually one or two in town centres as well. You'll also find **automatic exchange machines** at airports and train stations and outside many money exchange bureaux. They accept £10 and £20 notes as well as dollars and other European currency notes, but offer a very poor rate of exchange.

Opening hours and public holidays

Basic **hours of business** are 8 or 9am to noon or 1pm, and 2pm or 3pm to 6 or 7pm. In big city centres, shops and other businesses stay open throughout the day, and in July and August most tourist offices and museums are open without interruption. Otherwise almost everything closes for a couple of hours at midday, or even longer in the summer. Small food shops often don't reopen till halfway through the afternoon, closing around 7.30 or 8pm just before the evening meal. Supermarkets tend to stay open 9am to 9pm Monday to Saturday.

The standard **closing days** are Sunday and/or Monday, with shops taking turns to close with their neighbours; many food shops such as *boulangeries* (bakeries) that open on Sunday will do so in the morning only. In small towns you'll find everything except the odd *boulangerie* shut on both Sunday and Monday, while, even in cities, **restaurants and cafés** also often close on a Sunday or Monday.

Museums tend to open between 9 and 10am, close for lunch at noon until 2 or 3pm, and then run through to 5 or 6pm, although in the big cities they will stay open all day: **closing days** are usually Tuesday or Monday, sometimes both. Many state-owned museums have one day a week (often Sun) when they're free or half-price. **Cathedrals** are almost always open all day every day, with charges only for the crypt,

Public holidays

There are thirteen **national holidays** (*jours fériés*), when most shops and businesses (though not necessarily restaurants), and some museums, are closed. May in particular is a big month for holidays: as well as May Day and Victory Day, Ascension Day normally falls then, as sometimes does Pentecost.

January 1 New Year's Day

Easter Sunday

Easter Monday

Ascension Day (forty days after Easter)

Pentecost or Whitsun (seventh Sunday after Easter, plus the Monday)

May 1 May Day/Labour Day

May 8 Victory in Europe Day

July 14 Bastille Day

August 15 Assumption of the Virgin Mary

November 1 All Saints' Day

November 11 1918 Armistice Day

December 25 Christmas Day

treasuries or cloister and little fuss about how you're dressed. **Church** opening hours are often more restricted; on Sunday mornings (or at other times which you'll see posted up on the door) you may have to attend Mass to take a look. In small towns and villages, however, getting the key is not difficult – ask anyone nearby or seek out the priest, whose house is known as the *presbytère*.

Phones

The easiest option – though by no means the cheapest – is to use a **mobile phone**. France operates on the **European GSM standard**, and mobiles bought in the UK, Australia and New Zealand should work here, though US cellphones won't unless they're tri-band. If you plan to make a lot of calls you might consider buying a French mobile (*portable*) using pre-paid charge-up cards (*mobicartes*); inexpensive deals are always on offer from one of the big companies. Mobile phone **reception** is generally good throughout Languedoc and Roussillon although in isolated mountain valleys coverage may be poor and in summer months relays can become saturated.

It's cheaper to make both domestic and international phone calls from a **telephone box** (*cabine*), most of which use **phone cards** (called *télécartes*), available in €5 and €10 increments from *tabacs*, newsagents,

post offices, tourist offices and some train station ticket offices. You can also use credit cards in many call boxes. **Coin-only boxes** still exist in cafés, bars, hotel foyers and rural areas; they take 10, 20 and 50 cents and €1 pieces; put the money in after lifting up the receiver and before dialling.

Local calls cost €0.30 for four minutes; long-distance calls within France cost up to €1.20 for three minutes depending on the distance. **Off-peak charges** apply on weekdays between 7pm and 8am and after noon on Saturday until 8am Monday.

For **calls within France** – local or long-distance – simply dial all ten digits of the number. **Numbers** beginning with ☎08.00 are free numbers; those beginning with ☎08.36 are premium rate (from €0.34 per minute), and those beginning with ☎06 are mobile and therefore also expensive to call.

For **international calls**, it's cheaper to buy one of the private companies' pre-paid phone cards (*carte à codes*) from *tabacs*, newsagents and post offices, which can be used with any public or private telephone: Tiscali's "L'Astuce Internationale" (🖳www .prepaye.tiscali.fr), for example, gives you roughly three and a half hours to the UK, USA or Canada for €15.

To make a **reverse charge** or collect call – known in French as *téléphoner en PCV* ("pay-say-vey") – contact the international operator (see box below). For an English-speaking operator call ☎08.00.89.00.33 (in the UK) or ☎00.00.11 (in North America).

Swimming pools

Swimming pools (*piscines*) are well signposted in most French towns and reasonably priced, usually around €2.50–4 for a swim. Tourist offices have their addresses. You may be required to wear a bathing cap, whether you are male or female, so come prepared. Another common requirement is that all bathers wear lycra-style ("Speedo-type") bathing apparel only, with no "boxer"-style trunks or women's wear with flaps or panels allowed.

Time

France is **one hour ahead** of the UK, six hours ahead of Eastern Standard Time, and nine hours ahead of Pacific Standard Time. This also applies during daylight savings seasons, which are observed in France (as in most of Europe) from the end of March through to the end of October.

Toilets

Ask for *les toilettes* or look for signs for the WC (pronounced "vay say"); when reading the details of facilities outside hotels, don't confuse *lavabo*, which means wash basin, with lavatory. Usually found downstairs along with the phone, French **toilets** in bars are still often of the hole-in-the-ground squatting variety, and tend to lack toilet paper. Standards of cleanliness are often not high, and men shouldn't expect much privacy in the urinal, which often won't have a door. Both bar and restaurant toilets are usually free, as are toilets in museums, though toilets in railway stations and depart-ment stores are commonly staffed by attendants who will expect a bit of spare change. Some have coin-operated locks, so always keep change handy for these and for the frequent Tardis-like public toilets found on the streets. These beige-coloured boxes have automatic doors which open when you insert coins and are cleaned automatically once you exit. Children under 10 aren't allowed in on their own.

Useful numbers within Languedoc and Roussillon

Weather ☎08.36.68.02 + the number of the department: Ariège, 09; Aude, 11; Haute Garonne, 31; Hérault, 34; Pyrénées-Orientales, 66; Tarn, 81.
Traffic and road conditions ☎08.36.68.20.00.
Telegrams by phone Internal ☎36.55; external ☎08.00.33.44.11 – all languages.
Time ☎36.99.
International operator For Canada and the US ☎00-33-11; for all other countries ☎00-33 followed by the country code.
International directory assistance For Canada and the US ☎00-33-12-11; for all other countries ☎00-33-12 followed by the country code.
French operator ☎13 to signal a fault.
French directory assistance ☎12.

Calling France from overseas
International access code + 33 + ten-digit number (minus the initial 0).

Calling overseas from France
Note that the initial zero is omitted from the area code when dialling the UK, Ireland, Australia and New Zealand from abroad.
US and Canada 00 + 1 + area code.
Australia 00 + 61 + area code.
New Zealand 00 + 64 + area code.
UK 00 + 44 + area code.
Republic of Ireland 00 + 353 + area code.

Tourist information

Practically every town and many villages in Languedoc and Roussillon have a tourist office – usually an **Office du Tourisme (OT)** but sometimes a **Syndicat d'Initiative (SI)**. For the practical purposes of visitors, there is little difference between them: SIs have wider responsibilities for encouraging business, while Offices du Tourisme deal exclusively with tourism; sometimes they share premises and call themselves an OTSI. In small villages where there is no OT or SI, the *mairie* (mayoral office), frequently located in the Hôtel de Ville (town hall), will offer a similar service.

From all these offices you can get specific local information, including listings of hotels and restaurants, leisure activities, car and bike rental, bus timetables, laundries and countless other things; many can also book accommodation for you. Most offices can provide a free town plan (though some places charge a nominal €0.75–1.50), and will have maps and local walking guides on sale. In mountain regions they display daily meteorological information and often share premises with the local hiking and climbing organizations. In the larger cities you can usually also pick up free *What's On* guides.

Regional and departmental tourist offices

Comité Départemental du Tourisme Ariège-Pyrénées 31bis av de Général-de-Gaulle, BP 143, 09004 Foix ☎04.61.02.30.70, ⓦwww.ariegepyrenees.com.
Comité Départemental du Tourisme Aude Conseil Général, 11855 Carcassonne ☎04.68.11.66.00, ⓦwww.audetourisme.com.
Comité Départemental du Tourisme Gard 3 pl des Arènes, 30010 Nîmes ☎04.66.36.96.30, ⓦwww.tourismegard.com.
Comité Départemental du Tourisme Haute-Garonne 14 rue Bayard, BP 845, 31015 Toulouse ☎05.61.99.44.00, ⓦwww.tourisme-haute-garonne.com.
Départemental du Tourisme Hérault en Languedoc Maison du Tourisme, av des Moulins, BP 3067, 34043 Montpellier ☎04.67.67.71.71, ⓦwww.herault-tourisme.com.
Comité Régional du Tourisme Languedoc-Roussillon 20 rue de la République, 34000 Montpellier ☎04.67.22.81.00, ⓦwww.cr-languedocroussillon.fr.

Comité Régional du Tourisme du Midi-Pyrénées 54 bd de l'Embouchure, BP 2166, 31022 Toulouse ☎05.61.13.55.55, ⓦwww.tourisme-midi-pyrenees.com.
Comité Départemental du Tourisme Pyrénées-Orientales 16 av des Palmiers, 66005 Perpignan ☎04.68.51.52.53, ⓦwww.cdt-66.com.
Comité Départemental du Tourisme Tarn BP 225, 81006 Albi ☎05.63.77.32.10, ⓦwww.tourisme-tarn.com.

Websites

Tourism and recreation

ⓦ **www.cr-languedocroussillon.fr** Languedoc-Roussillon's official website, with links to activities, accommodation, gastronomy and culture. One of the best starting points, but limited to the boundaries of the modern administrative *région*.
ⓦ **www.europe-today.com/france** English-language master-site for outdoor activities in Languedoc and Roussillon. Features contact details for a variety of sports and pursuits, from canyoning to parachuting.
ⓦ **www.little-france.com** Roussillonais weekly webzine with information on culture, tourism, art, politics and economy.
ⓦ **www.monuments-france.fr** Information on over two hundred national monuments and museums – many in Languedoc and Roussillon – including news on special events.
ⓦ **www.pagesjaunes.fr** The complete French *Yellow Pages*, unbeatable for hunting down goods and services.
ⓦ **www.pyrenees-online.fr** The homepage of Pyrénées-Online, with information on accommodation, sights, recreational activities and regional specialities.
ⓦ **www.tourist-office.org** Useful database of France's municipal and local tourist offices arranged by *région and département*. Town listings have practical and cultural information and links to local websites.
ⓦ **www.viamichelin.com** The Euro-version of MapQuest allows you to map out detailed point-to-point driving itineraries around France and Europe, and gives you complete trip information and driving directions, free.

News and information

ⓦ **www.france2.fr** France TV 2's daily web page has the latest on news, weather and road conditions, as well as listings and reviews of cultural events. Also has a youth section.
ⓦ **www.francedaily.com** English-language web newspaper covering French, European and world news.
ⓦ **www.gksoft.com/govt** Gateway to English-language listings of all French government websites, including embassies, departmental

and regional tourist boards, political parties, municipalities and media.

ⓦ**www.lemonde.fr** The French-language version of one of France's most reputable daily newspapers. Includes national and international news, culture and sports.

ⓦ**www.midilibre.fr** French-language newspaper for Languedoc and Roussillon; good travel features, including ski information.

ⓦ**www.radio-france.fr** Radio France's official page has national and international news coverage, current affairs, as well as music, culture and the latest in French sports. French language only.

Arts and culture

ⓦ**www.bpi.fr** Home page of the Bibliothèque Pompidou, with good links to media and a very comprehensive list of arts and humanities pages for France.

ⓦ**www.cathares.org** Everything you ever wanted to know about the Cathars. A French-only site featuring information on culture, history and historical sites, as well as regular updates on related events and exhibitions.

ⓦ**web.culture.fr** French Ministry of Culture's page, with information on everything from monuments to exhibitions and also comprehensive links to organizations related to the whole gamut of artistic media.

ⓦ**www.ladanse.com** Multilingual site with comprehensive information on French and international dance including news, links, and a database of artists and companies.

ⓦ**www.occitanet.free.fr** A French-only site dedicated to the cuisine of Languedoc, and featuring weekly recipes, information regarding food-oriented events and festivals, and links to other culinary sites.

Travellers with disabilities

For people in wheelchairs, the haphazard parking habits of the French and stepped village streets can be serious obstacles, while public toilets with **disabled access** are rare. In the major cities and coastal resorts, however, ramps or other forms of access are gradually being added to hotels, museums and some theatres and concert halls: look out for the label National Tourisme Handicap (an APF initiative) affixed to disabled-friendly services and businesses.

Public transport is certainly not wheelchair-friendly, and although many train stations now have ramps for wheelchair-users to board and descend from carriages, at others it is still up to the guards to carry the chair. The high-speed TGVs (including Eurostar) have places for wheelchairs in the first-class carriage, which you must book in advance, though no higher fee is charged; on other trains, a wheelchair symbol on the timetable denotes whether that service offers special features, and you and your companion will again be upgraded to first class with no extra charge. The *Guide du Voyageur à Mobilité Réduite*, available free at main train stations, details all facilities. **Taxis** are obliged by law to carry you and to help you into the chair, also to carry guide dogs. Specialist taxi services are available in some towns: these are detailed in the *Guide des Transports à l'Usage des Personnes à Mobilité Réduite*, available at airports, main train stations and some tourist offices.

Contacts for travellers with disabilities

APF (Association des Paralysés de France) Head office, 17 bd Auguste-Blanqui, 75013 Paris ☎01.40.78.69.00; 116 bis, rue des Amidonniers, Toulouse ☎05.62.30.64.00; 1620 rue St Priest, Parc Euromédecine, 34097 Montpellier ☎04.67.10.03.25; ⓦwww.apf.asso.fr. National organization providing reliable information and lists of accessible accommodation. Their guide *Où Ferons-Nous Étape* is available at the office or by post to a French address.

CNRH (Comité National Français de Liaison pour la Réadaptation des Handicapés) 236 bis rue de Tolbiac, 75013 Paris ☎01.53.80.66.66; 91 rue de Fenouillet, 31200 Toulouse ☎05.61.13.48.00. Information service that publishes various useful guides, including *Touristes Quand Même!*, which lists facilities throughout France, though it's not updated regularly.

Fédération Française Handisport ☎01.40.31.45.00, ⓦwww.handisport.org. Provides information on sports and leisure facilities for people with disabilities.

Guide

Guide

1

Toulouse and around

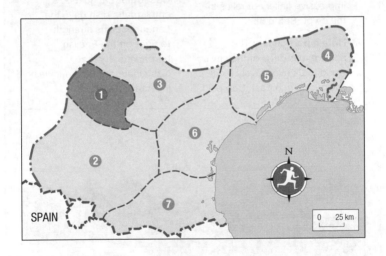

CHAPTER 1

Highlights

✳ **Place du Capitole** The square at the centre of Toulouse has been the heart of the city for eight hundred years; a bustling weekend market place, it is ideal for people-watching. **See p.67**

✳ **St-Sernin Basilica** Romanesque Toulouse's finest monument has been a stopping point for tourists and travellers since the twelfth century, as testified by the impressive gallery of relics in the crypt. **See p.68**

✳ **Hôtels particuliers** The ancient mansions of the city's woad lords evocatively recall Toulouse's rich past. **See p.71**

✳ **Les Abattoirs** This converted slaughterhouse is home to a world-class contemporary and modern art museum, the best in Southwest France. **See p.73**

✳ **La Montagne Noire** The western arm of the massif is a France time has left behind, where half-forgotten villages punctuate verdant hills. **See p.85**

✳ **Cassoulet** Languedoc's emblematic dish gave the Languedocians strength to fight off the English barbarians; try it at Castelnaudary, where it was invented. **See p.85**

▲ Place du Capitole, Toulouse

Toulouse and around

M idway between the cool shores of the Atlantic and the sun-baked Mediterranean coast, **Toulouse** and its surrounding area form the gateway to Languedoc. The city itself is a dynamo, undoubtedly the liveliest and most interesting on the west side of the Rhône; in addition to several notable museums, including the Musée des Augustins and Les Abattoirs, it has a vibrant cultural life and café and art scene and its medieval streets make for some of the most satisfying strolling in the south of France.

Among the gently undulating wheat fields of the **Lauragais** region, heartland of Toulouse's traditional agricultural prosperity, are little-known but colourful medieval towns like **Lavaur** and **Revel**. Scattered between these is an array of villages and castles whose ancient stones have witnessed both the success of the region's famous dye trade, and the violence and terror of Crusades and Wars of Religion. South of Revel is **Castelnaudary**, birthplace of the celebrated Langue-docian staple, cassoulet, and the largest town in Toulouse's environs; it not only contains a number of unique historical buildings, but is also the main inland port of the **Canal du Midi**, an engineering marvel which stretches from Toulouse to the sea and is one of the emblems of the Southwest.

Toulouse is a major rail centre, with regular **trains** in all directions; these are complemented by SNCF and local buses, the former following several east–west routes across the Lauragais and the latter fanning out from Toulouse. Moving north to south across the area is more difficult, although the quiet roads make for good, if hilly, **biking**.

Toulouse

Although it falls into the modern administrative *région* of Midi-Pyrénées, **TOULOUSE** has a long tradition as the capital of Languedoc, while a solid indus-trial base, notably as the centre for French aeronautics, helps maintain it as the sixth-largest city in the nation. It's a lively, cheerful place, with a vibrant arts community and a distinct Mediterranean look – as the sun edges towards the horizon, the hallmark pink brick buildings soak up the soft light and glow with a muted luminescence (hence its traditional nickname, *La Ville Rose*). The city has much to offer: aside from fine medieval churches and mansions, and first-rate galleries, there's an almost constant succession of **festivals** (see box, p.61); in addition, it's the most cosmopolitan city in the Southwest, with a vigorous nightlife fuelled by the massive student population of its famous university, and a range of immigrant cultures reflected in a variety of restaurants.

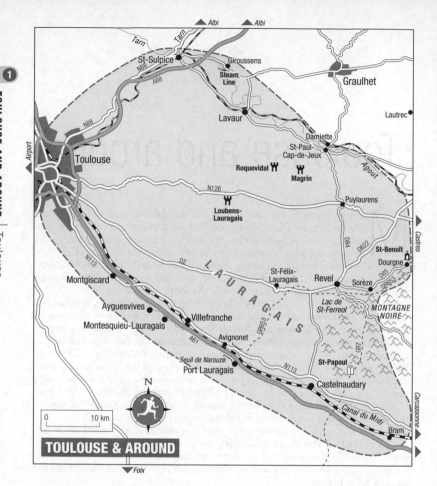

It's hard not to enjoy Toulouse, whether you are sitting in one of its multitude of outdoor cafés, strolling through its ancient streets or taking in some of the best museums west of the Rhône. A stay here is the easiest way to introduce yourself to southwest France, and you could easily spend a week exploring. If you're short of time, the two sights that should not be missed are the Romanesque **Basilique de St-Sernin** and the modern art gallery, **Les Abattoirs**.

Some history

Originally located a bit further upstream on the Garonne from the present city centre, Toulouse (then called Tolosa) was moved to the plain it currently occupies when the Romans took it over in 120 BC. Ruled after the decline of the Empire by Visigoths and Franks in turn, the town stagnated until the eleventh century, when the local **counts** (who were almost without exception named Raymond) began to encourage the nascent carpentry and leather industries. A century later a city council, or **Capitolo**, was set up to handle administration and justice and the wealthiest townsfolk – merchants and landholders – served as its members (the *capitouls*); the resulting convergence between their economic interests and political power allowed the city to flourish.

Festivals in and around Toulouse

Toulouse and the surrounding area aren't the best places to look for folk or traditional festivals – for these you're better off heading for the uplands of Languedoc or the Pyrenees to the south. Toulouse's strength is the arts – its splendid galleries and museums are complemented by a series of **music**, **dance** and **art festivals** that bring in top-notch names from around the world. Where we haven't given contact details, enquire at the tourist office (see p.64).

Mid-Jan to mid-Feb Toulouse: *C'est la Danse Contemporaine* ☎05.61.59.98.78, ⓦ www.cdctoulouse.com. A month-long programme of innovative contemporary dance featuring choreographers and ensembles from around Europe.

Late Feb to mid-March Toulouse: *¡mira!* ☎05.61.62.80.72, ⓦ www.toulouse .cervantes.es. An exciting programme of Spanish and Portuguese music, dance and other cultural events held at the TNT and other venues.

First or second Sat in Feb Toulouse: *Fête de la Violette* (International Violet Meeting). The city's massive violet market features exhibitions relating to flower production, as well as a market and events.

Late March Toulouse: *Festival Flamenco* ☎05.62.25.81.21. A new addition to the city's cultural calendar, featuring live performances, exhibitions and film.

Late June Toulouse: *¡Río loco!* ☎05.61.32.77.28, ⓦ www.rio-loco.org. An annual international festival featuring dance, music, film and a variety of events. Each year focuses on a different country; recent selections have included Senegal and Morocco.

Late June and early July Toulouse: *Les Siestes Électroniques* ☎05.61.23.80.57, ⓦ www.les-siestes-electroniques.com. A celebration of electronic and ambient music, featuring performers from around the world. Free afternoon concerts (Sat & Sun 4pm) are held in the Jardin Raymond VI, behind Les Abattoirs on the left bank of the Garonne.

Mid-July and early Aug Toulouse: *Toulouse d'Été* ☎05.62.27.60.71, ⓦ www .toulousedete.org. Eclectic programme of concerts held in the Couvent des Jacobins, Notre-Dame-de-la-Daurade and Zénith on Tuesday and Thursday nights, featuring a diversity of styles – from classical, to gospel and flamenco.

Throughout Sept Toulouse: *Piano aux Jacobins* ☎05.61.22.40.05, ⓦ www .pianojacobins.com. Nightly recitals in the cloister of the Jacobins by pianists from around the world. For programme details, contact the Piano aux Jacobins, 61 rue de la Pomme, 31000 Toulouse.

One weekend in Sept Toulouse: *Estrambord Garones* ☎05.61.29.80.01. Traditional Occitan water-jousting (see p.233) matches are held on the Garonne, amidst a lively street-festival.

Late Sept to early Oct Toulouse: *Festival Occitania* ☎05.61.11.24.87, ⓦ www .festivaloccitania.com. A week-long festival of Occitan and Mediterranean culture, featuring music, food, arts and crafts.

Late Sept to mid-Oct Toulouse: *Le Printemps de Septembre* ☎01.43.38.00.11, ⓦ www.printempsdeseptembre.org. A three-week-long visual arts festival, in which artists invited from around Europe use the city as their canvas.

End Oct Toulouse: *Jazz sur Son 31* ☎05.24.45.05.92, ⓦ www.jazz31.com. The world-class festival of the Haute Garonne attracts the biggest and best names in jazz, blues and salsa. Past performers include Miles Davis, Campay Segundo and Carlos Santana. Programme available early September.

Second week in Nov Toulouse: *Salon des Antiquaires* ☎05.61.21.93.25, ⓦ www .salon-antiquaires-toulouse.com. Internationally renowned antiques fair, featuring 300 pre-selected antiques dealers from around Europe. Held at the Parc des Expositions.

Meanwhile, the counts – for all intents and purposes independent sovereigns – began to extend their influence over the other major families of the south, including the Trencavels (see p.98). By the late twelfth century they effectively controlled all of Languedoc, and adopted the surname of "St-Gilles", in honour of one of their favourite fiefs. Both the counts and the city prospered until the reign of Raymond VI, by which time Cathar beliefs, considered heretical by the Church, had taken firm root in the region (see *The Land of the Cathars* colour section). Raymond may or may not have been a Cathar himself, but was content to let his subjects choose their religious beliefs, thus provoking the ire of the papacy and providing the northern French aristocracy with a justification for war against him. When their knights stormed into Languedoc on a campaign of religious and political conquest – the **Albigensian Crusade** – Toulouse fell to forces led by the cruel Simon de Montfort. With the help of Catalan allies, Raymond recovered it in 1217, but it fell under the power of the French Crown in 1271. One of the consequences of the Catholic takeover early in the thirteenth century was the foundation of Toulouse's **university**, which thanks to the Dominican Order became the most important theological centre in France after Paris. Despite suffering grievously from a series of plagues, the city prospered with the booming woad **dye** industry in the 1400s (see box, p.81), and in the sixteenth century it became the official capital of Languedoc, although it later suffered – along with the whole of the South – as a result of the Wars of Religion, and as a consequence of the failed **revolt** against Cardinal Richelieu led by Henri de Montmorency (1595–1632), Governor of Languedoc. The Revolution of 1789, which the city fervently supported, heralded a new age of affluence as industry recovered and the Canal du Midi provided better market access for the agricultural hinterland. The good times were interrupted only by the Napoleonic Wars, during which the English general, Wellington, pursued the retreating Soult to the city in 1814; the French field marshal broke through the near encirclement, dealing the English a minor defeat before escaping towards the Montagne Noire.

Occupied by the Germans during World War II when it was an important centre of the Resistance, Toulouse passed through the war more or less unscathed, and today the city is best known for its thriving aerospace industry. It is home to Airbus Industries, where the successful A340 and A440 crafts, the first "fly-by-wire" (entirely electronically-controlled) planes are assembled, and where the A380, a daringly designed two-level super-liner, was launched. In recent times Toulouse was hit by the riots which spread across France in late 2005 in which young French of North African origin reacted against their marginalization. On a brighter note, since 1985 the city's violet cultivation industry – once a major concern, but dormant for nearly a century – was revived thanks to "test tube" technology. The annual flower fair (see box, p.61) is once again a major event.

Arrival, information and getting around

Toulouse's **airport** (℡05.34.61.80.00, ⓦ www.toulouse.aeroport.fr) is 6km northwest of the centre in the suburb of Blagnac. It has better services than many

Getting from the airport to the centre

A **shuttle bus** runs from Toulouse's airport to the centre (5am–8.20pm every 20min, returning 7.35–12.15am). The journey takes approximately twenty minutes, and you can buy your ticket directly from the driver (€4 one-way, €6 return). The bus makes various stops in town, including the Compan-Caffarelli, place Jeanne d'Arc (near St-Sernin), place Jean-Jaurès (near place Wilson) and the *gare routière*. A **taxi** (℡05.61.30.02.54) to or from the centre will cost around €25.

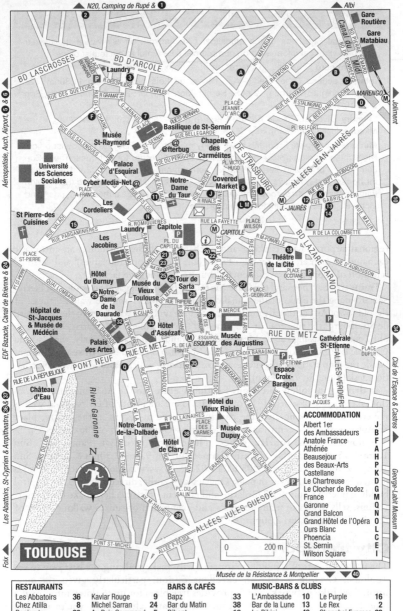

TOULOUSE

0   200 m

ACCOMMODATION

Albert 1er	J
des Ambassadeurs	B
Anatole France	F
Athénée	A
Beausejour	H
des Beaux-Arts	P
Castellane	K
Le Chartreuse	D
Le Clocher de Rodez	G
France	M
Garonne	Q
Grand Balcon	N
Grand Hôtel de l'Opéra	O
Ours Blanc	L
Phoencia	C
St. Sernin	E
Wilson Square	I

RESTAURANTS

Les Abbatoirs	36	Kaviar Rouge	9
Chez Atilla	8	Michel Sarran	24
Benjamin	23	Au Pois Gourmand	5
Le Chateaubriand	15	Saveurs Bio	18
Le Colombier	4	Le Sept Place	
La Côté de Doeuf	25	St-Sernin	7
Chez Émile	27	La Table de la	
Faim des Haricots	28	Bascule	39
Le Genty Magre	30	Le Ver Luisant	17
Les Jardins			
de l'Opéra	0		

BARS & CAFÉS

Bapz	33		
Bar du Matin	38		
Bibent	19		
Le Café des Artistes	29		
Le Donjon	20		
Le Florida	21		
The Frog and Rosbif	14		
Jour de Fête	11		
Au Père Louis	31		
St-Philipe	3		
Le Sherpa	11		

MUSIC-BARS & CLUBS

L'Ambassade	10	Le Purple	16
Bar de la Lune	13	Le Rex	2
Le Bikini	40	Shanghai Express	22
Bodega-Bodega	12	L'Ubu	26
Café Classico	35		
Le Cri de la			
Mouette	6		
Erich Coffie	37		
La Luna Loca	1		
Le Petit Voisin	32		
Puerto Habana	34		

Essentials

Bike rental Subscribe to the municipal bike network on Ⓦwww.velo.toulouse.fr (see below), or get information on commercial bike rental at the tourist office.

Discount card "Toulouse en liberté" card; see box opposite.

Internet access Cyber Media-Net, 19 rue de Lois (Mon–Fri 9am–11.30pm, Sat 10am–midnight); @fterbug, 12 pl St-Sernin (Mon–Fri noon–2am, Sat noon–5am, Sun 2.30–10.30pm).

Laundry Lavomat, 20 rue Arnaud-Bernard (daily 7am–10pm); Lavaria Auto, 7 rue Mirepoix (daily 7am–9pm).

Markets A complete list of the city's many markets is available at the tourist office. Highlights include: pl St-Sernin and allées Jules-Guesde, for **antiques** (Thurs–Sun 8am–4pm); pl Arnaud-Bernard (Thurs morning) and pl St-Étienne (Sat 10am–5pm) for **books**; pl du Capitole (Wed & Sun 8am–1pm) and bd de Strasbourg (Sun & Mon 8am–1pm) for **clothes**, **food** and general items; and pl des Carmes, St-Cyprien and Victor-Hugo (all Tues–Sun) for fresh **produce**.

regional airports, with banking and exchange facilities, including an automatic exchange dispenser, car rental offices (all the major companies) and a small selection of shops and travel agencies, but no left-luggage facility.

Trains arrive at the grand old **Gare Matabiau** (no left luggage) on boulevard Pierre-Sémard along the banks of the Canal du Midi – a twenty-minute walk northeast of the old town. Any of the city buses that stop here will take you down to the boulevard de Strasbourg (the ring road around the old town), while bus #2 carries on through old Toulouse, passing rue de Metz and the Grand Rond; alternatively, the place du Capitole is just two stops away from Gare Matabiau on the métro. **Buses** pull in right beside the train station at the modern **gare routière**, which has an excellent information desk (Mon–Sat 7am–8pm).

If **driving** in, follow directions for the "Centre" to the A61 ring road – from this take any one of exits 14–17 or 21–30. There are plenty of car parks, as well as metered street parking and free parking in place St-Sernin in the centre, place St-Auban east of the centre and les allées Jules-Guesde south of the centre.

Toulouse's main **tourist office** (June–Sept Mon–Sat 9am–7pm, Sun 10am–5.15pm; Oct–May Mon–Fri 9am–6pm, Sat 9am–12.30pm & 2–6pm, Sun 10am–12.30pm & 2–5pm; ℡05.61.11.02.22, Ⓦwww.toulouse-tourisme.com) is housed in a restored tower in place Charles-de-Gaulle, directly behind the Capitol building (métro Capitole). This large and efficient office can help make hotel reservations, sells tickets to many festivals and events and organizes walking tours of the city (in English, Fri 2.30pm; €7.50).

City transport

The narrow streets of the old town necessarily make **walking** the best way to see Toulouse. **Cycling** is also an excellent option, particularly given the new **municipal bike network**, which provides free bikes for up to thirty minutes at a time from over two hundred automated stations, after which you're charged approximately €2 per hour. Subscribe for €1 per day or €5 per week at Ⓦwww .velo.toulouse.fr, and pick up a map of cycle paths, sightseeing routes and details on commercial bike rental at the tourist office.

Both **métro** and **buses** – which you're only likely to use when travelling from the bus or train station to the hotel districts, or to visit outlying sights like the Cité de l'Espace – are operated by the urban transport agency Tisseo-Connex

(☎05.61.41.70.70, ⓦwww.tisseo-connex.com), whose **information** office is at 7 pl Esquirol (métro Esquirol). **Tickets**, available from métro stations, tobacconists and bus drivers, cost €1.40 (one-way), €2.50 (return), and €4.20 (*ticket tribu*, good for up to six persons). The métro and buses run till about 10pm, with a nightbus network, operating from the gare SNCF, continuing until 1am. You can pick up a transport **map** from the tourist office or any métro station.

If you're short of time, **tourist taxis** offer 75-minute (€45) and two-hour (€60) itineraries: call Capitole Taxi (☎05.34.25.02.50), Taxi Radio Toulousain (☎05.61.42.38.38) or La Tolousaine (☎05.61.20.90.00).

Accommodation

There's no shortage of **hotels** of every bracket of price and comfort. The cluster of establishments around the station are good value but the zone is rather nondescript and far from the centre. Closer in, there are cheap options around place de Belfort, which is also a sort of red-light district. In the old town, the hotels around place Victor Hugo (just up from the Capitole and pl Wilson) are an easy bet, with a wide selection of two-star options in the ❸ bracket. Rooms in the city and the surrounding area can also be booked through a **free reservation service** (☎08.92.70.02.97, ⓦwww.reserv-hotels .fr). For **discounts** and deals use the "Toulouse en liberté" discount card (see below), or check out the "short breaks" and "weekends" packages on the tourist office website. The only **campsite** close enough to be of use is the well-equipped *Camping de Rupé*, just a few kilometres north of the centre on chemin du Pont du Rupé (☎05.61.70.07.35, ⓔcampinglerupe31@orange.fr; bus #59 from pl Jeanne-d'Arc to "Rupé").

Budget hotels

des Ambassadeurs 68 rue Bayard ☎05.61.62.65.84, ⓦwww.hotel-des -ambassadeurs.com. Very friendly little hotel run by a young couple, just down from the station. Its rooms all have wi-fi, cable TV, en-suite bath and phone – a surprisingly good deal given the price. Family rooms and parking are available. ❸

Anatole France 46 pl Anatole-France ☎05.61.23.19.96, ⓦwww.hotel-anatolefrance .com. Another excellent bargain, the *Anatole-France* boasts wi-fi, a TV and WC in each room, and is located in a quiet section of the old city. ❷

Beauséjour 4 rue Caffarelli ☎05.61.62.77.59, ⓔhotel.beausejour@hotmail.fr. Basic, but dirt cheap and with a great copper-balconied facade and sound-proofed rooms. This is the best of the hotels in this slightly dodgy but engagingly gritty neighbourhood around place de Belfort. ❷

Le Chartreuse 4 bis bd Bonrepos ☎05.61.62.93.39, ⓦwww.chartreusehotel.com. Efficiently modern choice, right by the station, with a cute little interior patio. Great amenities: each room has wi-fi, private shower, toilet and TV. ❷

Mid-priced hotels

Albert 1er 8 rue Rivals ☎05.61.21.17.91, ⓦwww.hotel-albert1.com. Set in a quiet side-street just off the Capitole and close to the central market in place Victor-Hugo. A small, comfortable and good-value establishment, with wi-fi, foreign

---

Toulouse en liberté card and "Toulouse Festivals"

The "en Liberté" **discount card** (€10 adult, €25 family of four) gives ten percent discount in many shops, fifty percent off museum tickets, and a thirty to sixty percent discount on many hotels (indicated on the tourist office website). "Toulouse Festivals" is a package offered by the tourist office timed for the city's major events; it includes one to four nights of accommodation and breakfast, events tickets and an "en Liberté" card. Prices vary with length of stay and category of hotel. Both can be ordered online in advance.

cable TV and a/c. Special weekend deals are sometimes available. ➍

Athénée 13 bis rue de Matabiau ☎05.61.63.10.63, ⓦwww.athenee-hotel.com. This well-renovated hotel offers all mod cons, including TV, garage parking and a cocktail bar, amid a carefully chosen contemporary decor. Quiet, despite its location between the station and the old town. Wheelchair-accessible. ➏

Castellane 17 rue Castellane ☎05.61.62.18.82, ⓦwww.castellanehotel.com. A cheerful hotel with a wide selection of room types and sizes, most of which are bright and quiet. All rooms have a/c and wi-fi, and breakfast is free for under-12s. Rooms for up to six people are available. It is wheelchair-accessible, and has parking. ➎

🏃 **Le Clocher de Rodez** 14 pl de Jeanne-d'Arc ☎05.61.62.42.92, ⓦwww.hotel-clocher-toulouse.com. Comfortable and central, with secure parking and a solid range of amenities. Most rooms have a/c and wi-fi (ask), and the breakfast is excellent. Despite its size, it exudes a very personal hospitality. Wheelchair-accessible. ➎

France 5 rue d'Austerlitz ☎05.61.21.88.24, ⓦwww.hotel-france-toulouse.com. Excellent value-for-price option in the rue d'Austerlitz/place Wilson area. Clean and functional, if nondescript, rooms with wi-fi, cable TV and a/c. ➍

Ours Blanc Victor Hugo 25 pl Victor-Hugo ☎05.61.21.62.40, ⓦwww.hotel-ours-blanc.fr. Right by the covered market and steps from the Capitole, this welcoming hotel is a good deal, although room quality varies. The entire building has been renovated and each room has wi-fi, TV, a/c, telephone and a private bath. The owners run two other similar-standard hotels nearby, the *Ours Blanc Centre*, 2 rue Porte Sardane, and the *Ours Blanc Wilson*, 2 rue Victor Hugo. ➎

Phoenicia 7 bd Bonrepos ☎05.61.63.81.63, ⓦwww.hotel-phoenicia-toulouse.com. Weird retro decor but good service and facilities in this three-star place near the station. The staff are friendly, and it has a small cocktail bar on the main floor. Free wi-fi. ➎

St-Sernin 2 rue St-Bernard ☎05.61.21.73.08, ⓦwww.hotelstsernin.com. Well-renovated old hotel in one of the best districts of the old town, around the basilica – close to all the action, but far enough

away to provide peace in the evening. The decor is modern and coolly understated; amenities include wi-fi, a/c and flatscreen TV. ➎

Wilson Square 12 rue d'Austerlitz ☎05.61.21.67.57, ⓦwww.hotel-wilson.com. Clean and well-kept classic-style hotel at the top of rue d'Austerlitz, with internet, TV, a/c and a lift; steps from the airport *navette* stop. Also has a great *pâtisserie* on street level. ➍

Expensive hotels

des Beaux-Arts 1 pl du Pont Neuf ☎05.34.45.42.42, ⓦwww.hoteldesbeauxarts.com. Located in a 150-year-old building, this hotel's contemporary but refined interior contrasts well with its ageing facade, making for solid, old-world elegance. Each room is individually decorated, some have views of the Garonne, and all have wi-fi and satellite TV. Weekend discounts are available as is free use of city bikes. ➐

🏃 **Garonne** 22 descente de la Halle-aux-Poissons ☎05.34.31.94.80, ⓦwww.hotelgaronne.com. A chic little hotel tucked away down an alley near the Pont Neuf, with fourteen rooms of understated luxury looking out over the river and the old town. Warmly decorated rooms have DSL and flatscreen TV; check the website for excellent-value weekend and off-season specials. The most romantic of the city's hotels. ➒

Grand Balcon 8 rue Romiguières ☎05.61.21.48.08, ⓦwww.grandbalconhotel.com. Just off place du Capitole, this ageing classic was frequented by the aviation pioneers, such as "*Little Prince*" author St-Exupéry (see p.75). Recently re opened as an arty, luxury hotel, it provides the city's most modern and chic accommodation. Rooms come in five ranges from "cosy" to "suite", all with ultra modern decor and facilities. ➒

🏃 **Grand Hôtel de l'Opéra** 1 pl du Capitole ☎05.61.21.82.66, ⓦwww.grand-hotel-opera.com. The *grande dame* of the city's hotels presides over the place du Capitole in the guise of a seventeenth-century convent. The rich decor, peppered with antiques and artwork, underlines its sophisticated atmosphere. This is the city's deluxe option, with crisp, formal service of the finest Gallic style. Also has a fitness centre for working off that second helping of foie gras. ➒

The City

Toulouse's **old town**, straddling a curve in the River Garonne and hedged by a busy, roughly hexagon-shaped ring road (which marks the course of its former defensive walls), is where you'll find most of the city's points of interest. Its heart is the majestically broad **place du Capitole**, the town hall square near the northeastern edge, from which crooked streets radiate out, web-like, to a

Toulouse museums

The normal **entrance fee** for Toulouse's historical museums is €3, except for the first Sunday of each month, when they are free. You can also buy museum **passeports** for three or six visits (€6 and €9 respectively) to the following museums: the Augustins, the Musée St-Raymond, the Musée Paul-Dupuy, the Musée Georges-Labit and the Jacobins.

series of *places*. East from the place du Capitole is primarily a business district, where the city's offices, hotels and restaurants are concentrated. To the north, the area around the wonderful **Basilique de St-Sernin**, with the nearby archeological museum, forms the university quarter, while west of the Capitole towards the river lies the bulk of medieval Toulouse – major sights here include the Dominicans' **Les Jacobins** complex, plus a number of noteworthy churches such as St-Pierre-des-Cuisines and Notre-Dame-de-la-Daurade. It's also home to most of the city's majestic Renaissance-era **hôtels particuliers** (private mansions), some of which, like the magnificent **Hôtel d'Assézat**, are now open as museums; most, though, are simply worth seeing for their striking and varied facades. The city's shopping district, focused on rue d'Alsace-Lorraine and rue St-Rome, stretches south to intersect with rue de Metz, south of which again, after the **cathedral**, a further series of *places* leads down to the formal gardens, the **Grand Rond** and **Jardin des Plantes** at the southeast corner of the old town. Beyond this, you'll find the town's canal port and a couple of small museums. Across the Garonne to the west, the neighbourhood of **St-Cyprien** is of interest for its stunningly renovated, cutting-edge modern art gallery, **Les Abattoirs**, while the only reason to visit the **suburbs** is to see two modern exhibitions revolving around the city's aeronautical tradition.

Place du Capitole and place Wilson

Place du Capitole, the sweeping plaza containing Toulouse's historical seat of government, the **Capitole**, forms the administrative and civic hub of the city. Apart from when it fills up with market stalls on Wednesday and Sunday mornings, the *place* is host to a constant surge of pedestrian traffic – great for people-watching. Prettiest at sunset, when permeated by a pink glow reflected off the huge Capitole's brickwork, the square is best appreciated from one of the numerous cafés which line its western side – the perfect spot from which to contemplate the Neoclassical symmetry and elegance of the building's 130m-long facade. Deriving its name from the twelfth-century administration of the city (see p.60), the palace dates back to the sixteenth century, although the frontage you see today was raised in the mid-eighteenth. There's not much to see in the cavernous seventeenth-century **foyer** (Mon–Fri 9am–7pm, Sat & Sun 9am–5pm; free), aside from a gallery of paintings extolling the glories of France and celebrating the execution of revolt-leader Montmorency, which took place in the square. On the far side of the palace a small patch of green is presided over by Viollet-le-Duc's (see box, p.104) restored 1529 pseudo-medieval *donjon* – the only remnant of the original Capitole and now the tourist office.

East of here is the oblong **place Wilson**, which, edged by modern, expensive hotels, retains a certain grandeur. Directly north of place Wilson is the lively triangle of streets centred on the town's main **indoor market** (Tues–Sun 6am–noon) in place Victor-Hugo. The surrounding area is home to an array of cheap hotels and restaurants, as well as some great places to pick up regional culinary goodies – look out for the Ducs de Gascogne delicatessen at 1 rue des Remparts

Villeneuve, and the Chocolatier de Bayonne, next door. **Rue d'Alsace Lorraine**, the western boundary of the triangle, is Toulouse's principal shopping street, lined by stately nineteenth-century apartments whose magnificent facades, with their monumental doorways, elaborately carved cornices and wrought-iron balconies, exude *fin-de-siècle* elegance. Just west of the market the seventeenth-century **Chapelle des Carmélites** (Tues–Sun: May–Sept 9.30am–1pm & 2–6pm; Oct–April 10am–1pm & 2–5pm; free), once part of a sprawling Carmelite convent, is richly decorated with period murals.

North to the Basilique de St-Sernin and beyond

Leading north out of place du Capitole, rue de Taur is a street full of lively studenty cafés and shops, a reminder that Toulouse has long been a university city. Past the turreted **Notre-Dame du Taur** sprawls the sixteenth-century Palace d'Esquiral, now home to the city's main cinema and a meeting place for student literary groups.

A few steps from here is the **Basilique de St-Sernin** (July–Sept Mon–Sat 8.30am–6pm, Sun 8.30am–7.30pm; Oct–June Mon–Sat 8.30–11.45am & 2–5.45pm, Sun 8.30am–12.30pm & 2–7pm; free), which, with its wedding-cake bell tower – an emblem of Toulouse – is arguably southern France's greatest Romanesque church and the largest of its style in Western Europe. It was begun in 1080 to hold the remains of the city's first bishop, who was killed by the Romans in 250 AD – dragged to death by a bull (hence the name of the street). Later, the church was an important stop on the pilgrimage to Santiago de Compostela. Despite the fact that the present building was not completed until the fourteenth century, it has almost no Gothic elements: it's this stylistic purity combined with its sheer mass that makes it such a singular monument. The most striking feature of its exterior is the early twelfth-century **Miégeville door**, whose restrained but expressive biblical sculptures mark it as a product of the pivotal era in the evolution of medieval art. Inside, the uniform simplicity of the cavernous nave is impressive; the plain marble altar, still used today, was consecrated by Urban II in 1096. But the real attraction is the church's incredible collection of **reliquaries** (daily 10am–6pm; €2), which it amassed over the years under the patronage of kings and with the financial help of donations from Santiago-bound pilgrims. Body parts of all the major saints can be found here, reposing in carved and gilded boxes set into the walls and chapels of the ambulatory and stored in the crypt below the altar,

Zebda and the Toulouse scene

Toulouse has a deeply ingrained, grass-roots tradition of **social activism**, linked both to its university and its multicultural heritage. One especially visible (and audible) manifestation of this was the popular music group **Zebda**, founded in 1985 by local activist Magyd Cherfi and six other musicians of various ethnic backgrounds. The group's energetic combination of reggae, rai, rock and rap led to a string of hits (notably 1998's *Tomber la Chemise*), but members did not abandon their political goals, which focused largely on the marginalized inhabitants of France's *banlieues* (suburbs). The group saw political as well as musical success when a party they were associated with took twelve percent of the vote in the 2001 municipal elections. Although Zebda itself broke up two years later in 2003, its members' activism has continued: **Tactikollectif**, a music and dance group featuring former Zebda members, carries on the tradition today. Of course, Zebda and its successors represent only the most visible tip of the city's dynamic youth art and culture scene, which embraces art forms as diverse as graffiti and urban dance, as well as a thriving lesbian and gay culture.

including a spectacular bust of James the Greater, whose thirteenth-century painted effigy is decked out in pilgrim's garb.

On the other side of place St-Sernin, which is unfortunately used as a car park, is the **Musée St-Raymond** (daily 10am–6/7pm; €3), which holds the city's archeological finds. The best part of this collection is the prehistoric and Bronze Age section on the first floor, which includes an impressive range of pre-Roman jewellery, weapons and even chariot wheels. The Roman religious sculpture and third-century portraiture is also worth seeking out.

North from the *place*, up rue Gatien-Arnoult, there's a small but lively **African quarter**, populated by immigrants from the Maghreb, in particular, and the shops and restaurants of rue Trois Pilliers exude wafts of mint and parsley. Nearby streets meander through a series of quiet neighbourhood squares – des Tiercerettes, St-Julien and Peyrou – each of which has a couple of small café-restaurants.

Les Jacobins

The most colourful part of Toulouse's old town is found in the labyrinth of streets radiating west and south from the place du Capitole, and dominated by the former Dominican headquarters, known as **Les Jacobins** (daily 9am–7pm). Built in 1230, this was the first-ever permanent convent of St Dominic's Order of Preachers (the Dominicans), founded in the city in 1215 to combat the Cathar heresy. From its humble beginnings the order quickly grew in power, soon taking charge of the Church's Holy Inquisition and exercising, for a time, a near monopoly over the bishoprics and universities of the medieval West. This building is, in fact, Toulouse's original university, home of the theology faculty established by the Dominicans to strengthen Catholic orthodoxy. Its cavernous fourteenth-century **interior** (free) contains a single file of seven enormous supporting columns, from which a web of delicate interlacing ribs fan out across the vaulted ceiling. These ribs, still bearing their original painted pattern of red and black bands, contrast beautifully with the cream-coloured brick they support. In a modest gilt box under the grey marble altar in the centre of the nave rest the remains of **St Thomas Aquinas** (1225–74), the great Dominican philosopher who strove to introduce the thought of Aristotle – as interpreted by the Muslim philosopher Ibn Rushd – into Catholic theology. There's still a pilgrimage here on his feast day (Jan 28). Leaving the church, you enter a low Gothic **cloister** (€3), its stubby and unadorned columns as sober in style as the order that built it. In fact, the cloister isn't original, but the structures along its north side are, including the large **chapterhouse** and the fourteenth-century **chapel of St-Antonin**. The old **refectory**, also accessed from the cloister, now houses high-quality temporary art exhibitions of a decidedly secular character.

Place St-Pierre and west

Close by on the banks of the Garonne sits placid little **place St-Pierre**, home to a couple of small pubs and **St-Pierre-des-Cuisines** (June Mon 10am–1pm; Aug daily 10am–noon & 2–7pm; €2), an ancient church reputed to be the oldest ecclesiastical building in Southwest France. A substantial Gallo-Roman necropolis sits beneath it, accessed via the church's **crypt** (guided tours Mon 11am, Aug daily 4.30pm; €2.50).

Just west of the *place*, the languid **Canal de Brienne** angles away from the river through a nineteenth-century industrial area, where newly erected student apartment buildings abut old warehouses and cigarette factories. The River Garonne has been exploited for industrial purposes since grain mills were first set up here in the twelfth century. They became a symbol of the city's prosperity, which was at that time based on local wheat production, and achieved such renown that the sixteenth-century satirist Rabelais cited them as the most powerful in the world. In 1890 the **EDF Bazacle** (Wed–Mon 2–7pm, Thurs to 9pm; free), a generating plant that powers up Toulouse to this day, was built on the banks at the former site of the mills, about a ten-minute walk from St-Pierre. Here you can see both the modern and original turbines churning away, have a look at the cascading fish ladder, and take in the local and international art exhibits, displayed in the main foyer.

Place de la Daurade and around

Back upstream from the power plant, **place de la Daurade** makes a great spot to take a break and loll by the riverside – or better still, take one of the cruises that depart from here (see "Listings", p.79). Across the Garonne you can see Toulouse's medieval hospital, the Hôtel-Dieu St-Jacques, with the stub of the old bridge still poking out from its walls, while on the flood banks above the square you'll find the city's oddest church, **Notre-Dame-de-la-Daurade** (opening times vary), a curious compound of disparate architectural styles, disguising a church said to have originated as a pagan temple. Today, the centre of attraction is its *Vierge noire*, or **black Madonna** – a medieval polychrome sculpture of Christ (of the type produced throughout the area in the eleventh and twelfth centurires) seated on Mary's knee, showing Mary's skin tone as black, due to changes in pigment over time. Reputedly empowered to cure ailments and bring good fortune to the unborn child, it is still the object of popular pilgrimage, with many devotional plaques fixed around the entrance.

Also off the place de la Daurade is the sixteenth-century **Hôtel de Burnuy**, one of Toulouse's famed *hôtels particuliers* (see box, opposite), and once the home of Jean de Burnuy. The town's wealthiest woad merchant, de Burnuy was rich enough to literally afford a king's ransom, paying for Francis I's release from captivity at the hands of the Habsburgs in 1526. The palace's 1504 **facade** features an array of sculpted window-frames featuring delicate Gothic details, while its cherub-topped main entrance completes the strange stylistic mix. Stepping back from the building, you'll see its slender tower rising high above the street.

Hôtel d'Assézat

Between place de la Daurade and place du Capitole lies the woad merchants' neighbourhood, the site of the **Hôtel d'Assézat** – once home to the *jocs florals* (see p.356). This is Toulouse's most famous and possibly most luxurious *hôtel particulier*, home to a hugely successful Pierre d'Assézat; his wealth is evident in the predominance of stone over brick, which endows the building with a sense of majesty that many of the town's best mansions lack. It was built in 1555 in cutting-edge style – the weighty, columned facade anticipates the Neoclassicism that would soon dominate European architecture. Inside, the patio is no less splendid, with a magnificent covered porch and columns. Despite his riches, d'Assézat suffered a tragic fate: having taken up Protestantism, he was deprived of his fortune, and Catholic repression forced him into exile.

Today the building is home to an impressive art gallery, the **Foundation Bemberg** (Tues–Sun 10am–12.30pm & 1–6pm, Thurs until 9pm; €4.60; Ⓦwww .fondation-bemberg.fr). On the first floor up you'll pass through a collection of Renaissance furniture, reaching a gallery displaying fifteenth- and sixteenth-century Flemish art, dominated by portraiture. Works by Lucas Cranach the Elder, in particular *Venus and Cupid*, and his portrait of a young woman, stand out. Further along there's a collection of sixteenth-century decorative statuary, whose kinetic realism bears an odd but striking resemblance to early twentieth-century

Toulouse's hôtels particuliers

One of the hallmarks of Toulouse is its multitude of luxurious private mansions, or **hôtels particuliers**, scattered throughout the old town, and testament to the tremendous prosperity the town enjoyed in the fifteenth and sixteenth centuries when the *pastel* dye industry turned local merchants and bankers into veritable princes (see box, p.81). The earliest mansions have some sections of timber and daub, but the majority are constructed from local brick, which – ageing badly – detracts somewhat from their majesty. There is often, however, wonderful **masonry**; the mansions' splendour tends to reside in their stone doorways and window frames, embellished with carved figures, statues, coats of arms and floral designs. Stone was relatively expensive here, so more masonry was a sign of greater wealth; the most opulent

buildings have facades constructed entirely from stone. In later examples, you'll find Renaissance flourishes, and some of these "mature" *hôtels* have graceful **turrets**, built to reflect the status of the owner; only the chartered elite – those who were wealthy enough to serve as *capitouls* – could add a tower. By the late sixteenth century, however, declining *pastel* production precipitated the end of the woad lords, leaving their magnificent homes to fall into gradual decay. Today they serve a variety of functions, including apartments, offices, schools and museums.

Art Nouveau. Upstairs you'll find a worthy collection of more recent art, with the Impressionists and their successors well represented, among them Monet, Gauguin, Matisse and Bonnard, who has a whole roomful of works here, including *Still Life with Lemons*. On the museum's covered porch you can enjoy a coffee or light snack from the in-house café and soak up the atmosphere of the courtyard.

Along rue St-Rome

Pedestrianized **rue St-Rome** leads south from place du Capitole to some noteworthy buildings, including – just off the street on rue du May – the sixteenth-century **Hôtel du May**, built by a regent dean of the university's medical faculty, and now home to the rather basic **Musée du Vieux Toulouse** (mid-May to mid-Oct 2–6pm; €2.50). One of the town's least ornate *hôtels* – with only a simple door decoration to boast – it is proof that even then academics were underpaid. More elaborate is the old timber-and-brick mansion down adjacent rue Tripière, studded with stone decorations in the form of rabbits, while a little further south squats the three-storey **Tour de Sarta**, another former palace. **Rue des Changes**, the continuation of rue St-Rome, is evocatively lined by overhanging sixteenth-century homes. South of the modern rue Metz are more *hôtels*, including the Neoclassical **Hôtel de Clary** and the compact but beautiful fifteenth-century **Hôtel du Vieux Raisin.** Nearby, the old Hôtel Pierre-Bresson houses the **Musée Paul-Dupuy** (daily: June–Sept 10am–6pm; Oct May 10am–5pm; €3), an applied arts museum containing the knick-knacks collected by its nineteenth-century namesake. It is particularly worth visiting on the first Wednesday of the month at 3pm, when the ornate nineteenth-century Orientalist-themed automaton, "The Singing Lesson", is put in motion.

Towards the river, **place du Salin** opens up in front of the massive brick Palais de Justice, built on the site of Toulouse's medieval castle, and its predecessor, the Roman fort. On the adjacent place du Parlement, at no. 7, you'll find the house where St Dominic and his early disciples stayed when they arrived in Toulouse in 1215 to preach against Catharism.

The Musée des Augustins

Southeast of the place du Capitole, the former home of the city's powerful canons of the Augustinian Order now houses Toulouse's second-largest museum, the **Musée des Augustins** (daily 10am–6pm, Wed to 9pm; ⓦ www.augustins.org; €3), with an important collection of medieval sculpture. The quality of work here is superb and the building itself is well worth a look. An externally featureless fourteenth-century brick precinct, covering an area almost as big as the place du Capitole and dominated by a strikingly huge bell-tower, the monastery was founded in 1309 on the authority of Pope Clement V. The extensive southern French Gothic style cloister and large chapterhouse are original construction, while its smaller Neoclassical cloister dates from the seventeenth century. The refectory *looks* medieval, though this is, in fact, one of Viollet-le-Duc's (see p.104) dubious nineteenth-century reconstructions.

The museum's **collection** consists of two disparate sections: superb medieval sculpture and less remarkable eighteenth- and nineteenth-century paintings. The former is made up of high-quality stone carvings – a legacy of the city's twelfth-century counts. The complex was only restored to its original size in the last thirty years, and in the course of these works, more medieval treasures were discovered and added to the displays. The main floor houses pieces from around France, and as far afield as northern England. The star attraction here is the forest of Romanesque **columns** on the bottom floor of the refectory, found just off the cloister on the west side. Rescued from the ruins of the town's various churches, these were crafted by a school of Toulouse sculptors that thrived under the patronage of the counts in the first half of the twelfth century, their consummate skill evident in the impressively carved capitals. Moving through the refectory, you can follow the development of the Toulouse school of sculpture, as the elaborate vegetal forms of the 1120s to 1140s give way to busy narrative scenes in increasingly high relief as the century progresses and draws to a close. The latest examples are the most spectacular – wonderfully carved scenes centred around episodes such as the death of John the Baptist. From the refectory, a monumental staircase leads to the upper floor, which, along with the stifling third storey, contains a collection of less impressive **paintings**, amassed by city councillors of the post-Revolution period. On your way out, back on the ground floor, you'll walk past a series of grounded gargoyles set upright on the floor and apparently yawning, unimpressed by their surroundings.

The cathedral and around

East of the Musée des Augustins, rue de Metz brings you to the curious **Cathédrale St-Étienne** (Mon–Sat 8am–7pm, Sun 9am–7pm; free), which, despite holding ecclesiastical priority, has always played second fiddle to its rival St-Sernin. The discord between its average-sized brick entrance, which dates from the beginning of the thirteenth century, and the incongruously massive choir plonked on the back some seventy years later is obvious, and continues when, on entering, you discover that the huge ambulatory isn't even lined up squarely with the older church. The reason for this lack of harmony is that the cathedral was slated to be rebuilt on a much grander scale – the original nave demolished and a new one of the same proportions as the entrance added on – but money ran out, and the church was left as it is today. The **interior** of the cathedral holds few surprises, but is worth a quick look, if only for the Renaissance tapestries which line the walls of the nave, the sixteenth-century carved walnut choir, and the details of some of the chapels behind the main altar: there are several good **stained-glass windows**, going back as early as the fifteenth century, and some carved ceiling medallions date from the 1200s.

Adjacent place St-Étienne itself is surprisingly quiet, boasting little more than the city's oldest fountain – the Griffoul – dating from 1546. South from the cathedral you'll find a peaceful neighbourhood of old houses and narrow streets. There are fewer shops and restaurants here, although each of the small *places* – and there seems to be one at every intersection – has somewhere to sit and have a drink or bite to eat. Rue Perchepinte, the continuation of rue Nazareth, leads to the pretty place Ste-Scarbes, the centre of Toulouse's antique furniture trade.

St-Cyprien and Les Abattoirs

Across the river, the west bank of the Garonne is the site of the old neighbourhood of **St-Cyprien**, which, although enclosed within the medieval city's defensive walls, was always marginalized, owing to its location. Home to tanners and butchers, professionals banned from the main town for sanitary reasons, from the Middle Ages it was also the home of Toulouse's hospitals, where the sick were kept in semi-quarantine. Thus, on this side of the river, you won't find the grand mansions of *capitouls* and merchants.

You will, however, find the excellent **Les Abattoirs** (Tues–Sun 11am–7pm; €6, free first Sun of month; ⓦ www.lesabattoirs.org) on allées Charles-de-Fitte, the avenue which marks the precinct of the city's former western wall, just behind the great cupola dominating the river's left bank. This splendid venue, opened in 2000, is not only one of France's best contemporary art museums, but also an inspired piece of urban regeneration. The hulking brick complex was constructed in 1828, and functioned as an abattoir until 1989, when environmental concerns forced it to close. The space itself is massive, with huge chambers perfectly suited to display even the largest canvases. Comprising over two thousand works by 130 artists, the collection covers everything from painting to multimedia exhibits. Most European and American schools are well represented, with the major postwar French movements, including Support-Surface, Art Brut and Figuration Libre, plus Italian and Spanish works a particular strength. The most striking piece is undoubtedly **Picasso**'s massive 14m-by-20m theatre backdrop, *The Stripping of the Minotaur in the Harlequin Suit*, painted in 1936 for Romain Rolland's *Le 14 Juillet* and towering over the lower gallery. Other avant-garde works which stand out are the untitled canvases of **Tàpies** and **Barceló**, **Bettencourt**'s provocative mosaic *The Conversion of St Paul* and a large collection of **Dubuffet**'s paintings. More unusual exhibits include a sculpture made up of transparent pipes into which you drop coins, but the collection is so large and varied that, whatever your tastes, you're unlikely to come away disappointed. The complex also includes libraries and a resource centre, interactive terminals on which you can manipulate digital images and a fantastic children's play area. Behind the museum, the grassy Jardin Raymond IV stretches out towards the river, along an impressive section of the city's fourteenth-century **walls**.

South of this is the old **hospital of St-Jacques**. Modern hospitals grew out of the hospices which cared for pilgrims en route to the Holy Land or Santiago, and which eventually took over the care of sick people in general. Toulouse, being on the pilgrim route and the site of a major university, was a pioneer in medieval medicine. In the plague-ridden centuries preceding the Revolution, the most contagious patients arrived at the hospital directly by boat, so as not to infect the town. Today, these buildings house the administrative offices for Toulouse's centralized medical services, as well as two small **medical museums** (Thurs & Fri 1–5pm, first Sun of the month 10am–6pm; free) with collections of surgical instruments and pharmaceutical equipment. Finally, on the western side of the Pont Neuf which crosses over to the old town, you'll see the **Château d'Eau** (Tues–Sun 1–7pm; €2.5), a former pumphouse, now a small photographic museum holding very worthwhile monthly exhibitions.

The New Town and the Canal du Midi

If you have the time and energy, the areas south and east of the old town are also worth exploring. The southern district is marked off from old Toulouse by the wide allées Jules-Guesde, the southernmost stretch of the former walls and site of an **antiques market** from Thursday to Sunday. The town's main park, the formally styled **Jardin des Plantes** (daily 7.45am–dusk), can be entered through a large arch off Jules-Guesde. The park itself is a lively place, complete with kids' rides, ice-cream stands and an ersatz mountain and waterfall. Near the entrance stands the city's vast **natural history museum** (Tues–Sun 10am–6pm; €7), featuring a jaw-dropping 12m-wide *quetzalcoatlus* skeleton and an eclectic array of curiosities from the plant and animal world.

Further along, among the fading glory of the Art Deco mansions, you'll come across plaques marking the spots where Resistance fighters were shot dead by the Germans in the street-fighting of 1944. Finally, at no. 52, you'll arrive at the **Musée de la Résistance et de la Déportation** (Mon–Fri 9.30am–noon & 2–6pm, Sat 2–6pm; free), which through photos, artefacts and dioramas commemorates the life of the maquis, the plight of those living under occupation and the crimes of the occupiers.

A short walk up rue du Japon, just outside the museum's doors, brings you to the tiny mansion belonging to the traveller and collector **Georges Labit**. This nineteenth-century pavilion is pure Orientalist fantasy, a Gilbert and Sullivanesque vision of the East, while the **museum** (daily: June–Sept 10am–6pm; Oct–May 10am–5pm; €3) holds a small but incredibly varied collection of Asiatica, including Chinese artefacts dating from the tenth century, temple carvings from Northern India and two complete samurai suits of armour.

Just a stone's throw away, a canalside path leads up to the remains of the old Canal du Midi port, **Port St-Saveur**, now being refitted as a modern pleasure port. The towpath running parallel forms the first leg of the canalside bike and walking route from Toulouse to the **Seuil de Naurouze** (see box, p.89).

The suburbs

A number of specific sights may tempt you to leave old Toulouse and its immediate environs and head for the suburbs. Most popular of these is the **Cité de l'Espace**

Toulouse: the future of air travel

Toulouse's aviation industry is best known for Airbus, which has been giving stiff competition to major American airline manufacturers like Boeing, and has now upped the ante with its development of a new **super-liner**, the A-380. With a passenger capacity of 853, this two-storey colossus almost doubles the size of Boeing's 747; each plane contains over 500km of wiring. The creation of the super-liner hasn't been an entirely smooth ride, however: the plane's titanic components – manufactured in Germany, Britain and elsewhere in France – can be shipped to Bordeaux, but their size has meant that 250km of highway have had to be altered or built anew to accommodate trucks bearing loads up to 13m in height and 300m long (travelling at the break-neck speed of 20km per hour). While the A-380 entered into passenger service in 2007, a combination of rising fuel prices, company scandals, and an uncertain economy continue to cast doubts on the plane's viability.

An aviation legend

Toulouse has long been a centre of innovation in aviation. An early hero was **Antoine de Saint-Exupéry** (born 1900 in Lyon), a pilot who joined a local company and pioneered airmail routes over Africa and the South Atlantic, but is better known today as an author and journalist. Joining up in 1939 to fight the Germans, and despite physical disabilities, he flew reconnaissance missions for the Free French forces from 1940 onwards. A man of courage and conviction, he soon fell out with the authoritarian de Gaulle and, despite his exemplary record, became the subject of accusations of disloyalty. Meanwhile he authored a string of acclaimed books, the most famous of which, the children's fable *The Little Prince* (1943), has become a worldwide classic. A year after the book's publication Saint-Exupéry vanished during a flight over the Mediterranean, and his ultimate fate remained a mystery until 2004, when a Corsican fisherman turned up the pilot's identity bracelet; remains of his plane were found soon after. In 2008, a former German fighter pilot, who was even then a fan of the author, regretfully confessed to having shot down Saint-Exupéry's P-38 Lightning on July 31, 1944.

(daily 9am–5/7pm; Ⓦwww.cite-espace.com; €22, children under 5 free), east of the city centre by exit 17 of the *périphérique est* ring road. This massive high-tech science centre is packed with scores of exhibits on the theme of space and its exploration, including satellite communications, space probes, a real Ariane rocket and, best of all, a walk-in mock-up of the MIR space station – a fascinating, but absolutely chilling and inhuman, environment. Many of the exhibits are interactive and, though it's on the pricey side, you could easily spend half a day here, especially if you've got children in tow. Unfortunately, getting here by public transport is tricky: the closest bus lines (#16 and #19, from place Esquirol and Gare Matabiau respectively) leave you a good twenty-minute walk north of the park.

Only slightly more down to earth is the tour of **Aérospatiale**'s huge assembly plant in Colomiers, near the airport. In 1970 Toulouse became home to the French branch of the European conglomerate Airbus Industries, which manufactures passenger jets. The planes are assembled, painted and tested in a vast hangar, L'Usine Clément Ader, before taking their maiden flights from next-door Blagnac airport. You can choose between a ninety-minute **guided tour** (Mon–Sat; €14) of the assembly bays, where crews of one hundred people churn out five Airbuses a week, assisted by scores of computerized robots, or a Mach 2 flight experience on a Concorde (€22.50 with assembly tour): tours must be booked well in advance (July & Aug contact the tourist office; Sept–June ring Ⓣ05.61.18.06.01, Ⓦwww .taxiway.fr). The closest bus route to the factory is #64 (from métro Arènes), and the bus driver will direct you to the site.

In the northern suburbs, you'll find the scant remains of Roman Toulouse's **amphitheatre**, constructed in the first century and used through to the end of the fourth. There are also the vestiges of Roman baths and you can visit a small archeological centre (mid-May to Oct 2–6/7pm; €3). The site is about halfway to the airport, 5km downstream from the centre on the Garonne, on avenue des Arènes-Romaines, and can be reached by buses #66 (from métro St-Cyprien to "Cautarets") or #70 (from place Jeanne-d'Arc to "Purpan").

Eating and drinking

There's no shortage of good **eating** options in Toulouse, although on Sundays you will find your choice drastically reduced. The city's ethnic mix has engendered a culinary cosmopolitanism, and for French cooking you'll find a multitude of choices in every category of style and price. Toulouse is also a city that loves its **cafés** and **bars** – not surprisingly, given that the population swells by almost a quarter with the annual inundation of university students. The establishments listed below are only a fraction of what's out there – whichever part of town you find yourself in, you're never far from a drink or a meal.

Restaurants

There are several good areas for **restaurants**. Rue de la Colombette in the St-Aubin district, just across boulevard Carnot, has some attractive and fashionable choices. The area surrounding St-Sernin is particularly good; just north, place Arnaud-Bernard and the tiny adjacent place des Tiercerettes have appealing options; between the basilica and place Bernard there's a compact knot of **Arabic** and **Maghrebi** restaurants; and rue du Taur has a number of **Vietnamese** places and sandwich bars. Should you feel stuck for a choice, you can always head south of place Wilson to place St-Georges, where you'll find a gaggle of typical terraced eateries, or to the bottom end of rue des Filatiers where there's a cluster of late-night restaurants and tapas bars. Several of the bistrots on place Wilson are distinguished not so much by their fare, but by the fact that you can eat as late as 1am. As a last resort, you'll find a late-night grocery store at 67 rue des Pargaminières. The best lunchtime bargain is in the covered **market** on place Victor-Hugo (closed Mon), whose upper floor has a group of very cheap food counters.

Budget

Les Abattoirs Chez Carmen 97 allée Charles-de-Fitte ☎05.61.42.04.95. A family-run restaurant for two generations, the last of the traditional slaughterhouse-side meat emporia, with a reputation for top-of-the-line intestinal delicacies such as calves' brains and pigs' feet, as well as solid and generous cuts of lovingly roasted red meat. *Menus* from €18. Closed Sun, Mon & Aug.

Benjamin 7 rue des Gestes ☎05.61.22.92.66. A long-standing local institution for economical *terroir* food, such as cassoulet and foie gras; service is professional, and the atmosphere pleasant and airy. A wide selection of copious lunch and dinner *menus* at €11–19.

Le Châteaubriand 42 rue Pargaminières. Named after the politician rather than the steak, this casual but warm little restaurant serves an excellent cassoulet, made with flavourful *haricots Tarbais*, excellent side of beef, and scrumptious home-made desserts. Lunch *menus* from €13, or €19–27 for dinner. Closed Aug, Sat lunch & Sun.

Chez Atilla In the market at pl Victor-Hugo. The best of the market restaurants, this no-nonsense lunch-time establishment is a local institution and one of Toulouse's best options for seafood – their Spanish *zarzuela* stew is a fish-lover's dream. *Menus* from €12. Closed Mon & part Aug.

Faim des Haricots 3 rue du Puits Vert ☎05.61.22.49.25. An excellent and unpretentious vegetarian option, with generous all-you-can-eat salad and dessert buffets, "bottomless" bowls of soup and a *plat du jour* (€11–13). The recipes are

an eclectic mix based on various ethnic cuisines, and are welcome relief after one cassoulet too many. Open Mon–Sat lunch & Thurs–Sat dinner; closed first half Aug.

Saveurs Bio 22 rue Maurice-Fonvielle ☎05.61.12.15.15. Toulouse's best vegetarian place, offering everything from spinach quiche to alfalfa salads, made with certified organic produce. You can choose from the casual all-you-can-eat buffet (€9) or a range of set meals from €16–22 served in formal sit-down style. Closed Sat eve & Sun.

Le Ver Luisant 41 rue de la Colombette ☎05.61.63.06.73. A bar and simple restaurant frequented by the arty set. The good food – featuring *gastronomique* spins on regional fare – is copious and the atmosphere fun. Look for dishes such as pigs' feet, duck *aiguillette* and heart *confit*. *Plat du jour* €10 at lunchtime, or €18–30 for an evening meal. Closed Sat lunch & Sun.

Moderate

Le Colombier 14 rue Bayard ☎05.61.62.40.05. This elegant restaurant, set in the eighteenth-century former stables of the *capitole*, is widely regarded as having the best cassoulet in town. Other regional delights include *gésiers* ("gizzards") and foie gras, as well as seafood and game, all prepared and presented in an imaginative and modern style. *Formules* from €21. Closed Sat lunch & Sun.

La Côte de Boeuf 12 rue des Gestes ☎05.61.21.19.61. This simple and compact street-side restaurant is not the cheapest in the neighbourhood, but the quality of its wood-fire home-cooking (superb duck and foie gras, not to mention the namesake side of beef) and the genuine friendliness of the family who run it put it a step above its neighbours. Extras (such as coffee and wine) are pricey. Expect to spend €18–47. Closed Sun, Mon & Aug.

Le Genty Magre 3 rue Genty Magre ⊤05.61.21.31.60. A perfect blend of economy and elegance, this restaurant is well-known to locals for its warm service, excellent *gastronomique* cuisine, and superb, well-priced wine list. Evening *menu* from €22, lunch from €13.50. Closed Sun eve & Mon.

Kaviar Rouge 21 pl Nicholas Bachelier ⊤05.61.62.31.19. At Toulouse's Russian restaurant you can sample a wide selection of Caucasian delicacies, including caviar (€25–160 per 50g) and the city's best selection of Polish and Russian flavoured vodkas (from €5) in the cosy atmosphere of a *faux* Siberian log cabin. Generous dinner *menus* at €21 and 25, and frequent live shows of Rusian dance and music.

Le Sept Place St-Sernin 7 pl St-Sernin ⊤05.62.30.05.30. This intimately romantic restaurant set in a small house behind the basilica serves inventive and original cuisine based on regional ingredients, with a constantly changing *carte*, followed by dazzling desserts. It is justly acclaimed by the local and national press, and perhaps the best value for money in the city. *Menus* from €23 and a lunchtime *formule* for €9. Closed Sat lunch & Sun.

La Table de la Bascule 14 av Maurice-Hauriou ⊤05.61.52.09.51. A Toulouse institution, this outfit's chromy interior is pure Art Deco and the food well prepared and presented. The diverse *carte* includes regional dishes like cassoulet, *foie de canard* and oysters from the Bay of Arcachon. *Menus* from €23, and a lunch-time *formule* for €9. Closed Sat lunch & Sun.

Expensive

Chez Émile 13 pl St-Georges ⊤05.61.21.05.56. One of Toulouse's best restaurants, and well situated on this busy oblong square. Regional cuisine downstairs and *gastronomique* with a strong seafood accent upstairs, and a selection of well-reputed "agapes" – recipes unique to *Chez Émile*. Lunch *menu* from €20, dinner from €41. Closed Sun & Mon, but open Mon eve in summer; reservations essential.

Les Jardins de l'Opéra 1 pl du Capitole ⊤05.61.21.05.56. The *Grand Hôtel*'s restaurant is Toulouse's best and most luxurious. If you fancy a splurge this is a good place to do it – the food is outstanding – but you will pay for it: a basic *menu* starts at €29 at lunch; expect to pay €100 à la carte. Closed Sun & Mon lunch & part Aug.

Michel Sarran 21 bd Armand-Duportal ⊤05.61.12.32.32. This famous *gastronomique*, universally acknowledged as the city's best restaurant, is a fifteen-minute walk from the place du Capitole (follow rue des Lois and rue des Salenques to the end, and turn left). Imaginative dishes with a strong Mediterranean streak are served with style and warmth. The desserts are decadent in both constitution and price (€18). Well worth the price, this is the Toulouse dining experience not to be missed. *Menus* from €44 at lunch and €95 at dinner. Closed Sat, Sun, Wed lunch & part Aug.

Au Pois Gourmand 3 rue Émile Heybrard ⊤05.61.31.95.95. Great location in a nineteenth-century riverside house with a beautiful patio. The quality French gastro cuisine does not come cheap here (*menus* from €22–64), but is of a predictably high standard, and the *carte* presents a pleasant departure from purely regional dishes, including specialties such as "stuffed pigeon Mont Royal", and "shrimps and langoustines in Tandoori essence." If you're too full to make it back home, rooms are available for €120. Bus #66 or #14 from métro St-Cyprien-République. Closed Sat & Mon lunch, Sun & Aug.

Cafés and bars

Many establishments cater to a mellow coffee and beer clientele during the day and put on the music after 10pm. Regular daytime **café**-lounging can be pursued around the popular student/arty hangout of place Arnaud-Bernard, while place du Capitole is the early evening meeting place. Place St-Georges has been somewhat inundated by restaurant terraces but remains another option, while the more elegant terraces of place Wilson are good if you don't mind the traffic.

Bapz 13 rue de la Bourse. English-style bakery and tearoom – definitely not your typical "caff", with good breakfasts and snacks. Smart service (and prices). Closed Sun.

Bar du Matin 16 pl des Carmes. Great old street-corner bar in the finest beer, peanuts and *pastis*

tradition. A friendly and deservedly popular place. Closed Sun.

Bibent 5 pl du Capitole. On the south side of the square, this is Toulouse's most distinguished café, with exuberant plasterwork, marble tables and cascading chandeliers.

Le Café des Artistes Pl de la Daurade. Lively, young café overlooking the Garonne. A perfect spot to watch the sun set on warm summer evenings, as floodlights pick out the brick buildings along the quays.

Le Donjon Bar 2 rue du Poids de l'Huile. Tiny bar on the south side of the Capitole building. Impossibly crowded but great fun for watching rugby or having a drink. Open until 2am. Closed Sun.

Le Florida 12 pl du Capitole. Relaxed café with a nicely retro air. One of the most pleasant places to hang out on the central square.

The Frog and Rosbif 14 rue de l'Industrie. Stop by this friendly British pub, just off bd Lazare-Carnot, for a pint of Darktagnan stout, or one of their other excellent home brews. Quiz nights, football, and fish and chips draw an international crowd. Open until 2am, Sat until 4am. Closed part Aug.

Jour de Fête 43 rue de Taur. Funky tearoom and brasserie with a small street-side patio. Friendly service and a young studenty crowd. Open until 2am Fri & Sat.

Au Père Louis 45 rue des Tourneurs ☎05.61.21.33.45. A lively, old-fashioned bar with chansons and music some nights. Open till 10pm. Closed Sun.

St-Philipe 19 rue Arnaud-Bernard Escoussières. Just off place Bernard to the north of the St-Sernin, on the edge of the Maghrebi neighbourhood, this bar attracts a mixed crowd of locals, students and business people. There's a pool table, table football and video games to keep you busy over your beer. Open daily.

Le Sherpa 44 rue de Taur. Another of the city's many tea rooms. Popular with the university crowd and conveniently located by the Cinémathèque. Closed Sun.

Nightlife

The annual influx of university students ensures that the city's **nightlife** is active, sustaining a whole range of **music-bars** and **clubs**; if the French are not famous for exuberant partying, Toulouse helps belie the stereotype. Things slow down from July to September, when the academic year breaks, but even in the summer you'll have no trouble drinking and dancing as late as you like. Unfortunately some of the city's best venues lie in the suburbs, which means paying for a taxi, though there's no shortage of options closer to the old town. Entrance fees to discos and clubs may be charged depending on the night and event, but generally you're expected to buy a rather expensive drink (€8–10), while at venues which are essentially bars you can enter free of charge.

Music-bars and clubs

L'Ambassade 22 bd de la Gare. Downbeat club where funk and soul rule. Live jazz on Sunday nights. Open Tues, Fri & Sun until 2am, Sat till 5am.

Bar de la Lune 24 rue Palaprat. This evening drinking spot in St-Aubin draws an arty crowd with its occasional exhibitions and concerts. Daily from 7pm.

Le Bikini 55 chemin des Étroits, rte de Lacroix-Falgarde ⓦwww.lebikini.com. On the city's southern outskirts, this is *the* hangout of Toulouse rockers, and a prime venue for live gigs. Open Thurs–Sun.

Bodega-Bodega 1 rue Gabriel-Péri. The old *Télégraphe* newspaper building makes a superb venue for this bar-restaurant, with its hugely popular disco after 10pm. Daily until 2am, Sat 4am.

Café Classico 37 rue des Filatiers. Trendy, designer-ish establishment that's a café by day and music-bar by night. House, hip-hop and jungle. Daily until 1am, Sat 4am.

Le Cri de la Mouette Pl Héraklès ⓦwww .lecridelamouette.com. Popular disco featuring

reggae, rock, funk and soul. Cover from €5. Daily 11pm–5am.

Erich Coffie 9 rue Joseph-Villèle. West of the river, far beyond the *quartier* St-Cyprien, this is one of the city's liveliest and most enjoyable music-bars, with an eclectic music policy. There's food available and live bands most evenings. Open Tues–Sat from 10pm.

La Luna Loca 15 rue Pierre Rubens. Cultural centre and club for lesbians. Men admitted on Wed & Fri only. Daily 8pm–late.

Le Petit Voisin 37 rue Peyrolières. A neighbourhood place, just like the name, "the little neighbour", says. Laidback during the day when workers and businessmen stop for a drink, and livelier at night, when it fills with a student crowd. Open until 2am, Sat 4am. Closed Sun & mid-Aug.

Puerto Habana 12 port St-Etienne. Toulouse's hottest salsa venue, in a superb setting beside the Canal du Midi. Also has an excellent restaurant and a house band Thurs–Sat. Mon–Fri until 2am, Sat till 5am.

Le Purple 2 rue Castellane ⓦwww.purepurple.fr. Southwest France's temple of cool and Mecca of House, with food, drinks and dancing. Tues–Sat 11pm to dawn.
Le Rex 15 av Honoré-Serres ⓦwww.le-rex -toulouse.com. Located in a converted cinema, just north of the old town, this bar/concert hall usually features ska and punk acts. Opening hours vary – check the website or local listings magazines for concerts and events.

Shanghai Express 12 rue de la Pomme. One of the city's most established gay and lesbian clubs, which attracts a mixed crowd including transvestites and transsexuals. Wed–Sun 11pm–late (on Sat right through to Sun 1pm).
L'Ubu 16 rue St-Rome. Long-standing pillar of the city's dance scene that remains as popular as ever. Mon–Sat 11pm till dawn.

Entertainment and festivals

Drinking and dancing aside, there's plenty to do in Toulouse. Several **cinemas** regularly show v.o. ("version originale", undubbed) films, including ABC, 13 rue St-Bernard (☎05.61.29.81.00), Cinémathèque, 68 rue de Taur (☎05.62.30.30.10, ⓦwww.lacinemathequedetoulouse.com), and Utopia, 24 rue Montardy (☎05.61.23.66.20, ⓦwww.cinemas-utopia.org). The city also has an extremely vibrant **theatre** culture. The official Théâtre de la Cité, 1 rue Pierre-Baudis (☎05.34.45.05.05, ⓦwww.tnt-cite.com), is home to the Théâtre National de Toulouse Midi-Pyrénées, which has a narrative theatre programme livened up by occasional dance performances, while the workshop Nouveau Théâtre Jules-Julien, 6 av des Écoles-Jules-Juliens (☎05.61.25.79.92), has a reputation for staging provocative drama, with a particular emphasis on Absurdist productions. The large venue Odyssud, 4 av du Parc Blagnac (☎05.61.71.75.15; bus #66), features both theatre and **opera**, but the place to head for the latter, as well as **ballet** and **contemporary dance** performances, is the Théâtre du Capitole, housed in the Capitole building (☎05.61.63.13.13, ⓦwww.theatre-du-capitole.org), a highly acclaimed venue where you can also hear recitals and chamber music. **Classical music** fans also have the Orchestre National du Capitole, with its base in the Halle aux Grains in place Dupuy (☎05.61.99.78.00, ⓦwww.onct.mairie-toulouse.fr). The city's biggest **rock music** venue, with nine thousand seats, is Zénith, at 11 av Raymond Badiou (☎05.62.74.49.49; métro Arènes), which features both French and foreign groups, including visiting jazz and blues performers; while for something a little less energetic, Cave-Poésie, 71 rue de Taur (☎05.61.23.62.00), is home to various **literary workshops** and gatherings of a decidedly bohemian spirit.

Toulouse's **festivals** calendar is packed out, with a back-to-back programme of artistic, musical or literary events throughout the year. For a rundown of the highlights, see the box on p.61. To get up-to-date **information** on the latest cultural events check the weekly magazines *Toulouse Hebdo* (€1) or *Flash* (€3), which have detailed concert and event listings and are available at newsstands. The monthly *Ramdam* (€2.20; ⓦwww.ramdam-magazine.com) has listings for the whole region of Midi-Pyrénées, while the *mairie* distributes a free magazine, *Cultures Toulouse*, and has comprehensive event listings at ⓦwww.mairie-toulouse.fr.

Listings

Boat trips and rental Various outfits offer tours on the Garonne and the canals du Midi and de Brienne. Le Capitole has several daily and night-time departures from pl de la Daurade for a ninety-minute journey on the Garonne (€8; reserve at the tourist office; ⓦwww.toulouse-croisieres.com). Baladine (ⓦwww.bateaux-toulousains.com) has a variety of full-day programmes, as well as a 75-minute cruise of historic Toulouse departing from the Quai de la Daurade (2.30pm, 4pm & 5.30pm daily in summer otherwise Wed, Sat & Sun; €8). For houseboat rental, contact Navicanal, 139 rue Bonnat (☎05.61.55.10.91, ⓦwww .navicanal.com).

Books The best general bookshops are Castéla, on place du Capitole, and FNAC, at 16 allées F-Roosevelt. Toulouse Presse, 60 rue Bayard, stocks a good range of IGN maps and guides while Ombres-Blanches at 50 rue Gambetta is a good choice for travel literature. For English-language books, head for The Bookshop, 17 rue Lakanal. There are book markets on Thursday mornings in place Arnaud-Bernard, and all day Saturday in place St-Étienne.

Car rental A2L, 81 bd Déodat-de-Séverac ℡05.61.59.33.99; Avis, gare SNCF ℡05.61.63.71.71; Budget, 49 rue Bayard ℡05.61.63.18.18; Europcar, 15 bd Bonrepos ℡05.61.62.52.89; Hertz, gare SNCF ℡05.61.62.94.12.

Gay and lesbian For information contact the gay and lesbian students' group Jules et Julies, Comité des Étudiants, Université du Mirail, 5 allée Machado, 310589, or Gais et Lesbiennes en Marche (℡06.11.87.38.81, ✉gelem@altern.org).

Hospitals There are two major hospitals, both outside the A61 ring road: CHR Ranguiel, chemin du Vallon (℡05.61.32.25.33), to the south, and CHR Purpan, pl du Dr Baylac (℡05.61.77.22.33), to the west. Emergency ℡15 or 05.61.12.77.77.

Pharmacy The Pharmacie de Nuit, 70–76 allées Jean-Jaurès (entry on rue Arnaud Vidal), is open Mon–Sat 8pm–8am & Sun 8pm–9am.

Police 23 bd de l'Embouchure ℡05.61.12.77.77; emergency ℡17.

Rugby Toulouse is a centre of excellence for French rugby – many players in the national team hail from these parts. You can see their first-rate Stade Toulousain team in action at their stadium at 114 rue de Troènes (℡05.61.57.05.05, ⍟www.stadetoulousain.fr; bus #16 to "Stade").

Swimming There are several public pools in town. Alfred Nakache is open year-round, allées Paul-Bienes (℡05.61.22.31.35).

Around Toulouse

Predominantly flat, and ribbed by a multitude of small streams, the hinterland fanning out to the north and east of Toulouse has long been the source of the city's wealth. The woad boom of the fifteenth and sixteenth centuries may have powered its prosperous golden age, but the **cereal farming** carried out in this immensely fertile region has been Toulouse's traditional mainstay. Field after field of wheat dominates the rolling landscape, cut across by narrow bands of woodland, and dotted by the church steeples of modest, introverted hamlets – havens of determined rural existence where elderly farmers speak French with a rounded Occitan accent. The region is hedged to the north by the River Agout and to the west by the rising peaks of the **Montagne Noire** (see p.170), but is most notable for its southern boundary, the **Canal du Midi** – the engineering marvel constructed in the seventeenth century to link the Mediterranean and the Atlantic, and now a favourite with boating enthusiasts and cyclists.

The northern stretch of the region, known as the "pays de Cocagne" (see box opposite), is dominated by **Lavaur**, once a stalwart Cathar centre, with its beautifully preserved old town. The easternmost town in the area, sitting on the edge of the Parc du Haut Languedoc, is the old *bastide* of **Revel**, with an impressive medieval covered market place. Just south of here, at **St-Ferreol**, you'll find part of the incredible catchment system of the Canal du Midi. The flat **Lauragais** district stretches southwest of Revel: **St-Félix** is its prettiest town, but **Castelnaudary** – the area's capital – contains a surprising number of monuments and mansions. More significantly, it is also the main town on this stretch of the Canal du Midi.

Lavaur and around

Thirty-seven kilometres east of Toulouse, **LAVAUR** is the biggest town on the Agout west of Castres, and the traditional capital of the surrounding pays de Cocagne. It's also a key town in the history of Catharism, the twelfth-century heretical movement (see *The Land of Cathars* colour section). The town was brutally conquered by Simon de Montfort's crusaders after a two-month siege in

The woad to riches

From the mid-fifteenth to the mid-sixteenth century Toulouse and Albi experienced an unprecedented wave of prosperity, based on the humble **woad** plant (*Isatis tinctoria* or in French, *pastel*). When craftsmen in Albi discovered that the innocuous weed, which was used for medicinal purposes across the Mediterranean, yielded a rich blue **dye**, they knew they were onto a good thing: blue was one of the colours most in demand for clothing by the growing middle class, and up to that point it could only be produced from rare and expensive raw materials.

With capital from Toulouse, intensive woad cultivation operations were set up across the Lauragais, which had ideal soil and climate conditions for the plant. Once harvested, the process of dye production lasted some four months, involving crushing and rolling the leaves into balls (*coques*) and fermenting them for two weeks. After this the sticky dye was pressed out and rolled into balls (*cocagnes*). Demand from textile manufacturers across Europe brought staggering wealth to the region, which became known in common parlance as the **pays de Cocagne** (a play on words, also meaning "the land of plenty"). Some 30,000–40,000 tonnes were shipped annually, while the woad **merchants**, many of whom became *capitouls* of Toulouse, erected fine mansions, the **hôtels particuliers**, which even today bear witness to their former wealth. By the late sixteenth century, however, *pastel* began to be superseded by cheaper indigo-based dyes from the Indies. The violent upheavals of the Wars of Religion, ravaging fields and interrupting transport, provided the final blow, and the dye, along with the incredible affluence it generated, became a thing of the past. Today, you can purchase traditionally dyed items at La Fleurée de Pastel at 20 rue de la Bourse in Toulouse, near the Hôtel d'Assézat.

1211 – Guiraude de Laurac, widow of the town's lord and leader of the defense, was thrown down a well and pelted with stones; her brother, along with nearly a hundred knights, was put to the sword; and some four hundred Cathars were burnt at the stake. But the heresy persisted, prompting the papacy and Crown to establish a series of religious foundations here, starting with a Dominican house to run the local Inquisition and finally, in the fourteenth century, a cathedral. In the sixteenth century the town was a Huguenot hotbed, pitting itself once more against the Catholic establishment and the powers of the North. Nevertheless it prospered, profiting first from the lucrative woad industry and, later, silk manufacture. Today Lavaur is an attractive if quiet rural centre, surrounded by the wheat fields of the Agout valley.

The town's main landmark, the brick-built former **cathedral** of St-Alain, stands on a wide plaza above the river. The present structure was built in 1254, replacing that destroyed by the Crusaders. Some notable features include a wooden door on the south side, which survives from the original pre-Crusade building, an eleventh-century marble altar, a highly stylized fifteenth-century doorway and an incredible mechanical clock, perched high above the ground in one of its two towers. This *jacquemart* – a clock that strikes using a mechanical figure in the form of a soldier wielding a hammer – dates back to 1523 and still marks every half-hour. Close by in the old town, you'll find the fourteenth-century **church of St-François**, dedicated to St Francis of Assisi, founder of the Franciscans, the first group established to preach against heretics and the Dominicans' great rivals. Set in the town's old main street, the Grande Rue, this church has weathered the centuries, but the graceful simplicity of its single nave and surviving columns make it worth a look. In the adjoining **garden** keep an eye out for the old dovecote, one of the first along the route des Colombiers (see p.82). Nearby, the **church of the Cordeliers** also merits a visit for its elegant Gothic interior.

As you walk around the town you'll see a number of timber-and-brick houses, many dating from the fourteenth to sixteenth centuries, and the narrow old streets make for a pleasantly atmospheric whole.

Practicalities

Trains and buses stop at Lavaur's **gare SNCF**, located northeast of the old quarter on the place de Stalingrad. From here it's a fifteen-minute walk to the **tourist office** (Tues–Sat 9am–noon & 2–6pm; ☎05.63.58.02.00, ⓦwww.ville-lavaur.fr), which is housed in a small turret on the riverside quai Tour de Rondes. There's also an information kiosk by the cathedral (July–Aug daily 10am–12.30pm & 3.30–6.30pm). As for **hotels**, the cosy *Les Pasteliers* (☎05.63.58.04.16, ⓔlespasteliers@orange.fr; ❸) in 7 rue Alsace-Lorraine is a good choice, but better still is the **chambres d'hôtes** ☀ *Les Chambres du Pastel*, 5 rue du Père Colin (☎05.63.58.38.95, ⓔpierrick .broustet@free.fr; ❹), an ancient house located just a short walk from the old cathedral with four small but homey rooms. It also has a great bar, worth a visit whether you're staying there or not. For eating, the best choice is the **restaurant** at *Le Jacquemart* (☎05.63.58.04.17, ⓦwww.le-jacquemart.com; closed Sun eve & Mon), 3 pl Stalingrad, which does good local food from €14 and also has basic rooms (❷). You'll also find a clutch of places in the elongated square stretching up from the tourist office, the most interesting of which is *Pitcholina* (closed Sun), a Basque restaurant with excellent tapas. Lavaur's **country market** is on Saturday morning throughout the old town, and there's a **horse fair** held on the third Saturday of each month near the *gare*.

Giroussens and St-Sulpice

Some 15km northwest of Lavaur, the ancient village of **GIROUSSENS** huddles on the slope of a high ridge. It's been a centre of pottery production for thousands of years – local wares can be purchased at the museum/shop **Maison de la Céramique Contemporaine** (May–Aug Tues 2–6pm & Wed–Sun 10am–noon & 2–6pm; Sept–April daily 2–6pm; €2.5) and at the huge **ceramics market** held on the last weekend of April. Just across the river on the south bank of the Agout, you'll find the hamlet of **ST-LIEUX-LÈS-LAVAUR**, site of a much-touted **steam train** (mid-April to mid-July, Sept & Oct Sun 2.30–5.30pm; late July Sat–Tues 2.30–4.30/5.30pm; Aug daily 2.30–4.30/5.30pm; Nov to mid-April Sun & school hols 2.30–4.30/5.30pm; subject to cancellation if less than ten tickets sold; €6), which runs a one-hour return trip eastwards along the river valley. Its highpoint is crossing over a 20m-high viaduct: note that sometimes the steam train is substituted with a regular diesel engine. Nearby, the **Jardin des Martels** (late March Sun

---

The route des colombiers

If you're cycling or driving from **Lavaur**, you should take time to explore the **route des Colombiers**, a loose circuit of approximately 20km which you can start on the southern bank of the Agout heading east out of the town. *Colombiers*, elaborate and varied **dovecotes**, have been constructed here among the farm fields since the Middle Ages to house the pigeons which formed a valuable part of the rural economy, providing food and fertilizer. The tourist office in Lavaur has a map with directions to all of the dovecotes (many are private and hardly visible from the road) as well as some explanatory text. If you don't want to do the whole circuit, which leads about 10km east before looping back, you'll pass a good number of dovecotes by taking the small riverside road from Lavaur towards St-Paul (follow signs for "Flamarens"). There are also plenty to see right along the main D112 highway which runs between Lavaur and Castres, in addition to half a dozen in Lavaur itself.

1–6pm; April, Sept & Oct Mon–Fri 1–6pm, Sat & Sun 11am–6pm; May–Aug daily 11am–6pm; Nov Sat & Sun 1–6pm; €6), a botanical garden with thousands of varieties of flowers and plants, as well as a petting zoo. The train and garden make a good combination if you are travelling with children. Good **accommodation** can be found at *L'Échauguette* (℡05.63.41.63.65, ℻05.63.41.63.13; ❸), in the lower part of Giroussens. This beautiful thirteenth-century building has several well-furnished rooms and a small, intimate dining room, featuring the *gastronomique* creations of a – gasp! – English chef (*menus* from €26 at dinner).

You're only likely to make a stop in tiny **ST-SULPICE**, 8km further west, if changing buses or trains en route to Toulouse or Albi from Lavaur or the Montagne Noire, or to dine at ⚓ *L'Auberge de la Pointe* (variable closing days; ℡05.63.41.80.14) just by the bridge over the Tarn. This is one of the region's highest-rated *gastronomiques*, where you can enjoy subtle and elaborate five-course *menus* in an eighteenth-century inn overlooking the river for €23–46, but call in advance to check opening and to reserve.

East of Lavaur

East of Lavaur, the plains are dotted by occasional hamlets: **St-Paul-Cap-de-Joux**, **Puylaurens** and **Damiette**, the latter with a **gare SNCF** on the Toulouse–Revel line and a **campsite** (mid-June to mid-Sept; ℡05.63.70.66.07). There are several **castles** in the area – most dating back to the Middle Ages, and most lived in – including **Roquevidal**, **Magrin**, and **Loubens-Lauragais**; each are interesting and open to visit, but none are exceptional.

Revel and around

Situated at the westernmost point of the long **Montagne Noire** massif, **REVEL** is a tiny but busy district capital which serves as a regional bus hub and a good base for

▲ *Colombier near Lavaur*

exploring the surrounding area. It was founded as a *bastide* in 1342 by Philip IV, and the deliberate plan of the town is reflected in its octagonal layout and regular streets; indeed, Revel's original charter prescribed a uniformity which even regulated the size of the houses which could be built. Today, it is still dominated by the immense fourteenth-century covered market which covers the entirety of the town's central square, its rows of stout pillars supporting a single-gabled roof, converging at a stone-constructed tower. Revel was the region's principal market town before becoming a centre for furniture manufacture in the nineteenth century. Local workshops still turn out exceptionally crafted wooden furniture, and if you're interested in how it used to be done check out **Sylvéa**, the "Woodworkers' Conservatory", at 13 rue Jean Moulin (Nov–April Tues–Sat 2–6pm; May–Oct Mon–Fri 10am–noon & 2–6pm, Sat & Sun 2–6pm; €4.50) on the northeast corner of the main square. Many medieval houses remain in the compact old town, making Revel an atmospheric stop and a good place to spend a comfortable night and get your laundry done if you're heading to or from the Montagne Noire.

Seven kilometres west of Revel, on the road back to Toulouse, the tiny pictur-esque hill-top hamlet of **St-Félix-Lauragais** – birthplace of the composer Déodat-de-Séverac (1872–1921) – dominates the flatlands stretching west towards the capital of Midi-Pyrénées. Nothing remains of the time when the town was a meeting place for Cathar clergy, but it does retain a fine wooden **market** with a small stone tower, a curious Gothic-style **church** tucked away among the buildings of the main street and a profusion of timber-frame houses.

Practicalities

Buses to Revel stop on the place de la République, on the main road just north of the town's covered market, where there is a small SNCF ticket office (Tues–Fri 9am–noon & 1.30–6.30pm, Sat 9am–noon; ℡05.61.83.53.73). The **tourist office** (July & Aug Mon–Fri 9am–6.30pm, Sat 9am–7pm, Sun 10am–12.30pm & 3–6pm; Sept–June Mon–Sat 9.30am–12.30/1pm & 2.30/3–6.30pm, Sun 10am–12.30pm & 3–6pm; closed Sun in Jan; ℡05.34.66.67.68, Ⓦwww.revel-lauragais.com), located in the tower in the market's centre, can give you information about neighbouring towns too.

The best of the **hotels** here is the *du Midi*, set in a refined old nineteenth-century mansion at 34 bd Gambetta, just north of the market (closed late Nov to early Dec; ℡05.61.83.50.50, Ⓦwww.hotelrestaurantdumidi.com; ❸), which also has the best restaurant (*menus* €19–45; closed Sun and Mon noon). Close by, at 7 rue de Taur, the *Commanderie Hôtel* (℡05.34.66.11.24; closed part Feb, part June, part Sept; ❹) is a good second choice, with an old timber-framed facade and a remod-elled interior. The municipal **campsite** is walking distance from the main square (mid-June to Aug; ℡05.61.83.32.47). For a chance to see the old covered *halles* in use, try to catch the Saturday-morning **market**. That said, if you have transport, call to reserve at the excellent **hotel-restaurant** ♃ *Auberge du Poids Public* (closed Jan & part Nov; ℡05.62.18.85.00, Ⓦwww.auberge-du-poidspublic.com; ❹) in St-Félix-Lauragais. Located in a large old house beside the town's public weigh-bridge, the hotel has been restored and decorated in warm luxury, while the restaurant is widely praised for its regional gastronomic creations – try the rabbit and pigeon dishes (*menus* from €32) – served up with fine Gaillac vintages.

Approaching the Montagne Noire

Three kilometres southwest of Revel is **Lac de St-Ferreol**, an artificial reservoir created in 1672 with the completion of a massive 780m-long dam. This was part of the incredible Canal du Midi project (see p.86), and took some seven thousand workers five years of hard labour to construct. It was here that run off from the

Montagne Noire was collected to feed the canal, flowing down the Rigole de Canal du Midi to Naurouze, approximately 25km to the southwest. Nowadays it's a popular weekend spot: the woods make for easy walking, and you can **swim** or **sail** on the lake. A variant of the **hiking** trail GR7 swings by the reservoir, linking up with the G653 west at the Rigole, and passing close to Castelnaudary to the south.

Lac de St-Ferréol has a profusion of **hotels** and **campsites**, most of them clustered along the northwest corner, where the road from Revel meets the lake. Two of the better places to stay are the *Hôtellerie du Lac* – turn right coming from Revel – (T05.62.18.70.80, Wwww.hotellerie-du-lac.com; ❹; closed late Dec to early Jan), which also has suites with kitchenettes, and *La Renaissance* (closed mid-Dec to mid-March; T05.61.83.51.50, Wwww.hotellarenaissance.fr; English spoken; ❸), right at the main intersection. The *Hôtellerie* also has a decent **restaurant** (*menus* from €15). The campsites around the lake tend towards the deluxe multi-facility type, with the closest to the water being *En Salvan* (April–Oct; T05.61.83.55.95). You can rent **bikes** and **sailboats** through *Le Bivouac* (T05.61.27.53.94), in rue des 4 Vents, behind the *Hôtellerie*.

Heading east from Revel, the D85 – the scenic road to Castres – takes you through an idyllic expanse of rolling green pasture, with the wooded ridge of the **Montagne Noire** rising up sharply along the south side of the road. Along the way you'll pass low key Sorèze and Dourgne, handy jumping-off points for exploring the western reaches of the massif. In **SORÈZE**, just 6km east of Revel, a Dominican **convent-school** – once a military academy in which the Latin American hero Simón Bolívar trained – is now home to a luxurious **hotel-restaurant**, the *Abbaye-École* (T05.63.74.44.80, Wwww.hotelfp-soreze.com; ❸) with great old timber-beamed rooms and *menus* from €34. The town's **tourist office** (June–Sept daily 10am–noon & 2–6pm; Oct–May Mon–Fri 10am–noon & 2–5.30/6pm, Sat & Sun 2–5.30/6pm; T05.63.74.16.28, Wwww.ville-soreze.fr) is off the main square, in rue St-Martin, though more up-to-date information on the Parc Naturel Régional du Haut Languedoc, which begins in the hills above the town, can be found at the former **Maison du Parc**, on the main road at the west end of town, which now houses the **municipal museum** (July & Aug Wed–Mon 2–6.30pm; Sept–June Sat, Sun & hols 2–6pm; €2). The **campsite**, *St-Martin* (T&F05.63.73.28.99) is open in summer months, and there is a lively country market on Friday mornings.

Just beyond Sorèze, **DOURGNE** is home to two Benedictine communities. The larger of the two is the **Monastère de St-Benoît**, which you can visit to sit in on any of the five daily services and hear a chanted Mass; the smaller convent of **Ste-Scholastique** is the home of nuns who pass the time in devotion and weaving. The **hotel-restaurant** *Hôtellerie de la Montagne Noire*, 15 pl des Promenades (closed part Feb, part Sept & part Nov; T05.63.50.31.12, Wwww.montagnenoire-81 .com; ❸) serves up hearty *terroir*-inspired food (*menus* €21.50–31; closed Sun eve & Mon). Alternatively, the bucolic **chambres d'hôtes** *Domaine de Béthanie* (T05.63.50.15.92; ❸) is ideal for families, and there is a tiny one-star municipal **campsite** (mid-June to mid-Sept; T05.63.50.31.20).

Castelnaudary and around

The biggest stop on the Canal du Midi between Carcassonne and Toulouse, **CASTELNAUDARY** holds the joint honours of being the legendary birthplace of that most Occitan of dishes, **cassoulet**, and the capital of the Lauragais region, the flat grain-producing hinterland of Toulouse. With its wide **Grand Bassin**, or reservoir, the town is the major pleasure port on the canal, and a great place to start a waterborne trip towards the Mediterranean. Like the surrounding region, Castelnaudary's past is intimately linked with Cathar history – the town endured

The building of the Canal du Midi

The **Canal du Midi** runs for some 240km from the River Garonne at Toulouse, via Castelnaudary, Carcassonne and Béziers, to the Mediterranean at Agde or Sète, and via its subsidiary, the **Canal de la Robine**, to Narbonne, entering the sea at Gruissan. The waterway was the brainchild of **Pierre-Paul Riquet**, a minor noble and the holder of the lucrative salt-tax concession for Languedoc (the *gabelle* – a tax levied on the sale of salt – was one of the royal treasury's most lucrative sources of income). Riquet succeeded in firing the imagination of Louis XIV (and more importantly, his first minister, Colbert) with the idea of linking the Atlantic and the Mediterranean via the Garonne.

The **main canal**, begun in 1667, took fourteen years to complete using tens of thousands of workers. At the start, an engineering problem automatically presented itself: how to feed the canal with water when the Mediterranean was obviously at sea level, the Garonne at 132m above sea level, and, in the middle, the Col (or Seuil) de Naurouze at 201m. Riquet's solution was to build a system of **dams** and **reservoirs** at St-Ferréol, Lampy and on the Alzeau in the Montagne Noire, channelling run off water from the heights down to Naurouze. He spent the whole of his fortune on the canal (sacrificing even his daughters' dowries) and, sadly, died just six months before its inauguration in 1681. But the waterway, built to accommodate barges of up to 30m in length, was a success and sparked a wave of prosperity along its course, thanks to the access it provided local farmers, manufacturers and raw material industries to foreign markets (via the Mediterranean). Traffic increased steadily until 1856, when it carried 111,000 metric tonnes of material as well as one million passengers, and the official link-up to the Garonne and the Atlantic opened. The next year the Sète–Bordeaux railway opened and, rail transport being faster and more cost-effective, traffic on the canal dropped to all but nothing almost immediately.

no fewer than three sieges during the Albigensian campaigns, and was also the birthplace of Pierre de Castelnau, the papal legate whose murder prompted Pope Innocent III to proclaim the Crusade. When the Inquisition arrived here in 1235, the grey-robed Dominicans' efforts to root out heretics were thwarted by the solidarity of the townsfolk, who refused to implicate their fellows. It was also just outside the town that the last dream of Languedocian independence died, with the capture in 1632 of the rebellious Henri de Montmorency, who was borne away to Toulouse and executed on orders of Cardinal Richelieu.

Arrival, information and accommodation

Trains arrive at Castelnaudary's **gare SNCF**, located on the south side of the Canal du Midi. The **gare routière**, on the other hand, is on the north side of town, on avenue Frédéric-Mistral, not far from the central *place* and the town's **tourist office** (June & Sept Mon–Sat 9am–12.30pm & 2.30–6pm; July & Aug daily 9am–1pm & 2–7pm; Oct–May Mon–Fri 9am–12.30pm & 2.30–6pm & Sat 9am–12.30pm; ☎04.68.23.05.73, ⊛www.castelnaudary-tourisme.com). **Bicycles** can be rented at Bateau St. Roch (☎06.62.03.49.40), on quai du Port. For **internet** access, head to CAFE.NET in 10 rue Soumet, or Cyberc@fe, 22 rue Dunquerque.

There are several **hotels** to choose from in town, the best of which is the friendly, canalside *Hôtel du Canal* (☎04.68.94.05.05, ⊛www.hotelducanal.com; ❹), at 2 av Arnaut-Vidal – a comfortable place with all mod cons (including wi-fi and satellite television) and a garage; family rooms are also available. Second choice is the *Hôtel du Centre et du Lauragais* (closed Jan to mid-Feb; ☎04.68.23.25.95, ⊛www.hotel -centre-lauragais.com; ❹), a converted nineteenth-century house, centrally located at 31 cours de la République. The municipal **campsite**, *La Giraille* (July to mid-Sept; ☎04.68.23.11.28) can be found west of town, a twenty-minute walk along avenue Georges-Pompidou from the bridge at the foot of cours de la République.

The Town

Although Castelnaudary's main attraction is its canal port, the Grand Bassin, there are a number of sights worth seeing in the town itself. The first you're likely to encounter is the **halle aux grains**, the former cereal market, with a plain but dignified arcaded front on the west side of place de la République. Heading uphill from the *halle* along allée du Cassieu you can follow the main road west to the thirteenth-century **church of St-François**, inside which you'll find a well-crafted statue of the Virgin and Child, dating from the same period. Another 800m further on (turn up towards the cemetery on the impasse Claude-Chappe), is the curious **Tour Chappe**. This tower was once part of the immense semaphore network that covered much of France. Napoleon used the system extensively, and on a clear day messages could be passed from Strasbourg to Paris in just over three hours, using over 180 of these signal stations. The network was a huge success, until the introduction of the electric telegraph in 1859 rendered it obsolete.

Alternatively, continue straight uphill from the *halle* to rue du Château; this will take you to the old **Moulin de Cugarel** (July & Aug Tues–Sat 10am–12.30pm & 3–6.30pm; free), the last of the town's wind-powered grain mills. With the building of the Canal du Midi, farmers suddenly had access to markets as far afield as Toulouse and the Mediterranean, and so 32 mills were built to process the wheat which they brought to be sold. The *moulin* is an attractive stone structure; its superb grinding mechanism was fully restored in 1962. Below the mill in the heart of the old town, **place de Verdun** was medieval Castelnaudary's main square. Ringed by handsome mansion facades, the *place* is home to the town's main **covered market**, as well as the site of the colourful Monday market originally instituted in June 1268 by order of Alphonse de Poitiers, Count of Toulouse. Not far off sits the southern-Gothic-style, collegiate **church of St-Michel**, built in the fourteenth century. Its exterior is notable for its beautiful steeple, towering 55m above the neighbouring place de St-Just, as well as two fine doorways on the north side. Following the steps up from place Auriol takes you to the **Présidial**, a sombre stone building raised on the site of the town's castle in 1585, when Henri III made Castelnaudary capital of the Lauragais; it served in turn as a courthouse and a prison. Further north, in rue

---

Cassoulet

One of the great pillars of southern-French *terroir* ("country" or "local") cuisine is the humble **cassoulet**. A simple but tasty baked dish, made up of white beans and garlic cooked with bits of pork and sausage, cassoulet is a staple you'll find just about everywhere between the peaks of the Pyrenees and the banks of the Rhône. Legend has it that the dish originated in **Castelnaudary** in the mid-fourteenth century, when the Black Prince, Edward, besieged the town during the course of the Hundred Years' War. The defenders, gathering their last provisions, which amounted to some beans and scraps of meat, not only managed to concoct a culinary triumph under extreme duress but, thus fortified, put the English troops (whose own inferior syrupy brown baked-bean diet could not compete) to flight. Today the "original" recipe is safeguarded by the amusingly solemn **Confraternity of the Grand Cassoulet**, a collective of local chefs who occasionally dress up in distinctive medieval-style robes for culinary events and fairs. You'll have plenty of chances to eat cassoulet in Languedoc and Roussillon, but be warned, local wisdom (and common sense) says that it is a dish best avoided in the summer.

de l'Hôpital, the chapel of **Notre–Dame–de–Pitié** should not be missed. Founded in the eleventh century and a popular stop on the medieval pilgrimage route to Santiago de Compostela, its dazzling interior (which you can peek at through the grilles), contains a feast of gilt wooden low-relief panels depicting angels and biblical scenes in the most outrageously flamboyant Baroque style. The town's best restaurant, *Le Tirou* (see below) is just a short walk beyond.

The Grand Bassin

Castelnaudary's biggest draw is the section of the **Canal du Midi** which runs through town, punctuated by the broad **Grand Bassin**. This roughly oblong pool, some seven hectares in area, is the largest reservoir along the length of the navigable canal. Constructed as a port, where barges could turn around, get repaired and load up with the grain harvested in the Lauragais, it now serves as a **pleasure port** and point of embarkation for tours and trips along the inland waterways of the Midi and Languedoc. To the west, the Grand Bassin empties into the Petit Bassin, marked by the two road bridges over the canal, before narrowing to wind its way towards Toulouse. On the east side, a remarkable series of six locks, the **Écluse de St-Roch** lowers barges and boats bound for the Mediterranean. If you want to rent a boat for a few hours or a few weeks, take a tour or simply take in the variety of modern and historical craft that you can find on the canal, this is the place to do it (see box, p.90).

Eating and drinking

There is no shortage of **restaurants** where you can sample cassoulet and other *terroir* treats. The best, and most expensive, is undoubtedly ⅋ *Le Tirou* at 90 av Monseigneur de Langle (☎04.68.94.15.95; closed Wed, Thurs & Sun eve & late Dec to late Jan & part June), in an old stone house with a pleasant garden and an excellent *terroir carte* (€16–32). Of the hotel restaurants, the best is the *Centre et Lauragais* (see p.86), with a traditional Midi dining room (closed Mon–Fri eve; *menus* from €25), while *La Belle Époque* (closed Tues eve & Wed; ☎04.68.23.39.72), at 55 rue Général-Dejean, serves a great cassoulet (basic *menu* €12).

You can also pick up **take away** cassoulet and other regional delicacies from the town's well-reputed *traiteurs* and *conservateurs*, artisanal butchers and confectioners. There are a number of them in the old town, including Le Regal, at 30 rue Dunkerque, Escudier at no. 9, and Au Gourmet Chaurien at 38 cours de la République. The local **market** is held on Mondays.

St-Papoul

Just 8km from Castelnaudary, the **abbey of St-Papoul** (April–June, Sept & Oct daily 10–11.30am & 2–5.30pm; July & Aug daily 10am–6.30pm; Nov–March Sat, Sun & hols 10–11.30am & 2–6.30pm; €3.50, reduction with "Carte Inter-site" – see p.102) sits on the edge of the Lauragais plain. Founded in the eighth century by Pepin the Short, it became a powerful monastic site after 1317 when its abbot was elevated to the status of bishop. The church itself is impressive, with some sections dating back to the twelfth century. The most important feature, however, is the **carved capitals** on the upper rim of the exterior of the apse (which can be viewed without entering and outside of opening hours), executed by the "Master of Cabestany" (see box, p.297) and depicting Daniel in the lions' den.

Along the Canal du Midi from Toulouse to Carcassonne

The **Canal du Midi** cuts a roughly straight path through the wheat-producing lands of the Lauragais, clearing the compact suburbs of Toulouse and steering its

Biking and hiking the Canal du Midi

Whereas renting a boat (see p.90) may be the ideal way to enjoy the Canal du Midi, there are other eminently enjoyable options which involve considerably less time and expense. The easiest part of the canal's route along which to **bike** or **hike** is the initial – paved – stretch from **Toulouse to the Seuil de Naurouze**, following a path from Port St-Saveur (see p.74). The surrounding farmland, which gradually ascends the further you go, doesn't make for the most spectacular of backdrops, but the canal – its tree-lined placidity interrupted only by the "putt-putt" of passing boats – is beautiful in its own right. The total distance along the paved path is 50km, which can be biked in about five hours and walked in under twenty. If you decide on the latter course of action you need not commit yourself to going the whole way – you can stop at Ville-franche-Lauragais at the 30-kilometre mark to catch a bus back or onwards, or there are several places where you can break the journey and **spend the night** (see p.91). From Port-Lauragais, a further 12km from Villefranche, you have the option of continuing the rest of the journey to Naurouze on a boat cruise (see p.91). The paved path ends at Écluse Océan, shortly after the port, and a gravel towpath (fine for mountain bikes) continues to Carcassonne, a further 35km along the canal; should you wish to continue beyond Castelnaudary you will find good accommodation and **dining** options in Bram (see p.91).

tree-lined course east, parallel to the River Hers, towards its highest point, at the **Seuil** (or "threshold") **de Naurouze**. From here it descends to the basin at Castelnaudary, as the Montagne Noire, the source of the canal's water, comes into view to the north. From the Grand Bassin, the waterway travels eastwards across the plain, bridging the 32km to **Carcassonne**, where it begins to adapt to the contours of the Aude valley, and start in earnest its descent towards the sea (see Chapter 6). The total distance travelled by the canal from Toulouse to Carcassonne is 90km.

The canal today

Following the dramatic collapse of canal traffic in the mid-1800s (see box, p.86), the Canal du Midi languished and decayed. In the last fifteen years or so, however, it has been revived as a course for pleasure craft, and it's not difficult to see why. It remains a marvel of engineering and beauty, incorporating no fewer than 99 **locks** (*écluses*) and 130 **bridges**. The various topographical challenges were met with imagination, including the construction of **canal tunnels** and bridges, the latter allowing water to cross valleys and gullies, suspended in the air. No less beautiful are the stone foot and road bridges, most of which date back to the first era of construction. The graceful oval lock-basins, built in that shape for more strength, are guarded by uniform *maisons d'éclusier*, where the controls of the mechanism are housed; and, as along any major route, inns and restaurants punctuate the canal's course. Even the double file of plane trees which lines most of the waterway's length, giving it a distinctive "Midi" look, serves a technical as well as an aesthetic purpose: to shade the water and impede its loss through evaporation. The canal was designated a **UNESCO** World Heritage Site in 1996, ensuring its conservation.

You can follow it by road, and most sections have **foot** or **bicycle paths**, but the best way to travel it (and an ideal way to spend a family or group holiday) is, of course, **by boat**. It's a gentle, restful chug down a tunnel of greenery enhanced in spring by the bloom of yellow iris and wild gladioli, with occasional glimpses of a world beyond: a distant smudge of hills or the pinnacles of Carcassonne. There are outfits in all of the major ports which **rent houseboats** and barges – most of which will also rent bikes as an extra, perfect for exploring the sights along the waterway. Or, if you prefer to be driven rather than drive, there are many **cruises** too.

Navigating the Canal du Midi from Toulouse to Carcassonne

The canal is navigable from March to November, but the high season of July and August is best avoided – boat availability declines, prices rise and the canal gets quite crowded. Finally, if you don't want to commit the time and money to rent a houseboat, most ports also rent smaller **electric boats**, suitable for one to six people by the hour (usually €20) or half-day (around €50). Navigation itself is straightforward (quite literally) and an orientation session by the boat rental company is all you need to get you on your way – no licence is required. Generally, **locks** are open from 8am to 12.30pm and 1.30pm to 5.30/7.30pm: they open daily from mid-March to early-November, and Monday to Friday from mid-December to mid-March, but close on major holidays. There's no charge for passage, and you can count on about a quarter of an hour for a basin to fill or empty. With a maximum permitted speed of 6km per hour, you should expect to travel no more than 250km in a week of cruising. **Canal information** can be found at the port offices of Voies Navigables de France, the government organization in charge of inland waterways. Their head office is at 2 Port St-Étienne in Toulouse (℡05.61.36.24.24, ⱳwww.vnf.fr), with English-speaking port offices at Carcassonne (℡06.84.81.96.20), Castelnaudary (℡06.84.81.96.23) and Port St-Saveur (℡06.84.81.96.21). For port information and administration in Toulouse contact La Capitannerie, 7 Port Saint-Saveur (℡05.61.14.17.25, ℮infos @toulouse-croisieres.com)

To organize **boat rental** in Toulouse, contact Navicanal, 139 rue Bonnat (℡05.61.55.10.91, ⱳwww.navicanal.com). In Castelnaudary the biggest boat rental company is Crown Blue Line, Le Grand Bassin (℡04.68.94.52.72, ⱳwww.crown blueline.com); their fleet consists mostly of modern craft, so if you're hoping for a more authentic-looking barge, you may have to shop around and book well ahead. Another option in Castelnaudary is Connoisseur (℡04.68.94.09.75, ⱳwww.connoisseur.fr), also at Le Grand Bassin. At Carcassonne you can rent from Nautic (℡04.68.71.88.95, ⱳwww.nautique.fr), while Locaboat (℡03.86.91.72.72, ⱳwww.locaboat.com) rents out *pénichettes* (traditional canal boats), and also has a branch in Montesquieu-Lauragais (℡05.61.81.36.40) between Toulouse and Castelnaudary. Castel Nautique (℡04.68.76.73.34, ⱳwww.castelnautique.com) in Bram rents out both traditional and electric boats, as well as bicycles. At any of these firms expect to **pay** between €500 and €1500 per week for a three- to five-person boat depending on the model, amenities and time of year. For a **green option**, try the solar-power, handicapped-accessible 14-berth barges available from Naviratous, based in Sallèles d'Aude (see p.270) starting at €700 per week (℡04.68.46.37.98, ⱳwww.naviratous2.com).

For information on navigating the canal east of Carcassonne, see the box on p.268.

Along the canal

Whether you are drifting, rolling or strolling along, the quiet and unassuming hamlets along the Canal du Midi will afford you a glimpse of rural France at its most antiquated and peaceful. The first village of any size you'll pass is the old *bastide* of **Montgiscard**, some 10km from the port of Toulouse. There's not much to see here, but if you're tempted to stop, take a look at the medieval church, part of which was remodelled by the same architect who designed Toulouse's Hôtel d'Assézat. Next along you'll come to **Ayguesvives** and **Montesquieu-Lauragais**, both of which have impressive nineteenth-century *châteaux*. Eighteen kilometres from Toulouse you'll reach the **écluse de Négra**, which is where you leave the canal to reach **Villefranche-Lauragais**, and was once the first post-stop on the way to Agde – several of the old canalside buildings survive. Just to the east, **Avignonet-Lauragais** was once a wealthy woad town, and is notable for being the place where, in 1242, the Cathars, holed up in Montségur, launched an attack on and massacred a contingent of the Dominican Inquisition; the resulting counterattack brought about the destruction of Montségur castle and the mass execution of its garrison and population (see p.112). Today the town has a fourteenth-century church with a fine retable dating from 1632. The last stop before you reach Naurouze is the modern **Port-Lauragais**, built specifically for pleasure boating. It is of no particular interest in itself, aside from amenities including a restaurant and *capitannerie*. **Naurouze**, the highest point on the canal's path, is where the Rigole, or feeder canal, arrives bearing the water gathered on the slopes of the Montagne Noire; it has long been a point of transit, as the vestiges of Roman road here testify. The area around the canal junction has been set up as a **picnic area** and **park** (unfortunately with no toilets), and nearby you'll find a rather sombre monument to the canal's founder, Pierre-Paul Riquet. Incidentally, this is also the site where Soult signed his surrender to Wellington in 1814. From Naurouze it's another 12km to Castelnaudary (see p.85).

The main place of interest between Castelnaudary and Carcassonne is the ancient village of **BRAM**, a thirteenth-century *circulade* (see box, p.162) where the houses are arranged in tight concentric circles around the church. Bram's villagers resisted the Albigensian Crusaders in 1210, and when the town eventually fell to the Catholic forces, the inhabitants came to a grisly end. The Crusaders' leader, Simon de Montfort, ordered a hundred prisoners to be blinded and mutilated; the refugees, carrying their amputated body parts, were then sent to the as yet unvanquished fortress of Cabaret, led by the one villager who had been left with a single eye ungouged.

Practicalities

For general **information**, as well as plenty of details on navigating the canal, see Ⓦwww.canaldumidi.com. If you're boating, **accommodation** will not be a concern, but for cyclists and walkers there are various possibilities along the way. At Ayguesvives, 20km south of Toulouse, head for *La Pradesse* (Ⓣ05.61.81.55.96, Ⓦwww.lapradesse.com; ❺), a well-equipped *chambres d'hôtes* at 39 chemin de Toulouse (meals €29). About 5km east at Montesquieu-Lauragais, look for the welcoming *La Maison d'Hôtes de Bigot* (Ⓣ05.61.27.02.83; ❺), which does excellent home-made meals for €20. *L'Obélisque* (Ⓣ.05.61.27.24.30; ❷), a further 12km or so along, near the centre of Avignonet, is another excellent choice for both a room and a meal. There are a number of options at Castelnaudary (see p.86). Further along, at Bram, there's a bucolic *chambres d'hôtes*, *Domaine de Pigné* (Ⓣ04.68.76.10.25, Ⓦwww.ferme-auberge-du-pigne.com; ❸), on the outskirts of the village, and a simple but comfortable hotel, the *Clos Saint Loup*, at 69 av des Razes, just south of the old *circulade* (closed Dec 24–28; Ⓣ04.68.76.11.91, Ⓔleclossaintloup@orange.fr; ❸), which also offers filling local *menus* from €14. From here, if you can't make the last 25km to Carcassonne in one go, stop at *Domaine de l'Espitalet* (Ⓣ04.68.71.66.75) in **Caux et Sauzens**, which provides cosy rooms (❸) and meals (€20).

Options for **canal tours** include *Le St Roch*, in Castelnaudary's Grand Bassin (Ⓣ04.68.23.49.40, Ⓦwww.saintroch11.com), which offers excursions of between thirty minutes and two hours (€4–12 per person), while *Croisières Cathy* (Ⓣ06.09.33.15.96, Ⓦpagesperso-orange.fr/croisierescathy), also in Castelnaudary, runs full- and half-day programmes (9am, €30 including lunch, and 2.15pm, €9.50, respectively). Additionally, just west of Naurouze at Port-Laugarais, the *Lucie* runs a thirty-minute circuit to the Seuil and back (April–Sept daily; €5), as well as other longer itineraries whenever ten or more passengers assemble.

Travel details

Trains

Toulouse is the rail hub for this region, on the Narbonne–Bordeaux/Paris trunk line, with smaller lines going to Albi and Carmaux, and Latour-de-Carol/Enveitg, which hooks up with the Train Jaune (p.92) to Perpignan, as well as services to Revel and Castres. SNCF buses may run in lieu of trains on some of these lines; services are reduced on Sundays and holidays. TGV stations are indicated with an asterisk.

Toulouse* to:

Albi (connections to Carmaux), via Rabastens, Lisle and Gaillac (many hourly; 1hr–1hr 30min).

Latour-de-Carol/Enveitg (connections to Train Jaune & Perpignan), via Pamiers, Foix, Tarascon-sûr-Ariège, L'Hospitalet-près-l'Andorre and Porte-Puymorens (several daily; 3hr–3hr 15min).

Mazamet, via Lavaur and Castres (many daily; 2hr–2hr 15min).

Nîmes* (connections to Grau & Tarascon/Beaucaire), via Bram, Castelnaudary, Carcassonne* (connection to Quillan), Narbonne* (connections to Perpignan), Béziers* (connections to Bédarieux), Agde, Sète and Montpellier* (several hourly; 2hr 45min–3hr 45min).

Paris* (several daily; 5hr 30min+).

St-Girons/St-Lizier, via Boussens (several daily; 1hr 45min–2hr).

Vindrac (Cordes), via Rabastens, Lisle and Gaillac (several daily; 1hr).

Buses

In the Haute Garonne most lines have no Sunday service; holidays and school holiday periods often have little or no service (see partial schedule of regional lines at ⊕ www.cg31.fr/bus.asp).

Castelnaudary to: Alet-les-Bains (daily; 1hr 5min); Axat (daily; 1hr 50min); Bram (several weekly; 30min); Carcassonne (several daily; 45min); Limoux (daily; 1hr); Quillan (several weekly; 1hr 30min); Sorèze (at least 1 weekly; 30min); Villefranche (several daily; 20min).

Lavaur to: Castres (several daily; 45min–1hr); Gaillac (several daily; 35min); Toulouse (several daily; 50min).

Revel to: Castres (several daily; 1hr); St-Félix (several daily; 20min).

Toulouse to: Albi (several daily; 2hr 40min); Avignonet (many daily; 1hr 25min); Ax (daily; 2hr 11min); Carcassonne (daily; 2hr 20min); Castelnaudary (many daily; 1hr 25min); Castres (several daily; 1hr 40min–2hr); Foix (several daily; 1hr 30min); Gaillac (several daily; 1hr 25min); Grauhlet (several daily; 1hr 35min); Lavaur (daily; 1hr 10min); Lavelanet (daily; 2hr 30min); Mas d'Azil (daily; 1hr 50min); Mazamet (daily; 2hr); Mirepoix (daily; 2hr); Pamiers (several daily; 1hr–1hr 30min); Revel (several daily; 1hr 10min); St-Félix-de-Lauragais (daily; 1hr 5min); St-Girons (daily; 2hr 30min); St-Sulpice (daily; 30min); Sorèze (daily; 1hr 20min); Villefranche (several daily; 44min).

Carcassonne, Upper Aude and Ariège

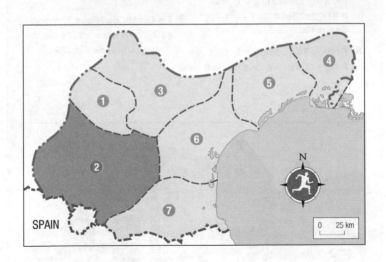

CHAPTER 2 # Highlights

* **Carcassonne** Southern France's most visited monument, this reconstructed medieval citadel is a must-see. **See p.96**

* **Carnaval** Limoux's famous Lenten festival draws crowds from around the Southwest to see its elaborately costumed dancers. **See p.97**

* **Rennes-le-Château** A mecca for occultists and conspiracy theorists following the trail of a nineteenth-century priest. **See p.108**

* **Rafting** The upper Aude and Ariège rivers provide excellent opportunities for a range of skill levels. **See p.111**

* **Montségur** The legendary site of the heretic Cathars' last stand enjoys as dramatic a setting as you're likely to see anywhere. **See p.112**

* **Mirepoix** The region's best-preserved medieval town features a stunningly carved fourteenth-century town hall, now converted into a hotel. **See p.115**

* **La Grotte de Niaux** The best prehistoric cave art still open to the public. **See p.129**

▲ Carcassonne

Carcassonne, Upper Aude and Ariège

The citadel of **Carcassonne** is quintessential Languedoc: a medieval fortress with the foothills of the Pyrenees rising off to the south, the peaks of the Montagne Noire looming to the north, and the languid waters of the Canal du Midi gliding past towards the Mediterranean. Although it fell to Catholic forces early in the Crusade, Carcassonne was held to be the epicentre of the Cathar heresy in Languedoc: the castles which form a far-flung ring in the Corbières and the Pyrenean slopes to the south were referred to as the heretic capital's "sons". The land fanning southwest of the city rises in a series of ridges and plains, cut through by two rivers. The first, the **Aude**, runs north to Carcassonne, skirting the highlands of the **pays de Sault** on its way down from the mountains. Journeying up this valley and into the *pays*, a region littered with narrow gorges and high passes, is like flipping through the pages of Cathar history – from the site of their greatest fortified city to the ruins of their last redoubt, **Montségur**. The second river, flowing down from Andorra to Toulouse, gives its name to the *département* – **Ariège** – constituting the remainder of this chapter. **Foix**, once the thriving capital of a proudly independent county, sits at the centre of the *département*, standing sentinel over the course of the rapid river, after it has twisted through the northern slopes of the Pyrenees past the skiing and hiking country around the spa of **Ax-les-Thermes** and **Tarascon-sur-Ariège**, with its incredible array of **prehistoric caves** – justification alone for a trip to the region. The plain northeast of Foix was once the haunt of troubadours and men of religion: Cathar *parfaits* (see *The Land of Cathars* colour section) and the Inquisitors sent to hunt them. Reduced to a ruin in the Wars of Religion, today its ancient, near-abandoned villages with their arcaded squares and crumbling walls offer the only faded record of the district's rich past. At the southwestern limits of the *département*, the **Couserans**, whose snowcapped peaks are ranged in breathtaking cirques, form a virtually impenetrable barrier to Spain beyond.

Today, the Aude valley – with the exception of ever-popular Carcassonne – and the Ariège *département* are two of the least developed regions in the French Southwest. Isolated by difficult terrain, and afflicted for generations by the emigration of youth to the better prospects of the northern cities, they offer few opportunities apart from farming and herding. In recent years, tourism has rescued the area from its relentless decline, and to a certain extent, the construction of **ski resorts**, spas and local museums has served to improve the region's prospects.

Toulouse ▲ ▲ Toulouse

CARCASSONNE,
THE UPPER AUDE
& ARIÈGE

But these recent initiatives, if they have stimulated the local economy, have not detracted from the essential flavour of the area – a refuge of mountain tradition.

As you'd expect, the region is not the best for public transport. There's a good **rail** service running up the Ariège valley, from Toulouse (hooking up with the Tech service of Roussillon), while the other line, from Carcassonne to Quillan, has considerably fewer services. **Bus** services, even between larger towns, are infrequent: consult the "Travel details" on p.133, and obtain current local information before planning a route.

Carcassonne

Your first view of **CARCASSONNE**, its fairy-tale citadel perched high above the grassy verges of the River Aude, is likely to be a memorable one. The famous **cité**, declared a UNESCO World Heritage Site in 1997, enjoys must-see status on any trip through southwest France, and if it has suffered through the ages – beaten, burnt and dismantled – you'd never guess from looking at it. Aside from the walled town, with

Festivals in Carcassonne and Ariège

July and August are the best months for **festivals** in Ariège. The biggest festival is Carcassonne's Bastille Day, but bear in mind that the town gets packed out for the event, with parked cars lining the *route nationale* for several kilometres from the *cité*. Limoux's *Carnaval* is also a unique event, worth planning for if you're in the area.

Mid-Jan to Easter Limoux: *Carnaval*. An extended Lenten celebration featuring vividly costumed dancers in the old town squares. Three sets of performances (11am, 4pm & 10pm) on Saturdays and Sundays.

June Couserans: *Transhumances en Couserans* ⓦ www.transhcouserans.free.fr. In a revival of the ancient tradition, four thousand sheep are driven up the valleys of the Couserans into the high pasturelands. See box on p.126.

19–23 June St-Girons: *Sent Joan Beth e Gran* ⓣ 05.61.04.65.53, ⓦ www.ville-st -girons.fr. Celebration of St John's Day culminating in the traditional bonfire: four days of folk concerts and dances feature groups of the Couserans as well as foreign troupes.

Throughout July Carcassonne: *Festival de Carcassonne de la Cité & Festival de la Bastide* ⓣ 04.68.25.33.16. Month-long festival of dance, music and theatre with nightly performances in the castle's amphitheatre and free performances in the squares of the *cité*, with huge fireworks on Bastille Day (July 14).

Third weekend of July Mirepoix: *Les Médiévales de Mirepoix* ⓣ 05.61.68.83.76. Medieval horsemanship, pageantry, market and fair in the arcaded squares around the cathedral.

Late July Limoux: *Festival du Folklore*. Five-day international festival featuring traditional storytelling, theatre, dance and music.

Late July Quillan: *Festival du Folklore International*. Held over six days, this international festival features storytelling and theatre with an impressive repertoire of groups from as far afield as East Asia and South America.

Late July Ax-les-Thermes: *Spectacles de Grands Chemins* ⓣ 05.61.64.38.00, ⓦ www.ax-animation.com. A three-day festival of street theatre celebrating local *montagnard* culture and featuring over twenty French companies.

Early Aug Mirepoix: *Festival de la Marionette* ⓣ 05.61.68.20.72, ⓦ www.filentrope .free.fr. Three-day festival of puppetry along with a large craft and produce market.

First week of Aug St-Girons: *Rite* ⓣ 06.07.32.77.58, ⓦ www.bethmalais.org. Ten-day festival of traditional culture, including music, song and dance, and featuring over two hundred performers drawn from countries as diverse as Mongolia and Angola.

First weekend of Aug St-Girons: *Autrefois le Couserans* ⓦ www.ville-stgirons.fr. Two days celebrating the region's rural traditions, including performances, a market and horse and donkey races.

Mid-Aug Carcassonne: *Spectacle Médiéval* ⓣ 04.68.71.35.35, ⓦ www.terredhistoire .com. Medieval costumes and pageantry and a theatrical re-enactment with a different theme each year.

First two weeks of Aug Limoux: *Vigne et Terroir* ⓣ 05.61.96.67.89. A celebration of local culinary traditions, with concerts, street performances and good food and drink in abundance.

Last weekend of Aug Carcassonne: *Fiesta y Toros*. A weekend of taurine events including bullfights and *abrivados*, equestrian displays, and a Spanish-style street party (bullfights €30; ⓣ 04.68.71.01.00).

First two weeks of Sept Foix: *Fêtes de Foix*. An annual festival, with produce markets, music and a medieval theme, centred on the illustrious figure of Gaston Fébus (see p.121).

Sept 21 Vicdessos: *St-Matthieu*. Transhumant livestock fair, formalized by the Count de Foix in 1313. Nowadays, the tradition continues with a lively market and celebration.

Early Oct Couserans: *Transhumances en Couserans* (see June, above).

its castle and basilica, there's the medieval lower town, or **ville basse**, set on the far side of the Aude. Together, the two complement each other: the first is outstandingly beautiful, while the latter is lively and practical. Comparatively good transport links by bus, rail, canal and air also make Carcassonne the best starting point for exploring the surrounding areas: the uplands of the Ariège and the Aude covered later in this chapter, and to the north, the isolated Montagne Noire (see p.170).

The city was settled as far back as the sixth century BC, passing through the hands of Romans and Visigoths before its golden age under the great Languedocian family, the **Trencavels**. This family, vassals of the counts of Toulouse (the "St-Gilles" family) from 1163, used Carcassonne as their principal residence, ensuring the town's prosperity. The town was besieged and taken in 1209 by anti-Cathar Crusaders, eventually passing to the notorious Simon de Montfort, who made it his "**capital**". After the feared warrior died outside the walls of Toulouse in 1218, the Trencavel Raymond-Roger VII briefly recovered the town, only to see it pass to royal control in 1229. Some twenty years later, King Louis IX laid out the *ville basse*, a *bastide* that would serve as a regional market and increase the town's wealth. Carcassonne thus prospered until the Hundred Years' War, when the English **Black Prince** (see box, p.266), frustrated by his inability to seize the citadel, burnt the *ville basse* to the ground in 1355. Despite this, the citizens rallied and rebuilt, and for the rest of the Middle Ages Carcassonne was an important market town, profiting from its location on the frontier of the Kingdom of France. With the annexation of Roussillon in 1659, however, the border shifted south and Carcassonne stagnated. The citadel was abandoned and eventually quarried for its stones. This is how it remained until it was rediscovered in the nineteenth century by **Viollet-le-Duc**, whose visionary fifty-year restoration project rescued it from obscurity.

Today Carcassonne continues to flourish largely because of that vision, which brings in masses of visitors every year, making it the country's most visited city after Paris. Despite the fact that the citadel is the only sight as such, and there is essentially very little to do here, it is nevertheless a great place to spend a relaxing few days. Additionally, the *cité* has become something of a symbol of medieval France; its yearly **pageants** and spectacular Bastille Day celebrations (see box, p.97), featuring the second-largest fireworks display in France, keep the streets full of both French and foreign tourists.

Arrival and information

Carcassonne's small **airport** (Ⓦ www.carcassonne.aeroport.fr) is just west of town. A shuttle bus, or *navette* (hourly; 15min; €5), leaves from outside the terminal and stops in town at the train station, place Gambetta, and the *cité*; a **taxi** to the centre costs €8–15. The **gare SNCF** (Ⓣ08.36.35.35.35) is on the north side of the *ville basse*, just over the Canal du Midi from boulevard Omer Sarraut. From the station you can catch the *navette*, or simply head south until you hit rue de Verdun where the

---

Essentials

Bike rental Évasion 2 Roues, 85 allée d'Iéna (Ⓣ04.68.25.28.18); Espace 11, 3 rte de Minervoise (Ⓣ04.68.25.28.18, Ⓔespace11@orange.fr), also has motorbikes and scooters. Both are closed Sun & Mon.

Internet access Alert Rouge, 73 rue de Verdun (Mon–Fri 10am–1am, Sat 2pm–3am).

Laundry 5 sq Gambetta & 31 rue Aimé-Ramond.

Market pl Carnot, Tues, Thurs & Sat mornings.

Taxi Radio Taxi Ⓣ04.68.71.50.50.

The Legend of Dame Carcas

The origin of Carcassonne's strange-sounding name has given rise to a number of interesting stories, the most enduring of which is that of **Dame Carcas**. Legend asserts that when the town was under Muslim control in the early Middle Ages, the Emperor Charlemagne arrived to lay siege, knowing that if his army attacked for long enough, eventually the town would run short of food. However, just when defeat looked inevitable, Carcas, the Muslim ruler's wife, ordered a pig to be force-fed with the last of the town's precious grain and tossed over the battlements. When it hit the ground and split open , Charlemagne's troops despaired, believing that the town was well supplied. They lifted the siege and retreated, and as the town's church bells pealed in celebration, the townsfolk cried "Carcas, sonne!" ("Ring, Carcas!"). It is pure fantasy of course. A Muslim ruler would never have kept pigs. Nevertheless it is more evocative than the true origin of the name, which derives from the Occitan *carac* ("rock") and *sonne* ("wood").

main **tourist office** can be found at no. 28 (Mon–Sat 9am–6pm & Sun 9am–noon; ☎04.68.10.24.30, ⓦ www.carcassonne-tourisme.com); there's a second tourist office (daily: June & Sept 9am–6pm; July & Aug 9am–7pm; Oct–May 9am–5pm; ☎04.68.10.24.36) in the *cité*, just inside the main entrance. Both branches sell the handy *Rando-Guide* (€1), outlining six walks and hikes in the Carcassonne area. Finally, there's a canalside information office (daily: April–June, Sept & Oct noon–6pm; July & Aug 9am–6pm) at the town's port. Carcassonne has no *gare routière* as such; **buses** arrive along the broad boulevard de Varsovie on the west side of the *ville basse*. If you're arriving **by car**, there's a car park up by the *cité*, but there are cheaper options ringing the *ville basse*, as well as free and metered street parking.

Place Gambetta is the **local transport** hub; all city buses and *navettes* (€1.10) leave from here – a *navette* to the *cité* (€1.50 return) and campsite departs from near the Caisse d'Épargne bank (mid-July to mid-Sept 7am–10.30pm, every 15min).

Accommodation

Although your first impulse may be to get a room in the *cité*, beware that if you are hoping to pass the evenings in a medieval idyll you will most likely be disappointed. What little **accommodation** there is here is expensive; furthermore, the citadel is very busy – verging on lunacy in high season. You may be more satisfied with a room along the slopes down towards the riverbank, or in the *ville basse* (from where you get the view of the *cité*). From November to March the tourist office operates a "Bon week-end" programme, which gives you two nights for one at participating hotels.

Cité hotels

All the hotels below are marked on the *cité* map on p.101.

🏃 **De la Cité** Pl de l'Église ☎04.68.71.98.71, ⓦ www.hoteldelacite.com. If you can afford it, this luxurious hotel with its beautiful enclosed courtyard will separate you from the maddening crowds of the *cité*. Service and amenities are deluxe; rooms, which are serviced twice daily, have satellite TV and DVD (with an in-house library) and they'll lend you a laptop if you don't bring your own. The price matches the opulence. Closed mid-Jan to mid-Feb. ❾

Le Donjon 2 rue du Comte Roger ☎04.68.11 .23.00, ⓦ www.hotel-donjon.fr. The other *cité* hotel

is surprisingly affordable for what you get: a thoroughly renovated establishment with excellent service and an atmosphere of refined luxury. A much better value-for-money choice than the *De la Cité*. Just a stone's throw from the *donjon*. ❼

Éspace Cité 132 rue Trivalle ☎04.68.25.24.24, ⓦ www.hotelespacecite.fr. With its motel ambience, what this hotel lacks in charm it tries hard to make up for with amenities such as a/c, TV and garage parking. A comfortable option and an excellent deal. Just downhill from the main gate to the *cité*; wheelchair-accessible. ❹

Montmorency 2 rue Camille St-Saëns ☎04.68.11.96.70, ⓦ www.lemontmorency.com. A plain exterior conceals a welcoming and well-kept respite, with sound-proofed rooms, a/c and a good range of services. Well located for visiting the citadel, as it's just one street north of the *cité*. Wheelchair access and a swimming pool. ❹

du Pont Vieux 32 rue Trivalle ⓣ04.68.25.24.99, ⓦwww.lacitedecarcassonne.fr. Perhaps the best all-round choice in town, this friendly, traditional-style hotel is on a lively, atmospheric little street which winds up from the medieval bridge towards the *cité*. Expect to pay more for rooms with a view of the city. TV and parking; pets are welcome. ❹

Ville basse hotels

All the hotels below are marked on the *ville basse* map on p.103.

de la Bastide 81 rue de la Liberté ⓣ04.68.71.96.89, ⓔhoteldelabastide@wanadoo .fr. A great deal in this family-run establishment in the *ville basse*, down a quiet side-street not far from the station. The clean rooms come equipped with TV, wi-fi and a/c; there's also a lift and car park, all at one-star prices. ❸

Ibis Centre 5 pl Gambetta ⓣ04.68.72.37.37, ⓦwww.ibishotel.com. This well-kept establishment is convenient for the old town. The rooms are compact but modern and comfortable; all have a/c and wi-fi and some are wheelchair-accessible. ❺

Montségur 27 allée d'Iéna ⓣ04.68.25.31.41, ⓦwww.hotelmontsegur.com. Comfortable rooms in an impressive-looking nineteenth-century townhouse. Located a fifteen-minute walk west of the cathedral, off boulevard Barbès, it is not the closest hotel to the *cité*, but it's competitively priced. The decor is decidedly "olde worlde" but all

rooms have satellite TV, a/c and wi-fi. Closed late Dec to Jan. English spoken. ❻

🏃 **Du Soleil Terminus** 2 av de Maréchal Joffre ⓣ04.68.25.25.00, ⓕ04.68.75.53.09. Fading steam-age luxury in this station-side hotel, which has a splendid *fin-de-siècle* facade. Excellent value for money with a range of amenities including a good bar, an indoor pool, sauna and whirlpool. Larger rooms and suites are available. ❹

Hostels and campsite

All the listings below are marked on the *cité* map opposite.

Camping de la Cité Rte St-Hilaire ⓣ04.68.25.11.17, ⓦwww.camping-carcassonne .info. Exceptional ground with good shady sites, some bungalows and a shop. Tucked away in parkland to the south of town, it can be reached by local bus #8 or by a twenty-minute walk from the *cité*. If you point your tent in the right direction you get a view of the citadel poking up over the trees. Open mid-March to mid-Oct.

HI hostel rue Trencavel ⓣ04.68.25.23.16, ⓔcarcassonne@fuaj.org. Excellent, modern hostel in the heart of the citadel. Its dorms (€16) and 4–6-person rooms are clean and bright, and there's a large patio for respite from the crowds outside, plus a bar. Membership (available on site) required in summer. Closed last two weeks of Dec.

Notre Dame de l'Abbaye 103 rue Trivalle ⓣ04.68.25.16.65, ⓦwww.abbaye-carcassonne .com. A second choice for hostel-style accommodation. Great location in a beautiful street; comfortable dorms (€16) and sheet rental available (€3).

The Town

Carcassonne is divided into three main parts. The oldest is the **cité**, the compact citadel perched on a hill on the east bank of the Aude. Descending from here you pass through the medieval suburb of La Barbacane before crossing the river to the **ville basse**, formally La Bastide de St-Louis – a typical grid of thirteenth-century streets, once contained by a wall. Splayed out around this is the nondescript **new town**, a series of uninteresting suburbs with nothing to tempt you out there.

The Cité

From whichever direction you approach, Carcassonne's magnificent **citadel**, its stout ramparts and pennant-capped towers piercing the sky, presents one of the South of France's most striking images, straight out of a medieval fantasy. However, much of Carcassonne is, in fact, fabrication – a piece of imaginative reconstruction by the nineteenth-century restorer Viollet-le-Duc, whose enthusiasm for "the medieval" inspired him to invent inaccurate features like the conical towers and arrow-slits, which the original medieval fortress lacked.

Nevertheless, as you cross over the moat, passing the wide grassy verges between the thick double walls, you do feel as though you're entering another world. You can

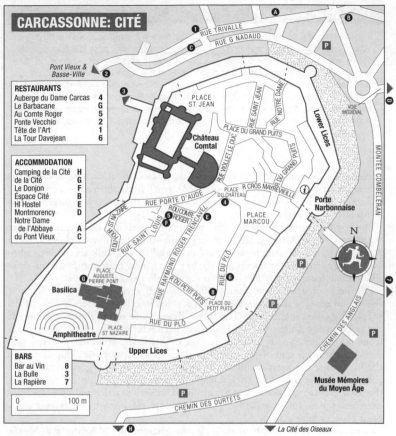

CARCASSONNE: CITÉ

Pont Vieux & Basse-Ville

RESTAURANTS

Auberge du Dame Carcas	**4**
Le Barbacane	**G**
Au Comte Roger	**5**
Ponte Vecchio	**2**
Tête de l'Art	**1**
La Tour Davejean	**6**

ACCOMMODATION

Camping de la Cité	**H**
de la Cité	**G**
Le Donjon	**F**
Espace Cité	**B**
HI Hostel	**E**
Montmorency	**D**
Notre Dame	
de l'Abbaye	**A**
du Pont Vieux	**C**

BARS

Bar au Vin	**8**
La Bulle	**3**
La Rapière	**7**

0   100 m

PLACE ST JEAN

VOIE MÉDIÉVAL

Château Comtal

RUE PORTE D'AUDE

PLACE DU CHÂTEAU

R CROS MAYREVIEILLE

Porte Narbonnaise

PLACE MARCOU

RUE RAYMOND ROGER TRENCAVEL

PLACE AUGUSTE PIERRE PONT

Basilica

PLACE DU PETIT PUITS

RUE DU PLÔ

Amphitheatre

PLACE ST NAZAIRE

Upper Lices

MONTÉE COMBELERAN

CHEMIN DES ANGLAIS

Musée Mémoires du Moyen Âge

CHEMIN DES OURTETS

La Cité des Oiseaux

enter through the **Porte d'Aude**, on the citadel's western side, but a more visually impressive option is the main **Porte Narbonnaise** on the far side of the *cité*, where the local *navettes* and main car park are found. From here, rue Cros Mayrevieille, with its phalanxes of souvenir shops and ice-cream stands, leads to the entrance of the twelfth-century **Château Comtal** (daily: Oct–March 10am–5pm, April–Sept 10am–6.30pm; by guided tour only; €8), the castle where Raymond-Roger Trencavel made his last stand against the northern knights, and surrendered, in 1209. The ticket office for the castle is just inside the Porte Narbonnaise, to the left, and you can pick up handsets for self-guided audio tours (€3) here as well. **Guided tours** (35–40min, occasionally in English in summer) of the castle begin in the main castle courtyard, leading through the now roofless keep, and along a section of the citadel's three kilometres of walls including three of its 31 towers. Take care along the walls, as stairways can be slippery and the inadequate railings are no match for curious children. The views from the walls are excellent, and the guides' frank account of the history of the town is lively and informative. Appropriately, the castle also hosts an exhibition on the life and work of Viollet-le-Duc (see box, p.104).

The tour ends behind the **basilica** of St-Nazaire (Mon–Fri 8.45am–12.45pm & 1.45–5/6pm, Sat & Sun 8.45–10.30am & 2–5/6pm; free), a late eleventh-century Romanesque church that has undergone major Gothic and neo-Gothic remodellings.

The Cathar "Passport"

If you're planning on visiting a few of the Cathar sites in the region, consider buying a **"Carte Inter-site"** or "Le Passeport des sites du Pays Cathare" pass (€3) from participating sites or local tourist offices. Valid for a year, it gives you reductions on the entrance fee to selected castles and monuments of the Aude *département*, including the abbeys and castles of Aguilar, Arques, Carcassonne, Caunes-Minervois, Fontfroide, Lagrasse, Lastours, Minerve, Montségur, Peyrepertuse, Puilaurens, the Puivert museum, Quéribus, St-Hilaire, St-Papoul, Saissac, Termes, Usson, Villelongue and Villerouge. Total savings, if you visit all of these sites, is €18 for adults, €28.70 for children.

Look out for a stunning series of **gargoyles** along the eaves of the apse, as well as the amusingly carved heads above the door. Inside, you'll find a thirteenth-century choir and rosette window – while propped up against a wall in the south transept is Simon de Montfort's original tombstone.

The best thing to do in the *cité,* after visiting the castle and church, is to wander the narrow, crooked streets, and absorb the convincingly medieval ambience. You'll pass a smattering of small, tourist-trap "museums" as you walk about, devoted to Middle Age torture instruments and the like, but you're better off bypassing these and heading for the grassy *lices* between the citadel's two sets of walls.

The *lices* – a narrow space some 1100m in length, created with the building of the second set of walls in the 1200s, and divided into two sections – makes for a beautifully atmospheric stroll. The **lower lices** run from the Porte Narbonnaise to the Porte de l'Aude around the northern perimeter of the citadel; starting out from the former, you'll notice a section of brick-and-stone-constructed wall dating back to the end of the period of Roman occupation. Walking along the slightly longer southern circuit of the **upper lices** gives you good views of the elaborate towers added to the citadel's defences under Philip III in the late thirteenth century. Once a space for medieval archery practice and other military exercises, the *lices* now provide a favourite route for horsedrawn *calèches* and a great place to have a picnic.

Outside the Porte Narbonnaise, on the chemin des Anglais, the **Musée Mémoires du Moyen Âge** (Museum of Memories of the Middle Ages; 10am–7pm; €3) houses a collection of dioramas depicting battalions of medieval soldiers hacking and slashing at each other – strictly for kids.

The ville basse

When you leave the *cité*, instead of backtracking through the main gates and past the car park, a better option is to take the gate at the end of rue Notre Dame, off place du Grand Puits, and cut down to rue Trivalle, a world away from the touristy scrum in the fortress above. Spanning the Aude is the picturesque fourteenth-century **Pont Vieux**, adorned on its far side by the small and simple Gothic structure of the twelfth-century Notre Dame de la Santé **chapel**. The riverbanks on the *cité* side have been kept free of building and make a nice grassy spot to relax or have a picnic.

Across the river, **place Gambetta** – the southern hub of the **ville basse** – has an airy feel, despite the traffic, as well as some attractive nineteenth-century facades. Keep an eye out for the impressive Art Deco facade of the Groupe Scolaire Jean-Jaurès on the northwest corner. Close by on rue de Verdun is an eighteenth-century *hôtel* housing the **Musée des Beaux-Arts** (mid-June to mid-Sept Wed–Sun 10am–6pm; mid-Sept to mid-June Tues–Sat 10am–noon &

2–6pm; free), which has a large collection of eighteenth-century landscapes, and sometimes hosts interesting temporary exhibitions. At the far end of rue de Verdun, the **Maison des Mémoires** at no. 53 (Tues–Sat 9am–noon & 2–6pm; free) pays homage to local-born surrealist poet Joë Bousquet (1857–1950). Left paraplegic by battle wounds received at Vailly in 1918, Bousquet lived out the rest of his life bedridden in this house in Carcassonne, comforted by opium and producing dark and mystical poetical reflections which attracted the attention of the interwar intelligentsia. **Place Carnot** is the heart of the old *bastide* – a wide square with shops, cafés and bars as well as a good **market** (Tues, Thurs & Sat mornings). A couple of blocks south, near the fourteenth-century **cathedral** of St-Michel on boulevard Barbès, you'll find the most substantial remains of the town's once stout defences; the **Porte des Jacobins**, a medieval gate which was widened and remodelled in Neoclassical style in 1778, is in good shape, while beside it lie the remains of the old ramparts. Otherwise, look for some of the impressive old private *hôtels*; on rue Aimé-Ramond you'll find the plain, medieval-styled facade of the fourteenth-century Maison du Sénéchal, at no. 70, and a more flamboyant Renaissance *hôtel* at no. 50.

Eating, drinking and nightlife

You'll never have a problem getting something **to eat** in Carcassonne, whether in the *cité*, where every other facade seems to belong to a bistro, or in the *ville basse*, which has a good selection of simple and smarter establishments. Place Marcou in the *cité*, in particular, is home to a mass of indistinguishable patios all of which have *menus* in the €12 range.

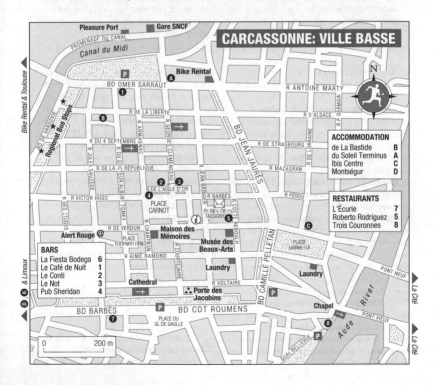

It may come as a surprise that many of the buildings of medieval France are, in fact, nineteenth-century reconstructions. Up until then, the Middle Ages was considered a barbaric period best forgotten, but in the early 1800s European intellectuals began to look back at the medieval era as the time when their nations were born, and projects were undertaken to recover its neglected art and architecture. The major figure in this movement in France was Eugène Emmanuel **Viollet-le-Duc**, the prolific restorer-extraordinaire who left his – often fantastical – mark all over the country, but particularly in Languedoc and Roussillon.

Having studied art history at the Sorbonne, Viollet-le-Duc began his career assisting in the renovation of Paris's glorious **Sainte-Chapelle**, and established his reputation as a restorer. In the years that followed he was inundated with contracts to restore buildings such as Narbonne's Hôtel de Ville (see p.258) and the basilica of St-Nazaire in Carcassonne, and in 1853 Louis-Napoleon granted him supervision of the restoration of all of France's medieval buildings. By this time he had already begun the massive reconstruction of the **cité** – a fifty-year project he would not live to see finished.

Viollet-le-Duc's idiosyncratic **theory** of restoration dictated that buildings should not necessarily be returned to their exact previous state, but rather modified according to their essential underlying architectural principles (as he saw them, naturally). As a result, the elaborate restorations – in which he sometimes started from nothing more than a pile of stones – are reflections of Viollet-le-Duc's imagination. In Carcassonne's *cité*, for example, he not only made "improvements", such as adding arrow-slits and crenellation to the walls, but adopted features which are aesthetically pleasing but, quite simply, inaccurate: the pointed roofs on the towers are German-style as opposed to the flat Languedocian version. Whatever you think about Viollet-le-Duc's easy attitude to verisimilitude, as you travel around Languedoc and Roussillon, bear in mind that – for better or worse – almost all the great medieval monuments here have "benefited" to some degree from his endeavours.

Cité restaurants

All the restaurants below are marked on the *cité* map on p.101.

Auberge de Dame Carcas 3 pl du Château ☎04.68.71.23.23. Large restaurant with several dining rooms, serving up excellent-quality traditional and regional cuisine. With *menus* at €15–26, this is one of the best-value places in town, so book ahead. Closed Sun eve, Mon lunch & Feb.

Le Barbacane Pl de l'Église ☎04.68.71.98.71. The most elegant (and expensive) of the three restaurants operated by the *Hôtel de la Cité*. Adventurous Mediterranean-grounded *gastronomique* cuisine with four-star service, and the only Michelin star in Carcassonne. You'll pay upwards of €75, although for €160 chef Jérôme Ryan will treat you to an eight-course meal matched up with local wine selections. Evenings only.

Au Comte Roger 14 rue St-Louis ☎04.68.11.93.41. Renowned chef Pierre Mesa imaginatively combines local Lauragais basics with subtle *gastronomique* touches. The roast lamb in an earthenware pot makes an ideal end to a day in the *cité*. *Menus* €20–45. Closed Sun & late Jan to late Feb.

Ponte Vecchio 22 rue Trivalle ☎04.68.71.33.17. Fine Italian dining and hospitable atmosphere in the shadow of the *cité*. Good old comfort food (pasta!) if you are tiring of the duck and goose liver. *Menus* €14.50–17.50. Closed Mon & mid-Nov to mid-Dec.

Tête de l'Art 37 bis rue Trivalle ☎04.68.71.23.11. Located on the atmospheric thoroughfare which connects the old bridge and the *cité*, the *Tête de l'Art* sports an unassuming exterior girded by a tiny sidewalk patio, and an interior festooned with contemporary paintings and sculpture. Excellent *terroir* fare at €16–34 with a filling vegetarian option at €13.

Le Tour Davejean 32 rue de Plô. One of the best deals in the *cité*: small, friendly and cheap with good local, home-style cooking. You can dine well here on regional fare for about €20, in a quiet little interior patio. Closed Jan.

Ville basse restaurants

All the restaurants below are marked on the *ville basse* map on p.103.

L'Écurie 43 bd Barbès ☎04.68.72.04.04. Elegant, excellent-value dining in a converted eighteenth-century stable, with *menus* from €15 to €30. Serves local cuisine as well as dishes with adventurous touches, such as mackerel brochettes in thyme sauce. Popular with gays and lesbians. Closed Sun eve & Wed.

Roberto Rodriguez 39 rue Coste Reboulh ☎04.68.47.37.80. Another excellent alternative to local cuisine is this Spanish-run gastronomical laboratory. Nothing like a *sushi de brandade* to shake off your culinary complacency. After-dinner theatre and dance shows make this a venue for an excellent evening out. Not informal, but serious fun. *Menus* €40–70. Closed Wed eve & Sun.

des Trois Couronnes 2 rue des Trois Couronnes ☎04.68.25.36.10. Tasty regional cuisine served on a riverside terrace or in an enclosed dining room, both with panoramic views of the medieval bridge and the walls of the *cité*. Expect to spend about €21–28. Closed Jan.

Bars and nightlife

For a small city, Carcassonne does quite well for **nightlife**, with a good selection of late-night **bars** (normally open until 2am, sometimes 4am or 5am at weekends) in the *ville basse*. *Le Café de Nuit*, 32 bd Omer Sarraut, livens up later with a mixed gay/straight crowd, while *La Fiesta Bodega*, at 49 av Henri Goût, is a rather pricey Spanish-Mexican restaurant by day, but stays open late as a lively tapas bar. Tiny rue de l'Aigle d'Or, just off place Carnot, is the centre for local hipsters, with bars like *Le Conti*, at no. 16, which has two dancefloors (daily till 5am), and the rockish *Le Not*, at no. 18 (Tues–Sat till 2am), while the cosy British *Pub Sheridan* can be found nearby at 13 rue Victor-Hugo. In the *cité* itself, *Bar au Vin*, in rue Plô, is the best place for a drink – a post-show favourite for visiting actors and musicians. For **dancing**, try *La Bulle* (closed Mon & Tues), just below the *cité* at 115 rue Barbacane, or *La Rapière*, a house-sound disco popular with under-25s, just outside the main gates.

Listings

Boat rental Nautic (☎04.68.71.88.95, ⓦwww.nautique.fr) and Locaboat (☎03.86.91.72.72, ⓦwww.locaboat.com), both located in the pleasure port, where Voies Navigables de France also has an office (☎04.68.71.74.55).

Bus departures Tickets for long-distance buses and Eurolines can be bought from Verdier Voyages, 1 av Maréchal-Joffre (☎04.68.25.09.06).

Car rental Avis, 52 rue Antoine Marty ☎04.68.25.05.84; Budget, 5 bd Omer Sarraut ☎04.68.72.31.31; Europcar, 7 bd Omer Sarraut ☎04.68.25.05.09; Garage la Bouriette, 58 bd Denis Papin ☎04.68.47.80.00; Location Occitan de Véhicules, 36 av Franklin Roosevelt ☎04.68.11.74.10. All of these companies, except for Garage la Bouriette, also have offices at the airport.

Hospital Centre Hospitalier Général, rte de St-Hilaire ☎04.68.24.24.24.

Pharmacy There are several: try Pharmacie Serin, 56 rue de Verdun; after 8pm enquire at the police station.

Police 4 bd Barbès ☎04.68.11.26.00.

Swimming pool Grazailles, rue du Moulin de la Seigne (☎04.68.47.81.83), is the one municipal pool. Covered and open year-round (bus #2 or #3), you'll need to bring a bathing cap. Locals also head for the Lac de Cavayère, signposted from the Narbonne road, just east of the *cité* (#7 bus).

The upper Aude valley

Carcassonne's river, whose course can be followed due south from Carcassonne through the **upper Aude valley**, is like a highway of Catharism – the majority of the most famous sights and ruins associated with the heretical sect lie along its path as it ascends into the Pyrenees. The river's lower regions are less visited, making quiet towns like **Limoux** and **Alet-les-Bains** good places to get away from the summer crowds, but as the valley winds its way up to the modern service centre of **Quillan**, more relics of the area's history reveal themselves. On the way you'll pass the myste-rious site of **Rennes-le-Château**, a favourite of occultists and treasure-hunters. Just south, the so-called "Cathar castles" form a rough chain stretching from Foix in the west to the hills of the Fenouillèdes to the east (see p.298). South of Quillan, the valley narrows into a series of gorges as you begin the climb into the mountains, eventually reaching the isolated **Donezan** region – a great area for **hiking**.

Limoux and around

LIMOUX, the first major town you'll arrive at as you follow the course of the Aude upstream from Carcassonne, is known for its sparkling white *blanquette* ("little white") wine, first vinted in 1531, and – pre-dating the sparkling wines of Champagne by a century – claimed as the original "Brut." The town is most famous for its Lenten *Carnaval* **festival**, held from January through to March in the town's main place de la République, which features displays of masked, harlequin-style dancers and live music. Limoux makes an excellent first stop on an ascent up the Aude, as well as a base for visiting St-Hilaire to the north.

Arrival, information and accommodation

Trains arrive at Limoux's **gare SNCF**, on the east bank of the river, a good twenty-minute walk from the old town, while **buses** (☎04.68.31.09.64) stop outside the cinema on allée des Marronniers, in the old town. The **tourist office** (July & Aug daily 9am–7pm; Sept–June Mon–Fri 9am–noon & 2–6pm, Sat & Sun 10am–noon & 2–5pm; ☎04.68.31.11.82, ⓦwww.limoux.fr) is on promenade de Tivoli, just south of the main roundabout.

The best **accommodation** option is the splendid and stately ⚓ *Moderne & Pigeon* (☎04.68.31.00.25, ⓦwww.grandhotelmodernepigeon.fr; ❽) in place Général-Leclerc, with its large, comfortable rooms, which include wi-fi and cable TV. At the other end of the price scale, but still good quality, is the humbler *des Arcades* (closed mid-Dec to mid-Jan; ☎04.68.31.02.57, ⓦwww.logis-de-france.fr; ❸), south of the church at 96 rue St-Martin, overlooking the old town's arcaded square. Limoux's municipal **campsite** (June–Sept; ☎04.68.31.13.63) is on the east bank of the river, south of the old bridge. **Bike rental** is available from Cycles Taillefer (☎04.68.31.02.01) at 18 esplanade François Mitterrand. The weekly **market** is held on Fridays.

The Town

Limoux has dominated this neck of the woods since the Middle Ages and the same **bridge** which spans the Aude today brought prosperity in the form of merchants and traders as far back as the fourteenth century. Thanks to this, the local consuls were able to construct a formidable set of **defensive walls**, part of which can still be seen along the riverside. But these did not prove strong enough to keep out either the Black Death or the Black Prince in the 1300s, and a century and a half later Calvinism arrived, bringing religious strife, quickly followed by a poverty from which it never quite recovered.

Today, Limoux's tranquil old town provides an opportunity to stretch your legs on the way towards the Pyrenees. The heart of the town is the **place de la République**, a wide square with some fine old stone arcading, a number of timber-frame houses and the requisite café and restaurant patios. Just down rue St-Martin, the town's main **church** has some top-notch stained-glass windows and remarkably restrained sixteenth- and seventeenth-century decor in the side chapels. On the promenade de Tivoli, the Carcassonne–Quillan highway, you'll find the small **Musée Petiet** (July & Aug daily 9am–12.30pm & 2–7pm; Sept–June Mon–Fri 9am–noon & 2–6pm, Sat & Sun 10am–noon & 2–5pm; €3) in the same building as the tourist office. Its collection of paintings, dominated by local nineteenth-century pointillism and allegory, contains some works of surprising quality. If you're interested in the local *blanquette*, head to the *domaine* Caves Sieur d'Arques

(Mon–Sat 10–11am & 3–5pm; free) on avenue de Mauzac, 1km west of the centre on avenue Charles de Gaulle from the main roundabout. Here you can learn about the history of the vintage, as well as sample and buy some to take home.

Eating and drinking

Restaurants in Limoux range from the excellent but expensive dining room of the *Moderne & Pigeon* (closed Sat lunch & Mon), with elaborate and broad-ranging *menus* (€38–117), to the cluster of brasseries on place de la République. Otherwise, *Maison de la Blanquette*, at 46 bis promenade de Tivoli, is a good place to wash down regional cuisine with some bubbly white (from €18), or try *l'Hibiscus* (closed Mon), a *gastronomique* restaurant at the edge of town en route to St-Polycarpe (€13–45; closed Mon).

North to St-Hilaire

Heading north of town, after 12km the winding D104 skirts **Notre-Dame de Marceille** (9am–7pm), a Romanesque church with a fine painted interior and an eleventh-century Virgin and Child still reputed by local Catholics to perform miracles. Next, it passes through tiny and quiet **ST-HILAIRE**, home to an ancient **abbey-church** (daily: April–June & Sept–Oct 10am–noon & 2–6pm; July & Aug 10am–7pm; Nov–March Sat, 10am–noon & 2–5pm; €4) whose monks invented Blanquette de Limoux. This sixth-century foundation, once the choice burial place of the counts of Carcassonne, contains a splendid sarcophagus, carved in vivid relief by the Master of Cabestany (see box, p.297), and depicting the martyrdom of Toulouse's first bishop, St Sernin. On the right-hand side of the main panel, there is a representation of Toulouse's medieval Capitole building. From here, the winding backroads lead north to Carcassonne.

Alet-les-Bains

Sixteen kilometres upstream from Limoux, **ALET-LES-BAINS** is also an excellent stop. This ancient village still owes its modest prosperity to the **hot springs** that bubble out of the ground on the north side of the town, first harnessed for curative purposes by the Romans, and now harnessed by a spa. From the ninth century the town flourished as the site of a Benedictine abbey, and from the fourteenth as a bishopric, before declining into obscurity with the Wars of Religion. Largely overlooked today, it preserves an atmosphere of antiquity, and its quiet streets conceal some surprising relics. A seventeenth-century **bridge** still connects Alet with the Limoux–Quillan highway, and just across it loom the ruins of the **abbey of Notre-Dame** (Easter–Oct daily 10am–noon & 2.30–6/7pm; rest of year same hours, closed Sun; €3), destroyed in 1577 and subsequently plundered to strengthen the town walls. Nearby, the town's main **square** is boxed in by timbered houses and the stone **Maison des Consuls**. Along the village's outskirts you'll find **Roman relics**, including a scrap of ancient road, a long section of twelfth-century wall, and a row of tiny **medieval houses**, which housed merchants' families eight hundred years ago.

Practicalities

Buses stop on the main road by the old bridge, a short walk from the **tourist office** beside the ruined abbey (Easter–Oct daily 10am–noon & 2.30–6/7pm; Nov–Easter Mon–Sat 10am–noon & 2.30–6pm, except late Dec to mid-Feb, when it's closed; ☎04.68.69.93.56, ⓦinfo.aletlesbains.free.fr). Next door, an excellent **hotel**, the ⚘ *Hostellerie de l'Évêché* (closed Nov–March; ☎04.68.69.90.25, ⓦwww.hotel-eveche.com; ❹), shelters in a wooded garden. If this is full, head for the friendly, English-run *Maison Val d'Aleth* (☎04.68.69.90.40, ⓦwww.valdaleth .com; ❸) on the same street, which has cosy rooms and a well-equipped riverside

campsite (book far ahead in summer), open year-round. The only **restaurant** in town is *L'Évêché*'s dining room (closed Sun; *menus* €22–50), which serves high-quality regional cuisine.

Rennes-le-Château and Arques

Almost mid way along the Alet-to-Quillan road, two short detours will take you to the ancient abbey-town of **Rennes-le-Château** – Languedoc's most intriguing site – and the picture-perfect castle at **Arques**, east of the main highway.

RENNES-LE-CHÂTEAU (not to be confused with the nearby spa town of Rennes-les-Bains) sits at the end of a four-kilometre mountain road winding up from the little village of Couiza. It was here that the enigmatic Bérenguer Saunière, Rennes' parish priest, died in 1917 after having lived in luxury for nearly thirty years, building himself a private villa, conservatory and library, and renovating the church in garish style (see box opposite). Together these sites form the mysterious **Espace Bérenguer Saunière** (March, April, mid-Sept to mid-Nov & mid-Dec to mid-Jan daily 11.30am–4/4.30pm; May to mid-Sept daily 10.30am–6pm; mid-Nov to mid-Dec Sat & Sun 11.30am–4pm; €4.50), a magnet for treasure-seekers, occultists and crop-circle aficionados, and inspiration for *The Da Vinci Code*. Entry to the **church** is free, and to the pavilion beside it, which served as Saunière's office. Behind this you'll find the cemetery where he lies next to his "housekeeper", Marie Denardaud. The compact church is entered through the side door, above which a Latin inscription welcomes you to this "terrible place" – perhaps a reference to the decor. Inside, you're greeted by a rather sinister wooden carving of a grimacing demon surmounted by four angels. The interior is painted in medieval style and filled

▲ Carving, Rennes-le-Château

Bérenguer Saunière arrived to serve as the priest in the tiny and backward hamlet of Rennes in 1885 – at 33, a cranky, royalist reactionary whose political views had already earned him the ire of the Church authorities. But his exile was to take an unexpected turn. Within a few years the humble priest was renovating the tiny and ancient **parish church**, decking it with a collection of eccentric fineries bought on order in Paris. By 1891 he'd begun buying up considerable tracts of land, placing the title under the name of **Marie Denardaud**. Marie, the daughter of his housekeeper, and sixteen years his junior, became his lifelong companion. In 1899, Saunière began work on the house and gardens of **Béthania**, as he called the smartly appointed villa which he raised next to the church. Luxurious by local standards, it was finished in 1904. Meanwhile, the *abbé* and his consort lorded it over the hamlet, dispensing generous donations and throwing magnificent *fêtes*, while keeping an iron grip on its affairs. Such was the awe Saunière inspired that when villagers begged Marie for access to the priest's cistern to put out a fire, she refused them, rather than rouse him from a nap to get his permission.

By 1907 Saunière's activities and outspoken politics provoked an investigation by the bishop of Carcassonne and he was deposed on a string of charges, ranging from abuse of power and finances to traffic of Church offices. His initial appeal failed in 1911 and, **defrocked**, he filed a second appeal to the Holy See in Rome. Meanwhile, work on the villa continued; banned by canon law from celebrating Mass in church, he performed the sacraments in the stained-glass annexe built onto Béthania. On January 22, 1917, after giving his last confession, Saunière died of a heart attack and was buried in the cemetery behind the church. Marie Denardaud, much to Saunière's family's disappointment, was his only heir, and she remained faithful to her *"chèr disparu"* till her end, refusing to divulge his secrets. Since her death in 1953, they have lain in adjacent graves.

The secret, of course, was where Saunière's money came from. It is generally believed he stumbled upon a cache of medieval coins, perhaps after finding ancient parchments either in the hollow stone **Visigothic** altar-support, in a secret compartment in a wooden column or under a carved flagstone that sat before the altar. After his death, Marie made cryptic references to the "gold" over which the "villagers were walking", which would be enough to "support the village for a hundred years". These tales attracted the attention of a steady string of **treasure-hunters** who became so troublesome and disruptive that even today signs forbid any digging in the vicinity of the town.

The story of the treasure and the bizarre symbolism of the church's decor have spawned scores of occult theories over their origin and significance, including possible links to a secret society called the Priory of Zion, the Templars, **Solomon's treasure**, Cathars, the **Holy Grail** and a Christ who escaped crucifixion. In the last decades this has turned into a small industry and there are dozens of books written on the subject. Most are full of the kind of incoherent and self-contradictory pseudo-scientific ramblings that typify this genre, notably Lincoln, Baigent and Leigh's *Holy Blood, Holy Grail* – an inspiration for Dan Brown's *The Da Vinci Code*. Inevitably, the town has sparked a series of reports of parapsychological and extra terrestrial events, including a miraculous image of the Virgin and Child, discernible in a 1967 aerial photograph, UFO visitations and crop circles. The controversy continued in 2009, when Rennes' mayor went public with new documents showing that Saunière died in poverty; more or less simultaneously a new documentary, *Bloodline*, trumpeted claims that a tomb (perhaps of Mary Magdalene...?) had been discovered nearby.

with a healthy contingent of carved Baroque saints. Although these may seem rather ordinary church furnishings, enthusiasts have uncovered a complex code in their details and arrangement, one which corresponds either to Kabbalistic theory, UFO influence or the secret "Priory of Zion" society (depending on who you ask).

Next door to the church is the house in which Saunière lived, now converted into a **museum** and containing important relics, such as the hollow Visigothic pillar that once supported the church's altar. From there you enter Saunière's spacious garden, girded by a fanciful fortified wall capped by two turrets, one of which once served as his library, while adjacent to the farmhouse sits "Béthania", a more luxurious house where he entertained guests and – banned from conducting the Catholic Mass – installed his own chapel.

Arques

The **donjon d'Arques** is around 10km east of Couiza along the D613, which winds slowly uphill following the course of the Orbieu. Coming into view, the perfectly preserved square **keep** (daily: March & Oct–Nov 10.30am–12.30pm & 1.30–5pm; April–June & Sept 10.30am–6pm; July & Aug 9.30am–8pm; €5) is unmistakable as it rises 25m above the surrounding fields. The castle – undoubtedly the most beautiful in the region – was built in perfect northern-French Gothic style by its new lord, Pierre de Voisins, after the Cathar original had been destroyed. Pierre's local reputation was cemented when he burned a 60-year-old local woman as a witch soon after he arrived. The central *donjon*, which dates back to the thirteenth century, is extremely well preserved, with graceful Gothic vaulting sustaining two of its great chambers. The third-floor hall is dominated by an impressively huge fireplace. Outside, there's a group of beehives clustered just to the side of the entrance, where you can buy fresh honey.

About 1.5km east of the castle, the village of **ARQUES** is a little hamlet with a fourteenth-century church, some contemporary buildings and a small exhibition on Catharism housed in the **Maison de Déodat Roché** (same hours and ticket as castle). From Arques the road continues (no public transport) through ever more untamed and isolated terrain towards the castles at Termes and Villerouge-Termenès (see p.263), and the abbey-town of Lagrasse (see p.264), a route very much worthwhile exploring either by car or bicycle.

Practicalities

If you have no transport, you can reach Rennes-le-Château and Arques by **taxi** (about €12) from Couiza (℡04.68.74.25.36), although, if you are up to it, the demanding six-kilometre uphill walk is enjoyable. Alternatively, Au Fil de l'Aude (℡04.68.74.16.69) in Couiza rents **bikes**. There's a **tourist office** in Rennes (daily: mid-June to mid-Sept 10am–7pm; mid-Sept to mid-June 10am–5.30pm; ℡04.68.74.72.68, ⓦwww.rennes-le-chateau.org).

The only **accommodation** in Rennes is the excellent *Les Labadous* guesthouse (℡04.68.74.25.16, ⓦwww.labadous.com; ❹), which has several doubles and a large common room set in a beautifully renovated eighteenth-century farmhouse, and provides excellent meals (€12–15). They also have apartments. Nearby in the village of Esperaza, you'll find the attractive, English-run *Maison du Chapelier* **chambres d'hôtes** (℡04.68.74.22.49, ⓦwww.esperazabedandbreakfast.com; ❹), complete with wi-fi, while the spectacular *Château des Ducs de Joyeuse* (℡04.68.74.04.20, ⓦwww.chateau-des-ducs.com; ❽), set in a picture-perfect sixteenth-century castle, is below in Couiza. In Arques, there's the **campsite** *Relais Soleil* (℡04.68.69.88.30, ⓦwww.relaisoleil.com; Feb–Oct), which also has bungalows, and there's also a campsite in Rennes (℡04.68.74.09.32, ⓔcamping .rennes-les-baines@orange.fr; May–Oct).

Good *terroir* **restaurants** are scattered throughout the area, the best being the *Château des Ducs* in Couiza, which sometimes has a dinner-theatre show (closed Sun & Mon eve mid-Nov to March; *menus* from €30). Also worth trying are *Jardins de l'Abbé* in Rennes, with live music on Friday evenings (closed Sun & Mon lunch

& Nov–April; ☎04.68.74.31.16; from €20), and *Auberge du Moulin d'Arques* in Arques (☎04.68.69.80.61; closed Sun & Mon & Jan–March).

Quillan and around

Set on the west bank of the Aude about halfway along its course, **QUILLAN** is the gateway to the spectacular **Aude gorges**, providing ample canoeing and rafting possibilities. It's also a jumping-off point for the isolated region just to the south, known as the **Donezan** and home to two historically important, but decayed, Cathar sites at the hamlets of Usson and Quérigut. The area makes for excellent hiking and driving, but public transport is almost non existent.

Quillan itself is a picturesque town, though the only monument of interest is the ruined **castle** on the east bank of the Aude – here a sturdy torrent – just across the Pont Vieux; long reduced to rubble and remnants, it is nevertheless a romantic spot. Shrinking and semi-abandoned **USSON**, 31km to the south along a winding D188, sits in the shadow of its dilapidated **château** (Feb–April hols & Sept daily 2–6pm; July & Aug daily 10am–1pm & 3–7pm; €3.50), which was the first place of safety for the four Cathars who escaped the massacre at Montségur (see *The Land of Cathars* colour section), and dates back to at least the eleventh century. The hamlet of **QUÉRIGUT**, 7km further south, stands at the head of a slope of neglected terraces, notable only for the stump of the **Château de Donezan**, the last stronghold of the Cathar leadership, who held out here for eleven years after the fall of Montségur.

Practicalities

Quillan's **gare SNCF** and **gare routière** are both central, on boulevard Charles-de-Gaulle. The **tourist office** occupies a prominent kiosk beside the train station (Jan–June Mon–Fri 9am–noon & 2–6pm, Sat 9am–1pm; July to mid-Sept Mon–Sat 9am–noon & 2–7pm, Sun 9am–1pm; mid-Sept to Dec Mon–Fri 9am–noon & 2–6pm, Sat 9am–1pm; ☎04.68.20.07.78, ⓦ www.aude-en-pyrenees.fr), and can help with Grotte de l'Aguzou reservations (see box below), as well as provide information on rafting and canoeing. The **Donezan tourist office** (July & Aug daily 8.30am–12.30pm & 2–6pm, Sat 3–7pm & Sun 9am–noon & 4–7pm; Sept–June Mon–Fri 8.30am–12.30pm & 1.30–4.30/5.30pm; ☎04.68.20.41.37, ⓦ www.donezan.com) is in **Le Pla**, a hamlet 5km north of Quérigut on the D16. Staff here can provide detailed information on hiking and outdoor activities.

Quillan's best **hotel**, the *Cartier* (☎04.68.20.05.14, ⓦ www.hotelcartier.com; ❸) is on the main street near the tourist office. The comfortable and newly renovated

---

Spelunking in the Grotte de l'Aguzou

While the prehistoric caves around Foix are stunningly impressive, if you are hankering after doing some real cave exploring in one of the region's famous caves, visit the **Grotte de l'Aguzou**, 27km south of Quillan towards the upstream end of the Gorges de l'Aude. The guided tour of this magnificent complex is the real thing – equipped with overalls, helmet and lamp, groups of four to ten people are taken into the unlit **cave system** at 9am, to be conducted through the *grandes salles* of stalactites, stalagmites, columns and draperies, some of which are 20m high. Lunch (you bring your own) is taken 600m underground, and then it's on to the so-called "gardens of crystals" – a fantastic array of forms and shapes, some growing from the rock in long, thin needles, or like pine cones dusted by hoar frost, and others clear and convoluted like a Venetian glass-blower's accident. The full-day **excursions** led by veteran speleologist Philippe Moreno are very popular, so book well in advance, and check the website for details (€50; ☎04.68.20.45.38, ⓦ www.grotte-aguzou.com).

rooms offer flat-screen TV, wi-fi and similar amenities. In the heart of the Donezan, the best (and almost the only) choice is the excellent *Relais de Pailhères* (☎04.68.20.46.97; ❸) 3km from Usson in **Mijanès**, with well-sized, wooden-floored rooms; reservations advisable at weekends. In Quérigut, the simple *Auberge Donezan* (☎04.68.20.42.40, ⓦwww.auberge-du-donezan.com; ❷) is the place to stay. **Campsites** include *La Sapinette* (☎04.68.20.13.52, ⓦwww.camping-la -sapinette.com; April–Oct) on rue René-Delpech in Quillan, and the simple riverside *Le Bousquet*, in Quérigut. Quillan's **market** is held on Wednesdays (8am–4pm), and **bikes** can be rented from Cycles Bénassis (☎04.68.20.18.91) on boulevard Charles de Gaulle.

Montségur and around

After Carcassonnne, **Montségur** is undoubtedly the most widely known monument of Languedoc and Roussillon, a fame which owes far more to the mythology and history that grew up around it than to its present condition. The castle was the setting for the Cathars' "last stand" – a site where over two hundred heretics chose to be burnt to death rather than abjure their faith. It is set amid the magnificent **pays de Sault** – the upland area more or less bounded by the rivers Aude and Ariège and, to the north, the main road (D117) from Quillan to Foix. This is the most accessible route into the area, and offers some of Languedoc's most outstanding scenery, as well as Cathar castles at **Puivert** and **Roquefixade**. The other main road, the D163, runs southwest from Quillan to Ax-les-Thermes, passing the famous heretic village, **Montaillou**, and the dramatic limestone crevice, the **Gorges de la Frau**.

Although motoring is by far the best way to explore the region, there is a **bus service** on each of these routes. This is also excellent **hiking** terrain; you can cross the area in a few days, using a network of walking itineraries – the "Tour du Pays de Sault", the "Tour du Massif de Tabe", the "Piémont", the GR107 and the popular "**Sentier Cathare**". This gentle trail can be followed from Foix to Montségur, and all the way down to the Mediterranean.

Montségur

The ruined castle of **MONTSÉGUR** looms dramatically atop a towering, pillar-like hill, its plain stone walls poised mutely above the straggling village at its foot. The original fortifications were built in the eighth century by Guillaume "Short-Nose", duke of Aquitaine, but between 1204 and 1232 it was reconstructed as a bastion of the Cathars under the direction of Guilhabert de Castres, leader of the sect, who imagined the sheer rocky cliffs of the *pog* ("hill") would render it untakeable. The only access to the ruin (daily: May, June & Oct 10am–6.30pm; July & Aug 9am–7.30pm; Sept 9.30am–7.30pm; Nov–April 9/10am–4.30/6pm; €4.50) is along the western side, where it is possible to walk up to the summit (about 30min) through what is now called the *prat dels cremats* ("meadow of the burned"). It was here the surviving Cathars were put to the stake after the castle fell (see p.334) – a modern stone memorial pays tribute to them.

The beauty of the site – the crumbling curtain-wall perched on a toothlike outcrop – is what hits you first; the original walls were reduced by half after the siege, and all internal structures are gone except the simple keep, now open to the sky. Then you begin to wonder how that last Cathar community of five hundred people could have held out so long in such a small space. Even given that some

The Land of the Cathars

From the rolling hills around Albi to the coasts of the Mediterranean it's impossible to travel through Languedoc without crossing paths with the Cathars. Mixing Christianity with Middle Eastern philosophies, the Cathar cult was brought to the region by returning Crusaders in the twelfth century, and gained popularity as a reaction to the wealthy and corrupt Catholic Church. Cathars believed in the struggle between the good spirit world and the evil material world, and practised asceticism (self-denial and abstinence) as a path to salvation. Monk-like perfecti (or parfaits) presided over the believers, who aspired to become perfecti themselves just before death, so that they could die pure and escape the material universe.

The rise of Catharism

By the 1140s, the sect had become a formal church, which spread rapidly throughout northern France and the Low Countries, with Italy, Spain and, of course, **Languedoc** all becoming important centres. In Languedoc, the religion was welcomed by urban tradesmen, by the regional nobility (who resented the papacy's political expansion and feared a Church-backed takeover by the French Crown), and by peasants who were attracted by the dedication of the *perfecti* and the Cathar cosmology. Thus, Cathar beliefs fused with **Occitan identity**, and came to be associated strongly with the region. By 1200, the Catholic Church could no longer ignore the rival religion, and **Pope Innocent III** (1198–1216) undertook a series of initiatives against them, culminating in a military campaign.

Québribus ▲

Madeleine church ▼

The Albigensian Crusade

On July 22, 1209, the papacy sent an army of knights to surround **Béziers**, led by Arnaud-Amaury, Abbot of Cîteaux, the most powerful monastery in northern France. As the noose around the town tightened, a band of Béziers citizens, both Catholic and Cathar, took refuge in the **Church of the Madeleine**, within which, according to Catholic law, no blood was to be shed. Arnaud-Amaury, however, gave the order to set fire to the church, exclaiming, "Burn them all, God will know his own!"

This was the start of the **Albigensian Crusade**, a ferocious campaign waged against the Counts of Toulouse, who were tolerant of their Cathar population, by the papacy and the northern French nobility. **Simon de Montfort** was one

of the leaders of this brutal campaign of terror: his treatment of the populace was pitiless, with massacres and mutilation commonplace. De Montfort came to an appropriate end in June 1218 at the **Siege of Toulouse**, when a missile from a catapult fired by a squad of women and children bashed his brains out. His relentless attacks, however, left Languedoc unable to withstand the pressure of the French Crown, and led ultimately to the destruction of Catharism and the fall of independent Languedoc.

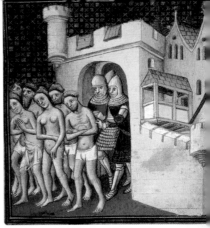
▲ The expulsion of the Albigensians from Carcassonne

The Inquisition

In the aftermath of the Crusade, the papacy set about converting the "hearts and minds" of the Cathars and their supporters. This was taken on by two new religious orders, the **Franciscans** (1209) and **Dominicans** (1215), backed up by the **Inquisition**, part secret police, part travelling court.

▼ Minerve

▼ Lastours

Top 10 Cathar sites

▶▶ **Montségur:** the defiant Cathar redoubt. See p.112.
▶▶ **Carcassonne:** De Montfort's headquarters. See p.96.
▶▶ **Lavaur:** the capital of the Cathar heartland. See p.80.
▶▶ **Les Jacobins:** the Dominican headquarters in Languedoc. See p.69.
▶▶ **Lastours:** Cathar fortresses that defied de Montfort. See p.172.
▶▶ **The Madeleine church, Béziers:** the site of the massacre. See p.274.
▶▶ **Minerve:** breathtaking, canyon-girded Cathar village. See p.267.
▶▶ **Quéribus castle:** the rebel's last refuge. See p.298.
▶▶ **Villerouge:** site of the last burning in 1321. See p.263.
▶▶ **Montaillou:** a Cathar hamlet in the Pyrenees. See p.114.

Inquisitors went from town to town investigating locals' religious leanings and sniffing out secret heretics; guilt was frequently assumed, and torture frequent. Once condemned by the Church, the victim was handed over to local authorities for execution. Not surprisingly, the Inquisition did little to endear the people of Languedoc to the Catholic authorities, and it contributed to the region's residual distrust of "foreign" authority.

Painting of St Dominic burning Cathar books ▲

The summit of Montségur ▼

The Siege of Montségur

In 1242 a band of Cathar warriors struck out from **Montségur** castle and attacked and killed a party of Dominican Inquisitors at **Avignonet-Lauragais**, sparking a series of rebellions across the region. The royal response was swift: a massive force was raised and in May 1243 they laid **siege** to the castle. Inside, 150 knights, led by **Pierre-Roger of Mirepoix**, and several hundred Cathars endured eight months of siege and bombardment, before Pierre-Roger negotiated for clemency in exchange for surrender. But the Cathar faithful would not betray their cause and when the castle was opened to the French, some 225 were led out to a field below the fort and **burnt alive**. Nevertheless, it took the Inquisition over a century to finish the job. In the early 1300s the brothers **Pierre and Guillaume Autier**, trained as *perfecti* in northern Italy, preached secretly until caught and executed. The last known Cathar *bon homme*, **Guillaume Bélibaste**, was burnt at **Villerouge-Termenès** in 1321, and shortly afterwards the last remaining community of Cathars was discovered in the village of **Montaillou** and prosecuted in an Inquisition led by the Bishop of Foix.

lived in now-vanished houses at the foot of the walls on the north and west faces, there was still a sizeable garrison to be accommodated, together with the *faydits* – local aristocrats dispossessed by the crusade. What's left of the castle takes no more than a few minutes to explore, and the walls are now off-limits, but it isn't so much what you see at Montségur that makes the trip unforgettable, as what your imagination can re-create from its remnants.

Down in the village, 1km below, a one-room **archeological museum** (daily: May–Sept 10am–1pm & 2–6/7pm; Oct–April 2–5/7pm; free) displays artefacts excavated since the 1950s from the original village beside the walls, from both pre- and post-Cathar periods – mostly food, bones, personal effects, tools and surviving fragments of houses.

Practicalities

Despite its small size, tourist numbers at Montségur village have led to the establishment of a **tourist office** (Feb–June & Oct–Dec Wed–Sun irregular hours; July–Sept daily 10am–noon & 2–6pm; ☎05.61.03.03.03, ⓦwww .montsegur.fr). If you'd like to stay the night – and the beautiful scenery certainly appeals – there are a couple of good **hotels**: the old-fashioned *Couquet* (☎05.61.01.10.28, ⓦwww.montsegur-village.org; ❸), a rambling country *pension* of wood-furnished rooms with washbasins, and the welcoming and comfortable *Costes* (☎05.61.01.10.24, ⓦwww.chez-costes.com; ❷), just uphill, which has basic accommodation as well as (slightly pricier) deluxe rooms with jacuzzis. The closest **campsite** (tents only) is the *Point Accueil Jeunes* (April–Sept; ☎05.61.01.10.27), at the lower end of the village on the Bélesta side. The *Costes* has a reasonably priced organic **restaurant** attached (from €14) featuring game and *Ariègeois terroir*.

Puivert

Half an hour east of Montségur (and twenty minutes west of Quillan) on the D117, the ancient village of **PUIVERT** sits among mountain meadows planted with corn and sunflowers. Set above it, 1km to the east, is its romantically sited **château** (daily: April to mid-July 10.30am–12.30pm & 2–6pm; mid-July to Aug 10.30am–7pm; Oct 2–5pm; €4), which fell to the Albigensian Crusade in 1210, and was rebuilt in the 1300s. More a place of culture than of arms, it was closely associated with the troubadour poets (see p.355), whose preoccupation with love might seem incompatible with the asceticism of the Cathars. What united them was the Occitan language, then spoken all across southern France.

The most interesting part of the castle is its *donjon*. Within it is a chapel with vigil seats at the north and south windows, a wall font and rib-vaulting on the ceiling, culminating in a keystone embossed with images of the Virgin and St George. The highest chamber is dubbed the "musicians' room" after its eight *culs-de-lamps* or torch sockets at the termini of more rib-vaulting, each sculpted in the form of a figure playing a different period instrument. In the village below, a small **museum** (same hours as castle; €4) displays reproductions of medieval instruments copied from the castle's sculptures.

If you want to spend the night, stay at the funky and welcoming **chambres d'hôtes**, *L'Irenée* in the village centre (☎04.68.20.95.79, ⓦwww.irenee-puivert .com; ❸) – an ideal stop for families with its welcoming atmosphere and large rooms – or at the lakeside **campsite** (☎04.68.20.00.58, ⓦwww.campingpuivert .com; May–Sept), 1km to the south, which also has a public swimming area (daily except Mon).

Roquefixade

ROQUEFIXADE, the westernmost of the Cathar castles and first stop on the "Sentier Cathare" after Foix, is about twenty minutes to the northwest of Montségur, and 2km off of the main D117 highway. Destroyed during the Albigensian Crusade, the village was subsequently refounded as a *bastide*. From the high end of the village it's a twenty-minute climb to the unenclosed castle (free), which takes its name (originally *roca fissada*) from the vast natural fissures augmenting its defences. Perched at the western end of a long ridge, it's bigger than it appears from below but utterly ruined; your main reward is the view over the valley below with its clustered villages, and south – weather permitting – to the high Pyrenean ridge. There is an excellent **hotel** here, the homey three-star *Relais des Trois Châteaux* (closed late Nov & mid-Jan to mid-Feb; ℡05.61.01.33.99, Ⓦwww.troischateaux.com; ❸), which has a very good *gastronomique* **restaurant**, as well as a small indoor pool.

Montaillou

Sitting on the narrow and sparsely travelled road from Quillan to Ax-les-Thermes, the village of **MONTAILLOU** is only 15km southeast of Montségur, but – unless you're hiking – is reached from it via a forty-kilometre tortuous route through remote territory that vividly evokes a past of heresy and isolation (allow an hour each way by car). Montaillou subscribed to the Cathar heresy long after the fall of Montségur, until the Inquisition set to work here during the early 1300s. Fewer than twenty people live here permanently now, all of them descendants of the Cathars, as you can see by comparing their surnames (such as Clergues and Belot) with those on the headstones in the ancient graveyard. The village's crumbled **castle** was once the home of Béatrice de Planissolles (see box opposite), and the village church is the same one in which she was seduced by the parish priest. Services are nearly non existent on this stretch of highway, although the nearby village of **Camurac** has a **hotel**, *Auberge du Pays de Sault* (℡04.68.20.33.69, Ⓦwww.paysdesault.com; ❷), which serves home-cooked meals for €14, and a **campsite**, *Les Sapins* (℡04.68.20.38.11, Ⓦwww.lessapins -camurac.com).

Hiking from Camurac to Montségur

The **GR107 trail** north from the village of **Camurac** – close to Montaillou on the D613 – leads north and west to **Montségur**, a hike of a little over four hours, tracing a stretch of the **Chemin des Bonhommes** ("The Goodmen's Trail"), which re-creates the path by which Cathar *perfecti* (see *The Land of Cathers* colour section) crossed back and forth over the Pyrenees. Shortly after leaving Camurac, you'll arrive at the hamlet of Comus. Here, the trail drops down as a mule track between fields to a wide gorge that suddenly becomes a defile – the **Gorges de la Frau** – where thousand-metre-high cliffs admit the sun only during the early afternoon. When the gorge widens again, you meet the dead end of the D5 coming south from Bélesta and Fougax-Barrineuf. There are two options for continuing to Montségur: either westwards along the GR107, which runs along a shaded riverbank (turn off at the first farm, "Pelail", 45min along the D5), or via a bridle trail beginning about an hour along the tarmac, offering higher, more open ground. If you want an early start, you can stay at the **gîte**, *de Montaigne*, in Comus (℡04.68.20.33.69, Ⓦwww.gites-comus.com; ❷). Should you wish to continue on from Montségur, **Roquefixade** is a moderate five-hour hike beyond along the GR107.

Montaillou's secret heretics

In July 1320, **Béatrice de Planissolles**, a woman of the lower nobility of the Ariège and widow of the lord of Montaillou, was summoned to appear before Jacques Fournier, Bishop of Pamiers, Inquisitor, former abbot of Fontfroide (see p.263) and future Pope Benedict XII on charges of **heresy** and **witchcraft**. Under Fournier's interrogation, Béatrice, who had had a string of lovers, confessed her Cathar tendencies and those of her townsmen. This only served to confirm longstanding suspicions – already in 1308 the entire village of Montaillou had been arrested and hauled off by the **Inquisition** for interrogation. The resulting confessions revealed a village in the grip of heresy, harbouring an adulterous and vengeful parish priest, free-thinking itinerant shepherds, a hypocritical and philandering Perfectus, and the sorts of petty intrigues, violent struggles, and illicit liaisons not untypical of an isolated and insular mountain peasant community. In the end, the villagers suffered various fates: a few were put to death, others condemned to wear yellow crosses on their clothes as a sign of their heresy, while most were absolved after completing some relatively minor penance. Béatrice herself was **immured** ("walled in") for one year, before being freed under the condition that she would wear the yellow crosses.

The copious and detailed records compiled by the inquisitors were so precise that historian Emmanuel Le Roy Ladurie was able to re-create every aspect of the villagers' lives from them, from the minutiae of domestic economics to the details of their sexual habits and their conceptions of god and the universe, in his book, *Montaillou* (see p.346).

Mirepoix and the lower Ariège valley

The **lower Ariège valley** winds a leisurely course through a broad, rolling upland, whose rich dairy and wheat farms set it apart from the dry, vine-dominated scrub of most of Languedoc and Roussillon. East of the river, a broad plain straddles the banks of its tributary, the **Hers**. Centred on **Mirepoix**, these flatlands were home to Cathars and castles; today a series of surprising and unique medieval **monuments** remain. Dominating the Ariège itself is **Foix**, capital of France's smallest *département*, bearing the same name as the river. The town's strikingly positioned castle is the only testament to Foix's former role as the centre of a proudly independent principality – now a casualty of history, like the neighbouring County of Toulouse.

Mirepoix and around

The town of **MIREPOIX** is tucked away among the undulating hills of the Hers valley, 48km from Carcassonne and 24km from Pamiers. History was not kind to this Cathar stronghold: first its townsfolk suffered a massacre at the hands of the Crusaders, then a generation later it was all but destroyed by flood. The present town dates back to 1290, when the noble Jean de Lévis laid out a new *bastide* in a safer location. At the centre of the village sits the broad **place Maréchal-Leclerc** (or place de Couverts), arguably the most beautiful town square west of the Rhône. Almost the entire perimeter is rimmed by broad arcades supported by stout old beams, above which rise two storeys of pastel timber-frame houses. Although the *place* as a whole is beautiful, its star attraction is the fourteenth-century **Maison des Consuls** (now a hotel, see p.116) in the centre of the north side, at no. 6. This former town hall, courthouse and prison dates from the fourteenth century and is decorated by nearly 150 **wooden heads**, carved in high relief at the ends of the beams supporting the second storey. Each carving is individual, the portraits ranging across the gamut of medieval social classes and professions and including exotic and foreign peoples (notably some very early portrayals of black Africans), as well as demons, monsters, animals and assorted grotesques. They make a singular masterwork.

By passing through an attractive nineteenth-century wrought-iron **market hall** on the south side of the square, you arrive at another arcaded *place*, Philip-de-Lévis – not as stunning as its larger counterpart, but also impressive. In the middle stands the fourteenth-century **cathedral of St-Maurice** (Mon–Sat 9am–noon & 2–6pm), whose broad single nave is the widest of any Gothic-style church in France. Local lore attributes the absence of supporting columns to the clergy's desire to monitor parishioners, checking that they were not carrying out forbidden Cathar practices, but this is doubtful given that the cathedral was not consecrated until 1509.

There is little in particular to do here, but the beauty of the town makes it the perfect spot to relax on a terrace, have a drink and soak up the atmosphere. On Monday mornings both of the *places* fill with the **market** stalls of local farmers – an excellent opportunity to prepare a picnic lunch.

Practicalities

Buses passing through Mirepoix stop within sight of the cathedral, from where it's a short walk to the **tourist office** (Mon–Sat 9am–noon & 2–6pm; ☎05.61.68.83.76, ⓦwww.tourisme-mirepoix.fr), located in the only modern building on place Leclerc. There are two upmarket **hotels** to choose from: the *Relais Royal* (☎05.61.60.19.19, ⓦwww.relaisroyal.com; ❾) in an splendid eighteenth-century mansion in rue Maréchal Clauzel, and the gorgeous, and more affordable, ⅍ *Maison des Consuls* (English spoken; ☎05.61.68.81.81, ⓦwww.maisondesconsuls.com; ❻) at 6 pl Maréchal Leclerc, where the best rooms are the "Marquis" and the "Dame Louise." Both hotels have wi-fi, air conditioning and satellite TV. There is also a two-star **campsite**, *Les Nysades* (mid-June to mid-Sept; ☎05.61.68.28.63), on the road to Fanjeux. Mirepoix's best **restaurant** is in the *Relais Royal*, which features simple but luxurious variations on local and international cuisine (€30–90) and has an in-house sommelier. Good-value options are *Le Comptoir Gourmand*, on cours Maréchal de Mirepoix (closed Mon; ☎05.61.68.19.19), and *La Flambée*, 17 rue Porte d'Amont (closed Sun eve & Mon; ☎05.61.68.16.59), both of which are in the €15-and-up range and specialize in cassoulet and dishes based on locally raised beef.

Camon

CAMON, 13km southeast of Mirepoix, is a tiny settlement, of exceptional charm and rich in atmosphere. Founded by Charlemagne himself, it is still dominated by its thousand-year-old **abbey-castle** and surrounded by parts of its two sets of walls (fourteenth and sixteenth century). The castle is private and operates as a hotel, but its richly appointed sixteenth-century interior, arranged around a vine-draped courtyard, can also be taken in as part of a guided tour (€5), arranged by the small **tourist office** on Grand Rue (Mon–Sat 9am–noon & 2–5pm; ☎05.61.68.88.26, ⓦmairiecamon.ifrance.com).

The best way to make the most of the castle is, of course, to **stay** here: ⅍ *L'Abbaye-Château* (☎04.61.68.31.23, ⓦwww.chateaudecamon.com; ❽) is a one-of-a-kind hotel, featuring luxurious decor and a sumptuous restaurant (dinner only, closed Wed) offering elaborate variations on local staples such as duck, foie gras and riverfish. If you're only passing by, you should at least enjoy a drink in its *salon de thé*, *La Tartine*. The other option is north of town at *La Besse Farm* (☎05.61.68.84.63, ⓦwww.camping-labesse.com), which has a **campsite** as well as **rooms** (☎05.61.68.13.11; ❷). The rural atmosphere is unbeatable and you can buy farm-fresh produce and swim in the outdoor pool.

Vals

Perhaps the most interesting sight in the vicinity of Mirepoix is the little-known church at **VALS**, a cluster of a half-dozen farmhouses 12km west of town on the north bank of the Hers. About 20m from the main road a small and incredibly ancient **subterranean church** (daily 9am–6pm), once a stopping-point on the pilgrims' route to Compostela, is built on a rocky spur. Entering through a hobbit-sized doorway you climb a staircase carved in the rock, passing through a pseudo-crypt of pre-Roman origin before reaching the church itself. When you enter, grope for the light switch to the left of the door to illuminate the curious three-chambered vertical structure; in the arches of some of its windows you'll find well-preserved late eleventh- and early twelfth-century frescoes of saints and angels, which recall the styles of painted churches of the Pyrenees.

Fanjeux

By contrast with Vals, **FANJEUX**, an uninspiring village halfway between Mirepoix and Carcassonne, is steeped in historical renown but of virtually no interest today. It was here that in 1206 St Dominic de Guzmán experienced the vision that inspired him to found the Dominican Order, and here that the trouba-dour competition known as the *jocs florals* ("the floral games") was first convened in 1323. These days, the only vestiges of Fanjeux's medieval splendour are the old Dominican headquarters and the town's church, where you can look out over the same vista as St Dominic did over eight hundred years ago.

Pamiers and the Grotte du Mas d'Azil

The town of **PAMIERS** is loaded with history, but suffered so gravely in the Wars of Religion that there is virtually nothing left to see here. Founded by returning Crusaders – who named it after the ancient city of Apamea in Syria, which they had captured – Pamiers later played the role of headquarters for the anti-Cathar Crusaders. In 1321, the Inquisition burned the last Cathar *parfait* Guillaume Bélibaste here. Now, of the town's vanished medieval glory only a scattering of old bell towers survive, poking above the rooftops in the tight knot of streets on the east bank of the Ariège, which make up Pamiers' unremarkable old town.

More appealing is the **bike ride** (if you're in good shape) or drive (if you're not) that starts just outside town, following a great route across the western spur of the low Plantaurel mountains to the Grotte du Mas d'Azil (reached by way of some gruelling hairpin curves), and on to St-Girons. Pick this up by crossing the Ariège west of Pamiers' old town on the D110 (direction St-Victor); 7km later you'll hook up with the main D119, which leads to Mas d'Azil and beyond.

The cave and village of Mas d'Azil

The village of **MAS D'AZIL**, 33km west of Pamiers, is the site of a massive cavern, noteworthy not only for being the most northerly and largest of the great Pyrenean prehistoric *grottes* (see p.129), but also as Europe's only **drive-through cave**. The gaping maw (some 50m in height) opens up just to the south of the village, swallowing the D119 road whole, before disgorging it several hundred metres later. Once a lair of the giant cave-bears which populated the south of France in the days of the great mammals, and roughly thirty thousand years ago, a home for our own humble ancestors, historically the cave has provided refuge for a whole series of endangered species, including early Christians, Cathars and Huguenots. Indeed, it was here and in the village that a group of Protestants made a valiant and desperate stand in 1625, fending off a Catholic army which outnum-bered them fifteen to one. If you're interested in seeing more than simply what passes by your window, other sections of the cave are **accessible by foot** (March,

The Return of Martin Guerre

In 1548 **Martin Guerre**, a surly young farmer who had been accused of theft, suddenly vanished from his home in **Artigat**, abandoning his teenage wife Berthrande and their infant son. Eight years later Martin returned, to the joy of his wife and family. By 1559, however, domestic bliss had given way to family tensions; when Martin sued his uncle for part of his father's inheritance, Pierre Guerre countered with the incredible charge that Martin was, in fact, an **imposter**. After a series of suits and counter-suits the case was brought before the *capitouls* of Toulouse in 1560. Martin was in closing arguments with legal victory in his grasp, when suddenly a man claiming to be the true Martin Guerre appeared in court. And so it was that the defendant was found guilty and sentenced to be **hanged** at the very doors of the house he had fraudulently inhabited. This tale was brought to international attention in the 1980s thanks to historian Natalie Zemon Davis's *The Return of Martin Guerre* (see Books, p.346), incredible for its historical accuracy, and the excellent film of the same name, starring Gérard Depardieu and Nathalie Baye – a vivid evocation of rural life in the sixteenth-century Pyrenees and a must-see for travellers to the region. Sadly, little remains of the Artigat of Martin Guerre; the town was captured and all but destroyed by Protestants on March 7, 1621.

Oct & Nov Sun 2–6pm; April & May Tues–Sun 2–6pm and sometimes 10am–noon; June & Sept Tues–Sun 10am–noon & 2–6pm; July & Aug daily 10am–6pm; Dec–Feb school hols 2–6pm; €6.10; Ⓦ www.grotte-masdazil.com), and you can stroll through galleries littered and decorated with the vestiges of its former inhabitants. The visit is best combined with the **Musée de la Préhistoire** (same hours, €4.60) on place d'Église. Nearby on the north bank of the Arize, another museum, **La Forêt aux Dinosaures** (hours vary widely, consult Ⓦ www.ariege-dinosaure .com; €7) has an outdoor exhibition of living reptiles, fossils and dinosaur replicas that will delight children.

The **village** itself, at the north mouth of the cavern, seems to be little more than an extension of cave-centred tourism and some local agriculture. The **tourist office** (April–Sept daily 10am–1pm & 2–6pm; Ⓣ 05.61.69.97.22, Ⓔ tourisme .arize.leze@orange.fr) is at 15 rue Temple, near the church. There are two **hotels**, both good. The family-run *Hôtel Gardel* (closed mid-Nov to mid-March; Ⓣ 05.61.69.90.05, Ⓦ www.ariege.com/hotel-gardel; ❷) is set in an old farmhouse on the main road, and retains the curious mix of rustic charm and bourgeois propriety of the French countryside. For something with more character, there's the small *Le Jardin de Cadettou* (Ⓣ 05.61.69.95.23, Ⓦ www.cadettou.fr; ❸), 200m south of town off the main highway, with three well-kept rooms. Both have internet access. There's a good **campsite**, *Le Petit Pyrénéen* (April to early Oct; Ⓣ 05.61.69.71.37, Ⓦ www.lepetitpyreneen.com) with a pool, about 1km east of the town centre on the D119. The place to eat is at the **restaurant** of the *Cadettou* (closed Sat lunch time, Sun eve & Mon), which serves excellent *menus* of Ariègeois cuisine from €15.

Emerging from the south entrance of the cave, the road meanders through attractively forested uplands before meeting the main highway at Lescure, just 8km east of St-Girons (see p.123). Fans of the film and book *The Return of Martin Guerre* (see box above) will want to visit **Artigat**, a bucolic little village west of Pamiers, over 20km of winding lanes, which is best reached via the D919.

Foix and around

Eighteen kilometres upstream from Pamiers, **FOIX** has few specific sights itself but is the most agreeable base in the valley, with connections by train and bus into the mountains. It has a good range of services, and is surprisingly lively for a relatively small town. What's more, people tend to hurry past, so that although Foix is located in the midst of the greatest concentration of prehistoric caves in France, it is never overwhelmed by visitors and retains an appealing intimacy and freshness.

Arrival and information

The **gare SNCF** sits on the right bank of the Ariège, a ten-minute walk north of the centre; most **buses** stop on the central cours Gabriel-Fauré, near the Resistance monument, although some will drop you off behind the post office. The **tourist office** at 45 cours Gabriel-Fauré (July & Aug Mon–Sat 9am–7pm & Sun 9.30am–12.30pm & 2–6pm; Sept–June Mon–Sat 9am–noon & 2–6pm; ⓣ05.61.65.12.12, ⓦwww.ot-foix.fr) can be reached from the train station by walking south along the river and then crossing the Pont Neuf. If you plan on doing any hiking, pick up a free *randonnées* booklet here, published by the *département* of Ariège.

Accommodation

Most **accommodation** is in the old town, west of the Ariège, with several solid, if unexceptional, options. The three-star municipal **campsite**, *du Lac* (year-round; ⓣ05.61.65.11.58, ⓦwww.campingdulac.com), is 3km north of town, along the banks of the Ariège.

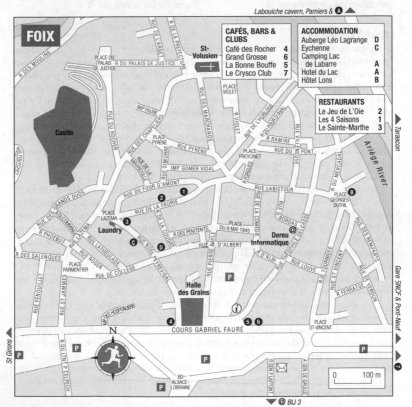

Essentials

Internet access Best done via a hotel. The Bureau d'Information Jeunesse (Mon, Wed & Fri 10am–noon, Tues & Thurs 1–5pm; closed Aug) at 3 rue Longue is expensive (€5 per hour). An alternative is Dereu Informatique, 18 rue Delcassé (Tues–Sat 9am–noon & 2–6pm; €3 per hour).

Laundry Pl Lazéma.

Market Fridays.

Auberge Léo Lagrange 16 rue Noël-Peyrevidal ☎05.61.65.09.04, ⓦwww.leolagrange-foix.com. This family-friendly hostel has rooms for one to four persons, each with an en-suite WC and shower. Other options include studios with a hot plate and fridge and an apartment for up to seven people. ❷

Eychenne 11 rue Noël-Peyrevidal ☎05.61.65.00.04, ⓦwww.hotel-eychenne.com. Located in the heart of the old town, this few-frills hotel has clean and functional rooms. Light sleepers should beware: the bar on the ground floor can get noisy in the evening. ❸

Hôtel du Lac N20, Labarre ☎05.61.65.17.17, ⓦwww.hoteldulac-foix.fr. This is the best option in the neighbourhood, if you don't mind heading 3km north of the old city along the former highway. Comfortable rooms with a/c, wi-fi, satellite TV and DVD players, as well as a spacious garden, make this an excellent base. ❺

Hôtel Lons 6 place Duthil ☎05.34.09.28.00, ⓦwww.hotel-lons-foix.com. The quietest and most comfortable option in Foix is this three-star, set in an old postal *relais*. Amenities include wi-fi and a buffet breakfast, and bikes can be rented here. Closed late Dec to early Jan. ❸

The Town

Foix has a well-preserved **old town** of narrow alleys, wedged in the triangle between the Ariège and the Arget rivers. A few of the overhanging houses here date from the fourteenth to sixteenth centuries, and especially attractive are **place Pyrène** and **place St-Vincent** with their fountains, though many junctions in the old quarter sport some sort of water feature. All lanes seem to lead eventually to the conspicuously large **church of St-Volusien** in the east of the old town, originally Romanesque but almost completely reconstructed after being razed during the Wars of Religion. Its eponymous square, along with the Halles des Grains just off cours Gabriel-Fauré, hosts lively Wednesday and Friday **markets** – farm produce and plants at the *place*, and meat, cheese, savouries and pastries at the metal-roofed *halles*, which on other days is a prime drinking venue.

Presiding over the old town is Foix's grey hilltop **castle** (Feb–April, Nov & Dec Wed–Sun 10.30am–noon & 2–5.30pm; May daily 10.30am–noon & 2–6pm; June & Sept daily 9.45am–noon & 2–6pm; July & Aug daily 9.45am–6pm; €4.30), not so much a single fortification as three magnificent, dissimilar towers from different eras: a slender twelfth-century **turret**, a bulky square fourteenth-century **keep** and a broad and rounded fifteenth-century tower – dramatic when viewed from any angle. From 1012 the castle on this site was the seat of the counts of Foix, whose association with the Cathar faith led to its being besieged four times by Simon de Montfort, who failed to break the fort's resistance.

The castle is reached by ascending a steep flight of stairs. Inside, two of the three towers hold exhibits relating to the history of the building and the County of Foix; the other is home to rather uninspiring interactive displays of local crafts and products. On a clear day the **views** from the crenellated turrets reward those who puff up the narrow keystone staircases. If the castle seems rather too cramped to have served as a noble residence, bear in mind that the counts' regular residence was the roomier castle of Orthez in Béarn – they just stopped in here on occasion to reassert their power over the town.

Foix's greatest hero is **Gaston Fébus** (or Phébus, in French), Count of Foix and Viscount of Béarn (just to the west). Fébus is a local legend, revered as a leader who fought hard for regional independence, epitomizing medieval ideals of chivalry. A soldier and poet, he was born in 1331 and died sixty years later. With his dashing, aristocratic image he naturally became a subject for the songs of troubadours and, a relentless self-promoter, he did everything he could to encourage and embroider tales of his own valour and prowess, even inviting Jean Froissart, the great chronicler of the Hundred Years' War, to write his biography. His surname, Fébus, was his own invention, derived from the Occitan word for sun and celebrating his long, golden hair. As a ruler he was very much a medieval nobleman – he had no time for the legislative town councils, which he abolished, and he set himself up as the highest judicial authority in his realms.

Fébus' great ambition was to create an **autonomous kingdom** in the Pyrenees, a goal that was made impossible by the continuing Hundred Years' War, which divided the loyalties of his subjects between the English and French, and emboldened his restless underlings. Despite successes in battle, his ambitions were clearly untenable, and his dreams of **dynastic dominance** were dealt a final, crushing blow in 1380, when he is said to have killed his only son on discovering the latter's role in a conspiracy to assassinate him. After this, he threw in his lot with the French king.

Despite his failures, Gaston Fébus' ideals and endeavours have come to represent all that is romantic about the medieval era, and, in Foix especially, he is celebrated with festivals in July and August and remembered fondly for **l'hypocras**, a spiced wine drink which he invented and which is enjoyed in the region to this day.

Eating, drinking and nightlife

The best area for **eating** is rue Lafaurie, the old blacksmiths' bazaar at the centre of the medieval town, where an excellent choice is *Les 4 Saisons* at no. 11 (closed Sat & Sun in season, plus Sun–Thurs eve off-season), whose gimmick is to bring to your table a hotplate – a *pierrade* – on which you cook fish and meat yourself; they also do a wide range of crêpes (from €14). *Le Jeu de l'Oie* (closed Sun & Mon in winter), nearby at no. 17, is also worth trying for more traditional fare (about €12). A pricier, but worthwhile option is *Le Sainte-Marthe* (☎05.61.02.87.87; closed Wed off-season), at 21 rue Peyrevidal, which has a range of specialities (*menus* €22–51) including cassoulet, with a dog-free dining room and street-side terrace.

There is a row of café-restaurants which occasionally double as night-time **music-bars** on the west side of the cours Gabriel-Fauré, on either side of the old market hall. *Café des Rochers*, *Grand Grosse* and *La Bonne Bouffe* all have decent if unspectacular dinner *menus* for €10–15, and stay open for **drinking**. Later on, you can head to the **disco** *Le Crysco Club* (Wed–Sat 10pm–3am) at 3 cours Irénée Cros, on the far side of the Pont Vieux over the Ariège.

Listings

Car rental ADA (59 av du Général-Leclerc ☎05.61.68.38.38, ⓦwww.ada.fr), Europcar (Route d'Espagne ☎05.61.02.32.74) and Hertz (RN20 Peysales ☎05.61.65.15.99) have offices in or near town.

Hospital The nearest hospital is the Centre Hospitalier du Val d'Arriège (☎05.61.03.30.30) in St-Jean-de-Verges, 7km north of Foix on the N20.

Pharmacy Pharmacie Loubes, 15 rue Bayle.

Police 2 rue Lakanal ☎05.61.05.43.00.

Swimming pool Indoor and outdoor swimming pools are located at place du Champs de Mars, behind the main post office (€2.50 admission).

Watersports The narrow Lac Labarre reservoir, just north of town, has the usual gamut of waterside facilities; ASPTT (☎05.61.02.62.99) rents kayaks and canoes, and organizes rafting trips.

West of Foix

Heading west from Foix, the main road – the D117 – climbs rapidly to the **col de Bouich** (599m) before descending through the Aujole and Baup valleys to arrive at St-Girons and St-Lizier, near the western limit of the *département*. On this particular road, there's little to detain you, although you might stop at **La Bastide-de-Sérou**, just under halfway, to have a drink in the square outside its old market building. Just past the village, a treacherous forest road cuts up towards Mas d'Azil (see p.117).

If, however, you take the Vernajoul road from the town centre, which eventually links up with the D117, you'll come to the subterranean **river-cavern of Labouiche**, some 3km northwest of Foix (daily: Easter–June & Sept–mid-Nov 10–11.15am & 2–5.15pm; July & Aug 9.30am–5.15pm; €8). It claims to be the longest such navigable cave in western Europe, although the water levels in winter are so high as to block access completely. The same amusement-park atmosphere prevails here as at Lombrives (see p.131): twelve-person boats travel for 75 minutes in opposite directions along the 1500m of galleries open to the public. Entry is either via the natural entrance, or an artificial one bored at the upstream end, on either side of the ticket office – you're told which to assemble at. Highlights of the cavern are the **waterfall** at the upstream end of the river and a small chamber full of formations below the artificial entry; these and other oddities along the way are described by the guides, who do their best to keep up a witty patter while hauling the craft via ceiling-mounted cables.

There are a couple of highly recommended **accommodation** options in the area. Heading south from La Bastide de Serou towards Massat, you'll come upon the ✱ *Auberge les Myrtilles* (☏05.61.65.16.46, ⓦwww.perso.orange.fr/auberge.les .myrtilles; ❹; closed Nov–Feb) in Col des Marrous, a beautiful, rustic hotel with an indoor pool and jacuzzi, as well as a fine *terroir* restaurant (from €22). Further west along the main highway, at Rimont (34km from Foix), there is – a rarity in France – excellent and reasonably priced vegan accommodation, at English-run ✱ *Le Guerrat*, Suzanne Morris's and Trevor Warman's working organic farm (mid-May to mid-Oct; ☏05.61.96.37.03; ❹), where you can enjoy a three-course dinner with wine for €20.

The Couserans

Southwest of Foix, the peaks and the northern slopes of the Pyrenees shelter a series of high river valleys known collectively as the **Couserans**. As the Garbet, Salat, Arac and Alet rivers drain off the high glaciers, they flow down through a country traditionally as poor and isolated as it is majestically beautiful. Cattle farming, herding and forest industries were the original means of subsistence for the meagre population of this area, while later, mineral exploitation and spa development brought tenuous fits of humble prosperity and sustain the area today. The two towns that dominate this region, **St-Girons** and **St-Lizier**, are worth a visit if only to appreciate the subtle cultural shift offered by the mid-Pyrenees – the western-most zone of Occitan influence coloured by contacts with Navarre, the Basque country and the flatlands of Gascony. The lowlands around the two towns were prosperous in the Middle Ages, as the cluster of Romanesque churches in the countryside around them testifies to. If you have the time, energy and perseverance, exploring the highlands to the south will lead you through some of the most remote and splendid scenery, and distinctive culture, the Pyrenees have to offer.

Given the area's isolation, it should come as no surprise that there is little by way of public **transport** in the region. There are bus links from Toulouse and Foix to St-Girons, and a regular service up into the Couserans, but unless you have a car, to do any real exploring you'll have to resort to **hiking** – cycling in these hills is strictly for the dedicated.

St-Girons and St-Lizier

The two complementary towns of **St-Girons** and **St-Lizier**, 45km west of Foix along the D117, and separated from each other by only 1500m of riverbank, to all intents and purposes form a single unit. The former is the administrative and commercial centre, which, with good transport links to Toulouse and a range of services, is most useful as a base for exploring the mountains. The latter, which was the capital of the Couserans until the role was ceded to St-Girons, is where you'll find the sights.

St-Girons

Apart from its long association with making cigarette papers, the most striking thing about **ST-GIRONS** is its pavements, made of a local dark-grey marble veined with white, and with finely chiselled gullies to carry away the rainwater. And although there are no other memorable sights, it's a far from unpleasant place, with a couple of decent **festivals**: folklore in mid-July and theatre in early August. The simplest centre for orientation is the **Pont Vieux**. Straight ahead on the right bank of the River Salat, the bridge points you into the old commercial centre of the town, with some marvellously old-fashioned shops, their fronts and fittings unchanged for generations. To the right is the typically provincial **place des Poilus**, its cachet largely derived from the faded elegance of the *Grand Hôtel de France* and the equally old-fashioned *Hôtel de l'Union*, opposite, where you can still stay. The *Grand Café de l'Union* on the square is a splendidly balconied period café that faces the *mairie*. Beside it, along the riverbank, a wide gravelled *allée* of plane trees, the **Champ de Mars**, provides the site for a big general **market** on the second and fourth Mondays of every month, and for a regular produce market every Saturday morning.

St-Lizier

ST-LIZIER, St-Girons' older and prettier sibling, occupies a little hillock, still partially enclosed by walls and towers built under the Romans in the third and fourth centuries. Strolling along its narrow streets, keep an eye out for the carved facades of its numerous fifteenth-century palaces, particularly around the places de l'Église and des Entends, and on the rues des Nobles and de l'Horloge. Of special note is the late seventeenth-century **bishop's palace**, on route de l'Évêché, from the terrace of which you get a great view over the Couserans rising to the south, with the snowcapped peaks of the Pyrenees as a backdrop. Inside, the **museum** (April–June, Sept & Oct Tues–Sun 2–5.30pm; July & Aug daily 10am–12.30pm & 2–7pm; €4) contains an uninspiring collection of local handicrafts, bric-a-brac and household items.

The main attraction here is the **cathedral of St-Lizier** (Mon–Sat 9am–noon & 2–6/6.30pm, Sun 2–6/6.30pm), an eleventh-century structure built on Roman foundations, with a magnificent array of Romanesque frescoes on the walls and ceiling of its twelfth-century apse; the figure of Christ, as Pantocrator ("Lord of all") presides over angels, apostles and various other figures who descend in hierarchy towards the floor. The adjacent **cloister** is particularly noteworthy for the carvings of its capitals – in addition to the usual floral motifs and monsters are extraordinary narrative scenes illustrating the highlights of the Old and New Testaments. Over the five centuries after its founding the church was completed piecemeal, with sections added on in a strange higgledy-piggledy manner, and though there hardly seems to be a right angle in the floor plan, somehow it all holds together. Apart from the building itself, the church's **treasury** is host to a

▲ St-Lizier

stunning sixteenth-century reliquary bust of St Lizier, as well as other pieces dating back to the eleventh century.

Four kilometres northeast of St-Lizier, just off the highway to Foix, the tiny, beautifully preserved *bastide* hamlet of **Montjoie** evokes a sense of history which the larger villages and towns of the region have all but lost. Hunkered down within fourteenth-century walls, it boasts a striking fortified church. There's also a notable Romanesque church in **Eycheil** (contact the tourist office in St-Girons; €1.50), 3km southeast of St-Girons on the Massat/Aulus route.

Practicalities

Buses from Toulouse and the Couserans arrive in St-Girons on the left bank of the river at place des Capots. There's a **tourist office** here, in the central place Alphonse-Seintein (July & Aug Mon–Sat 9am–6.30pm, Sun 10am–1pm; Sept–June Mon–Sat 9am–noon & 2–6pm; ☎05.61.96.26.60, ⓦwww.ville-st-girons.fr), and a seasonal one up in St-Lizier (June–Sept Mon–Sat 10am–noon & 2–6/7pm, Sun 2–6/7pm; ☎05.61.96.77.77, Ⓔot.saintlizier@orange.fr). The best **accommodation** in town for both atmosphere and comfort is St-Lizier's *Hôtel de la Tour* (☎05.61.66.38.02, ⓦwww.ariege.com/hoteldelatour; ❹) in an ancient building attached to a twelfth-century tower overlooking the river. In St-Girons, there's the elegant but rather over priced *Hotel Eychennes*, on avenue Paul-Laffont

(T05.61.04.04.50, Wwww.ariege.com/hotel-eychenne; ❸), with a large garden and swimming pool, but a better choice is ⚔ *Château Beauregard* (T05.61.66.66.64, Wwww.chateaubeauregard.net; ❺). This is a nineteenth-century estate with its own park, set on the south edge of town. It has a swimming pool and an exquisite little spa which can be reserved by the hour (€40). In St-Lizier, the three-star year-round **campsite** *Parc des Palettes* (T05.61.66.06.79, Wwww.parcdepaletes.com) also rents out bungalows. The *département* website (Wwww.ariege.com) also has comprehensive listings of *gîtes*, B&Bs and hotels in the isolated hinterlands.

There are two excellent **restaurants** here: that of the *Château Beauregard* (closed Sun eve; from €33), set in a magnificently renovated barn, and that of the *de la Tour* (also closed Sun eve; *menus* from €19); both have superb *gastronomique* chefs. **Bikes** can be rented at Horizon Vertical in St-Girons (T05.61.96.08.22; off-season T05.61.04.71.42), who also do caving, canyoning and rock-climbing trips, and at Cycles Solana in St-Lizier (T05.61.66.84.71).

Over the Couserans to Tarascon

Looping back to Tarascon (see p.128) in the Ariège valley provides an opportunity to take in the stunning terrain of the **COUSERANS**, which buttress some of the highest peaks in the Pyrenees and, culturally, remains a unique and independent zone, quite different from Languedocian Foix. Gascon is still spoken here, and if you have the good fortune to visit during local festivities, you'll be treated to the area's singular costume and music: men wearing white embroidered jackets and red *baretos* (hats) sport curious wooden shoes with high (up to 30cm) pointed toes, while women wear long dresses draped with colourful scarves. The Couserans has traditionally been a difficult area to access and even more so to govern, the proud mountain people resentful of any infringement of their liberties or threat to their way of life. As late as the nineteenth century, the villagers waged a guerrilla war against the French government – the so-called Guerre des Demoiselles ("war of the girls"), when they dressed up as women in a surprise attack on local property owners, government foresters and police.

The magnificent landscape is accessible by road and trail, with a number of rewarding circuits. Most of the villages of the Couserans have tourist offices, but hours can be irregular and confirmation is best made at the office in St-Girons, which has information and **walking** itineraries for the whole region. You may also want to contact the Ariège tourist board for **information** (CDT Ariège Pyrénées, 31 bis av Général de Gaulle, BP 143, 09004 Foix; T05.61.02.30.70, Wwww .ariegepyrenees.com). There are three main **routes** that traverse the Couserans from west to east, none of them served by public transport.

Donkey-trekking in the Pyrenees

Perhaps the best and most authentic way to explore the amazing mountain trails of the Couserans is to go traditional and avail yourself of one of the low-emission ATVs that have been popular in the region for over a thousand years. Walking with a **pack donkey** frees you from shouldering your own pack and allows you to enjoy the countryside unencumbered. Panoram'âne, a family-run outfit (English spoken) based in Aleu (just west of Massat), can set you up. After an "initiation walk" (€50), you can **hire** a donkey and pack saddle for between one and nine days (€35 and €250, respectively), or opt for a more expensive **guided tour**. This is a one-of-a-kind experience, and families will be pleased to hear that **children** up to 40kg can ride instead of walk. **Camping** in tepees with half-board options is also available. Contact Panoram'âne at T05.61.04.43.19, Wwww.ariege.com/panoramane/.

Via Massat

Striking out from the River Salat, south of St-Girons, through the dramatic **Gorges de Riabouto** will bring you to the confluence of the Arac and Riabouto rivers. Here, you can take the more direct of the two routes to Tarascon by heading due east to the village of **MASSAT**. As you approach, the fifteenth-century bell tower of its church rises 60m above the village in a marvellous Pyrenean tableau. There's a **tourist office** here (Tues–Fri 10am–noon & 2–6pm, Sat 10am–1pm & 4.30–6pm; ☎05.61.96.92.76, ✉otmassat@orange.fr) and good shops and services. The bright and airy *Hôtel Le Globe* (☎05.61.96.91.39, ⓦwww .ariege.com/le-globe; ❷), on the main square, is an excellent place to stay, and the **market**, held on the second and fourth Thursday of every month, and Sundays in summer, features superb local produce. Continuing east, the road climbs in a seemingly endless succession of hair-raising bends until you reach the 1250m-high **Col de Port**. On the left rise the wooded slopes of the **Montagnes de l'Arize**, while on the right the barren **Pic des Trois Seigneurs** (2199m) scratches the clouds. A steep eighteen-kilometre descent then brings you to Tarascon, passing the Parc de la Préhistoire (see p.129) at the entrance to the town.

Via Seix

From the mouth of the Riabouto gorge, the road heads further up the Salat to the hamlet of **OUST** (ⓦwww.ariege.com/oust). The squat twelfth-century **church** in neighbouring **VIC** (contact the tourist office in St-Girons; €1.50) is the only real attraction, but there are some good **accommodation** options, including the charming, two-star *de la Poste* (☎05.61.66.86.33, ⓦwww.ariege .com/hoteldelaposte; ❸), with an outdoor pool, and a restaurant where the

---

Transhumance in the Pyrenees

Since at least the early Middle Ages, shepherds have capitalized on the change of seasons by moving their herds of sheep and goats up into high mountain pastures to graze for the summer. This practice, **transhumance**, became a focus of social and economic life and a lifeline to the world outside for isolated, rural zones, and continues to be a living tradition in the Couserans, where flocks are taken up in late May and early June and descend in September or October. Both events were causes for **celebration** in peasant villages, and several towns have developed the occasion as an organized event. There is probably no better way for visitors of all ages to experience the rural culture of the Pyrenees.

The best-organized transhumance **festival** takes place at **Seix** on the second weekend of June. On the Friday, herds gather in St-Girons and make their way up the Salat valley. On Saturday morning they arrive at the meadow of Oust, 2km south of Seix. Meanwhile, a series of celebrations are held in Seix including a small livestock fair and demonstrations of **equestrian skill** and mountain **folk-traditions**, including companies from the Basque country performing a traditional **bear pageant** (see p.315) and Landais shepherds **dancing on stilts**. Far from being a packaged tourist event, this is a genuine local celebration and the real protagonists are the townsfolk and shepherds. There is a communal BBQ lunch (€15) and a dinner and show in the evening (€24). On Sunday morning, crowds of walkers accompany the herds south up to the hills, fêted with liqueurs at every hamlet and culminating in a **picnic lunch** (€15) in the high meadow where the herds are loosed.

Book well ahead to ensure accommodation, and contact the very amenable tourist office in Seix (see opposite) to arrange to buy **tickets** for Saturday lunch and dinner and the Sunday picnic (all of which sell out ahead of the date). See ⓦwww.transhcouserans .free.fr for further information.

house speciality is stuffed pigeon. Nearby is the year-round **campsite** *Quatre Saisons* (T05.61.96.55.55, W www.camping4saisons.com), which also has bungalows.

At Oust, two routes lead to Aulus-les-Bains – a relatively straight road going up the Garbet valley, and a longer route which swings south, via **SEIX** (pronounced "sex"), where the peaks of the **cirque** at the valley's head come into view. This market town, lorded over by a fifteenth-century castle and with a distinctive church tower, makes a good base if you plan to do some hiking in the region: the welcoming and comfortable *Auberge du Haut Salat* (English spoken, family-sized rooms available; T05.61.66.88.03, W www.aubergedu hautsalat.com; ❷) is an excellent place to **stay**. There's also a **campsite**, *Cos de Bergerac* (T05.61.66.87.33). The **tourist office** (T05.61.96.52.90, W www .haut-couserans.com) in the town centre provides up-to-date hiking information and free wi-fi, and can tell you about the **mountain-biking** circuit just south of town; bikes can be rented at La Marmotte (T05.61.66.91.60), in place Joffre. In summer a **market** is held on the second and fourth Wednesday of the month, and local products are also sold at the annual **horse fair** on October 18. The best time to visit, however, is undoubtedly during the spring **transhumance** (see box opposite).

From Seix, the bus continues up the River Alet to its terminus at **AULUS-LES-BAINS**, a spa village and adjunct to the mediocre ski station of **Guzet-Neige** (T05.61.96.00.11, W www.guzet.com), separated from Spain's Vall de Cardós by a 10km-wide mountain wall, and lying among lush and fragrant meadows ringed by dramatic peaks. In summer the station becomes a centre for a variety of sports including para gliding, rafting and hiking. The most remote point of the traditionally poor Couserans, Aulus was once famous for its bear trainers, who toured the wealthier lowlands. The classic **walk** here involves heading south along the GR10 to the **Cascade d'Ars** waterfall, a round trip of about five hours. Aulus' **tourist office** on allée des Thermes (daily 9am–noon/12.30pm & 2/3–6/7pm; T05.61.96.00.01, W www.haut-couserans.com) can provide detailed information. The best **accommodation** is the *Hôtel les Ousaillès* (T05.61.96.03.68, W www.ariege.com/les-oussailles; ❸), and the nearest **campsite** is *Le Couledous* (year-round; T05.61.96.00.87) in a holiday complex neighbouring the town. Sunday is **market** day (morning).

From Aulus, a narrow mountain road and the GR10 wind separate paths along the northern fringe of the **Pic Rouge de Bassiès** (2676m), weaving in and out of the tree line. Looking back, you'll see the high-walled crenellated cirque formed by the peak and its nearest neighbour, the Pic des Trois Comtes. The road rises to the east, then the north, skirting the small Étang de Lers and passing herds of grey cows grazing the alpine meadow, to arrive at the pass, the **Port de Lers** (1517m). Eventually passing the waterfall, the **cascade d'Arbu**, some 3km beyond, you begin a sharp descent towards Vicdessos.

There is little to detain you in **VICDESSOS**, the capital of a remote and poor *canton*, and nearby **AUZAT** is remarkable chiefly for the large and ugly aluminium factory that dominates it. It is, however, at these villages that the footpath and road route converge again, and where the main road descends the river valley, passing the Grotte de Niaux (see p.129), shortly before entering **Tarascon**. Vicdessos' **market** is held on Thursdays, and there is an annual fair on September 21. For further information on the area, check W www.pays-du-montcalm.com.

Via Castillon-en-Couserans

The longest but most rewarding route over the Couserans to Tarascon begins by heading southwest from St-Girons along the broad Bouigane valley to

CASTILLON-EN-COUSERANS. This is the most populated and prosperous part of the region, as evidenced by the ancient **churches** clustered around the town. The best are at **Arrout** and **Andressein**, en route to Castillon, and **Ourjout**, just beyond: all can be visited (€1.50) by prior arrangement with the St-Girons tourist office.

While hardly a bustling metropolis, Castillon's central position means it has long been an important market town. It is set at the crossroads ("Cruz de Camisses" in Gascon) of the four "B" valleys – Biros, Bethmale, Balaguères and Bellongue – and, as such, is the Couserans heartland. Its **tourist office** (hours vary; ☎05.61.96.72.64, ⑩www.ot-castillon-en-couserans.fr) provides detailed information on the whole area, including local B&Bs. The main reason to stay here is to use the town as a base for hiking, with the best **accommodation** being at the chambre d'hôtes *Le Clos Enchanté*, a magnificent townhouse at 58 rue Peyrevidal (☎05.61.04.64.47, ⑩www.chambre-hote-ariege-pyrenees.com; ❹).

From Castillon, it's a tense 35km drive of hair-raising switchbacks up the **Vallée de Bethemale** to Seix, where you'll join the route described on p.127. However, you'll be rewarded by spectacular views, both in the tree-lined valley and, once the road breaks into open ground, at the **Col de la Côte**, just past the halfway mark.

The upper Ariège valley

South of Foix, the Ariège river narrows rapidly, and forest slopes rise sharply on either side as the riverbed twists and cuts down through gneiss and schist of the Pyrenean foothills towards **Tarascon**. It is along this part of the river that you'll find in thick concentration many of France's best and most famous prehistorically inhabited **caves**, decorated by hand prints, etchings and animal figures left by our ancestors up to a quarter of a million years ago. This, along with the beauty of the countryside, has made the **upper Ariège valley** an extremely popular destination, especially for French tourists. High season, particularly August, is mayhem, and if you're hoping to see the renowned cave art you should plan (and reserve) as far ahead as possible. Further up in the hills towards the Spanish and Andorran frontiers, the high peaks of the Pyrenees loom ever closer. Here, around **Ax-les-Thermes**, there is breathtaking mountain scenery and great possibilities for **walking**.

Tarascon-sur-Ariège and the caves

A small, utilitarian mining and metallurgy centre with traffic roaring past on the bypass highway, **TARASCON-SUR-ARIÈGE** has nothing about it to suggest that this is the heart of one of the most fascinating areas in Europe. Yet any account of the emergence of the human species must include the **caves** around the town, which, taken as a group, constitute an unequalled display of prehistoric painting and artefacts. The *grottes* served as shelters – and, arguably, as places of worship – for early humans, later coming in handy as hideouts for religious dissidents during the Christian era. Their high concentration in the Ariège is due to the limestone which constitutes the hillsides here – permeable rock ideally suited to the work of cavern creation. There are four main sites, all accessible in a single day if you have your own transport.

Tarascon itself is a small but very attractively set town, with riverside cafés providing pleasant vantage points over the Ariège, and a narrow pedestrian lane leading past a string of craft shops into the old quarter. Here the church of St-Michel presides over a partly arcaded square, and various surviving bits of the medieval walls, razed in 1632, crop up here and there: the **Tour St-Michel** and the **Porte d'Espagne** with a fountain inside. From this former town gate, the short hike past walled orchards up to the **Tour du Castella**, now a clock tower, is worthwhile for the views over the five valleys which converge here. Tarascon is the site of two lively livestock **fairs**, on May 8 and September 30, timed for the passing of the transhumant herds. A regular **market** is held on Wednesday morning in the place de l'Horte, and Saturday morning in the place de l'Ayroule as well as during the annual fairs on May 8 and September 30. On Sundays there is a flea market scattered throughout the town centre.

If you haven't managed to make reservations at the caverns, you can still experience the Neolithic era, albeit vicariously, at the **Parc de la Préhistoire** (April–June & Sept to early Nov Mon–Fri 10am–6pm, Sat & Sun 10am–7pm; July & Aug daily 10am–8pm; €9.70), 5km outside Tarascon – take the N20 north, and you'll see it signposted at the junction for St-Girons. This rambling park contains nature trails and prehistory-related exhibits including replica bison and reproductions of some of the more important and inaccessible cave art – a good alternative to the real thing if you have children.

Practicalities

Buses and trains call frequently from nearby Ax-les-Thermes and Foix, on the line from Toulouse to Latour-de-Carol; the **gare SNCF**, which also serves as the bus stop, is on the left bank of the Ariège, in the northern half of town. The **tourist office** (July & Aug daily 9am–7pm; Sept–June Mon–Sat 9am–6pm; ☎05.61.05.94.94, Ⓦwww.paysdetarascon.com) is inside the multipurpose hall known as the Espace François Mitterand, on avenue des Pyrénées in the centre.

There are two basic but reasonable **hotels**, both along the riverside. The *Confort*, on quai Armand-Sylvestre (☎05.61.05.61.90, Ⓔhotel.comfort@orange.fr; ❸), makes a good base, with a half-pension option (€40 per person), and the better rooms set on an inner courtyard. The nearby *Hostellerie de la Poste* (☎05.61.05.60.41, Ⓦwww.hostellerieposte.com; ❸), set in an eighteenth-century postal stop, has a cosy fireside lounge and a shady bankside garden. It also offers special rates for skiing at Beille (see box, p.132). The best option, however, is the eighteenth-century manor house, *Domaine Fournie* (☎05.61.05.54.52, Ⓦwww.domaine -fournie.com; ❸), 1km from the town centre on the road to Saurat, now a **chambre d'hôtes** featuring five unique rooms, a fine *table* and an indoor pool, all set within impressive private grounds. There are several **campsites**, the best of which is the four-star *Pré Lombard* (☎05.61.05.61.94, Ⓦwww.prelombard.com), set along the riverside, on the south side of the old town. All the hotels have attached **restaurants**, with the best food and service at the *Hostellerie de la Poste*, which offers a reasonably priced Gascon *menu* featuring *auzinat*, a rich hotpot of cabbage, potato, sausage, game and other goodies; the *Domaine Fournie* is another good bet, with an €18 *menu*. **Markets** are held Tuesday and Saturday morning, as well as during the annual fairs on May 8 and September 30.

Grotte de Niaux

Unquestionably the finest of the Pyrenean caves is the **Grotte de Niaux**, 2km southwest of Tarascon. Rivals like Lascaux in the Dordogne and Altamira in Spain are now closed or very nearly so, but the only restriction on access to Niaux is the mandatory **reservation** for places on the twenty-person ninety-minute **guided tour** (daily: April–June & Oct 10.30am–5pm; July–Sept 9.10am–5.30pm; Nov–March 11am–4.15pm; July & Aug English tours at 9.10am & 12.45pm; €9.40).

The current entrance to Niaux is a tunnel created in 1968 near the low and narrow natural opening under an enormous rock overhang. Using flashlights (provided) for illumination, you penetrate 900m (from a total 4km of galleries) to

Pyrenean cave art

The **painted caves** of the Pyrenees are known to have been created by nomadic and semi-nomadic communities of *Homo sapiens* during the Late Paleolithic period, between 10,000 and 35,000 years ago. Almost everything else about them is conjecture.

An early hypothesis was that cave art served a **magical function**, to ensure an abundance of game. The frequency with which animals appear on the walls seems to back up this theory, but the animal remains found in the caves show that the species most frequently depicted were not in fact the main food supply. Other theories focused on the **layout** of cave designs. It was observed, for example, that horses were depicted only at the entrance to caves or in the centre, and that mammoths and bison were confined to the centre. To some, this suggested that the arrangement reflected a **sexual polarity**, with bison symbolizing the female element, and horses the male. However, poor lighting would probably not have allowed the artists to see the cave decorations as a unity. Moreover, successive paintings were superimposed to the extent that they became indecipherable, even though suitable areas of blank rock were available nearby. Recently paleo-anthropologists have suggested that the paintings were executed by **shamans** in a **trance state**, and they reflect the spirit world rather than reality, or that they are the testosterone-charged **graffiti** of teenage Cro-Magnons.

What is certain is that they did not serve as wallpaper for Neanderthal living rooms, nor were they casual stone-age doodlings. The zones that are painted are extremely difficult to access, reachable only after hundreds of metres of scrabbling through pitch-black tunnels and galleries. The sense, even today, is that you are in the belly or the womb of the world, and that these works of **art** were executed at great sacrifice to serve a very deliberate purpose – and that they would seldom be seen by human eyes. This, together with the manifest **technical skill** and artistic sensibility displayed by our ancestors tens of millennia ago, makes visiting the caves an intensely moving experience.

see just some of the famous black outlines of **horse** and **bison**, minimally shaded yet capturing every nuance. Analysis has established that these drawings, and those of the ibex and stag in the recess further back, were produced around 10,800 BC with a "crayon" made of bison fat and manganese oxide. A line of **footprints** left by the artists can be seen in a part of the cave that was opened up in 1970, while their primitive form of **writing** is represented by the dots and bunches of lines on the wall of the main cavity.

NIAUX village itself, between the cave and Tarascon, has a small, private **Musée Pyrénéen** (daily: July & Aug 9am–8pm; Sept–June 10am–noon & 2–6pm; €8) which displays a splendid collection of tools, furnishings and archival photos illustrating the vanished traditions of the Ariège. Exhibits also explain local Pyrenean architecture, with its use of *lauzes* (stone slabs), *ardoise* (slate) and occasionally *chaume* (thatch) for roofing. About halfway between Niaux and Tarascon, keep your eye peeled also for the picturesque remains of a medieval smelting works by the riverside.

Grotte de la Vache

The **Grotte de la Vache** (daily: April–June, Sept & off-season school hols 2.30–4pm; July & Aug 10am–5.30pm; ☎05.61.05.95.06, ⓦwww.grotte-de-la-vache.org; €8) at **Alliat** is well worth the 2km journey across the valley from Niaux, south on the road to Vicdessos: walkers can slightly shortcut the road, by taking the path beginning 150m or so before the Niaux museum. Excavations here over two decades sifted through the detritus of ten thousand years of habitation, beginning between 15,000 and 12,500 BC and ending in the Bronze Age. In one of the chambers, scientists have uncovered and reconstructed a complete hunting camp dating back some fourteen thousand years. Around thirty thousand fragments of flint tools were unearthed and over six thousand complete tools, mainly for engraving in rock; some pieces are displayed in the cave. Tracing your way through the various tunnels, the visit lasts ninety minutes.

Grotte de Bédeilhac

To reach the **Grotte de Bédeilhac** (Easter–June & Sept Mon–Sat 2.15–5pm; July & Aug daily 10am–5.15pm; Oct–Easter Sun 3pm; winter school hols daily 2.30pm & 4.30pm; ℡05.61.05.95.06, Ⓦwww.grotte-de-bedeilhac.org; €9) above the eponymous village, you have to return to Tarascon and cover 5km along the D618 towards Saurat. This cave, a hollow in the ridge of Soudour, contains examples of every known technique of Paleolithic art, including polychrome painting (now faded to monochrome). The imposing entrance yawns 35m wide by 20m high, making it easy to understand how the Germans managed to adapt the cavern as an aircraft hangar during World War II. Although the art within is not as immediately powerful as that at Niaux, its diversity compensates, with low reliefs in mud, paintings of bison, deer and ibex, and stalagmites used to model figures. The visit is 75 minutes in length.

Grotte de Lombrives

The **Grotte de Lombrives** (April school hols, late June & Oct daily 10am–5pm; May, early June & Sept, Mon–Fri 2–5pm, Sat & Sun 9am–7pm; July & Aug daily 9am–7pm; winter school hols daily 2–5pm, ℡05.61.05.98.40, Ⓦwww.grotte-lombrives.fr), 3km south of Tarascon along the N20, near Ussat-les-Bains, could only disappoint if you've already seen Niaux, Vache and Bédeilhac. The access by underground train gives it something of an amusement-park feel – as do the nocturnal *spectacles* regularly staged here in July and August – but the stalagmite formations are superb, and the sheer size of the complex is impressive. It is, in fact, the largest cavern in Europe, and would take five days' walking to see it in its entirety. Lombrives was inhabited around 4000 BC, but all the material found here now rests in museums such as that at Foix. Its later history is embellished by legends of the last Cathars walled up inside in 1328, and of 250 soldiers subsequently disappearing without trace, the victims of cave-dwelling bandits. There are various **routes for visitors**, ranging from a one-hour visit to a seven-hour underground odyssey (€7.50–44).

Ax-les-Thermes and around

AX-LES-THERMES, 26km southeast of Tarascon on the main N20 road, is an unobjectionable spa resort with little specifically to see – owing to frequent disastrous fires in centuries past – other than a lively Monday market along the river promenade. However, it makes a good base for skiing or walking in the Ariège region, with **hikes** routed in circuits from the town, and several **ski resorts**, both downhill and Nordic, within a convenient distance.

Ax dates back to at least Roman times, while the commercial exploitation of its **hot springs** dates from the thirteenth century; the smell of sulphur that early twentieth-century travellers commented on can still be whiffed from the spring water coursing through the gutters, and the ambience of a spa remains. In total there are more than forty *sources*, producing a volume of water in excess of 600,000 litres per day, some at temperatures hotter than 70°C. Just off the main square,

Skiing and mountain biking around Ax-les-Thermes

The nearest **ski station** to Ax is **Station d'Ax** (Ⓦwww.ax-ski.com), 8km south up the D820 – an agglomeration of three resorts, Bonascre, Saquet and Campels. The station itself is a hideous knot of high-rises, but once you get into the *télécabine* (€6.50 to Bonascre; €10 to Saquet) and up to the **Plateau du Saquet**, with the beautiful Andorran frontier peaks as a backdrop, it's a different matter. The snow record here is good, there are 75km of pistes (some over 3km long), and the top lift is at 2305m. There's an alternative station 13km east of Ax at **Ascou-Pailhères** (Ⓦwww.ascou-ski .com), with fifteen downhill runs and a top station of 2020m. It's a pretty drive up to the station, and though it only has one black piste, it's quite a challenging one.

Three valleys west of Bonascre, the **Plateau de Beille** (Ⓦwww.beille.fr) has been developed for **cross-country skiing**. The 55km of pistes range in length from one to twenty kilometres, at an altitude of just under 2000m – which should ensure adequate snow. The station can be reached by *navette* (weekends in the ski season and daily during school hols) from the village of Les Cabannes, 15km north of Ax along the main N20 road. There's also good cross-country skiing to the north of Ax around the **Col de Chioula** (1431m). You can also try **dogsledding** here.

When the snow goes, several ski stations switch over to become summer recreation centres specializing in hiking, paragliding and **mountain biking** (or **VTT**: Vélos Tout Terrain), with runs up to 21km in length, colour-coded for difficulty. See Ⓦwww .vtt-vallees-ax.fr or the Ax tourist office for details.

place du Breilh, you can join the locals and dangle your feet for free in the **Bassin des Ladres**, a pool of hot sulphurous water (up to 77°C) dating to 1250, which was once incorporated into the now-vanished hospital founded in 1260 by St Louis for leprous soldiers returning from the Crusades. For a twenty-first-century **spa** experience, the best option is the **Bains du Couloubret** (during school hols Mon–Thurs 10am–8pm, Fri 10am–9pm, Sat 10am–10pm, Sun 10am–7pm; otherwise Mon–Thurs 2–8pm, Fri 2–9pm, Sat 10am–10pm & Sun 10am–7pm; Ⓦwww.bains-couloubret.com) on the central promenade Paul Salette. The spa offers a range of therapies (none of which require you to be ill) with a basic rate of €3 per half-hour.

The town itself is small and pleasant enough, but there's little to see once you've wandered a couple of streets in the quarter to the south of the N20, which forms the main street. Rue de l'École and rue de la Boucarie retain a few medieval buildings, and above place du Breilh, the **church of St-Vincent** is of architectural interest for its Romanesque tower.

Practicalities

The **gare SNCF** is on the northwest side of town, just off the main avenue Delcassé; **buses** stop in the town centre. On the north side of the main road, half way through town, the helpful **tourist office** (daily 9am–noon & 2–6/7pm; ℡05.61.64.60.60, Ⓦwww.vallees-ax.com) provides information on hiking, can contact guides, and sells a range of *Topoguides* and maps. The Bureau des Guides et Accompagnateurs Montagne des Vallées d'Ax (℡05.61.64.31.51) next door provides details on seventeen walks around the town, ranging in length from twenty minutes to seven hours, with varying ranges of difficulty. Thanks to the baths and the local skiing, there is a number of **hotels** in and around town: the best are *L'Auzeraie* in avenue Delcassé (℡05.61.64.20.70, Ⓦwww.auzeraie.com; ❸) at the north end of town, and the three-star *L'Orry le Saquet* (English spoken, internet; ℡05.61.64.31.30, Ⓦwww.auberge-lorry.com; ❹), a little over 1km south of the town centre on the main highway. The vast municipal **campsite**,

Malazéou (year-round; ☎05.61.64.69.14, ⓦ www.campingmalazeou.com), is beside the Ariège, 500m from the train station.

The most noteworthy **restaurant** in town is the hip *La Petite Fringale*, on rue Piétonne, for its *montagnard* cuisine (from €16) and shady terrace. Otherwise the *Grand Café*, on the same square as the Bassin des Ladres, serves light fare in an atmospheric setting. The **market** is held on Tuesday and Sunday mornings (also Thurs in summer), and **bikes** can be rented at L'Eskimo Sport, in nearby Savignac (☎05.61.64.02.85).

Around Ax

Extending east from Ax, the damp, leafy **Oriège valley** is a jumping-off point for hikes into the Carlit peaks and the **Réserve Nationale d'Orlu**, created south of the road in 1975 to benefit a growing herd of isards (Pyrenean chamois, a goat-like animal) as well as roe deer, golden eagles and lammergeiers (Europe's biggest birds of prey, also known as the bearded vulture). Under the shadow of the distinctive Dent d'Orlu, the D22 road heads up the valley to **ORLU**, where there's camping at the *Municipal* (☎05.61.64.30.09) and a popular *gîte d'étape* aimed at walkers, the *Relais Montagnard* (☎05.61.64.61.88, ⓦ www.aurelaismontagnard.com; ❶), with half- and full pensions available. At a popular picnic area some 8km beyond Orlu, the asphalt ends and a jeep track, prohibited for all private cars, climbs south into the *réserve* through the En Gaudu valley.

South of Ax, the road leads to alternatively Andorra, Spain and the upper reaches of Roussillon's Têt River (see p.307). In between there is fine alpine scenery, but little else to detain you. **Mérens-les-Vals**, 8km south of Ax, is known for the stocky **Mérenguais horse**, whose characteristics can be discerned in the prehistoric cave drawings at Niaux (see p.129), but little else. A few kilometres beyond, **L'Hospitalet-près-L'Andorre** is the site of a modern monument to engineering – a 7km-long road tunnel which pierces the Col de Puymorens (1915m), and saves drivers from 10km of hair-raising hairpin curves and dizzying switchbacks.

Travel details

Trains

The main rail corridors in this region are Toulouse/ Narbonne, and Toulouse/Latour-de-Carol/Enveitg which hooks up with the *Train Jaune* (p.307) to Perpignan. A spur line runs from Carcassonne to Quillan and the Fenouillèdes line (p.300) from Rivesaltes terminates at Axat. SNCF buses may run in lieu of trains on these lines; services are reduced on Sundays and holidays. TGV stations are indicated with an asterisk.

Carcassonne* to:
Nîmes* (connections to Grau & Tarascon/ Beaucaire), via Lézignan, Narbonne* (connections to Perpignan), Béziers* (connections to Bédarieux), Agde, Sète and Montpellier* (several hourly; 2hr 15min–2hr 45min).
Paris* (several daily; 6hr 30min+).
Quillan, via Limoux and Alet-les-Bains (several daily; 1hr 15min).
Toulouse*, via Castelnaudary and Bram (several hourly; 1hr–2hr 30min).

Foix to:
Latour-de-Carol/Enveitg (connections to *Train Jaune* & Perpignan), via Tarascon-sûr-Ariège, L'Hospitalet-près-l'Andorre and Porte-Puymorens (several daily; 1hr 50min).
Toulouse*, via Pamiers (several daily; 1hr 10min–2hr).

Latour-de-Carol/Enveitg to:
Toulouse*, via Porte-Puymorens, L'Hospitalet-près-l'Andorre, Tarascon-sûr-Ariège, Foix and Pamiers (several daily; 3hr–3hr 15min).
Villefranche-de-Conflent (several daily; 2hr 30min).

Limoux to: Quillan (several daily; 45min).
Pamiers to: Lavelanet (daily; 45min).
St-Girons/St-Lizier to: Toulouse*, via Boussens (several daily; 1hr 45min–2hr).

Buses

In the Aude and Ariège, weekend services are much reduced, with most lines having no buses on Sundays, and holidays and school holidays often having little or no service; for full schedules and map, see ⊛www.cg09.fr.

Ax-les-Thermes to: Toulouse (daily; 2hr 10min).

Axat to: Castelnaudary (daily; 1hr 50min); Limoux (daily; 50min).

Carcassonne to: Albi (daily; 2hr); Axat (daily; 1hr 45min); Castelnaudary (several daily; 45min); Castres (several daily; 1hr 50min); Homps (daily; 55min); Lézignan (several daily; 45min); Marseillette (daily; 22min); Narbonne (daily; 1hr 25min); Quillan (daily; 1hr 20min); St-Hilaire (daily; 45min); Toulouse (daily; 2hr 20min); Trèbes (several daily; 15min).

Comus to: Quillan (daily; 1hr 5min).

Foix to: Auzat (daily; 1hr 50min); Ax-les-Thermes (several daily; 1hr 20min); La Bastide (several daily; 25min); Lavelanet (daily; 35min); Lescure (several daily; 40min); Niaux (daily; 1hr); Pamiers (daily; 30min); St-Girons (daily; 50min); Quillan (daily; 2hr); Tarascon (several daily; 35–55min); Toulouse

(daily; 1hr 30min); Ussat (daily; 55min); Vicdessos (daily; 1hr 20min); Villeneuve d'Olmes (several weekly; 30min).

Latour-de-Carol/Enveitg to: Font-Romeu (daily; 50min); Perpignan (daily; 3hr).

Lavelanet to: Belesta (several weekly; 20min); Foix (daily; 35min); Mirepoix (daily; 20min); Pamiers (daily; 1hr); Quillan (daily; 1hr); Toulouse (daily; 2hr 30min).

Limoux to: Castelnaudary (daily; 35min).

Mas d'Azil to: Toulouse (daily; 1hr 50min).

Pamiers to: Niaux (daily; 1hr); Tarascon (daily; 55min); Vicdessos/Auzat (daily; 1hr 20min).

Quillan to: Axat (daily; 15min); Carcassonne (daily; 1hr 20min); Comus (daily; 1hr); St-Paul-le-Fenouillet (daily; 30min); Quérigut (weekly in summer; 1hr 30min).

St-Girons to: Aulus-les-Bains (daily; 45min); Castillon (several daily; 13–25min); Foix (several daily; 50min); Lescours (several daily; 25min); Mas d'Azil (daily; 35min); Massat (daily; 35min); Oust (daily; 30min); Seix (daily; 25min); Toulouse (several daily; 2hr 30min).

Tarascon-sur-Ariège to: Niaux (daily; 1hr); Vicdessos/Auzat (daily; 1hr 25min).

3

Albi and Haut Languedoc

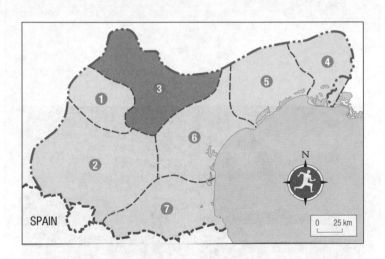

SPAIN

N

0   25 km

CHAPTER 3　**Highlights**

✳ **Albi cathedral** Distinctive brickwork construction gives this medieval cathedral a surreal look. **See p.143**

✳ **Toulouse-Lautrec** See the world's largest collection of the diminutive Impressionist's unmistakable work. **See p.144**

✳ **Cordes-sur-Ciel** Once a refuge for heretics, now a town of artisans, perched "on the sky" west of Albi. **See p.150**

✳ **Gaillac wines** Sample one of the country's oldest and most venerable AOCs. **See p.153**

✳ **Rabastens** Don't miss this village's brilliantly restored, painted church set by the tranquil banks of the Tarn. **See p.155**

✳ **Parc du Haut Languedoc** A wild and under populated area, perfect for hiking and cycling. **See p.162**

▲ Albi cathedral

Albi and Haut Languedoc

arn, the *département* to the east of Toulouse, consists of two contrasting zones. The northwest is wine country: the rolling landscape on the banks of the river which is its namesake is punctuated by towns nurtured on the modest prosperity of the grape and other products of the soil, including garlic and woad. The southeast, on the other hand, is a rugged upland where herding and wool have sustained a precarious living for the villagers of the high valleys as far back as can be recalled. Today Tarn is not the most dynamic of regions, having fallen victim to the rural depopulation that typifies much of southern France. Nevertheless, there's much to see here and though, like Toulouse, it falls outside the modern administrative *région* of Languedoc-Roussillon, it is culturally and historically inseparable from the Occitan coastal lands.

In the northwest, **Albi**, Tarn's principal town, was ruled for centuries by the counts of Toulouse, and its name is synonymous with the Cathar sect, or "Albigensians," with which modern *languedociens* still proudly identify. The undulating lowlands which surround the town are defined by the flow of the Tarn: to the east, descending from the Grandes Causses, it follows a rapid, rocky course, cutting down through forested hills and meandering dramatically around the ancient hamlet of **Ambialet**; north of the capital, gritty **Carmaux** sits atop a coal-rich landscape, the Ségala, scarred by the centuries-long search for the black stuff; to the west, the stunningly preserved medieval citadel of **Cordes** marks the transition to the Aveyron valley; and finally, passing Albi, the Tarn flows west toward **Gaillac** and one of the most praised wine regions of the South of France, veering south, past the ancient *bastides* of **Lisle** and **Rabastens**, before being met by the tributary Agout. The region's interior, south of Albi, has a scattering of sleepy old towns set amid fields of corn and wheat, slumbering since the leather industry that sustained them in the Middle Ages declined. Moving away from the river past the unassuming *bastides* of **Graulhet** and **Réalmont**, the land becomes more hilly, and here you'll find **Lautrec**, the most beautiful town of the Albigeois.

To the southeast, **Haut Languedoc** ("Upper Languedoc"), a wild hinterland of rocky hills that provides an unexpected contrast with the bustle of the nearby coast, has a history of religious and political nonconformity – it was once a remote hotbed of Protestant Huguenots. At its base lies **Castres**, Albi's poorer cousin, a lively little provincial town, birthplace of the socialist hero Jean Jaurès

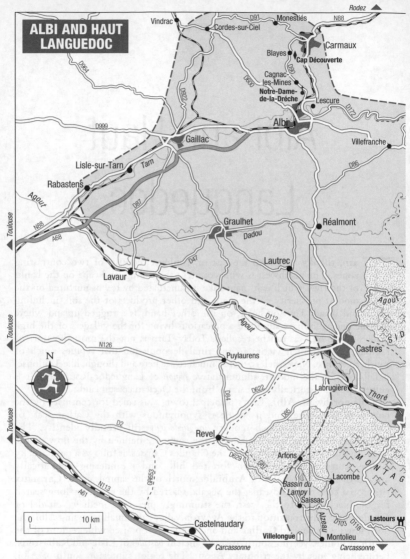

ALBI AND HAUT LANGUEDOC

Rodez ▲

Vindrac   D91   Monestiés   N88

          Cordes-sur-Ciel

                    Blayes   Carmaux
                          Cap Découverte
                    Cagnac-
                    les-Mines
                    Notrè-Dame-
                    de-la-Drèche
                              Lescure
D964
          D922   D172

D999   **Albi**

          ▼ Gaillac   Villefranche
                                              D86
Lisle-sur-Tarn   Tarn
                  D87
Rabastens   Agout

                    Graulhet   Réalmont
          N88   Dadou
          A68
Toulouse ◄   D47

                    Lautrec
Lavaur

                    Agout   D112

N126   Puylaurens   Castres
                                          S I D
Toulouse ◄   N   O
                                    Labrugière Thoré
                  D84   D622
          D2   D85
Revel   M O N T A G
          D629   Arfons
Toulouse ◄ GR653   Bassin du   Lacombe
          N113   Lampy
          A61   Saissac   D103 D118
0   10 km   **Lastours** ⚒
                              Montolieu
          Castelnaudary   **Villelongue** ⌂
                    ▼ Carcassonne   Carcassonne ▼

and home to an important collection of Spanish art. It's a good place in which to unwind and chill out, while the rest of the region features rugged countryside, ideal for rambling or back-road motoring and cycling. In the uplands, most of which have been incorporated into the **Parc Naturel Régional du Haut Languedoc**, dark woods and high pasture are interspersed with a series of largely forgotten villages, including **Lacune**, **La Salvetat** and **St-Pons**. This is easy walking terrain, crisscrossed by *grandes randonnées* and local trails such as the Gijou Valley Railway Path. Further south the densely forested massif of the **Montagne Noire**, rising south of **Mazamet**, presents an even more isolated and

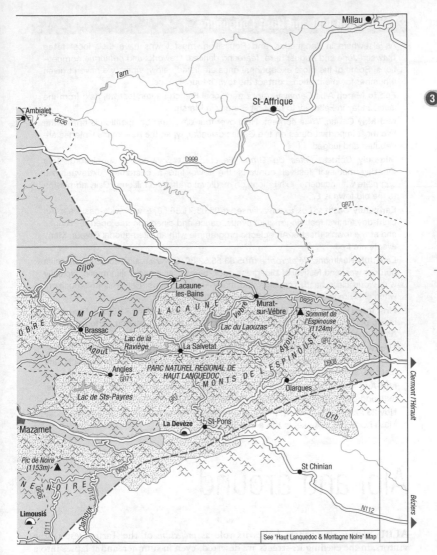

See 'Haut Languedoc & Montagne Noire' Map

untamed landscape, guarded on its southern side by the ruined fortress of **Saissac** and the Cathar castles of **Lastours**.

Despite its general isolation, the area of Albi and Haut Languedoc is well served by public transport. The main Toulouse–Rodez **rail** line follows the course of the Tarn up to Albi and Carmaux, with branch-offs to Cordes and Castres. Cordes acts as a **bus** hub for the western part of the Parc Naturel, and there is good transport to St-Pons, which gives access to the heart of the park. In general, while major routes are served by regular SNCF buses or local lines, getting to smaller villages can be difficult without your own transport.

Festivals in Albi and Haut Languedoc

As elsewhere in Languedoc and Roussillon, most towns have their local **fêtes** between June and August here, featuring dances, fireworks and *pétanque* competitions. Some of the more exceptional ones are listed below; where we haven't given a number for information, contact the town's tourist office.

Feb to March Albi: *Carnaval*. Albi's traditional French Lenten festival, held from the last Sunday in February to the first Sunday in March.

Mid-May Gaillac: Wine contest. Held over four days, this competition is one of the two most important dates on the Gaillac calendar, when the new year's vintages are debuted and judged.

Mid-July Cordes: *Fêtes du Grand Fauconnier* ⓦwww.cordes-sur-ciel.org. This four-day medieval festival converts the town into a costumed extravaganza, complete with concerts, exhibitions on medieval crafts and falconry. Daily admission to the old town is €7.

Early July Castres: *Les Extravadanses* ☏05.63.71.56.58, ⓦwww.ville-castres.fr. An eight-day festival featuring music, circus, dance and cinema in free open-air venues and at the town's theatre. An eclectic programme with an international flavour. Many events are free.

Late July Réalmont: *Ré'alcroche* ☏05.63.55.52.89, ⓦwww.realcroche.com. Massive outdoor weekend festival of bluegrass, rock, blues, Celtic and Cajun music, typically with world-class headlining acts and many French groups. Delicious juxtaposition: when else are you going to see Occitan bluegrass?

First three weeks of Aug Castres: *Couleurs du Monde* ☏05.63.71.59.84. Free world music performances held nightly in the place du 1er Mai, featuring performers from Africa, the Caribbean, Latin America and across Europe.

First weekend of Aug Gaillac: *Fête du vin*. Gaillac's second wine festival is timed to coincide with the beginning of the grape-harvest season, with wine contests and tastings, as well as concerts and cultural events.

Mid-Aug Rabastens: *Grande Cavalcade*. Typical village *fête* held for two days, featuring dancing, fireworks, and a parade through the town centre.

Nov 23 Albi: Ste Cécile Day. Feast of the patron saint of the cathedral, with a special Mass held, and a market in the adjacent square.

Albi and around

ALBI's sleepy atmosphere belies its role as *préfecture* of the Tarn. Despite the visitors, in the evening its streets are deserted, even in summer, and it lapses into a village-like slumber. The highlights are the hulking brick-built **cathedral** and the **Toulouse-Lautrec museum**, which houses the world's largest collection of paintings by the native artist. In addition, the town offers a well-preserved **medieval quarter** of winding cobblestone alleys and centuries-old mansions. Albi is easily explored on foot, and you can take in the main sights in a single day.

After the decline of Roman power, the former Celtic settlement here passed through Visigothic and Frankish hands before coming under the power of the counts of Toulouse in the eleventh century. It was under them that the Pont Vieux was built over the Tarn, stimulating the town's growth as a centre for trade and attracting immigrants from as far away as the Rhine. The anti-Cathar Crusade provided an opportunity for the town's burghers and bishops to play the counts

ALBI

CAFÉS & BARS

Café de la Poste	6
No Name	10
O'Sullivans	9
Picadelli	8

LA MADELEINE

Musée Lapérouse

Centre d'Art du Lait Ⓑ

Old Mills

Tarn River

Gabares Pier

Laundry

Jardins de L'Évêché

Palace de la Berbie

Musée de Toulouse-Lautrec

Covered Market

Cathédrale Ste-Cécile

PLACE SAINTE CECILE

Church of St-Salvy

Pharmacie des Pénitents

Maison de Vieil-Albi

Hôtel de Ville

Ludi.com

Hôtel du Bosc

PLACE DU PALAIS

PLACE LAPEROUSE

Jardin National

Gare Routière

PL JEAN-JAURÈS

RUE DE LA RÉPUBLIQUE

ACCOMMODATION

Camping Caravaning du Languedoc	C
Georges V-La Régence	G
Hostellerie St-Antoine	F
Mercure Albi Bastides	B
La Réserve	A
St-Clair	D
Le Vieil-Alby	E

RESTAURANTS

La Calèche	5
L'Esprit du Vin	3
Le Jardin de Quatre Saisons	1
Le Robinson	2
La Tête de l'Art	4
La Viguière d'Alby	7

0   200 m

Essentials

Bike rental Basile Sarl, 28 av Maréchal-Foch ☎05.63.38.43.09.

Discount card The Albi Pass gives free entry into the Toulouse-Lautrec museum and the cathedral choir and provides reductions for other sights, as well as discounts on restaurants, boat tours, shopping and other activities. It's available at the tourist office and costs €6.50.

Internet access Les Royaumes Virtuels, 44 rue Croix Verte (daily 2pm–midnight); Ludi.com, 62 rue Séré de Rivère (daily 11am–midnight).

Laundry Lavatop, 10 rue Émile Grand (daily 8.30am–8pm).

Shopping and markets Flea market in the Halle de Castelviel (Sat 8am–noon), just west of the cathedral, and produce markets in pl Ste-Cécile and pl du Marché (Tues–Sun 8am–noon). Organic foods are sold at an open-air market in pl F-Pelloutier (Tues 5–7pm) and at Aliments Naturels, 1 rue Puech Bérenguier (☎05.63.54.44.86).

Taxi Albi Taxi ☎05.63.54.85.03.

and kings against each other, increasing their own autonomy, and under the rule of the bishops from the 1300s onwards, Albi rode a wave of prosperity, based on the same woad trade that powered Toulouse (see box, p.81). But the town's fortunes diminished with the demand for the dye, and by the 1700s the adventurous were turning to the sea, some becoming renowned navigators. Industrialization came with the development of coalfields to the north; glass-working and textiles soon became the mainstay. These industries persist in Albi on a modest scale, and today the town is something of a backwater, living on under the shadows of its cathedral and the legacy of its most famous son, the artist Henri de Toulouse-Lautrec (see box, p.144).

Arrival and information

Albi's **gare SNCF**, midway along the Toulouse–Rodez line, is southwest of the old town on place de Stalingrad; you can walk to the town centre in fifteen minutes, or take a local bus (#1; every 30min; €0.80) from the station to place du Vigan. The *gare* has a car rental office and small café, but no left-luggage service. The **gare routière** is on place Jean-Jaurès, southeast of the old town, from where it's a little over ten minutes by foot to the cathedral and the **tourist office** (July & Aug Mon–Sat 9am–7pm, Sun 10am–12.30pm & 2.30–6.30pm; Sept–June Mon–Sat 9am–12.30pm & 2–6/6.30pm, Sun 10am–12.30pm & 2.30–5pm; ☎05.63.49.48.80, ⓦwww.albi-tourisme.fr), which is housed next door in the Palace de la Berbie.

Accommodation

Given its size, Albi offers a wide selection of good **hotels**, especially at the higher end. The two-star **campsite**, *Camping Caravaning du Languedoc*, is a thirty-minute walk east of the centre in Parc de Caussels (Easter–Oct; ☎05.63.60.37.06; Albibus #5 to "Camping" from place Jean-Jaurès). Check the tourist office website for details on the "Albi Destination" **set-price hotel package**, offering a double room for €61 for the one night, €109 for two, and including an Albi Pass (see box above), with various optional add-ons.

Georges V & La Régence 27 & 29 av Maréchal-Joffre ☎05.63.54.24.16, ⓦwww.laregence -georgev.fr. Two adjoining small hotels near the train station in a couple of converted, hundred-year-old townhouses. Each room is individually decorated in modern pastel tones, and there's a garden to breakfast in. Both have junior suites available. This is excellent value for money, and you'll need to book ahead. **③**

Hostellerie St-Antoine 17 rue St-Antoine ☎05.63.54.04.04, ⓦ www.saint-antoine-albi.com. Classy establishment founded in 1734 and run by the same family for five generations. Louis XI once slept here. The sumptuous rooms are appointed with antique furnishings, complemented by modern facilities such as parking, wi-fi and a/c. The garden courtyard is stunning. **⑦**

Mercure Albi Bastides 41 rue Porta ☎05.63.47.66.66, ⓦ www.lemoulin-albi.fr. A large, luxury hotel in a restored eighteenth-century mill, with modern amenities including a/c and wi-fi, and a highly rated and well-priced restaurant. The room decor is understated and unremarkable, but the views of the town and cathedral – if you can get a riverside window – are spectacular. **④**

La Réserve rte de Cordes ☎05.63.60.80.80, ⓦ www.relaischateaux.com/reservealbi. Opulent luxury for those willing to pay. More resort than mere hotel, the *Réserve* is set on a rambling green estate at the northwest end of town, and offers a wide range of facilities including tennis, swimming, horseriding and childcare. The service is first-rate, as you'd expect of a Relais & Châteaux hotel. Open May–Oct. **⑨**

St-Clair 8 rue St-Claire ☎05.63.54.25.66, ⓦ www.hotel-albi-saintclair.com. Occupying a converted old brick-and-timber house in the heart of the old town, only 50m from the cathedral, this friendly place is clean and well maintained. Also has wi-fi and a garage (€8). Closed part Jan. **③**

Le Vieil-Alby 25 rue Toulouse-Lautrec ☎05.63.54.14.69, ⓦ www.levieilalby.com. Comfortable, quiet and set in a renovated medieval house in the centre, this hotel is possibly the best deal in town. It also has a great *terroir* restaurant (closed Sun & Mon off-season) with *menus* at €15–35 and very friendly management. Closed part Jan & early July. **④**

The Town

Albi's sights are within or adjacent to the compact limits of the once-walled **old town**, whose northern boundary is formed by the steep banks of the Tarn, and which is now completely surrounded by the sprawl of the new town. Across the river, the eighteenth-century suburb of **La Madeleine** is also worth a look, primarily for the spectacular views of the Tarn which it affords, with medieval Albi perched above.

The Cathédrale Ste-Cécile

The rounded arches and towers and red-brick construction of the **Cathédrale Ste-Cécile** (daily: June–Sept 9am–6.30pm; Oct–May 9am–noon & 2.30–6.30pm; free) dominate Albi, evoking a mix of the Middle Ages and Art Deco that makes it without doubt the most curious medieval cathedral you are likely to see. Today, it vies with London's Battersea Power Station for the title of world's largest brick building. Financed by the proceeds of the Inquisition, the first bricks were laid in 1282, some fifty years after the Cathar defeat, but the 30m-wide nave and 78m-tall tower were not completed until more than a century after. The cathedral's clean lines, narrow windows and hulking mass reflect its role as a bastion of militant Catholicism in a region plagued by heresy, but two alterations spoil its unity: a gaudy and incongruous sixteenth-century stone porch, and a Baroque frenzy of *trompe l'oeil* festooned about the interior. In better harmony with the structure are the fifteenth-century **statues** of saints and biblical figures which decorate the rood screen to the right of the entrance, while the west wall is dominated by a giant contemporary **mural** of the Last Judgement – sadly marred by the later construction of a chapel – replete with nasty devils carrying off teeth-gnashing souls to the Inferno. To the immediate right of the entrance, a doorway leads to the **choir** (€3), consisting of wooden stalls backed by elaborately carved stonework and more statuary, similar to that of the nave. The **treasury** (€3), reached by a spiral staircase on the north wall, is disappointingly small. If you can, catch the **organ recitals** held in the cathedral in July and August (Wed 5pm & Sun 4pm; free).

The Palace de la Berbie and the Musée de Toulouse-Lautrec

Next to the cathedral, the matching brick-built **Palace de la Berbie** ("bishop", in local parlance), the fortified redoubt of Albi's lord-bishops, squats over the slow-passing Tarn. This complex began as a simple keep in the thirteenth century, but was elaborated in succeeding centuries by its wealthy owners, who strengthened its fortifications, linked it to the cathedral and laid out a classical garden. Today the palace houses the **Musée de Toulouse-Lautrec** (April–June & Sept daily 9/10am–noon & 2–6pm; July & Aug daily 9am–6pm; Oct–March Wed–Mon 10am–noon & 2–5/6pm; €5.50), the most important public collection of the works of the nineteenth-century painter, Toulouse-Lautrec, and the only part of the palace interior open to the public. Conceived and endowed by the artist's mother and opened in 1922, the museum is comprehensive (boasting both his first and last works) – a must for any fan of the diminutive Albigeois. His famous depictions of the entertainers and prostitutes of *fin-de-siècle* Paris, such as the provocatively matter-of-fact *In the Salon in Moulin Street*, or the erotic *Woman Disrobing*, are

Henri de Toulouse-Lautrec

Undoubtedly the most famous of Languedoc's artists is the painter and illustrator **Henri de Toulouse-Lautrec**. Born into the venerable family of the Viscounts of Toulouse-Lautrec in 1864, Henri was deprived of a traditional aristocratic upbringing due to a congenital bone condition; his frailty kept him out of school, and after two falls at his home in Albi resulted in broken legs, any hope of pursuing a "normal" life ended. He thus turned to painting, and his earliest works, scenes from his family's milieu such as *Artilleryman Saddling a Horse*, and portraits – particularly of his mother – showed great promise. With the support of his family and the encouragement of their friend, the painter René Princeteau, Henri moved to Paris to study under Bonnat and Cormon, two successful conservative artists. Settled in bohemian Montmartre and accompanied by his friend and fellow student **Vincent Van Gogh**, he came under the spell both of the Impressionists and of the seedy underside of the city, and it was here that his own vivid style began to flourish. Seduced by the subversive Parisian **nightclubs**, he began to convey their dynamism in charcoal sketches like *Gin-Cocktail* and *Chocolate Dancing*, which were published in popular newspapers and magazines. By the early 1890s he was renowned as an illustrator, doing colourful line-drawn adverts, posters for the famous **Moulin Rouge** cabaret and covers for magazines like *La Revue Blanche*. By 1894, when he began his series of sketches and paintings of Paris **brothels**, including *In the Salon in Moulin Street* and *The Two Girlfriends*, he was already successful.

Henri's disabilities did not prevent him from living life to the full: he travelled widely, drank copiously and, of course, patronized with gusto the brothels he depicted (he was known to Parisian prostitutes as "the teapot", owing to his short rotund figure and excessive endowment). One of the creations attributed to him was "the Earth-quake" – half cognac, half hallucinogenic absinthe. In the end his vices aggravated his already fragile state, and by 1899 he was seeking treatment for **alcoholism**. In September 1901, at the age of 37, he died in a family castle near Bordeaux. What compelled Lautrec's dissolute lifestyle is uncertain (it wasn't his family relations, as he remained close to his parents throughout his life) but his contribution to the artistic world is unquestionable; with a unique illustrative style – a peculiar outgrowth of Impressionism – he not only influenced successive movements such as the Fauvists, but set the precedent for innovative poster design: to this day his Moulin Rouge adverts remain some of the most reproduced pictures in the world. His other great legacy is the **chocolate mousse**, a dessert invented by the painter, for whom culinary experimentation was also a passion.

complemented by many **posters** and lesser-known works inspired by his family life in the local countryside. Off in a corner up a spiral stairway, you'll find a sumptuous thirteenth-century **chapel**, with a beautiful ceiling of gold-painted stars on a blue background – once the audience chamber of the bishops. The top floor of the museum's three storeys houses works by other modern French artists, including Brayer (see also Cordes, p.152), Gauguin and Matisse.

The palace also has a partly covered gallery with a shady outdoor **café** providing views of the old bridge and the far riverbank, as well as access to the **garden** (July & Aug 9am–6pm; Sept–May 8am–noon & 2–6pm); you enter it from the place de l'Archevêché, on the east side of the complex.

The old town

Albi's **old town** is a chaotic jumble of narrow streets spreading east and south of the cathedral-palace complex. Its most conspicuous landmark is the red-brick spire of the much mistreated **church of St-Salvy**, which marks the old town's centre. Between 474 and 584, it served as Albi's first cathedral, while after the Revolution it was used as a shed for fodder. Its simple Romanesque **cloister** is a great place to read or just take a break (daily: 7am–8pm; free). Just east, in rue Timbal, sits the sixteenth-century brick-and-timber **Pharmacie des Pénitents**, once a wealthy merchant's mansion and now a pharmacy, with playfully carved faces on its wooden beams. South and west of here, narrow cobbled streets overhung with the balconies of medieval houses evoke the age when the bishops and woad merchants held sway. On rue de la Croix Blanche you'll find the medieval **Maison du Vieil Alby** (Mon 3–7pm, Tues–Sat 10.30am–12.30pm & 3–7pm; €2), a museum displaying items of local interest, including memorabilia of the young Toulouse-Lautrec, and – more interestingly – a period townhouse interior. Close by, on rue Lautrec, is the artist's childhood home, the **Hôtel du Bosc** (no entry), an otherwise indistinguishable middle-class townhouse.

La Madeleine

Across the river from the main body of the old town lies the eighteenth-century suburb of **La Madeleine**, best reached by the oft-repaired eleventh-century Pont Vieux to the east of the bishop's palace. Before you cross over, however, you might want to explore the banks of the Tarn, where, under the shadow of the palace walls, *gabares* (traditional riverboats) depart downriver for **excursions** around town (30min; May–Sept 11–11.45am & 2–6pm; €6) or to Aiguelèze (2hr; July & Aug Mon & Wed 5.45pm & Sun 9am; €23 return), about halfway to Gaillac. La Madeleine itself is a compact knot of residential houses, with a number of disused eighteenth-century mill buildings clustered along the riverbank on its eastern side. Part of the mill complex, back from the river, holds the **Musée Lapérouse** (July & Aug Mon–Fri 9am–noon & 2–6pm, Sat & Sun 10am–noon & 2–7pm; Sept & Oct Tues–Sun 9/10am–noon & 2–5/6pm; €3), named in honour of the adventurous navigator (1741–88) who fought the British in New France before embarking on a scientific voyage to South America, Japan, Siberia and the East Indies, where he perished in a shipwreck. The museum reviews the admiral's career in a lively display of personal and period artefacts, maps and dioramas. This area is also home to Albi's newest cultural institution, the very worthwhile **Centre d'Art du LAIT** (Wed–Sun 2–7pm; €2) at 41 rue Porta, which features temporary exhibitions by contemporary artists from around the world.

Eating, drinking and nightlife

Food in Albi is very good and economical, if rather uniform: most **restaurants** specialize in local *terroir* ("country cooking"), with the usual cassoulet, foie gras and duck, accompanied by fine Gaillac wine. Also widely available are "lou tastou", tapas-sized portions which permit you to sample a variety of dishes without breaking the bank. Numerous **cafés** and **bars** lining place de l'Archevêché and place du Vigan have terraces for a daytime drink, including *Café de la Poste* on the north side of place du Vigan, with a good selection of Belgian beers. For nighttime **music** (predominantly Latin), there's *Picadelli* (nightly till 2am) at 44 rue Séré des Rivières, and *No Name* (weekends till 2am) in 25 pl Edmond-Canet. *O'Sullivans*, 44 pl Jean Jaurès, is the Irish-style option.

Restaurants

La Calèche 8 rue de la Piale ⓣ05.63.54.15.52. Comfy dining room built under the supporting vaults of the cathedral, with a wide range of lunch and dinner *menus*, including cassoulets, escargots, excellent salads and Moroccan dishes (three-course lunches from €15). The service is fast and professional, yet friendly. Wheelchair-accessible. Closed Wed off-season.

L'Esprit du Vin 11 quai Choiseul ⓣ05.63.54.60.44. Under the shadow of la Berbie, this place scores on both decor and quality with imaginative *gastronomique* cuisine, balancing sweet and savoury with duck, lamb and fish dishes as well as excellent home-made desserts. This is one of the town's top-end restaurants: expect to pay €30 at lunch and €80 at dinner. Closed Sun & mid-Feb to May.

Le Jardin des Quatre Saisons 19 bd de Strasbourg ⓣ05.63.60.77.76. Hearty *terroir* fare prepared with market-fresh ingredients. Dine in air-conditioned comfort inside the ancient vaulted dining room, or on a shaded terrace. Also has a very good humidor for cigar-lovers. *Menus* from €17. Closed Sun eve & Mon.

Le Robinson 142 rue Edouard-Branly ⓣ05.63.46.15.69. Top marks for atmosphere at this charming restaurant, occupying a rambling old house in a wooded riverside park, reached by a footpath from the new bridge. Come in the afternoon for a cocktail and enjoy the selection of grilled meats and other *terroir* treats. *Menus* from €17. Closed Mon, Tues & Nov–March.

La Tête de l'Art 7 rue de la Piale ⓣ05.63.38.44.75. The decidedly unrestrained atmosphere and wacky decor make a pleasant change from this restaurant's more formal rivals. *Menus* featuring generous portions of local cuisine start at €14. Closed Tues & Wed off-season & Aug.

La Viguière d'Alby 7 rue Toulouse-Lautrec ⓣ05.63.54.76.44. Long an Albigeois *terroir* institution, the cuisine here has now taken a *gastronomique* twist with an emphasis on fish. Off-season dining is cosy in the fire-warmed dining room. *Menus* from €15 at lunch to €60 in the evening. Closed Wed eve & Thurs off-season.

Listings

Bus information ⓣ05.63.53.31.28.
Car rental Auto Gita, 6 rte de Millau ⓣ05.63.47.79.30, ⓦwww.rentacar.fr; Avis, 70 av François Verdier ⓣ05.63.54.76.54; Budget, rte de Castres ⓣ05.63.47.97.00; Cars Coulom, 4 av Gambetta ⓣ05.63.54.18.39, ⓔcarscoulom @orange.fr; Europcar, 24 av François-Verdier ⓣ05.63.48.88.33.
Hospital Centre Hospitalier, bd Général Sibille (ⓣ05.63.47.47.47), southwest of the old town.

Pharmacy At-Grimal, rue des Pénitents.
Police Police Municipale, Hôtel de Police, 11 licés Georges-Pompidou.
Swimming Espace Caussels is a waterpark just north of town on the Cordes road with an Olympic-sized pool and activities for children. Daily June–Aug 10am–8pm; €4 (€3 children).

Around Albi

An excellent vantage point from which to take in the panorama of Albi is the nineteenth-century octagonal sanctuary of **Notre-Dame-de-la-Drèche**, set on a rise 6km north of town. Founded by returning missionaries, it houses a small museum (Mon–Sat 9.30am–12.15pm & 4–6pm; free) recalling their efforts overseas; the grassy grounds outside the church are a popular picnic spot, and make an ideal rest stop for those returning by foot or bike from Cagnac (see p.149).

The Albi–Castres rail line trail

The best way to get from Albi to Castres is to follow the former rail line, now converted into a **trail**, perfect for **hiking**, **cycling** and **riding**. There are no major sights on the way, but the landscape – gently rolling hills with alternating pastures, wheat fields and sunflowers – is beautiful if not breathtaking. The walk is suitable for all ages and fitness levels. The total **distance** is 45km, which can be walked in approximately sixteen hours, making an overnight stop at Lautrec (see p.156), 26km from Albi. The trail can be picked up 1km south of the Albi ring road, on rue Bourgelat, near the old cemetery, just off the southbound N112.

After 800m you'll meet the D71, which should be followed south for 900m to regain the trail. A further 7km will lead you past the ruined church of Montsalvy and along the N112 until you reach a car park. Following the yellow trail markings you'll take a small lane on your right, and continue straight, over the quiet N120, as the trail once again becomes dirt. After 400m, branch off to the right (southeast) to regain the rail line. Turning right it continues for 3.5km, passing below the hamlet of Lombers, and continuing 12km to Lautrec, the turn-off for which is marked by a disused crossing-house. Leaving Lautrec the trail can be regained at the same point, or by taking the D83 (direction Castres) south for 1.5km, where you'll pass a grain silo on the left. From here the trail continues for the remaining 16km to Castres, emerging near the town's *gare*.

You could also call in at the old hamlet of **Lescure**, on the northeast edge of Albi, whose draw is the must-see eleventh-century **chapel of St-Michel** (hours vary), a daughter-house of the monastery of Gaillac. Currently used for photography and art exhibitions, the ancient church boasts a striking twelfth-century Romanesque doorway and is festooned inside and out with carvings of gargoyles, animals and biblical scenes. Die-hard **Toulouse-Lautrec** fans will want to trek 45km north to **Château du Bosc** (guided tours in French: 45min; daily 9am–7pm; €5), the family's principal estate, easily accessible from Albi by car or train to Naucelle-Gare, and then 3km southeast (follow signs for "Bosc"). The rambling estate is presided over by a magnificently appointed manor house still owned by the painter's family. In addition to family furnishings and *objets*, there are galleries featuring temporary exhibitions.

Ambialet

Some 21km east of Albi, the Tarn bends back on itself in a dramatic oxbow only 25m wide at its narrowest point. Here, perched on a rocky isthmus in a truly striking location, is **AMBIALET**, a tiny hamlet dominated by its still-active monastery. First mentioned as a monastic centre in 924 AD, Ambialet was seized by Simon de Montfort during the Albigensian Crusade, and over the following centuries declined; by the nineteenth it lay abandoned and even today it exudes a certain sleepy desolation. The main sight here is the austere Romanesque **church** (daily 7.15am–10pm; free), still used by the resident monks whose chanted masses are open to the public. Set on the top of the hill, it provides an impressive panorama of the town below. You reach the church by climbing up a path from the "old town", which sits at the narrowest part of the river's meander (the "new town" is above the road tunnel), and return either the same way, or by following the road behind the monastery for 2km.

Buses stop in the car park on the south bank, near which you'll find Ambialet's summer **tourist office** (July & Aug Tues–Sun 10am–noon & 3.30–7pm; ℡05.63.55.39.14, ⓦwww.si-ambialet.fr). On the north bank, the only **hotel** here, the well-appointed *du Pont* (closed Jan–Feb; ℡05.63.55.32.07, ⓦwww .hotel-du-pont.com; ❹), has been run by the same family for almost two centuries. The rooms are homey, and have wi-fi; a separate bungalow is available for families. Its **restaurant** offers excellent *menus*, featuring elaborate regional dishes, such as lamb and rice with chanterelles, from €24–50. **Bikes** can be rented at the hotel, while **kayaks** and **canoes** can be rented near the bridge on the same side of the river, and at other locales along the length of the river on the way to Albi. Wednesday's "country" **market** (July & Aug) is strictly a tourist affair.

Carmaux and around

Lying 16km north of Albi, down-to-earth **CARMAUX** owes its existence to the thirty-square-kilometre coalfield over which it sits, and its few visitors are drawn by the relics of the defunct mining industry around the town: the open pit of **Sainte-Marie** and the museum of **Cagnac**. These sights can be taken in by car, bicycle or even by foot, and, combined with a visit to the church of Notre-Dame-de-la-Drèche (see p.146), make a good day's outing from Albi. The countryside hereabouts is flat, scarred by excavation, and not particularly welcoming, but it improves as you head west towards Cordes, passing through **Monestiés**, a small village that's home to a well-preserved ensemble of late medieval statues. If you're relying on public transport, you'll have to catch one of the frequent buses which follow the old Carmaux–Albi highway to see the mining sites, but there's no public transport between Carmaux and Monestiés.

The town's **coal** vein has been used since the twelfth century, but mining on a grand scale didn't begin until the 1700s, when the local squire, Georges Solages, received a royal licence to exploit the deposit. Late in the nineteenth century, the massive coalface at nearby Cagnac was discovered and became the focus of a boom. By the end of that century, though, brutal conditions prompted miners, supported by **Jean Jaurès**, to unionize; in the half-century that followed the mines enjoyed their greatest period of production. In the 1970s things began to wind down, and the last mine, the great open pit, closed in 1997.

Carmaux itself offers little to visitors aside from a refreshing roughness – a relief after the pretensions of one too many polished-up *bastides*. In fact, the only attraction is the **Musée du Verre**, a modest mining and glass-working museum set on the former Solages estate 1km west of the centre (French-only 1hr guided visits: June–Aug Mon–Sat 9am–noon & 2–6pm, Sun 3–6pm; Sept–May Mon–Fri 9am–noon & 2–6pm, Sat & Sun 3–6pm; €5). With little else to detain you in town, Carmaux is best used as a jumping-off point for visiting the coal country to the south.

Practicalities

Carmaux's **gare SNCF**, on the Albi–Rodez line, sits on the west side of the town centre. Turning left out of the station, boulevard Malroux leads north 100m to avenue Jean-Jaurès, the main street; at the junction turn right and you'll arrive three minutes later at the *place* of the same name, the town's centre. Two streets beyond lies place Gambetta, where the same kiosk serves as the **gare routière** and **tourist office** (Mon–Sat 10am–noon & 2–6pm; ℡05.63.76.76.67, ⓦwww .carmaux.fr). There's no need to stay in Carmaux, which is an easy day-trip from

Albi, but if you're stopping for lunch, you'll find the town's best **restaurant**, *La Mouette* (closed Sun & Mon eves & mid-Feb; T05.63.36.79.90), on place Jean-Jaurès; it offers original and varied *menus* featuring grilled meats and *confits* starting at €15. **Bikes** can be rented from Patrick Gelac (T05.63.56.05.64) at 23 bd Augustin-Malroux, near the station.

Blaye-les-Mines, Cap Découverte and Cagnac-les-Mines

With the land sloping down towards Albi, it makes the most sense to start a trip through the once coal-filled landscape to **Cagnac** from Carmaux. Just 2km south of town on the D90, the mining hamlet of **BLAYE–LES–MINES** is now a centre for industrial-history tourism, and a remarkable example of creative economic rehabilitation of what had become a post industrial wasteland. It makes an interesting stop, particularly if you are travelling with children. The first thing you'll come upon is the abandoned *découverte*, or **open pit**, of Sainte-Marie, now transformed into the amusement park **Cap Découverte** (July & Aug 10am–8pm, Sept–June consult website for days, 11am–6.30pm; W www.capdecouverte.com), with a wide range of activities including go-karting, water skiing and a beach: the activities are payable individually, or with a day-pass (adults €20, children €13, and €30 for the whole family). The site also plays host to various concerts and cultural events. The day-pass includes entrance to the adjacent **Jardins du Carbonifère** (same hours) featuring nature trails among the local fauna, while the silent hulks of rusting machinery parked along the rim of the pit can be explored in the **Parc des Titans** (free).

Further along the D90 you'll pass the **Cité du Homps**, an industrial suburb of single-storey wooden huts, built for the Polish miners who immigrated in the 1950s. Beyond this, in **CAGNAC-LES-MINES**, you reach the excellent **Musée de la Mine** (also part of the Cap Découverte complex), a vivid re-creation of the world of the coal mine, and undoubtedly the region's most original museum. It consists of a stimulating, if claustrophobic, ninety-minute guided tour through 350m of galleries, excavated by out-of-work miners, and over a century of mining history, as you're shown different types of tunnels and machinery, a broad coal face and the miners' day quarters. From Cagnac, the D90 begins a rapid descent, reaching Notre-Dame-de-la-Drèche (see p.146) after 3km, before continuing to Albi.

Monestiés

Some 8km west of Carmaux the village of **MONESTIÉS** owes its fame to a magnificent set of fifteenth-century religious **statues** housed in its **Chapelle St-Jacques** (July & Aug daily 10am–12.30pm & 2–6.30pm; Sept–June daily 10am noon & 2–5/6pm; mid-Dec to mid-March closed mornings Mon–Fri; €3, €4 with museum). The stone carvings on display are a set of four works representing a group of figures in Christ's tomb, the Crucifixion and a *pieta* (Mary holding a dead Christ in her arms). Commissioned in 1490 by the Bishop of Albi to grace this humble stop on the Chemin de Saint-Jacques, the vivid polychrome statues mark an intermediary step between medieval formalism and humanistic realism – they are not quite portraits, but they are lifelike, individualized representations. The village is also home to the small **Musée Bajén-Vega** (same hours as Chapelle St-Jacques; €3, or €4 with chapel), displaying unexceptional works by the two locally based twentieth-century artists after whom it is named. Next door, a small open-air excavation of Iron Age remains completes the village's attractions. Monestiés' **tourist office** is in the same building as the Musée Bajén-Vega (same hours; ℡05.63.76.19.17, Ⓦwww.tourisme-monesties.fr). The only **hotel** is the *Hostellerie de Saint-Jacques* (℡05.63.76.11.72, Ⓦwww.logis-de-france.fr; ❸), opposite the *chapelle*. There is a basic riverside municipal **campsite** (mid-June to mid-Sept) off the road to Cordes. Friendly *Auberge Occitane* (closed late Aug to Sept & Wed) on the main street serves two-course **meals** from €12; the grocery store rents **bikes** (℡05.63.76.11.51).

Cordes-sur-Ciel

CORDES-SUR-CIEL, 27km northwest of Albi and just west of Monestiés, is the most spectacularly preserved of the Albigeois fortified planned towns, or *bastides*. Dramatically situated on a steep hill, the origin of the town's surname *sur-ciel* ("in the sky") can be appreciated on mornings when fog cloaks the foot of the hill and the medieval *cité* pokes through, apparently suspended in the clouds. No single sight brings people to Cordes; rather, the town as a whole, girded by several concentric medieval walls and endowed with a score of old houses, is something of an open-air museum and artisanal centre. It can be seen in an afternoon, but if you can afford the relatively expensive hotels, it makes for an atmospheric place to spend a night or two.

Founded in 1222 by Count Raymond VII of Toulouse at the height of the war against his Cathar subjects, Cordes provided a durable and defiant stronghold against Simon de Montfort's attacks. Its forename comes from the **leatherworking** industry (a craft associated with Islamic Córdoba, in Spain) that supported and enriched the town, bringing rapid growth; in the 1200s alone the walls had to be enlarged no fewer than seven times. Things took a downturn, however, with the arrival of the plague in the 1300s. Although Cordes later recovered, and had a notable lace industry in the nineteenth century, its real renaissance didn't come until the 1970s, when hippies, including the **craftsmen** and **artisans** whose wood, metalwork and other studios now cram the upper town, arrived to put Cordes back on the map, attracted by the place's beauty and air of antiquity.

Hiking through the Cérou valley

From Monestiés to Cordes-sur-Ciel the **Cérou river** meanders down from the scrubby highlands of the Ségala towards the rocky hills of the Tarnais *causses*, before emptying into the Lot. The pleasant and unchallenging sixteen-kilometre trip along the wooded riverbank can be made by car or **bicycle**, but can also be **hiked**, following a gentle path, in four to five hours. Leaving from the sports ground on the north side of Monestiés, follow the disused rail-bed which runs parallel to the D91 highway for 6km to the hamlet of Salles. Crossing the river, follow the directions through town for Virac, but turn right when you come to Salles' medieval church. At the end of that street follow the sealed road which ascends towards the Vignasse farm. After 200m or so, take the first trail branching off to the right. After a further 800m or so, following the yellow trail markings, you should reach the top of a T-junction. Cross this and proceed 30m, before the trail turns off left through the trees. Regaining a country lane 60m later, turn right, passing a bridge on your right, and a turn on your left, before coming to a T-junction. Here, take the left branch, which descends, becoming a dirt trail for 250m before reaching the D7 road. Cordes should now be in view. Descending along the D7 for just over 1km you'll pass a sign saying "virages sur 2000m"; here you can pick up the trail which leads to the town itself (1km further).

▲ Cordes-sur-Ciel

Arrival, information and accommodation

Trains stop 5km to the west of Cordes at **Vindrac** (☎05.63.56.05.64), from where it's a pleasant hour-long walk, or a short ride on the *navette* (€4.50). **Buses** arrive in the lower town, near the summer-only **tourist office** (May to mid-June & early Sept Sat 2–6pm, Sun 10.30am–12.30pm & 2–6pm; mid-June to Aug Mon 2–6pm, Tues–Sun 10.30am–12.30pm & 2–6pm), while the main tourist office (Jan Sun 2–6pm; Feb, March, Nov & Dec Tues–Fri & Sun 2–6pm; April–June, Sept & Oct daily 2–6pm, plus Tues–Fri 10.30am–12.30pm, Sat–Mon 2–6pm; July & Aug daily 9.30am–1pm & 2–6.30pm; ☎05.63.56.00.52, ⓦwww.cordes -sur-ciel.org) is in the heart of the *cité*. If you're driving, **parking** can be a challenge – in the summer months the area a few metres east of the lower tourist office soon fills up and cars line the roads leading into town. Don't be tempted to drive into the old town.

Famed Tarnaise pastry chef and chocolatier Yves Thuriès presides over several of Cordes' **hotels**, including the lavish four-star ⚑ *Grand Écuyer* (closed mid-Oct to

Easter; ☎05.63.53.79.50, 🅦www.legrandecuyer.com; ❸), housed in Raymond's former palace on Grand Rue Raymond VII; the atmospheric three-star *Vieux Cordes* (closed mid-Oct to May; ☎05.63.53.79.20, 🅦www.vieuxcordes.com; ❸); and the two-star *Hôtel de la Cité* (closed Nov–April; ☎05.63.56.03.53, 🅦www .vieuxcordes.com; ❹), both also on the same street. There's also a decent **campsite**, *Le Garissou* (open April to Oct; ☎05.63.56.27.14, 🅦www.aquadis -loisirs.com), in the nearby village of Les Cabannes, to the west of town.

The Town

The traveller, who from the terrace of Cordes regards the summer's night, knows that he has no need to go further, and that if he allows it, day after day, the beauty here will raise him out of any solitude.

Albert Camus

Camus' words give some idea of the town's allure, and hard though it may be to achieve such a placid state when the streets are packed during summer days, in the evening or out of season the romance of Cordes returns. To watch the sun rise from the ramparts is worth getting up for, and with every other building a medieval mansion, walking the town before the crowds arrive is a delight. Its layout is simple: the old citadel – the "**upper town**" – runs along and down the sides of the long and narrow ridge which juts up from the plain, while the modern "**lower town**" consists of a clump of streets at the foot of the old town's eastern tip. The best route to the upper town is the knee-cracking Grande Rue Basse ascending from the lower tourist office (see p.151), although at busy times, it is more pleasant to take one of the picturesque but less crowded side-streets. Alternatively, a *petit train* (July & Aug; €3) makes frequent trips from outside the tourist office. Along the way a series of medieval **gates** leads to the compact upper town.

Entering the last of the fortified entrances, you'll reach the **Musée Charles-Portal** (July & Aug daily 2–6pm; Sept–June Sat & Sun 2–5/6pm; €2.50), housing a display on the medieval wells that riddle the town, which were used in time of siege for water supply or to store grain. Further along, on Grande Rue, the elegant and symmetrical arcaded face of the fourteenth-century Maison du Grand Fauconnier houses the **Musée d'Art Moderne et Contemporain** (daily: Feb, March, Nov & Dec 2–5pm; April, May & Oct 11.30am–12.30pm & 2–6.30pm; June–Sept 11am–12.30pm & 2–7pm; €4). The museum's high points include works by the figurative painter Yves Brayer, who lived in Cordes from 1940, as well as a motley collection of modern art, including minor pieces by Picasso, Miró and Klee. Across the street squats the ancient **covered market**, where you can peer down one of the town's famously deep wells, which allowed it to endure the Crusaders' seiges. Close by is **L'Historama de Cordes** (March, April, Oct–Dec Sat & Sun 2–6pm; May daily 2.30–7.30pm; June–Sept daily 10.30am–12.30pm & 2.30–7/7.30pm; €4), a wax museum and diorama re-creating life in the medieval town; it's a little cheesy but a good stop nonetheless, especially if you're travelling with kids. Continuing along Grande Rue, you'll pass the **Maison du Grand Veneur** ("House of the Great Hunter") whose otherwise plain stone facade is festooned with amusingly sculpted and extremely well preserved medieval caricatures of beasts and hunters. You'll find another impressively carved frontage a few doors down at Raymond of Toulouse's old palace, now home to the hotel *Grand Écuyer* (named after the finely sculpted horse figure) while, just beyond, the contemporary **Porte des Ormeaux** ("Gate of the Elm Saplings") takes you out of the old town.

There are more than forty **boutiques** in Cordes, including some which are thinly disguised as "museums". If price is not an issue, you could easily spend an

❸

afternoon or two here shopping for leatherwork, metal and handicraft items. Many of the stores double as workshops, so even window-shopping is quite interesting. One of the better deals is Le Petit Bois, in the place de l'Église, which has ingenious toys and gifts.

Eating and drinking

The best **restaurants** are in the hotels, including that in the *Grand Écuyer*, a one-star Michelin restaurant known for its foie gras and its "trilogy cuisine", in which each plate contains three separate mini-dishes cooked three separate ways (*menus* from €35). There's plenty of choice for more economical fare around the central place de la Halle and adjacent place de la Bride, while *Les Ormeaux*, at 3 rue St-Michel (closed part Jan; *menus* from €25), offers an appetizing middle ground. If you don't want to splash out for dinner at the *Grand Écuyer*, then you should definitely head there for an evening **drink**, to soak up the medieval atmosphere.

Gaillac and around

Twenty-three kilometres west of Albi along the Tarn, **GAILLAC**, located at the heart of the wine region bearing its name, is a town built on the grape. It has an ideal climate for viticulture, and its inhabitants started putting corks in bottles more than 2500 years ago. The industry really took off in the eighth century with the founding of the Benedictine abbey of St-Michel – as part of their rule, monks were given a healthy daily ration of wine which, along with that needed for Holy Communion, ensured a high demand for the local product. In the tenth century the entrepreneurial order decided to guarantee the quality of their vintage by laying down rules specifying which wines could qualify as Gaillacoises – and thus one of France's most famous AOCs was born. Today, Gaillac continues to live off the deserved reputation of its wine, although perhaps the success of such a class-conscious product has led the town to affect a certain air unmerited by its provincial character. Aside from being a great place to buy wine, Gaillac makes a handy stepping-off point for exploring the old *bastide* villages of **Lisle** and **Rabastens**, further downstream.

The town, with its compact medieval core, sits on the north side of the river. The focal point is the ponderous **abbey-church of St-Michel**, built in the eleventh century, and impressively large for its era. The interior is unadorned, apart from a fourteenth-century painted Virgin and Child on the left-hand side of the nave. The **Musée de l'Abbaye de la Vigne et du Vin** (daily 9am–noon & 2–5/6pm; €2.50), next door, is dedicated to wine making, with displays of old presses, barrels, tools and bottles, located in the cellars of the old monastery. The real centre of attraction in Gaillac, however, is the **Maison des Vins** (daily 10am–noon & 2–6pm; free) in the same complex, where you can sample and buy local vintages.

Beyond this, the old town retains a number of storybook-style brick-and-timber houses, while a few minutes' walk northwest of the church, across the old Pont Château-de-Homps, sits the **natural history museum** (July & Aug daily 10am–noon & 2–6pm; Sept–June Fri–Sun same hours; €2.50), with a collection of specimen cases stacked with the usual stuffed birds, dead bugs and sea creatures. Behind the monastery, off place Eugénie de Guérin, lies the medieval *faubourg*, whose twisting lanes lack grand monuments but are loaded with atmosphere. On its eastern side, in shady **Parc Foucaud**, the surprisingly good **Musée des Beaux-Arts** (July & Aug daily 10am–noon & 2–6pm; Sept–June Fri–Sun same hours;

③

A quick guide to wine tasting

Wine in France is far more than a mere drink, and its intoxicating effects are seen not so much as the reason to buy wine, but rather an (eventual) impediment to its full enjoyment. The following quick guide to **wine tasting** is offered to prevent you from reinforcing lingering French stereotypes of Anglo lack of couth and invest you with an air of sophistication which will elicit admiration from even the most haughty Gallic *sommelier*.

Proper wine tasting can be accomplished in **ten easy steps**. When you visit a *domaine* that advertises *dégustation* ("tasting"), you will be offered a selection of different types of wine that are produced there. When your host pours you a glass, be sure to **pick it up by the stem**. Cupping the wine glass will cause your body-heat to warm the wine, which the vitner has taken care to present at the ideal temperature. Next, **study the wine**. Swirl it gently in the glass. Keep an eye out for particulate matter, and for "legs" – the viscous drops that slide slowly down the glass (an indicator of sugar content). **Examine it** against a white background for consistency of colour; hold it up to the light. For the **"first nose,"** press your nose deep into the glass and take several short, sharp snorts. Pause, and proceed to the **"second nose"**: sniffing the wine slowly while swirling it in the glass. Next, the **taste**. Sip the wine, pursing your lips and slurping loudly, forcing it to mix with air as it enters your mouth. Concentrate on the texture and feel of the wine, but don't swallow yet. **Slosh** it around your mouth, to feel the wine's effect on the different zones of your palette. There are three distinct phases to the taste: the initial "attack," as the wine hits your mouth, the "evolution," as it circulates, and the "finish," or the after-tastes. If you cannot resist, swallow the wine; but a true connoisseur will **spit it out** into the bucket provided. Repeat. **Concentrate** on the sensations you have experienced. Finally, **declaim** your impressions in a stream-of-consciousness deluge (preferably in French, although an evidently enthusiastic English will also serve). While *sommeliers* might employ a specific vocabulary, any adjectives are fair game – the point is to remember your impressions. Then have a cracker and move on to the next vintage.

Tasting is all about **taking your time**, enjoying the taste of the wine, and hopefully finding something special you'll be happy to take home. In the end, what matters most is not the price tag or what others say, but whether you like the wine you are buying. After a week or so of making the rounds of the ubiquitous *caves* which dot the Occitan countryside, you too will be a connoisseur (or at least pass as one). Beware that buying expensive wines carries an inherent risk: it's impossible to know whether an individual bottle is "corked," or fouled, until it's opened. Be safe, and buy two.

€2.50), houses some contemporary art that rises well above the usual quality of a country museum: the nineteenth- and twentieth-century Impressionist works of local artists Raymond Tournon and Henri Loubat, in particular, deserve a look.

Practicalities

Gaillac's **gare SNCF**, which is also where **buses** stop, is to the north of the old town, a good twenty-minute walk from the wine centre and the **tourist office** (daily July & Aug 9.30am–1pm & 2–7pm; Sept–June 10am–noon & 2–5/6.30pm; ☎05.63.57.14.65, ⓦwww.ville-gaillac.fr) at the heart of things. **Accommodation** is plentiful and relatively cheap: the best is at ☀ *La Verrerie*, rue de l'Égalité (closed mid-Oct to mid-April; ☎05.63.57.32.77, ⓦwww.la-verrerie.com; ❹; English spoken; wheelchair-accessible), a converted glass factory in its own grounds, with a pool set amid a 150-year-old bamboo garden. Another good option is the well-equipped, no-nonsense *Hôtel Occitan* (☎05.63.57.11.52, ⓦwww.hotel-occitan-gaillac.com; ❸) at 41 rue Georges-Clémenceau, while

Lucile Pinon, 8 pl St-Michel (℡05.63.57.61.48, ⓦlucile.pinon.hotes81.monsite
.orange.fr; ❸), has **chambres d'hôtes** in her comfortable sixteenth-century
faubourg house. The municipal **campsite** (June to mid-Sept; ℡05.63.57.18.30) is
nicely situated along the river, beneath the shadow of the abbey, and has
bungalows available. The best **restaurant** in town is *Les Sarments* at 27 rue Cabrol
(closed Sun eve & Mon; ℡05.63.57.62.61; *menus* from €36), a *gastronomique* place
tucked away in a fourteenth-century storehouse in the *faubourg*. The local **market**
is held on Tuesday, Friday and Sunday mornings.

Lisle-sur-Tarn

Only a ten-minute ride (7km) south on one of the frequent buses or trains from
Gaillac, **LISLE-SUR-TARN** is a tranquil twelfth-century *bastide* known for its
pountets, the overhead covered passages which connect many of its brick-built
medieval houses. The best way to take it in is with a stroll through the town and a
relaxed drink in the arcaded place Saissac, at its centre. The small local **museum**
(April to mid-Oct Tues–Sun 10am–noon & 2–6pm; €2) is tucked away to the
southeast of the square and contains works by the native designer Raymond Lafage
(who studied under Michelangelo). To the east, a street descends to the riverside to
what was long ago the town's pier – an evocative spot. A strikingly bold fourteenth-
century brick **church** sits just downstream near the modern bridge.

Lisle's **tourist office** (May, June, Sept & Oct Tues–Sun 10am–noon & 2–6pm;
July & Aug daily 10am–12.30pm & 2.30–7pm; Nov–April Tues–Fri 2–5pm, Sat
& Sun 10am–noon & 2–5pm; ℡05.63.40.31.85, ⓦwww.tourisme-bastide.com)
is on the east side of place Saissac. At present the town's only accommodation is a
tiny one-star **campsite** (July–Sept; ℡05.63.33.35.18) on the road to Rabastens.
Bikes can be rented from the local mechanic, Fauroux (℡05.63.33.35.06).

Rabastens

RABASTENS, 8km downriver from Lisle, can be reached easily by bicycle or on
foot along the river course, and is a better choice than Lisle for an overnight stop.
On weekend evenings the village's streets fill with young people, giving it a vivacity
surprising for its size and making it a welcome contrast to the sleepier villages of
the Albigeois. Still guarded by vestiges of its brick ramparts, Rabastens was founded
in the time of the fifth-century barbarian invasions, when it served as a refuge for
the inhabitants of a huge Gallo-Roman villa. In the Middle Ages, the tanning
industry brought it considerable prosperity, reflected in its surprisingly rich architecture. The sight that makes Rabastens an obligatory stop is its twelfth-century
church, **Notre-Dame du Bourg** (Mon–Sat 10am–noon & 2–6pm, Sun 2–6pm),
designated a UNESCO World Heritage Site. Its incredible painted interior was
rediscovered and restored in the 1860s: the magnificent, vibrant **frescoes** cover
virtually every surface, and provide a rare chance to see what medieval churches
really looked like, before the "puritans" of the Catholic Reformation scrubbed
them clean. Also of note is a chapel dedicated to St James, donated by the
archbishop of Santiago, grateful for the wealth the pilgrimage route was bringing
his diocese. The **Musée du Rabastinois** (Feb–Nov Mon–Sat 10am–noon &
2–6pm, Sun 3–6pm; €2.50) is just down the street and contains pieces from the
Gallo-Roman and medieval periods.

Buses pass through the centre of Rabastens, while the **gare SNCF** is located just
across the river in **Coufouleux** – about a ten-minute walk from the centre. The
tourist office (March to mid-June, Sept, Oct Tues–Sat 10am–noon & 2–6pm;
mid-June to Sept daily 9.30am–2pm & 3–6.30pm; Nov–Feb Tues–Sat 10am–noon
& 1.30–5.30pm; ℡05.63.40.65.65, ⓦwww.cc-paysrabastinois.fr), at 12 rue Pont

del Pâ, is by the old bridge and the church. The best **hotel** in Rabastens is the *Hostellerie du Pré-Vert* (℡05.63.33.70.51, Ⓦwww.leprevert.com; ❸), an eighteenth-century mansion on the promenade des Lices. The one-star **campsite**, *Les Auzerals* (May–Aug; ℡05.63.33.70.36), is 3km northwest of town, by a small lake. As for food and drink, any of the bistros and **restaurants** on the main promenade can provide solid Tarnaise sustenance, but for something different head to the *Hôtel de la Poste*, on place St-Michel (just off the main road), which has authentic Andalucían ambience and *menus* from €15, including wine (closed Sun eve & Mon).

Lautrec and around

The most beautiful and inviting of the towns between Albi and Castres, **LAUTREC** enjoys a picturesque setting on a windmill-capped spur, once the site of a twelfth-century castle. The little town gathered around it is a warren of steep, twisting streets, interspersed by compact arcaded squares, making this an agreeable place to spend an afternoon or evening. It was here that a marriage alliance in 1196 established the family of the counts of Toulouse-Lautrec (the artist Henri's forebears). Nowadays the town prides itself on its pungent pink **garlic**, first brought here by Spanish merchants in the eighteenth century. Four thousand tonnes of the stuff are harvested here every year, but smaller quantities can be purchased at the town's Friday-morning **market**, and it even has its own festival (Aug 6).

Entering the old town through rue du Mercadial, where the main road passes on the north side, the *mairie* is just on the left, in a building which also houses a humble two-room **archeological museum** (Thurs–Sun 3.30–6.30pm; €2). A low-key affair, the museum has a display on local medieval burial customs and information on the scores of wells that perforate the old town and served primarily for grain storage. Lautrec's main attraction is the functioning seventeenth-century **windmill** perched above the town (Sat, Sun & hols 2.30–6.30pm; €2). As you enter the mill on a windy day, the sight and sound of the large, rapidly spinning wooden mechanisms are exhilarating. The hilltop also offers a superb panoramic **view** towards the south.

There are a number of **chambres d'hôtes** in or near the town: the most homely is Alain Rouquier's very French house in place du Monument (℡05.63.75.30.02, Ⓦwww.cadalen81.com; ❸), while the grander *La Terrasse* (℡05.63.75.84.22, Ⓦwww.laterrassedelautrec.com; ❺), in rue de l'Église, is a seventeenth-century mansion with an impressive French garden. A lavish dinner is provided for guests only at €28. For more options, head for the **tourist office** in rue du Mercadial (mid-June to mid-Sept Tues–Sat 10am–noon & 2–6.30pm, Sun & Mon 2–6.30pm; mid-Sept to mid-June Tues–Sat 10am–noon & 2–5/5.30pm, Sun & Mon 2–5.30pm; ℡05.63.75.31.40, Ⓦot.lautrec.free.fr). Lautrec's best **restaurant** is *Le Garde Pile* (℡05.63.75.34.58; Fri noon to Sun noon only), located in a converted granary, just outside town on the Castres road, which serves a selection of lively dishes, strong on the local pink garlic (*menus* from €19); otherwise there are a couple of snackbars/cafés in the centre.

Graulhet and Réalmont

The other couple of *bastides* near Lautrec – Graulhet and Réalmont – are less appealing, though better served by public transport. Indeed, the only compelling reason to visit **GRAULHET** is to change buses en route to Lautrec, 16km away. Sitting on the Dadou river, between Gaillac and Castres, it's a grim, unsmiling town, whose unremarkable old quarter has decayed into a shambles. The town's name is derived from *groule*, the Occitan word for leather, which has been the source of its meagre prosperity since the Middle Ages – as early as the twelfth century raw hides from the pasture lands of the Montagne Noire were brought here to be tanned and finished. If you're passing through, it's worth heading for the acclaimed **restaurant** 🍴 *La Rigaudié*, set in a nineteenth-century mansion 2km east of town on the St-Julien-du-Puy road (closed Mon, Sat & Sun eves, Aug & late Dec; ☏05.63.34.49.54), with an excellent fish *menu* from €24.

Seventeen kilometres east of Graulhet, **RÉALMONT** is one of the "royal *bastides*" founded by the twelfth-century Capetian kings to weaken the power of the local nobility. Today, only a few vestiges of its medieval past – the arcades of the main square and the grid of streets typical of medieval "new towns" – survive. There's little to see, although it's worth stopping here on a Wednesday morning in July or August – the country **market** has local produce at excellent prices: a great opportunity to stock up for a picnic.

Castres and around

Southeast of Lautrec, the rolling agricultural landscape comes to an abrupt end as the land begins to rise and you approach Haut Languedoc, a highland ridged by peaks rising up to 1100m. **CASTRES**, on the western edge of the uplands, 42km south of Albi, began some two thousand years ago as a Roman military base (as its name, from the word for "camp" or "fort", recalls). An important Benedictine monastery was built here in the seventh century but, like the Roman town, its traces have all but vanished. In the twelfth century Castres was swept up in the Cathar movement, and it was here that the first Albigensian **martyrs** were burned at the stake in 1209. The ever-rebellious population took up the Protestant banner four centuries later, and the town became an important centre of **Huguenot** administration. Today, still supported by the textile industry which boomed in the eighteenth century, Castres is a town with energy – worth visiting in its own right and an ideal point of access to the northern and western parts of the Parc Naturel Régional du Haut Languedoc (see p.162). Boasting a colourful medieval core and a pleasantly diverse populace, it is also enlivened by two summer **music festivals** (see p.142). In addition, it has a couple of good museums: one dedicated to Castres' native son, the nineteenth-century socialist Jean Jaurès, and the other to Spanish art. The **Sidobre**, a granite massif to the east famed for its peculiar rock formations, makes an easy excursion. Castres is also the end-point of the **Gijou Valley Trail**, a hiking, riding and mountain-bike route, leading up into the isolated heights of Haut Languedoc (see p.166).

Essentials

Boat trips The *Miredames* riverboat does a 45min round trip down the Agout, leaving from the pier outside the tourist office (May–Oct at noon, 2.20pm, 3.40pm & 5.10pm; €5).

Discount card The "Passe tourisme en ville" (€3.50), valid for one month, gives admission to the town's four museums. You can buy it at the tourist office.

Internet access Multimedia Cultural Centre, 2 av de Sidorbe ☏05.63.62.41.60.

Laundry Lavanderie Express, 8–9 rue Fuzies (daily till 9pm).

Market Tues, Thurs, Fri & Sat in pl Jean-Jaurès and pl l'Albinique.

Taxis ☏05.63.59.99.25.

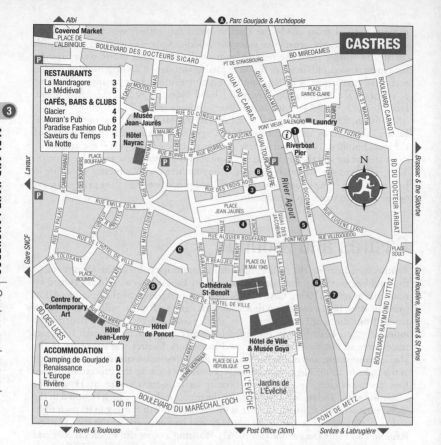

On the map:

▲ *Albi* ▲ **ⓐ**, *Parc Gourjade & Archéopole*

Covered Market
PLACE DE
L'ALBINIQUE

BOULEVARD DES DOCTEURS SICARD

CASTRES

PT DE STRASBOURG

BD MIREDAMES

QUAI DU CARRAS

QUAI MIREDAMES

RUE CORNEBASSE

PLACE
SAINTE-CLAIRE

BOULEVARD CARNOT

RUE ST MARTIN

RESTAURANTS
La Mandragore 3
Le Médiéval 5

CAFÉS, BARS & CLUBS
Glacier 4
Moran's Pub 6
Paradise Fashion Club 2
Saveurs du Temps 1
Via Notte 7

**Musée
Jean-Jaurès**

**Hôtel
Nayrac**

RUE DU CONSULAT

RUE MALBEC

R DES CAPUCINS

RUE HENRI IV

R MALPAS

RUE BORREL

RUE BORREL

PONT VIEUX SALENGRO

PLACE
SALENGRO

Laundry

RUE FUZIES

ⓘ **ⓘ**
**Riverboat
Pier**

RUE ST MARTIN

PLACE
BOUFFAD

R CAMILLE RABAUD

R LES BOURSIERS

RUE FRÉDÉRIC THOMAS

RUE DES TROIS ROIS

QUAI TOURCAUDIÈRE

River Agout

RUE DE L'ÉGLISE

RUE F FERRER

RUE MILHAU DUCOMMUN

BD DU DOCTEUR ARIBAT

N

RUE EMILE ZOLA

RUE DE TURENNE

R BRITTES

RUE MONTLEDIER

PLACE
JEAN JAURÈS

QUAI DES
JACOBINS

RUE EUGENE LERIS

PLACE
SOULT

RUE DU PALAIS

RUE TOLOSANE

RUE DE L'HÔTEL DE VILLE

RUE ALQUIER BOUFFARD

R CALER

PONT NEUF

RUE VILLEGOUDOU

PLACE
ROUMIVE

RUE VICTOR HUGO

RUE SABATIER

R BEAUJEU

R ST BENOIT

PLACE DU
8 MAI 1945

RD DE LA LIBERATION

**Centre for
Contemporary
Art**

RUE CHAMBRE DE L'EDIT

**Hôtel
Jean-Leroy**

**Hôtel
de Poncet**

RUE DE GUY

**Cathédrale
St-Benoît**

RUE DE L'HÔTEL DE VILLE

RUE BARRAL

RUE BARRAL

QUAI DU MOULIN

**Hôtel de Ville
& Musée Goya**

BOULEVARD RAYMOND VITTOZ

RUE GAMBETTA

RSQUE MATIMAR

PLACE DE LA
RÉPUBLIQUE

RUE DE L'ÉVÊCHÉ

**Jardins de
L'Évêché**

RUE D'EMPARE

ACCOMMODATION
Camping de Gourjade A
Renaissance D
L'Europe C
Rivière B

0 ──── 100 m

BOULEVARD DU MARÉCHAL FOCH

PONT DE METZ

▼ *Revel & Toulouse* ▼ *Post Office (30m)* *Sorèze & Labrugière* ▼

◄ *Lavaur*

◄ *Gare SNCF*

► *Brassac & the Sidobre*

► *Gare Routière, Mazamet & St Pons*

BD DES LICES

Map labels: A, B, C, D markers; numbered markers 1–7.

Arrival, information and accommodation

Castres' **gare SNCF** is at avenue Albert 1er, a 25-minute walk west of the old town (bus #7; €1). The **gare routière** on place Soult is on the far eastern edge of the centre – a short walk from the river. For those driving, **parking** on the street in old Castres is possible, but check the signs carefully: between the market days and street-cleaning schedule, you could easily get your car towed away. The **tourist office** is at 3 rue Milhau-Ducommun, along the riverbank in the old town, by the Pont Vieux (July & Aug daily 9.30am–12.30pm & 1.30–6.30pm; Sept–June Mon–Sat 9.30am–12.30pm & 2–6pm; ☎05.63.62.63.62, ⓦwww.ville-castres.fr).

Castres has two marvellous seventeenth-century mansions converted into luxurious but affordable **hotels**: the deluxe ⚜ *Renaissance* at 17 rue Victor Hugo (☎05.63.59.30.42, ⓦwww.hotel-renaissance.fr; **❹**), and the very comfortable *L'Europe* (same contact details); both have a/c, free wi-fi and a video library. Alternatively, the *Rivière*, 10 quai Tourcaudière (☎05.63.59.04.53, ⓦpagesperso-orange.fr /hotelriviere; **❸**), has pleasant views over the Agout, free wi-fi and helpful staff. The three-star **campsite** in Parc Gourjade (April–Sept; ☎05.63.59.72.30, ⓦwww .campingdegourjade.net) also has bungalows, with walking trails and watersports facilities in the Parc itself: get there by buses #3, #6 or #7 (direction Borde-Basse) or by the *Miredames* riverboat (see "Essentials", p.157).

The Town

Don't be fooled by the drab suburbs that surround it – Castres' **old town**, spilling over the River Agout to the east, its rough square outline reflecting the Roman layout, is a delight. The brightly painted riverside **dyers' houses** are the town's hallmark, while the impressive sixteenth-century mansions hidden among its narrow streets make the medieval quarter a pleasure to stroll through.

Place Jean-Jaurès to the Goya museum

Castres' centre is marked by café-girded **place Jean-Jaurès**, home to a bustling produce market four days a week, while just south of the square, the unprepossessing **Cathédrale St-Benoît**, constructed in 1677, stands on the site of the old monastery church. It's a squat and not especially noteworthy Baroque building, although the marble statues of saints around the choir are worth a look.

Across the street, the **Hôtel de Ville** reposes within the former bishop's palace, a dour, hulking square edifice, whose grey sobriety contrasts with the bright formal gardens, the **Jardins de l'Évêché**, which stretch out on its southern side. The building also houses Castres' foremost museum, the **Musée Goya** (July & Aug daily noon–6pm; Sept–June Tues–Sun 9am–noon & 2–5/6pm; €2.30), which was established a century ago by private donation, and now holds the biggest collection of Spanish paintings in France outside the Louvre. Dominating its largest salon, the core of the exhibition is, as you'd expect, taken up by the artist after whom it is named, but the paintings here are not the dark, sinister visions for which **Francisco Goya** is most famous, but rather his portraiture, including his *Self-portrait with Glasses*, and politically inspired works like *The Junta of the Philippines Presided over by Ferdinand VII*. A separate room features several series of his satirical pen-and-ink cartoons, depicting vices and virtues and popular adages, as well as series on bullfighting and war. Other rooms contain numerous pieces by other seventeenth-century Iberian masters – including **Velázquez**'s *Portrait of Philip IV*, **Murillo**'s *Virgin with Rosary* and **Zurburán**'s *Carthusian Martyr*. Flemish-influenced medieval paintings by fifteenth-century Catalan and Spanish artists round out the collection. There are also displays of old coins, royal seals and assorted archeological knick-knacks, as well as a room dedicated to the local wartime Resistance. An adjacent gallery (separate admission) houses temporary exhibitions of impressive quality.

The hôtels particuliers

West of the Goya museum along rue Chambre de l'Édit are three palatial **hôtels particuliers** – mansions dating from the sixteenth and seventeenth centuries. On rue Guy, the first street on the right, the seventeenth-century **Hôtel de Poncet** stands out, with its classically inspired Renaissance facade and caryatid columns supporting an elegant Ionic-columned loggia. Further along rue Chambre de l'Édit you'll find the earlier **Hôtel Jean-Leroy**, notable for its stately carved casement windows and topped by a defensive tower. Next door to that, **Hôtel de Viviès**, built along the now-vanished city walls, was once the seat of the town's Huguenot judicial court and now houses the small **Centre for Contemporary Art** (Wed–Sun 2–7pm; €2), which hosts temporary exhibitions of local and international modern works. Castres' **shopping** district stretches north from here, on the far side of which, in rue Thomas, you'll find Castres' grandest *hôtel particulier*, the **Hôtel de Nayrac**, built in the brick-and-stone style of the Toulouse mansions, with three sober facades boxing in a broad, symmetrical courtyard.

Musée Jean-Jaurès and beyond

Just beyond the Hôtel de Nayrac is the **Musée Jean-Jaurès** (same hours as Musée Goya; €1.50), which pays homage to the life of Castres' favourite son,

Jean Jaurès, the nineteenth-century labour activist, politician and martyr, is a figure whose presence travellers can scarcely escape in Languedoc. Nearly every town has at least one street or square – usually a main one – and a building or two named after this **socialist hero**, whose tireless struggle for workers' rights and international peace eventually cost him his life.

Born in Castres in 1859, Jean Jaurès showed exceptional promise as a student and won a scholarship to complete his studies in Paris. When these were finished, rather than stay in the capital he returned to his home *département* of Tarn and took a post teaching philosophy in **Albi**'s *lycée* (high school), and giving lectures at the University of Toulouse. But the miserable conditions under which his **working-class** neighbours toiled drew him out of the academy; their dangerous working environment, underpayment and near-total lack of rights and representation could have been lifted straight from the pages of **Émile Zola**'s contemporary *Germinal*. Jaurès ran for political office and at the young age of 26 was elected a legislative representative for the Tarn. One of his first projects was to help the glass-workers at Albi found the collectively run V.O.A. bottle factory, which still operates today. Continuing in politics and the cause of social justice, in 1893, as socialist deputy for **Carmaux**, he supported the miners' struggle for better working conditions, and his renown as a social reformer began to spread.

However, Jaurès' desire for reform went beyond simply improving the lives of those around him. Five years later he joined other liberals, including Zola, in defence of the Jewish army captain, **Alfred Dreyfus**, convicted on unfounded charges of espionage. National feelings of resentment against Dreyfus were running high, but despite this Jaurès persisted in his defence of the underdog, and – eventually – helped him obtain a pardon. The patriotically charged issue temporarily cost Jaurès his popularity, but he was soon back on the stage, founding the Communist daily *L'Humanité* in 1904 (still one of France's major newspapers; ⓦwww.humanite.fr) and the following year helping found the socialist SFIO party. With the dawn of World War I, however, Jaurès' internationalist brand of socialism revealed itself again in an outspoken and unpopular **pacifist** stand – and led to his **assassination** in Paris by a nationalist extremist in July 1914. On his death he was hailed as a martyr, the perfect hero for the Tarn – a local politician who improved the quality of life in this underdeveloped and marginalized region, and who wasn't afraid to take on the political establishment of Paris in order to defend a higher justice.

recounting the martyred activist's career with newspaper reports, memorabilia and contemporary artefacts. Castres' newest museum, **Archéopole** (Mon–Sat 2–6pm, €2), which features exhibitions on local archeology as well as finds from across Europe, is in the Gourjade park, north of the city, best reached by boat (see "Essentials", p.157).

Over on the far side of the river, the scruffier east bank of the Agout is home to a number of interesting little restaurants and cafés, and although it lacks historical buildings the neighbourhood's proletarian feel is refreshing. The sparsely adorned medieval **fountain** in place Fagerie, just north of the Pont Neuf, is also worth seeking out, if only for the "undiscovered" atmosphere of the square in which it sits.

Eating, drinking and nightlife

For its size, Castres has an impressive range of **restaurants**. The *l'Europe* hotel has an excellent all-you-can-eat buffet (€12) both at lunch and dinner-time (daily noon–2pm & 8.30–10.30pm), featuring a range of *terroir* fare and an impressive selection of desserts. *La Mandragore*, 1 rue Malpas (closed Sun & Mon lunch;

05.63.59.51.27), is praised both for its *gastronomique* cuisine and selection of wines *(menus* range from €13–36), while for a no-nonsense quality **brasserie**, try *Le Médiéval* at 44 rue Milhau-Ducommun (closed Sun & Mon; ℡05.63.51.13.78), whose eleventh-century dining room sits poised above the Agout, with a funky pseudo-medieval decor *(menus* from €18). Along rue Fuzies, which runs east from the Pont Vieux, you'll find a number of cheaper options.

A good **café** is *Saveurs du Temps*, 4 rue Fuzies, and you can get a pint at the very un-Irish *Moran's Pub* at 18 rue d'Empare. Aside from this, any of the **bars** around place Jean-Jaurès will do for a coffee or drink, with *Glacier*, on the south side, being particularly popular with locals for its gigantic ice-cream sundaes (€7.50), and sometimes hosting live music. Late-night diversion is provided by the rock **club** *Paradise Fashion Club* (after 11pm), through the graffitied door (no sign) in passage Henri IV, and the disco, *Via Notte*, at 16 rue d'Empare (Wed–Sat 11pm–5am).

Listings

Bus information ℡05.63.35.37.31.
Car rental Ada, 32 av Charles de Gaulle
℡05.63.51.10.26; Avis, rte de Toulouse
℡05.63.72.82.21; Budget, rue Albert 1er
℡05.63.71.31.28; Europcar, 67 rue Maillot
℡05.63.72.24.69; Hertz, av François Mitterand
℡05.63.59.01.14; Lavail, rte d'Albi
℡05.63.71.93.34.

Hospital The Centre Hospitalier is on place Alsace-Lorraine, just south of the Hôtel de Ville
(℡05.63.71.15.15).
Pharmacy Des Arcades, 2 pl Jean Jaurès.
Police 2 av Charles de Gaulle ℡17 or
05.63.35.40.10.
Swimming Piscine Bisséous, 49 rue Frédéric Mistral, is an outoor pool.

Around Castres

Castres is not only a comfortable place to stay for a day or two, but an ideal base for exploring a number of day-trip destinations in the vicinity. Just to the east lies the hundred-square-kilometre granite plateau known as the **Sidobre**. This heavily promoted area is known for the boulders that litter it, either eroded into evocative shapes or balancing precariously. Many, including the rock-strewn waterfall, **Saut de la Truite**, are found within a three-kilometre radius of **Lacrouzette**, a nondescript town 15km northeast of Castres. While some of the formations are truly remarkable, others are really rather lame – the **Trois Fromages** ("Three Cheeses"), for example, merely comprises a group of three roundish boulders set on top of each other. South of these groups lies the **Peyro Clabado**, an 800-tonne boulder perched on a smaller stone, and the **Rochers de Sept-Faux**, "logan stones" – two giant rocks balanced in such a way that the upper one, 900 tonnes in mass, can be rocked simply by pushing on it. The wooded paths leading to the sites are well maintained and make for pleasant walking, although on weekends they're crowded with families. Bring sufficient water or be prepared to pay over the odds at the cafés and drinks stands near the trails. To explore the region by foot or bicycle, pick up the free *Les Circuits du Tarn* brochure in Castres, which provides detailed descriptions of routes.

All the sights of the region are easily accessed by **bus** from Castres, but if you want to stay locally, **accommodation** can be found at *L'Auberge du Crémaussel* (Easter–Nov; ℡05.63.50.61.33; ❸), in the middle of Lacrouzette, which also has a restaurant serving generous *menus* from €16 (closed Sun eve & Wed all year, Jan & winter weekends), or *Au Relais du Sidobre* (℡05.63.50.60.06, Ⓦwww.hotel-restaurant -sidobre.com; ❸), at 8 rte de Vabre. Alternatively head to nearby **Burlats**, where there's great *chambres d'hôtes* accommodation in a luxurious fourteenth- to sixteenth-century castle (℡05.63.35.29.20, Ⓦwww.lecasteldeburlats.fr.st; ❺), at 8 place du 8 mai 1945. *Le Clos du Roc* **restaurant** at 1 av du Sidobre in nearby **St-Salvy** serves

Circulades

A curious feature of southern Languedoc is its **circulades**, or circular villages: concentric rings of streets at the centre of which is, or was once, a castle or fortified church. The origin of these hamlets, thought to date from the ninth century, is uncertain, but it seems likely that their peculiar design was the result of the military uncertainties of the era and the challenges posed by defence in flat countryside. A circular town, the entrances of which can be barricaded, is more easily defensible than a dispersed settlement. Few of these towns contain much of interest beyond their peculiar design, but it's worth stopping in one or two if only to take in the unmistakable medieval character of their streets. Aside from **Labrugière**, some good examples of *circulades* include **Aigne** (see p.267), **Balaruc-le-Vieux** (p.236), **Bram** (p.91), **Frontignan** (p.202), **Gruissan** (p.261), and **Poussan** (p.236). You can check out aerial views on Google Earth and other satellite mapping sites.

excellent food at economical prices, in a converted barn, (closed Wed eve, Sun, Mon & part Feb; ℡05.63.50.57.23; *menus* €12–30; book ahead).

South of Castres: Labrugière

South of Castres on the way to Mazamet, you may pass through **LABRUGIÈRE**, a quaint *circulade*, or "round village", laid out in concentric circles around the village church. Dating back to 985 AD, the town owes its notoriety to the 1484 **witch trial** of Péronne Bachère. Accused of making a pact with the Devil, casting spells and killing a neighbour with magic powder, she confessed all when interrogated and was burnt at a nearby crossroads. The original parchment recording her trial can be seen today in a display at the *mairie* on the town's main square.

The Parc du Haut Languedoc

The southeastern half of the *département* of Tarn is dominated by the mountain-ridged highlands of Upper Languedoc. In this region of isolated hamlets the scant population has traditionally subsisted on herding and agriculture, supplemented nowadays by a growing outdoor recreation industry. Long a backwood of proudly self-sufficient Calvinist Huguenots, these hills later proved a fertile recruiting ground for anti-German resistance after the occupation of Vichy France. The zone is dominated by the sprawling and imprecisely bounded **PARC NATUREL RÉGIONAL DU HAUT LANGUEDOC**, which over the thirty years or so since its establishment has been expanding almost yearly. Its designation as a park is primarily administrative, which can lead to confusion – the boundaries aren't well marked, and there's no change in the landscape or villages which distinguishes it from the surrounding area. Essentially, it is defined by the mountains which cross it: the **Monts de Lacaune** in the north, the **Monts de l'Espinouse** to the east, and the north face of the **Montagne Noire** range (see p.170), tacked onto the park's southwest. The man-made **lakes** dotting the highland near **La Salvetat** and **Fraïsse** are popular summertime vacation spots, each ringed by campsites and boat-rental outfits. Public **transport** across the park is poor, but it serves **hikers** and **cyclists** well, crisscrossed by a network of footpaths, notably the **Gijou Valley Railway Trail** linking **Lacaune-les-Bains**, **Vabre** and **Brassac**. Native wildlife, including some wild boar and deer, is less frequently encountered, thanks to the park's popularity – but you may see the ancient breed of mouflon sheep if you cross the Monts de l'Espinouse. Although straddling the border of the Atlantic and

Mediterranean climatic zones, the bulk of the park lies in the cooler, humid northern zone, typified by forests of sturdy oak and chestnut. Detailed park **information** can be obtained at the **Maison du Parc** offices in **St-Pons**, the "capital" of the park, and **Murat**; local tourist offices sell a guide to fifteen **bicycle** itineraries in the area.

Lacaune-les-Bains and around

On the northern edge of the park, slate-roofed **LACAUNE-LES-BAINS** lies east from Castres, at a distance of either 67km along the tortuous Agout and Gijou valley road, or 46km along the mountainous route which passes through Brassac. At 885m, this lively little village sits just below the source of the Gijou river in the **Monts de Lacaune**, whose sheep are the exclusive source of milk for the famous blue cheese of Roquefort. The town was a curative spa (specializing in urinary tract ailments) in the Middle Ages, a role commemorated by a fourteenth-century iron **fountain** in the town centre known as "Les Pisseurs", featuring four tiny but impressively endowed male figures peeing into a pool below. Beside the fountain, in place du Friggoul, is the **Musée du Vieux Lacaune** (April to mid-June & Nov Tues–Sun 2–6pm; late June & Sept–Oct Tues–Sun 10am–noon & 2–6pm; July & Aug daily 10am–noon & 2–6pm; free), which offers a look at local nineteenth-century rural life. In similar vein, on rue Rhin et Danube, the **Filature** is a wool workshop from the same era, where you can watch various old tools and machines in use (mid-June to mid-Sept 3pm; €2). It's also worthwhile taking in the Sunday-morning local **market** or the larger regional **fair** held on the 21st of each month. The town has good bus connections, but the best way to explore the area is on foot or by bike along the Gijou Valley Trail, a disused narrow-gauge railway line heading west towards Castres (see p.166).

▲ Les Pisseurs, Lacaune-les-Bains

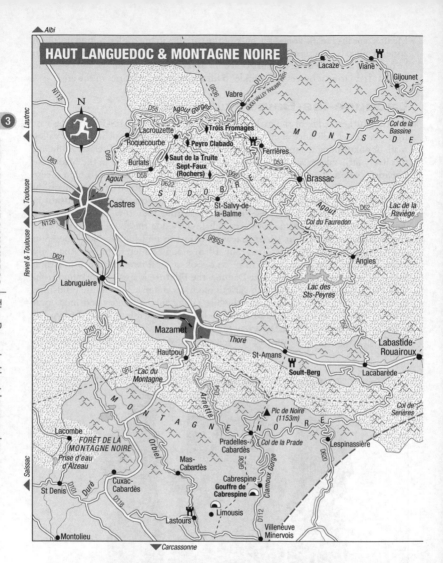

Buses stop at place de la République, where a small **tourist office** (mid-June to mid-Sept Mon–Fri 9am–noon & 2–6.30pm, Sat & Sun 10am–noon & 2–6.30pm; mid-Sept to mid-June Mon 2–5pm, Tues–Fri 9am–noon & 2–5pm, Sat 10am–noon & 2–5pm; ☏05.63.37.04.98, Ⓦwww.lacaune.com) rents out **bikes**. If you want to **stay** the night, the *Relais de Fusies*, on rue de la République (☏05.63.37.02.03, Ⓦwww.hotelfusies.fr; ❹), offers three-star amenities, though the small family-run hotel *Calas*, tucked away in the place de la Vierge (closed mid-Dec to mid-Jan; ☏05.63.37.03.28, Ⓦwww.pageloisirs.com/calas; ❷), is more attractive, cheaper, and boasts a pool. Its owner, Claude Calas, a fourth-generation chef, also runs a highly praised **bistro** (closed Fri & Sat eves Oct–Easter; *menus* €11–45), offering house speci-alities such as pigeon, or pigs' feet with truffles. The local municipal **campsite** is on the Murat road (all year; ☏05.63.37.03.59, Ⓦwww.pageloisirs.com/le-clot).

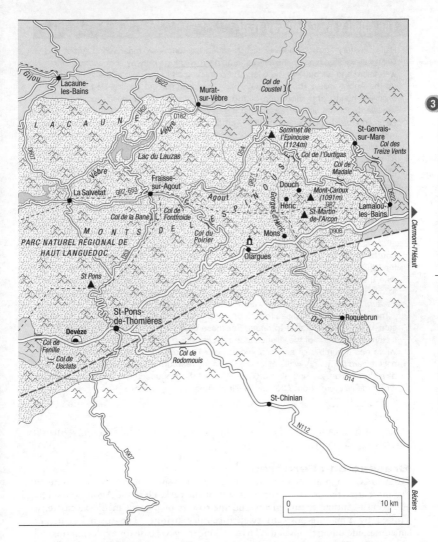

Labels on map: Gijou, Lacaune-les-Bains, D622, Murat-sur-Vèbre, Col de Coustel, D162, Vèbre, D62, Sommet de l'Epinouse (1124m), St-Gervais-sur-Mare, Col des Treize Vents, Col de l'Ourtigas, Lac du Lauzas, Col de Madale, D14, Fraisse-sur-Agout, Douch, Mont-Caroux (1091m), GR7, La Salvetat, GR7-653, Agout, Héric, St-Martin-de-l'Arcon, Lamalou-les-Bains, D908, Col de la Bane, Col de Fontfroide, L E S P I N O U S E S, Gorges d'Héric, GR71, D908, M O N T S   D E, Col du Poirier, Mons, Clermont-l'Hérault, PARC NATUREL RÉGIONAL DE HAUT LANGUEDOC, Olargues, St Pons, Orb, Roquebrun, St-Pons-de-Thomières, Devèze, Col de Fenille, Col de Usclats, Col de Rodomouls, D14, St-Chinian, N112, D907, Béziers, 0   10 km

Murat-sur-Vèbre

Twenty-six kilometres east of Lacaune lies **MURAT-SUR-VÈBRE**, an ancient hamlet bisected by a tributary of the Vèbre, which undoubtedly saw its heaviest traffic passing through when it was a way-stop on the pilgrim route to Santiago. Hikers who want to relive a bit of the Middle Ages can follow the Chemin de St-Jacques (now the GR653; see box, p.203) east to Castres. If you stop in Murat it will most likely be to pick up information from the **Maison du Parc** (July & Aug Mon–Sat 10am–noon & 2–6pm; Sept–June 10am–noon & 2–5pm; ☎05.63.37.45.76), an annexe to the local **tourist office** (same hours; ☎05.63.37.47.47), which also rents out **bikes**. The only **hotel** is the rather basic *Durand* (☎05.63.37.41.91, ⓦwww.pageloisirs.com/durand; ❸), with a reasonable but unexceptional **restaurant** (closed Fri eve & Sat out of season), and

The Gijou Valley Railway Trail

Half a century ago locomotives still threaded the tortuously meandering Agout and Gijou valleys, steaming up the cliff-hanging **narrow-gauge railway** connecting Castres with Vabre and Lacaune to the east, and branching off to Brassac to the south, 16km up the Agout valley. The trains have long disappeared, but the rail-bed is now an excellent **hiking and mountain-biking** trail – a route best travelled from Lacaune westwards for the simple reason that it's downhill. This defunct railway winds along steep and forested banks, dramatically crossing the riverbed on ancient trestle bridges and only rarely passing tiny hamlets of slate-shingled houses and solitary farmsteads.

Leaving Lacaune, the trail arrives at tiny **Gijounet** after a couple of hours' walk, just after a small waterfall. Continuing along for 5km, it skirts the slightly larger **Viane**, with a ruined *château* perched above, and then at **Lacaze**, several hours beyond, a medieval bridge spans the river, beside a once-stately fifteenth-century mansion. From this point the river gains force and begins to wind erratically through the cliffs girding it; fifteen kilometres now remain to **Vabre**, a larger town with a twelfth-century bridge. The distance from Lacaze to Vabre is 40km, which will take around **eleven hours on foot**.

Here the mainline converges with a spur coming from **Brassac**. A few kilometres after Vabre, the Gijou empties into the Agout, and the rail line continues to **Roquecourbe**, threading the gorges which mark the northern limit of the Sidobre; from here the D89 can be followed for 8km to Castres. Alternatively, 3km out of Roquecourbe, take the tarmac road towards Le Carla generating station to regain the river and follow it to Castres via **Burlats** (adding 12km to the route). The Topoguide *Le Tarn...à pied* details the trail with accompanying **maps**.

There are few opportunities to pick up **supplies** en route – Lacaze, with a store and café, is the first good spot to refuel. For those planning on making the journey over a night or two, each of the villages along the line has a very basic and free **campsite**. Vabre has a number of services, including a Thursday-morning **market**, while the best reward for hungry walkers (or drivers) is the **restaurant** *La Chaumière* (closed all day Mon & Sun, & Tues eve; ☎05.63.75.60.88) in Roquecourbe, featuring superb *terroir* meals (from about €20) and Gaillac wines.

there's also a **campsite**, *Les Adrets* (June–Sept; ☎05.63.37.41.16, Ⓔⓜairie .murat81@orange.fr).

Brassac and Ferrières

BRASSAC, lying about halfway between Castres and Lacaune, is undoubtedly the most attractive town on the west side of the park. Here the Agout, girded by nineteenth-century textile plants and the towers of a small medieval **castle**, is crossed by a picture-postcard twelfth-century **bridge**. The town has decent amenities, including shops and ATMs, making it a good base for exploring this end of the park. The former staging post, the *Café de Paris* (☎05.63.74.00.31; ❸) is a pleasantly old-style **hotel**, with a **restaurant** serving *menus* from €15 (Sept–June closed Sun). Across the street, the *Centre* (☎05.63.74.00.14; ❷) also offers unsophisticated but functional rooms and meals, and has a little **bar**. You'll find a basic municipal **campsite** just north of the village (☎05.63.74.09.11, ⓦwww .camping.brassac.fr).

Five kilometres downstream, you'll pass the still fiercely Huguenot village of **FERRIÈRES**, home to a private **castle** (closed) and the small **Musée du Protestantisme** (April–June, Sept & Oct Sun & hols 2–6pm; July & Aug Mon & Wed–Sat 10am–noon & 3–7pm, Tues & Sun 2–6pm; €3) – remarkable as a manifestation of enduring local pride and memory.

La Salvetat and around

LA SALVETAT-SUR-AGOUT, set in the middle of the rambling upland of the park, forms the hub of the **Plateau des Lacs**, so called for the reservoirs that now punctuate the landscape. The attractive little town has not been spoiled by the souvenir shops which dot its centre, and when the daily hubbub subsides, the tangled knot of streets which makes up the old town evokes the eleventh century, when La Salvetat was founded. There is nothing in particular to look at here, but two historical relics lie just outside: a twelfth-century Romanesque **chapel** (July & Aug daily 3–7pm), which contains a "black Virgin" – a Romanesque statue discoloured by time – and the stone bridge next to it, used by medieval pilgrims en route to Santiago. The town is a short walk from the 10km-long **Lac de la Raviège**, which has been extensively developed as a holiday spot – here you'll find **beaches**, and plenty of **canoe**, **sail** and **motorboat** rental outlets. Those wishing to explore the surrounding area on foot can purchase a booklet (€1) with twelve well-laid-out *petites randonnées* from La Salvetat's **tourist office** (Mon–Fri 9am–noon & 2–6pm, Sat & Sun 10am–noon & 2–5pm, Sept–June closed Sun; ℡04.67.97.64.44, ⓌVwww.lasalvetatot.com), which can also help find furnished flats and cottages to rent.

Alternatively, inexpensive **rooms** and generous portions of home-cooked local food (for guests only) can be found at *La Plage* (℡04.67.97.69.87, Ⓦwww .pageloisirs.com/hotel-la-plage; ❸), a small, lakeside hotel 1km from the town centre. **Bikes** can be rented at *Évasion Raviège* (℡04.67.97.53.96). There are four **campsites** within walking distance; the nearest is *La Blaquière* on allée St-Étienne de Cavall, just north of the centre (June–Aug; ℡04.67.97.61.29, Ⓦwww .campingblaquiere.com), while down by the lake there's the small *Des Cèpes* (℡04.67.97.63.45, Ⓦwww.camping-des-cepes.com). Of the several **restaurants** in town, the only notable one is the excellent *La Table Forestière* (℡04.67.97.56.01), on the route de Lacaune, which is open all year and whose elaborate meat and seafood dishes are a favourite among locals.

Fraïsse-sur-Agout and Lac de Lauzas

East of La Salvetat, **FRAÏSSE-SUR-AGOUT** is set at a hilly crossroads only 2km south of **Lac de Lauzas** as the crow flies, though the winding road which crosses the intervening hills clocks in at nearly 10km. This hamlet has become rather touristy in summer, but still retains its bucolic air, thanks to its diminutive size and the isolated beauty of its surroundings. From the ancient bridge over the Agout, a short trail leads southwards uphill for 2km through wooded hills to the **Prat d'Alaric,** a traditional working **farm museum** (Thurs 10am–noon; free) with buildings and technology going back to the eighteenth century.

Fraïsse has a **tourist office** (May, June & Sept Sat & Sun 10am–12.30pm & 2–5pm; July & Aug daily same hours; ℡04.67.97.61.14), and you can **stay** at the homey *Auberge de l'Espinouse* by the bridge (℡04.67.95.40.46, Ⓦwww.aubergespinouse.net; ❷), which also has a good *gastronomique* **restaurant** (May–Nov; *menu* €18). Nearby Lac de Lauzas is devoted to developed waterside **camping**, with a full gamut of activities: its main campsite is *Rieu Montagné* on the north side of the lake (mid-June to mid-Sept; ℡05.63.37.15.42, Ⓦwww.village-centre.fr), or there's *Le Pioch* (May–Oct; ℡04.67.97.61.72, Ⓦwww.lepioch.com) in Fraïsse itself.

St-Pons-de-Thomières

Deep in the folds of the Jaur valley, 35km due east on the N112 from Mazamet, sits **ST-PONS-DE-THOMIÈRES**, separated from the Plateau des Lacs to the north by a high ridge, the western spur of the Monts de l'Espinouse (see p.162).

The Huguenots of Haut Languedoc

The rugged and isolated hills of Haut Languedoc remain a bastion of France's once much-mistreated but stubborn community of Protestants, or **Huguenots**. During the sixteenth century, Protestantism, like Catharism before it, exercised a strong attraction over the inhabitants of Languedoc. In an age when political and religious obedience were perceived as parallel, the people of the south felt exploited, on the one hand by an absolutist monarchy in Paris and on the other by a Church which manifested itself most visibly as a tax collector.

The new faith arrived in the Haut Languedoc close on the heels of Martin Luther's defiance of Church authority in 1519; the first Protestant was burned in Toulouse only eight years later. The Huguenot movement – named after an obscure Swiss political event – however, tended to follow the Frenchman **John Calvin**'s teachings, which had a more politically revolutionary message. When the Crown and Church reacted by attempting to eradicate it, arresting reforming theologians and preachers and impounding French-language versions of the Bible, the people of the South, backed by the equally dissatisfied local nobility, retaliated, and the long and bloody **Wars of Religion** ensued. In a dynamic reminiscent of the Cathar era, the nobility, already divided into factions, used the theological conflict as justification for open warfare: the princely house of Guise and their allies championed Catholicism, while the rival Bourbons took up the Protestant flag. After a prolonged series of military campaigns and massacres the wars ended, or rather paused for a while, with a compromise when the formerly Protestant Henri IV passed the **Edict of Nantes** in 1598, recognizing limited Huguenot rights. Castres became a "protected zone" for Protestants, and eventually home to one of four courts empowered to mediate disputes between Catholics and Huguenots. This uneasy accommodation ended when the supreme autocrat Louis XIV outlawed Calvinism in 1685, setting off a harsh **repression** in Haut Languedoc. Soldiers were billeted in suspected Protestant homes, and possession of the Bible in French (instead of Latin) became a criminal offence. Huguenots escaped into exile or went underground, like the community in Ferrières, which hid Bibles in secret wall-compartments or women's bonnets, and held clandestine services in the forest. Eventually many villages fled *en masse* to the isolated Cévennes to the east, out of reach of royal officials and the army. Many returned only after 1787's **Edict of Toleration** established Protestant liberties. With the foundation of the secular revolutionary government two years later, Catholicism ceased to be an official measure of "Frenchness". Despite the centuries of persecution, nearly every hamlet in the highlands and every sizeable town in Languedoc still has a Huguenot church (or *temple*), and country folk of Haut Languedoc recall the stalwart nonconformity of their ancestors with pride.

The park's principal information centre, it is also a transport hub, with two main **bus** routes (Béziers–La Salvetat and Castres–Montpellier) intersecting here. This ancient town's curious compound name originates with local count Raymond Pons, who founded a monastery (hence, the "St" part of the name) across the river, north of the hamlet of Thomières in 936.

St-Pons' **old quarter** is worth a walk around – on the edge of it, on the north side of the modern road, is poised the twelfth-century **cathedral** (€3), with its incongruous, slapped-on seventeenth-century facade, around the back of which you can still see the statues on the medieval tympana, faces chipped off by iconoclastic Huguenots in the sixteenth century. The bulk of the old town, however, lies south of the main road on both sides of the Jaur, which is crossed by a medieval **bridge**. Amid the ancient alleys, the square fourteenth-century defensive tower, the **Tour de l'Évêché**, pokes above the rooftops. To the west of the old town, the **Musée de la Préhistoire** (April to mid-June & mid-Sept to Nov Tues 10am–noon & 3–6pm,

Wed–Sun 3–6pm; mid-June to mid-Sept daily 10am–noon & 3–6pm; €3.50) has information on the area's *menhirs* (standing stones) as well as an exhibition of local Flintstonian relics, and also arranges speleological **safaris** in the neighbouring Ponderatz cave complex (℡05.67.97.22.61; check for availability of English-speaking guides). Cave fans will also want to check out the **Grotte de Devèze**, 5km west of St-Pons on the N112, and its **Musée Français de la Spéléologie** (Feb–March & Oct–Nov Sun 2.30–4pm; April–June & Sept daily 2.30–4pm; July & Aug daily 10.30am–6.30pm; €7). Opened in 1932, the cave contains a variety of rock forms, including an impressive stone cascade and several calcite "draperies".

Practicalities

Buses pull up near the main crossroads of St-Pons, on the south side of which is the town's **tourist office** (July & Aug Mon–Sat 9.30am–12.30pm & 2.30–7.30pm, Sun 9.30am–1pm; Sept–June Tues–Fri 10am–noon & 2–6pm, Sat 9am–noon & 2–5pm; ℡04.67.97.06.65, ⓦwww.saint-pons-tourisme.com), which also houses the central information office for the park, the **Maison du Parc** (ⓦwww.parc-haut-languedoc .fr). The best of the town's two unremarkable **hotels** is *Le Somail*, near the tourist office (℡04.67.97.00.12, ℱ04.67.97.05.84; ❶), though more luxurious accommodation can be found 1km east of town on the route de Narbonne at the ⚸ *Bergeries de Ponderach* (℡04.67.97.02.57, ⓦwww.bergeries-ponderach.com; ❼), a seventeenth-century country estate with a fine restaurant, a swimming pool and sumptuous accoutrements. The municipal **campsite** (reserve through the tourist office) is open in summer only, while the year-round *Cerisiers du Jaur* (℡04.67.97.06.65, ⓦwww.cerisierdujaur.com) is just out of town on the road to Bédarieux. There are a number of **restaurants** in St-Pons, the best of which is *La Route de Sel* (lunch daily; ℡04.67.97.05.14) at 15 Grande Rue, which has an excellent *terroir carte*; local smoked-trout *carpaccio* and chicken in Muscat are two specialities. Another option is the *Auberge le Juge*, a working farm 4km west of town at Courniou, offering abundant home-cooked meals featuring local produce. Reservations must be made in advance (℡04.67.97.11.11, ⓔcontact@ferme-auberge-languedoc.com).

Olargues and around

From St-Pons, the River Jaur snakes northeast, skirting the **Monts de l'Espinouse** that loom over the north bank, to arrive at **OLARGUES**. Approached from the west, this hamlet presents an impressive vista: a high and gracefully arched medieval **bridge** backed by the steep hill where its castle once stood. From a covered staircase just west of the parking area along the main street, a ten-minute climb through the steep medieval alleys leads up to the lonely **clock tower**, the only remaining vestige of the eleventh-century fortress. Nearby, the Romanesque **priory** of St-Julien makes a good hike or a short drive, its shady wooded surroundings providing a great picnic spot and wonderful **views** of the Jaur valley; take the Bédarieux road east for 2.5km and climb steeply on the left up the narrow signposted road a further 1500m.

Olargues' **tourist office** (July & Aug Tues–Sat 10am–12.30pm & 4–7pm, Sun 9.30am–noon; Sept–June Tues–Sat 9.30am–12.30pm & 3–6pm; ℡04.67.97.71.26, ⓦwww.olargues.org) is on the main street. There's a deluxe country **hotel**, the *Domaine de Rieumégé* (March–Dec; ℡04.67.97.73.99, ⓦwww.domainederieumege .fr; ❻) just outside town on the St-Pons road, but a better deal is Pauline Giles' homely ⚸ *Les Quatr' Farceurs* in rue de la Comporte (℡04.67.97.81.33, ⓦwww .olargues.co.uk; ❸), which serves huge meals with free-flowing wine for €25, or *Au Fil de l'Eau* (℡04.67.97.27.04, ⓦlefildeleau.online.fr; ❹), in an old house at the foot of the bridge, with a €21 *menu*. In nearby **Mons**, at the base of the Gorges d'Héric, there's a comfortable B&B, *Manoir le Trivalle* (℡04.67.97.85.56,

3

Ⓦ www.monslatrivalle.com; Ⓐ). Olargues has a seasonal municipal **campsite** (July to mid-Sept; ☏04.67.97.71.50) and **bikes** can be rented from Oxygène (☏04.67.97.87.00), in chemin de Coulayro.

The Monts de l'Espinouse

Olargues is a natural place to begin a circuit of the **Monts de l'Espinouse**, an area whose isolated beauty is preserved in part by its inaccessibility; there's no public transport here. From the village, the D14 switchbacks steeply up past slate-covered hamlets clinging to near-perpendicular slopes until you reach the central pass of the **Col de Fontfroide** (971m). Here, **trails** (including the main GR7-71) crisscross the barren hillsides, and a sombre **monument** commemorates the German occupation. To the east on the lonely D53 the forest gets thicker (a picnicker's paradise) as you approach the 1124-metre **summit** (sommet de l'Espinouse). A few kilometres later, rounding the **Col de l'Ourtigas**, the country opens up dramatically into a series of broad gorges, the vibrant green landscape contrasting with dull grey rock. Continuing for 4km, you come to the turn-off for **Douch**, after which the road descends to **Lamalous-les-Bains**. Douch is a good place to pick up the GR7 trail to reach either **Mont Caroux** (1091m; 2hr round trip) or the **Gorges d'Héric**, which you access via the tiny stone hamlet of Héric, 2km west of Douch. The deep and narrow gully of sparkling red granite shaded by thickly covering oak descends rapidly to the River Orb, 6km below, and the beauty of the gorge accounts for its popularity with day-trippers. Easier access to the trails of the gorge is found at **Mons la Trivalle**, just off the main St-Pons–Bédarieux highway.

Mazamet and the Montagne Noire

The highlands of Haut Languedoc are bounded on their southwest side by the deep valley of the River Thoré, which empties into the Agout just west of Castres. A separate massif, the **MONTAGNE NOIRE** stretches in a narrow 50km band along the south side of the river course and westwards to Revel (see p.83), its highest peak, the **Pic de Noire** (1153m), located more or less at the centre of the range.

The two sides of the Montagne Noire present a stark contrast: the north face, which has been incorporated into the Parc Naturel Régional du Haut Languedoc, is thickly covered in a mixed forest of oak, beech and spruce, while the south presents a scrubby Mediterranean landscape of brush and vine. This whole district has traditionally been even poorer and more isolated than Haut Languedoc proper: near-subsistence farming and herding continue to be the only activities through most of the zone now that the mining of Salsigne and cloth industry of **Mazamet**, which boomed in the nineteenth century, have been reduced to relics. The Montagne Noire's chief attraction is its isolated wilderness, and you'll find that the outdoor facilities that have sprung up in the main park are lacking here. South of Mazamet, the ruin of medieval **Hautpoul** is a popular stop.

There are two direct **routes** over the mountains: the first starts at Hautpoul before continuing to the Pic de Noire and Carcassonne via the **Clamoux Gorges**; the second, 10km west and roughly parallel to this route, follows the dark and evocatively lush Orbiel valley down to the Cathar castles of **Lastours**. Further west still, on the far side of the main Mazamet–Carcassonne road, you can skirt the massif to medieval **Saissac**, a good base from which either to ascend to the forests around Arfons, or descend via **Montolieu** – known for its bookshops – past the ruined abbey at **Villelongue** and on into the open country around Carcassonne. Public **transport** in this neck of the woods is more or less non existent, the only regular service being the Mazamet–Carcassonne bus.

Mazamet and around

Lying 17km southeast of Castres, lacklustre **MAZAMET** is an old industrial town whose single sight is the **Musée Mémoire du Catharisme Occitan** (Feb–May & Sept–Dec Tues–Sun 2.30–5.30pm; June–Aug Mon–Fri 10am–noon & 2–6pm, Sat & Sun 3–6pm; €3) in the old Fuzier family mansion in rue de Casernes, near the tourist office – an unimpressive exhibition consisting mainly of a fifteen-minute French-language slide show lamenting the fate of the Cathars. More interesting is the short trip to **Hautpoul**, a Cathar redoubt perched on a hillside, which was all but levelled by the unstoppable de Montfort in 1212. The trip up to the village follows the serpentine **Route des Usines**, climbing the course of the Arnette river, where windowless relics of hulking nineteenth-century factories lurk at every hairpin. Now consisting of nothing more than one winding street and the sparse vestiges of the **castle**, Hautpoul is lorded over by the **Maison du Bois** (July & Aug daily 2–7pm; Sept–June Wed, Sat & Sun 2–6pm), an artisanal operation churning out wooden toys. There's nothing else to see here, but Hautpoul is nevertheless a popular spot because of the strong Cathar connection and its breathtaking setting, with views over the seemingly endless forested hills. If you don't have a car, take one of the tourist office's **organized trips** (regular departures March–Oct; €5).

Practicalities

Mazamet's **gare SNCF** is located just off the Castres road, a fifteen-minute walk from the town centre; **buses** stop here or 300m further south on avenue Rouvière, by the post office. The **tourist office** (Mon–Sat 9/9.30am–noon/12.30pm & 2/3–6.30/7pm, Sun 2/3pm–5/6pm; Jan closed Sun; ☎05.63.61.27.07, ⓦwww.ville-mazamet.com) is further south on the cours René Reille, where you can park. Inexpensive **hotels** are plentiful in Mazamet, the best one in town being the comfortable *Le Boulevard*, 24 bd Soult (closed late Dec; ☎05.63.61.16.08, ⓔdegruel@aol.com; ❸). The three-star campsite *La Lauze* (May–Sept; ☎05.63.61.24.69, ⓦwww.camping-mazamet.com) lies some 5km east of town. Once again, the hotel **restaurants** are the best bet for food here – *Le Boulevard* has a good-value *menu* with wine included (€12–24).

St-Amans-Soult and the Thoré valley

Climbing east from Mazamet, the **Thoré valley** still maintains its long-established role as a transport link between Castres and the Mediterranean coastlands, now the N112. Not far east of Mazamet you reach **ST-AMANS-SOULT**, a nondescript town which changed its name in honour of its native son, Field Marshal **Nicolas Soult** (1769–1851), Wellington's would-be nemesis of the Peninsular War. The warrior's sombre and monolithic tomb is hardly worth stopping to see, but not so his palatial estate, **Château de Soult-Berg** (June–Sept Wed & Sun guided tours at 3 & 4pm; €5), set amidst a wooded park. The sumptuously furnished rooms here are immaculately preserved, and the mansion's richly endowed library reflects the eighteenth-century ideal of the Renaissance man: aristocratic, learned and soldierly. From here the highway continues, passing through tiny **Labastides** and eventually reaching St-Pons. St-Amans and Labastides will be of interest to hikers in need of supplies or yearning for a hotel. The former is crossed by the **GR36** on its way to the Pic de Noire, and the latter by the **GR7**, descending from the Monts de l'Espinouse. In St-Amans the only **hotel** is the *Hostellerie des Cèdres* (☎05.63.98.36.73, ⓦwww.hostellerielescedres.com; ❸), set in a park among centenary trees, while 1.5km north of Labastides at 84 av de la Méditerranée, *La Bouriotte* offers comfortable and cheap **farm accommodation** and plentiful home-cooked food (☎05.63.98.07.64, ⓦwww.gite-bouriotte.com; ❷). Both St-Amans (☎05.63.98.87.31, ⓔcamping.valleethore@orange.fr) and Labastides (mid-June to mid-Sept; ☎05.63.98.49.74, ⓔtourisme@labastide-rouairoux.com) have **campsites**.

South via the Pic de Noire

If you're heading towards Carcassonne from Mazamet, and you have your own transport, there are a couple of interesting routes which you can take across the Montagne Noire. To cross via the **Pic de Noire**, continue up the Arnette valley past the turn-off to Hautpoul, for 3km, until you reach a junction from which the massive transmission tower crowning the summit should be in easy view. An arm-wrenching series of switchbacks then takes you to the flat and barren mountaintop around the antenna's base, and a breathtaking combination of cool, thin air and sweeping panorama. From the peak, the tortuous road descends several kilometres to the hamlet of **Pradelles-Cabardès**, with its medieval **church**, before threading through the steep and forested cliffs of the **Clamoux gorges**, where, after 12km, you'll pass the turn-off for the **Gouffre de Cabrespine** (daily: Feb–March & Nov–Dec 2–5.30pm; April–Oct 10.15am–5.30/6pm; €8.40), a huge, vertical subterranean cavern with a main chamber 250m in height ("higher than the Eiffel Tower!"). The route continues to **Villeneuve-Minervois**, a quiet little town with some traces of medieval buildings, including the remains of its **castle**. Services along this route are minimal and you should plan to complete it before nightfall. In Pradelles there is a basic **campsite** on a nearby reservoir, and a **café** which also serves simple meals, while in Villeneuve the **restaurant** *La Clamoux* (*menus* €13–24) also has **rooms** (☎04.68.26.15.69, ⊛clamoux.free.fr; ❸).

The Châteaux de Lastours and around

An alternative route across the Montagne Noire, which you pick up by turning east off the D118 just after Lac du Montagne, is via the **Orbiel valley**, and south to the castles at Lastours. As you descend the valley, the blanket of iridescent green forest threatens to swallow the steep and narrow stone-buttressed road, and the hairpin curves make the 11km to Mas-Cabardès seem at least twice as long as it should. Driving here is an effort, however, which the scenery makes worthwhile.

After the long descent you'll pass the romantically ruined church of St-Pierre-de-Vals, just outside **Mas-Cabardès**, a village that makes a good spot to stretch your legs before the tortuous second leg of the trip. While here check to see if the medieval **church**, crowned by a fifteenth-century bell tower, is open; if it is, step inside to see the fourteenth-century statuary within. Onwards from Mas-Cabardès, the road bends sharply as you approach **LASTOURS**, where the old textile mill which serves as the entrance to the grounds of the **Châteaux de Lastours** (Feb, March, Nov & Dec Sat, Sun & hols 10am–5pm; April–June & Sept daily 10am–6pm; July & Aug daily 9am–8pm; Oct daily 10am–5pm; €5) looms on the right. A cluster of four separate forts, perched dramatically on the points of the rocky hill dominating the river-bend, these are the northernmost of the Cathar castles, although in fact only two of them, eleventh-century Cabaret and twelfth-century Surdespines, date from the era of the Crusade. When Simon de Montfort had conquered Minerve to the east and Termes to the south, the survivors took refuge in these forts, which were the redoubt of the Cathar-protecting lord, Pierre-Roger Cabaret. Efforts to besiege them proved vain and de Montfort only took the castles in 1211, when Pierre-Roger surrendered in exchange for a pardon. Two more castles were built in the fourteenth century. A path climbs the steep and scrubby hill, and leads from one small castle to the next – an exhilarating walk which takes about two hours. The *châteaux* are quite ruined, and really their location is more evocative than their remains, so if you don't want to climb, you can drive to the look-out point (same ticket), set on a ridge to the west, which affords the best perspectives. There's a basic **campsite** (June–Sept; ☎04.68.77.56.01) beside the belvedere in Lastours, which has a great location overlooking the castles, and simple **restaurants** in Mas-Cabardès and Lastours.

Before continuing south, take the five-kilometre detour on the D111 to **Limousis**, whose **cave complex** (tours late March & Oct daily 2–5pm; April–June & Sept daily 10am–noon & 2–6pm; July & Aug daily 10am–6pm; Nov Sun 2.30–4.30pm; €8) boasts impressive calcite formations, including the largest known cluster of the crystalline mineral, aragonite. The lively English-speaking guides make the visit particularly enjoyable.

Saissac and around

By traversing the Montagne Noire and heading west along its lower slopes you'll arrive at **SAISSAC**, an ancient hamlet whose steeply sloping lanes lead downhill from the main road to a large ruined fortress looking out towards Carcassonne – the medieval walls and towers can be clearly made out in the distance. Although little remains of the fifteenth-century **castle** (Feb, March, Nov & Dec Sat, Sun & hols 10am–5pm; April–June & Sept daily 10am–6pm; July & Aug daily 9am–8pm; Oct daily 10am–5pm; €5), which can be reached from the road in about ten minutes, the hollow ruin is evocative – and a great place for viewing sunsets – but there's virtually nothing to see inside.

Leaving Saissac by car, you can easily reach the **Bassin du Lampy**, the smallest of the Park du Haut Languedoc's reservoirs, and a quiet place to have a swim, 5km up the D4 (picked up just west of Saissac). From the reservoir, the road continues north, through ever-thickening forest, to **Arfons**. Set among a series of grassy clearings, this little hamlet has an enchantingly forgotten air and is a great place to buy freshly picked mountain produce, including splendid wild mushrooms in late summer. The forest road continues north, eventually forking off to Dourgne and Sorèze. South of Arfons, a turn-off to the east leads towards Lacombe, following a narrow path through the **Forêt de la Montagne Noire**, lush and dark woods which make for another prime picnicking zone. In the heart of the *forêt*, at the hamlet of La Galaube, a path leads south for twenty minutes to the **Prise d'eau d'Alzeau**, the uppermost reservoir of the Canal du Midi's catchment system. The easy-to-follow trail to the site, where you'll find a statue of Pierre-Paul Riquet, the canal's visionary engineer, is a good way to get a feel for the forest of this region.

Practicalities

Saissac's **tourist office** (July & Aug daily 10am–12.30pm & 2–6.30pm; ℡04.68.24.47.80) is up on the main road, housed in a solitary tower surviving from the village's now-vanished walls. Its only **hotel**, *Montagne Noire*, on the main road through town (℡04.68.24.46.36; ❸), is nothing special. You're better off heading out to the bucolic Bassin du Lampy, where the *Domaine du Lampy-Neuf* (℡04.68.24.46.07, ⓦwww.domainelampy-neuf.com) offers deluxe **chambres d'hôtes** (❹) and *gîte* dorms (€15) as well as meals (€20). Another excellent option is *La Galaube*, set amid dense forest by the Prise d'eau d'Alzeau (closed mid-Sept to mid-Jan; ℡04.68.26.51.23, ⓦwww.lagalaube.com; ❸), which offers comfortable, rustic-styled rooms and an inexpensive year-round **restaurant**. There are basic **campsites** at the Bassin du Lampy and at Arfons (ask at the bakery in Arfons), which also has a bar and restaurant.

Montolieu and Villelongue

Set between Saissac and Carcassonne, once-sleepy **MONTOLIEU**, an attractive village of eighteenth-century terraced houses, has striven to make a mark since 1990 as a "town of books", a deliberate (if pale) imitation of England's famous Hay-on-Wye. One shop, the aptly titled English Bookshop in rue de la Mairie, specializes in English-language titles, while several of the rest concentrate on New Age and occult books. You can also look round a collection of old presses and book-binding tools in the **Musée Michel Braibant** (Jan–March daily 2–5pm; April–Dec Mon–Sat 10am–noon & 2–6pm, Sun 2–6pm; €2) at the north end of the village. West of Montolieu, tucked away in a wooded vale down a seemingly endless country lane, lie the ruins of the twelfth-century Cistercian **Abbey of Villelongue** (April–June, Sept & Oct Tues–Sun 10am–noon & 2–6.30pm; July & Aug daily 10am–noon & 2–7pm; €4) – worth driving to if only for the picturesque location on the banks of the Vernassonne. The remains of the abbey include a thirteenth-century vaulted cellar, a fourteenth-century Gothic cloister and the ruins of the abbey-church, now surrounded by a garden.

Montolieu's **tourist office** is in the *mairie* (Mon–Fri 10am–noon & 2–6pm; ✆04.68.24.80.80, Ⓦwww.montolieu.net), in the street of the same name, and you can **stay** at the bright and cheery B&B *Les Anges au Plafond* (✆04.68.24.97.19, Ⓦwww.lesangesauplafond.com; ❹) in the same street, or in greater luxury at the *Château de Villeneuve* (✆04.68.24.84.08, Ⓦwww.chateauvilleneuve.com; ❻), a wine *domaine* just north of town on the D8, whose amenities include a pool and an excellent *table* (*menu* at €25; reservation required). There's a three-star **campsite** in Montolieu (✆04.68.76.95.01, Ⓦwww.camping-de-montolieu.com).

Travel details

Trains

A regional train line runs along the Tarn from Toulouse to Albi and Carmaux, while Castres and Mazamet are also served from Toulouse. SNCF buses may run in lieu of trains on these lines; service is reduced on Sundays and holidays. TGV stations are indicated with an asterisk.

Albi to:
Naucelle, via Carmaux (several daily; 1hr).
Toulouse*, via Gaillac (connections for Cordes), Rabastens and Lisle-sûr-Tarn (hourly; 1hr).
Gaillac to: Vindrac/Cordes (several daily; 15min).
Mazamet to:
St-Pons, via St-Amans (daily; 40min).
Toulouse*, via Castres and Lavaur (many daily; 2hr–2hr 15min).

Buses

Many lines in Tarn-et-Garonne have reduced or no service on Saturdays, Sundays and holidays, and in the summer months. For regional lines see Ⓦwww.federteep.org; for buses to Béziers, see Ⓦwww.herault.fr.

Albi to: Ambialet (several daily; 30min); Blayes (several daily; 15min); Cagnac (daily; 30min); Carcassonne (daily; 2hr); Carmaux (daily; 20min); Castres (several daily; 40min–1hr 40min); Cordes (daily; 35min); Gaillac (several daily; 35min); Graulhet (several daily; 40min); Lacaune (daily; 1hr 35min); Lavaur (daily; 1hr 20min); Lisle (daily; 1hr); Rabastens (several daily;

1hr 15min); Toulouse (daily; 2hr 40min).
Carmaux to: Blayes (several daily; 10min); Cagnac (daily; 20min).
Castres to: Béziers (daily; 2hr 50min); Brassac (several daily; 50min); Carcassonne (several daily; 1hr 50min); Dourgne (several daily; 40min); Gaillac (daily; 1hr 15min); Lacaune (daily; 1hr 15min); Lautrec (daily; 30min); Lavaur (several daily; 45min–1hr); Mazamet (several daily; 20–30min); Revel (daily; 45min); St-Pons (daily; 1hr 15min); the Sidobre (local service; 20min); Sorèze (daily; 45min); Toulouse (daily; 1hr 40min–2hr); Vabre (daily; 45min).
Gaillac to: Graulhet (several daily; 30min); Lavaur (daily; 40min); Lisle (several daily; 10min); Rabastens (several daily; 20min); Toulouse (several daily; 1hr 25min).
La Salvetat to: Béziers (weekly; 2hr); St-Pons (several daily; 40–55min).
Mazamet to: La Salvetat (daily; 45min); Lavaur (daily; 1hr 10min); Revel (daily; 45min); St-Amans (daily; 20min); St-Pons (several daily; 45min); Toulouse (daily; 2hr).
Revel to: Dourgne (daily; 5min); Sorèze (daily; 10min).
St-Pons to: Bédarieux (several daily; 1hr 20min); Béziers (several daily; 1hr 20min); Lamalou-les-Bains (several daily; 55min); La Salvetat (several daily; 40–55min); Montpellier (daily; 2hr 25min).
Sorèze to: Castres (daily; 45min); Castelnaudary (weekly; 30min); St-Félix (daily; 20min); Toulouse (daily; 1hr 20min).

Nîmes and around

SPAIN

N

0   25 km

CHAPTER 4

Highlights

* **Nîmes amphitheatre** Once the scene of gladiatorial combats, this twenty-thousand-seat stadium still functions after two thousand years. **See p.187**

* **Pont du Gard** France's most famous Roman monument, a testament both to brilliant engineering and slave labour. **See p.196**

* **The Monastery of St-Roman** An underground monastery cut from the living rock, tucked away in the hills above the Rhône. **See p.201**

* **La Petite Camargue** Durrell's "Little Argentina", an open expanse of saltpans and meadows, populated by horses, bulls and a wide array of birdlife. **See p.205**

* **Aigues-Mortes** A picture-perfect medieval walled town, set among the swamps and dunes of the Mediterranean coast. **See p.207**

* **Tauromachie** The "art of the bull" is practised in the Gard with a passion and intensity unparalleled north of the Pyrenees. **See p.209**

▲ Pont du Gard

Nîmes and around

N îmes is Languedoc's most revitalized city, on the way up after an eighteen-hundred-year slump following its decline as an imperial settlement. Chock-full of the region's most impressive Roman monuments, and a showcase for its most exciting new architecture, it's a busy little place, embodying an intriguing combination of ancient glory and modern style. The lands around the city comprise the southern half of **Gard**, the easternmost *département* of Languedoc-Roussillon – hemmed in on the east by the mighty Rhône river and on the west by the humble River Vidourle. On the Mediterranean coast, the **Petite Camargue**, the western section of the Rhône delta, rises tentatively out of the sea. This is desolate and windswept country, dominated by bull and horse farms near the seaside, and vineyards closer inland. As you move away from the sea, the sand dunes gradually give way to the brushy hills known as the **garrigues**, around Nîmes itself and to the north. These in turn are cut through by the deep gorge of the Gardon river, on the far bank of which runs the band of flatland once dominated by the ducal castle of **Uzès**. Vineyards cover the river valley, but in the scrub-covered hills stunted holm oaks compete with hardy thistles, lavender and thyme.

Although the numerous and majestic **Roman ruins** of southern Gard, including Nîmes' **Les Arènes** and the magnificent **Pont du Gard**, attest to the area's prosperity in Roman times, this corner of the south has for centuries been something of a poorer cousin of neighbouring Provence, relegated to secondary status in the wake of the Albigensian Crusade. This marginalization is reflected in the faded glory of the former medieval port towns of **Beaucaire** and **St-Gilles**, although further south, recent revival has drawn developers to the **beaches** and **pleasure ports** of the Camarguais coast. To the west, the gentle Vidourle is still spanned by **Roman bridges** and dotted by all but forgotten hamlets.

The weather in Gard tends to extremes: hot summers and mild winters, punctuated by violent rainstorms in autumn and the merciless buffeting of the cold mistral wind in spring. The best season to visit is undoubtedly summer, but if you want to see Nîmes and Gard at their most traditional, try to visit during the local **festivals**, which invariably entail *tauromachie* – bullfighting and horsemanship, both Camarguais- and Spanish-style.

Getting around in southern Gard presents some difficulties if you're reliant on **public transport**, and want to get off the main routes. Nîmes is the hub, with good train and bus services to most of the region's towns, services to the coast becoming more frequent in summer. The flattish terrain makes for relatively easy walking; unfortunately for **cyclists**, heavy traffic makes the roads of the coastal plain unpleasant and dangerous, but among the *garrigues* and along the Vidourle there are some excellent and not overly challenging routes.

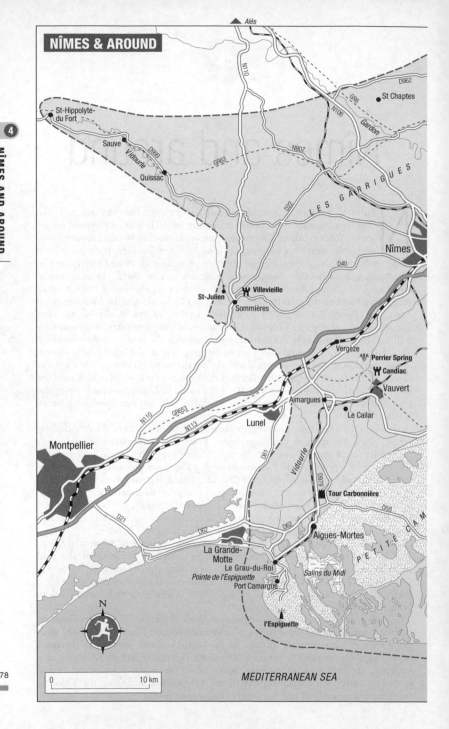

Alés

St Chaptes

St-Hippolyte-
du Fort

Sauve

Vidourle

Quissac

LES GARRIGUES

Nîmes

Villevieille

St-Julien

Sommières

Vergèze

Perrier Spring

Candiac

Vauvert

Aimargues

Le Cailar

Lunel

Montpellier

Vidourle

Tour Carbonnière

Aigues-Mortes

PETITE CAM

La Grande-
Motte

Le Grau-du-Roi

Pointe de l'Espiguette

Port Camargue

Salins du Midi

l'Espiguette

N

0   10 km

MEDITERRANEAN SEA

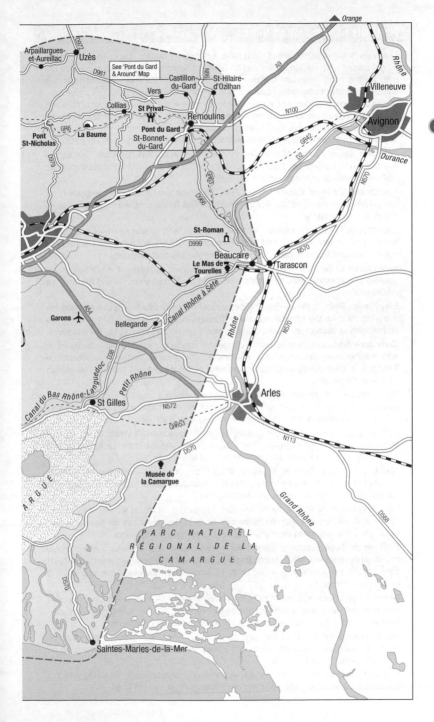

Festivals in the *département* of Gard have a decidedly bullish flavour to them. In the bigger places – Nîmes, Beaucaire and St-Gilles – full-blown Spanish-style *corridas* are held for the most important occasions, but otherwise, nearly every small town will somehow involve **bulls** in their celebrations, whether *courses camarguaises* (see box, p.209) or simply a running of the bulls. Aside from these there are a number of fairs and events which commemorate the area's medieval past or its regional products. Where no specific information number is given, contact the relevant tourist office for details. For the spectacular festivals of **Saintes-Maries-de-la-Mer**, see the box on p.206.

Late Jan Nîmes: *Festival Nîmes Flamenco* Ⓦ www.theatredenimes.com. This annual five-day event gathers top flamenco stars for performances of music and dance, as well as a series of conferences and exhibitions.

Fourth week before Easter Nîmes: *Feria de Primavera*. The local celebration for pre-Lenten *Carnaval*, and the first of Nîmes' famed *ferias*, a street festival including music and *tauromachie*.

Late March St-Gilles: *Carnaval*. Held for one week and similar to the Nîmes event, but on a much smaller scale and with emphasis on the traditions of the Camarguais cowboy culture: horsemanship, *courses camarguaises* and *corridas*.

Late March to Sept Le Grau/Port Camargue: *Courses camarguaises* are held every weekend in order to decide the year's winners of the Trophée des As and the Trophée de l'Avenir.

May Nîmes: *Feria de Pentecôte*. The city's most important festival and a frenzied rite of spring, held on the fifth weekend after Easter. The festival has a heavy emphasis on bullfighting, along with music, dancing and a large street market in the old town.

Early June Beaucaire: *Fête du Drac*. A three-day medieval festival, held in conjunction with neighbouring Tarascon, and celebrating the legend of the river beast, La Tarasque, a child-eating amphibious monster of local medieval folklore. Admission charge of €9 per day.

Mid-June Le Grau-du-Roi: *Fête de la Mer*. Along with the traditional *courses camarguaises*, water-jousting competitions are held in the harbour and canals in this four-day celebration of Le Grau's fishermen and their traditions.

Late July Uzès: *Autres Rivages* Ⓦ www.autres-rivages.com. A World Music festival featuring primarily African groups. Performances are held in sites of architectural and archeological interest in the countryside around town.

Mid-Aug St-Gilles: *Feria de la pêche et de l'abricot*. A one-week harvest festival, celebrating two of the area's major agricultural products, peaches and apricots, with the emphasis on ranch culture and *tauromachie*.

Late Aug Aigues-Mortes: *Fête de St-Louis*. Held on the closest weekend to August 25, a medieval pageant and reconstruction of St Louis' departure for the Crusades, celebrating the day when the saint-king set out to fight the Muslims.

First week Sept Fourques (near Beaucaire): *Foires aux Chevaux*. A traditional two-day horse market, which brings together ranch-owners and *gardians* ("cowboys") from across the Camargue, in addition to some ten thousand spectators, for a boisterous carnival.

Second week Sept Le Grau/Port Camargue: *Fête locale*. A major event on the taurine calendar, the twin towns' festivities include bull-running, *courses camarguaises*, water-jousting and the usual markets, street parties and general exuberance.

Third week Sept Nîmes: *Feria des Vendanges*. The third great *feria* in Nîmes, celebrating the wine harvest. Another *tauromachie* extravaganza, with live open-air concerts, parades and a market.

Mid-Oct Aigues-Mortes: *Fête locale*. A three-day annual party featuring Gardois *tauromachie* performed alongside the medieval walls of the old town.

Nîmes

NÎMES is a city inextricably linked to its Roman past. Its location on the Via Domitia – the main chariot route from Spain to Rome – helped make it a favourite with a series of emperors of the first and second centuries AD, who endowed it with the outstanding collection of monuments which dominate the place today; the **Maison Carrée**, the **amphitheatre** (or "Arènes") and the **Temple of Diana** are all testament to the city's bright, if short-lived, splendour. Since then, over the last eighteen hundred years, Nîmes has had something of a tough time of it, having to vie with neighbouring rivals Arles, Avignon and Montpellier, which each in their time stole the city's limelight. In the 1980s and 1990s, however, two flamboyant socialist mayors drove a local renaissance, engaging in a series of audacious building projects (including a retractable cover for the Roman amphitheatre), and sponsoring grand cultural events. Their efforts kindled a spark that not even the massive mudslide of 1988, which covered the city in two and a half metres of muck and claimed the lives of seven people, could extinguish. Nowadays, crowds come not only to see the shrines of the Caesars and the dusted-off **mansions** of the cloth-making bourgeoisie, but a collection of provocative contemporary urban architecture in a city that is redefining itself. Nîmes also has two surprisingly good **art galleries**, and hosts some of the South of France's most colourful **festivals**, when the arena fills with **bullfighting** aficionados and the bars and restaurants are packed late into the night with noisy revellers.

Some history

Nemausus had been a Roman colony since 40 BC, but didn't really take off until Augustus Caesar (then, Octavian, and not yet emperor) defeated Mark Antony and Cleopatra at Actium in 31 BC, bringing Egypt under his power. As a reward, he settled his veterans here, laying out a Roman grid-plan city and endowing it with powerful fortifications. In honour of their victory in Egypt, his soldiers adopted the ensign of a crocodile (the Nile) chained to a palm tree, which subsequently became the city's **symbol**. As the town grew, water-demand outstripped the resources of its sacred spring and, under Claudius, a 50km-long canal, of which the Pont du Gard (see p.196) is part, was constructed to supply water. A century later the city was at its zenith, enjoying the special patronage of the emperor Antoninus Pius, whose mother's family hailed from these parts. It was a sprawling city enclosed by some 7km of thick walls (which survived as late as 1786), reinforced by thirty stout towers and pierced by seven monumental gates. From that glorious era, however, things went rapidly downhill. Within a decade of Antoninus's death, the Roman Empire spun into a temporary political crisis, and by the time the situation had restabilized, Christianity had replaced paganism in the empire, and Christian Arles had supplanted pagan Nîmes as the local capital.

With the Roman decline, Nîmes passed to the Visigoths, in turn displaced by Muslims who came up from Spain in about 724. Only seven years later the Muslims were forced out, and for the next four hundred years the town was incorporated into a series of rapidly dissolving Germanic principalities. In 1185 it came under the control of the **counts of Toulouse**, and briefly flirted with Catharism; the mere sight of de Montfort's powerful army, however, was enough to make it "repent" and return to the Catholic fold. Nîmes was

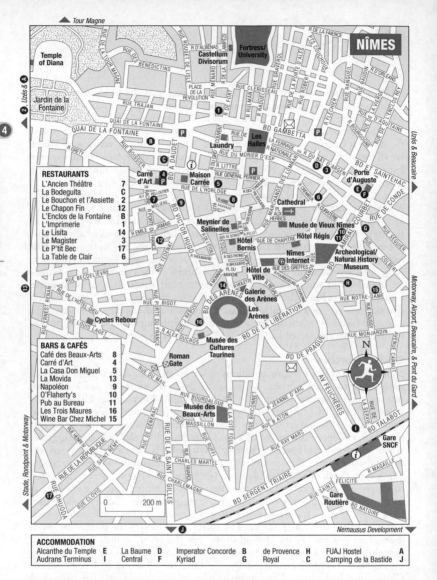

NÎMES

RESTAURANTS

L'Ancien Théâtre	7
La Bodeguita	C
Le Bouchon et l'Assiette	2
Le Chapon Fin	12
L'Enclos de la Fontaine	B
L'Imprimerie	1
Le Lisita	14
Le Magister	3
Le P'tit Bec	17
La Table de Clair	6

BARS & CAFÉS

Café des Beaux-Arts	8
Carré d'Art	4
La Casa Don Miguel	5
La Movida	13
Napoléon	9
O'Flaherty's	10
Pub au Bureau	11
Les Trois Maures	16
Wine Bar Chez Michel	15

0   200 m

ACCOMMODATION

Alcanthe du Temple	E	La Baume	D	Imperator Concorde	B	de Provence	H	FUAJ Hostel	A
Audrans Terminus	I	Central	F	Kyriad	G	Royal	C	Camping de la Bastide	J

absorbed by the French Crown in 1226, but by this time little was left of the glorious Roman city – only two clusters of houses huddled around the cathedral and amphitheatre.

After three sleepy centuries, Nîmes discovered a new vocation as a textile centre – until the **Wars of Religion** wracked the region. Calvinist preachers found eager ears among Nîmes' prosperous cloth-makers, to the extent that local Huguenots destroyed the eleventh-century cathedral and, on St Michael's Day of 1567, massacred some two hundred clergy. Following their repression in the wake of the Wars, Protestants from Nîmes as well as exiles from Haut Languedoc rose up together in the Camisard rebellion, brutally suppressed by royal forces in 1704, following its leader's defection to the Catholic forces at Nîmes. Many Protestants fled, while others persevered, having to disguise their faith. After the Revolution, religious issues were laid aside, and Nîmes, still predominantly Protestant, got back down to making money, which it did by spinning silk and cotton. The town's product became so successful that the cotton cloth "de Nîmes" (thus, "denim") went west, where in 1848 an American, Levi Strauss, hit upon the idea of attaching small red labels to trousers made out of the material.

Arrival and information

Located 10km south of the city, Nîmes **airport** (Ⓦ www.nimes-aeroport.fr) has few facilities other than an ATM and car rental desks. From here the trip to the city can be made by *navette* ("Gambetta" or "Imperator" stop; €5), or by taxi (at least €30, or €35 at night). Nîmes' **gare SNCF** and **gare routière** are both about a ten-minute walk south of the old town. Arriving **by car** on the A9, take either exit for the city and follow signs for the centre (north of the *autoroute*); there are underground parking spaces on the ring road, and street parking is also legal, if often difficult. The **main tourist office** (Mon–Fri 8.30am–7/8pm, Sat 9am–6.30/7pm & Sun 10am–5/6pm; Ⓣ04.66.58.38.00, Ⓦ www.ot-nimes.fr) is centrally located at 6 rue Auguste; you can get there from the stations on bus #8 (the "Antonin" stop). Up-to-date information on Nîmes and other places covered in this chapter can be found at Ⓦ www.tourismegard.com.

Essentials

Bike rental Cycles Rebour, at 38 rue Hôtel Dieu (Ⓣ04.66.21.20.20), as well as from the youth hostel (see p.184) and campsite.

Buses (Ⓦ www.tangobus.fr). The bus network's hub is avenue Feuchères; line #8 circles the city centre. Single ticket €1.

Discount card If you plan on visiting more than one of the Roman sights, consider buying a "Billet Romaine", a combined ticket allowing entry to Les Arènes, La Maison Carrée and the Tour Magne for €9.80: it can be bought at Les Arènes and the tourist office. Alternatively, a similar ticket (€9) gives entry to all Nîmes' museums.

Hotel package The "Pass Romain" includes admission to the city's museums, the Pont du Gard, a "Roman" meal, and one night's accommodation (from €79 per person, depending on hotel rating).

Internet access Nîmes Internet, 4 rue des Greffes (Mon–Fri 10am–10pm, Sun 3–10pm).

Les Jeudis Thursday-night street markets with live music held in nearly every square during the month of July.

Laundry Rue du Grand Couvent, at the corner of rue de l'Agau (daily 7am–9pm).

Markets Farmers' market (Fri) and flea market (Mon morning) on boulevard Jean-Jaurès; also general open-air crafts market throughout the old town in July & Aug (Thurs 6–10pm).

Taxi TRAN (Ⓣ04.66.29.40.11, Ⓦ www.taxinimes.com), besides operating as a regular taxi, runs an excursion to the Pont du Gard with a 30min wait for €40.

Accommodation

Accommodation options in Nîmes are plentiful, although rock-bottom budget places aren't so easy to come by, and you should book ahead as far as possible for any of the city's celebrations, when you may have to resort to the cluster of chain motels around the Nîmes-Ouest exit of the A9. A useful resource is the central hotel **reservation service** (℡04.66.36.96.30, ✉groupes@ot-nimes.fr.com), operated by the tourist office. In addition to the HI hostel (see below) there are several private **hostels** (*résidences*), some for under-25s, others with self-catering suites (contact the tourist office for details).

Hotels

Alcanthe du Temple 1 rue Charles Babout ℡04.66.67.54.61, ⓦwww.hotel-du-temple .com. One of the old town's best bargains: friendly, well-kept and quiet, set in an eighteenth-century house. Rooms have fans, TV and en-suite showers. Closed Jan. ❸

Audrans Terminus 23 av Feuchères ℡04.66.69.20.14, ⓦwww.hotel-terminus-nimes .com. Right by the train station, this is a well-decorated and lively hotel, with attentive staff. Amenities include cable TV and wi-fi. Wheelchair-accessible. ❷

La Baume 21 rue Nationale ℡04.66.76.28.42, ⓦwww.new-hotel.com. Located in a tastefully decorated former mansion with an in-house bar and friendly and professional service; pricey, but worth it. Junior suites available. ❽

Central 2 pl du Château ℡04.66.67.27.75, ⓦwww .hotel-central.org. Just behind the temple and the Porte d'Auguste, with English-speaking management, this small but cosy hotel features simple but comfortable rooms and also has secure parking. ❷

Imperator Concorde Quai de la Fontaine ℡04.66.21.90.30, ⓦwww.hotel-imperator.com. Nîmes' best and most prestigious hotel, with first-rate service and amenities in an atmosphere-loaded *fin-de-siècle* mansion with a stately garden. Prices quadruple during *ferias*. ❾

Kyriad 10 rue Rossy ℡04.66.76.16.20, ⓦwww .hotel-kyriad-nimes.com. One of Nîmes' newer hotels, the *Kyriad* is a solid two-star option with an impressive range of amenities including a/c, cable TV and wi-fi, and comes with a generous breakfast buffet. Its location just outside the old town makes street parking a convenient possibility. ❺

de Provence 5/7 square de la Couronne ℡04.66.76.04.92, ⓦwww.provencehotel.net. Well located near the train and bus stations and the amphitheatre. Rooms have cable TV but other than that bear a rather spartan old-fashioned-continental-hotel character; parking is extra. ❸

Royal 3 bd Alphonse-Daudet ℡04.66.58.28.27, ⓦwww.royalhotel -nimes.com. The *Royal* has a cool Spanish-style decor which draws in passing *toreros*. The rooms are individually decorated with a distinctly Iberian flavour, and the place exudes a certain cool chic. Amenities include HDTV and wi-fi. It's also home to the *Bodeguita* tapas bar. ❹

Hostel and campsites

Camping de la Bastide ℡04.66.62.05.82, ⓦwww.camping-nimes.com. Open year-round, on the route de Générac, 5km south of the centre, beyond the A9 *autoroute* (bus #D: "La Bastide" stop). Facilities include a laundry, grocery store, bar and restaurant, as well as a playground for kids.

FUAJ/ HI hostel chemin de la Cigale ℡04.66.6803.20, ⓦwww.hinimes.com. A comfortable hostel 2km northwest of the centre (take bus #2, direction Alès or Villeverte, to "Stade"), with dorm beds for €9; also has camping facilities and private rooms. July & Aug membership required; Sept–June no curfew; free wi-fi.

The City

The heart of Nîmes is a *place* where an august two-thousand-year-old temple, the **Maison Carrée**, faces off against its gleaming twentieth-century doppelganger, the **Carré d'Art**. Fanning out from here to the east, a compact warren of pedestrian streets makes up the city's **old town**, where you'll find most of the sights. Nîmes' **Roman monuments** lie for the most part on the edge of the old town, and off to the north and east, clustered around the blunt Mont

Cavalier. The town's famous modern architecture is concentrated in the far south, in the newer suburbs.

The Maison Carrée

The **Maison Carrée** ("square house"), a tiny but perfectly proportioned temple, once the centrepiece of the city's forum, was likely founded in 16 BC. Size, of course, is not everything, and as Henry James remarked, it is precisely because of its compactness that "it does not overwhelm you, you can conceive it." This is perhaps the world's best-preserved Roman temple (rivalled only by the Temple of Apollo at Baalbek), and can still boast all of its columns, an intact roof and *cella* (inner sanctum). If, over the ages, its functions – including use as a stable – haven't always done it justice, its aesthetic perfection has long drawn admirers: Colbert, Louis XIV's powerful finance minister, wanted to carry it off lock and stock to Versailles; Thomas Jefferson modelled the Virginia Capitol building on it; and Napoleon took it as inspiration for the Magdalene church in Paris. Today it houses a small **museum** (daily: March & Oct 10am–6pm; April, May & Sept 10am–6.30pm; June–Aug 10am–7/8pm; Nov–Feb 10am–1pm & 2–4.30pm; €4.50) on the history of Nîmes.

The Carré d'Art

On the far side of boulevard Victor-Hugo towers Norman Foster's 1993 **Carré d'Art** (Tues–Sun 10am–6pm; free), a twentieth-century *riposte* to the Roman temple. Four fine columns support its high portico with seeming effortlessness, contrasting the chunkier Ionic columns of the smaller Maison Carrée, reflected in the inscrutable glass face of Foster's building. Home to a library and resource centre, the top two floors house the city's **Musée d'Art Contemporain** (€5), which contains an impressive survey of French and Western European art of the last four decades. Emphasis is on Gallic movements such as Nouveau Réalisme and Support-surfaces, but Mediterranean and northern European art is also strongly represented. The l'Accrochage exhibition (changes annually), which highlights the collection's new acquisitions and lesser-seen works, is a good option if you are short on time.

Nîmes' avant-garde architecture

Through the mid-1980s and 1990s Nîmes embarked on an audacious project of **urban renewal**, contracting high-flying architects from around the world to construct public housing developments, sports centres and civic spaces. These new buildings – Nîmes' modern pride – vary in originality and effect; you may judge them to be either wonders or monstrosities. Some of them you'll pass as you make the rounds in the centre, while the rest (which are really only of interest to hard-core modern architecture fans) are scattered around the southern edge of the city and are best visited either by bike or taxi.

The best work by far is Norman Foster's great **Carré d'Art** (1993; see above). Also in the old town are two remodelled urban *places*: Martiel Raysse's **la place d'Assas** (1989) and Philippe Starck's **Arbibus** (1987), both offering simple landscape architecture and decidedly underwhelming modern sculpture. The peripheral sites include the whale-like and rapidly ageing social housing development **Nemausus 1** (Jean Nouvel, 1987), its monstrous rejoinder, **Nemausus 2** (Alain Amedeo and Jacek Padlewski, 1989), and three sports complexes – **Stade des Costlères** (Vittorio Gregotti and Marc Chausse, 1989), **Salle Omnisports** (Gregotti, 1993) and already-dated **Le Colisée** (Kisho Kurokawa, 1991) – which, with their lungeing surfaces of concrete and glass, complete the discordant collection.

The cathedral and around

With the core of the Roman city long built over, and most of the medieval buildings destroyed in the course of the Wars of Religion, Nîmes' **old town** is testament to the success of the local cloth merchants of the seventeenth to nineteenth centuries – the builders of the grandiose *hôtels particuliers* which pepper the streets south and west of the **Cathédrale de Notre-Dame et St-Castors**, a five-minute stroll east of the Maison Carrée. This church was constructed on the foundations of the former temple of Apollo; of the original cathedral, founded in 1069, only the bell tower and the badly chipped friezes of the facade survived the Huguenots' wrath – the rest was rebuilt in the 1700s. The new building is rather nondescript and the interior of little interest. On the south side of the square sits the **bishop's palace**, now home to the **Musée du Vieux Nîmes** (Tues–Sun 10am–6pm; free), whose lively collection focuses on the city's artisanal and industrial past, including, of course, denim, and will appeal to both adults and children. It is a well-organized exhibition, rounded out by a noteworthy furniture collection, including a nineteenth-century billiard table and sedan chairs.

Northeast of the cathedral is the excavated **Porte d'Auguste**. This surprisingly well-preserved triumphal entryway into the city, sunk by the rising ground level, was only discovered in the eighteenth century with the destruction of a later palace that had been built around it. The **Via Domitia** entered Nîmes through this gate: the larger central passages were for chariots and the smaller side entrances for pedestrians.

The hôtels of the denim lords

South of the cathedral on rue du Chapitre is **Hôtel Régis**, a former merchant's house with a stately sixteenth-century courtyard. Close by, on Grande Rue, you'll be confronted by the clean Neoclassical lines of the former **Jesuits' Chapel** (Tues–Sun 10am–6pm; free). Inside, there's a spacious and luxuriously appointed Baroque interior, now used for exhibitions and concerts. In rue des Greffes, to the south, sits the late Renaissance **Hôtel de Ville**, built in 1700 – look for the stuffed crocodiles suspended above the staircase inside the entry hall, gifts to the city from contented (and rich) eighteenth-century burghers.

West from here, the saurian theme continues in place du Marché, where a twentieth-century homage to the city's emblem has been paid in a **fountain** designed by Martiel Raysse and Silvio and Vito Tongiani. A couple of blocks north sits **Hôtel Bernis**, one of the town's earliest surviving mansions, its fifteenth-century facade studded by casement windows and concealing an atmospheric old courtyard with a well in the centre. Nearby, at 8 rue l'Aspic, you can see three early Christian sarcophagi incorporated into the walls of the **Meynier de Salinelles** mansion, as well as a splendid staircase leading up from its courtyard. Further along rue l'Aspic is the place de l'Horloge, whose solitary eighteenth-century **clock tower** is now crowded by the tables of café terraces.

The Museum of Archeology and Natural History

Abutting the back of the Jesuits' Chapel is the **Museum of Archeology and Natural History** (Tues–Sun 10am–6pm; free), housing two collections with little in common. The archeological section is disappointingly poor in Roman artefacts considering the city's ancient Latin glory; items are limited to a sizeable but visually monotonous collection of Latin epigraphy and an assortment of household goods, though it does have some fine Greek lacquerware and Etruscan statuary.

The quirky natural-history exhibition comprises a jumbled collection of Polynesian masks and spears, and a hotchpotch of stuffed animals, including a Royal Bengal Tiger. In fact, the museum rather resembles a large curio cabinet – a journey into the nineteenth-century European mind, which saw the world beyond its borders as a hunting ground for collectables.

Les Arènes and around

The city's most famous Roman monument squats at the south end of boulevard Victor-Hugo, and although not the largest surviving Roman amphitheatre, **Les Arènes** (daily: March–May & Sept–Oct 9am–6/6.30pm; June–Aug 9am–7/8pm; Nov–Feb 9.30am–5pm; €7.70) is one of the best preserved. Dating from the first century AD, the 133m-long and 101m-wide oval surges 21m above the street, thanks to its uniquely intact upper galleries, and still holds the crowds of twenty thousand spectators for which it was designed. An ingenious access system allows the public to enter and exit through the *vomitoria* – the great arched entryways that ring the building – quickly and with minimal jostling. Before the Christians banned gladiatorial matches in the fourth century, these entertainments, along with spectacles involving killing exotic animals, were the big draw. Since the decline of these games the building has managed to escape destruction thanks to its more or less continued use. Starting with the Visigoths it was used as a fortress (in the east section, two contemporary windows remain), and beginning in the twelfth century it filled up with houses, shops and churches, coming to constitute a veritable slum, which was only cleared out when restoration work began in 1809.

Since the nineteenth century the amphitheatre has been used again for public spectacles, including bullfights. Visiting today you can't fail to be impressed by the vast, near-identical passages, stairways and bench-rows – a tribute to Roman engineering. Unfortunately, concerts and events often obscure the building with scaffolding and stage-works, and the retractable cover added in the late 1980s frustrates efforts to imagine the building's ancient ambience. The best way to visit Les Arènes is to come for a **bullfight** (see box, p.188) during one of Nîmes' *ferias*. Outside the main entrance of the arena you'll see a sombre reminder of the seriousness of the *corrida*, the statue of Christian Moncouquiol, a promising young *torero* known as "el Nimeño II", who was gored to death in 1991.

▲ Les Arènes, Nîmes

Bullfighting

The traditions of the **bullfight**, which seem now to be so essential to the spirit of Gard, are in fact almost exclusively recent innovations. The first real **corrida** (Spanish bullfight) in France was held in 1853 at Bayonne under the patronage of a Spanish nobleman. It was a great success and soon spread throughout the Midi and into Provence. Nîmes' first official *corrida* was held at Les Arènes in 1865, and by 1880 the spectacle could be seen across the south.

The standard Spanish-style *corrida* is a highly ritualized **ceremony** – a fatal dance in which the bull is an unwitting but respected partner. In a typical afternoon, three matadors will dispose of six bulls, each of which will face a series of torments: first, after a few initial passes with the large cape (*capote*), the bull is subjected to the long, barbed spear of the mounted *picadores*; next, the graceful *banderilleros* run at the bull and plant their colourful barbs in its shoulder; and finally, the matador executes a series of choreographed passes with his small red *mula* until, to the minor strains of a *paso doble*, the president of the *corrida* gives the order for the bullfighter to finish off his partner. Crowds at the event are extremely vocal and demonstrative: a poor matador and bull will be pelted with seat cushions, while a very successful matador will be greeted with cheers, showered with roses, rewarded with a gift of the bull's ears and tail and borne out of the ring on the shoulders of the crowd. The happiest ending, however, is the rare *indulto*, when the bull is also rewarded for his performance, and retired, to be used for breeding and allowed to die of contented old age.

For more **information** on bullfighting in Nîmes, contact the Bureau de location des Arènes, at 4 rue de la Violette (℡08.91.70.14.01, ✆www.arenesdenimes.com).

Musée des Cultures Taurines and Galerie des Arènes

If you don't manage to see a matador in action, be sure to check out the **Musée des Cultures Taurines**, close to the Arènes at 6 rue Alexandre Ducros (late May to Oct Tues–Sun 10am–6pm; €5.23). Dedicated to *tauromachie*, it houses a permanent collection of posters and relics, and engagingly themed annual exhibitions. Not far from here, on the north side of the boulevard des Arènes, the **Galerie des Arènes** (Tues–Sun 11am–6pm; free) houses temporary exhibitions of works by local artists and photographers.

Musée des Beaux-Arts

From the amphitheatre, it's a five-minute jaunt south along rue de la Cité Foulc to the **Musée des Beaux-Arts** (Tues–Sun 10am–6pm; €5.23), whose highlight is a huge Roman mosaic depicting the mythical "marriage of Admetus". The rest of the collection – mostly Flemish, Italian and French paintings from the sixteenth to eighteenth centuries – is endowed with works of surprising quality, including Rubens' uncharacteristically static *Portrait of a Monk*, and a fine example of the transition from medieval to humanist style in Giambono's *Mystical Marriage of St Catherine*.

Along the way, in rue Porte de France, you'll pass through the **Roman gate** of the same name. It's worth pausing here to consider the immense size of the Roman city – the whole area between here and the Tour Magne was contained by its walls.

The castellum divisorum, la Tour Magne and Temple of Diana

Tucked away north of boulevard Gambetta, beside the cold and sinister facade of the town's eighteenth-century **fortress**, now the Centre Universitaire du Vauban (free), sits one of Nîmes' most important but least known Roman artefacts – the **castellum divisorum** (daily: mid-March to mid-Oct 7.30am–10pm; mid-Oct to mid-March 7.30am–6.30pm; free), the rare remains of a first-century waterworks (the only similar ones are at Pompeii in Italy and Tiermes in Spain). It was from this innocuous-looking open basin that the water carried to the town via the Pont du Gard was distributed to the various parts of the Roman city by lead pipes, which are still partly visible – multimedia installations at the Pont du Gard museum (see p.199) show how the complex worked. Following the quiet residential streets west from here takes you to the **Jardin de la Fontaine**, a formal eighteenth-century garden with a complex series of fountains and pools, at the foot of the forested **Mont Cavalier**.

La Tour Magne and Temple of Diana

From the *place* at the foot of the Mont, a serpentine path leads up to the ruins of the **Tour Magne**. This **watchtower** (daily: March & Oct 9.30am–1pm & 2–6pm; April, May & Sept 9.30am–6.30pm; June–Aug 9am–7/8pm; Nov–Feb 9.30am–1pm & 2–4.30pm; €2.70), based on an earlier Celtic structure, dates from about 15 BC, and as the Roman settlement grew, was eventually incorporated into the city walls. The tower has suffered its share of indignities, including the loss of the top fifteen of its original 45m height and the frantic diggings around the foundations by a treasure-hunting seventeenth-century gardener deluded by a prediction of Nostradamus, but it is impressive even in its ruined state. Broken off and eroded, the tower evokes the romantic etchings of the nineteenth-century travellers who marvelled at it, and it is still the best place from which to survey Nîmes and its surroundings.

As you return to the foot of the hill, to the right of the Jardin sit the shambolic ruins of the "**Temple of Diana**" (daily: mid-March to mid-Oct 7.30am–10pm; mid-Oct to mid-March 7.30am–6.30pm; free). Originally a *nymphaeum*, a sacred fountain dedicated to Nemausus (the god of the spring), the structure was taken over by Benedictine monks in the Middle Ages, in whose care it remained until destroyed by Huguenot mobs. Today the hulking half-arches and ruined walls are the only remnants of the temple, but are enough to give you an impression of the scale of the building in Roman times.

Eating, drinking and entertainment

Three culinary traditions – Spanish, *gastronomique* and, of course, Gardois *terroir* – dominate Nîmes' **restaurants**, with Indian and North African establishments adding a cosmopolitan flavour. The cuisine of Gard has a distinctly Mediterranean taste, with a strong current of olive and garlic, plus rosemary, basil, bay and mint, all of which sprout up in the *garrigues*. Look out for *boeuf à la Gardianne* (slow-cooked marinated beef), *soupe au pistou* (vegetable soup with pesto), and *brandade de morue* (cod and olive-oil purée); wash these down with the wines of the Costières, or with the famous Côtes-du-Rhône vintages.

Restaurants

Many of the cheapest **restaurants**, including self-service cafés and budget sandwich stands, can be found along the boulevard Amiral-Courbet, and the whole of the old town is thick with small restaurants and brasseries, with a veritable colony of street-side bistros in the narrow alleys around place du Marché (many in the €12–20 range). When weather permits, you'll be threading through the tables that spread into the streets and squares.

L'Ancien Théâtre 4 rue Racine ☏04.66.21.30.75. Just a five-minute stroll west from the Maison Carrée, with solid Gard cuisine, and featuring home-made breads and pastries. *Menus* from €18. Closed Sat noon, Sun, Mon & early Aug.

La Bodeguita 1 pl d'Assas, in the *Royal Hotel* ☏04.66.58.28.27. A reliable choice for Spanish food and tapas – Manchego cheese, octopus, *patatas bravas* – with a good view of the Maison Carrée. A meal costs about €25, tapas from €5. Closed Sun off-season.

Le Bouchon et l'Assiette 5 bis rue de Sauve ☏04.66.62.02.93. Worth the walk out past the Temple of Diana – come here for elaborate *gastronomique* variations on traditional *tarnaise* themes, such as a "hamburger" of game fowl, or venison with pepper sauce. Very reasonably priced, with *menus* at €17–45. Closed Tues & Wed, part Jan & most of Aug.

Le Chapon Fin 3 rue Château Fadaise ☏04.66.67.34.73. Basic but hearty *terroir* cuisine in simple surroundings; a good value-for-money choice. Closed Sun; open late till 11pm many nights. *Menus* €11–30.

L'Enclos de la Fontaine Quai de la Fontaine ☏04.66.21.90.30. Set in the luxurious *Hotel Imperator*, with a shady garden, its *carte* treads a line between *terroir* and *gastronomique*. Splurge on the *Menu Dégustation* for €53.

L'Imprimerie 3 rue Balore ☏04.66.29.57.16. A favourite of local artists, and set in a former printing shop, this restaurant features a *carte* that changes daily according to the whims of the market and its chef, grounded in the south but drawing on influences as far off as North Africa. Open Mon–Fri, with *tapas* till 10pm on Friday.

Le Lisita 2B bd des Arènes ☏04.66.67.29.15. Hands-down the city's best *gastronomique*, run by two former staff of Michel Roux's famous London restaurant *Le Gavroche*. High points include salt cod dishes and local beef, which can be enjoyed on a terrace with views of the Arènes. *Menus* start from as little as €35.

Le Magister 5 rue Nationale ☏04.66.76.11.00. Daring experimentation is the order of the day at this good *gastronomique* restaurant. Cod and salmon act as a springboard for the most adventurous combinations, which blend tangy herbs with the sweetness of fruit, while the lamb cutlets are also of exceptional tenderness. The €30 *menu* is a solid option, and includes wine; otherwise à la carte is pricey. Closed Sat lunch & Sun, part of Feb, July & Aug.

Le P'tit Bec 87 bis rue de la République ☏04.66.38.05.83. The best mid-range place for typical Gardoise cuisine, including the ever-present *boeuf à la gardianne* and *brandade de morue*. *Menu* options from €18, plus children's meals. The dining room is pleasant and airy and the service is friendly. Closed Sun eve & Mon.

La Table de Clair Pl des Esclafidous ☏04.66.67.55.61. This funky and unprepossessing restaurant has a hip feel and several awards to its name. The cuisine is eclectic, and everything is good. The house speciality is local beef, grilled and smothered in Cassis mustard sauce. *Menus* at €19 & €32. Closed Mon, Wed lunch & Sun eve.

Bars and cafés

Since 2008's smoking ban went into effect, the blue haze of Gaulloise and Gitane smoke that used to hang in the air of Nîmes has disappeared, and with it, a piece of local heritage – the person who introduced tobacco to France in the sixteenth century was Nîmes native Jean Nicot (also the drug's namesake). Nevertheless, the city's traditional drinking establishments remain lively, if somewhat less atmospheric. A generous selection of quiet, neighbourhood **café-bars**, and louder and larger **music-bars** is scattered throughout the city. Nimes' **clubs**, on the other hand, tend to be in far-flung suburbs or out of town, making them all but impossible to get to without a car.

Café des Beaux-Arts Pl aux Herbes. A cheerful and airy place with a good patio that's well located for people-watching, or simply for soaking up the ambience of the old medieval heart of Nîmes. Closed Sun.

Café Carré d'Art Bd Daudet. Great views of the city from inside the glassed-in interior or outside on the patio atop the museum of the same name. Open the same hours as the museum (see p.185).

La Casa Don Miguel 18 rue de l'Horloge. This popular and late-opening Spanish-style *bodega* is known for its cocktails and large variety of tapas. Occasional flamenco, salsa and jazz shows. Closed Sun.

La Movida 2 la Placette. A Spanish bar with decent tapas and a Romany/flamenco atmosphere that explodes during the *ferias*. Closed Sun & most of Aug.

Napoléon Top end of bd Victor Hugo. Famous old neighbourhood café – complete with faded wood decor, cigar-chomping old men in cardigans and unbeatable Gallic ambience. Great place for a refreshing mid-afternoon *pastis* break and right on the edge of the old town. Closed Sun.

O'Flaherty's 26 bd Amiral-Courbet. British beer – seven kinds on tap – plus food and regular

Thursday concerts of Irish, country and bluegrass (except July & Aug). Open till 2–3am daily.

Pub au Bureau 24 bd Amiral-Courbet. Massive bar and pool hall which also features live music on most weekends from Oct to May. Open late.

Les Trois Maures 10 bd des Arènes. Fantastic old high-ceilinged bar beside the Arènes, festooned with bullfighting and rugby memorabilia and exceptionally busy during *ferias*. Open late. Closed Sun in July & Aug.

Wine Bar Chez Michel 11 square de la Couronne. This is *the* place to begin your acquaintance with the wines of Languedoc (at €20–200 a bottle), served with traditional Gard cuisine. Closed Mon & Sat noon & Sun.

Entertainment and festivals

The city's highbrow cultural programme is disappointing, possibly because of its proximity to more prestigious centres like Avignon and Montpellier. That said, there's a steady stream of theatre groups and musicians, ranging from symphonies to rock and blues acts, coming to town – drawn primarily by the presence of an excellent venue in the Roman amphitheatre. The **cinema**, Sémaphore, 25 rue Porte de France (℡04.66.67.83.11, Ⓦwww.lesemaphore.free.fr), shows films in *version originale*.

The most important dates in the Nîmes calendar are those of the **ferias**, lively street festivals featuring parties, music and *tauromachie*. The city is the French capital of the *corrida*, and during the three great annual *ferias* – **Primavera** (Feb), **Pentecôte** (seven weeks after Easter) and **des Vendanges** (mid-Sept), the best local and Spanish *toreros* come to Les Arènes to practise the brutal pageantry of their art. During the *ferias*, particularly Pentecost, the centre of Nîmes becomes a massive round-the-clock party, and the best hotels get booked a year in advance.

Listings

Books Secondhand English books can be bought and sold at Bouquinerie, 21 av Amiral-Courbet (beside *O'Flaherty's* pub).

Car rental ADA, 2614 rte de Montpellier (℗04.66.04.79.99; Avis, 1800 av du Maréchal Juin ℡04.66.29.05.33; Budget, 1800 av du Maréchal Juin ℡04.66.38.01.69; Europcar, 1bis rue de la République ℡04.66.21.31.35; Hertz, 5 bd de Prague ℡04.66.76.25.91. Avis, Europcar, National and Hertz also have airport offices, and Avis has an office at the train station as well.

Children's activities A good place to take the kids is Parc Aquatropic (℡04.66.38.31.00), a waterslide theme park near the Nîmes-Ouest

autoroute exit, accessible by bus #D from outside the Halles shopping centre on boulevard Gambetta. Adults pay €4.90, kids €1.30. Open summer only 9am–10pm.

Hospital Carremeau Hospital is at Nîmes University (℡04.66.68.68.68). Emergency ℡15.

Pharmacy Grande Pharmacie de l'Horloge, 1 pl de l'Horloge. To find a 24hr pharmacy, call the emergency number ℡3237.

Police *Mairie*, rue Hôtel de Ville (℡04.66.76.70.54). Emergency ℡17.

Swimming Piscine Pablo Neruda is a covered pool at 1 pl Hubert Rouger (℡04.66.36.98.50).

Around Nîmes

For such a small area, the southern portion of Gard contains a surprising number of attractions. Just across the River Gardon to the north of Nîmes lies **Uzès**, the "First Duchy" of France, its castle still in the hands of a family which traces its roots back to Charlemagne. A few kilometres east of the city lies the **Pont du Gard**, perhaps the most famous of all Roman aqueducts, now developed into a major attraction, while along the Rhône, medieval **Beaucaire**'s castle and the uniquely sculpted facade of the church of **St-Gilles** deserve a visit. The southern edge of the *département*, sweeping west of here, is dominated by the westernmost branch of the swampy Rhône delta, the **Petite Camargue** – an important way-station for migratory birds. On the edge of the Camargue, the medieval walls of **Aigues-Mortes**, once attacked by allies of the English, are now besieged only by invading sun-seekers who crowd the beaches south of the town, around **Le Grau-du-Roi** and **Port Camargue**. Upstream from Le Grau, on the River Vidourle, **Sommières** and **Sauve** lie quietly languishing in forgotten obscurity, far from the bustle of the coast.

Public transport in the region is fairly good and, with the unfortunate exception of Uzès, the main towns are served by frequent bus and train routes. Distances, however, are not great, and the generally even landscape makes **hiking** a good option. Unfortunately, south of the *garrigues*, **cycling** is made hazardous by the intense and rapid traffic on the area's narrow highways.

Uzès

Long disdained by the French literati as the proverbial "middle of nowhere", **UZÈS**, nestled among the rocky *garrigues* 20km north of Nîmes, has now been discovered. Like so many of Gard's towns, Uzès traces its history back to the time of the toga, when it served as an agricultural and local market centre. It became the seat of a bishop in the fifth century, eventually coming under the control of the counts of Toulouse. Under the kings of France, who took over in 1229, the lords of Uzès distinguished themselves as loyalists and were rewarded in 1632 with the title "First Duchy of France," which the Dukes of Montmorency had held until Henri de Montmorency's failed revolt (see p.337). Like Nîmes, Uzès violently embraced Calvinism – becoming the fifth most important Huguenot centre in France – but once the movement was suppressed and the majority of Protestants fled, those "Catholics" that remained turned it into a wealthy silk town, which it remained for the next three hundred years. The early twentieth century brought depression, and when the railway bypassed the town, the writing of Uzès' decline was on the wall. The history of the town's celebrities is also one of near misses: Guillaume de Grimoard, later to become Pope Urban V, was not from Uzès, but did live here for a while; the great seventeenth-century poet Jean Racine had an uncle from the town, and spent a year and a half here; and Charles Gide, father of Nobel-laureate author André, was a native – the junior Gide passed his childhood summers here.

But Uzès' historical marginalization belies its beauty. As André Gide remarked, "O little town of Uzès! Were you in Umbria, the tourists of Paris would rush to see you!" In fact, today the town fairly packs out with tourists in summer months; each medieval stone arcade now conceals a bistro, and when the weather is good the restaurant patios that dominate the squares are frequented by buskers of

Map labels:

UZÈS

0   50 m

RUE BENOÎT

RUE K. SALON

BOULEVARD CHARLES GIDE

AV. MAXIME PASCAL

Bike Rental

PLACE ALBERT 1er

RUE DU SALIN

RUE ST-ROMAN

RUE DE LA FERTÉ-MILON

PROMENADE DES MARRONNIERS

GAMBETTA

RUE DE SÉNÉCHAL

PLACE DU DUCHÉ

RUE JACQUES DUPÉS

RUE DU PLAN DE L'OUM

RUE DU Dr-BLANCHARD

RUE ST-JULIEN

BOULEVARD

RUE DE LA RÉPUBLIQUE

Le Duché

BOUCARIE

Hôtel des Monnaies

Municipal Museum

RUE AMIRAL-DE-BRUEYS

RUE G-CODIN

RUE RAFIN

PLACE DAMPARTIN

RUE ENTRÉES-LES-TOURS

RUE G-CHAUVET

RUE DE LA CALADE

PLACE DE L'ÉVÊCHÉ

Cathedral

RUE DE FER

RUE PELISSERIE

RUE CORI ROYAL

RUE DE L'ÉVÊCHÉ

PASSAGE DE MARCHANDS

Medieval Gardens

RUE ST-THÉODORIT

Tour Fenestrelle

PLACE AUX HERBES

Pavillion Racine

BOULEVARD DES ALLIÉS

RUE DU 4 SEPTEMBRE

PLACE AUSTERLITZ

LE PORTALET

Gare Routière

RUE ST-ÉTIENNE

PLACE MALRAUX

Cyberland @

BARS
Au Suisse d'Alger   3
Bar l'Encas   2

RUE N-FROMENT

RUE P-FOUSSAT

St Étienne

BOULEVARD VICTOR HUGO

R. GRANDE BOURGADE

RESTAURANTS
L'Abbaye   1
Le Bec à Vin   4
Les Jardins de Castille   C
L'Oustal   5

ACCOMMODATION
Château d'Arpaillargues   D
Général d'Entraigues   C
Hostellerie Provençal   E
Campsite La Paillote   A
La Taverne   B

surprising quality. Saturday's traditional **market** is particularly lively, while gourmands will want to sample the **truffles** for which the town is renowned. If you're reliant on public transport and short on time the town is best visited on a day-trip from Nîmes that also takes in the **Pont du Gard**, 20km southwest.

Arrival and information

Uzès' **gare routière** is located just west of the old town, a short walk from the **tourist office** (June–Sept Mon–Fri 9am–6/7pm, Sat & Sun 10am–1pm & 2–5pm; Oct–May Mon–Fri 9am–12.30pm & 2–6pm, Sat 10am–1pm; ℡04.66.22.68.88, ⓦwww.uzes-tourisme.com) in place Albert 1er, just north of the Duché. **Bikes** can be rented one block west of the tourist office, at Et Paysan, on avenue Général Vincent, where you can also pick up a free brochure of bike routes, including one to the Pont du Gard. Cyberland **internet** café is on place Austerlitz (noon–2am).

Accommodation

Most of the town's **hotels** reflect its noble past – which is to say, luxurious but pricey. If you're **camping**, head for *La Paillote*, a small campground on rue Xavier Sigalon (℡04.66.22.38.55, ⓦlapailloteuzes.monsite.orange.fr; mid-March to Sept), with pitches set among wooded lots and a pool.

Château d'Arpaillargues 4km southwest of town, on route d'Uzès (℡04.66.22.14.48, ⓦwww.chateaudarpaillargues.com). Owned by the same people as the *Général d'Entraigues*, this rural mansion converted into a hotel boasts high ceilings, elegant furnishings, manicured gardens and a swimming pool. Closed Nov–March. ❼

Général d'Entraigues 8 rue de la Calade ☎04.66.22.32.68, ⓦwww.hoteldentraigues .com. Set in a converted fifteenth-century mansion opposite the cathedral, this hotel has character without being overbearing. The rooms are ample and comfortable and amenities include a small swimming pool and the best restaurant in town. **❻**

Hostellerie Provençale 1 rue Grande Bourgade ☎04.66.22.11.06, ⓦwww.hostellerieprovencale .com. A simple-looking facade disguises one of the area's most highly praised hotels, with personal service and comfortable rooms featuring state-of-the-art amenities. See the web page for discounts and promotions. **❻**

La Taverne 4 rue Xavier Sigalon ☎04.66.22.13.10, ⓔlataverne.uzes @orange.fr. This easy-going hotel is the best value for money in Uzès. An excellent location within the old town, with a small shaded garden, perfect for escaping the high-season hordes. **❹**

The Town

Uzès' compact **old town** can be walked in about an hour. It is still dominated by the twelfth-century castle, **the Duché**, just south of the tourist office, while its other focal point, the **place aux Herbes**, lies southwest of the fortress. The **cathedral** overlooks the Alzon river on the eastern edge of the old town, as if pushed aside by the power of the town's dukes.

The Duché

The old **ducal castle** of the de Cressol family (daily: July & Aug 10am–12.30pm & 2–6.30pm; Sept–June 10am–noon & 2–6pm), remains the centrepiece of Uzès, and the sight of its towering *donjon* topped by the family's red-and-yellow-banded pennant makes a Hollywoodesque but authentic tableau. The compact walled *enceinte* rises dramatically from amid the old town's buildings, concealing a courtyard presided over by a majestically columned Renaissance facade, and a small garden, as well as the bulky and crude keep. Claiming roots that go back to Charlemagne and St Louis, the de Cressols are proud of their long lineage, and their motto *ferro non auro* – "by iron [i.e. the sword], not gold" – sets them apart from the later families who bought rather than fought their way into the aristocracy. Their stay in Uzès has not been continuous, however, as the Revolution precipitated a hiatus which lasted until 1954. Among the most colourful of the family's members was the Duchess Anne, grandmother of the present duke: monarchist, suffragette and enthusiastic hunter (she killed over two thousand animals), she rode until the age of 87, and was France's first female driver – and the first to receive a speeding ticket. Still a part-time residence for the dukes, the castle can be visited on a lively hour-long **guided tour** (€15; an English-language handout is provided), although the budget-conscious may opt only to climb the tenth-century **Tour Bermonde** (€10), whose summit gives fine views from between the battlements. The main tour through the family's apartments is entertaining and offers an intimate look at a disappearing aristocratic world, with personal effects set among the rare furnishings and ancient books. The visit ends in the castle's ancient cellars, where guests are invited to taste the duke's own vintage (also on sale, of course) and buy over priced Provençal statuettes.

The rest of the old town

The castle is far from Uzès' only attraction, and a wander through the dense and evocative alleys of the old town is a true pleasure. Close by is the arcaded **place aux Herbes**, a popular gathering place for buskers. South of the St-Étienne **church**, with its thirteenth-century belfry, sits the old Gide house, among pleasantly quiet streets, unlike the café- and boutique-crammed area around the *place* to the west. In rue Port Royal, east of the Duché, is the entrance to a re-created

André Gide was born in Paris in 1869, the son of a wealthy Huguenot family from Uzès. A sensitive, nervous soul, the young Gide's introspection and uncertainty was nourished by tensions he felt regarding his sexual identity. His disquietudes came to be expressed through literature, and his exceptional promise was reflected in the fact that he published his first work at the age of 20. His *Si le grain ne meurt* ("If It Die"; 1924–26), recalls in part the summers of his youth, spent in Uzès. Like so many nonconformist contemporaries he was drawn to exotic and liberating French North Africa, where he confronted and eventually came to celebrate his bisexuality, as in the landmark *The Fruits of All Earth* (1897) – a work that decisively influenced both Camus and Sartre. In the English-speaking world his best-known **novels** are *The Immoralist* (1902) and *The Counterfeiters* (1926). He died in 1951, recognized as a seminal moral and social iconoclast of the modern age, four years after having received the Nobel Prize for Literature. In 1952 his books were placed on the Catholic Church's Index of forbidden reading.

medieval garden (daily: April–June & Sept Mon–Fri 2–6pm, Sat & Sun 10.30am–12.30pm & 2–6pm; July & Aug 10.30am–12.30pm & 2–6pm; Oct 2–5pm; €4). Set in the courtyard of the former bishop's palace, it contains the herbs and plants that were collected or cultivated in the area during the Middle Ages and makes a great stop for children. Further east, past the dour entrance to the plain **Hôtel des Monnaies** (the former bishop's mint), you'll find the cathedral.

Like so many in the region, the medieval **cathedral** of Uzès fell victim to the violence of the Wars of Religion but, thankfully, the twelfth-century bell tower, the **Tour Fenestrelle**, survived. Rising 42m, the six levels of arched windows on this round structure – unique in France – strongly recall the Leaning Tower of Pisa. The new cathedral, on the other hand, is hardly of interest, apart from its flamboyantly styled seventeenth-century organ. On the north side of the cathedral, the sombre and hulking episcopal palace houses the **municipal museum** (Tues–Sun: March–June, Sept & Oct 3–6pm; July & Aug 10am–noon & 3–6pm; Nov, Dec & Feb 2–5pm; €2), which holds Polynesian relics carried home by local missionaries, some decent eighteenth-century portraiture and a room full of Gide family memorabilia. If the kids are bored of monuments and churches, head east out of town on the road towards St-Quentin-de-Poterie, to find a huge sunflower field **labyrinth** (July & Aug 3–8pm; €8, under-4s free); even if they don't speak French, and miss out on some of the theatrical aspects of the attraction, they'll enjoy running around through the fields.

Eating and drinking

Uzès' recent tourist boom has been good news for diners, as the town has a surplus of **restaurants** – stiff competition meaning good prices. Among the terraces that clutter the old town and line the ring road, a number of establishments stand out (see below). For a **drink**, try the lively terrace at *Au Suisse d'Alger* on rue République. Later in the evening *Bar l'Encas*, at the corner of Gambetta and République, is the place to head for – in addition to its pool table and good selection of beers, it has a terrace where off-duty buskers often sit down for an impromptu jam.

L'Abbaye 24 bd Charles-Gide ☎04.66.22.91.21. For good-value *terroir* cuisine, try the traditional family-run bistro with *menus* from €15. Closed winter.

Le Bec à Vin rue Entre-les-Tours ☎04.66.22.41.20. Well regarded by locals for its innovative Mediterranean fare (from €15–30), you

The black diamonds of Uzès

The eighteenth-century Brillat-Savarin, one of the founders of modern gastronomy, called them "the diamonds of cuisine" – *tuber melanosporum*, or the **Black Truffle**, is a dark lumpy fungus which grows underground in certain oak forests of southern France. Growing only **wild**, and all but undetectable to the human eye, gatherers use trained pigs and dogs to sniff out these truffles, some of which grow to 7cm in diameter, and which can easily sell for €1000 per kilo. All of this for a pungent, earthy taste which *épicures* the world over worship. Fortunately, not much is needed, and modest quantities of Black Truffle can raise a pasta, rice, egg or meat dish from *quotidien* to *extraordinaire*.

Nevertheless, Uzès and the truffle trade that is so much a part of the town's soul is under threat from much cheaper **Chinese** truffles (a distinct species), grown at a fraction of the cost, but a mere shadow of their Gallic cousins. Not only are they sold fraudulently as "real" truffles, but even local restaurateurs have been caught substituting them. The problem is, so few people have tried real Black Truffles, not many can spot the difference.

If you want to be sure to get the real thing (and are prepared to pay), go to the Maison de la Truffe at 27 pl aux Herbes, to buy your own, or dine at *Les Jardins des Castille* (see below), which is certified as using only true wild truffles of Uzès. Or best of all, come to town in the third weekend of January for the truffle festival, which includes live demonstrations of truffle hunting and, of course, the best and freshest "black diamonds" for sale.

can dine indoors or in one of several outdoor court-yards. Closed Sun.

Les Jardins de Castille 8 rue de la Calade
℡04.66.22.32.68. Uzès' best dining is here at the *Général d'Entraigues* hotel, where you can enjoy deluxe versions of the local *terroir* on a panoramic terrace *(menus* €25–50). If you're going to try Uzès Black Truffles, this is the place to do it.

L'Oustal 23 pl aux Herbes. One of the more solid choices on the restaurant-packed *place* at the heart of the old town. Generous salads and otherwise dependable *terroir* from €13.

The Pont du Gard and around

No one with even a passing interest in history or architecture should travel through Gard without seeing what is arguably the world's most famous Roman aqueduct, the **PONT DU GARD**, 20km northeast of Nîmes. The area around the Pont was devastated by serious flooding in 2000, but since then the site has been developed as a major tourist attraction, with an activities centre and an impressive modern **museum** which, together with the stony but pleasant river-beach, excellent **picnic** and **hiking** possibilities and a wide range of nearby accommodation and activities, make it a good base, particularly if you are travelling with children. Several of the **surrounding hamlets** are worth checking out too, as is the **medieval bridge of St-Nicholas**, further up the Gardon river.

Some history

When the Romans needed to supply growing Nîmes with water, they found that the nearest suitable source was some 50km away on the Eure river, near Uzès. Despite the deep Gardon gorge which cut through the route, with Roman single-mindedness (and slave labour), they set about constructing a waterway. This remains nothing short of a technical marvel, descending only 17m in altitude along its course and bridging the Gardon with a monumental aqueduct, the **Pont du Gard**. Most likely constructed in the mid-first century, the Pont's three tiers of arches span an incredible 275m in length, carrying water 49m above the riverbed below. Pillaged for stone through the ages, and first used as a bridge in 1295, the aqueduct has suffered various misfortunes, including an earthquake of 1448, but there was enough of the structure remaining to begin a comprehensive restoration in the eighteenth century. Such was its impact that when Rousseau passed by shortly after this work had been undertaken, the sight of the monument was enough to make him say he wished he'd "been born a Roman". A visit here used to be a must for French journeyman masons on their traditional tour of the country, and many of them have left their names and home towns carved on the stonework. Among these, the markings made by the original builders to facilitate construction can also still be found.

Arrival and information

The Pont itself can be reached by **bus** direct from Nîmes (there is a stop on the south riverbank), or via the nearby town of **Remoulins** (a 45-minute walk away down a quiet lane), which is served by buses from Uzès and Nîmes. Those arriving by **car** can park in official spaces (€5 per day, or €13 for an annual pass) on either bank of the river, or for free in Remoulins, 3km from the site. **Tourist information** is provided at the ticket counter of the activity centre on the north bank (*la rive gauche*), where you'll find the closest parking, and in Remoulins there is a larger **tourist office** in place des Grands Jours (June & Oct Mon–Fri 9am–12.30pm & 2.30–6pm, Sat 10am–1pm; July & Aug Mon–Fri 9am–6pm, Sat & Sun 10am–1pm & 2–5/6pm; Oct–May Mon–Fri 9am–12.30pm & 2.30–6pm, Sat & Sun 9am–12.30pm; ☏04.66.37.22.34, ⓦwww.ot-pontdugard.com). For **canoe rental**, Kayak Vert on the south shore by the aqueduct (☏04.66.22.80.76, ⓦwww.canoe-france.com), can arrange trips (including pick-up or drop-off) in either direction, the best being the downstream paddle from the Pont St-Nicholas. They also rent out mountain **bikes**.

Accommodation

The websites of the Uzès (ⓦwww.uzes-tourisme.com) and Remoulins (ⓦwww .ot-pontdugard.com) tourist offices are great for **accommodation**: the former has

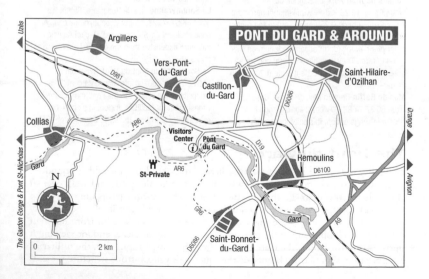

an excellent central **hotel** reservation system covering much of this area, and the latter has many options for rural accommodation. There are also many **campsites** in the area, most with cabins or trailers for rent, though in high season they get booked up very quickly.

Hotels

L'Arceau 1 rue de l'Arceau, St-Hilaire ☎04.66.37.34.45, ⊚www.hotel-arceau.com. One of the best value-for-money options in the region, this eighteenth-century home is set in a picturesque hamlet 3km from the aqueduct. Mid-Feb to late Nov. **⑤**

🏃 **Bégude St-Pierre** CD 981, Vers ☎04.66.63.63.63, ⊚www.hotel-saintpierre .fr. Excellent value, good location and a swimming pool make this seventeenth-century former post-house on the edge of Vers village a first-rate option. Suites available. **⑤**

Le Columbier Av Pont de Gard, Remoulins ☎04.66.37.05.28, ⊜hotelresto.columbier@free.fr. The best of Remoulins' hotels: a mid-sized establishment with good amenities and helpful staff. **③**

Le Gardon Collias ☎04.66.22.80.54, ⊚www .hotel-le-gardon.fr. Another excellent mid-range choice. An old farmhouse in a village just up river from Remoulins. Amenities include flat-screen TV, a/c, internet, and a pool. Mid-March to mid-Oct. **⑤**

Hostellerie Le Castillas Grand' Rue, Collias ☎04.66.22.88.88, ⊚www.lecastellas.com. Three luxuriously if idiosyncratically restored seventeenth-century houses are home to this small and welcoming hotel. All rooms have a/c, TV and internet, and there's an outdoor pool. Closed Jan & Feb. **⑧**

Le Mas de Mon Père La Bégude de Vers, Vers ☎04.66.37.16.25, ⊚www.masdemonpere.com. The cheapest beds (€28 per person) in the region around the Pont are here at the Turions' three-room *gîte d'étape* (dorm accommodation) on this working farm. They also have several comfortable private rooms, and an excellent table (€20). Open Easter–Oct. **④**

Mas de Raffin Chemin Mas de Raffin, Castillon ☎04.66.37.13.28, ⊜viccastillon@orange.fr. A good mid-range option, this small but stately restored five-roomed mansion sits at the heart of its own vineyard on the outskirts of the village. It also boasts a swimming pool, an in-house spa, and has English-speaking staff. Price includes breakfast. **⑤**

🏃 **Le Moulin** Av Pont-du-Gard, Remoulins ☎04.66.22.44.28, ⊚www.lemoulinduroy .com. Small but homey hotel set in a medieval mill on the riverside. One of the best bargains close to the aquaduct. Also has an excellent restaurant (menu €35). **④**

🏃 **Le Vieux Castillon** Rue Turion Sabatier, Castillon ☎04.66.37.61.61, ⊚www .vieuxcastillon.com. This gloriously restored, rambling country estate with a swimming pool provides pricey top-end accommodation. Closed Jan–March. **⑨**

Campsites

Le Barralet in Collias ☎04.66.22.84.52, ⊚www .barralet.fr. This site wins out on both location and value – set on the riverside, it is cheap and far from the crowds, and has excellent facilities. Open March to mid-Sept.

Gorges du Gardon Chemin de la Barque Vieille, Vers ☎04.66.22.81.81, ⊚www.le-camping -international.com. This is the cheapest campsite around, but has good amenities, including a pool. Open mid-March to Oct.

La Soubeyranne Rte de Beaucaire, Remoulins ☎04.66.37.03.21, ⊚www.soubeyranne.com. A good choice if *La Sousta* is full. Decent facilities, but more expensive than the others. Late March to mid-Sept.

La Sousta Av du Pont du Gard, rive droite ☎04.66.37.12.80, ⊜info@lasousta.com. This campsite is the closest to the Pont and has the widest range of facilities, including a shop, pool, recreational activities and wi-fi. Open March–Oct.

The Pont du Gard

Naturally, the whole point of coming here is to behold the incredible **aqueduct** which spans the Gardon. You can swim under it, hike alongside and walk over it, although for the moment the top tier is under renovation (reopening has been continually postponed), and you can only cross the broad lower level. The best way to enjoy this ancient engineering wonder, however, is to take it in from different perspectives, climbing up to the lookout areas at the top of either end, or viewing it upriver from the bed of the Gardon. Seen from here on a sunny day, the utilitarian but gracefully symmetrical beauty of the aqueduct's yellow-stone structure presents a striking contrast to the blue sky. If you're just going to splash around, keep your sandals on or buy some cheap plastic shoes to survive the pebbly bed of the Gardon; on the upriver side of the aqueduct there are places deep enough to dive in, but the river level varies considerably, so check carefully before taking the plunge.

In addition, the modern **Site du Pont du Gard** visitors' complex offers a whole range of activities and attractions. The **museum** (daily: 9.30am–5/7pm; €7) is an incredible multimedia installation, fully multi lingual and incorporating archeological finds, working models, film, sound effects and interactive terminals. Themes include the role of water in Roman society and culture, the building of the aqueduct, and its later decay and rediscovery. This is a must-see, not only for technology and engineering buffs and children, but for anyone remotely interested in the past. In the same building you'll find the Ludo, an interactive activity centre for **children** (same hours as museum, but closed Mon morning; €5), a resource centre, and a cinema. Out back, the **Mémoires de Garrigue** is a fifteen-hectare garden with **nature trails** highlighting the local fauna (daily 9.30am–6pm; free). Finally there are a number of activities and displays particularly suited to children including **workshops** for making Roman-style crafts and weapons (daily 10am–6pm), and **gladiator** demonstrations (daily noon & 5.30pm). The whole site is suitable for visitors with disabilities. A combined one-day **ticket** for all the permanent attractions costs €12 (family, €24), while the Site Pont du Gard **pass** (€15) gives unlimited access to all the attractions, including temporary exhibitions and parking.

Around the Pont du Gard

The Pont du Gard is a great place to cool down on a hot day (although the river slows to a trickle in August), and this part of the Gardon is an easy stretch for **canoeing** and **kayaking** (see p.197). Two kilometres west of the aqueduct lies the **château de St-Privat**, the site where Cardinal Richelieu – Louis XIII's most powerful minister – signed the Peace of Alès with the Huguenots in 1629 (the lords of the castle, the Faret family, were Protestants). The château is famous for its elaborate formal garden, which dates back to 1644. One of its three sections, the "Avant-park", is home to the **War Sacrifice Chapel**, commissioned after World War I by then-owner Jacques Rouché; its walls are decorated with painted works of metaphysical allegory, mixing biblical figures with depictions of *poilus* (French common soldiers). Unfortunately the property can only be visited on a ninety-minute **guided tour** (contact the tourist office at Remoulins or Pont du Gard for details).

Moving on from the aqueduct, the best way to leave is to hike west along the **Gardon gorge** to the Pont St-Nicholas. The GR6 on the north bank and the AR6 on the south (passing St-Privat) lead to **Collias** 4km away, formerly a hippie mecca, from where the GR6 can be followed upriver. Aside from the rugged beauty of the riverbed's red cliffs, look out for the **Grotte de la Baume**, a cave with a medieval chapel set among what were once the rocky abodes of hermits, set on the north bank just west of Collias. Finally, some 10km after Collias, you reach the ponderous thirteenth-century **Pont St-Nicholas**, now incorporated into the main Uzès–Nîmes highway.

There are also some interesting hamlets along the Uzès–Remoulins road, the most intriguing of which (and also the one where the most buses stop) is **Vers**, 4km north of the Pont, where you'll find bits of ruined arches and chunks of Roman road lying around town, and an eleventh-century church. Other nearby villages include **St-Hilaire** and **Castillon-du-Gard**, ancient and picturesque farming settlements which don't have any particular sights, but are worth wandering around.

Eating and drinking

The most pleasant option for **eating** is to have a **picnic** on the banks of the river. However, if you're not equipped, the visitors' centre also has a couple of fast-food outlets, although there's better dining on the far bank, at the pleasant **restaurant** *Cuisiniers Vignerons* (*menus* from €18). All the hotels listed on p.198 have restaurants, most with *terroir menus* in the €15–30 price range – the most sophisticated are those at *Le Vieux Castillon*, which features an eclectic *carte* (from about €60) and *Bégude St-Pierre* in Vers (*menus* from €30), which features variations on local *terroir* themes (notable for the predominance of beef) as well as the surrounding country's best selection of wines. Alternatively, *Le Clos de Vignes* in Castillon-du-Gard (closed Mon & Tues lunch & mid-Jan to mid-Feb; ☎04.66.37.02.26) serves up good, inexpensive local food on two pleasantly situated terraces (€18–25).

Beaucaire and the Rhône

BEAUCAIRE doesn't necessarily merit making a special effort to visit, but can be a rewarding stop for those passing through. This is particularly worth considering if you have your own transport, as the interesting **Roman** and **medieval** vestiges around the town are better reached by car, although **hiking** and **biking** are possible as well. The best time to visit Beaucaire is during June's Fête du Drac, a traditional festival in honour of the town's dragon mascot, marking the arrival of summer and featuring parades and *tauromachie*, or July's Estivales, a medieval pageant celebrating the town's once-famous fair.

From the second century BC Beaucaire was a Roman wine entrepôt known as Ugernum, but this disappeared along with the empire. Centuries later, the town thrived under the patronage of the counts of Toulouse. During the Albigensian Crusade, it was the site of a rare defeat for the fierce Simon de Montfort at the hands of Raymond VII – the jubilant count granted the town the right to hold a yearly **trade fair** as a reward. Bringing merchants from all over Europe, the Middle East and North Africa, the market survived the town's transition to the French Crown in 1229 and continued to be held through the nineteenth century. Trade routes shifted, however, and by the time Richelieu ordered the castle torn down in 1632, Beaucaire was already a backwater.

Arrival, information and accommodation

Coming by **train** you'll arrive at the **gare SNCF** on boulevard Gustave-Desplaces in Tarascon, just across the Rhône footbridge from Beaucaire. Arriving by **bus** (information on ☎04.66.29.27.29), get off at the "Passerelle" stop (the footbridge). Beaucaire's friendly **tourist office**, 24 cours de Gambetta (Mon–Fri 8.45am–12.15pm & 2–6pm, Sat 9.30am–12.30pm; Easter–Nov also Sat 3–6pm; July & Aug also Sun 9.30am–12.30pm; ☎04.66.59.26.57, ⓦwww.ot-beaucaire .fr), is on the north side of the canal that runs along the southern edge of the old town, and can provide information on package excursions to the Camargue.

The best **hotel** in town is the three-star *Doctrinaires* (closed mid-Dec to mid-Jan; ☎04.66.59.23.70, ⓦwww.hoteldoctrinaires.com; ❸), in a seventeenth-century building on quai Général-de-Gaulle overlooking the port. Those with transport should head 6km south of Beaucaire to the luxurious and relaxing ⚡*Domaine des Clos* (☎04.66.01.14.61, ⓦwww.domaine-des-clos.com; ❺; English spoken), an eighteenth-century Provençal farm on the route de Bellegard.

The Town

Today, the tree-lined **canal** running through town is alive with waterfront restaurants and the busy leisure of the boaters who ply the canals to Sète and Montpellier, while the **old town** continues to languish in semi-neglect. The best time to visit is on Friday nights in July and August when there are open-air concerts, featuring live acts ranging from blues to World Music, as well as a lively canalside street-market.

Poised on a rocky promontory rising 35m above the Rhône, Beaucaire's partially ruined **castle** – the main attraction here – provides dramatic views of the surrounding countryside and Tarascon's own castle. Parts of the fourteenth-century **curtain wall** survive, as do several towers, including the striking **Tour Polygonale**, shooting dramatically skyward out of the living rock of the hill. The only way of visiting the castle ruins is to take in the entertaining medieval **falconry** display, "Les Aigles", with hourly live demonstrations (daily: late March & Sept–Nov 2.30–4.30pm; April–June 2–4.30pm; July & Aug 3–5.30pm; closed Wed off-season; €10). The eighteenth-century listed **gardens** which fill the outer courtyard, however, can be visited free of charge (daily: April–Oct 10am–noon & 2.15–6.45pm; Nov–March 10.15am–noon & 2–5.15pm). On Friday nights in summer the castle is the backdrop for the *son et lumière* "Raymond VII and the Siege of Beaucaire" (July & Aug daily at 10pm), which floods the castle buildings in garish colour while recounting the town's moment of medieval glory.

Eating and drinking

Beaucaire's best-value **restaurant** is the *Auberge de l'Amadin* on chemin de la Croix de Marbre (℡04.66.59.55.07; mid-April to Oct Tues–Sun lunch only), featuring market-fresh *menus* (from €18) with an accent on fish. For something more simple and central, several canalside bistros along quai de Gaulle have €8–14 *formules*, while the more formal *Doctrinaires* (see "Accommodation", opposite; closed Sat lunch) is as fancy as it gets here; service and atmosphere are good and there is a solid range of meat and fish options for up to €40.

Along the Rhône

Four kilometres northwest of Beaucaire, off the Remoulins road just before the dam on the Rhône, lies the turn-off for the **underground monastery of St-Roman** (March–June, Sept & Oct Tues–Sun 10am–1pm & 2–5/6pm; July & Aug 10am–1pm & 2–7pm; Nov–Feb Sun & hols 2–5pm; €5.50); to get there, follow the narrow road (no RVs) 3km to the monastery car park, then walk 500m to the site itself. This incredible complex, founded in the fifth century, is one of the oldest monasteries in France. Later covered over by a castle that was subsequently destroyed, the huge abbey was not rediscovered until 1966. The subterranean main chapel – built to house the sacred remains of St Roman – still contains the impressive carved seat from which the abbots presided over their community until the sixteenth century. Inside you'll also find small tombs carved in the floor, and set with recesses in which oil lamps were placed in honour of the dead. This church, the monks' cells and other chambers were cut into the living rock of the hill in what must have been gruelling labour. The terrace of the monastery offers a sweeping panorama of the Rhône, with the hills of Provence easily visible in the distance.

Eight kilometres west of Beaucaire on the D38 (no public transport) is the re-created Roman winery of **Le Mas de Tourelles** (April–June, Sept & Oct daily 2–6pm; July & Aug Mon–Sat 10am–noon & 2–7pm, Sun 2–7pm; Nov–March Sat 2–6pm; €5). It's an entertaining stop, where on the second Sunday of September

The Rhône–Sète canal

Although not as famous as its sister to the west, the **Rhône–Sète canal** is an inland waterway which also offers great sightseeing and leisure possibilities, either on its own or combined with a trip along the Canal du Midi. Not only is the Rhône–Sète waterway less crowded than its more popular counterpart, but the general evenness of the landscape means that there are no locks (on the main line) and fewer queues to contend with, even in high season. The various **subsidiary canals** also offer the opportunity to explore the backwaters of the Camargue in relative isolation.

The canal begins from the River Rhône at **Beaucaire**, heading southwest through the flat Camarguais wine-country to **St-Gilles**, where you can turn off on a secondary canal to **Vauvert**, a handy stop for supplies, particularly when its market is in full swing, on Wednesday and Friday mornings. Otherwise, the main canal crosses 30km of salty marshland, rich in birdlife, to pass the medieval **Tour Carbonnière**, just before **Aigues-Mortes**. From here, St Louis' thirteenth-century canal (or *grau*) can be followed to **Le-Grau-du-Roi** and **Port Camargue**.

Alternatively, from Aigues-Mortes follow the main canal west as it weaves its way past the Étang de Maugaio, before arriving at **Palavas-les-Flots**, which provides a handy base for exploring **Montpellier**, and whose branch canals lead inland to **Villeneuve-lès-Maguelone** and Lattes. Heading west, the canal threads a series of *étangs*, gliding past the ancient cathedral of **Maguelone**, and **Frontignan**, an ancient *circulade* with a **medieval church**. Finally the canal arrives at its terminus, **Sète**; from here you can continue into the broad expanse of the Bassin de Thau, skirting the oyster beds, to visit its colourful fishing towns: Balaruc, **Mèze** and Marseillan. At the far end of this saltwater lagoon, an access canal leads 5km to **Agde**, from where the **Canal du Midi** can be accessed.

Boats can be rented at most of the ports of call along the canal, which also have sanitary facilities and fresh-water supplies. At Beaucaire there is Arolles Marine (℡04.66.01.75.15, ⓦwww.camargue-fluvial.com) or Connoisseurs Cruisers (℡04.66 .59.46.08, ⓦwww.connoisseur.ie), and Crown Blue Line (℡04.66.87.22.66, ⓦwww .crownblueline.com) is in St-Gilles. In addition, L'Isle de Stel (℡06.80.83.82.01, ⓦwww .islesdestel.camargue.fr) runs organized **cruises** out of St-Gilles on various itineraries along the network of canals and the Petit Rhône. The local Capitainneries can also direct you to the nearest **bicycle** rental, handy for exploring the canal-side towns.

(2–6pm) you can watch toga-clad types making wine using first-century AD technology; you can taste the final result before drawing your own conclusions as to its Roman authenticity. From the vineyard it's a thirty-minute signposted walk north to a well-preserved eight-kilometre stretch of the **Via Domitia** that leads west from Beaucaire, and still boasts three Roman **milestones**; when you reach the road, turn right and you will arrive shortly at the milestones.

Finally, while visiting Beaucaire it would be a shame not to walk or drive across the bridge which spans the Rhône to visit the **castle** at **Tarascon** (June–Sept daily 9.30am–6.30pm; Oct–May Tues–Sun 10.30am–5pm; €6.50). This immaculately preserved thirteenth-century fortress, rising majestically from the banks of the Rhône, provides a stunning contrast to the ruins of Beaucaire's fortress. It was here that the anonymous medieval poem (possibly a musical play), *Nicolette and Aucassin*, was written, recounting the tale of the star-crossed love affair between Aucassin, a fictional heir of Beaucaire, and Nicolette, a beautiful Muslim slave girl who had been bought by the viscount of Tarascon and raised as a Christian. Close by, the **church** of St Martha features a masterful Romanesque portal on the south side, and in the crypt you'll find a carved third- to fourth-century sarcophagus.

St-Gilles and the Petite Camargue

Twenty-six kilometres southwest of Beaucaire and 20km south of Nîmes lies the former pilgrims' stop of **St-Gilles**, another town whose candle blew out in the late Middle Ages, and whose present attraction is the magnificent and fortunately preserved facade of its former **abbey-church** (a UNESCO World Heritage monument). St-Gilles is also one of the gateways to the vast and swampy **Petite Camargue** which surrounds it on the eastern and southern sides, stretching from Beaucaire to the northeast, to Aigues-Mortes to the southwest. As you move away from town, the stony ground becomes increasingly sandy and marshy, and vineyards give way to flower farms, rice paddies and bull and horse **ranches** (*manades*). Among the salty *étangs*, or lagoons, which mark the coast sits **Saintes-Maries-de-la-Mer**, a town famous for its annual Romany pilgrimage and other festivals.

St-Gilles

Perched on the edge of the Camargue, quiet **ST-GILLES** takes its name from a legendary sixth-century hermit who converted the Visigothic king Wamba to Christianity. The ever-astute Cluniac monks promoted the cult of the saint in order to make the town (already on the Arles-to-Santiago de Compostela pilgrim route) a lucrative stopping point early in the twelfth century. By this time it was a favourite of the counts of Toulouse – the Crusader Raymond IV used "de St-Gilles" as his surname. A good port and liberal market privileges further boosted prosperity and drew traders from around the Mediterranean, but within a few hundred years the unstoppable silt of the Rhône and the tide of the Reformation conspired to kill both the port and the pilgrim route. The **Wars of Religion** were especially bitter in St-Gilles – at one point a Protestant mob is said to have thrown

The Chemin de St-Jacques

The pilgrimage route to Santiago de Compostela (known in Spain as the Camino de Santiago and in France as the **Chemin de St-Jacques**) was Languedoc's and Europe's first grand tourism venture (and inspired the first European guidebooks). It all started in the ninth century when a priest in northwestern Spain miraculously "discovered" the burial site of **St James the Greater**, the Apostle, in a local cemetery. The remains were shifted to a nearby hamlet, which was subsequently renamed as **Santiago** (St James) de Compostela (from the Latin for "little burial ground"). The tomb became a rallying point for the Christians of northern Spain, but it was in the late eleventh century that things really got going. By this time the Church was prescribing pilgrimage as a way of doing penance for sins, and both common folk and nobles saw it also as a way to see the world and escape the banalities of daily existence. The volume of travellers brought wealth and prosperity not only to Santiago, but also to the churches and monasteries along the route which, like **St-Sernin** in Toulouse (p.68), **St-Guilhem** in Hérault (p.248) and **St-Gilles** in Gard, made showcases of their own relics to attract the faithful along the way. Other notable stops on the pilgrim route include **Vals** in the Aude (p.117), **St-Lizier** in Ariège (p.123), **Rabastens** in the Tarn (p.155), **Joncels** (p.281), **Murat** (p.165), **La Salvetat** (p.167) and **Clermont l'Hérault** (p.243) in Haut Languedoc, and **Santa María Vilar** in Roussillon (p.319). Today, hikers continue to follow the route, designated a UNESCO World Heritage Site in 1998, and a fascinating window into a world long past. Most towns and hamlets along the route have a **pilgrim hostel** where you can sleep for about €8. In the old days these might be signalled by a carved scallop shell, the symbol of the pilgrimage, but nowadays look for signs which say "accueil pèlerins".

Perrier

Set amid the shadeless countryside of vineyards and indistinguishable hamlets west of St-Gilles is one of France's proudest commercial institutions, the **Perrier spring and bottling plant**, located a few minutes' drive north of **Vauvert**. The source of France's second most famous bubbly stuff, the much-advertised **spring** (Feb–June & Sept–Dec Mon–Fri 9.30–10.30am & 1–4pm, Sat & Sun 1.30–5pm; July & Aug Mon–Fri 9.30–10.30am & 1–6pm, Sat & Sun 10–10.30am & 1.30–4.30pm; €5) is a site venerated by Gallic hordes who arrive daily, blissfully shelling out for the two-hour **tour**, sharing vicariously in the glory of the water which has come to signify France abroad. The spring was known in Roman times, but subsequently languished in obscurity until 1894, when a certain Dr Perrier of Nîmes bought the property and set up the Perrier Spring Company in partnership with a young, disabled English aristocrat, who came up with the distinctive shape for the bottle inspired by the dumbbells he used for his physiotherapy. The **guided tour** includes a walk through the vast and modern bottling complex, a visit to the spring itself and ends at the former owner's mansion, this last now the Perrier "museum" – a thinly disguised shop where you can pay inflated prices for various bits of merchandising.

the church's choristers down a well – and by the time the great abbey-church was virtually destroyed by Huguenot mobs in 1622, the town had already passed into history. Today the town's two principal roles have been revived: it has both a busy canalside **pleasure port** and the still-functioning pilgrim route to Compostela, which lives on as the GR653, coming into town from Arles and heading on west through the flat vineyards to Montpellier. The biggest festivities in St-Gilles take place in mid-August, with the Feria de la Pêche et de l'Abricot ("The Peach and Apricot Festival") featuring *abrivados*, *encierros* and full-blown *corridas*.

Arrival, information and accommodation

St-Gilles' **gare routière** is a fifteen-minute walk northeast of the centre, and 100m from the **tourist office** at place Frédéric Mistral (daily 8.30am–noon & 2–5.30pm; ☎04.66.87.33.75, Ⓦwww.ot-saint-gilles.fr). The best of the town's **hotels** are the cheery *Le Cours*, 10 allée Griffeuille (closed mid-Dec to Feb; ☎04.66.87.31.93, Ⓦwww.hotel-le-cours.com; ❸), and the three-star *Heraclée*, 30 quai du Canal (☎04.66.87.44.10, Ⓦwww.hotel-heraclee.com; ❹), a more subdued second choice; both have TV and wi-fi. The **campsite**, *Chicanettes* (mid-April to Sept; ☎04.66.87.28.32, Ⓔcamping.la.chicanette@libertysurf.fr), is in town, just behind the public car park.

The Town

The main attraction in St-Gilles is its spectacular **abbey-church** in the heart of the old town. Although the Religious Wars destroyed almost the entire building, fate spared the most interesting work of medieval art of the region: the great twelfth-century Romanesque **frieze** that graces the church's west entrance. Spreading between and over the three great doorways (reminiscent of a Roman triumphal arch), a series of bas-reliefs conveys the story of Jesus' return to Jerusalem and subsequent Crucifixion, representations of the Apostles, the three Marys and St Paul, and scenes based on the Old Testament and medieval iconography. These carvings are of superlative workmanship, a unique blend of Byzantine, Classical and medieval styling setting them apart from the mass of contemporary work. They're best viewed (and photographed) in the afternoon, when the sunlight plays across the carvings. Aside from this, two other noteworthy remains of the medieval church can be seen: the choir and the **crypt** (April–Oct Mon–Sat 9am–12.30pm & 2/3–6/7pm; Nov–March Mon–Fri 8.30am–noon & 1.30–5.30pm, Sat 9/10am–noon/1pm; guided visit €4), which contains the **tombs** of St Gilles and Pierre de Castelnau (see p.333). Located behind the modern building, the ruins of the former choir hint at the grandeur of the medieval church. On the north side stands the *vis* ("screw"), a massive self-supporting **spiral staircase** built in the 1100s to access the church's upper gallery. An architectural marvel, it was, like the Pont du Gard, a mandatory stop on the masons' tour of the country.

Opposite the church sits the **Maison Romane**, a restored medieval house in which it is claimed Gui Folques, who became Pope Clement IV in 1265, was born; it now houses a municipal **museum** (Mon–Sat: July & Aug 9am–noon & 3–7pm; June & Sept 9am–noon & 2–6pm; Oct–Dec & Feb–May 9am–noon & 2–5pm; free) of slight interest, featuring local bric-a-brac. Otherwise, it's well worth wandering around the narrow lanes and arch-covered streets of the old town – many of the tiny houses here retain their medieval details and it won't take long for you to discover small doors set in slowly sagging walls, and half-open windows revealing pastel-toned plaster walls and ceiling beams within.

Eating and drinking

The best place to eat is the **restaurant** at *Le Cours* (see "Accommodation", opposite), which serves up well-executed and imaginative cuisine for around €14–36; the local speciality is *taureau* (beef) *à la gardianne*. A produce **market** is held on Thursday and Sunday mornings in avenue Emil-Cazelles.

The Petite Camargue

The **PETITE CAMARGUE**, which Lawrence Durrell called "Little Argentina", is a forbidding expanse of marshes, crisscrossed by canals, and dominated by great saltwater *étangs* ("lagoons"), spreading out from the banks of the Petit Rhône, an off-shoot of the larger river. This is a lightly populated and unwelcoming area, with only a single village, **Saintes-Maries-de-la-Mer**, and a scattering of isolated ranches, rice farms and salt works. It is temporary home, however, to an incredible variety of **waterfowl** – some four hundred different species – including a steady stream of

Exploring the Petite Camargue

The easiest way to get around the Petite Camargue is with your own vehicle; however, don't be tempted onto the **unpaved roads** and lanes leading out through the fields – quite often they are deceptively soft and you may find yourself walking back to civilization. The best way to visit the more remote areas is on an organized one-day **safari** or **boat tour**: Le Gitan in 6 rue des Alliés, **Le Grau** (☎04.66.52.04.99, ⓔcamargue -decouverte@orange.fr), run four-wheel-drive expeditions and a tour of a working bull farm; *Isle de Stel* at the Bassin d'Evolution in **Aigues-Mortes** (April–Oct; ☎04.66.53.60.70, ⓦwww.islesdestel.camargue.fr) offers a half-day boat tour of the nearby *étangs* and canals (from €10); and Cabane de Boucanet in **Port Camargue** (☎04.66.53.25.64) organizes horseback rides of the area (€15 per hr). In addition, several of the horse farms near St-Gilles offer half- and full-day horseback and carriage tours around their land (ask at the tourist office there). Whether you approve of the *corrida* or not, a visit to a bull farm (or *manade*) is an interesting experience – a chance to see the traditional lifestyle of the ranches of the delta, and witness the impressive equestrian skills of the *gardians* ("cowboys") who manage the herds. The tourist office in **St-Gilles** (see opposite) has a list of the twenty or so ranches in the area and can indicate which have English-speaking guides and which charge admission to visitors.

migrating birds crossing the Mediterranean between Europe and Africa in spring and fall; look out especially for pink flamingos, herons, grand cormorants and egrets. The Rhône Delta is also where the Gard's strong traditions of **horsemanship** and *tauromachie* originate, on the great ranches where wild bulls are left to graze the salty scrub freely. The *gardians* (camarguais cowboys) whose simple huts dot the plain have been the proud masters of the delta since at least 1512, when they established a formal confraternity. Riding their distinctively small "Camargue" ponies they pursue and corral the black bulls, rounding them up for branding in the springtime *ferrade*.

The Parc Naturel Régional de la Camargue

A large slice of the Camargue proper, which lies officially in Provence, has been incorporated since 1970 into the **Parc Naturel Régional de la Camargue** (Ⓦ www.parc-camargue.fr), but there is no visible characteristic that distinguishes the official parkland from the rest of the delta. Set in the park, 5km east of the Petit Rhône on the D570, is the **Musée de la Camargue** (April–Sept daily 9am–6pm; Oct–March Wed–Sun 10am–5pm; €4.50), which provides an excellent orientation to the area. Located in an old sheep-farm, Mas Pont du Rousty, and surrounded by nature trails, the museum contains exhibits relating to the ecology and economy of the Camargue, as well as on the figure of Sara – the object of the annual Romany pilgrimage (see box below).

Saintes-Maries-de-la-Mer

The furthest the road will take you in the Petite Camargue is **Saintes-Maries-de-la-Mer**, an ancient seaside village the population of which swells to over fifty thousand in July and August, from the less than three thousand inhabitants it has the rest of the year. The windswept fishing village, dominated by its fortress-like medieval church, attracted the likes of Hemingway and Picasso in the early twentieth century, and now brings in crowds of summer sun-worshippers. The crypt of the ancient **church** (free) is worth visiting to see the statue of Black

---

Sara and the three Marys

A legend going back five hundred years recounts how after the Crucifixion, Joseph of Arimathea and three of Jesus' female followers – Mary Magdalene, Mary Salomé and Mary Jacobé – had set sail from Egypt and landed near the mouth of the Petit Rhône at the town of Ra. In 1838 the town's name was changed to **Saintes-Maries-de-la-Mer**, and soon after **Roma** ("Gypsy") peoples began to gather here to mark the feast of St Sara, or "**Black Sara**," who they hold to have been an Egyptian servant-girl belonging to Mary Magdalene, and considered to be their patron saint. Black Sara is still commemorated every year on May 24 and 25, when thousands of Roma from around Europe converge on the town for a **celebration** marked by baptisms, music and dancing, culminating in the statue of Sara (and subsequently with those of Mary Salomé and Jacobé) being taken from the town's church and carried in **procession** by crowds down to the sea. The following day, May 26, is celebrated with an *abrivado*, folk dancing and displays of **horsemanship** by *gardians*. A second, smaller pilgrimage is celebrated on the closest Sunday to October 22, but this is strictly a local affair.

In addition, four other major events take place in Saintes-Maries throughout the year. On June 20, as part of the Feria Biou, *gardians* show off their skills, and herds of horses are driven through the town. A larger, five-day **horse festival** is held around July 14, marked by equestrian contests and bullfights. Around August 15 an important three-day festival of *tauromachie* is held, featuring *corridas* and *courses camarguaises*. Finally, around November 11, over two hundred *gardians* and **one thousand horses** converge on the town for a spectacular beachside cavalcade.

Sara (see box opposite), bedecked in colourful robes and surrounded by offerings of the faithful.

The town's **tourist office** (daily: April–Sept 9am–7/8pm; Oct–March 9am–5/6pm; ☎04.90.97.82.55, ⓦwww.saintesmaries.com) is at 5 rue Van Gogh. Of the many **hotels** in town, the best deal is the three-star *Galoubet* (☎04.90.97.82.17, ⓦwww.hotelgaloubet.com; ❹) on route de Cacharel, on the northeast edge of town. If you are prepared to pay for luxury, head for *Mas de la Fouque* (☎04.90.97.81.02, ⓦwww.masdelafouque.com; ❾), a deluxe spa and hotel on route de Petit Rhône, set in a gorgeous parkland and with stunningly luxurious facilities. The best **campsite** is the four-star *Le Clos du Rhône* (☎04.90.97.85.99, ⓦwww.camping-leclos.fr) on the seafront on route d'Aigues-Mortes.

The Camarguais coast

Lying 35km south of Nîmes, set by the **Camarguais coast** amid the flat swampy land of the westernmost reaches of the Rhône delta, sits **Aigues-Mortes**, its perfectly intact rectangular walls rising out of the plain like a storybook image of a medieval town. From here, an ancient canal leads southwest to **Le Grau-du-Roi**, once a humble fishing town, now a teeming **summer resort**, exploiting the great unbroken band of dunes which stretches along the coast from the town's eastern limits all the way to the mouth of the Petit Rhône. **Port Camargue**, a modern adjunct to Le Grau, is a purpose-built yachting complex – the biggest pleasure-port on the whole of the Mediterranean.

Aigues-Mortes

Originally intended to be France's principal Mediterranean port, **AIGUES-MORTES** was swallowed up in short order by the silt of the Rhône, which pushed the sea south and consigned the town to stagnation among the "dead waters" surrounding it. Founded by Louis IX in 1246, it was from here that the saint-king embarked on two of his expeditions: to Cyprus on the Seventh Crusade of 1248, and to Tunis in 1270, where he met his death (by diarrhoea). His son, Philip, gave the medieval town its present form – commissioning Genoan engineers to build walls in emulation of those of Damietta in Egypt, the site of Louis' early (but Pyrrhic) triumph. Local salt beds and trade privileges brought initial success, but by the end of the fourteenth century it had become a backwater, stranded by the waves of silt brought downriver by the Rhône. Aigues-Mortes' misfortune, however, has preserved the town's striking profile, which may have otherwise been built over and around. Today it is a mandatory photo-stop, and a tour of the **fortifications** and the grid of thirteenth-century streets is a pleasant way to pass an hour or so, combining well with a trip to the **beaches** to the south. If you have the good fortune to visit during a festival, try to catch a bit of the *course camarguaise*; watching the crowds and the bulls beneath the medieval ramparts is a truly evocative sight.

Arrival and information

The **gare SNCF**, on the spur line that runs down from Nîmes to Le Grau-du-Roi, is on the route de Nîmes, just north of the old town, while **buses** stop on avenue de la Liberté, across the canal from the *gare*. The **tourist office** (June & early Sept Mon–Fri 9am–6/7pm, Sat & Sun 10am–noon & 2–6/7pm; July & Aug Mon–Fri 9am–8pm, Sat & Sun 10am–8pm; mid-Sept to May Mon–Fri 9am–noon & 1–6pm, Sat & Sun 10am–noon & 2–6pm; ☎04.66.53.73.00, ⓦwww.ot-aiguesmortes.fr) is just inside the Porte de la Gardette, one of the old town's five monumental gates,

▲ Aigues-Mortes

east of the Tour de Constance on the north wall. **Bikes** can be rented from BV Location at 7 rue du Vidourle (☎06.67.44.78.16), and there's **internet** access at Les Remparts, 2 rue Émile Zola.

Accommodation

There are a number of **hotels** in and around Aigues-Mortes, though they get booked up early in high season, and room prices are relatively high and don't offer great value for money – hotels in Le Grau, only 8km away (see p.210), tend to be more reasonable. *L'Escale*, right by the Tour de Constance (☎04.66.53.71.14, ⓦwww.hotel .escale.free.fr; ❶), is the best deal, with a traditional homely atmosphere, as well as a good restaurant and family-sized rooms. Moving upscale, *Les Arcades*, 23 bd Gambetta (☎04.66.53.81.13, ⓦwww.les-arcades.fr; ❼), is a small, tastefully appointed hotel in a beautiful twelfth-century building; the rooms are not huge, but the service is attentive. The **campsite**, *Fleur de Camargue* (April to late Sept; ☎04.66.88.15.42, ⓦwww.fleur-de-camargue.com), is a four-star super-site, a massive complex with a café-bar, laundry facilities and a gamut of other services, located 3km west of town.

The Town

Aigues-Mortes' **old town**, where the sights, hotels and restaurants are concentrated, is laid out on a rectangular grid, girded by stout walls. It is well maintained, but its success as a day-trip and weekend destination has cluttered the streets with postcard and souvenir boutiques, the regular street pattern adding to an air of artificiality and tweeness. Henry James's observation of a hundred years ago is equally valid today: Aigues-Mortes, he wrote, "can hardly be said to be alive; but it has been very neatly embalmed".

On the far side of the open *place* where the tourist office sits, looms the massive **Tour de Constance** (daily: May–Aug 10am–7pm; Sept–April 10am–5pm; €7), the main fortress of the town – once a lighthouse and for many years a prison for uncooperative nobles and stalwart Huguenots. Protestant women were confined in the cells on the top floor, including one stoic Marie Durand who spent almost forty years here in the eighteenth century, and whose graffiti remain etched in the stone to this day. It is also through the tower that you access the walk along the **town walls**, which provides sweeping views over the flat terrain of the delta and allows a close-up

Food and wine

With its perfect weather and excellent soil, Languedoc has been producing wine since Roman times, and continues to account for one third of France's production. Traditionally a region that produced affordable, everyday wine, Languedoc has seen a blossoming of small vintners and co-ops producing excellent high-quality wines using blends of grapes similar to those of Provence. Likewise, the local terroir cuisine, hearty and simple by tradition, is being transformed by innovative gastronomique chefs whose creations are raising it to culinary heights without forsaking its earthy roots.

Local apricots, Cordes-sur-Ciel ▲

Cassoulet ▼

Regional terroir

In the east, Provençal influence is strong – especially in the use of the herbs that spring up throughout the *garrigues* – while the ranches of the **Petite Camargue** ensure beef's central role, whether in sausage or the stew-like *brandade de la Gardienne*. Other local ingredients include truffles, gathered around **Uzès**, olives, and Camargue rice. The fair climate favours fresh produce, including asparagus, peaches and apricots.

Fish and seafood abound in the **coastal cuisine**: in brothy *coquillages* (shellfish dishes), the garlicky *bourride* (fish soup) of Sète, or simply baked or barbecued. Tuna, anchovies and sardines dominate, while mussels and oysters are intensively farmed in the shallow *étangs*. The transition to the cooler uplands is marked by an increase in sheep-based dishes (using both meat and cheese), along with fruits, such as figs. Tripe (*tripoux*) is another staple.

In **Haut Languedoc**, mountain and forest fare, including wild mushrooms, add variety. The Cabardès, just north of Carcassonne, produces superb mutton. Northeast, in the **Tarn,** high-quality foie gras, land snails (*escargots*) and duck (*canard*) are hallmarks. Cassoulet, a local bean stew from Castelnaudary, has colonized the whole of Languedoc. Carcassonne and the Aude are home to excellent sweets, ranging from the rosemary-tinged honey of the Corbières to the nougat of Limoux and candied chestnuts, a traditional late-autumn treat.

Roussillonais cuisine is Catalan- and Spanish-influenced – obvious in the prevalence of olive oil, and adaptation of tapas and paella. The dry and grilled pork sausages (*embutits* and *botifares*) are excellent,

Miel (honey) *de Languedoc*, Narbonne ▼

Cheeses of Languedoc and Roussillon

You can find the great **cheeses** from all over France here, but it is well worth hunting out local specialities, some of which have AOC (*appellation d'origine controlée*) status. Farm-produced cheese – the best – will be found in speciality shops (a *fromagerie*, or a regional produce outlet), country markets, or from the farms themselves. The milk which produces the famous Roquefort cheese comes exclusively from an ancient breed from Lacaune. A few noteworthy cheese varieties include: **Pélardon des Cévennes**, a flavourful goats' (*chèvre*) milk cheese; the creamy but acidic **Pélardon des Corbières**, coated in natural mould; and **Le Pérail**, a white sheep's cheese from the Gard, whose taste becomes tangier as it ages.

▲ Anchovies, Collioure

▼ Cheese stall, Pézenas market

▼ Wine barrels, abbey of Valmagne

as is hearty pork-based *ollada* soup – a rural stand-by. Special occasions are celebrated with a *cargolada* – an elaborate dish of grilled land snails. Moving towards the coast, fruit reappears with the cherries of Céret, as well as almonds, peaches and pears. The coastal hills are swathed in olive trees, while fishing has long been the mainstay of seaside villages like Collioure and Port-Vendres.

The tradition of the vine

The **Romans** brought wine to Languedoc in the fourth century BC and production has continued since then. Most of the oldest and best varieties, including Gaillac and Blanquette de Limoux, were first made by medieval **monks**, whose regime permitted them a daily ration of about half a litre each. For ordinary people, wine was safer to drink than water, and was prized for

Gaillac vineyard ▲

Corbières wines ▼

Fitou grapes ▼

Top 10 wine types

▶▶ **Gaillac:** established as an AOC over a thousand years ago; best known for its whites, but also excellent reds and rosés.

▶▶ **Corbières:** one of the great AOCs of Languedoc, producing a variety of high-quality reds and whites.

▶▶ **Cabardès:** a tiny zone (AOC) near the Minervois, where Mediterranean and Atlantic grapes can be combined for unique vintages.

▶▶ **Minervois:** located north of Béziers, famous for honey-tinted whites and fruity reds.

▶▶ **Listel:** a rosé; one of the best of the *vins de sable*, the "sand wines" of the Camargue.

▶▶ **Costières de Nîmes:** well-regarded reds from the marshes of the Camargue, known for strength and subtlety.

▶▶ **Blanquette de Limoux:** a light, sparkling white, invented five centuries ago by monks near Limoux.

▶▶ **Côtes du Roussillon:** fruity and exciting reds from the *garrigues* and foothills of the Pyrenees.

▶▶ **Fitou:** a recent AOC, founded in 1948, which combines characteristics of the heavy, robust vintages of the Roussillon hills.

▶▶ **Byrrh of Thuir:** a Muscat, or sweet wine, obtained by adding alcohol to local vintages during the fermentation process. Virtually every tourist office in the region has a brochure on local vintages and a list of *domaines* which can be visited for tasting. For a general orientation, consult Ⓦwww.vins-du-roussillon.com.

medicinal and therapeutic qualities. Centuries later it had become the drink of choice, with national output peaking in 1875. By 1887, with vine-killing disease **phylloxera** ripping through France, the nation's vineyards were saved by replacing native stock with plants from the United States (raised from cuttings taken earlier from France) – the basis of the region's wine production today.

look at the city's defences: arrow-slitted battlements, and stone ducts for pouring boiling oil on would-be attackers. Those on a budget, however, should skip this steeply priced visit; a pleasant (and free) option is to walk across town from the Porte de la Gardette and take in the walls from the fields to the south. Looking back at the town from here, the tower you see on the far left is "the **tower of the salted Burgundians**", the curious nickname dating back to a grisly episode of the Hundred Years' War. When the town was seized in a raid by English-allied Burgundian forces in 1418, royalist Armagnacs came to try to retake the town. They were foiled by the strong fortifications, but one night a local citizen opened one of the smaller gates to let their forces in. Sneaking up on the sleeping Burgundian garrison, the Armagnacs slaughtered them before they knew what was happening, but rather than bury the bodies (no easy task in the fetid marshes surrounding the town), the victorious forces stuffed them into this tower, and layered them with salt so they would not putrefy – leaving them, literally, in a pickle.

Eating and drinking

On the **restaurant** front the old town fares quite respectably, with the culinary champion being the highly praised *Café de Bouzigues* at 7 rue Pasteur (☎04.66.53.93.95), where you can enjoy plentiful, elaborate *menus* on the cosy interior patio or in the comfortable dining room (main courses from €20). *Le Galion*, 24 rue Pasteur (☎04.66.53.86.41), with its unique stone-cooked meat and fish dishes, is also a solid, reasonably priced option (about €14 at lunch). Otherwise, the country **market**, held on Wednesday and Sunday mornings on the broad esplanade of avenue Frédéric Mistral (just north of the town walls), sells excellent produce and prepared dishes, and you could do much worse than buy a **picnic** and enjoy it with a bottle of the local *vin de sable*, "sand wine", on the grassy verge by the ramparts.

Tauromachie and les courses camargaises

Bulls have been raised in the Petite Camargue and the plains to its north for centuries, and for the people of the ranchlands around St-Gilles, **tauromachie** or *la bouvine* – the art of bull-handling – has come to represent a measure of virility, testament to their proud rural roots. Its significance however, is also region-wide: the growing cultural awareness of the mid-nineteenth century prompted intellectual Occitan patriots to find in it a further mark of the uniqueness of their local culture, thus investing *tauromachie* with iconic status throughout Languedoc and Roussillon. Although the imported Spanish tradition of the *corrida* (see p.188) has come to dominate, the bloodless **course camarguaise** – an expression of what locals call *La fé di biòu* ("love of the bull") – is quite distinct.

Less expensive and elaborate, the *course* is common in village *fêtes*, such as at **Uzès** or **Aigues-Mortes**. Here, the bulls (or cows) are first led to the ring (an *abrivado*), herded by a tumult of mounted *gardians* – if this takes place within a confined area, it is called an *encierro* (a "running" of the bulls). Once in the ring the animals are outfitted with a rosette and tassels suspended between their horns, and for fifteen minutes *raseteurs* (named after the hooked handgear they wear) provoke the animal into charging, and attempt to snatch the rosette or tassels without getting trampled or gored. When all is complete, the bulls are herded out with great fanfare and frenzy (the *bandido*) and back to the pen.

Aside from these entertainments, a rather more workaday manifestation of *la bouvine* has also become a staple of local spring time festivals. This is the **ferrado**, in which year-old bulls are driven from their pens by mounted *gardians*, wrestled to the ground by their colleagues on foot and then branded with a hot iron, marking them with the arms or initials of the *manade* to which they belong.

Around Aigues-Mortes

Heading northeast from Aigues-Mortes towards the Petite Camargue will take you to the curious **Tour Carbonnière**. Once the guard-post on the only land access to the medieval port-town, this 20m-high tower, perched on a rare mound of terra firma and pierced by a gate through which the road once led, is now a popular place for a picnic. In the opposite direction, heading southwest from Aigues-Mortes down to Le Grau-du-Roi you'll see the salt pans of the **Salins du Midi**, which can be visited by *petit train* (1hr 15min; €8.20) or jeep (2hr 15min; €30), with a guide explaining their history and the techniques of salt harvesting. The train is booked at the tourist office in Aigues-Mortes (see p.207), but check in advance if you need an English-speaking guide. Just beyond the salt works are the **Caves de Listel**, a wine *domaine* where locally produced "sand wine" can be sampled and purchased.

Le Grau-du-Roi and Port Camargue

LE GRAU-DU-ROI and its sister **PORT CAMARGUE** merge seamlessly into one another, comprising, between them, a bustling contrast to Aigues-Mortes. Like its fortress neighbour, Port Camargue is also a purpose-built port complex, but one dedicated to pacific hedonism rather than violent idealism. Le Grau (Occitan for "sand bar") has been a fishing village since the time of Henri IV in the sixteenth century, but it was only with the building of Port Camargue in 1969 that prosperity finally arrived. Now summer months fill the town with boaters and sun-worshippers from around the world who seek out the duned expanses stretching off towards the mouth of the Rhône in the east. If on one hand the town resembles a package-tour nightmare, on the other, there's no shortage of bars, cheap food and beachside fun. Off-season, it's another story entirely; things wind down quickly and, as happens in so many seaside towns, a certain air of cold desolation sets in.

Arrival, information and accommodation

Both **buses** and **trains** approach Le Grau/Port Camargue along the narrow sand spit leading from Aigues-Mortes and deposit passengers more or less smack in the middle of Le Grau, at the small **gare SNCF**, just off the canal on the east side. The large and efficient **tourist office**, 30 rue Rédarès (daily: May & Sept 9am–7pm; June–Aug 9am–9pm; Oct–April 9am–12.15pm & 2–6pm; ☎04.66.51.67.79, ⓦwww.ville-legrauduroi.fr), is on the east side of Le Grau, five streets south of the train station. Vélo Évasion, 1291 rue de Camargue (☎04.66.51.48.65), is one of several local outfits which rent **bicycles**. The handiest **internet** café is cyber-t @Résidence Ulysse on route Marine beside the *Hôtel Mercure*. **Markets** are held every morning (except Sunday) either at place de la République or Boucanet on the far bank of the canal (the "grau").

The dozen or so **hotels** in Le Grau and Port Camargue range from smaller and more attractive places in the old town to larger (and more expensive) beachside establishments in the port. The best of the old-town hotels is *Bellevue et d'Angleterre* at Quai Colbert, Le Grau (☎04.66.51.40.75, ⓦwww.hotelbellevueetdangleterre .com; ➍), a family-run establishment that is pleasant, airy and clean, with an excellent location and good views; all rooms have air conditioning. Over in Port Camargue, the *Oustau Camarguen*, 3 rt des Marines (☎04.66.51.51.65, ⓦwww .oustaucamarguen.com; ➐), boasts beautifully decorated rooms and many amenities, including wi-fi, air conditioning, two swimming pools, a jacuzzi, hammam and a play area for children. Another attractive choice is *Le Spinaker*, Pointe de la Presqu'île (☎04.66.53.36.37, ⓦwww.spinaker.com; ➐), a cosy hotel featuring tastefully decorated rooms, all with a private terrace and most with a sitting room, discreetly set in a green patch in the midst of the port. A garden-bar and swimming pool add the finishing touch.

There are also several **campsites**, including *L'Eden* on route de l'Espiguette (℡04.66.51.49.81, Ⓦ www.campingleden.fr; April–Oct) – a four-star, four-hundred-pitch monster-site which also rents out chalets. It has the full gamut of amenities and services including swimming pools, playgrounds and so on.

The Town

Basically, the only reason to stay in Le Grau or Port Camargue – which to all intents and purposes form a single town – is the beach. West of the mouth of the canal which passes through Le Grau's centre, a narrow band of sand, hemmed in closely by road, leads 5km west to La Grande-Motte (see p.229), whose curious triangle-shaped buildings can easily be made out on a clear day. This is the most accessible swimming area, but the best **beaches** are east of town, once you pass the busy little bay between Le Grau and Port Camargue. Just beyond Pointe de l'Espiguette, the spur of land jutting westwards on the south edge of Port Camargue, is where the real sand starts – an uninterrupted swathe of dunes stretching 5km east to the lighthouse and from there towards the horizon. The busiest area is around the **lighthouse** itself, which can be accessed by road from Le Grau, and where you will be charged a €5 fee to park. The further east you go, the more the crowds thin out, and the more laidback the beach etiquette becomes. **Nudists** have staked their claim on one stretch of beach to the east of the lighthouse, and if you are prepared to go far enough away you can find seclusion even at the busiest time of year.

Other than the seaside, the main attraction in town is the **Seaquarium** (daily: May, June & Sept 10am–8pm; July & Aug 10am–midnight; Oct–April 10am–7pm; €10.30), one of the biggest indoor aquariums in Europe, located in the Palais de la Mer between the old town and the port. The fairly steep admission price also gives access to the **Musée de la Mer** ("The Sea Museum") in the same building, which features exhibitions on local marine life and nautical history.

Le Grau and Port Camargue have facilities for a wide range of **watersports**, including outfits which rent sail-boards, sailing boats, kayaks and jet-skis, many offering instruction, as well as waterborne jousting competitions during the *fêtes* of mid-June and September. For children, there are no fewer than three nearby **water parks**. Le Grau/Port Camargue is also a big centre for **bull**-related activities, including a series of *courses* (held every weekend from the end of March to September), the climax of which is the Trophée des As competition in mid-August, and *corridas* held throughout July and August.

Eating and drinking

Eating in Le Grau and Port Camargue means **seafood**, and on every corner there is a restaurant serving up bouillabaisse, *moules frites*, *coquillages* and fish. Competition means prices are good, even if the product is often indistinguishable from one restaurant to another – most establishments have *menus* in the €12–24 range. *Le Spinaker's* restaurant (see "Accommodation", opposite) is the best in the area, with *menus* priced accordingly (from €60). Of the towns' many **bars**, the only one that stands out from the crowd is *Leon*, at 2 av de la Gare, the home turf of the local bullfighting aficionados' association.

The Vidourle valley

West of Nîmes, the border of Gard is marked by the **Vidourle valley**, whose river begins as a trickle on the southern edge of the Cévennes mountains at the northwest of the *département*. This is a quiet corner of Gard, relatively unexplored, and on the whole the villages here, some of which are impressively ancient, lack both the sights and amenities to draw travellers. Notable exceptions, though, are **Sommières**, where the breadth of the river is still spanned by a Roman bridge and watched over by the richly preserved castle of Villevieille; **Sauve**, an ancient hamlet that makes a convenient stopping-point en route from Nîmes to Ganges, in the upper Hérault valley; and further on, at the edge of the *département*, just 15km short of Ganges, **St-Hippolyte-du-Fort**.

Sommières and around

SOMMIÈRES, the largest town along the Vidourle, lying halfway between Nîmes and Montpellier, is one point on the way west from Nîmes which definitely merits a stop. Its easy, unspoilt charm seduced the English author Laurence Durrell into spending the last 33 years of his life here, and prompted him to remark, in *Spirit of Place*, that he had seen "nothing prettier". Walking through the old town or along the riverbank it's hard not to sympathize with Durrell's judgement – Sommières remains a peaceful, idyllic village. Strongly Protestant, it was all but destroyed during the Wars of Religion as it repeatedly changed hands before being conquered personally by Louis XIII in 1622. Today Sommières makes a pleasant stop for a bite to eat and a wander around, and those looking for a few days of quiet relaxation could fare a lot worse than to spend some time here, away from the crowded beaches of Le Grau and the busy streets of Nîmes. April through to September is the season for *courses camarguaises*, held on Sunday afternoons.

The **Roman bridge** which spans the river remains an integral feature of Sommières, uniting the newer town on the west bank with the old town on the east. Something of a curiosity, it was built in the first century and originally consisted of seventeen arches, but half a dozen have been gradually covered over by the encroaching town. A testament to Roman engineering, it continued to carry all of the car and truck traffic passing through the town up until the recent opening of a new bypass. At the bridge's western end, the walled old town is entered by passing through the **tour de l'horloge**, home to a ponderous seventeenth-century clock. From here you can descend to the left to the **bas marché** (lower market), now the place des Docteurs M. et G. Dax, or proceed along the course of the old Roman road to the **haut marché** (upper market), the place Jean-Jaurès – both arcaded squares still serve as market places for local farmers. From the upper market, an alley leads to the steep stairs at the foot of the town's **castle**. Not much remains of this fortress, built in the tenth century and all but destroyed by Catholic forces in 1573, but you can climb to the top of the square **tower** (July & Aug daily 4–7pm; €3) for a dramatic panorama of the Vidourle plain. Aside from the confines of the old *enceinte*, the quai Griolet, between the town walls and the riverbank, makes for a particularly evocative stroll downriver, with the geese which mill about the small dam honking emphatically at each other and passers-by.

Practicalities

Buses arriving in Sommières drop passengers off at the place de la République, along the northern wall of the old town. The **tourist office** (Mon–Sat 9am–12.30pm & 2–6/7pm; July & Aug also Sun 9.30am–12.30pm & 2–5pm; ☎46.68.80.99.30, ⓦwww.ot-sommieres.fr), on rue du Général-Bruyère, just west of the place de la République, distributes a pamphlet detailing local walking routes. The best **hotel** in Sommières is the A *L'Estelou* (☎04.66.77.71.08, ⓦhoteldelestelou.free.fr; ❹), an arty hotel set in the town's old *gare*, with a swimming pool and good service. Next best is the **chambres d'hôtes** *l'Orange* (☎04.66.77.79.94, ⓦhotel.delorange.free .fr; ❻), a seventeenth-century mansion with a pool tucked away in rue de Baumes in the shadow of the castle. The **campsite** (Easter–Sept; ☎04.66.80.33.49, Ⓔcampingmunicipal.sommieres@orange.fr) is on rue Eugène Rouché, on the west bank of the Vidourle, heading north out of town.

Auberge du Pont Romain (℡04.66.80.00.58; closed part March & part Nov), set in a former nineteenth-century cloth factory at 2 av Émile Jamais, is the best **restaurant** in the area, with excellent cuisine drawing on influences across the Midi – specialities include *foie gras* and sea bass (*menus* from €36) and rooms are available, too (❺). Next up is *L'Olivette*, 11 rue Abbé Fabre (closed Tues & Wed; ℡04.66.80.97.71), serving exciting regional cuisine and a seasonally changing *carte*, with *menus* from €25. On Saturday morning a **market** is held in place du Marché. Cyber Plus in passage des Aires has **internet**.

The Château de Villevieille

Perched on the rise that dominates the old town of Sommières, the **Château de Villevieille** (April–June & Oct Sat, Sun & hols 2–7pm; July–Sept daily 2–8pm; €8) is in **VILLEVIEILLE**, a beautiful little hamlet of stone-built houses. Owned by the same family for some 750 years, it is one of the few noble castles to escape appropriation or destruction during the Revolution (due to the lord's friendship with Voltaire and Condorcet, who interceded on his behalf). Today it boasts a sumptuous interior: the furnishings, including sixteenth-century Flemish leather "wallpaper" and the first mirror in France, are classed as national monuments, and the beds in which three kings of France and Cardinal Richelieu slept are still in their respective rooms. One of the best things about the visit is that you're shown around by members of the family – an unassuming, friendly bunch who are disarmingly frank, and genuinely welcoming.

The best of the **local walks** (detailed in the tourist office's brochure) is an excursion to the twelfth-century **church of St-Julien**, 5km north of Sommières along the right bank of the Vidourle (the turn-off is marked on the left after 3km). It makes a good stop for a picnic, though the church itself is usually closed. The villages of the *garrigues* stretching north from Sommières do not contain any sights of particular interest, but the relative tranquillity of the highways makes for very pleasant **cycling**.

Sauve

Twenty-kilometres upriver from Sommières, **SAUVE** is a quiet little town, once fortified and still presided over by the castle which was centuries ago the summer retreat of the bishops of Maguelone. The **old town** is a maze of twisting alleys, some of which are covered, and the **view** from the other side of the bridge over the Vidourle is inspiring. In recent years an influx of cosmopolitan urban refugees has revived the town, opening up some interesting, ethnic restaurants and cafés, and organizing an annual African music festival in mid-July.

Sauve's only **bus** link is with Nîmes and Ganges. It has a small seasonal **tourist office** in place René Isouard (July & Aug Mon–Sat 9am–12.30pm & 2.30–6.30pm; Sept–June Mon–Fri 9/9.30am–noon & 2–5/6pm; ℡04.66.77.57.51, ⓦwww .vallee-vidourle.com). There are two very comfortable **hotels**, both with pools: *La Magnanerie* (℡04.66.77.57.44, ⓦwww.lamagnanerie.fr; ❹) and *L'Auberge Pousaranque* (℡04.66.77.51.97, ⓦwww.lapousaranque.com; English spoken; ❸), the latter with family-sized rooms; both are about 2km east of town on the Nîmes road. There are two good **restaurants** in town: *Le Micocoulier*, at 3 place Jean Astruc, (mid-April to Sept Thurs–Sun dinner only; ℡04.66.77.57.61; *menu* €26), a cosy little *auberge* serving up intriguing *terroir*-based dishes and lavish desserts, and Anne Tourneux's *Villa Eugénie*, route de Villesèque (closed Dec–March; ℡04.66.77.05.22), which provides excellent dinners and lunches (about €30) in a garden setting. Finally, you can stock up on your own supplies at Sauve's country **market**, held on Thursdays and Saturdays in the town centre.

St-Hippolyte-du-Fort

ST-HIPPOLYTE-DU-FORT, 8km west of Sauve, like so many old cloth towns of the Cévennes, switched over to silk production in the period before the Revolution, and prospered until a nineteenth-century epidemic wiped out the mulberry plants on which the silkworms depended. These days it's a sleepy little town which has tried to reinvent itself by encouraging residents to affix individually designed sundials to their houses; the main reason for stopping here is an interesting **silk museum** (April–June & Sept–Nov Tues–Sun 10am–12.30pm & 2–6pm; July & Aug daily 10am–12.30pm & 2–6.30pm; €5), a five-minute walk west of the main square, place de la Canourgue. Displaying reconstructed silk-weaving machinery and an exhibition of live silk worms doing their stuff, the museum makes for a good stop for both adults and children.

Travel details

Trains

Trains run west from Nîmes along the coast to Sète and Béziers, and east to Provence via Beaucaire (hooking up with the north–south Rhône rail corridor), while a secondary line runs north via Alès to the Massif Central. SNCF buses may run in lieu of trains on these lines; services are reduced on Sundays and holidays. TGV stations are indicated with an asterisk.

Beaucaire/Tarascon to: Montpellier* (hourly; 1hr 05min) and Nîmes* (hourly; 25min).
Le Grau-du-Roi to: Nîmes*, via Aigues-Mortes (several daily; 50min).
Nîmes* to:
Beaucaire/Tarascon (several daily; 24min).
Paris* (hourly; 3hr+).
Perpignan*, via Montpellier*, Béziers* (connections to Bédarieux) and Narbonne* (several hourly; 2–3hr).
Toulouse*, via Vauvert, Montpellier*, Sète, Agde, Béziers* (connections to Bédarieux), Narbonne* (connections to Perpignan), Carcassonne* (connection to Quillan) and Castelnaudary (several hourly; 2hr 45min to 3hr 45min).

Buses

The principal bus routes run from Nîmes to Uzès via Remoulins and the Pont du Gard, and to Grau. Services to the upper Vidourle, Sommières and Beaucaire are less frequent, and routes are often reduced or cancelled on Sundays and holidays. In summer extra services run from Nîmes to Aigues-Mortes, Grau and La Grande-Motte. For full schedules, see ⓦ www.stdgard.com.

Aigues-Mortes to: Le Grau-du-Roi (several daily; 10min); Montpellier (several daily, increased in summer; 1hr 20min); Saintes-Maries-de-la-Mer (daily in summer; 30min).
Beaucaire to: Remoulins (daily; 45min); St-Gilles (daily; 30min).
Nîmes to: Aigues-Mortes (several daily; 1hr 5min); Beaucaire (several daily; 35min); Collias (daily; 1hr 5min); Ganges (several daily; 1hr 15min); La Grande Motte (several daily; 1hr 30min); Le Grau-du-Roi (several daily; 1hr 15min); Montpellier (daily; 1hr 30min); Pont du Gard (many daily; 45min); St-Gilles (several daily; 50min); St-Hippolyte (several daily; 1hr); Sauve (several daily; 50min); Sommières (several daily; 45min); Uzès (many daily; 30min–1hr); Vauvert (daily; 35min); Villevieille (several daily; 40min).
Quissac to: Ganges (several daily; 35min).
St-Hippolyte to: Ganges (several daily; 15min); Montpellier (daily; 1hr 45min); Sauve (several daily; 30min).
Sommières to: Montpellier (several daily; 1hr 10min); Nîmes (several daily; 45min); Villevieille (several daily; 5min).
Uzès to: Nîmes (many daily; 30min–1hr); Pont du Gard (several daily; 25min); St-Hippolyte (daily; 25min).

Montpellier and around

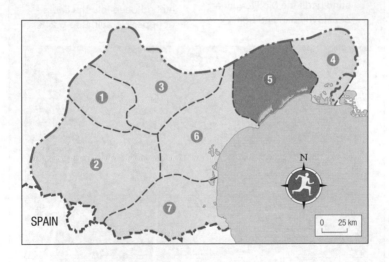

SPAIN

N

0   25 km

CHAPTER 5

Highlights

* **Place de la Comédie** This
expansive square is the
epicentre of Montpellier's
thriving cultural life.
See p.224

* **Seafood** Whether cultivated
in the Bassin de Thau or
fished from the sea, the
coastal cuisine of this area
is a gourmet's delight. See
p.228, p.231 & pp.235–236.

* **Beaches** A long swathe of
sand girds the Mediterranean
coast: you can find both

solitude and crowds here.
See pp.229–238

* **Water-jousting** This curious
Sètois sport has grown in the
last centuries into a regional
tradition. See p.233

* **Pézenas** Walk the streets of
Languedoc's old capital for
a taste of life in the age of
Molière. See p.239

* **Cirque de Navacelles** A
spectacular ox-bow canyon,
etched deep into the *causse*
of upper Hérault. See p.246

▲ Place de la Comédie, Montpellier

5

Montpellier and around

Together **Montpellier** and the surrounding country comprise the most varied and exciting region in Languedoc. The city is a capital in every sense of the word – a zesty centre of government, education, culture and economy for the whole of Languedoc-Roussillon *région* and, best of all, it is minutes from the beach. While Languedoc's **coast** may not be able to hold a candle to the likes of Provence's Côte d'Azur, if you can put up with the often strong wind, its forty kilometres or so of nearly uninterrupted sand-bar provide ample opportunities for sun-soaking and watersports – and plenty of scope for escaping the crowds, if you wish. Moreover, the seaside towns have not sunk into the irretrievable triteness of their Provençal counterparts; the continuing role of **Palavas**, **Mèze** and **Sète** as fishing ports balances their beach-town roles, endowing them with life and energy throughout the year. Just inland, **Pézenas** was the capital of Languedoc in the glory days of French Absolutism, and the many palaces that cram its old quarter preserve it as one of the most beautiful towns in the Southwest. The River Hérault gives its name to the *département* of which Montpellier is the administrative centre, and dominates its **interior**. Less travelled than the coast, its beautiful highlands are home to a wealth of natural wonders and historic sites. Dusty and provincial **Clermont-l'Hérault** acts as a gateway to the dramatically varied landscape at nearby **Lac du Salagou**, while **Lodève** – still lorded over by its hulking medieval cathedral – is the best place to set off for the breathtaking **Cirque de Navacelles**. East of the cirque, the quiet town of **Ganges** sits on the banks of the Hérault at the point where the river completes its descent from the high Cévennes mountains to the north; just downstream you can visit one of France's most celebrated caverns, the **Grotte des Demoiselles**, before following the dramatic Hérault gorge southwest past the ancient monastic centre of **St Guilhem le Désert**, or bearing due south towards the towering **Pic-St-Loup**, whose wooded outline can be seen for miles around.

Getting around by **public transport** in the region around Montpellier is easy. The city sits on the main coastal rail artery, uniting it with Sète to the west and Nîmes to the east, while the area of greater Montpellier, the *agglomération*, is served by the city's transport network (TAM), whose far-ranging buses reach Palavas and Maguelone on the coast. Inland, the lack of train lines is compensated by regular bus services connecting the bigger towns. Only the smaller villages, such as the hamlets around Lac du Salagou and Navacelles, do not have useful bus services; to explore these you'll need a car or bike, or be prepared to hitch-hike.

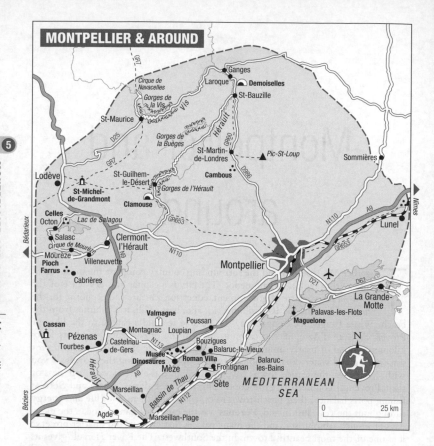

Montpellier

Home to a youthful and dynamic university culture and a host of artistic festivals and events, **MONTPELLIER** is the most exciting city in Languedoc proper. In addition, it boasts a beautiful architectural fusion of the classical and the avant-garde, and is even close enough to the Mediterranean to have the beach within reach of public transport. With fine museums, a charming old centre and a bouncy rhythm of life, Montpellier offers an ideal place for either a longer, relaxing stay, or a whirlwind two-day tour of its highpoints, notably the many Renaissance **mansions** of the old town.

Montpellier is a medieval city, and can't claim the same venerable Roman past of rival Nîmes. Starting off as a market town for nearby **Maguelone** in the tenth century, in 1204 it was acquired by marriage by the count-kings of Barcelona, who favoured it as a residence – both Jaume I "the Conqueror" and his son Jaume II of Mallorca were born here. By the late thirteenth century it had become second only to Paris in size, thanks partly to its famous **university**, and a major centre for medicine, law and the arts. With Jaume I's posthumous division of his realms, the city was incorporated into the Kingdom of Mallorca until 1349, when Jaume II sold it – afflicted with plague, banditry and famine – to the French Crown. In the era that followed the city was sustained by its university, through whose doors passed the pioneering Renaissance poet **Petrarch** and, later, the satirist **Rabelais**, who received his doctorate here in 1537. Despite the transfer of the bishopric of Maguelone here in 1537, Montpellier became strongly **Protestant** in the sixteenth and seventeenth centuries, losing many of its old church buildings in factionalist struggles, and was only saved from destruction at the hands of Louis XIII, who had personally waged war on the Huguenot stronghold in 1622, by an eleventh-hour truce.

The city's leftist tradition began with a bang in 1789, and the revolutionary anthem known as "La Marseillaise" was in fact first sung by a local medical student. Another wave of serious unrest came during the wine crisis of 1907, during which it was the strongest centre of popular agitation in reaction to plummeting grape prices (see p.267). The last shake-up was in 1962: with the dismantling of the Algerian colony, thirteen thousand French (*pieds-noirs*) and Maghrebi (*harki*) refugees arrived in the city, two groups whose integration into Montpellier society generated considerable friction, but whose presence brought a revitalizing dynamism to the city. Not long after this, Montpellier became the official capital of the administrative *région* of Languedoc-Roussillon.

By tradition solidly socialist, Montpellier has garnered kudos for its ecological initiatives, notably the development of its public transport system and most recently the effective banning of cars from the historic centre. Now you can stroll around the medieval city soaking up the atmosphere, free from exhaust fumes, tooting horns and traffic.

Arrival, information and city transport

The city's **airport** (Ⓦwww.montpellier.aeroport.fr) is 8km southeast of the centre, beside the Étang de Mauguio: from here a **navette** (timed for flights; 15min; €5.50) runs to a stop on rue de Crète beside the Antigone (by the Léon Blum tram stop), or a **taxi** (Ⓣ04.67.20.65.29) costs €14–30. The **gare SNCF** (no left luggage) and **gare routière** are next to each other at the southern end of rue Maguelone – it's a five-minute walk along this street to the central place de la Comédie. If you're driving, the simplest option for **parking** is to head for the "Comédie" car park, under the famous *place* – if, however, you want to avoid paying the hefty daily rate, outlying public car parks charge only €4 for parking (including a return tram fare for each passenger).

The main **tourist office** (Mon–Fri 9.30am–7.30pm, Sat 9.30am–6pm, Sun 9.30am–1pm & 2.30–6pm; Ⓣ04.67.60.60.60, Ⓦwww.ot-montpellier.fr) is on the northern edge of place de la Comédie, with seasonal branches at the gare SNCF (July–Sept Mon–Fri 9am–1pm & 2–6.45pm, Sat 9.30am–1pm & 2–5.30pm) and in the Antigone, at 78 av de Pirée (April–Oct Mon–Fri 9am–1pm & 2–6pm). All these offices can reserve the official **guided tours** (July–Sept Mon–Fri 10am & Sat 5pm; advance reservation obligatory; English audio guide; €7) that give you access to certain sights that are normally off-limits, such as the medieval *mikveh* (Jewish ritual bath) or the interior of the Arc de Triomphe. They also sell one-, two- and three-day "**City Cards**" (covering buses and trams, admission to many city sights and other discounts; see box, p.221), as well as handing out the free student guide *L'Indic*, the fortnightly *Sortir*, with entertainment listings, and *Montpellier Côté Coeur*, which also lists shops.

Montpellier's eco-friendly **tramlines**, which converge at the Corum, are the signature of its efficient and modern **public transport** system, run by TAM (short for "Transports de l'Agglomération de Montpellier"; Ⓦwww.tam-way.com). **Tickets** valid on trams and buses (single €1.30) can be purchased from drivers or

5

Festivals in and around Montpellier

Most of the action in Hérault *département* is centred on Montpellier, which is renowned for its cultural vitality, hosting a range of annual **festivals**. Also worth looking out for are the *fêtes* on the coast, which invariably feature the local tradition of **water-jousting** – throughout July and August in Palavas and Sète (see box, p.233) – as well as *tauromachie* (both Spanish and Camargue styles; see box, p.209). The uplands of the Hérault valley also have a few small local festivals. Where no specific information number is given, contact the relevant tourist office for details.

Feb or March Pézenas: *Carnaval*. Lent kicks off with a three-day Mardi Gras (Shrove Tuesday) festival here, featuring folkloric displays and a parade led by the local totem-animal, Le Poulain.

May Pézenas: *Cavalcade*. A popular festival with a bustling handicrafts market, culminating in a medieval period-costume parade led by Le Poulain. Held over one weekend in May.

Late June to mid-July Montpellier: *Montpellier Danse* ☎04.67.60.83.60, ⊛www .montpellierdanse.com. A three-week festival of traditional music and dance from around the world, held in various venues around town.

First weekend in July Sète: *Fête de la St-Pierre*. Traditional fishermen's festival with a religious procession, street party and jousting.

Second Sun in July Palavas: *Fête de la Mer* ☎04.67.07.73.34, ⊛www.palavas lesflots.com. Religious procession and blessing of fishing boats, followed by jousting, fireworks and *tauromachie*. Also night-time *joutes* on July 14.

Mid- to end July Montpellier: *Electromind* ⊛www.electromind.fr. The Languedocian version of Barcelona's *Sónar*, held outdoors at the beachside Espace Grammont, and featuring an impressive line-up of DJs and musicians from France, Europe and North America.

Mid- to end July Montpellier: *Le Festival de Radio-France et de Montpellier* ☎04.67.02.02.01, ⊛www.festivalradiofrancemontpellier.com. Music festival repre-senting styles from classical to jazz. Half the concerts are free.

July 21–23 St-Guilhem: *Fête*. Local town *fête*, featuring costumes, music and tradi-tional market.

Late July Bassin de Thau: *Festival de Thau* ☎04.67.18.70.83, ⊛www.festivaldethau .com. Annual week-long World Music festival, held in Mèze, Marseillan, Loupian and Frontignan. Recent headliners have included Salif Keita and Willy DeVille.

Aug 15 Palavas: Feast of the Assumption. Water-jousting.

End Aug Sète: *Fête de St-Louis*. One-day extravaganza of fireworks, street parties, jousting and medieval pageantry.

Sept 29 to Oct 1 Palavas: *Feria d'Automne* ☎06.61.46.68.85. Local Camarguais-style festival of horsemanship and *tauromachie*.

at the vending kiosks, while **passes** (one-day pass €3.20; weekly pass €11.10) are available at the TAM office, 27 rue Maguelone. Unless you're planning on visiting specific outlying sites, however, you won't need to use the system, as the centre of town is compact and eminently walkable.

Accommodation

With its roles as a student and administrative centre, Montpellier has abundant **hotel** facilities in all price ranges. Most accommodation is concentrated in the compact grid of streets between the *gares* and the place de la Comédie, but there are options in the old town, too, which are worth searching out.

The closest **campsite** to Montpellier is *L'Oasis Palavasienne* (April to mid-Oct; ☎04.67.15.11.61, @www.oasis-palavasienne.com), just south of town on the D21 to Palavas (bus #28), though you'll have much more choice in Palavas itself (see p.230).

Abasun 13 rue Maguelone ☎04.67.58.36.80, @www.abasunhotel montpelliercentre.com. Centrally located and newly renovated, this basic and functional hotel is a bargain for those on a budget. ❷

des Étuves 24 rue des Étuves ☎04.67.60.78.19, @www.hoteldesetuves.fr. Simple, spotless rooms in the south of the old city, all with en-suite bathrooms, free wi-fi and TV. ❷

Le Guilhem 18 rue J-J-Rousseau ☎04.67.52.90.90, @www.leguilhem .com. Beautifully restored sixteenth-century townhouse whose cheerful rooms mostly overlook quiet gardens, and with a sunny breakfast terrace. Free wi-fi. A good alternative to the *du Palais*, if full. ❻

HI hostel Impasse Petite Corraterie, off rue des Écoles Laïques ☎04.67.60.32.22, @www.fuaj.org. Fifteen minutes' walk from place de la Comédie in a renovated old building, this hostel has a bar, billiards room and a luggage check; the curfew is at 2am. Closed mid-Dec to mid-Jan. Dorm beds €15.50, some doubles ❷

L'Hôtel 6 rue Jules-Ferry ☎04.99.13.33.44, @www.l-hotel-montpellier.com. Newest and best of the station-side hotels – modern, clean and soundproof, with good amenities, including free wi-fi, flat-screen TV and a/c. Some rooms have bathtubs (others only showers). ❹

Le Jardin des Sens 11 av St-Lazare ☎04.67.79.63.38, @www.jardindessens .com. The best of the upper-bracket hotels, and the epitome of restrained and tasteful luxury, the four-star *Le Jardin* boasts a swimming pool, elegant rooms and one of the region's most acclaimed restaurants. ❾

Majestic 4 rue du Cheval-Blanc ☎04.67.66.26.85, ©majesticmontpellier@yahoo.fr. Very basic but clean, quiet and central, with rooms with en-suite showers. Larger rooms available too. ❷

Le Mistral 25 rue Boussairolles ☎04.67.58.45.25, @www.hotel-le-mistral.com. Comfortable and clean, an excellent economy-range option, offering satellite TV, free wi-fi and garage parking (€5 extra). ❸

New Hôtel du Midi 22 bd Victor-Hugo ☎04.67.92.69.61, @www.new-hotel.com. A rather pricy, luxury option with a great view of the Comédie. Service is top-notch, although its amenities are no match for those of the *Jardin des Sens*. ❾

du Palais 3 rue du Palais ☎04.67.60.47.38, @www.hoteldupalais-montpellier.fr. Tastefully renovated eighteenth-century mansion on the west side of the old town, blending modern and antique touches. Cosy rooms, most with en-suite facilities. An excellent mid-range option. Free wi-fi. ❹

Royal Hôtel 8 rue Maguelone ☎04.67.92.13.36, @www.royalhotelmontpellier.com. Good amenitIes

Essentials

Bike rental Montpellier's municipal Vélomagg (@www.tam-way.com) stations around town rent bikes for four hours (€1) and by the day (€2).

Discount card The "City Card", available at the tourist office, is good for one to three days (€15–28) and offers free public transport, museum entry, a free guided tour, and assorted discounts.

Internet access There are lots of cybercafés around town, including Cybersurf, 22 pl du Millénaire in Antigone (Mon–Fri 8am–9pm, Sat & Sun 10am–6pm).

Laundry 11 rue Sérane (daily 7.30am–10pm).

Markets Covered markets: Castellane, rue de la Loge, and Laïssac, pl A. Laïssac (both Mon–Sat 7.30am–1pm). Outdoor markets (Mon–Sat 7.30am–1pm): bd des Arceaux (organic food); av de Heidelberg (flea market, also Sun); cours Gambetta (food and clothes); pl de la Comédie (food and clothes); and Antigone (Wed & Sun only).

Taxis Allo Taxi d'Oc ☎04.67.47.26.80; Taxi 2000 ①04.67.03.45.45; Taxi à Montpellier ☎04.67.20.35.20; Taxi Bleu or 5 ACTM ☎04.67.03.20.00.

(including cable TV) in this three-star hotel between the Comédie and the *gare*, with an old-world ambience. ❺
Suitehotel 45 av du Pirée ☎04.67.20.57.57, ⓦwww.suite-hotel.com. This new three-star hotel in the Antigone offers roomy suites with all mod cons and excellent service. Amenities include free wi-fi and a swimming pool. There are discounts for weekends and for stays of four nights or more. Great for families. ❼

The Town

More or less everything you will want to see in Montpellier can be found in or on the edge of its compact and largely pedestrian **old town**, which spreads out north and west from the **place de la Comédie**, at the heart of the city. Bounded on the

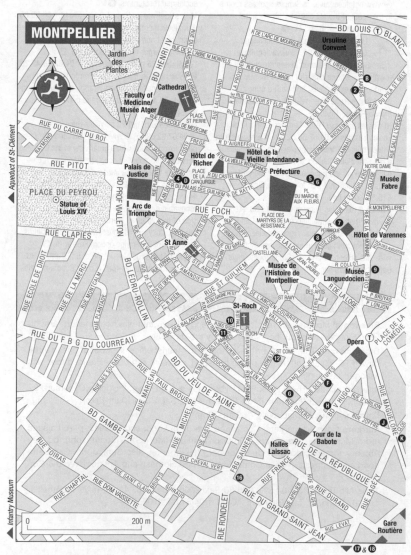

◀ Aqueduct of St-Clément

◀ Infantry Museum

0   200 m

north by the boulevards Pasteur and Louis Blanc, on the east by the **Champ de Mars** park and on the west by the **Jardin des Plantes** and **place du Peyrou**, the terminus of the town's old aqueduct, the old centre is marked off into two unequal halves by the avenue made up of rues de la Loge and Foch. The north side was the most prosperous part, as the **mansions** which pepper it testify, and is also home to the city's old university buildings and **cathedral**. The crowded lanes of the south side were inhabited by the city's workers and artisans; its buildings are correspondingly less showy. East of the place de la Comédie you'll find the sprawling **Antigone** development, Montpellier's boldly designed but sterile modern quarter. Beyond the old town are mixed commercial and residential quarters, which

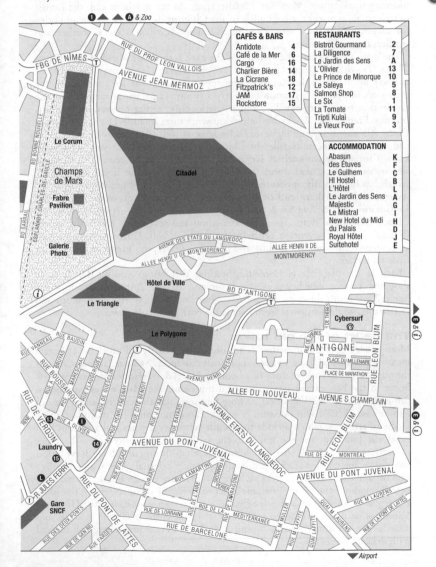

CAFÉS & BARS
Antidote	4
Café de la Mer	6
Cargo	16
Charlier Bière	14
La Cicrane	18
Fitzpatrick's	12
JAM	17
Rockstore	15

RESTAURANTS
Bistrot Gourmand	2
La Diligence	7
Le Jardin des Sens	A
L'Olivier	13
Le Prince de Minorque	10
Le Saleya	5
Salmon Shop	8
Le Six	1
La Tomate	11
Tripti Kulai	9
Le Vieux Four	3

ACCOMMODATION
Abasun	K
des Étuves	F
Le Guilhem	C
HI Hostel	B
L'Hôtel	L
Le Jardin des Sens	A
Majestic	G
Le Mistral	I
New Hotel du Midi	H
du Palais	D
Royal Hôtel	J
Suitehotel	E

provide interesting backdrops to stroll past, if lacking in significant sights, while further out still, various **châteaux** ring the town.

Place de la Comédie and the Champs de Mars park

The **place de la Comédie** is a broad plaza that was opened up in the mid-nineteenth century with the inauguration of the then new **opera hall** at its southern end. Although superseded by the new Corum hall, the gaily domed building still hosts music and theatre performances. Today the *place* to its northeast is a busy crossroads for both pedestrians and trams, and is lined on each side by a series of old cafés and fast-food joints, although it retains its traditional role as morning marketplace (Mon–Sat 7.30am–1pm). At the northern end, the tourist office's pavilion marks the beginning of the **Champs de Mars**, a park with both a formal promenade and a network of paths and ponds which attract sunbathers and strollers in good weather.

The main attraction in the vicinity of the park is the huge **Musée Fabre** (Tues, Thurs, Fri & Sun 10am–6pm, Wed 1–9pm & Sat 11am–6pm; €6), situated halfway up its west side. Recently reopened after a decade-long makeover, the museum's important collection of nearly a thousand paintings ranges from the renaissance to the present day, and is particularly strong on post-eighteenth-century French art. Works by better-known names include David's *Portrait of Doctor Alphonse Leroy* and Delacroix's *Fantasia*, as well as pieces by Dufy, Maillol and the local Frédéric Bazille. In addition to these, there are works by well-known foreign artists such as Reynolds, Zurbarán and Rubens. The museum also owns a palace next door, the **Hôtel Cabrières** (same hours and ticket), which has luxuriously appointed rooms in eighteenth- and nineteenth-century styles. At the northern end of the park looms the concrete-and-pink-granite **Le Corum** (July & Aug Sat & Sun 2–7pm; Sept–June Sat 2–7pm), designed by Claude Vasconi to house the city's two-thousand-seat opera hall – the Opéra Berlioz – plus a convention centre and exhibition hall. During opening hours you can poke around the building and take in the sweeping **views** of the old city from its terrace.

Back at the place de la Comédie, heading east brings you to the Triangle shopping centre, which marks the beginning of the Antigone development (see p.226); south down to the *gares* is a bustling neighbourhood of shops and restaurants, while northwest from here is the core of the old town.

The heart of the old town

Montpellier's greatest attraction is its **old town**, richly adorned by elaborate mansion facades and home to a series of small museums. At 7 rue Jacques-Coeur is the impressive fifteenth-century facade of the Hôtel des Trésoriers de France, now home to the best of the city's historical museums, the **Musée Languedocien** (Mon–Sat 2/2.30–5.30/6pm; €6), whose fine seventeenth-century courtyard can also be visited (€2). This museum is worth a look not only for its collection of medieval artefacts, which include thirteenth-century ceramics and a curious lead baptismal font, but for the impressively vaulted Gothic interior of the main exhibition room. You'll also find luxurious Flemish tapestries, pre-Revolution furniture – including a seventeenth-century Italian celestial globe – and a collection of *faïence* (tin-glazed pottery) whose manufacture was an important industry here throughout the 1700s. Just northwest of here, the compact, triangular place Pétrarque is closed in by a clutch of palaces, the largest of which is the **Hôtel de Varennes**, at no. 2, whose ground floor is almost entirely Gothic in style, and includes the beautiful fourteenth-century **salle de Pétrarque**, a long hall vaulted with delicate stone ribs.

South of place Pétrarque, the lively café-lined place Jean-Jaurès is home to the **Musée de l'Histoire de Montpellier** (Tues–Sat 10.30am–12.30pm & 1.30–6pm; €1.50), set in the ancient Romanesque crypt of the Notre-Dame-des-Tables church. In this area you'll find a concentration of mansions, particularly on **rue du Cannau** (north of the colourful place du Marché aux Fleurs), whose string of facades, decked out with ornately carved doorways and casement windows, attest to the wealth of this street – a prestigious neighbourhood three centuries ago. Further west, the **Hôtel de la Vieille Intendance**, the former governor's mansion at no. 9 on the street of the same name, is a stately palace which was later home of the philosopher Auguste Comte and writer Paul Valéry. Close by, the larger **place de la Canourgue** served as the eighteenth-century administrative hub of the city. Its eastern side is dominated by the huge **Hôtel de Richer**, the former town hall, whose broad, square courtyard is decorated in the finest Neoclassical pomp of the late 1700s.

The cathedral and around

On the north side of the old city sits Montpellier's **cathedral** (Mon–Sat 9.30am–noon & 2.30–7pm, Sun 9am–1pm), with its strikingly bizarre entrance, a porch flanked by two straight towers capped with a high conical roof, dating back to its fourteenth-century foundation. Next door in rue de l'École de Médecine is the **Faculty of Medicine**, a stately Neoclassical faculty building which is home to the **Musée Atger** (Mon, Wed & Fri 1.30–5.45pm; free), named after the local collector Xavier Atger, whose acquisitions include paintings by important Flemish artists such as Rubens and Van Dyck.

At the end of rue de l'École de Médecine, which is lined with nineteenth-century university buildings, the **Jardin des Plantes** (July & Aug noon–8pm; Sept–June 2–5pm; free) marks the transition to the new town. The garden dates back to 1593, when it was founded by order of the former Huguenot king, Henry IV, in order to cultivate and study herbal remedies. Today, you can stroll orderly lines of botanical specimens, cool down beside the pond of its English garden, and wander among tropical and Mediterranean trees – a quiet respite from Montpellier's normal bustle.

Place du Peyrou and south of rue Foch

Rising above the Jardin des Plantes on the edge of the old *enceinte*, the flat paved expanse of the **place du Peyrou** stretches west, dominated by a Roman-style equestrian statue of the "Emperor" Louis XIV – an 1838 replacement of the original statue of 1692, which was destroyed during the Revolution. The great bronze king is frozen in motionless stride towards the **Arc de Triomphe**, opposite the eastern end of the park, at the head of rue Foch. The arch, designed on the ancient Roman model, consists of a single, free-standing entryway, whose sides are covered with low-relief sculptures celebrating the military victories of the "Sun King" over the Dutch and the Huguenots, the revocation of the Edict of Nantes and the construction of the Canal du Midi. Behind Louis' statue, at the western end of the place du Peyrou, an octagonal, colonnaded pavilion marks the terminus of the 880m-long aqueduct of St-Clément, built in the late eighteenth century to carry water to the city from a nearby spring.

From place du Peyrou, passing through the triumphal arch you'll come face to face with the striking Neoclassical **Palais de Justice**, which features a Doric-columned facade capped by an impressive tympanum in relief. The nearby plain stone nineteenth-century **church of St-Anne** is only really of interest for the occasional art exhibitions it houses; it's also the epicentre of the "L'Isle aux Créateurs", a collective of a dozen or so designers of decorative goods who have set up workshop-boutiques throughout the zone. South of the church on rue de l'Huile, you'll enter the city's old **artisanal quarter**, containing houses that survive from as early as the thirteenth century.

This neighbourhood is bounded on the east by rue St-Guilhem, a street of functional, quotidian shops, beyond which you'll find a succession of squares – good territory for restaurant-hunting. At the northernmost of these, place St-Ravy, are the scant remains of the **palace** of the kings of Mallorca. To the south and east you'll come upon a final small *place*, set in the shadow of the **Tour de la Babote**, the only surviving portion of the town's twelfth-century defences. Crowned by an observatory in the 1700s it was also incorporated into the same semaphore system used at the Tour Chappe in Castelnaudary (see p.87).

The Antigone

Cut off from the main part of the old city by the sprawl of the Le Polygone shopping complex and defended on the north and south by a whizzing expressway, the **Antigone**, twenty-first-century Montpellier, is a world apart from that of the eighteenth. Laid out on an esplanade stretching east from the city for almost 2km, this self-contained and car-free development of residences, shops, services and restaurants is endowed with an uncompromising unity of form and design. The Catalan architect **Ricardo Bofill** has created a massive low-rise building complex, drawing largely on Classical motifs, including smooth columns, triangular window lintels and roof cornices reminiscent of ancient temples, but with a net effect that looks somehow futuristic–Georgian. The first section, the westernmost part of the complex, was inaugurated in 1984, and the latest, a library designed by Paris-born architect Paul Chemetov, opened in 2000. The whole thing, a striking if not entirely convincing Utopian landscape of broad cypress-lined courtyards, culminates in the monumental Esplanade de l'Europe on the bank of the River Lez, across which it gazes at the recently inaugurated Hôtel de Région, the governmental seat of Languedoc-Roussillon. It's an ambitious project, and you cannot deny it a certain graceful beauty, but it is somehow disappointing – perhaps it just needs some weathering to shake off the air of contrived novelty.

The suburbs

There are a number of sights scattered around the outskirts of the city. To the north, the city's eighty-hectare **Parc Zoologique de Lunaret** (daily: July & Aug 9am–7pm; Sept–June 9am–5pm; free) is a sprawling park with nearly 10km of paths leading through to spacious animal enclosures (reached on bus #9 to "René Bouginol"). A little further north, at 951 av d'Agropolis, **Agropolis** (Mon & Wed–Fri 10am–12.30pm & 2–6pm, Sat & Sun 2–6pm; €5) is a multimedia museum exploring the history of agriculture and food, with the emphasis on Languedoc; its interactive displays make it an entertaining stop for children (there's a shuttle bus from tram stop "St-Eloi"). To the south, in Lattes (bus #18 to "le Stade"), an **archeological museum** (Mon & Wed–Fri 10am–noon & 1.30–5.30pm, Sat & Sun 2–6pm; €2.50) contains important relics from the Greco-Roman settlement, Lattara.

The main attraction of Montpellier's hinterland, however, is the series of **follies** raised by the town's wealthiest citizens as summerhouses in the 1700s. In a game of social one-upmanship, merchants and aristocrats vied to construct ever more luxurious estates, a few of which have been opened to the public, and are accessible by city transport. To the east of the centre at 2235 route de Vaugières (tram #1 to "Odysseum"), the eighteenth-century **Château de la Mogère** (June–Sept daily 2.30–6.30pm; Oct–May Sat & Sun 2.30–6pm or by appointment; €5; ⓦ visite -guidee.lamogere.fr) is one of the most sumptuous mansions, and contains a considerable collection of period furniture and artwork. The oldest and most elegant, however, is the **Château de Flaugergues** (July & Aug daily 2.30–7pm; Oct–May by appointment; €7.50; ⓦ www.flaugergues.com), north of la Mogère at 1744 av Albert Einstein (bus #12 to "Louis Lépine"). Still owned by the original family who built the palace in 1696, the luxurious apartments, decked out with contemporary tapestries and objets d'art, and accompanying formal French gardens, sit amid the vineyards of its *domaine* (Mon–Sat 9am–12.30pm & 2.30–7pm; July & Aug also Sun 2.30–7pm; €5).

Eating, drinking and nightlife

No other city in Languedoc and Roussillon, with the possible exception of much larger Toulouse, can compete with Montpellier in terms of either dining possibilities or cultural life. **Eating** in Montpellier is a pleasure, with local cuisine combining the bounty of the sea, the rich garden produce of the plain and the meats of the hills. Fish lovers should look out for the savoury, tomato-based seafood stew known as *tielle*, or crab-stuffed squid tails (*enocrnets farcis*) while *gâteau d'aubergine* (aubergine cake) makes a delicious meat-free option. Far from the *manades* of Gard, pork makes a triumphant reappearance here as sausage, cured ham and pâté, with duck and goose in strong supporting roles. Practically all the squares in Montpellier's old town have a restaurant or two, so if you don't feel like searching out something special, just wander around and pick from among the many terraces.

The **nightlife** in Montpellier is also excellent, with an incredible number of **bars**, **clubs** and **live music** options. You'll be able to find everything you need in the old town and its environs, but die-hard clubbers will want to head for the string of nightclubs (*boîtes de nuit*) on the route de Palavas in Lattes. Fortunately, many of these are served by l'Amigo, TAM's night bus (till 5am), so you may not have to take a taxi home (TAM can provide a list of nightclubs served by the route). These clubs are supplemented by a profusion of **cafés littéraires** on a variety of themes: *Le César*, 17 pl du Nombre d'Or (ⓣ 04.67.20.27.02), holds two regular *cafés littéraires* – an astrology colloquium on the third Thursday of each month (8.30pm), and a feminist one once a month (days vary, 6pm). **Concerts**, ranging from chamber music to classical, as well as opera, are held at L'Opéra de la Comédie (ⓣ 04.67.60.19.99, ⓦ www.opera-montpellier.com), L'Opéra Berlioz in Le Corum (ⓣ 04.67.61.66.16), which also serves as a major venue for pop music, and at other venues – the tourist office has a complete list. The **theatre** scene thrives here too, with nearly a dozen regular stages scattered throughout town. Major performances are held at the Opéra, while you'll also find informal *cafés-théâtre* like *La Cicrane*, on 9 rue St-Ursule (ⓣ 04.67.60.74.11, ⓦ www.theatre-cicrane.com). The Diagonal complex at place Pierre-Enaidel (ⓣ 04.67.58.44.74) is the best place to go for **cinema**.

Restaurants

Bistrot Gourmand / pl de la Chapelle Neuve
ⓣ 04.67.66.08.09. Excellent-value Languedocian cuisine (both inland and coastal varieties) with a wonderful shaded terrace. The *pâtés de canard* are particularly notable, and the wine list is excellent. *Menus* €12 at lunch and €10 at dinner. Closed off-season Sun & Wed.

La Diligence 2 pl Pétrarque
ⓣ 04.67.66.12.21. Atmospheric, vaulted medieval setting for innovative French dishes

infused with Asian influence. Look out for cod cooked in banana leaf and mango fried duck. *Menus* are €36–60 (€20 at lunch), and offer a good-value dip into the finest French cuisine. Closed Sat lunch, Sun & Mon.

Le Jardin des Sens 11 av St-Lazare
ⓣ 04.67.79.63.38. One of the top restaurants in Languedoc and universally acclaimed as Montpellier's best, just north of Le Corum. Excellent *terroir*-based creations of the famed Pourcel brothers, served in elegant

227

surroundings. *Menus* €50–190. Closed Sun, Mon & Wed lunch.

L'Olivier 12 rue Aristide-Olivier ☎04.67.92.86.28. Pretty little restaurant north of the station offering excellent-value and imaginative cuisine, such as salmon with oyster tartare, and leg of rabbit stuffed with wild mushrooms. *Menus* €32–47. Closed Sun, Mon and Aug.

Le Prince de Minorque 1 rue des Tessiers ☎04.67.66.05.77. Great-value Mediterranean food, in a cheerful setting with a streetside patio. Solid *plats du jour* at only €8, and *menus* from €16 featuring grilled meat and fish. Closed Sun (but open Sun eves in summer).

Le Saleya Pl du Marché aux Fleurs ☎04.67.60.53.92. In fine weather, join the locals at the outdoor tables to feast on a daily selection of market-fresh fish and regional fare for €12. A long-standing Montpellier institution. Closed Sun and when it's raining.

Salmon Shop 5 rue de la Petite-Loge. Novel "mountain cabin" interior offering oak-smoked salmon main courses in half a dozen guises from €14 to €30 (including wine). Just off place Jean-Jaurès. Closed Sun lunch.

Le Six 55 bis rue de la Cavalerie ☎04.99.58.18.91. Elegant, modern restaurant featuring a range of dishes, from fresh shellfish to specialities of Aveyron. Open for dinner till 11.30pm with *menus* from €15 to €25.50 and a lunch special for €10. Closed Sat & Sun lunch.

La Tomate 8 rue Four de Flammes. Unmissable with its tomato-coloured facade, this restaurant serves solid, *terroir* standards from only €9 at lunch and from €13 at dinner. Closed Sun and Mon.

Tripti Kulai 20 rue Jacques-Coeur. Quirky, friendly women-run vegetarian/vegan restaurant. Dishes with oriental flair, including a good choice of salads, from €9. The lassis and home-made chai are superb. Closed Sun.

Le Vieux Four 59 rue de l'Aiguillerie ☎04.67.60.55.95. Carnivores will love this cosy, candlelit place specializing in *grillades au feu de bois* – meats roasted on an open spit. The *carte* is dominated by beef, but the *andouillette* (offal sausage) is excellent. *Menus* €14–25. Eves only; closed Sun in summer.

Cafés, bars and clubs

Antidote Pl de la Canourgue ⊛www.lantidot.fr. This snappy bar attracts the arty set. Techno-music dominates, and there are occasional art exhibitions. Mon–Thurs till 1am, Fri & Sat 2am.

Café de la Mer 5 pl du Marché-aux-Fleurs. Popular gay-friendly establishment with a busy terrace. Mon–Sat 8am–1am, Sun 3pm–1am, open till 2am in July & Aug.

Cargo Pl St-Denis ☎04.67.92.56.05. Montpellier's best nightclub and live venue for blues, funk and soul. A ten-minute walk south of the old town. Tues–Sat 7pm–1am. Entry free, up to €4.50 at weekends, or for concerts or special events.

Charlier Bière 22 rue A. Ollivier. Grungy beer-bar for under-25s. The slogan "Helping ugly people have sex since 1862" says it all.

Fitzpatrick's 5 pl St-Côme. The place to go if you're craving Guinness. Often has live music. Daily 10am–1am.

JAM (Jazz Action Montpellier) 100 rue Ferdinand-Lesseps ☎04.67.58.30.30, ⊛www .lejam.com. Jazz bar, concert venue and home of the regular *café littéraire* "Ethnologue" on the first Wed of month (8pm–midnight).

Rockstore 20 rue Verdun ⊛www.rockstore.fr. Legendary Montpellier club and concert venue. You can't miss the half-Cadillac protruding from the front of this former Calvinist temple. Free except for concerts. Mon–Sat 6pm–4am.

Listings

Books English books at Book in Bar, 8 rue du Bras de Fer, and Book Shop, 4 rue de l'Université.

Car rental ADA, 58 bis bd Clémenceau ☎04.67.58.34.35; Avis, 900 av des Prés d'Arènes ☎04.67.92.51.92; Europcar, 6 rue Jules-Ferry ☎04.67.06.89.00; Hertz, 18 rue Jules-Ferry ☎04.67.58.65.18; Rent-a-Car, 111 av de Palavas ☎04.67.22.42.52.

Hospital Centre Hospitalier de Montpellier, 555 rte de Ganges (☎04.67.33.93.02) – take bus #16 from the *gare* to "Route de Ganges" or the tram to "Hôpital Lapeyronie".

Medical emergencies ☎04.67.22.81.67 or ☎15.

Pharmacy Pharmacie de la Comédie, 1 rue de Verdun.

Police Hôtel de Ville ☎04.67.34.71.00.

Regional products Maison Régionale des Vins et des Produits du Terroir, 34 rue St-Guilhem (Mon–Sat 9am–8pm).

Swimming Piscine Olympique d'Antigone, av Jacques-Quartier (☎04.67.15.63.00; tram to "Léon Blum") is part of a massive indoor swimming and sports complex.

The coast: La Grande-Motte to Marseillan-Plage

From its narrowing point at Le Grau-du-Roi, south of Nîmes, the Petite Camargue trails off westwards in fits and starts – a string of salty *étangs* and scrubby flats populated by birds and bulls respectively, passing close by Montpellier and continuing as far as Agde (see p.275). The easternmost town along this stretch is **La Grande-Motte**, a bizarre 1960s planned resort. The other towns along this coast – **Palavas**, **Sète** and **Mèze** – have been fishing centres for generations, and their maritime heritage lives on in popular local traditions, such as the water-joust. Only **Maguelone**, once a bustling port, was unable to stand the test of the ages, and has been reduced to an ancient and romantically sited **cathedral**. Extremely popular and flooded with people in the summer months, all of these towns offer the makings of a good beach holiday, but they are far from being merely soulless seaside resorts.

La Grande-Motte

Separated by only a few kilometres of sandy beach from Le Grau-du-Roi to the east and less than 20km southeast of Montpellier's centre, **LA GRANDE-MOTTE** is undoubtedly the oddest resort town on the French Mediterranean. A Sixties-era beachside version of Montpellier's Antigone development, this "futuristic" planned community, executed by Jean Balladur, has aged about as gracefully as the beanbag chair and eight-track tape. Begun in 1967, the town consists of an immense array of weirdly shaped sand-coloured condos and apartment complexes with evocative names like "Le Calypso" and "Temple du Soleil", set on a long boardwalk. Traffic is banished to the background; you park (if you can find space) in the back streets, and reach the beach on foot. The strange aspect of the seafront is compounded by the absence of trees – nothing breaks up the pale beige landscape sandwiched between sea and sky – and, to cap it off, the proliferation of

▲ La Grande-Motte

restaurants and shops on the promenade makes the whole place feel like an enormous shopping mall that just happens to have a beach. Aside from its peculiar looks though, the town is a run-of-the-mill family-holiday seaside resort, where apartments and hotels are usually booked for two- to four-week blocks. It's as good a place as any to stop for a swim, and if you want to spend a couple of days on the beach, you'll find all the facilities and services you would expect.

Practicalities

Buses arrive at the *gare routière* on avenue de Melgueil, just to the east of the **tourist office** (daily: July & Aug 9am–8pm; Sept–June 9.30am–noon/12.30pm & 2–6/6.30pm; ℡04.67.56.42.00, Ⓦwww.ot-lagrandemotte.fr) on allée des Parcs, at the entrance to the town. The most appealing among La Grande-Motte's dozen or so near-identical **hotels** is the *Azur* (℡04.67.56.56.00, Ⓦwww.hotelazur.net; ❹), dramatically set on the extremity of the town's quay. Amenities include a heated pool, family-size rooms, and a babysitting service. A cluster of seven **campsites** sits just west of the tourist office, among them the four-star super-site, *Le Garden* (March–Oct; ℡04.67.56.50.09, Ⓦwww.legarden.fr), on the beaches with excellent facilities. The only **restaurant** that stands out above the uniform beachside fare is the renowned *Alexandre Amiraute* (closed Sun eve & Mon; ℡04.67.56.63.63) on esplanade de la Capitainerie. The food is excellent, but you will pay (*menus* from €50). **Bikes** and scooters can be rented at Bumpcycles, 172 rue des Artisans (℡04.67.29.87.73), and at several other beachside outfits.

Palavas and Maguelone

PALAVAS-LES-FLOTS is Montpellier's own beach town, now absorbed into the metropolitan *agglomération* and even served by regular city buses. The town has been a popular seaside destination for almost a century, a fact attested to by the satirical caricatures of its inhabitants and visitors drawn by Montpellier artist Albert Dubout (1905–76). It's not as dismal as first impressions suggest, either, for once you penetrate the surrounding developments you'll find that the oldest part, where the banks of the canalized River Lez reach the sea, still retains the air of a pretty old fishing town. Like so much of the coast, the town is built on a sand bar which encloses a series of *étangs*, the smallest of which, the Lac du Levant, on the north side of the old quarter, has a small eighteenth-century fort, La Redoute, in the middle. Reached by a long

---

Maguelone's past glory

You wouldn't guess it, but the Romanesque **cathedral** that looms over the green peninsula of Maguelone was for centuries one of the most important churches in medieval Christendom. Before accumulating silt linked it to the mainland, **Maguelone** was an **island**, most likely first settled by the Phoenicians. In the early eighth century, the town here was taken by Muslim forces, but Charles Martel, court chamberlain and de facto ruler of France, pushed back the Muslim advance and destroyed the settlement in 737 to prevent its recapture and use as a forward base for further attacks. Refounded in 1030, the strongly fortified church became an important **religious centre** and a place of refuge for bishops and popes in their quarrels with the nobility and kings of Europe. In 1096, Pope Urban II proclaimed Maguelone as the second church after Rome – an indulgence which guaranteed the complete forgiveness of sins of whoever was buried there. With the papal blessing and in its recovered role as **port**, the town thrived from the Middle Ages until the Wars of Religion, when Louis XIII destroyed it for its unrepentant Protestantism. Nowadays, all that remains is the ancient church.

causeway, the fort now houses the **Musée Albert Dubout** (Jan & Dec Sat & Sun 2–6pm; Feb–June & Sept–Nov Tues–Sun 2–6pm; July & Aug daily 4pm–midnight; €5 including the Musée du Train), where you can see the artist's work. Back on the mainland, a **Musée du Train** (same hours and ticket as Musée Dubout) houses the steam locomotive which used to run between here and Montpellier and was a favourite subject of Dubout's (you'll see it in several of the works on display in the museum). The *étangs* themselves are replete with birdlife, and are one of the few places on the French coast where you will see flamingoes in their habitat; the tourist office can arrange **birdwatching** trips (Mon–Fri 9am–noon; €5).

The most interesting section of **beach** and the best for swimming and sunbathing lies west of the main town, past the campsite. You can get there by TAM bus from Montpellier or, if you drive, you will be obliged (mid-June to mid-Sept) to use the free car park. From the parking area, a narrow sand-spit stretches west, separated from the *étang* behind by a shrubby embankment; the beach here is a popular gay spot and given over generally to **nude bathing**. A road runs along the inland side of the embankment on which a free *petit train* runs every twenty minutes, ferrying people from their cars to the beach and on to the peninsula of **MAGUELONE** (TAM buses do the route out of season), dominated by its twelfth-century **cathedral** – a lone survivor of the days when the former port was an important religious centre (see box opposite). The building is still a place of worship, so you can't enter it in beachwear, although you'll be able to see its marble **portal**, with excellent mid-twelfth-century low-relief carvings of apostles Peter and Paul. The most striking feature of the **interior** (10am–6/6.30pm; free), which has suffered total looting through the ages, is its huge overhanging gallery. You'll find some ancient tombstones down by the altar, and from the gallery you can look down through the sluices over the entrance, which were intended to have hot oil poured through them onto the heads of attackers. The rest of the peninsula is a verdant idyll, and on the north shore some restored fishermen's huts evoke the Maguelone of the early twentieth century, when it was a poor fishing hamlet.

Practicalities

TAM **buses** (route #17 from tram stop "Port Marianne" in Montpellier) circulate throughout the town. Palavas' **tourist office** (July & Aug daily 10am–8pm; April–June & Sept daily 10am–1pm & 2–6pm; Oct–March Mon–Sat 10am–1pm & 2–6pm; ℡04.67.07.73.34, ⓦwww.palavaslesflots.com) is in the unmistakable lighthouse building that towers above the port. For **accommodation**, try the central *Le France*, at 9 quai Clémenceau (℡04.67.74.00.35, ⓦwww.lefrancehotel.com; ❹), or the downbeat *du Midi*, 191 av St-Maurice (℡04.67.68.00.53, ⓦwww.hotel-palavas.com; ❹), half of whose rooms look out over the beach; both are good value with excellent locations, although the *Midi* has more amenities. There are several well-equipped **campsites** around town, most along avenue St-Maurice, but the best situated is the beachside *Palavas Camping* (mid-April to mid-Sept; ℡04.67.68.01.28, ⓦwww .palavas-camping.fr) at the westernmost end of town. You'll have no problem finding a **restaurant** here: the ones that stand out include the riverside *Le New Marine*, 1 quai Paul Cunq (℡04.67.68.00.05), for its original seafood creations (*menus* from €14), and *Les Flots Bleus*, at 21 quai Georges-Clémenceau (℡04.67.68.01.73; closed part Jan), for its grilled monkfish (*menu* from €19).

Sète

Some 38km west along the marshy coast from Maguelone, and a twenty-minute ride by train or car from Montpellier, the cranes and winches of **SÈTE**'s busy port rise above the expanse of *étangs*. Entering town from this direction you find

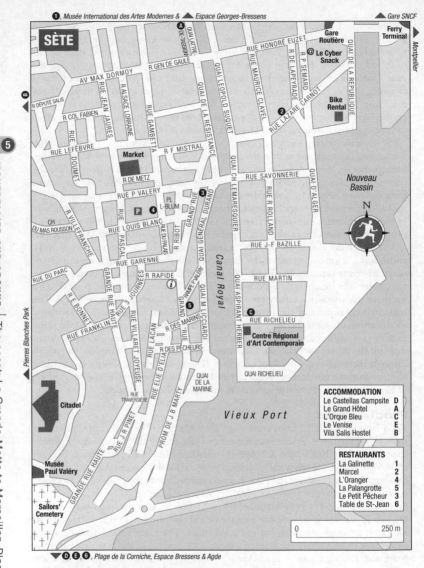

①, Musée International des Artes Modernes & ▲ Espace Georges-Bressens ▲ Gare SNCF

SÈTE

Gare Routière
@ Le Cyber Snack
Ferry Terminal
Montpellier

Bike Rental

Market

Nouveau Bassin

N

Canal Royal

PL L-BLUM

ⓘ

Centre Régional d'Art Contemporain

Vieux Port

Citadel

Musée Paul Valéry

Sailors' Cemetery

Pierres Blanches Park

ACCOMMODATION
Le Castellas Campsite D
Le Grand Hôtel A
L'Orque Bleu C
Le Venise E
Vila Salis Hostel B

RESTAURANTS
La Galinette 1
Marcel 2
L'Oranger 4
La Palangrotte 5
Le Petit Pêcheur 3
Table de St-Jean 6

0   250 m

▼❶,❷,❸, Plage de la Corniche, Espace Bressens & Agde

yourself surrounded by grey warehouses, fenced-in storage yards and stacks of freight containers. Once across the wide Canal Maritime, however, you'll arrive at the colourful **old quarter**, which straddles the westernmost of the two north–south canals, the Canal Royal. On the west bank, the land rises dramatically, hedging in the historical centre. This slope is the eastern side of the 175m-high rocky promontory, **Mont St-Clair**, whose presence has determined the growth of the town. Sète grew as a long corniche completely circling the *mont*, but recently suburbs have begun to climb its steep slopes. The attractive town has a couple of small museums and a park, but primarily makes a good base for enjoying the 20km-long unbroken stretch of beach west towards Agde – it also

Water-jousting

The origins of the curious Sètois sport of **water-jousting** are lost, but the practice seems to have originated in the late seventeenth century, when Sète was thriving as a port thanks to its link to the Canal du Midi and the Canal du Rhône. The sport consists of two sleek boats, each manned by eight oarsmen, charging at each other on a near head-on course. At the stern of each boat, a long, raised tail supports the platform on which a jouster stands, dressed in white. Six other jousters provide a counterweight to the platform, while the rest of the crew, a coxswain and two musicians, keep the boat on course and in time. As the boats approach each other, the jousters steady their small shields, aim their long lances and attempt to strike their adversary from his mount. The spectacle is repeated seven times in each **tournament**, or *joute*, and the winning team is the one that unseats its opponents the most times. There are about a dozen *sociétés des joutes* in Sète (other Languedocian ports also have their own teams). The **season** runs from late spring through early autumn, with more frequent tournaments taking place in the summer. The most important championships are held here on August 25, the Fête de St-Louis.

has accommodation, excellent pleasure-port facilities and lively nightlife in summer. It's worth trying to time your visit to coincide with one of the many **water-jousting** tournaments (see box above) held on the town's canals; the quaysides jam with people watching the boat-borne combatants, and afterwards the bars fill with boisterous revelry.

Arrival and information
Sète's **gare SNCF** is on quai Maréchal-Joffre, on the north bank of the Canal Latéral; from here it's a forty-minute walk into town so your best bet is to take bus #3 to the "Les Pénitents" stop, near the tourist office. The **gare routière** is a little bit closer in, on quai de la République, from where it's a twenty-five minute walk to the tourist office, or you can take bus #4 to the Hôtel de Ville, at the northern end of the old town. Across the Canal Maritime, to the east of the *gare routière*, you'll find the **ferry terminal**, Gare Maritime Orsetti (☎04.67.46.68.00; bus #4), which has regular departures for Mallorca and Morocco. The centrally located **tourist office** at 60 Grand'rue Mario Roustan (April–Oct daily 9.30am–6/7.30pm; Nov–March Mon–Fri 9.30am–6pm, Sat & Sun 9.30am–12.30pm & 2–5.30pm; ☎04.67.74.71.71, Ⓦwww.ot-sete.fr) has exchange facilities, and sells local bus tickets (€1; also available from drivers). You can rent **bikes** at Déferlantes, 6 quai Commandant-Samary (☎04.67.74.82.30), and **scooters** at Cabello, 9 quai Vauban (☎04.67.74.50.29). There's **internet** access at Le Cyber Snack, 10 av Victor-Hugo (Mon–Fri 9am–noon & 2–6pm). For glass-bottom **boat** tours, Sète Croisières on quai Général-Durand runs a number of regular trips in the summer for €10–15.

Accommodation
Surprisingly, given its seaside setting and the activity of its port, Sète is not overflowing with **accommodation**. As a consequence, booking ahead is crucial in summer, and far in advance should you be planning to stay during one of the town's festivals. The biggest and best **campsite** in the area is *Le Castellas*, 12km west of town on the RN112 (☎04.67.51.63.00; Ⓦwww.le-castellas.com; open April to late Sept). Situated on the seaside and ringed by a pine forest, it is a veritable village, with large pitches and all the services you can imagine; you can also rent campers and chalets.

Le Grand Hôtel 17 quai de Lattre de Tassigny ☎04.67.74.71.77, ⓦwww.legrandhotelsete.com. Alongside the northern part of the Canal Royal, this elegant hotel has good views over the canal, and secure parking. An apartment is also available, and there is free wi-fi. ❼

🏃 **L'Orque Bleu** 10 quai Aspirant-Herber ☎04.67.74.72.13, ⓦwww.hotel-orquebleue-sete.com. At the southern end of the Canal Royal, this converted nineteenth-century mansion is the best deal in town – try to get a quayside room (€30 supplement), as the views over the canal to the old town are great. All beds are king-size and rooms have DSL. ❺

le Venise Plage de la Corniche ☎04.67.53.02.86, ⓦwww.hotellevenise.com. Steps from the sand, this family-run hotel makes a good alternative to staying in the centre of town. Few amenities, but clean rooms and friendly service. Closed Dec & Jan. ❸

Villa Salis Hostel rue du Général-Revest ☎04.67.53.46.68, ⓦwww.fuaj.org. Unhospitably basic, and a stiff half-hour walk west of the *gare routière* on the eastern slopes of the Mont. Open mid-Jan to Nov. €20 per person for compulsory half-board in summer. ❷

The Town

You're likely to spend most of your time in Sète along the **Canal Royal**, which is lined on the west side by restaurants and bars, or in the tight scrum of streets between the water and the hill. On the waterfront, the **Centre Régional d'Art Contemporain**, at 26 quai Aspirant-Herber (Mon & Wed–Fri 12.30–7pm, Sat & Sun 3–8pm; free), houses a varied collection of local art, while the quirky **Musée Internationale des Arts Modestes** at 23 quai Maréchal-Lattre (July & Aug daily 10am–noon & 2–6pm; Sept–June Tues–Sun same hours; €6) contains a collection of art made from cast-off goods. Apart from this, the closest attraction to the old quarter is the **Musée Paul Valéry** (July & Aug daily 10am–noon & 2–6pm; Sept–June Wed–Sun same hours; €4), southwest of the canal on rue François-Desnoyer, about a ten-minute walk west of the old port. As well as editions and manuscripts written by the eponymous, renowned local writer, you'll find a small but impressive collection of contemporary paintings, including works by Dufy and Matisse. It also doubles as a municipal historical museum, whose collection focuses on the nautical traditions of the town and includes documents, models and paintings relating to the sport of water-jousting. Valéry's (see box below) remains lie in the **sailors' cemetery** across

Paul Valéry

Though of Corsican and Italian parentage, **Paul Valéry** was born in Sète in 1871, and spent his childhood and adolescence in the town. An introspective youth, he whiled away his hours contemplating the sea. On reaching adulthood, he moved to Paris, where he took up work as a legal clerk; by this time he had already begun writing **Symbolist poetry** influenced by Poe and Mallarmé. His great and largely unrequited love, however, was for science, and despite his literary successes, he turned towards more pragmatic intellectual pursuits in the sciences. He was a great admirer of da Vinci, in whom he saw the "universal man" – a cerebral Renaissance figure whom he brought to life in his stylized novel *Monsieur Teste* (1895). Valéry did his best to live up to the da Vincian ideal which he professed. In his forties, at the urging of André Gide, he returned to poetry, while his scientific pursuits brought him into personal contact with contemporaries such as Albert Einstein. His acute observational powers and political insights made him a popular *salon* guest in inter war Paris, and official accolades followed with his election in 1925 to the Académie Française and his appointment to the Collège de France as the first Professor of Poetry. Valéry remained in Paris through the Nazi occupation and, having lived to see the Liberation, died the following year and was buried as a national hero.

the street from the museum, along with those of many Sètois fishermen who have lost their lives at sea.

Looking over the Valéry museum, on a broad plateau on the west of Mont St-Clair, you'll see the park of **Pierres Blanches** (bus #5 from the Hôtel de Ville or the museum), a scrubby habitat for lavender, thyme and rosemary, which provides impressive views over the shellfish beds of the Bassin de Thau to the north, particularly towards sunset. This is also a great spot for a picnic, but if you come without supplies, you can get a snack at the small on-site café. Further east, at the summit of the *mont*, you'll find the nineteenth-century church of **Notre-Dame-de-la-Salette** (bus #5), built on the remains of a medieval fort; the church is nothing special but the views from here over the ports, old and new, are spectacular. The best **beach** reachable by public transport (buses #6, #7 and #9) – with showers and other amenities – is the **Plage de la Corniche**, where you'll also find restaurants and accommodation.

From the canal front, it's a long ride (bus #3) to the northwest side of Mont St-Clair, where you'll find another local shrine, the **Espace Georges-Brassens** (June–Sept daily 10am–noon & 2–7pm; Oct–May Tues–Sun 10am–noon & 2–6pm; €5). Local-born Brassens (1921–81) was perhaps France's most popular folk singer of the postwar era, a sort of Gallic Bob Dylan, whose simple guitar melodies served as platforms for irony-edged sentimental lyrics.

Eating and drinking

There's a barrage of restaurants along quai Général-Durand, from the pont de la Savonnerie right down to the pleasure port, all offering seafood in the €15–30 bracket.

La Galinette 26 pl des Mouettes ☎04.67.51.16.77. On the north side of town, this restaurant serves great-value seafood, with *menus* from €15. Dinner only in summer; otherwise closed Sun & Thurs eve, Fri & Sat noon.

Marcel rue Lazare-Carnot ☎04.67.74.20.89. A great deal with grilled fish and local wines from €15–50. Closed Sat lunch & Sun.

L'Oranger 5 pl de la Mairie ☎04.67.51.96.12. An excellent Sètois *terroir*, known for its fresh squid "foie gras", as well as a delicious fish soup. *Menu* at €20.

La Palangrotte 1 rampe Paul Valéry ☎04.67.74.80.35. A local favourite, famous for its mussels and bouillabaisse (€23–36) and

solid wine list. Reservations are recommended, especially on weekends. Closed Sun eve & Mon off-season.

Le Petit Pêcheur 12 quai Général-Durand ☎04.99.46.10.99. This port-side restaurant is famous for its Sètois seafood, including stuffed mussels and squid and monkfish, as well as excellent *coquillages*. *Menus* from €13–36. Closed Sun & Mon.

Table de St-Jean Plage de la Corniche ☎04.67.53.02.57. A good bet next door to *Le Venise* hotel. Serves local specialities including *la tielle*, a spicy octopus pie, and biscuits, such as the sweet *zézette*, best washed down with muscat or champagne. *Menus* starting from €12. Closed Mon.

Around the Bassin de Thau

North and west of Sète lies the shallow expanse of the **BASSIN DE THAU**, which, at 18km long and some 5km wide, is one of the biggest **salt lakes** in Languedoc. From its northeastern end above Sète it extends along the town's 14km stretch of beach southwest to Agde. The Bassin is a major centre of shellfish cultivation, particularly oysters and mussels, with approximately thirteen thousand tonnes of oysters raised here annually, ninety percent of which are the larger Pacific variety. At the eastern end of the lagoon, between Bouzigues and Sète, the wooden **oyster racks** protruding from the water make a curious aquascape. The oysters are harvested using a nineteenth-century technique of cementing them to ropes which hang from the racks: the strong winds which blow along the surface of the water compensate for the lack of tidal movement, which the shellfish depend on to move water through their gills. The water itself is a tepid, murky green – safe enough to swim in, although most prefer the clearer waters of the Mediterranean side. The closest you'll probably get to the oysters, however, is a steaming bowl of *coquillages*, enjoyed on a pier-side terrace.

There are two ways around the *étang* from Sète. The most direct **route** is to follow the windswept and narrow strip of dunes separating the lagoon from the sea, a deserted stretch of highway punctuated only by the massive *Camping Castellas* (see p.233) and by windsurfers' camping vans. There are parking areas along the length of the road (with two-metre-height barriers to prevent RVs from entering) and you can swim anywhere along its sandy length, though there are no showers, so you'll have to put up with a salty, post-swim crust until you reach accommodation. The **inland** route, while it has no major tourist sites, is a unique area well worth exploring, especially for its gastronomical delights such as the locally farmed oysters and mussels. Either route can be managed by **bike** (the whole circuit is about 40km), but the usual warnings regarding the high-speed traffic on the narrow secondary roads apply and strong winds add to the challenge.

Balaruc and Poussan

Coming from Sète, after 3km you'll arrive at **Balaruc**, which actually consists of two villages: **BALARUC-LES-BAINS**, an ancient fishing port turned spa town, and **BALARUC-LE-VIEUX**, a tiny *circulade* set dramatically on a low spur just inland. Here you can see the remains of a third-century paleo-Christian **basilica** (free). Don't let the built-up agglomeration of holiday flats around Balaruc-les-Bains put you off: its compact old town has managed to retain its charm, even in high season, and the views over the *étang* towards Sète and Mont St-Clair are striking. Five kilometres north is another ancient *circulade*, **POUSSAN**, dating from the tenth century. Its streets make for excellent strolling, with several fourteenth-century palaces, a still more ancient church, and a picturesque, early twentieth-century metalwork **market** building.

Balaruc-les-Bains makes a good base for exploring the area, with a small **tourist office** in the old spa complex (Mon–Sat 9am–noon & 2–6/7pm, Sun 10am–12.30pm; June–Sept also Sun 4–7pm; ☏04.67.46.81.46, ⊛www.balaruc -les-bains.com). It also has several good **hotels**, including the central *Neptune* at 3 rue Montgolfier (March–Nov; ☏04.67.48.53.17, ⊛hotelneptune-balaruc .m6blog.fr; ❹), with a pool, and the quieter, more modern *Arcadius* in the new town (☏04.67.80.90.00, ⊛www.arcadius.com; ❹), also with pool. The municipal **campsite**, *Du Pech d'Ay* (March–Dec; ☏04.67.48.50.34, ⊕pechday@wanadoo .fr), is on avenue de la Gare, just south of the central pedestrian area. There's a raft of **restaurants** along the waterfront: two of the best, both with good seafood *menus* and views across the bay, are *La Barge* (*menus* from €14–25), next to the campsite, and the more upmarket *Le Saint Clair*, on Quai du Port (from €28–49), whose *bouillabaisse* is hard to beat. Weekly **markets** are held on Tuesday in Balaruc and Friday in Poussan.

Bouzigues and Loupian

A few kilometres from Balaruc on the north shore, **BOUZIGUES** has the appearance of a fishing town that's slept through the last century, with its narrow, laundry-strung streets and strong salt air. It is also *the* place to eat **shellfish**, and the long waterfront boulevard, avenue Louis-Tudesq, is girded by a phalanx of colourful **restaurants** offering generous, fresh *coquillages* (normally €36 for two): *Le Grand Bleu* is one of the best here, serving *coquillages* since 1926. After lunch, head to the **Musée de l'Étang de Thau** (daily: July & Aug 10am–12.30pm & 2.30–7pm; Sept–June 10am–noon & 2–5/6pm; €4), whose array of imaginative multimedia displays explains the art of shellfish-raising (including tanks with live specimens) as well as traditional fishing techniques. If you want to stay, there's a surprisingly chic **hotel**, *À la Voile Blanche* on avenue Louis-Tudesq (℡04.67.78.35.77, Ⓦwww.alavoileblanche.com; ❺).

Heading inland 5km to the west, the medieval hamlet of **LOUPIAN** is the site of an excavated **Gallo-Roman villa** (July & Aug daily 1.30–6pm; Sept–June Wed–Mon same hours; guided tours €4.60), dating from the tail end of the Roman period and containing some impressive figurative and geometric mosaics.

Mèze and around

The largest village on the Bassin de Thau's northern shore, **MÈZE** is an ancient fishing village whose old quarter is a dense maze of narrow streets flanked by low houses. As it isn't directly on the sea it gets relatively few visitors, and provides some respite from the crowded coastal towns. The village has a pleasant, laidback feel, with two beaches, a beautiful old fishing port and a fine **market** building, making it an excellent stop for families. It's also the main service centre for the Bassin de Thau: its **tourist office** (July & Aug Mon–Sat 9am–12.30pm & 2–7pm, Sun 9am–12.30pm; Sept–June Mon–Fri 9am–noon & 2–5/5.30pm, Sat 9am–12.30pm; ℡04.67.43.93.08, Ⓦwww.ville-meze.fr) is near the village centre on rue Massaloup. The best **hotel** here is the *étang*-side *La Pyramide*, on the main promenade (℡04.67.46.61.50, Ⓦwww.hoteldelapyramide.fr; ❻), with excellent facilities, including wi-fi and a pool. The sprawling **campsite** *Beau Rivage* (April–Sept; ℡04.67.43.81.48, Ⓦwww.camping-beaurivage.fr) is located off the highway RN113. For dining, there's a string of near-identical **restaurants** along the waterfront quai Descournut, all serving up shellfish fresh from the *bassin*: *Le Chabichou* and *Le Coquillou* are well regarded by locals, but any of them will do (*menus* from €15). **Sailboats**, ideal for exploring the broad and calm *étang*, can be rented at Le Taurus in rue de la Méditerranée (℡04.67.43.59.51).

Three kilometres southwest of town along the shore is the three-hectare **Écosite** (daily: April–June, Sept & Oct 2–6pm; July & Aug 10am–7pm; €4.60). Set up to preserve the habitat of the salt lagoon, it has exhibitions on the flora and fauna of the *étang*, and on techniques of aquaculture. Also nearby, 5km north of Mèze, just off the main RN113 road towards Pézenas, is the **Musée-Parc La Plaine des Dinosaures** (daily: July & Aug 10am–7pm; Sept–June 2pm–5/7pm; €7.50), a museum and excavation area established on the site of a major paleontological find: its highlights include a 12m-tall Brachiosaurus skeleton and one of the biggest caches of dinosaur eggs yet discovered.

Marseillan and Marseillan-Plage

Marseillan and Marseillan-Plage, which anchor the southern end of the Bassin, reflect how the economy of the region has shifted in the last generation. Once a flourishing fishing town, **MARSEILLAN** now lies all but forgotten, ignored by the masses of weekenders who inundate the seashore at its namesake, Marseillan-Plage. This is good news for the few who do come to Marseillan, now the most picturesque and atmospheric town in the area, with a very evocative **old port** and a fine seventeenth-century **market**. There's little to do here aside from soak up the atmosphere, although a trip to the famed **Noilly Prat distillery** at 1 rue Noilly (see box below; daily 9.30am–noon & 3.30–7pm; €3.50) is a good excuse to soak up the local vermouth as well. Separated by nearly 10km of marshy reeds, **MARSEILLAN-PLAGE**, by contrast, is the epitome of noisy Mediterranean hedonism. Its one sight, other than the hordes of near-naked bodies that crowd its beaches, is the **débouché**, the terminus of the great Canal du Midi, whose earthworks protrude strikingly into the Mediterranean here. It's a quick drive or a nice, level bike-ride between the two towns, but buses are limited to two per day in each direction.

Marseillan-Plage's **tourist office** (July & Aug daily 9am–7pm; June & Sept daily 9am–noon & 2–6pm; Oct–May Mon–Fri 9am–noon & 1.30–5pm; ☎04.67.21.82.43, ⓦwww.marseillan.com) is right after the main roundabout at the entrance to the resort.

In Marseillan, there are just two **hotels**, the economical *Le Boulevard* in rue de Gaulle (☎04.67.77.21.11; ❷), and the ultra-luxurious *Rive Gauche* (☎04.67.11.87.15, ⓦwww.garrigaeresorts.com; ❾), a suites-only establishment overlooking the Bassin du Thau, and including a deluxe spa and tearoom. In Marseillan-Plage, the best hotel is sprawling *les Dunes* (☎04.67.21.91.50, ⓦwww.marseillan-hotel.com; ❻) in rue Arc en Ciel, where each room has a large balcony overlooking the sea. There are also over a dozen **campsites** near the beach, the largest of which, *Les Méditerranées* (April–Sept ☎04.67.21.94.49, ⓦwww.lesmediterranees.com), is on the appropriately named avenue des Campings.

There's no shortage of **restaurants** to choose from in Marseillan-Plage, although few rise above the beach-town standard: one of the better ones is *Chez Philippe* at 20 rue de Suffren (☎04.67.01.70.62; closed Sun–Tues Sept–June), an excellent traditional-style bistro where you'll spend €15–30. In the old town, the best

---

Stirred, not shaken...

The dry martini is not an association most of us would make with Languedoc, but, in fact, Marseillan-Plage is home to what British author and lifelong cocktail researcher **Somerset Maugham** described as a "necessary component" of the drink – and connoisseurs around the world agree. The secret is **Noilly Prat** (pronounced "nwah-lee Prah") vermouth, created in 1813 by taking white Languedoc wine, aging it in vats for eight months, and then for a further year outdoors in oaken barrels. The *aperitif* gets its distinctive taste from the twenty **herbs and spices** with which it is infused. For those in the know, it is the best vermouth for cocktails, although locals typically enjoy it on a hot day alone **on the rocks** with seafood. You can tour the Noilly Prat facility (see above) and buy some to take home; be warned, however, it is best consumed within a month of opening. Bond fans, incidentally, will be interested to know that according to Somerset Maugham, shaking a dry Martini destroys its "molecular characteristics" – Martinis should *always* be stirred.

Treasure-hunting in Languedoc

Thanks to the healthy rural middle-class which characterized southern France throughout the twentieth century, the **flea markets** (*marchés aux puces*) of Languedoc are a perfect place to find rare and distinctive antiques (*brocanterie*). In recent years, holding informal local sales (usually on Sundays) has become a popular passion – locally referred to as *vide greniers*, or "attic-clearing." Even in the smallest hamlets, the pickings are excellent – far better than the typical North American flea market or British boot sale. Housewares, furniture and vintage clothing can be found, often at bargain prices (and it's always worth haggling).

Big cities like Toulouse have regular markets which often run on weekdays, and there's a major market by the tourist office in **Marseillan-Plage** (Saturday 6am–6pm), but the real gems (and prices) are found in country towns, particularly in the Hérault and Gard. A comprehensive and up-to-date directory of local markets and sales can be found at ⓦ vide-greniers.org.

---

restaurant is *La Table d'Emilie* at 8 pl Carnot (closed lunch Mon & Thurs; ℡ 04.67.43.84.99), set in a twelfth-century chamber, and featuring combinations of local seafood and *terroir*, such as a tart of cured Iberian ham and scallops (*menus* from €19).

Pézenas and around

More or less halfway between Mèze and Béziers, and 54km southwest of Montpellier along the N113, **PÉZENAS** is the last large inland settlement on the Hérault river, as it meanders south to Agde through the vineyards of the Languedoc plain. One of the most singularly beautiful towns in the French Southwest, endowed with an almost overwhelming concentration of grand architecture, it is also a centre for **arts and crafts**, and thus very popular – packing out with tourists in July and August.

Although it had been an important market centre for centuries, Pézenas catapulted to glory when it became the seat of the Languedoc parliament and the residence of its governors in 1456, and reached its zenith in the late seventeenth century, when Armand de Bourbon, prince of Conti and governor of Languedoc, made it a "second Versailles", drawing artists and writers of the stature of Molière to his court with his wealthy patronage. On and off, the playwright spent a good four years here performing for the prince and garnering inspiration for the plays that would later make him famous. But with the prince's death in 1666, stagnation soon set in, and Pézenas reverted to the sleepy provincial town which – outside high season – it remains today. The rolling countryside around Pézenas is dotted with atmospheric old villages, such as **Tourbes**, as well as medieval castles and the country's largest wine-producing monastery, the **abbey of Valmagne**.

Arrival, information and accommodation

Buses stop in Pézenas at the open-air *gare routière* on place Molière, from where it's a five-minute walk west to the main **tourist office**, on place Gambetta (July & Aug Mon, Tues, Thurs & Sat 9am–7pm, Wed & Fri 9am–10pm, Sun 10am–7pm; Sept–June Mon–Sat 9am–noon & 2–6pm, Sun 10am–noon & 2–5pm; ℡ 04.67.98.36.40, ⓦ www.ot-pezenas-valdherault.com). On Saturday, the town centre is taken over by a busy **market** from 10am to 6pm. You can rent **bikes** at

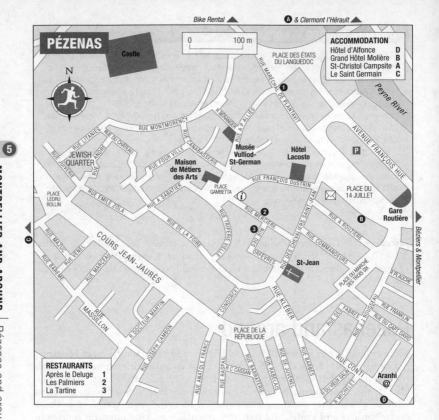

Planet Vélo in avenue Émile-Combes (☎04.67.98.34.04). For **internet**, head to Aranhi at 30 rue Conti (daily 10am–10pm).

Despite the town's charms and attraction, there is a limited choice of **accommodation** and rooms must be booked well ahead in summer. Set in a grand old nineteenth-century mansion on the main square, place du 14 Juillet, the *Grand Hôtel Molière* (☎04.67.98.14.00, ⓦwww.hotel-le-moliere.com; ❹) is a comfortable, atmospheric option, and offers TV, air conditioning and internet. While lacking the charm of the *Molière*, the *Saint Germain*, 6 av Paul-Vidal (☎04.67.09.75.75, ⓦwww.hotel-saintgermain.com; ❸), beats it outright on amenities and value for money. Rooms have wi-fi and cable TV and there is a pool. Another good bet is the *Hôtel d'Alfonce*, 32 rue Conti (☎04.67.90.71.89; ❹), a simple but elegant two-room *chambres d'hôte* set in the eighteenth-century *hôtel* where Molière put on his plays, offering unbeatable atmosphere, if basic amenities. One kilometre northwest of town on the chemin de Saint Christol, the *St-Christol* **campsite** (☎04.67.98.09.00, ⓦwww.campingsaintchristol.com; mid-April to mid-Sept) is set in a vineyard, and has a pool and on-site restaurant, with a buffet lunch for €11.

The Town

Pézenas' compact **old town** is set on the west bank of the Peyne river, occupying the area between the hill on which the town's castle once stood, and the village church. Of the several fine *hôtels particuliers* dotted around town, the first you'll likely encounter is the **Hôtel Lacoste** (10am–noon & 3–7pm; free) at 8 rue Oustrin, a fifteenth-century palace with a beautiful but compact vaulted courtyard framed by a monumental staircase. Close by, place Gambetta is home to the tourist office (see p.239), once the shop where Molière idled away his afternoons. Across the narrow, cobblestoned *place* stands the handsome sixteenth-century council house, whose broad and square vaulted interior once held sessions of the Estates of Languedoc, but now houses the **Maison des Métiers d'Arts** (daily 10am–noon & 3–7pm; July & Aug also Wed & Fri 9–11pm; free), a showcase for local crafts, including painting, decorative sculpture, stained-glass items and the like.

From here, wandering off in any direction will lead you to the carved stone facades that graced the homes of the wealthy merchants and nobles of Renaissance Pézenas; a glance up as you stroll around will almost certainly reveal a playful human face, a stately lion or regal sun carved out of a window casement or doorframe. North of the square, down rue Alliés, is the mansion housing the **Musée Vulliod-St-German** (June–Sept Tues–Sun 10am–noon & 3–7pm, plus Wed & Fri 9–11pm in July & Aug; Feb–May & Oct to mid-Nov Tues–Sun 10am–noon & 2–5.30pm; €2.50) containing all manner of sixteenth- and seventeenth-century artefacts, from classically themed Aubusson tapestries to displays dwelling on the daily life of the humbler classes. On the hill at the end of rue Béranger lie the ruins of the **castle** (closed) destroyed by Richelieu and dating back to as early as 1500 BC.

On the far side of the castle's base through rue Litanies, is the town's old **Jewish quarter**, marked off by gates, as was the custom during the Middle Ages – there's not much of interest here but snaking east, between the gate of rue Juiverie and place Gambetta, is a warren of narrow streets jammed with magnificent *hôtels*; make sure you check out the doorway of the **Hôtel Grave** on rue du Château, the fifteenth-century **Hôtel de Jacques Coeur** at 7 rue Émile-Zola and the impressive ironwork railing in the courtyard at 12 rue Sabatier. On the far side of town at 32 rue Conti, the **Hôtel d'Alfonce** (July & Aug Mon–Fri 10am–noon & 2–6pm; €2) features a spacious courtyard girded by an ornately balustraded stone balcony; it was here that Molière's players put on performances during the winter of 1655–56.

Finally, if you happen to be around for one of the local festivals (see box, p.220), keep an eye out for **Le Poulain** – the town's traditional totemic animal. A mock horse constructed of a cloth-draped wooden frame, borne through the streets by a bunch of burly men, Le Poulain was adopted in honour of a foal that King Louis VIII's favourite mare gave birth to here in 1226.

Eating and drinking

There are a couple of highly rated **restaurants** in Pézenas: *Les Palmiers*, 50 rue de Mercière (mid-April to mid-Sept; ☎04.67.09.42.56), is a beautiful and welcoming establishment serving inventive Mediterranean-style cuisine from about €28, while the excellent *Après le Déluge*, 5 rue Maréchal de Plantavit (☎04.67.98.10.77; closed Mon eve), is in a fourteenth-century building with several separate dining-rooms (*terroir menus* €14–45). The wine lists at both places are superb. For lunch, the comfortable *La Tartine* at 17 rue des Orfèvres serves home-style meals in a funky, informal atmosphere (lunch only; about €12). One of the local specialities is the *petit pâté*, a bite-sized mince tart based on the recipe of an Indian cook in Lord Clive's household – the British Governor of India holidayed here in 1768 and the recipe stuck. The best place to pick these up, piping hot, is at Maison Aleary, 9 rue des Chevaliers de St-Jean. Another speciality, the "Berlingot", is a hard candy that comes in a variety of flavours and continues to be made in the town.

5

Around Pézenas

The immediate surroundings of Pézenas offer good possibilities for walking, cycling or exploring by car. The attractive old town of **Montagnac**, with a well-preserved fourteenth-century church, lies halfway between Pézenas and the twelfth-century Cistercian **abbey of Valmagne** (daily: mid-June to Sept 10am–noon & 2.30–6pm; Oct to mid-June 2–6pm; closed Tues in winter; guided tours in English available; €7). Set in a romantic wooded park, Valmagne was once one of the richest abbeys in the South of France and is now the largest wine-producing monastery in the country. It has a well-preserved cloister, a gothic church and chapterhouse, three gardens, and hosts temporary art exhibitions and occasional concerts.

To the south of Pézenas, **Castelnau-de-Guers** was once a way station on the Roman Via Domitia, while 3km southwest on the road to Béziers, the medieval village of **Tourbes** boasts a maze of narrow alleys with a porticoed square and a medieval church. More impressive, however; is the priory, **Château de Cassan** (daily: May–June, Sept & late Oct 2–7pm, July & Aug 11am–7pm; €7), 10km west of town, just beyond Roujan. Founded in 1080, its abbots ruled over extensive territories in the 1200s, answering only to the pope. Following the Hundred Years' War and Wars of Religion, it fell into decline until the 1700s, when it was rebuilt as a huge Neoclassical palace. Aside from the Romanesque church, and the remains of a medieval hospital, the main attraction today is its immense cloister, which contains a fine iron-forged staircase. Also in the grounds is an elaborate Oriental garden founded by Armand de Bourbon.

Inland from Montpellier

The area **inland from Montpellier** is dominated by two rivers: the mighty **Hérault**, which cuts down southwest from the Cévennes mountains through the plains above the city, and the **Vis**, which runs along the northern rim of the *département* and into the Hérault at Ganges. Between them, their underpopulated and lesser-travelled valleys – a world apart from the fishing towns and beaches of the coast – offer some remarkable scenery and attractions and, taken in conjunction with a couple of absorbing towns, also form a naturally circuitous tour of the region by car, with plenty of hiking opportunities along the way.

The circuit starts with quiet **Clermont-l'Hérault**, poised on the eastern edge of the Haut Languedoc uplands 40km west of Montpellier, which provides access to the nearby reservoir **Lac du Salagou** and an array of interesting sites: the old industrial centre of **Villeneuvette**; **Cabrières'** prehistoric copper mines; and the eerie landscape of **Cirque de Mourèze**. North of here is **Lodève**, an eminently explorable town which boxes in the Orb valley to the west and provides a good base for local excursions, as well as for the route eastwards across the high plateau des Garrigues to the beautiful **Cirque de Navacelles** in the Vis valley. From here, you pass down through the Vis gorge to link up eventually with the Hérault just north of **Ganges**. Ganges provides easy access to the cavernous chambers of the **Grotte des Demoiselles**, which open up under the calcite plateau – you'll pass the *grotte* on either of two routes south to Montpellier. The first follows the **Hérault valley** itself, veering southwest to the deep Hérault gorge and the ancient hamlet and UNESCO World Heritage Site of **St-Guilhem-le-Désert**, while the second, more direct route heads straight south via the **Pic-St-Loup**, standing sentinel above the coastal plain, and the old town of **St-Martin-de-Londres**.

Clermont-l'Hérault and around

Some 40km west of Montpellier, a short distance from the banks of the River Hérault, lies quiet **CLERMONT-L'HÉRAULT**, a dull little cantonal capital whose only recommendation is as a jumping-off point for visiting the area around **Lac du Salagou**. The town itself merits little more than a brief walk, with a stop to look at the thirteenth-century **church**, fortified in the fourteenth century to defend it against the English, and the small Gothic chapel of **Notre-Dame-du-Peyrou**, at 8 rue Louis Blanc, once a way station on the Chemin de St-Jacques.

More interesting is nearby **VILLENEUVETTE**, 4km west. A model factory town founded by Colbert (Louis XIV's finance minister) in the seventeenth century to produce high-quality wool for sale in the Mediterranean, Villeneuvette stayed in business until 1954 and still has 85 inhabitants. The walled-in compound is entered through a monumental gate bearing the legend *Honneur au Travail* ("honour to work"), and inside, a square, flanked by the church and *mairie*, opens onto neat rows of low, flower-bedecked workers' houses. In its wooded surroundings, the little settlement presents a curious but enchanting idyll. A further 5km south of Villeneuvette, at Cabrières, you can visit the site of the **copper mines** of **Pioch Farrus** (April–Nov daily 2–7pm; €8), which were exploited by the region's Neolithic inhabitants over five thousand years ago – the engaging hour-long tour takes you through 200m of galleries. Be sure to wrap up: the temperature in the mine is a cool 15°C.

Northwest of Villeneuvette is the village of **MOURÈZE** in the midst of an eerie zone of eroded dolomite known as the **Cirque de Mourèze**, featuring a landscape of ancient seabed eroded by rainfall into a forest of rocky pinnacles. You can stroll though the myriad paths that crisscross the area, or enjoy an impressive panoramic view from the **Courtinales** (daily: July & Aug 10am–7pm; Sept–June 10am–6pm; €5), a private park whose footpaths lead through a garden of local fauna and reconstructions of the prehistoric dwellings of the region – good fun for adults and children. Mourèze was also the first town that the Resistance group, the Maquis Bir Hakeim (see box below), liberated from the Germans – a monument to 140 of their dead (including one English officer) sits a kilometre or two south of the entrance to town.

The war in Languedoc Rouge

In 1942, with the dissolution of the puppet **Vichy regime**, the formal **German occupation** of Languedoc began, and once again the natives of the region found themselves fighting an outside power against enormous odds. Embittered by labour conscriptions that had sent local men to German factories and concentration camps, many locals joined or supported the Communists, deserters and refugees who made up the local **Resistance** – called "*maquisards*" or "**maquis**", in reference to the scrubby Mediterranean landscape which was their home and refuge.

The main resistance group here, "the Maquis Bir Hakeim", was extremely active until surprised by German forces and wiped out in May 1944. In the Sidobre and Tarn, the feared "Maquis de Vabre" carried out a campaign of raiding and sabotage despite the brutal retaliations such acts provoked. Two months after D-Day, fifteen OSS (the forerunner of the CIA) commandos parachuted into Vabre, one day before a British agent, Major Davies, arrived. Davies' notebook, which he called a report on "the war in Languedoc Rouge", recalls the fighters as "mainly youths...upstanding fellows with fresh keen faces, from all social classes". Despite their lack of arms and equipment, in August 1944, *maquis* action turned the German withdrawal from Albi into a military debacle – many vehicles were lost and the 4500-strong garrison of Castres surrendered.

Continuing towards **Salasc**, a tiny crossroads hamlet 4km further west, the landscape looks Martian, as the ground gives way to red iron-rich dunes. From Salasc, the road marked for Liausson leads to the south shore of **Lac du Salagou**, a reservoir whose shallow waters teem with birdlife, as well as fish and tiny crabs. The north shore, east of the larger village of **Octon**, is more developed and the landscape less striking. As the road follows the cliffs above the shore, it passes the ghost town of **Celles**, which was expropriated in the 1970s when the reservoir was built. The waters, however, never reached the hamlet, which now sits abandoned. Today, it is the scene of a lively mix of families on outings, and nude bathers. After another 8km of winding road, you'll join up with the busy *route nationale* just north of Clermont.

Practicalities

Trains and **buses** arrive in Clermont-l'Hérault at the **gare SNCF** on place Frédéric-Mistral, five minutes' walk south of the town centre. The **tourist office** (Mon–Fri 9am–12.30pm & 2–7pm, Sat 9am–noon & 2–5/6pm; July & Aug also Sun 10am–noon; ☎04.67.96.23.86, ⓦwww.clermont-l-herault.com) for the town and surrounding area is in the central place Jean-Jaurès. There are several good **accommodation** options around Lac du Salagou. A solid budget choice is the comfortable old *La Calade* (☎04.67.96.19.21, ⓦwww.hotel-lacalade.com; March to mid-Dec; ❸), which also has an excellent *terroir* restaurant (*menu* €15; closed Tues & Wed out of season). Not far off is the area's best hotel, the luxurious Swiss-run ⚇ *La Palombe* (☎04.67.95.40.07, ⓦwww.lapalombe.com; ❻), overlooking the lake, 4km from Octon in Hameau de Basse. Villeneuvette's *La Source* (☎04.67.96.05.07, ⓦwww.hoteldelasource.com; closed Jan to mid-Feb & late Nov; ❹) is picturesquely set at the entrance to town; with a pool, relaxing garden and good restaurant (*menus* €22–34), this is the best value-for-money option. **Bikes** can be rented at Ozone on route du Lac du Salagou in Clermont (☎04.67.96.27.17).

Lodève and around

Located on the eastern spur of the massif that forms the bulk of the Parc Naturel Régional du Haut Languedoc (see p.162), and just 10km north of Lac du Salagou, **LODÈVE** is everything that Clermont-l'Hérault is not – a pleasantly situated and friendly little town with a couple of surprisingly good sights. Heading southwest from the *gare routière*, you'll arrive in a few minutes at the greatest of these, the **Cathédrale St-Fulcran**, built in the town's second great period of prosperity in the twelfth and thirteenth centuries (the first was under Nero in the first century BC, when it had been important enough to have an imperial Roman mint). The current cathedral was raised on the riches of the woollen cloth industry. Although it's mostly late medieval, traces of an earlier cathedral's sixth-century foundations can be seen, while the **cloisters** preserve part of the cathedral building raised by the saint himself in the tenth century. The nave's dimensions are impressive – 58m in length and 25m high – and its biggest bell weighs in at 2000kg; in a small interior chapel opposite the door, you'll find where the remains of the town's 84 bishops lie interred.

From the cathedral, the **old town** spreads out east, bounded on three sides by a dramatic bend in the Lergue river. Just southeast of the church, you'll find the beautiful medieval bridge, the **Pont de Montifort**, while in the centre of town, up nearby rue de la République, is the surprisingly good **Musée Fleury** (Tues–Sun 9.30am–noon & 2–6pm; €3.50), a gallery which draws the best fine-arts exhibitions between Castres and Montpellier, as well as a good selection of archeological finds and historical items dating from the prehistoric to the post-Revolutionary. Just east of the museum, in the place du Marché, the nineteenth-century *halle* has

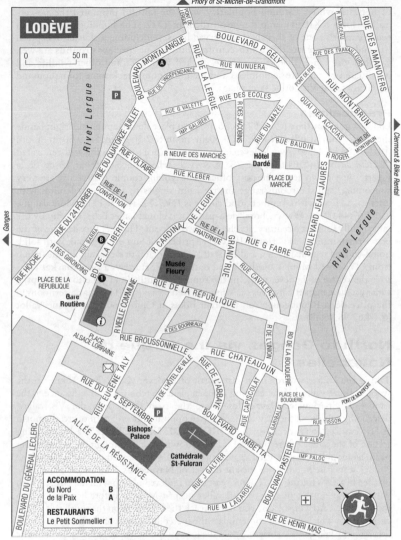

LODÈVE

0   50 m

Priory of St-Michel-de-Grandmont

Ganges

Clermont & Bike Rental

ACCOMMODATION
du Nord   B
de la Paix   A

RESTAURANTS
Le Petit Sommellier 1

been converted into the **Hôtel Dardé** (daily 9am–7pm; free), a showcase for local sculptor Paul Dardé (1888–1963). Unfortunately, little survives of medieval Lodève, as the town was nearly razed in retribution for its support of Montmorency's revolt.

Lodève makes a pleasant base for exploring the surrounding area, including the upper Orb valley to the west and Lac du Salagou to the south, but the nearest attraction is the **priory of St-Michel de Grandmont**, just 8km away, on a wooded rise to the east of town. The old monastery and its grounds can be visited as part of a **guided tour** or on your own (daily 10am–5/6/7pm; €5.60). Built in 1128, it was one of the first convents of the extremely strict Grandmontine Order of hermits, whose alarming popularity with the faithful prompted the power-jealous John XXII to clamp down on them in 1317. The buildings that remain today comprise one of their best-preserved houses, including a cloister, reception hall and an austere late thirteenth-century church. The spacious **grounds** are well worth a visit; their shaded woods are stocked with deer and other wildlife and punctuated by prehistoric dolmens and menhirs (going back some four thousand years) as well as Visigothic sarcophagi.

Practicalities

Lodève's **gare routière** (℡04.67.88.86.44) is on place de la République, right beside the town's **tourist office** (Mon–Fri 9.30am–noon & 2.30–6pm, Sat 9.30am–noon; ℡04.67.88.86.44, ⓦwww.lodeve.com). The best place to **stay** is the well-renovated ⚸ *Hôtel du Nord* (℡04.67.44.92.78, ⓦwww.hotellodeve.com; ❸) at 18 bd de la Liberté, just down from the post office. The young couple that run it are very welcoming, and the rooms range in size from singles to family-sized suites with kitchen; all have wi-fi. Another good choice is *Hôtel de la Paix* at 11 bd Montalangue (℡04.67.44.07.46, ⓦwww.hotel-dela-paix.com; closed Jan & Feb; ❸), run by the same family for over a century; its chief draw is its pool. The *de la Paix* has one of the better **restaurants** (*menus* from €18; Oct–April closed Sun eve & Mon), with solid, home-cooked regional dishes, and *Le Petit Sommelier*, at 3 pl de la République (*menus* from €17; closed Mon) is another good option. On Saturdays a large **market** takes over the centre of Lodève, while in the summer months (mid-June to mid-Sept) a *terroir* produce market convenes on Tuesday, Wednesday and Thursday afternoons in the place de la République. You can rent **bikes** at Club House, in avenue Vallot (℡04.67.96.46.48).

North to Ganges via the Cirque de Navacelles

Taking the D25 eastwards from just north of Lodève, you'll climb 15km up the wooded Brèze valley before reaching an open plain stretching a similar distance to the hamlet of **St-Maurice-Navacelles**. Here the road drops into the Vis valley, descending with it all the way to Ganges (see opposite). If you turn off to the north at St-Maurice, you'll come to the **CIRQUE DE NAVACELLES**, a breathtaking section of the valley where the river, carving down sharply through the surrounding plain, has doubled back on itself, leaving a small hillock stranded in the middle of the cirque; at its base huddles the ancient hamlet of **Navacelles**. The cirque can also be reached in a day's **hiking**; the GR653 east from Lodève links up with the GR7, which winds its way north, entering the Vis valley near St-Maurice before heading on into the Cévennes. Arriving by car, you'll first reach the belvedere on the south side of the cirque, from which you can contemplate the incredible sweep of the gorge and look down on the village 600m below. From the lookout point, the road follows a dramatic series of switchbacks descending to Navacelles itself – a tiny stone hamlet with a medieval bridge – before climbing to another lookout point on the north side. The **information centre** (daily 10am–noon & 2–6pm) for the cirque is located at the southern belvedere; it has a small exhibition explaining the formation of the curious canyon and conducts two- and three-hour walking tours (€5; frequently in English).

East of St-Maurice, the road snakes down into the **Vis gorges** for the remaining 26km to Ganges. Contrasting with the open scrub around Navacelles, this section of the valley is a steep and lush canyon, whose tree-clad banks at times close off the sky above with thick boughs. As you continue, it gradually widens, passing occasional signs of life – riverside *relais*, ancient bridges and abandoned factories – before opening up abruptly when it reaches the Hérault at Ganges.

As you'd expect, services are rather minimal in this neck of the woods: in Navacelles village, there's the homey **chambre d'hôtes** *Casa Lou Haîdouc* (℡04.67.81.51.54, ℮helene.nanciu@voila.fr; ❷). There are other possibilities along the Vis gorge, the most luxurious of which is the splendid *Château de Madières* (closed Nov–March; ℡04.67.73.84.03, ⓦwww.chateau-madieres.fr; ❾), a sumptuously renovated fourteenth-century castle with suites available.

Ganges and around

GANGES, the largest town in the upper Hérault valley, is primarily of interest as a transport hub and service centre for the more interesting places just to the south (which you can also access travelling along either of the two routes down to Montpellier – see p.218), and for the busy recreation industry which has grown up on the banks of the river. It was here, in August 1944, that the local *maquis* managed to repulse a column of three thousand German troops after a fierce ten-hour battle. Nowadays, there's little to see or do, although a walk through the old quarter will take you past a few remaining medieval houses, a pretty eighteenth-century market square and an imposingly dour Huguenot temple. All in all, though, these do not suffice to dispel a certain lingering air of stagnation.

The **gare routière** is on rue Jules-Ferry, just west of the central plan de l'Ormeau, which is where you'll find the **tourist office** (Mon–Fri 9am–noon/1pm & 2–6/7pm, Sat 9.30am–12.30am; July & Aug also Sat 3–7pm & Sun 10am–noon; ℡04.67.73.00.56, ⓦwww.ot-cevennes.com), and the **hotel** *de la Poste* (closed Jan; ℡04.67.73.85.88, ⓦwww.hoteldelaposteganges.com; ❷), with surprisingly good amenities and family-sized rooms. The *Domaine de Blancardy*, a working vineyard 7km out of town towards Nîmes (℡04.67.73.94.94, ⓦwww. blancardy.com; dorm beds €20, doubles ❹), operates a comfortable and well-equipped **gîte** with some private rooms and a good restaurant (from €13). The municipal **campsite** (mid-June to Aug; ℡04.67.57.92.97) is along the river at the southern end of Ganges, with the town's only laundry.

Of the local **restaurants**, the best is *Le Bon Coin* (closed Mon & Tues off season) at 32 cours de la République, featuring Savoyard cuisine, such as fondues and other mountain fare from €9. You'll find **internet** access at Pole Équateur, 17 rue Biron.

Laroque, the Grotte des Demoiselles and St-Bauzille

A couple of kilometres south of Ganges, the first place you come to is the hamlet of **Laroque**, attractively situated on a hillside along the Hérault river. It has a cheerful bankside promenade, with narrow medieval streets zigzagging up to the remains of its castle. A few kilometres further south, you'll come upon the area's biggest draw, the **Grotte des Demoiselles** (March & Oct daily 10am & 11am & 2–4.30pm; April–June & Sept daily 10am–5.30pm; July & Aug daily 10am–6pm; Nov–Feb Mon–Fri 2–4pm, Sat & Sun 10am & 11am & 2–4pm; €8.90), a little more than 2km east off the road. This incredibly vast cavern, discovered in 1770, stretches out below the plateau de Thaurac, the highland southeast of Ganges, and is famous for its huge stalactite and stalagmite formations. The obligatory one-hour **guided tour** (expect a long wait in high season; last departure 1hr before closing) is made aboard an underground funicular, which lends the whole thing an amusement-park air, and though the cave is spectacular, the whole experience can be a bit of a let-down, having to put up with all of the crowds and fuss.

Without doubt, the nicest place to stay in the area is **Laroque**, at the **chambre d'hôtes** *Le Parc aux Cèdres*, 120 av de l'Europe (℡04.67.73.82.63; ❹), in a park on the northern edge of town. There is also a **campsite**, the two-star *Le Tivoli* (June–Aug; ℡04.67.73.97.28), near the *Cèdres*. You can get excellent **food** at *Aux Trois*

Arches, on the main promenade (April–Oct; ☎04.67.73.86.80), while the nearby *Bar des Ramparts* has decent Belgian beers and home-made desserts.

St-Guilhem-le-Désert and the Grotte de Clamouse

The route from Ganges to St-Guilhem follows the course of the Hérault via the D4. Hugging the western bank of the river, the road follows the tortuous **Gorges de l'Hérault** to reach the stunningly situated village of **ST-GUILHEM-LE-DÉSERT**. There is no mistaking the great antiquity of St-Guilhem; nestled in a steep and wooded ravine rising from the gorge, the reddish roofs of its medieval houses contrast with the electric green of the surrounding trees. The village grew up around the abbey founded by Charlemagne's counsellor Guilhem, who returned from Rome in 800 with three pieces of wood said to be remnants of the Cross. Thanks to these relics, the monastery and the community around it thrived through the centuries that followed, both as a pilgrimage destination in its own right, as well as a stopping point on the way to Santiago de Compostela. Today, the immaculately preserved village, designated a UNESCO World Heritage Site, is still presided over by the eleventh-century **abbey-church of Gellone** (daily 8am–12.10pm & 2.30–6.20pm), up near the obligatory car park (€1.60 per hour). Crowned by a chunky, fifteenth-century bell tower, the church is the only surviving part of the once powerful monastic house. Its magnificent entryway, flanked by columns pillaged from Roman ruins, passes through a small vaulted narthex and opens into the cavernous but plain nave, ending in a curiously oversized transept and apse. Inside the church is the casket holding the remains of Guilhem (who was canonized after his death) and a reliquary holding one of the famous bits of wood. From the church you can climb down to the **crypt**, which dates from the eighth century, as well as the ruined **cloister**, whose north and west galleries are still in place. There is also a small **museum** here (July & Aug daily 11am–noon & 2/2.30–5/6pm; Sept–June Mon & Wed–Sat 2–5pm, Sun 2.30–5pm; €2), containing religious sculptures recovered from the destroyed abbey.

▲ St-Guilhem-le-Désert

The rest of the village consists of low, ancient houses which follow the narrow lanes leading down the ravine, interrupted by medieval pilgrims' fountains marked with the scallop-shell symbol of St James. Looking back as you descend past the church, you'll be treated to views of its impressive apsidal chapels. For the best **views** of St-Guilhem itself, take the one-hour hike from the car park up to the ruins of a castle, where you'll be rewarded by a beautiful vista of the village below.

Leaving St-Guilhem by road, the D4 continues 4km further along the dramatic canyon, passing the mouth of the **Grotte de Clamouse** (Feb–Nov daily 10.30am–5/7pm; €8.50), famous for its immense and delicate crystalline formations. Only 500m later, the gorge abruptly opens up at the beginning of the low Languedocian coastal plain; the transition is marked by a great medieval *pont du diable* (arched bridge) which crosses the river above a gravelly bank now serving as a popular river-beach.

Practicalities

St-Guilhem's **tourist office** (daily: July & Aug 9am–7pm; Sept–June 10.30am–12.30pm & 2–7pm; ℡04.67.57.44.32, Ⓦwww.saint-guilhem-le -desert.com) is at the foot of the village, just above the main road; the office has an ATM, and they can give you a coupon offering you €2 off entry to the Grotte de Clamouse (see opposite). The most comfortable of St-Guilhem's **hotels** is *Le Guilhaume d'Orange* at 2 av Guillaume d'Orange (℡04.667.57.24.53, Ⓦwww .guilhaumedorange.com; ❹), with ten individually designed rooms. The budget option is the English-speaking *gîte de la Tour* (℡04.67.57.34.00; ❶), located in a medieval tower in the village. The village's best **restaurant** is at *L'Auberge sur le Chemin* (Tues–Sun; ℡04.67.57.75.05), where you can enjoy an excellent *terroir menu* (€25) in an atmospheric medieval room. A dramatic approach to the town can be made from the riverbank 3km east of Causse on the D122, from where Canoë La Vallée des Moulins (℡04.67.73.12.45) runs **canoeing** excursions downriver to St-Guilhem. St-Guilhem's **rafting centre** is at the bottom of the hill, across the road (℡04.67.55.75.75) from the entrance to the village.

Pic-St-Loup and St-Martin-de-Londres

Some 30km due south of Ganges looms the great **Pic-St-Loup** (658m), a hulking limestone ridge which, dominating the plain of Hérault, can be seen from Béziers almost to Nîmes. **ST-MARTIN-DE-LONDRES**, 13km south from Ganges by road, makes the best base for hiking the remaining 10km to the *pic*'s wooded summit – a site from which you can enjoy impressive panoramas, but which can only be reached by foot (drivers can get as close as 4km away by taking the D113 to the hamlet of Cazevieille). St-Martin is another town of great antiquity and, contrary to appearances, its name has nothing to do with England's capital, London ("Londres" in French); it is named after the Plaine de Londres (from the Celtic word for "swamp") in which the town is located. Testament to the town's history is the beautiful knot of buildings focused around the eleventh-century Romanesque **church**, founded by monks from nearby St-Guilhem. Its interior is plain, but is more than made up for by the three-lobed Byzantine-style exterior, which blends in harmoniously with the surrounding buildings. Elsewhere in the town, you can see how the two concentric sets of walls and towers were swallowed up by houses over the centuries.

South of St-Martin (and also on the Montpellier bus route) is Viols-en-Laval, where you'll find the excavated **prehistoric village** of **Cambous** (May, June & Sept–Nov Sat & Sun 2–6pm; July & Aug Tues–Sun 2–7pm; €4), once home to the "Fontbouisse" culture, which practised copper-smelting and ceramic production as well as agriculture and herding some five thousand years ago.

St-Martin's **tourist office** (May, June & late Aug to mid-Sept Mon & Tues 9.30am–12.30pm; July to late Aug daily 9am–1pm; ☏04.67.55.09.59, ⓦwww .tourismed.com) is on the main road in the centre of town and there's a funky and friendly **chambre d'hôtes**, ⚶ *De ci…De là!* (☏04.67.86.36.83, ⓦwww.decidela .fr; ➍ includes breakfast) on the edge of town. The **campsite**, *Pic de Loup* (April–Sept; ☏04.67.55.00.53, ⓔpatrick.depelchin@orange.fr), is just east on the main road. ⚶ *Les Muscardins* **restaurant** at 19 rte des Cévennes (☏04.67.55.75.90; closed Feb, Mon & Tues) has superb Cevennoise *menus* from €29 featuring Aubrac beef, and an excellent selection of home-made desserts.

Travel details

Trains

The main coastal rail line (with TGV) connects Montpellier to Perpignan and Nîmes. SNCF buses may run in lieu of trains on secondary lines; services are reduced on Sundays and holidays. TGV stations are indicated with an asterisk.
Montpellier* to:
Nîmes* (connection to Beaucaire/Tarascon) (several hourly; 30min).
Paris* (many daily; 3hr 30min+).
Perpignan*, via Sète, Agde, Béziers* (connections to Bédarieux) and Narbonne* (several hourly; 2hr 15min).
Toulouse*, via Sète, Agde, Béziers* (connections to Bédarieux), via Carcassonne* (connection to Quillan) and Castelnaudary (several hourly; 2hr 15min–2hr 55min).

Buses

Hérault's bus hubs are in Montpellier and Béziers. Many lines have no Sunday service; service on Saturdays and holidays may be reduced. Summer lines, *lignes estivales*, serve St-Guilhem and other tourist sites. For a route map, full schedules and information on discount tickets, see ⓦwww .herault.fr or ☏08.25.34.01.34.
Clermont-l'Hérault to: Lodève (several daily; 25min); Pézenas (several daily; 35min).

Ganges to: Montpellier (several daily; 1hr 10min); Nîmes (several daily; 1hr 15min); St-Hippolyte (several daily; 15min); St-Martin-de-Londres (several daily; 25min); Sauve (several daily; 25min).
Gignac (summer only) to: Pont du Diable (daily; 20min); St-Guilhem (daily; 35min).
La Grande-Motte to: Lunel (daily; 35min).
Lodève to: Béziers (several daily; 1hr 50min); Clermont-l'Hérault (several daily; 25min); Pézenas (several daily; 1hr 20min).
Montpellier to: Aigues-Mortes (many daily; 1hr 5min); Bédarieux (several 6 daily; 1hr 45min); Béziers (several daily; 1hr 55min); Clermont-l'Hérault (many daily; 40min); Ganges (several daily; 1hr 10min); Gignac (for St-Guilhem; many daily; 40min); La Grande-Motte (many daily, in summer hourly; 30min); Lamalou (several daily; 2hr 5min); Le Grau-du-Roi (many daily; 45min); Lodève (several daily; 1hr 15min); Nîmes (daily; 50min); Pézenas (several daily; 1hr 25min); St-Bauzille (several daily; 55min); St-Hippolyte (daily; 1hr 45min); St-Martin-de-Londres (several daily; 45min); St-Pons (daily; 2hr 25min); Sète (several daily; 45min); Sommières (several daily; 1hr 10min).
Pézenas to: Béziers (several daily; 32min).
Sète to: Balaruc-les-Bains (many daily; 20min); Bouzigues (several daily; 35min); Loupian (daily; 40min); Marseillan (daily; 40min); Marseillan-Plage (daily; 30min); Mèze (daily; 45min).

6

Narbonne, Béziers and around

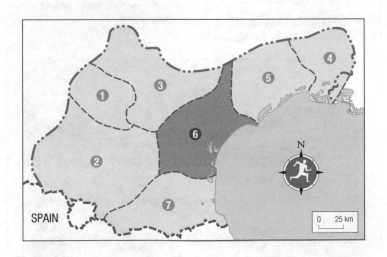

SPAIN

N

0   25 km

CHAPTER 6

Highlights

✳ **Lagrasse** This sleepy little walled village tucked among the hills of the Corbières sits beside an ancient and once-powerful monastery. See p.264

✳ **Canal du Midi** France's seventeenth-century engineering wonder is now a sublimely beautiful thoroughfare for cyclists, walkers and boaters. See pp.265–271

✳ **Oppidum d'Ensérune** These ruins of a pre-Roman settlement of "civilized" barbarians sit perched on a ridge above the vineyards of Béziers. See p.271

✳ **Old Béziers** A city of atmospheric streets whose splendid cathedral provides views as far west as the peak of the Canigou. See p.273

✳ **The Orb valley** Rarely visited, this river course boasts unique microclimate zones and near-forgotten hamlets. See p.278

▲ Canal du Midi

Narbonne, Béziers
and around

The provincial towns of **Narbonne** and **Béziers** dominate the flat expanse of marshy alluvial plain formed by the outpourings of the Hérault, Orb and Aude rivers, whose mouths all reach the Mediterranean within a 15km strip. The former town is the smaller, but generally livelier centre, with a compact medieval core and vibrant nightlife, while the latter is a historically proud and defiant place which, though somewhat more sedate these days, springs to life in the summer with its renowned *feria*. Poised just north of the Étang de Bages' long expanse, Narbonne is best situated for excursions into the **Corbières**, an isolated range of hills stretching south to Roussillon; once forming the Cathar heartland, they harbour the idyllic village of **Termes**, with its *château*, and the strikingly beautiful hamlet of **Lagrasse**. Swinging sharp east at Carcassonne, the River Aude makes its way along the northern edge of the Corbières, shadowed by the **Canal du Midi**, the incredible waterway which has dominated the whole of this area since the seventeenth century. The canal route takes you past the various monuments of the **Minervois** – the region squeezed in between the Corbières and Haut Languedoc – and attractive Languedocian scenery before it splits, with the Canal de la Robine heading south towards Narbonne and the main waterway meandering on, via Béziers, to the Bassin de Thau. Skirting Béziers, the route up the **Orb valley** threads north along the border of the Parc Naturel Régional du Haut Languedoc, passing a succession of villages which have survived the centuries thanks to the river's fertile banks. The coastal stretch curving between the two towns is, for the most part, an area of uninviting marsh, but at either end two chunks of terra firma, the Montagne St-Loup and de la Clape, provide anchors for a couple of old ports, **Agde** and **Gruissan**, each of which have modern beach-resort alter egos. Although those interested in sun and swimming will find prettier surroundings in the Côte Vermeille to the south (see Chapter 7), both of these old settlements are worth a visit for their gentle ambience – Agde from Béziers and Gruissan from Narbonne.

Public transport facilities in this region vary considerably. At Narbonne, the busy coastal rail line to Perpignan branches off from the main Toulouse–Marseille route, on which Béziers can be found. In the hinterland, you'll have to depend on bus services, which are fairly good for the major towns along the coast and the Orb valley. Out-of-the-way sites are more difficult: Minerve, for example, isn't served

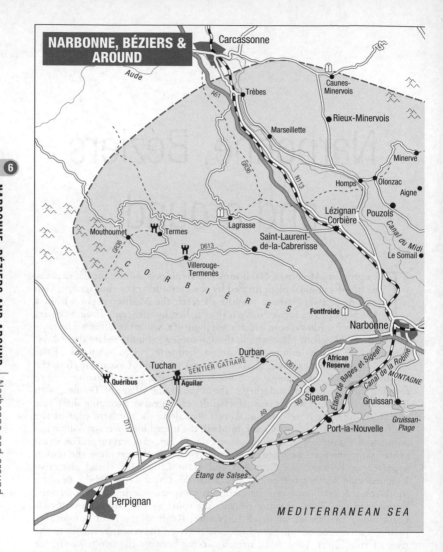

NARBONNE, BÉZIERS & AROUND

at all by public transport. But in any case – if you have time – the best way to travel through the region is by canal, either by piloting a houseboat, or biking or hiking along the towpath.

Narbonne and around

There's no mistaking **NARBONNE** as you approach it, its towering cathedral rising up over the rooftops and dominating the coastal plain for miles around. Once the capital of the Roman province of Gallia Narbonensis, it flourished as a port and communications centre from ancient times into the Middle Ages, and

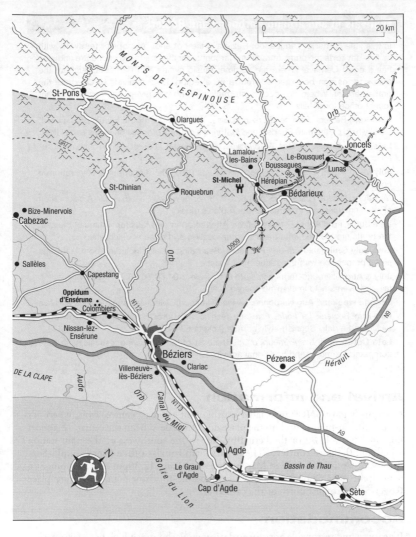

was home to an important Jewish university in the twelfth and thirteenth centuries. But in the mid-1300s things suddenly went awry: the Jews were expelled, the plague struck, the Black Prince burnt down the town, the dykes of the Aude burst and the port silted up, a series of disasters which brought ruin to Narbonne's economy. A tentative prosperity returned only in the late 1800s with the birth of the modern wine industry, which continues to support the town. Today, it's a pleasant provincial town with a small but well-preserved old core, centred on the great truncated choir of the **cathedral** and bisected by the **Canal de la Robine** (see p.269), whose banks provide a grassy esplanade running through the city centre.

Festivals in and around Narbonne and Béziers

In this little corner of Languedoc, Béziers is the hot spot for popular **festivals**, with its five-day **feria** the prime attraction. Narbonne, for its part, is big on theatre and also has a good Carnaval. There are summer music cycles and parties throughout the area and, as can be expected from a wine region, local festivals to celebrate the grape harvest. Where no specific information number is given, contact the relevant tourist office for details.

Late April Béziers: *Fête de la St-Aphrodise*. The feast day of the town's patron saint, usually held on the third Sunday, and featuring a curious procession with a camel float.

Late May Béziers: *Fêtes Médiévales*. A medieval market, with costumed re-enactments, food and fun.

July 7–10 Agde: *Grande Fête des Pêcheurs*. Three-day fishermen's celebration in honour of St Peter, patron saint of the sea.

Mid-July Béziers: *Festa d'Oc* ☎04.67.31.76.76, ⓦ www.ville-beziers.fr. A celebration of all things Occitan, in particular the region's music.

Late July Cap d'Agde: *Fête de la Mer*. After an open-air Mass for victims of the sea, the boats are blessed, and there's water-jousting and general celebration.

Late July Gruissan: *Fête des Pêcheurs*. Sea faring rituals, including boat blessings and a procession with the statue of St Peter.

July & Aug Villerouge-Termenès: *Fête Médiévale* ☎04.68.70.06.24. Medieval market, fair and events held in even-numbered years.

Second weekend Aug Narbonne: *La Via Mercaderia*. Medieval street market and fair.

Mid-Aug Béziers: *La Feria*. Five-day festival with street entertainment, fireworks, music and a daily Spanish-style *corrida* (tickets €24–83).

Late Oct Béziers: *Les Primeurs d'Oc*. The best of the local wine festivals, with wine competitions, music and traditional activities.

Arrival and information

Narbonne's **gare SNCF** is situated northeast of the city centre, from where it's about a fifteen-minute walk to the place de l'Hôtel de Ville in the centre, or a short hop on buses #1, #2 or the Petit Bus. Just to the southwest of the train station you'll find the **gare routière**. The town's main **tourist office** (April to mid-Sept daily 9am–7pm; mid-Sept to March Mon–Sat 10am–12.30pm & 1.20–6pm, Sun 9am–1pm; ☎04.68.65.15.60, ⓦwww.narbonne-tourisme.com) is on tiny place Roger-Salengro, just north of the cathedral.

Accommodation

It's easy to find reasonable **accommodation** in Narbonne, which has a fair number of good-value hotels, as well as a hostel and a couple of decent campsites.

Hotels

de France 6 rue Rossini ☎04.68.32.09.75, ⓦwww.hotelnarbonne.com. A quiet nineteenth-century establishment south of the old town, close to the covered market and the canal. It's basic but has a spread of amenities including TVs in the rooms, a/c and wi-fi and parking facilities, and is also wheelchair-accessible. ❷

Grand Hôtel du Languedoc 22 bd Gambetta ☎04.68.65.14.74, ⓦwww.hoteldulanguedoc.com. Located on the ring road, a five-minute walk south of the cathedral in an attractive old building converted from a nineteenth-century townhouse. Well-appointed and comfortable, this is one of the better deals in town; rooms have cable TV and wi-fi, and there's a good bar and private garage. ❹

La Résidence 6 rue du 1er Mai ☎04.68.32.19.41, ⓦwww.hotelresidence.fr. An early nineteenth-century converted house, in a great location on a quiet street near the Pont Voltaire. Comfortable rooms with a/c, and there's a garage and lift. **⑤**

Will's 23 av Pierre-Sémard ℡04.68.90.44.50, ⊛willshotel-narbonne .com. Friendly place and a travellers' stand-by set in a nineteenth-century townhouse right by the station. Accepts pets and has amenities like TV and cable, but fills up quickly. **③**

Hostel and campsite

Camping Club Les Mimosas Chaussée de Mandirac ℡04.68.49.03.72, ⊛www.lesmimosas.com.

Big three-star site with all mod cons, located 6km south of town on the Étang de Bages (no public transport). Open mid-March to Oct.

MJC Centre International de Séjour Pl Roger-Salengro ℡04.68.32.01.00, ⊛www.cis-narbonne .com. Modern hostel right by the tourist office, with dorm beds for €15.40 as well as some rather expensive private rooms (**③**). Nice lounge with TV and a simple restaurant.

The Town

If Narbonne's name lends itself to a certain sense of grandeur, you'll be surprised by its diminutive size. The whole of the **old town** – which is where all the sights

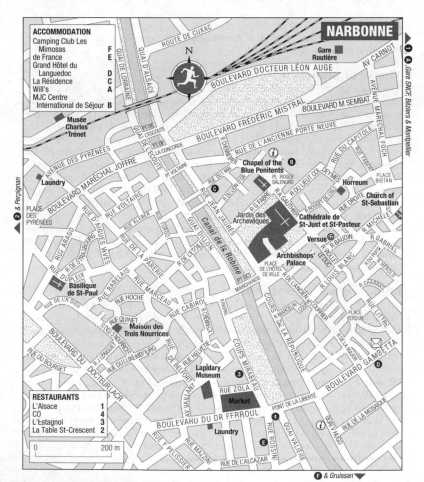

are – fits snugly into a 1km-by-750m rectangle, bisected north–south by the **Canal de la Robine**, with the **Archbishop's Palace**, its **museums** and the **cathedral** dominating affairs.

The Archbishop's Palace

The broad square of the place de l'Hôtel de Ville, in whose centre you'll find a recently uncovered section of the Roman Via Domitia, is overwhelmed by the great facade of the **Archbishop's Palace**, peppered by pointed ogival windows and decorated with Gothic-looking vegetal flourishes. But its "authentic" charms are the result of one of Viollet-le-Duc's imaginative repair jobs (see box, p.104) – an ersatz bit of medieval fantasy. Today the palace's rambling complex incorporates the city's two major museums, plus the entrance to the cathedral (see opposite). Passing through the main doors of the palace, which are directly on the square, on the left you'll find the entrance to the towering **donjon** (Mon–Fri 9am–noon & 2–6pm; free) commissioned in the late thirteenth century by the town's lord and archbishop, Gilles Aycelin. This ponderous 42m defensive tower is a fine example of late thirteenth-century military architecture – its splayed-out base was designed to prevent battering and undermining. There's not much to see inside, but after climbing the 162-step keystone staircase you can enjoy excellent **views** of the cathedral and the surrounding countryside.

Musée d'Art et d'Histoire

To the left of the *donjon*, you'll see the entrance to the **Musée d'Art et d'Histoire** (April–Sept daily 9.30am–12.15pm & 2–6pm; Oct–March Tues–Sun 10am–noon & 2–5pm; €3.70). The main attraction here is the luxurious interior of the palace itself, with its *artesonado* ceilings and other details; rooms to look out for in particular are the audience hall, the king's chamber – with seventeenth-century painted walls – and the grand salon. That said, the **Orientalist collection** in the Salle Hippolyte Lazerges alone almost justifies the admission price: paintings depicting sultry Berber girls staring enigmatically at the viewer, or eyes flashing from under turbans, as bearded men pose with cruel-looking swords on horse- or camel-back. On your way out, poke your head in the **Hall of the Synods**, accessed from the same grand staircase as the museum. Built by one of the archbishops in 1628, it was used for clerical meetings and sittings of the *parlement* of Languedoc and is decorated with impressive Aubusson tapestries.

Musée Archéologique

A much better collection can be found just across the courtyard in the **Musée Archéologique** (same hours as the art and history museum). It begins with the Neolithic period, represented by various skull parts and a series of footprints preserved in solidified muck, and follows with Bronze Age finds. The mainstay, however, is its **Roman collection**, whose strong maritime streak reflects the role Narbonne played as a major port of Roman Gaul. Various stone carvings illustrate ships of the period, and there's a towering 3.5-metre wood-and-lead ship's **anchor** on display. Combined with the seafaring items is a collection of first-century BC **Roman paintings** – the best of its kind in France.

The Cathédrale de St-Just et St-Pasteur

From the archeological museum a narrow alley, the passage de l'Ancre, leads further into the complex, towards the entrance to the **Cathédrale de St-Just et St-Pasteur** (daily: July–Sept 10am–7pm; Oct–June 9am–noon & 2–6pm; free). Christianity in the city dates back at least to the time of Constantine; as a provincial capital Narbonne became seat of an archbishop, and a cathedral was raised. Its exterior is pure Gothic – the tall and narrow core of the building, dominated by expanses of stained-glass window, is braced by sturdy buttresses, from which delicate-looking flying buttresses launch up to support the highest points on the walls. The building you see today was begun in 1272. With the completion of the hulking 49-metre choir some fifty years later, construction of the nave, which was meant to extend westwards, was held up after the first couple of stages, because extending it would have involved knocking down the old Roman defensive wall – still very useful in those uncertain times. Thus, as with Toulouse's cathedral, the project was never completed, leaving the church with its strikingly odd form. As you climb the short flight of stairs from the street you'll arrive first at the compact **cloister**, from where there's a good view of the flying buttresses. A door on the west side of the cloister leads to the formal-style **Jardin des Archevêques**, with even better views, and around to the so-called **Cour St-Eutrope**, which is in fact the sealed-off stub of the aborted nave. The entrance to the church itself is on the north side of the cloister.

On entering, the first thing that will strike you is the tremendous space inside the unfinished building – its soaring ceiling the third-highest for a French cathedral. Along with the upward dynamic of the design, the predominance of stained glass

---

Essentials

Bike rental From the municipal Vélostation by the boat moorings on cours de la République (℡06.21.49.61.95).

Boat tours and rental For canal trips, Berges de la Robine, cours de la République (℡06.11.75.36.98), rents electric boats by the hour (from €24); Connoisseurs Cruisers, promenade des Barques (℡04.68.65.14.55, ⓦwww.connoisseur.ie), has houseboats.

Discount cards Available at the tourist office and museums: one gets you into the art and history museums, the Horreum and the lapidary museum (€5.20), and another into all of the town's sights, including the cathedral treasury (€7.50).

Internet access Versus, rue Droite (Mon–Fri 10am–8pm, Sat 10am–2am, Sun 2–7pm).

Laundry 24 av des Pyrénées; 25 bd Docteur-Ferroul; 3 av Karl-Marx

Markets Flea market Thurs and Sun mornings in cours de la République; organic food Sat 8am–1pm, place du Forum.

Taxi Aude Taxi ℡04.68.41.65.56.

over stone on the walls is a hallmark of high Gothic style – some of the windows date from the original construction. Directly behind the altar, a badly damaged – but nevertheless beautiful – fourteenth-century stone **retable** illustrates themes of the Redemption with exceptionally carved and incredibly kinetic high-relief figures. Around this is a series of chapels hung with fine Gobelin and Aubusson tapestries. From the southernmost of these, a spiral stair leads up to the cathedral's **treasury** (July–Sept Mon–Sat 11am–6pm & Sun 2–6pm; Oct–June 2–5/6pm; €2.20), the centrepiece of which is a sumptuous fifteenth-century tapestry depicting the Holy Trinity, personified as three kings. Other fine pieces include a ninth-century ivory panel and an eleventh-century pyx of Muslim origin. Stop also in the gift shop, housed in the elegant **Salle au Pilier**, an airy fourteenth-century chamber whose Gothic vaulting is supported by a single delicate pillar, and in which you'll find rare carvings dating back to the Visigoths of the sixth century.

Around the palace and cathedral

It's worth taking time to explore the lesser sights in the vicinity of the palace and cathedral. First among these is the small **chapel of the Blue Penitents** (hours vary), just steps from the tourist office on the west side of place Salengro. South of the square two small streets lead directly away from the massive east wall of the cathedral into a compact **medieval neighbourhood**, once the *quartier* of the choristers and other functionaries of the great church: rue du Lieutenant-Colonel-Deymes and the next street along, rue Rouget de l'Isle, both contain houses with distinctly medieval windows and doors. On the latter street, at no. 7, is the **Horreum** (same hours as art museum; €3.70). Despite Narbonne's importance in Roman times, this is the only structure in the city to have survived from that era. Its name means "granary" in Latin, and that's precisely what it was: an underground grain store which was most likely attached to a market building or depot above the ground.

West of the Canal de la Robine

Narbonne's old town extends over the **Canal de la Robine** to the west, a humbler section of town even in the Middle Ages. Today, the narrow lanes and crooked streets are home to the city's marginalized North African community, and wear a certain air of neglect. Even so, it is eminently explorable; there are fewer shops and restaurants here, and the tiny windows of the ageing buildings hang with laundry, but the main reason for visiting is to see the two parish churches which share this side of the river. The first is the **Basilique de St-Paul** – a tall thirteenth-century construction, chipped and battered on the outside over the years, but inside possessing a pleasant mixture of Romanesque and Gothic. The main attraction is the **crypt** (Mon–Sat 9am–noon & 2–6pm, Sun 9am–noon; free): built over a paleo-Christian necropolis and dating back to the fourth century, it is where the town's first bishop was buried.

Close by you'll find the magnificent sixteenth-century facade of the **Maison des Trois Nourrices**, and back toward the canal, the former abbey-church of **Notre-Dame-de-la-Mourguié**. This is now home to the town's **lapidary museum** (same hours as art musem; €3.70), housing a large, but rather monotonous, collection of over a thousand statues, inscriptions, tombstones and sarcophagi, most dating back to Roman days. The town's beautifully restored nineteenth-century **covered market** (daily 7am–1pm) is beside the church on the banks of the canal.

Eating and drinking

While Narbonne is definitely not the culinary capital of the Southwest, you won't starve. There are a couple of **restaurants** which stand out, as well as an array of unexceptional brasseries and bistros where you can eat for under €18. The canalside is an excellent option for an afternoon aperitif, and late-night **bars** can be found in and around rue Marcelin-Courail in the old town.

🏃 **L'Alsace** 2 av Pierre-Sémard ☏04.68 .65.10.24. Just opposite the train station, this is undoubtedly Narbonne's best restaurant, featuring *terroir* and fresh fish dishes. Great decor, mammoth servings and *menus* from €14. Closed Tues & Wed.
CO 1 rue Rossini ☏04.20.39.12.91. Narbonne's swishest eating establishment is surprisingly sophisticated, with arty decor, modern furniture and subtle lighting. The *gastronomique carte* is a welcome relief from *steak frites. Menus* at €22–28.
L'Estagnol Cours Mirabeau ☏04.68.65.09.27. On the market side of the canal, this no-frills *terroir*

restaurant also has a good fish selection. Solid *menus* in the €12–28 range; less at lunch time. Closed Sun & Mon eve.
🏃 **La Table St-Crescent** Domaine St-Crescent-le-Vieil, 68 av Général-Leclerc ☏04.68.41.37.37. This excellent *gastronomique* is located in an ancient eighth-century oratory about 1km south of the canal, in the local wine producers' Palais des Vins, where you can shop for fine local vintages. Expect to spend about €40 per person. Closed Sat noon, Sun eve & Mon.

Listings

Car rental ADA, 12 av des Pyrénées ☏04.68.42.44.81; Avis, 21 bd Marcel-Sembat ☏04.68.32.43.36; Europcar, 52 bd Frédéric-Mistral ☏04.68.32.34.54; Locabest, 2 rue Romain ☏04.68.65.35.50.
Hospital Centre Hospitalier de Narbonne, bd Docteur-Lacroix (☏04.68.41.00.00; bus #1, #2 or #3 to "Hôpital").
Pharmacies Pharmacie de l'Hôtel de Ville, pl de l'Hôtel de Ville. For night-time and weekend opening hours, check the notice on the door.

Police Gendarmerie, rue Anatole-France ☏04.68.90.38.50.
Rugby Local team RCNM play at the Parc des Sports et de l'Amitié, southeast of the old town (☏04.68.41.76.93; bus #3 to "Parc des Sports").
Swimming Espace Liberté, rte de Perpignan (☏04.68.42.17.89; bus #3 to "Roches Grises" or "Hautes de Narbonne"). This complex includes both covered pools and a water park.

Gruissan and Gruissan-Plage

Some 20km southeast of Narbonne, the quiet fishing town of **GRUISSAN** cuts a striking figure from the distance, with its circular streets huddled around an ancient tower, and filling a dramatic-looking promontory in the inland *étang* which bears its name. Arriving, you may be surprised to find little sign of life among the fading colours of Gruissan's houses, or even around the ruins of the **watchtower** (no set hours; free entry) – development has turned its back on the town. The salty Étang du Grazier separates Gruissan from the narrow spit of sand marking the Mediterranean's shore. Here, about 1km from the old *circulade*, a concrete expanse of low-rise hotels has choked the banks of the inlet, and spreads north to the equally vacuous development of **GRUISSAN-PLAGE** (known locally as the "port"). Apart from the traditional array of beachside activities and sights for which the towns are admirably equipped, there is virtually nothing to see or do on this stretch of the coast. If you tire of wandering Gruissan's near-deserted streets and need a break from the beach, you can head to the tourist office, which distributes a series of **biking** and **walking** itineraries in the low but rugged mountain of La Clape, separating Narbonne from the coast.

Buses stop by the **tourist office** (July & Aug daily 9am–1pm & 3–7pm; Sept–June Mon–Sat 9.30am–noon & 2–6pm; ☏04.68.49.09.00, ⓦwww.ville-gruissan .fr) on boulevard Pech-Maynaud, between the old and new towns. There's no real reason to spend the night here, but if you are intent on a bout of beachside hedonism, you'll find a selection of modern, near-identical two- and three-star **hotels**. Right on the beachfront, *Le Floride* (℡04.68.49.04.06, Ⓦwww.legrandsoleil.com; ❸) is a reasonable choice with good amenities, including wi-fi, while the *Port* (mid-April to mid-Oct; ℡04.68.49.07.33, Ⓦwww.hotel-gruissan.com; ❺) is closer to the old town, on boulevard de la Corderie, and has a pool. The best-value of the several **campsites** in the area is the municipal site (April–Nov; ℡04.68.49.07.22, Ⓦwww .ville-gruissan.fr), on route de l'Ayrolle in the old town. If you're looking for a **meal** in town, well-priced seafood and fish can be enjoyed at *L'Estagnol*, on avenue de Narbonne (March–Sept; ℡04.68.49.01.27), whose patio dining area has good views (*menus* from €24), and *Le Phoebus* (℡04.68.49.03.05) in old Gruissan, at 4 rue Amiral-Courbet (*menus* €25–43).

Sigean and Tuchan

Heading south from Narbonne, the road hugs the base of the rising hills, separated from the sea by a wide buffer – a series of salty *étangs* – and accompanied by a landscape characterized by scrubby trees, red soil and an impossibly blue sky in summer. There's little along the coast to detain you until you arrive at unremarkable **SIGEAN**, 8km north of which is a large **African nature reserve** (daily 9am–4/6.30pm; €25). This immense drive-through park (no motorcycles) re-creates several equatorial habitats, including brushland, savannah and plain, and lazing around you'll see lions, giraffes, rhinos and hippos, as well as graceful oryx and springboks. For those without cars, a series of footpaths have been laid out among the habitats in a limited area.

In the hills southwest of Sigean, along the Cathar trail, the hamlet of **TUCHAN** is presided over by the **Château d'Aguilar** (daily: April to mid-June 10.30am– 5.30pm; mid-June to Sept 10am–7pm; Oct to mid-Nov 11am–5pm; €3.50), with a well-preserved thirteenth- and fourteenth-century curtain wall and keep. Tuchan is also home to the rather over priced *Relais d'Aguilar* (℡04.68.45.47.84, Ⓦwww.relaisaguilar.com; ❹), which also has a campsite, a restaurant (from €14) and a pool. Alternatively, *l'Amandier* (℡04.68.45.89.48, Ⓦhotel-restaurant-aude .com) in Durban, halfway between Sigean and Tuchan, can provide decent **accommodation** (❷) and a meal (from €14).

The Corbières

To journey into the heart of the hilly **Corbières** region, which fans out southwest of Narbonne, bordered to the west by the upper Aude valley and to the south by the Fenouillèdes hills of northern Roussillon, is to enter a world very distinct from the coastal plain. As the land rises, the roads narrow, twisting and writhing up into the forests of the low mountains, tenaciously following the stream beds which cut into the slopes. Once the heart of Cathar territory, this area has suffered centuries of abandonment and neglect, and many hamlets lack even a café or a proper payphone, let alone a restaurant or hotel. For all of this, it is a splendid place to drive through, offering the ancient monasteries of **Fontfroide** and **Lagrasse**, and the Cathar sites of **Villerouge-Termenès** and **Termes**. Without your own transport, however, the Corbières is difficult to access, the only bus route following the D613 from Narbonne.

Fontfroide

Passing through the rocky *garrigues* west of Narbonne, the D613 leads you past the narrow turn-off to the **Monastery of Fontfroide**, 22km out of town.

Following this road south for four kilometres, you'll come across the stout walls of the ancient Cistercian foundation, tucked inside a shallow valley hidden among cypress groves. Founded in the late eleventh century by a count of Narbonne, it saw its greatest prosperity in the two subsequent centuries, after which, like so many monastic centres, it began to decline. The monastery's best-known abbot was Jacques Fournier, who as Bishop of Foix commanded the Inquisition which investigated the Cathars of Montaillou (see box, p.115), and went on in 1337 to be elected pope as Benedict XII. In private hands for the last hundred years or so, the abbey can only be visited as part of a one-hour **guided tour** (daily: April–June & Sept 10am–12.15pm & 1.45–5.30pm; July & Aug 10am–6pm; Oct 10am–12.15pm & 1.45–4.45pm; Nov–March 10am–noon & 2–4pm; €9). It's best to come early in the morning or late in the day in order to avoid crowds; but be warned, this is a popular stop on bus tours, and in high season is frequently too busy to be enjoyable.

There's no accommodation at Fontfroide, so if you're travelling by **bus** you'll want to make sure you are at the main road in time to catch the last one back to Narbonne or further on up into the hills. There is, however, an excellent **restaurant** at the monastery, *La Bergerie* (closed Dec–Feb), which is divided into two parts: the less-expensive lunch-time dining room serves traditional but well-executed dishes (*menus* from €17); while the evening-only *gastronomique* will set you back €35 or more (closed Mon).

Villerouge-Termenès and Termes

West from Fontfroide along the D613, the road forks right for Lagrasse (see p.264), and left towards the hills. Following this second route will lead you into some of the wildest back-country of the region, where forested uplands are capped by the tumbled remains of nameless castles. As you round the top of the 404m-high Col de Villerouge you'll get a startling view of the village of **VILLEROUGE-TERMENÈS** below, dominated by the tall keep of its impressively restored **castle** (Feb, March & late Oct to Dec Sat, Sun & school hols 10am–5pm; April–June & Sept to mid-Oct daily 10am–6pm; July & Aug daily 10am–7.30pm; €6). The earlier Cathar fort here was destroyed in the wake of its conquest by Crusaders in 1210, and the present structure, dating from the 1300s, was designed not to protect but to dominate the inhabitants of the surrounding hills. A visit involves an engaging audiovisual show which recaps the history of the area and recounts the tale of Guilhem Bélibaste, the Cathar *parfait* who was burned at the stake here in 1321. Afterwards it's worth taking a walk through the village huddled around the castle; the town was almost certainly fortified in the twelfth century, but the walls that are visible today were built to fend off the English and their allies during the Hundred Years' War in the 1300s. South of the *enceinte* you'll find the **church** of St-Étienne, which houses an immense sixteenth-century retable.

Leaving Villerouge, another steep ascent takes you to the **Col de Bedos** (485m), where a narrow paved road veers off to the right. Carefully following this relentless succession of hairpin curves will take you over hill and into valley until you make a sharp descent to **TERMES**. Little more than a cluster of ancient houses set on cramped but orderly streets, this extraordinarily beautiful hamlet would be worth a visit even if it weren't for its famous castle. Trees crowd over the narrow stream, spanned by a centuries-old stone bridge, and the sharply rising slopes above are covered by a blanket of beech, ash and stunted oak. The only thing that ruins the effect is the modern reception centre across the river, where you begin the arduous ascent to the ruins of the **castle** (March & mid-Oct to Dec Sat, Sun &

school hols 10am–5pm; April–June & Sept to mid-Oct daily 10am–6pm; July & Aug daily 10am–7.30pm; €3.50), one of the "five sons of Carcassonne." You wouldn't know it from either the ruins or the village, but this castle was dominated by one of the greatest feudal domains of Languedoc. Ruled by an unrepentant heretic lord, Raymond, it was a prime target for de Montfort, who besieged it for four months, until the disease-ravaged garrison could resist no more. The castle remained in use until destroyed by Richelieu in the seventeenth century. Clambering among the remains of the two concentric sets of walls, you'll find the chapel and can take in breathtaking **views** over the hills around.

Practicalities

Services are extremely thin on the ground in this neck of the woods, with accommodation limited to an unofficial **campsite** on the riverside outside Termes, just before you enter town. **Eating** is a little better: in Villerouge you can enjoy a lively meal in the castle's *Rôtisserie Médiévale* (closed Sun eve & Mon except hols, open weekends by reservation only off-season; ℡04.68.70.06.06) for about €27.

Lagrasse

Just over halfway from Narbonne to Carcassonne and separated from the Aude valley by the low ridge of the Montagne d'Alaric, **LAGRASSE** is the largest and most beautiful village of the Corbières highlands. A compact walled settlement set idyllically where the Orbieu opens up in a broad hollow, it hugs the right bank of the shallow river, while its magnificent abbey squats on the far side. Delightfully, Lagrasse is not very touristy; the grid of streets in the old town is almost completely residential, and you'll hardly see a postcard stand or gift shop. Much of the old *enceinte* is intact, and as you cross the eleventh-century bridge, try to crane over its protective walls to look at the town's riverside fortifications, now pierced by the scores of windows of the houses built against them – an especially evocative sight at dusk. It's only about a five-minute walk from the far side of the river to the **abbey of Ste-Marie d'Orbieu** (daily: late Jan to June & Oct–Dec 10am–12.30pm & 2–5/6pm; July–Sept 10am–7pm; €4). This is one of the

▲ Lagrasse

region's oldest monastic houses, founded in an era when it was a dangerous, under-populated frontier of the eighth-century Carolingian empire. Cultivating the extensive lands with which they had been endowed, the monks slowly increased the monastery's wealth until its golden age in the fourteenth century. The complex is now a pastiche of styles, with components dating from the tenth to eighteenth centuries. The abbot's Renaissance **palace** and cloister were built during the monastery's second great period of revival – just before the storm of Revolution swept it away – whereas the bulk of the **abbey-church** and the old Romanesque-style **cloister** date from the thirteenth century, although both have since been substantially remodelled. Look for the distinctive mark of the "Master of Cabestany" (see box, p.297) in the cloister and on one of the abbey's entrances. You can also climb the Gothic-tinged fifteenth-century **clock tower**, whose heights afford impressive vistas of the town and valley. Leaving the abbey, continue along the riverside to a low dam bridging the river – you can walk across here and re-enter the town.

Heading on from Lagrasse towards Carcassonne, the most scenic route takes you west through the Gorges d'Alsou.

Practicalities

Lagrasse's services and shops are mostly strung along the tree-lined boulevard de la Promenade, including the **tourist office** (daily: July & Aug 10.30am–12.30pm & 2–7pm; Sept–June 10.30am–12.30pm & 2–5.30pm; ℡04.68.43.11.56, ⓦwww .lagrasse.com) at no. 6. Further along, at no. 9, you'll find the friendly **hotel** ⚥ *Hostellerie des Corbières* (℡04.68.43.15.22, ⓦwww.hostelleriecorbieres.com; ❻; closed Nov to mid-March), which also has an excellent restaurant (*menu* from €17). For something truly unique, head 10km east to Saint-Laurent-de-la-Cabrerisse, where you'll find the *Jardins de Saint Benoît* (℡04.68.44.18.70, ⓦwww .garrigaeresorts.com; ❾) – a village-like spa-complex where you can rent houses by the night or week, and where activities range from cooking classes given by locals to wild boar hunting, all in state-of-the-art luxury. At Lagrasse there's a basic municipal **campsite** (March–Oct; for details, contact the tourist office) on the edge of town. The most interesting **restaurant** here is *Les Temps de Courges* at 3 rue des Mazels (closed Tues & Wed lunch; ℡04.68.43.10.18), which has a great *cave*, and where you can order regional vegetarian or meat dishes and dine on a cosy little terrace (*menus* at €20–26).

Along the Canal du Midi east from Carcassonne

Heading east from Carcassonne, the **Canal du Midi** follows the course of the lower Aude valley, past the shady port at **Trèbes**, and on into the wine country of the **Minervois**, bounded by Haut Languedoc to the north and the hills of the Corbières to the south. Here the small port of **Homps** provides a jumping-off point for the old Cathar stronghold of **Minerve** and the monastery at **Caunes**, while bustling **Lézignan** is a hub for non-fluvial transport. Just after the old way-station of Le Somail the canal splits; the offshoot **Canal de la Robine** glides past the ancient wine centre of **Sallèles**, and on through Narbonne to reach the sea near Gruissan, while the main channel edges on to pass the magnificent **Oppidum d'Ensérune**, before reaching Béziers and, eventually, Agde (see p.275). As with the western leg of the canal system, you needn't commit yourself to boating to enjoy this archetypal southern French landscape, since the two towpaths which run along the canal's length make for wonderful **biking** and **walking**.

Trèbes

The first and prettiest port of call along the eastern stretch of the Canal du Midi is **TRÈBES**, just a few kilometres east of Carcassonne. The canal makes a broad curve here, following the wide meander of the Aude; arriving at Trèbes, two canal bridges, the second designed by the military architect Vauban in 1686, carry the watercourse over the Frequel and Orbiel rivers. Aside from being an attractive place with a canal port overlooked by the town walls at its western end, Trèbes is home to the remarkable **church of St-Étienne** (July & Aug Mon–Fri 10am–noon & 2–6pm; Sept–June 2–5/6pm), the wooden-beamed ceiling of which, dating back to the early fourteenth century, has over 350 individual faces painted on the ends of its roof supports, including caricatures of various professions and social classes, exotic foreigners and grotesques. For boaters the town is a well-equipped stage post, just as it was in the seventeenth century, with mooring facilities and a range of services.

Trèbes' **tourist office** is by the former canal *auberge*, on rue Pierre-Loti (March–April & Oct Mon–Sat 2–7pm; May–June & Sept daily 10am–noon & 2–7.30pm; July & Aug daily 10am–12.30pm & 2–8pm; ℡04.68.78.89.50, ⓦot-trebes.fr). The nearby Sautès Le Bas commercial zone, just west of the town centre, is home to a good **hotel**, *La Gentilhommière* at 6 Zac de Sautès Le Bas (℡04.68.78.74.74, ⓦwww .lagentilhom.com; ❺). Trèbes' **campsite** is on chemin de la Lande on the west side of town (April–Sept; ℡04.68.78.61.75, ⓦwww.campingmicocouliers.com), and has a pool. **Bike rental** is available at Loca Velos (℡04.69.78.68.81) in the village.

A further 8km on from Trèbes, the village of **MARSEILLETTE** makes another handy stopover if you need a place to stay. Here, *Hôtel la Muscadelle*, on route de Languedoc (℡04.68.79.20.90, ⓦwww.ferien-frankreich.com; ❸), has several clean and bright rooms set within an old, converted windmill.

The Black Prince: Languedoc's first English tourist

Not long after the dust of the Cathar Wars settled, events far off at the courts of Westminster and Paris brought warfare once again to the already severely devastated region. This time the occasion was the **Hundred Years' War**, which flared up in 1330 when Edward III of England claimed that he, rather than Philip VI, was the rightful king of France. At that time, Edward III's eldest son and heir, also named Edward, was only two years of age, but by the time he was 16, he was a veteran warrior.

Young Edward, Duke of Aquitaine, and the first heir to the throne to carry the title "Prince of Wales", was sent off to Bordeaux to take command of the province. Here the local Gascons were only too happy to join the English in looting and pillaging their neighbours. Edward, by then known as the **Black Prince** after the colour of his armour, would give them every opportunity, mounting a massive scorched-earth campaign into Languedoc in 1355. Striking out towards Toulouse, he and his men covered nearly 675 miles in 68 days of raiding. Castelnaudary, as well as the *bastide* of Carcassonne, Trèbes, Limoux and Narbonne, were just a few of the towns he and his troops sacked and torched, and his five thousand men laid waste to nearly eighteen thousand square miles of territory. The following year Edward went on to further glory by capturing the French king, John II, in battle at Poitiers. With Gallic aplomb, the contemporary chronicler, Froissart, summed up the expedition as proof of "the great haughtiness of the English, who are affable to no other nation than their own".

Wine wars

Despite the region's high-quality vintages and deep-rooted traditions, Languedoc's wine industry is in crisis: vineyards are being torn up; growers are demonstrating; wine stock sits backed up in *caves*; and in 2006 a mob armed with crowbars attacked a storehouse at Sète, and dumped **half a million litres** of wine in response to falling prices. A **militant vintner group**, CRAV (Comité Régional d'Action Viticole), has even attacked consignments of foreign wine arriving for sale. In 2007 **bombs** were set off at the headquarters of a major wine co-op, and a video manifesto was delivered by vintner-cum-terrorists in black balaclavas, reacting to an EU plan to destroy 200,000 hectares of vineyards by 2013. The main cause of this crisis is foreign competition, as once-marginal areas such as the US, Australia, South America and Eastern Europe now produce top-quality wines at a **cheaper** price. But changing **French habits** are also contributing to the problem: people are increasingly health-conscious and less likely to drink wine at lunch. Furthermore, with the rising price of wine and cost of living, fewer diners will order a bottle with lunch knowing they may leave much of it at the table. What the future holds is difficult to say, but wine-makers are being forced to become increasingly creative and selective and to reassess both **production** strategies and **marketing**: it is good news for consumers, but disquieting for a land proud of its *terroir* traditions.

The Minervois

As the canal arcs northward it passes **HOMPS**, a town which suffered destruction in the Crusade and the Wars of Religion, but revived with the construction of the waterway. It's main port of the **Minervois** region, a sun-bleached wine-producing territory stretching from the north bank of the Aude up to the hills of Haut Languedoc. The principal town of the Minervois, **OLONZAC**, lies just 2km north of the canal, linked to Homps by the D910. There are no sights here but it makes a convenient stop on the road to the former Cathar stronghold of **MINERVE**, a further 15km north. A tiny medieval hamlet, located at the cirque where the deep gorge of the River Cesse doubles back on itself, Minerve's main attraction is its stunningly dramatic location – only a single pile of stones remains of its **fortress**, which resisted Simon de Montfort for five months in 1210. When it was taken, 140 Cathars who refused to recant their beliefs voluntarily jumped into the fire the Crusaders had prepared for them. Neither of the town's museums merit much attention. Instead, head for the **canyon** that surrounds the town, where you can walk in natural tunnels bored through the cliffs – the trail can be picked up just over the bridge which enters town. It's best to avoid Minerve in high season and at weekends, when the volume of visitors threatens to obliterate its charms.

The Cesse river meanders eastwards for 10km from Minerve and can be followed by road, veering south and descending to the quiet, walled hamlet of **BIZE-MINERVOIS**. Although there are no specific sights, it's a pleasant and atmospheric spot, and in summer the canalized Cesse river here is a favourite local bathing spot. Halfway between Bize and Minerve, **AIGNE**, a beautiful little *circulade* (see box, p.162) wrapped snugly around the tenth-century church of St-Martin, has now been revived as an artists' colony.

CAUNES-MINERVOIS, the region's capital, lies 20km west of Olonzac on the far western edge of the Minervois. Its centre is dominated by a hulking **abbey** (daily: Feb–June & Sept–Dec 10am–noon & 2–5/6pm; July & Aug 10am–7pm; €4.50). There's not much to see here, although the crypt holds the foundation of the original fourth-century church, and some eleventh-century pavement has been uncovered in the cloister. Caunes is most famous for its marble quarries, which

Navigating the Canal du Midi east of Carcassonne

The section of the Canal du Midi east of Carcassonne is the most interesting, and the best for **biking**, **hiking** and **boating** (for the basics, see the boxes on p.89 and p.90). Almost all of the towns along the way have **boat rental** facilities. At Trèbes, head to the canalside boat basin, where the port office (T04.68.78.83.08) and Connoisseur (T04.68.78.73.75, Wwww.connoisseur.ie) have a selection of houseboats, and you can also rent electric boats for shorter trips (two hours €35). For **boat trips** contact Les Croisières Entre Deux Mers, also at the boat basin (T04.68.94.42.02, Ecroisiereentre2mers@net-up.com). Connoisseur (T04.68.91.24.00, Wwww.connoisseur.ie) in Homps' port, also rents out bikes as well as boats. In Le Somail, Minervois Cruisers, at 38 chemin des Patiasses (T04.68.46.28.52, Wwww.minervoiscruisers.com), rents out cruising boats for longer trips, while Comptoir Nature (T04.68.46.01.61, Wcomptoirnature.free.fr), at 1 chemin de Halage, hires electric boats by the hour. In Colombiers boats can be rented from the riverside Rive de France (T04.67.37.14.23, Wwww.rivedefrance.com); at Béziers' port contact Ad'navis-Amica Tours (T04.67.62.18.18, Econtact@adnavis.com). Voies Navigables de France, the government organization in charge of inland waterways (T04.68.11.81.30, Wwww.vnf.fr), has an office in avenue Duy Prado, Béziers, and is the best place for further **information**.

For those biking or walking, there are several good **accommodation** options along the way, which we detail in the Guide. Particularly handy for the canal are those in Trèbes (see p.266), Marseillette (see p.266), Le Somail (see opposite), Homps (see below) and Rieux (see below).

supplied stone for many of the churches throughout the region. Along the way you may want to stop in **RIEUX-MINERVOIS**, where the town's **Église de Sainte-Marie** is one of only three heptagonal (seven-sided) churches in the world, and contains a fine example of the handiwork of the "Master of Cabestany" (see box, p.297) in its chapel of the Assumption, as well as a fine fifteenth-century tomb.

Practicalities

There are seasonal **tourist offices** in the centre of Olonzac, at 9 bd Blazin (July & Aug daily 9am–noon & 2–6pm; T04.68.91.34.95), and behind the church in Minerve, at 9 rue des Martyrs (July & Aug daily 10am–noon & 2–6pm; T04.68.91.81.43, Wwww.minerve-tourisme.com). Comfortable **hotels** and **chambres d'hôtes** in the region include *L'Auberge de l'Arbousier* at 50 av de Carcassonne in Homps (T04.68.91.11.24, Wwww.auberge-canaldumidi.com; ❸), which offers accommodation – and great food – in a beautifully renovated eighteenth-century wine warehouse, handy for those hiking or biking along the canal. The excellent, English-owned ⚘ *Maison des Rossignols* in Pouzols, just east of Olonzac (T04.68.46.03.59, Wwww.maison-des-rossignols.com; ❸), has comfortable rooms and superb home-cooked meals (€18) for guests only. In Minerve, the only hotel is the appealing *Relais Chantovent* (T04.68.91.14.18, Wwww.relaischantovent-minerve.fr; ❸; closed mid-Dec to mid-March), which is also the best place for a local meal (*menus* from €19). Another great choice is the luxurious but well-priced *domaine*, ⚘ *La Bastide Cabezac* (T04.68.46.23.05, Wwww.la-bastide-cabezac.com; ❺), in Hameau de Cabezac, 3km south of Bize on the main road. If you feel like a splurge, there's the stylish, English-owned *Domaine aux Quat'Saisons* on avenue Général-Clémenceau in **Rieux** (T04.68.24.49.73, Wwww.auxquatsaisons.com; ❻), which also offers delicious home-cooked meals (Mon, Wed & Fri). At the other end of the scale, Caunes has a municipal **campsite** (mid-June to mid-Sept; T04.68.78.07.83).

Additional **restaurants** include Olonzac's highly rated *Du Minervois Bel*, 2 rue des Écoles (☎04.68.91.20.73; from €22; closed Sun & Mon), and *L'Olivier*, a renowned *gastronomique* at Hameau de Cabezac (closed Mon, Tues noon, Sat noon & Sun off-season; *menus* from €25), which is well worth a detour.

Lézignan-Corbières and Le Somail

Veering south and east after Homps, the Canal du Midi enters a particularly beautiful stretch, passing a series of castles as the landscape settles into vine-covered plain. Some 5km south of the canal sits **LÉZIGNAN-CORBIÈRES**, the capital of the rugged region rising gradually to the south. Lézignan has been in the business of wine production since the time of the Romans and today remains a small but bustling centre of the viticulture industry. There's no overwhelming reason to visit, although if you're dependent on public transport you may have to change buses or trains here.

Buses will let you off as they pass through the town's centre, while **trains** stop at the **gare SNCF**, 3 rue Turgot. There's a **tourist office** (July & Aug Mon–Fri 9am–7pm, Sat 10am–12.30pm & 2–6pm, Sun 10am–12.30pm; late Sept to June Mon–Fri 10am–noon & 2–6pm; May, June & Sept also Sat 9am–12.30pm; ☎04.68.27.05.42, ⓦwww.lezignan-corbieres.fr), at 9 cours de la République, on the southern side of the ring road which skirts the old town. You'll find a good selection of shops, services and **hotels** in Lézignan, the best of which is the *Tassigny* on rond-point de Lattre-de-Tassigny (☎04.68.27.11.51, ⓦwww.logis-de-france.fr; ❸), with clean rooms and good amenities. Its restaurant serves meat and fish grilled over a wood fire with *menus* from €14, *vin compris*. You can also get a bed at the local MJC **hostel**, 25 rue Marat (☎04.68.27.03.34, ⓦwww.mjc-lezignan-corbieres.com; dorm beds €11), and there's a well-equipped **campsite**, *La Pinède* (March–Oct; ☎04.68.27.05.08, ⓦwww.campinglapinede.fr), on the main road on the eastern edge of town. **Bikes** can be rented from Plancade, at 33 av Président-Wilson (☎04.68.27.29.13, Ⓔcyclesplancade@yahoo.fr). Wednesday morning is **market** day.

From Lézignan, this leg of the canal continues over the canal bridge of Répudre – France's first, and an invention of Riquet himself – on to **LE SOMAIL**, the last port before the Canal de la Robine splits off to head south towards Narbonne. Here a single-arched stone **bridge** dating from the eighteenth century spans the canal, still attached to the old post-house *auberge* on the east bank and a small **chapel** on the west. There's little to do here aside from enjoying a drink or meal and soaking up the canalside ambience before moving on.

There's a small canal **information office** (irregular hours; ☎06.84.81.96.20) by the old bridge, and decent *chambres d'hôtes* **accommodation** in an old canal *auberge* at *Chez Pierrette Bernabeu*, on the east side of the bridge (☎04.68.46.16.02, Ⓔpierrette.bernabeu@orange.fr; ❸). The neighbouring *Auberge Lou Somaillou* (March–Nov; ☎04.68.46.19.41) serves satisfying **meals** in a comfortable dining room or on the canalside terrace (*menus* €16–36).

Along the Canal de la Robine

From Le Somail, the **CANAL DE LA ROBINE**'s short trajectory heads almost directly south, crossing the course of the wide and, here, tame Aude, and contin-uing through Narbonne before penetrating the marshy extent of the Étang de Bages et de Sigean. After Narbonne there are two legs; the longer tracks the same spit of land as the railway, skirting the bird-lovers' paradise of Île de Ste-Lucie, before arriving at Port-la-Nouvelle and the sea, while the shorter cuts east past the vineyards of La Clape, passing Gruissan (see p.261) and the saltpans of St-Martin before reaching the Mediterranean.

The only major port of call on the Canal de la Robine, a few kilometres before it merges with the Aude, is **SALLÈLES**. Like Lézignan, Sallèles is a wine town of great antiquity, whose vintages graced the tables of Rome more than two thousand years ago. Bearing testimony to this are the town's Roman pottery works, now incorporated into the **Amphoralis** museum on Sallèles' northern edge (daily: July–Sept 10am–noon & 3–7pm; Oct–Dec 10am–noon & 2–6pm; Jan–June 10am–noon & 2–6pm; €4). Named after the distinctively tapered vessels (*amphorae*) once made here, it's a well laid out and entertaining museum, which includes the excavation site of the pottery itself. The walk out to the museum from the tourist office is interesting too, thanks to the six sets of **locks** which grace that part of the canal.

Sallèles' **tourist office** (Mon–Fri 10.30am–12.30pm & 4–6.30pm; ℡ 04.68.46.81.46, Ⓦ www.sallelesdaude.com) is in the centre of town right next to the canal at 3 Grand'Rue. The best **accommodation** is at the canalside B&B, *Les Volets Bleus* (℡ 04.68.46.83.03, Ⓦ www.salleles.net; English spoken; ❸; closed Dec to mid-March), a funky place set in a hundred-year-old canal master's house, with comfortable rooms and generous meals available (€24). There are a couple of **cafés** along the main road where you can get a meal, and **bikes** can be rented at Vélo's on quai Victor-Hugo (℡ 04.68.46.18.15, Ⓔ velos.salleles@free.fr).

The Canal du Midi from Le Somail to the sea

East of Le Somail, the Canal du Midi enters its most picturesque stretch, snaking through a rugged landscape of low and rocky vine-clad hills whose only reminder of civilization is an occasional bell tower. Beyond Béziers, the Canal finally empties into the Bassin de Thau, from where you can reach the sea or connect with the other great inland waterway of Languedoc, the Rhône–Sète Canal (see box, p.202), which carries on past the Petite Camargue into Provence.

Capestang

Sixteen kilometres before reaching Béziers, the Canal du Midi passes under the old hilltop town of **CAPESTANG**, whose small castle is capped by a distinctive tower. With a tree-lined square snuggled up against its medieval church, Capestang is an exceedingly pleasant little town, where you can climb the church's **bell tower** to enjoy sweeping views over the Aude valley, or simply enjoy a snack or drink and observe the unhurried life of the *place*. The nondescript-looking **castle** was once a residence of the archbishops of Narbonne. Despite centuries of neglect, the incredible artwork of the old great hall has survived the ages – the 161 fourteenth-century **ceiling paintings** are a must-see for those following the canal route. These vivid caricatures depict monsters, musicians, court ladies and even a mischievous jester pulling a rather exaggerated "moon" at the viewer: for entry details enquire at the **tourist office** on the main street, adjacent to the castle (May–Oct Mon–Sat 10am–noon & 3–6pm, Nov–April closed Sat; ℡ 04.67.93.34.23, Ⓦ www.ville-capestang .fr). Capestang has a couple of worthwhile **accommodation** options, both along cours Belfort, the main road through town: the two-star hotel *Le Relais Bleu*, at no. 39 (℡ 04.67.93.31.26; ❸), and the *chambres d'hôte*, *La Bellifontaine* at no. 44 (℡ 04.67.93.69.68, Ⓦ www.bellifontaine.com; ❹). The *mairie* runs a **campsite**, *Tounel* (May–Sept; ℡ 04.67.49.34.23). One of the best **restaurants** in town is the popular *La Grillade* on the main square, which serves succulent grilled meats from €9 on its large patio.

Colombiers and the Oppidum d'Ensérune

After cutting through the ancient hamlet of Poilhes, some 5km beyond Capestang, the Canal du Midi passes through a long tunnel, eventually arriving at the tiny village of **COLOMBIERS**, where you can visit the **Cave des Ducs de Castries** (daily 10am–12.30pm & 4–8pm; €2.50) in place du Millénaire, a sumptuous nineteenth-century *bodega* designed by woodcarvers who studied under Eiffel, which hosts art and archeological exhibitions. Colombiers is also home to the area's best **restaurant**, the elegant ✝ *Château de Colombiers* (☎04.67.37.06.93; closed Wed noon, Thurs & Sun off-season) set in the town's *château*, which uses local produce for its fine fare (from €25); chef Gilles Roca has earned the establishment a string of awards, making this a not-to-miss dining experience.

Two kilometres west of Colombiers and set on a long ridge towering over the surrounding plains, the site of the **OPPIDUM D'ENSÉRUNE** (*oppidum* being Latin for "town", referring generally to pre-Roman hilltop settlements) has attracted settlers for over 2500 years. Even before Hannibal and the Romans took it over in turn, it was an important centre for trade, maintaining commercial ties with Greece, while under the Romans it served as one of the postal way-stations on the busy Via Domitia. The site itself, a rocky spur crowned with cypress and brambles, is characteristically Mediterranean, and climbing to the top, looking north, you'll get a view of a strange array of fields resembling a spoked wheel. This was once the *étang* of Montady, one of the many salt lagoons of the lowlands here that were drained and cultivated in the thirteenth century. The **excavations** (April & Sept daily 10am–12.30pm & 2–6pm; May–Aug daily 10am–7pm; Oct–March Tues–Sun 9.30am–12.30pm & 2–5.30pm; €7) of the ancient ruins, covering most of the hilltop, are impressive, with remains of defensive walls, villas and a large number of cisterns and sunken grain stores. The small **site museum** inside the grounds holds a collection of statuary found here, including small devotional pieces and larger civic portraits.

Villeneuve-lès-Béziers and the neuf écluses

As it arrives at the foot of Béziers' ridge, the canal descends another set of multiple locks, the **neuf écluses**. Billed as a tourist attraction, and endowed with footpaths and snack bars, the lock complex draws families and tour groups who dutifully stand around watching the boats make their slow descent – altogether about as exciting as watching someone take the lift. Five kilometres further on, tiny **VILLENEUVE-LÈS-BÉZIERS** is the last mooring point on the Canal du Midi before it follows a flat and featureless course to Agde (see p.275) and empties into the Bassin de Thau. Also worth a stop is **SÈRIGNAN**, a further 4km south, and home to the region's first **contemporary art museum** (Tues–Sun: July & Aug 10am–6pm; Sept–June 1 6pm; €5), featuring works ranging in style from Abstract Landscape and Support/Surfaces to Narrative Figuration. In addition to the permanent collection, it hosts good temporary exhibitions.

Villeneuve's **tourist office** is on rue de la Fontaine (July & Aug daily 9am–7pm; Sept–June Mon–Fri 9am–noon & 2–6pm; ☎04.67.39.48.83, ⓦwww.villeneuve-les-beziers.fr). The municipal **campsite**, *Les Berges du Canal* (mid-April to mid-Sept; ☎04.67.39.36.09, ⓦwww.lesbergesducanal.com) is on Promenade des Vernets. The town's country **market** is held on Tuesdays and Sundays.

Béziers and around

Just inland from the mouth of the Orb river and dominating the strip of plain between the coast and Haut Languedoc, **BÉZIERS** could be held up as a metaphor for Languedoc – it's a town with a long and proud past, and a history of independent spirit, which it has more than once paid for in blood. Like neighbouring Narbonne, Béziers was already a sizeable settlement when the Romans took it over in the second century BC; it thrived under *pax Romana*, and was the seat of a bishop and a prosperous market town through the Middle Ages. The last great event here was the attack it suffered in the Albigensian Crusade, and since then it has been something of a sleepy bywater – Paul Riquet, the genius behind the Canal du Midi, is the town's biggest claim to fame. Still, its former grandeur is evident from afar; as you approach, its impressive **cathedral** towers over the Orb river, high up on a dramatic ridge. Until only recently the city had fallen into decay, its dusty streets and deteriorating shop-fronts betraying the slump into which the town has settled in the last century or so. Determined civic efforts have turned the situation around, however, and Béziers is once more a delight, its atmospheric **old quarter** now bustling with busy shops. Modern Béziers is the home of two great Languedocian adopted traditions: English **rugby**, and the Spanish **corrida**, both of which it follows with a passion. The best time to visit is during the mid-August **feria**, a raucous five-day party which you will enjoy even if you don't find bullfighting to your taste. Béziers is also a useful staging point for

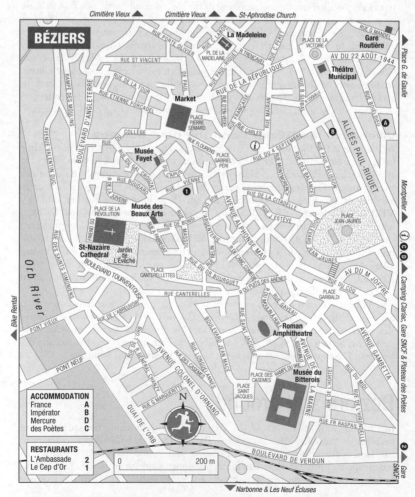

excursions up the **Orb valley** (see p.278) towards Haut Languedoc, or down to **Agde** and the coast.

Arrival and information

If you arrive at the **gare SNCF** on boulevard de Verdun, about fifteen minutes' walk southeast of the old town, the best way into the centre is through the landscaped gardens of the Plateau des Poètes, opposite the *gare* entrance, and up allées Paul-Riquet to place de la Victoire. The **gare routière** is on place Général de Gaulle, just to the east of place de la Victoire, while the **tourist office** is in the Palais des Congrès at 29 av Saint-Saëns (June & Sept daily 9am–12.30pm & 1.30–6pm; July & Aug Mon–Sat 9am–6.30pm, Sun 10am–1pm & 3–6pm; Oct–May daily 9am–noon & 2–5/6pm; ☏04.67.76.47.00, ⓦwww.beziers-tourisme .fr). There are also a couple of small seasonal offices: one in place Lavabre in the old town (April & May Mon–Sat 10am–12.30pm & 2–6pm; June & Sept Mon–Fri 10am–6pm & Sat noon–6pm; July & Aug Mon–Sat 10am–7pm), and one by the canal locks (April & May Fri–Sun 10am–12.30pm & 2–6pm; June–Sept daily 10.30am–1pm & 2.30–6pm).

Accommodation

Accommodation is not as plentiful as you might expect for a town so close to the coast, but there are good choices here in each price range. The nearest **campsite** is at Villeneuve-lès-Béziers (see p.271).

France 36 rue Boïédieu ☏04.67.28.44.72, ⓦwww.hotel-2-france.com. The rooms are clean and basic with few amenities (TV, fan), but the price and professionalism make this a great bargain. **❷**

Impérator 28 allées Paul-Riquet ☏04.67.49.02.25, ⓦwww.hotel-Imperator .fr. This is Béziers' best value for money: classy comfort, just shy of luxury, but with good amenities and breakfast included. **❺**

Mercure 33 av Saint-Saëns ☏04.67.00.19.96, ⓦwww.mercure.com. The town's best hotel offers free wi-fi, an indoor garage, bar, a/c and modern, if rather nondescript, rooms. **❼**

des Poètes 80 allées Paul-Riquet ☏04.67.76.38.66, ⓦwww.hoteldespoetes.net. An all-round excellent choice with good rooms and amenities including TV, wi-fi and bike loan, and a good breakfast for €7. Larger rooms available. **❸**

The Town

Béziers' vaguely semicircular **old town** snuggles into a gentle meander of the Orb, which, along with the canal – the Ruisseau de Bagnols – bounds it on three sides. The eastern limit is marked by allées Paul-Riquet, which has a broad pedestrian concourse running down its centre.

The Cathédrale St-Nazaire

Béziers' main attraction is undoubtedly the majestic Romanesque **Cathédrale St-Nazaire** (daily 10am–12.30pm & 2–6.30pm; free), about five minutes' walk west from place Péri on the western rim, just off place de la Révolution.

Essentials

Bike rental Locascoot, 3 pl des Alliés (☏04.67.28.34.99).
Museum pass Pass Forfait Musées (€3.40): valid for one visit to each of the town's museums.
Taxis ☏04.67.35.00.85.

Constructed in the thirteenth century, the cathedral's marriage of style and function is immediately apparent in its west face, which has a great rosette window flanked by two fortified towers. From the entrance here, the first part of the cathedral you enter is the cloister. Within its low and austere gallery, there's a collection of old funerary stones, including one with Hebrew characters, while on its east side a stairway descends into the airy gardens, the **Jardin de l'Évêché**, built off the south side of the great church. The cathedral's voluminous, predominantly unadorned **interior** is dominated by an outrageous Baroque retable – a gaudy starburst of saints and cherubs which clashes with the sobriety of the building. The high point of the visit is the dizzying climb to the **upper galleries** (free) – a rare opportunity to get a pigeon's-eye view of a cathedral's interior. Climbing the well-worn, narrow keystone staircase, you traverse a small landing before continuing up to the top – the balconies which circle the pinnacles afford spectacular **views**. Almost directly below the cliffs on which the cathedral stands, you'll see the evocative twelfth-century Pont Vieux as it crosses the Orb below and, beyond to the west, the whole of the Biterrois plain stretching off into a haze – on a clear day you might make out the form of Le Canigou on the horizon. Take care when climbing the stairs and circulating up top, particularly if you're travelling with children – the only protective fencing here is the old stone balustrade.

The rest of the old town

North of the cathedral, at the far end of the pleasant place de la Révolution – where republican protesters were fired upon in 1851 – is the Hôtel Fabrégat, a mansion which houses the **Musée des Beaux-Arts** (Tues–Sun: July & Aug 10am–6pm; Sept–June 9/10am–noon & 2–5/6pm; €2.70), a collection of works by local painters as well as better-known artists such as Delacroix and Dufy. The museum's sculpture annexe is lodged in another aristocratic residence, the nearby **Musée Fayet**, whose collection is dominated by nineteenth-century works, notably by local sculptor Injalbert (same hours and ticket). North of here, you'll see the beautiful wrought-iron covered **market** (Tues–Sun 7.30am–12.30pm), in attractive place Pierre-Sémard and, further on, the church of **La Madeleine** (irregular hours), scene of the murder of the Trencavel viscount in 1167 and the **massacre** of seven thousand Catholics by the Crusaders in 1209 (see *The Land of the Cathars* colour section). Further along, on place St-Aphrodise – follow the pedestrian signs – you'll come across **St-Aphrodise church** (Mass only), an incredibly old structure with a tenth-century nave and Gallo-Roman crypt. A further five minutes' walk north along rue de la Faïence brings you to the **cimetière vieux** (daily 8am–5.45pm; free), founded in 1838. It contains a series of impressive mausoleums and monuments raised by the town's prospering bourgeoisie, featuring sculptures by Jean-Antoine Injalbert (a native, whose ponderous works grace Paris's Hôtel de Ville and Palais de Justice) and other noteworthy artists.

Beyond the old town

Heading east from La Madeleine, rue Trencavel takes you towards the pretty Art Nouveau-style **Théâtre Municipal Molière** at the top end of **allées Paul-Riquet**, a broad, leafy esplanade lined with cafés, crêpes stalls and restaurants; on Friday mornings the weekly flower market is held here. The boulevard ends at the gorgeous little park of the **Plateau des Poètes**, whose ponds, palms and lime trees were laid out in the so-called English manner by the brothers Denis et Eugène Bülher, who created Paris's Bois de Boulogne. Finally, to the west of the park on rampe du 96ème, you'll find the impressive **Musée du Biterrois** (Tues–Sun: July & Aug 10am–6pm; Sept–June 9/10am–noon & 2–5/6pm; €2.70), housed in an old barracks and containing sections on natural history, ethnography and archeology. The first two, respectively illustrating the biological diversity of the marshy coast and the rural and craft traditions of the region, are passable, but it's the last section, most of which is given over to the Gallo-Roman period, which makes the museum well worth a stop. This important collection ranges from locally produced pottery and ceramics to funerary monuments and milestones, and there are also various artefacts dredged from ancient shipwrecks off the coast, but the highlight is the "treasure of Béziers" – a rich cache of **silver platters** found in a nearby field. The medieval period is represented by locally sculpted medieval capitals and bas-reliefs.

Eating and drinking

There's a whole string of economical **restaurants** (with patios) along the west side of allées Paul-Riquet, serving the usual steak-frites-type *menus* for about €12. Better fare can be found in the old quarter, where rue Viennet has a good choice of places. The best is ⅍ *Le Cep d'Or*, at no. 7, serving mostly local seafood dishes (*menus* €16–25; closed Sun eve & Mon out of season). The service is warm and the food is excellent. *L'Ambassade,* at 22 bd de Verdun (☎04.67.76.06.24; closed Sun & Mon), is another good choice for seafood; the *gastronomique* dishes are more elaborate than the *Cep's,* but much more expensive (€29–115). In addition to the town's covered **market** (Mon–Sat mornings), a regional produce market is held on Fridays in place du 14 Juillet.

Listings

Car rental ADA, 23 bd Verdun ☎04.67.62.65.39; Avis, 18 bd Verdun ☎04.67.28.65.44; Budget, 35 bd Verdun ☎04.67.35.84.54; Europcar, 70 allées Paul-Riquet ☎04.67.62.09.89; Hertz, 83 av Président-Wilson ☎04.67.62.82.00.
Hospital Centre Hospitalier, 11 rue Victor-Hugo ☎04.67.11.07.76.
Pharmacie Pharmacie de la Poste, 120 av Georges Clémenceau.

Police rue Georges-Mandel ☎04.67.49.54.00.
Rugby Béziers has one of the star rugby clubs in France, ASBH, based at the Stade de la Méditerranée in the eastern suburbs (☎04.67 .11.03.76, ⓦwww.asbh.net).
Swimming The covered *piscine municipale* Léo Lagrange (☎04.67.30.36.31) is open year-round.

Agde and the coast

Thanks to the few kilometres that separate it from the sea, **AGDE**, just 12km east of Béziers, is one of the most unspoilt towns on the Languedocian coast. It boomed as a port 2500 years ago under the Phoenicians and on through the Middle Ages, until competition from neighbouring towns and the silting up of the Hérault pushed the seashore from its walls. Today, its compact old town has resisted intensive development and remains a quiet respite from the crowds which certainly can't be said of nearby **Cap d'Agde**, on the coast. The best time to arrive in Agde is on one of the town's market days: Thursday for produce and Wednesday and Saturday for the flea market.

Arrival and information

Trains and **buses** arrive in Agde just across the river from the old town. To continue south to the Cap you can take a municipal bus (€0.60) from the *gare*, or use the superb network of cycle paths – once there you'll realize it's no place to walk and end up using one of the two *petits trains* which circulate around the town (€2), or the various **water taxis**. Agde's **tourist office** is on place Molière, near the main roundabout (daily 9am–noon & 2–6pm; ☎04.67.94.29.68; ⓦwww.capdagde.com), while in

6

Essentials

Bike rental La Cadotière, 1 pl Jean-Jaurès, Agde ℡04.76.94.26.20.

Boat rental Nautic, chemin de la Pagèze (℡04.67.94.78.93), and Locarama, in av Passeur Challiès (℡04.67.26.26.45).

Discount card The Agde Pass (€12), available at the tourist office, is good for one visit to each museum.

Internet access Globe Trotter, 4 pl de la Marine, Agde.

River trips Les Bateaux du Soleil at the port (℡04.67.94.08.79).

Cap d'Agde, you'll find the tourist office (daily: June–Aug 9am–7/8pm; Sept–May 9am–noon & 2–6/7pm; ℡04.67.01.04.04) on the huge roundabout in the centre.

Accommodation

The **hotel** situation is poor, especially in old Agde. By contrast, there are no fewer than 24 **campsites** in the area, most with good services and pretty indistinguishable from each other. One to try is *Sud Loisirs* on the route de Marseillan Ville, between Agde and Cap d'Adge (℡04.67.21.09.10, Ⓦwww.campingsudloisirs .com) – a large, three-star campground with excellent facilities and open year-round. Bungalows and campervans are available for rent.

L'Ephèbe 12 quai du Commandant-Méric, Grau d'Agde ℡04.67.21.49.88, Ⓦwww.lephebe.com. This small, family-run hotel in Grau has great service and a quaint atmosphere. The facilities are good (including bike rental) and many rooms have sea views. ⑤

Eve Impasse Siassan, Cap d'Adge ℡04.67.26.71.70, Ⓦwww.hoteleve.com. Decadent luxury at the *quartier naturiste*'s own hotel. Facilities include pools, sauna, a solarium and bar. The rooms are modern and comfortable, and suites and duplexes are available. Open April–Oct. ⑦

La Galiote Pl Jean-Jaurès, Agde ℡04.67.94.45.58, Ⓦwww.lagaliote.fr. This is the best hotel in Agde, located in the old bishops' palace. The Dutch owners are welcoming and the hotel has good amenities, including a/c and TV. There are family-sized rooms as well as rooms without en-suite baths, which have discounted rates. ⑤

La Voile d'Or Pl du Globe, Cap d'Adge ℡04.67.01.04.11, Ⓦwww.lavoiledor.com. This modern, resort-type hotel has lots of amenities, including two swimming pools. Prices reduce significantly outside high season. Open April–Nov. ⑥

Old Agde

Set along the now canalized river, the town is dominated by a twelfth-century fortified **cathedral**, St-Étienne, on its south bank, whose appearance is more castle than church, its three-metre-thick walls and hot-oil sluices having formed the strongpoint of the town's defences: you can climb the **bell tower** (Mon–Fri 10am, 11.45am & 4.30pm; €3) to get striking views of the town and coastal plain. A series of *places* follows the riverside from east to west: the lively Jean-Jaurès, with its sidewalk cafés; Picheire, where you'll find the small porticoed medieval **market**; and de la Marine, a grittily authentic fishermen's quarter. Heading south from place de la Marine, the residential rue de la Poissonnerie is a step back in time – a neighbourhood of fishermen's families living in modest and ancient houses. Following it to the end, you'll arrive at the old convent housing the **Musée Agathois** (daily 10am–noon & 2–6pm; €8.50). It's one of the better of the region's "local" museums, with exhibitions on life in the area from the prehistoric era to the present day; relics of the town's seafaring past range from ancient Greek amphorae to nineteenth-century navigational instruments. Continuing, you'll pass the new market building and the **church of St-André**, occupying a site on which there's been a church since as far back as 506 AD, when an episcopal council was held here.

Just south is the wide tree-lined La Promenade, with its multitude of terraced bars, while close by, rue de l'Amour and rue Jean-Roger are lined with tacky souvenir shops. If you're looking to escape the crowds, head to the shady nineteenth-century gardens of **Château Laurens**, set on Belle-Isle, a twelve-hectare park bordered by the Hérault and the Canal du Midi, just across the bridge from the old town.

Cap d'Agde and Grau d'Agde

Agde's evil twin, **CAP D'AGDE** lies to the south of Mont St-Loup on the seashore, some 5km south. A sprawling and characterless modern resort, its only redemption is the abundance of colourful plants and flowers which line its broad streets, only partially concealing a uniform sea of cream-coloured holiday villas behind. But the Cap has everything you would want for a mindless, cultureless beach holiday, with an abundance of nightclubs, watersports and restaurants – although here you will pay dearly for them. If you're just passing through, though, a worthwhile stop is the **Musée de l'Éphèbe** (daily 10am–noon & 2–6pm; €8.50) in the central Parc de la Clape, which holds a collection of Greek and Roman relics retrieved from the sea bed, including the beautiful little Hellenistic bronze statuette known as the *Éphèbe d'Agde*, formerly housed in the Louvre. There is also an **aquarium** at 11 rue des Deux-Frères (daily: June & Sept 10am–7pm; July & Aug 10am–11pm; Oct–May 2–6pm; €6.90), and a huge Aqualand **amusement park** (mid-June to mid-Sept 10am–6/7pm; €24.50) at the west end of town. The former prison of **Fort de Brescou**, built in 1680, lies just offshore and can be reached by ferries departing from the ports at either Cap d'Agde (Sarl Croisières: July & Aug Thurs–Mon 10.30am, 2.30pm & 6.30pm; €6) or le Grau d'Agde (Île de Brescou: July & Aug daily 2.30pm & 4.30pm; €7). The grim fortress, which evokes Marseille's famous Château d'Îf, can be visited on a **guided tour** (timed with boat arrivals from mid-June to early Sept; €3), or you can simply explore the rocky seagull-infested island for free.

Cap d'Agde's naked city

Founded in 1958 by a caravan-load of German naturists looking for a quiet place to strip off, Cap d'Agde's **quartier naturiste** has a population which swells to sixty thousand in summer – making it the world's largest nudist colony. The *quartier* took shape over the Sixties and Seventies and has now become a small town in its own right, with supermarkets, restaurants, cafés, bars, discos, a hotel and a campsite with more than 2500 places, all catering to a naturist clientele. Nudity is permitted – although not absolutely required – at all times anywhere within the confines of the resort.

Until about the early 1990s most of the people who came to Cap d'Agde's *quartier naturiste* did so simply because they enjoyed spending their time naked. Gradually, however, another type of naturist, described by French commentators as "*à poilistes*", began to arrive. For these people nudity and sex were inextricably linked, and soon the beach became unofficially segregated into various sections: for families, for sexually liberated heterosexuals and for gays. Now there are more boutiques selling X-rated clothing in the *quartier naturiste* than in most large cities, and some of the raunchiest and most famous **swingers' clubs** in Europe are located here.

The nudist **season** in Cap d'Agde runs from mid-March to mid-October. One-day access is €10 with a car or €5 for pedestrians and cyclists. No tickets are sold after 8pm. For more information, contact the Bureau d'Accueil (℡04.67.26.00.26, ⊛www .agdenaturisme.com), or read Ross Velton's *The Naked Truth About Cap d'Agde* (⊛www.wordcrafting.com).

6

If you fancy a dip, the best **beaches**, sheltered from the often overwhelming Mediterranean winds, are on the west side of the cape stretching over towards La Guirandette; on the east side there's a huge, self-contained **nudist colony** (see box, p.277). Nearby **GRAU D'AGDE** is the beach-town antithesis of the Cap: a dispersed settlement of weathered houses and ageing bungalows, this dissipating suburb distils into an old fishing town as you reach the lighthouse-capped wavebreak. Both Cap and Grau can be reached by local buses from the *gare* in Agde.

Eating and drinking

One of the area's best **restaurants** is at *Le Jardin de Beaumont* (☎04.67.21.19.23) set in a wine *domaine* 3km north of Agde, on route de Florensac, where you can dine on tapas and excellent wines inside or out (about €30). A good choice at the Cap is the seafood specialist, *Le Brasero*, Port Richelieu II (☎04.67.26.24.75; *menus* from €15). In Agde itself, there are a number of places right on the quayside or in rue Chassefière, which runs along it, but the best option is *La Table de Stéphane* (☎04.67.26.45.22) at 2 rue du Moulins à Huile, where you can enjoy elaborate creations such as jellied oysters in squids' ink (*menus* from €26; closed Mon, Sat lunch & Sun eve). One thing Cap d'Agde is good for is **drinking**; you'll find an abundant supply of more or less indistinguishable but serviceable bars among the resorts along the beach.

The Orb valley

The **River Orb** winds a twisting path down from its source in the hills of Haut Languedoc north of Béziers, descending some 120km through the highlands and across the broad coastal plain to skirt the city before emptying into the Golfe du Lion. Heading up its valley from Béziers provides rapid access from the coast to the lesser-travelled uplands of Haut Languedoc. Just after **Roquebrun**, a centre both for viticulture and rafting, the valley delves into the rugged uplands, wheeling off to the east to pass **Hérépian** and the old spa town of **Lamalou-les-Bains** – both good bases for walks into the Parc Naturel Régional du Haut Languedoc. From here the valley follows the park's edge round until the land opens up into a compact but fertile plane around **Bédarieux** – another possible departure point for exploring the highlands. Heading further north into the **upper valley** you eventually reach a series of tiny hamlets high up at the river's origins.

Roquebrun and around

Journeying 21km upriver from Béziers, the D14 joins the course of the Orb at tiny **Cessenon**, just before it ascends into the rugged uplands. The border of the Parc du Haut Languedoc (see p.162) has recently been pushed south to incorporate the area around **ROQUEBRUN**, less than 10km further along. This old town, clumped on a hillside beneath the ruins of its medieval tower, is located in an exceptionally mild microclimate, making the valley floor, which is still wide here, an ideal place for vine cultivation – indeed the town has produced several award-winning vintages (AOC Saint-Chinian), which you can sample and buy at the various *domaines* scattered around the valley. The good weather also provides a suitable climate for the town's **Jardin Méditerranéen** (daily: mid-Feb to June & Sept to mid-Nov 9am–noon & 1.30–5.30pm; July & Aug 9am–7pm; €4.50), a collection of exotic, primarily arid-climate plants from around the world, while in winter the valley around the town bursts into colour with the blooming of mimosas.

▲ Jardin Méditerranéen, Roquebrun

Roquebrun has a small **tourist office** (Mon–Fri 9am–noon & 2–5/6pm; ⊤04.67.89.79.97, Ⓦwww.roquebrun.org) in avenue des Orangers. There's a welcoming English-run **chambre d'hôtes**, *Les Mimosas* (⊤04.67.89.61.36, Ⓦwww.lesmimosas.net; ❹), in a nineteenth-century house in avenue Orangers, which also does meals (€28), and the *Le Nice* **campsite** (mid-March to mid-Nov; ⊤04.67.89.61.99, Ⓦwww.camping-lenice.com) in rue du Temps Libre.

Lamalou-les-Bains and Hérépian

Built on the hot springs which have brought it prosperity for the last thousand years, **LAMALOU-LES-BAINS** lies just a kilometre north of the river course. In the late nineteenth and early twentieth century it came into fashion, and notables such as the writers Alphonse Daudet and André Gide came to enjoy its curative waters. It's still a popular therapeutic spot today, and the more or less constant parade of ailing people moving among its faded *fin-de-siècle* mansions gives it the strange air of a large outdoor hospital. The town is most useful as a stopover for hikers making their way through the hills, but there is also a beautiful old parish church here, **St-Pierre-de-Rhèdes**, which dates back to the spa's earliest beginnings. The church's pastiche of stylistic touches, overlaying its basic Romanesque form, results from immigrants to the region, including Mozarabs from Spain, who left Christian inscriptions written in Arabic.

Lamalou's **tourist office**, on avenue Dr-Ménard (June to mid-Sept Mon–Fri 9am–noon & 2–6pm, Sat 9.15am–noon & 2–5pm, Sun 10am–noon; mid-Sept to May Mon–Fri 9am–noon & 2–5/6pm, Sat 9.15am–noon; ⊤04.67.95.70.91, Ⓦwww.ot-lamaloulesbains.fr), provides information on nearby towns and sells SNCF bus tickets. There is no shortage of **accommodation** here and the hotels *l'Arbousier*, 18 rue A-Daudet (⊤04.67.95.63.11, Ⓦwww.arbousierhotel.com; ❹), and *Galimar*, 17 bd St-Michel (⊤04.67.95.22.99, Ⓦwww.galimar.fr; ❸), are both good value. The *Arbousier* has an excellent **restaurant** (*menus* from €18.50); try the terrine of veal or the roasted black pudding with fried foic gras. The two-star municipal **campsite**, *Le Verdale*, is at Le Bois de Lon (March–Oct; ⊤04.67.95.86.89).

Hérépian

A few kilometres upstream, **HÉRÉPIAN** is a pleasant workaday town with a less clinical air than its neighbour, and limited services. It's home to one of the country's last functioning bell foundries, the **Bruneau–Garnier foundry** (July & Aug by appointment only; ☎04.67.95.07.96), and also makes a good base for the **hike** up to the ruins of the **castle of St-Michel**, 300m above the riverbed on the slopes of the **Pic de la Coquillade**. The trail head begins on the Orb's south bank, just west of the hamlet of Les Aires, and the gruelling 6km walk will take you first to the extensive ruins of the castle, which was founded in 990, and on to the summit, where you'll find a small chapel with dramatic views of the surrounding hills. The chief reason to come here, however, is the wonderful hotel-spa, *Le Couvent d'Hérépian* (☎04.67.23.36.30, ⓦwww.garrigaeresorts.com/le-couvent; ⓪), a deluxe all-suite hotel set in a seventeenth-century convent, and an excellent base for exploring the area. *L'Ocre Rouge* (open Mon eve to Sun lunch; ☎04.67.95.06.93), on 12 pl de la Croiz, is one of the area's best **restaurants**, serving up elaborate seasonal dishes based on local produce, such as pistachio-encrusted flank of lamb and chestnut *millefeuille* (from €24).

Bédarieux

Continuing from Hérépian, the valley broadens suddenly, forming a wide pocket of flat land dominated by **BÉDARIEUX**, the biggest place north of Béziers on the course of the Orb. The town is something of a transport hub and, as an administrative centre, it's also busy, but you're not likely to want to stay too long. Bédarieux's one tourist attraction is the mediocre **Maison des Arts** (Mon, Tues & Thurs 3–6pm; €3), on avenue Abbé-Taroux, whose collection is dominated by local painter Pierre-Auguste Cot. Otherwise, the tourist office can set you up with detailed information on **walks** in the local countryside (€1 for their booklet). One of the better short ones is the trail, through vines and bulrushes, to the twelfth-century pre-Romanesque **chapel** of St-Raphaël, on the far bank of the river, while a more challenging option is the ascent of the Pic de Tanajo (518m) to the southwest.

Bédarieux's **gare SNCF**, which is also where **buses** stop, is a good twenty-minute hike north of the old centre, where you'll find the regional **tourist office** on place aux Herbes (Mon–Fri 9am–noon & 2–6pm, Sat 9am–noon; ☎04.67.95.08.79, ⓦwww.bedarieux.fr). The town's only **hotel**, *Hôtel de l'Orb* (☎04.67.23.35.90, ⓦwww.hotel-orb.com; ❸) is on route de St-Pins, near the station, with the **campsite** *Trois Vallées* (mid-June to Aug; ☎04.67.23.30.19, Ⓔgites.bedarieux@orange.fr) on the south bank of the Orb, just west of town. There's an excellent **restaurant**, *La Forge* (Tues–Sun; ☎04.67.95.13.13), at 22 av Abbé-Tarroux, with a cosy, vaulted dining room and *terroir menus* from €16. **Car rental** is available from Wallgreen, 4 rue de la République (☎04.67.23.18.23), and Happy Car, 53 bis rte de Lodève (☎04.67.95.00.65), while Cycles Horizon, at 13 av Abbé-Tarroux (☎04.67.95.24.25), rents out **bikes**. There are **markets** in the town's *places* on Monday and Saturday mornings.

The upper Orb valley

Moving north, the valley continues to rise, with the river petering out to little more than a brook near its sources in the Monts d'Orb. Proceeding from Bédarieux, you should take the turn-off 6km north of town and ascend to tiny medieval **BOUSSAGUES**, an extremely well preserved, walled town, replete with church, fountain and *donjon*, which is surprisingly unvisited; the only service you'll find here is a (frequently closed) café. The ruins of its castles, on the hill above, are little more than foundations overgrown by vine and bramble, but the views they provide are great. **Hikers** on the GR7 will pass by Boussagues as they make their way between Lamalou and Lodève. **LE-BOUSQUET**, 10km further up the valley, has a strange air, as if everyone is waiting for something to happen – nothing ever does, however, and aside from taking a fleeting look at the old quarter gathered in a mound on the right bank, there is no reason to stay.

LUNAS, just a few kilometres further along the road, makes a much more pleasant option. Here the river glides past the walls of a pitched-roof *château*; you'll find an old bridge and a church which, it is claimed, dates back to the fifth century – nothing particularly stunning, but, with the low, forest-clad hills rising on either side of the river valley, an attractive and peaceful scene, and a good stop before braving the spectacular mountain road which leads east along the steep ridge to Lodève (see p.244). **Accommodation** in Lunas includes the *Auberge Gourmande* (℡04.67.23.81.41, ⓦwww.auberge-lunas.fr; ❸) at 52 Grand'Route, whose restaurant (closed Fri–Sun in winter) has *menus* at €17–27, or the more attractive and better-equipped *Manoir de Gravezon* on the route de Bédarieux (℡04.67.23.89.79, ⓦwww.hotel-manoir-de-gravezon.com; ❸). There's a seasonal **campsite** in nearby Le-Bousquet (mid-June to Aug; ℡04.67.23.80.89).

Five kilometres north of Lunas is the evocative mountain hamlet of **JONCELS**, which grew up around the seventh-century Benedictine monastery of St-Pierre, and became an important stop on the Chemin de St-Jacques pilgrim route (see p.203). In the thirteenth century the town was fortified, with further amendments made in the eighteenth century, but the monks still live there today (forbidden by papal order from leaving the confines of the abbey) and still provide rest for passing pilgrims. There's an excellent **hotel** in the village, ⚘ *Villa Issiates* (℡04.67.23.20.93, ⓦvilla.issiates.free.fr; ❸), which has a wide range of amenities including wi-fi, cable TV, laundry service and more; in addition, there's a **pilgrims' hostel** (℡04.67.23.80.89; dorm beds €15), and a **campsite** (mid-June to Sept; ℡04.67.23.89.89).

Travel details

Trains

Main lines link Narbonne to Béziers/Montpellier and Perpignan, as well as to Carcassonne/Toulouse, while a secondary line climbs the Orb from Béziers towards the Massif Central. SNCF buses may run in lieu of trains on these lines; services are reduced on Sundays and holidays. TGV stations are indicated with an asterisk.

Béziers* to:

Bédarieux (several daily; 35min).

Capestang (daily; 18min).

Nîmes*, via Agde, Sète and Montpellier* (several hourly; 2hr 10min–2hr 45min).

Paris* (many daily; 4hr+).

Perpignan*, via Narbonne* and Salses (hourly; 50min–1hr 25min).

Toulouse*, via Narbonne, Lézignan, Carcassonne* (connection to Quillan) and Castelnaudary (hourly; 1hr 30min–1hr 45min).

Narbonne* to:

Nîmes*, via Béziers* (connections to Bédarieux), Agde, Sète and Montpellier* (several hourly; 2hr 10min–2hr 45min).

Paris* (many daily; 4hr 30min+).

Perpignan*, via Salses (hourly; 35–50min).

Toulouse*, via Lézignan, Carcassonne* (connection to Quillan) and Castelnaudary (many daily; 1hr 20min–1hr 45min).

Buses

Main bus lines in the Aude *département* run up the valley to Quillan and down to Narbonne. Services may be reduced on Saturdays and school holidays. No buses run on Sundays in the Aude, and on many lines in the Minervois (for Hérault bus schedules, ℡08.25.34.01.34 or ⓦwww .herault .fr). In summer extra services run from Béziers and Narbonne to the beach towns.

Agde to: Cap d'Agde (winter several daily; summer local service; 15min); Pézenas (daily; 40min).

Bédarieux to: Le Bousquet (daily; 15min); Lamalou-les-Bains (daily; 20min); Lunas (1–2 daily; 15min); Montpellier (several daily; 1hr 45min); St-Pons (daily; 1hr 20min).

Béziers to: Agde (several daily; 30min); Bédarieux (daily; 1hr–1hr 20min); Capestang (several daily; 40min); Castres (daily; 2hr 50min); Colombiers (several daily; 20min); Lamalou (daily; 1hr 10min); Marseillan (several daily; 45min); Montpellier (several daily; 1hr 55min); Olonzac (daily on Fri; 55min); Pézenas (several daily; 32min); Roquebrun (several daily; 50min); St-Pons (several daily; 1hr 20min).

Carcassonne to: Caunes-Minervois (daily; 30min); Lagrasse (daily; 1hr 40min).

Narbonne to: Bize (daily; 40min); Carcassonne (daily; 1hr 25min); Gruissan (several daily; 30min); Lézignan (several daily; 35min); Perpignan (daily; 2hr 30min); Sallèles (daily; 30min); Salses (daily; 1hr 55min); Sigean (daily; 35min); Sigean Reserve (daily; 30min); St-Julien/Fontfroide (several daily; 40min); Villerouge-Termenès (daily; 1hr 40min).

Roussillon

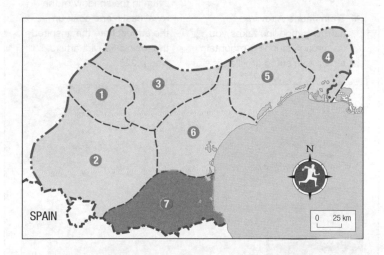

CHAPTER 7 **Highlights**

✳ Christmas festivals
Roussillon celebrates
Christmas in distinctive
Catalan style featuring
traditional folk art: *pessebres*,
caganers and *cagatiós*.
See p.293

✳ Le Canigou The Catalans'
sacred mountain towers
above Roussillon; join
the midsummer firelight
pilgrimage. See p.304

✳ Train Jaune A revived
narrow-gauge line takes you
up through stunning mountain
terrain to a string of villages
that make perfect hiking
bases. See p.307

✳ Romanesque churches
The slopes of the Pyrenees
are home to a series of
rural churches painted and
sculpted by local masters a
thousand years ago.
See p.319

✳ Collioure At the region's most
beautiful beach town you can
swim in the shadow of the
royal castle and soak up
the atmosphere that inspired
the town's Fauvist artists.
See p.320

▲ Collioure

7

Roussillon

R oussillon, bordered by the Mediterranean to the east, the hills of the Corbières along the north, and the upper Aude and Ariège valleys to the west, is France's southernmost region, sometimes known as French Catalonia; the peaks of the eastern section of the Pyrenees, which it shares with Spain, mark its southern limit. Although absorbed by France some three and a half centuries ago, and now known officially as the *département* of Pyrénées-Orientales, it hasn't entirely lost its **Catalan** flavour: in the mountains there are many people whose language of choice is Catalan, and even in the larger towns you'll find the survival of customs such as the *sardana* dance and unique Paschal rituals. You'll also notice the influence of traditional Catalan ingredients and recipes in the region's *terroir* cuisine. But despite these particularities, and recent efforts by Catalan speakers to broaden the currency of the language, Roussillon is fundamentally French in cultural orientation, and unlike other French regions, such as Corsica, it has no significant separatist movement or regionalist political party – most likely, your only encounter with the language will be overhearing the conversations of the many visitors to the region from Catalonia proper. Traditionally a poor and neglected area, Roussillon's people have historically lived off fishing on the coast; agriculture, herding and lumber in the hills; and, until recently, smuggling, which, with the region's frontier position and the inhospitality of its landscape, provided a meagre source of income. In the last decade or so, though, the mild climate has provoked its resurgence as a retirement spot for northern French, viewed by some of the local inhabitants with a jaundiced eye as "foreign" encroachers.

It is a beautiful region, marked by the variety and contrasts of its landscape. North of the cosmopolitan main city, **Perpignan**, a marshy coastline hems in the **Fenouillèdes** hills stretching up to the northeast corner of the *département* – home to the easternmost Cathar castles and a number of prehistoric caves. Southwest from the capital you can follow the course of Roussillon's jugular, the River **Têt** (or **Conflent**), up the valley to **Canigou**, the peak which still symbolizes all of Catalonia, and the scene of a patriotic torchlight procession on midsummer's eve. Roussillon's mountains begin with the Canigou massif and include the zones of the **upper Têt** (shadowed by the spectacular route of the *Train Jaune*), the **Capcir** plateau, stretching up to the Aude, the **Cerdagne**, tucked away in the far southwest corner of the *département* and, north of that, the forbidding **Carlit** massif; all of these regions – recently incorporated into the **Parc Régional Naturel des Pyrénées Catalanes** (see p.308) – offer excellent **hiking** and **skiing** amid superb scenery. There are also many architectural treasures worth seeking out here, in particular the sturdy Romanesque **monasteries** which cropped up

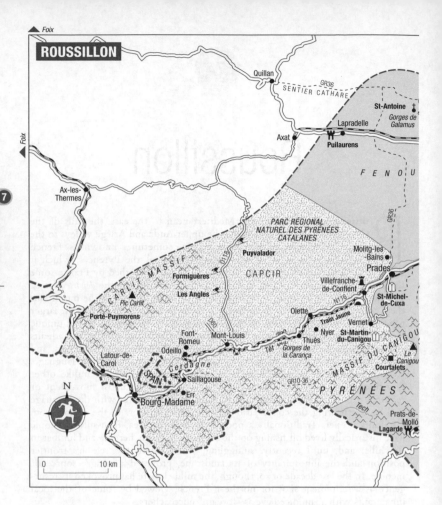

along this length of the Pyrenees in the eleventh and twelfth centuries. The **Tech valley** runs a vaguely parallel course to the Têt, leading up from the plains south of Perpignan and along the Spanish border; a favourite zone with refugees from Franco's repression, its villages are some of the most traditionally Catalan in the whole region. Finally, the rugged **Côte Vermeille**, the seashore to the north of the frontier, is ideal for swimming and relaxing, its rocky harbours, cut out of wind-blown precipitous hills, forming a mirror image of Catalan Empordà on the far side of the Pyrenees.

Despite its relative lack of development, Roussillon is fairly easy to get around, as long you stick to the main **transport** routes, which run along the coast, and up the major valleys – the Têt, Tech and rivers of the Fenouillet. Bus fares across the *departement* have now been set at €1. Travelling between the valleys is more problematic, and unless you have your own transport you'll have to resort to hiking or hitching. The main road and rail links to Spain head south from Perpignan, the latter passing through the towns of the Côte Vermeille.

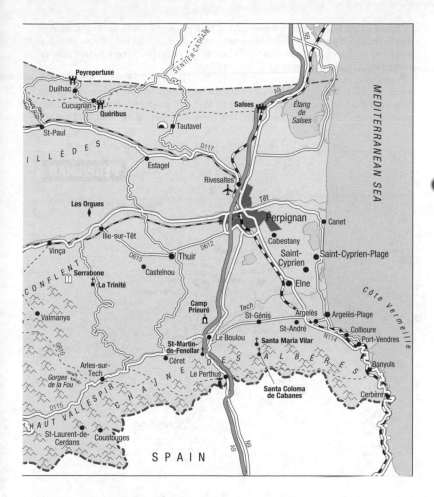

Perpignan and around

PERPIGNAN (or Perpinyà, in Catalan), the capital of Roussillon, is the most multinational city in the Southwest. A substantial part of its population is descended from Spanish Catalans who poured across the border in the final days of the Spanish Civil War, desperate to avoid reprisals at the hands of Franco's Castilian and Moroccan troops. There's also a sizeable Romany contingent, while some of the suburbs were settled by French colonists who fled the upheavals associated with the Maghrebi independence movements of the 1950s and 1960s. Finally, a run-down zone in the centre has become the quarter for recent arrivals from Morocco and Algeria, who moved here fleeing unstable and repressive political regimes or simply in search of a brighter economic future. The melting-pot atmosphere of the city makes it difficult for a distinctly Catalan ambience to coalesce, but the people are nonetheless happy to set themselves apart from the rest of their countrymen by promoting this identity – even if their own spoken Catalan is frequently nonexistent or limited to a few phrases pronounced with a distinctly Gallic accent. Unfortunately, though, Perpignan is far from a model of tolerance – Le Pen's Front National party and its derivatives have done well here at the polls, peddling a racist vision of white French nationals "swamped" by outsiders.

Perpignan has had a quiet history. Too far from the sea to serve as a port itself, it was a sizeable if unremarkable town until the thirteenth century, when it began to boom as a cloth-making centre. Jaume II of Mallorca and Roussillon enhanced this prosperity in 1276, when he made the town his alternative mainland capital

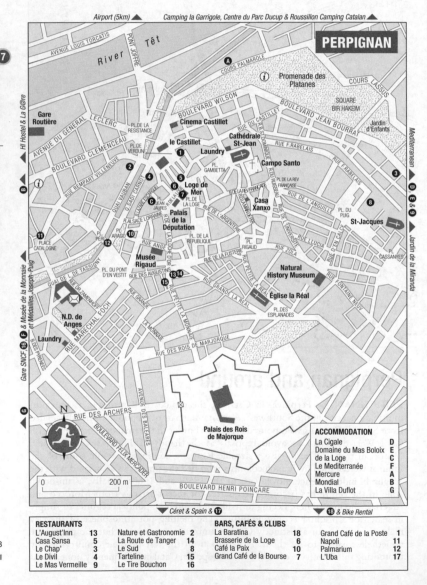

RESTAURANTS				BARS, CAFÉS & CLUBS			
L'August'Inn	13	Nature et Gastronomie	2	La Baratina	18	Grand Café de la Poste	1
Casa Sansa	5	La Route de Tanger	14	Brasserie de la Loge	6	Napoli	11
Le Chap'	3	Le Sud	8	Café la Paix	10	Palmarium	12
Le Divil	4	Tarteline	15	Grand Café de la Bourse	7	L'Uba	17
Le Mas Vermeille	9	Le Tire Bouchon	16				

Roussillon's festivals and traditions

The Roussillonais seem to have inherited a penchant for **festivals** from their Spanish cousins south of the Pyrenees, as just about every village has at least one cheerfully energetic celebration – usually the local saint's day, or *festa major* (*fête majeure*, in French). It is in these that the region's Catalan and Spanish character come to the fore, with *sardanas*, *corridas de toros* and Holy Week processions. The last of these, a solemn barefoot march by taper-carrying and hooded penitents, is best seen in places like Collioure (Aug 16), Arles-sur-Tech (first weekend in Sept) and Céret (early June).

First weekend in Feb Arles-sur-Tech and St-Laurent-de-Cerdans: *Fête de l'Ours*. This ancient festival, rooted in prehistoric shamanistic ceremonies and hunting traditions, marks the time when bears come out of hibernation (see p.315).

April 22 Perpignan: *San Jordi*. Festival of Catalonia's patron saint, St George. Men present their sweethearts with a red rose, and women reciprocate with a book.

Late May Perpignan: Medieval Market. The old town centre is transformed into a medieval open-air market replete with costumed vendors, jugglers and street entertainers.

June 23 Têt valley: *Nit de Sant-Jaume*. On the eve of St John's Day people come from all over Catalonia for the torchlight pilgrimage from the Castillet in Perpignan to the peak of Le Canigou – one of the symbols of the Catalan nation.

End June Arles-sur-Tech: *Fête de St-Éloi*. This three-day festival culminates in the blessing of the mules – traditionally indispensable as transport here.

Mid-July Céret: *Céret de Toros*. Three days of bullfights and bull running.

July 28–30 Arles-sur-Tech: *Festa Major*. Typically boisterous Catalan festival, featuring processions and loaded with medieval traditions.

End July to mid-Aug Prades: *Festival Pablo Casals* ☎04.68.96.33.07, ⓦwww .prades-festival-casals.com. A world-famous classical music festival.

First two weeks Sept Perpignan: *Visa pour l'Image* ⓦwww.visapourlimage.com. International festival of photojournalism held at the Palais des Congrès, with seminars, exhibitions and screenings of journalistic photos by leading photographers and rising stars.

Mid-Sept Céret: *Ronde Céretaine*. A Catalan music and culture festival with *correfocs* (fireworks parades) and *sardanas*.

Last two weeks Dec Perpignan: Christmas activities that include a market, *pessebres* (Nativity scenes), a public *cagatió* and concerts.

(Montpellier being the other, and Palma de Mallorca the king's principal residence). When that kingdom evaporated in 1349, however, the city was absorbed by the Catalan-Aragonese Crown, whose own main capital was nearby Barcelona, bringing an end to Perpignan's elevated status. In the centuries that followed it was the object of repeated campaigns of conquest by France, finally becoming French territory in 1659 with the Treaty of the Pyrenees.

Aside from taking in the pleasant Mediterranean ambience of the place, there are a number of interesting monuments and museums worth seeking out here, and the one sight that shouldn't be missed is the **Palais des Rois**, in the south of the old town. In addition, Perpignan is the principal transport hub of the region and serves as a handy base for exploring nearby **Salses**, as well as **Tautavel** on the way into the Fenouillèdes (see p.298), plus the beaches of the Côte Vermeille.

Arrival and information

Perpignan's small **airport**, Perpignan-Rivesaltes (☎04.68.52.60.70, ⓦwww .perpignan.cci.fr), 5km north of town, handles daily flights to and from Paris,

Essentials

Bike rental Véloland, 95 av du Maréchal Juin ☎04.68.08.19.99.

Buses The city buses cost €1.10 for a single journey; get tickets at the CTP kiosk in pl Péri, near the *Palmarium* café. A free *navette* circulates through the old town and to the *gare*.

Discount card Passeport Musées and Inter-site card; see box opposite.

Internet access La G@re, 62 bis av Général-de-Gaulle (daily 10am–2am).

Laundry Laverie Foch, 23 rue Maréchal Foch (daily 9am–7pm), and Laverie St-Jean, 3 rue Cité E. Bartisol, near Campo Santo (daily 7.30am–7pm).

Markets General market in pl de la République (Mon 7am–1pm, Tues–Sat 7am–12.30pm & 4.30–7.30pm), plus antiques in allées Maillol (Sat 8am–6pm) and organic food in pl Rigaud (Sat 8am–noon). The most colourful market takes place on Saturday and Sunday mornings in the tree-shaded pl Cassanyes, with a mixture of French, Arab and African traders selling cheap clothes, crafts and all sorts of local produce.

Taxis ☎04.68.35.15.15 or 06.09.36.96.86. There are also taxi stands at pl de Verdun, at the gare SNCF and on pl Arago.

Montpellier, Lyon and Strasbourg, as well as services from London in summer; its meagre facilities include shops, a bar and restaurant, and car rental offices. An airport **navette** (shuttle service) makes the twenty-minute trip (€4.50) into the centre up to six times daily (though it is rather tightly timed to meet the flights), stopping at the train station, place de Catalogne and the bus station. A **taxi** into the centre will cost around €14.

Perpignan's **gare SNCF**, at the west end of avenue Général-de-Gaulle, was once dubbed "the centre of the world" by Salvador Dalí, and is now topped by a large statue of the artist, falling over backwards or reaching out to embrace the heavens. To get into the heart of the city from here is a twenty-minute walk – or you can take one of the frequent #2 buses to "Castillet". Arriving by bus or airport *navette*, you'll be dropped at the **gare routière**, a short distance northwest of place de la Résistance. From the station a free *navette* does a circuit of the old town, but does not run during lunch hour.

The **tourist office** (mid-June to mid-Sept Mon–Sat 9am–7pm, Sun 10am–4pm; mid-Sept to mid-June Mon–Sat 9am–6pm, Sun 10am–1pm; ☎04.68.66.30.30, Ⓦwww.perpignantourisme.com) is in the Palais des Congrès, the white building at the eastern end of the leafy promenade des Platanes which runs parallel to boulevard Wilson – they can supply you with the free *Perpignan Mag* (monthly in summer, otherwise quarterly) for events listings.

Accommodation

Accommodation is plentiful in Perpignan, with a selection of establishments in all price ranges, although the most common are small and serviceable, few-frills hotels.

Hotels

La Cigale 78 bd Jean-Bourrat ☎04.68.50.20.14, Ⓦwww.hotel-cigale-perpignan.com. Renovated, comfortable two-star hotel at the far end of the promenade des Platanes, near the church of St-Jacques. Facilities are adequate (TV and internet) and service is friendly. ❸

Domaine du Mas Boluix Chemin du Pou des Colobres ☎04.68.08.17.70, Ⓦwww.domaine-de-boluix.com. Well-appointed B&B with five rooms, sitting room and garden on the outskirts of Perpignan (towards Cabestany). Breakfast included. ❻

de la Loge 1 rue Fabriques d'En Nabot ☎04.68.34.41.02, Ⓦwww.hoteldelaloge.fr.

A well-priced option in the heart of the old town with spacious rooms and good facilities. Best value-for-money option in town. ❸

🏃 **Le Mediterranée** 62 bis av Général-de-Gaulle ☎04.68.34.87.48, ⓦwww.hotel-mediterranee.com. Hip hotel near the station, very popular with the backpacking crowd. The building isn't the most modern and the service is relaxed to say the least, but its bar, cybercafé (wi-fi for guests) and laidback atmosphere more than compensate. The family rooms are a bargain. ❸

Mercure Perpignan Centre 5 bis cours Palmarole ☎04.68.35.67.66, ⓦwww.mercure.com. Ideal for families, this distinctive-looking hotel has five suites in addition to its well-equipped rooms, all with a/c and wi-fi. Located just within the confines of the old town, north of the tourist office. ❼

Mondial 40 bd Clémenceau ☎04.68.34.23.45, ⓦwww.hotel-mondial-perpignan.com. Solid two-star hotel with good amenities, near the Musée Joseph-Puig, a short walk from the Castellet. Rooms have wi-fi and cable TV. Steeply discounted from Sept to July, this is the best value off-season. ❹

La Villa Duflot Rondpoint Albert Donnezan (Serrat d'en Vaquer) ☎04.68.56.67.67, ⓦwww.villa-duflot.com. Halfway between the city centre and the airport, Perpignan's most luxurious hotel is set among a sixteen-acre spread of ancient olive gardens and has an excellent in-house *gastronomique* restaurant (*menu* from €30). Rooms have four-star amenities and Art Deco styling. Mini-suites and apartments available. ❽

Hostel and campsite

HI Hostel Av de la Grande-Bretagne ☎04.68.34.63.32, ⓦwww.fuaj.org. Modern, well-run hostel beside a park, fifteen minutes' walk from the centre, between the *gare routière* and the gare SNCF, but with a noisy road running behind it. Curfews 11am–4pm & 11pm. Open March to mid-Nov. Dorm beds €15.20 with breakfast. Camping is permitted.

Roussillon Camping Catalan Rte de Bompas ☎04.68.62.16.92, ⓦcamping-catalan.com. Large two-star site, 8km northeast of the city, with shop, swimming pool and laundry service. Also rents caravans and is wheelchair-accessible. No service by municipal bus. Open March–Oct.

The City

Perpignan's medieval walls, though spared by Richelieu, were demolished early last century to allow for expansion, and replaced by wide boulevards. This, in fact, maintained the separation of the city's older districts from the new, and it's still easy and enjoyable to get around the compact **old town** on foot. Most of the city's sights are concentrated in the dense clutch of pedestrian streets northeast of riverside **place Arago**, and stretching towards the geographical centre of the old town, while between **place de la Loge** and **place Rigaud**, just to the southeast, you could be on the Left Bank in Paris, the old streets now a maze of chic boutiques. On the north side of the pedestrian area you'll find the **cathedral**, from where you can follow the course of the old walls through the Romany and **Maghrebi quarter** to the church of St-Jacques, marking the eastern limit of old Perpignan. To the south of this the land rises towards the massive **Palais des Rois de Majorque**, crowning the hill which dominated the southern quarter of the medieval town. In the **new town**, to the west of the River La Basse, you won't

---

Museum discount passes

For €8 you can purchase a **Passeport Musées**, which gives you access to any four of Perpignan's museums, except the Palais des Rois. The latter, however, is covered by the **Inter-site discount card**, which gives reductions of fifteen to fifty percent on the entrance fees of up to eleven out of a total of 38 museums and monuments in Pyrénées-Orientales, including those on the coast and the most important fortresses and churches of the Tech and Conflent valleys. The Inter-site card is free and valid for one year after you have visited your first monument. Both passes are available at participating museums and monuments, and you can get the Inter-site at tourist offices throughout the *département*.

find many sights, but the avenues leading west towards the train station make for excellent hotel- and restaurant-hunting.

Place Arago to Le Castillet

The heart of the city is café-lined **place Arago**, on the flower-decked bank of the canalized Basse river. South of this is a tiny thirteenth-century *faubourg*, whose quiet grid of streets contains well-restored houses and the odd café. But you'll most likely prefer to dive directly east into Perpignan's historical centre. Close by, along rue Ange, you'll find the **Musée Rigaud** at no. 16 (Wed–Mon: May–Sept noon–7pm; Oct–April 11am–5.30pm; €4). The museum is housed in a seventeenth-century palace, originally the workshop of local artist Hyacinthe Rigaud, a favourite of Louis XIV, and it later served as studio and living space for Picasso, Dufy and Cocteau. Today it holds a good collection of modern art, including works by Maillol, Alechinsky and the aforementioned artists. From here, rue Cloche d'Or ("street of the Golden Bell") can be followed uphill towards the hulking Palais des Rois (see p.294), while turning left will lead you further into the medieval quarter.

The **place de la Loge** was the centre of activity in fourteenth-century Perpignan: on its southeastern side, you'll find three of the city's most important administrative buildings. The first of these is the fifteenth-century Gothic-style **Palais de la Députation**, where the Catalan count-kings once convened the Roussillon parliament, while next door, the sixteenth-century **Hôtel de Ville** is worth a peek for the Aristide Maillol bronze, *La Méditerranée*, which sits in the courtyard. The last of the three great buildings is Roussillon's famous **Loge de Mer**; built in 1397, it served as the region's stock exchange – the meeting place and court for its merchants. High on the south wall is a blazon bearing three arms, which stand for the three classes of city folk who ran the town council: merchants and drapers; doctors and notaries; and artisans and gardeners. The building remains a marvel, with a gracefully vaulted interior and gargoyles adorning the upper parts of its facade – a fine and rare example of Gothic civic architecture, and now home to a tastefully arty café-restaurant. The square, which spreads around the Loge, long served as the scene of grisly executions, notably of the rebels housed in Le Castillet (see below), while during World War II, the *place*'s busy pavement cafés were the place to find *passeurs*, the men and women who guided refugees across the Pyrenees into Spain.

If you feel like exploring around place de la Loge, take a wander through the series of ancient lanes which run off towards the river, including tiny **rue Fabriques d'En Nabot**, where you'll come across a number of notable thirteenth- and fourteenth-century houses, with magnificent doorways and ogival windows. Following any of these streets, or taking the wider rue Louis-Blanc at the north end of place de la Loge, will lead you to Perpignan's distinctive red-brick **Le Castillet**, the lone surviving tower of the old town walls. Also known as the Casa Païral ("The House of the Ancestors"), it now houses a **museum** celebrating Roussillonais rural culture (Wed–Mon: May–Sept 10am–6.30pm; Oct–April 11am–5.30pm; €2) and in particular commemorating the anti-French rebellions of 1661–74, when the tower held captured Catalan insurgents. The **place de Verdun**, on the south side of Le Castillet, is the setting for summer evening performances of the *sardana*, the perplexingly insipid Catalan folk dance. Nearby, at 1 bd Wilson, is the battered but splendidly ornate **Cinéma Castillet**, the oldest cinema in France, now converted into a seven-screen complex.

The cathedral and around

Two hundred metres east of Le Castillet, but most easily accessed from the north end of place de la Loge, is another ancient square, **place Gambetta**, scene of the

The Catalan Christmas cagatió

Among the many Catalan folkloric customs that have survived centuries of French domination are two rather strange practices associated with **Christmas**. Like the Provençals, the Roussillonais are known for their elaborate **Nativity** scenes (*pessebres*), populated by hordes of figurines. However, if you look carefully at the Catalan version, among the various shepherds, angel choirs and wise men you'll note a small figure, usually dressed in peasant garb and sporting a traditional Catalan red cap. This is the **caganer**, a crouching man, poised with pants around his ankles, in some stage of the act of defecation. Similarly, although Catalan children customarily receive presents on the Epiphany (Jan 6), the **cagatió** (literally, the "shitting log") ensures that they don't go completely empty-handed at Christmas. It consists of a log with a painted-on face, draped with a red cloth at its posterior end. As children gather round the *cagatió*, beating it with sticks and singing a song invoking bowel movement, the blanket is withdrawn to the delight of all, revealing the sweets it has apparently excreted. You can purchase your own *caganers* (which now come in various forms, including policemen, referees and political figures) and *cagatiós* at Perpignan's Christmas market, held in front of the cathedral during the four weeks of Advent.

7

town's open-air **market** since the Middle Ages. At its eastern end towers the **Cathédrale St-Jean** (daily 9am–noon & 3–6.30pm; free), commissioned in 1324 and elevated to cathedral status in 1602 when the diocese of Elne was transferred to Perpignan. Next door, its predecessor, the impressive Romanesque **St-Jean le Vieux** (currently closed for renovations), is linked to the cathedral by mammoth buttresses. The cathedral's striking exterior sports bands of rounded river stones sandwiched by brick, while inside there's a majestically columned nave, whose side chapels, though badly damaged, retain some elaborate sixteenth- and seventeenth-century retables. Leaving through the south transept, poke your head in the **chapel** on the left, which is presided over by an excellent fourteenth-century polychrome Crucifixion, known as the *Dévot Christ*, and most likely the work of a Rhineland sculptor. Past the chapel, on the left, is the entrance to the **Campo Santo**, one of France's oldest cemeteries, going back some six hundred years (Oct–April only Tues–Sun 11am–5pm; free) – it is now used for concerts in summer.

On the far side of Campo Santo, down the evocatively named rue de la Main de Fer is **Casa Xanxo** (Tues–Sun: April–Sept noon–7pm; Oct–March 11am–5.30pm; free), a luxurious residence constructed by the local merchant Bernat Xanxo and renovated in the seventeenth and eighteenth centuries; it now houses temporary exhibitions. Close by, the lively rue de la Révolution Française, populated by arty cafés and hip bars, runs east to the *place* of the same name.

East to the church of St-Jacques

East of place de la Révolution Française you can ascend into the slums of old Perpignan, which spread south from here almost as far as the great palace, and east to place Cassanyes, at the former limits of the city walls. Inhabited almost exclusively by recent arrivals from North Africa, with a Romany enclave centred on **place du Puig** (pronounced "pooch"), this can seem an intimidating district, although it has improved in recent years; the cramped quarters are littered with refuse and hung with washing, a stereotype of immigrant poverty. But it's worth persevering – the various squares dotted around are rich with history, such as **place Fontaine-Neuve**, which dates back some seven hundred years to the time when the "new well" after which it is named was dug here.

Northeast of place Fontaine-Neuve and just east of place du Puig is the fourteenth-century **church of St-Jacques** (daily: July & Aug 3–7pm; Sept–June 2.30–5.30pm), the nucleus of Perpignan's oldest parish, originally founded by Jaume I in honour of his patron saint (Jacques being French for Jaume) a hundred years earlier. The king was also a donor to the confraternity of Sanch – a parish-based social organization typical of the Middle Ages, dedicated to the Holy Blood of Christ ("sanch" means "blood" in old Catalan). On Maundy Thursday each year they hold a Spanish-style procession of penitents, who walk from the church through the town hooded (so as not to take pride in their piety) and barefooted, carrying heavy candles or crosses. Behind the church, the **Jardin de la Miranda** (daily 8am–noon & 2–5.30pm), built on a section of the city's old fortifications, provides an airy respite for the inhabitants of this quarter.

The Palais des Rois de Majorque

Perpignan's most famous sight, and the kernel around which the city grew, is the massive **Palais des Rois de Majorque** (daily: June–Sept 10am–6pm; Oct–May 9am–5pm; €4) on the southern fringe of the old city; the entrance is on the west side of the complex in rue des Archers, around fifteen minutes' walk from place de la Loge, and slightly longer from the church of St-Jacques.

The history of Perpignan is more or less synonymous with that of the palace, originally built in the late thirteenth century as a residence for Jaume II of Mallorca, son of Jaume I ("The Conqueror"), Count of Barcelona and King of Aragón and Valencia, who captured Mallorca from the Muslims. At his death "The Conqueror" divided his kingdom between his two sons: to the elder, Pere II, went the titles of King of Aragón and Valencia and Count of Barcelona, but only a portion of the actual kingdom; the remainder, including Roussillon and Mallorca, went to the younger Jaume. The two branches of the family were immediately at each other's throats, and stayed that way until Roussillon was reunited with Aragón and Catalonia in the early fourteenth century by the powerful Pere III. Having passed to the French, then back to the Catalans, Perpignan changed hands for the last time in 1642, a couple of years after France had occupied Roussillon in the wake of the Catalans' revolt against the Habsburg rulers of Madrid; in September, after a siege that was at times commanded personally by Louis XIII and Richelieu, Perpignan fell. Vauban, military engineer to Louis XIV, constructed the imposing outer walls in the fit of over-enthusiastic fortification that followed consolidation of French sovereignty accorded by the 1659 Treaty of the Pyrenees.

After ascending an impressive zigzagging ramp, large enough for several cavalry to ride abreast, you enter a grassy park, with the square thirteenth-century **castle** ahead of you, standing incongruously with its curious stone-and-mortar construction. Passing into the splendid two-storey **courtyard**, whose upper level opens into graceful Gothic galleries on the east and west sides, you ascend the stairs to the former kings' apartments, now a boutique for Roussillon vintages. Across from these you'll find the unsullied but sparsely furnished queens' apartments, which have delicately vaulted period ceilings and windows. Between the two sets of royal apartments are the so-called king's and queen's **chapels**, one on the upper floor and one on the lower, and both with interesting details in Gothic style, from carved corbels to fading frescoes. The palace frequently holds temporary exhibitions on local history and culture (included in admission).

Just below the fortress is the **Église la Réal** (hours vary; free); set in the street of the same name, this fourteenth-century foundation was the parish church of the castle, and contains contemporary frescoes, fifteenth-century wooden polychrome sculpture and a fine, carved baptismal font. Northwest of here, back by the canal, is another royal church, the stunningly decorated **Chapelle Notre-Dame des Anges** (June–Sept 10am–12.30pm & 1.15–6pm; Oct–May 9.30am–5.30pm; free), originally the chapter house of a monastery founded by the Kings of

Majorca in the thirteenth century and featuring a tympanum attributed to the Master of Cabestany.

Eating, drinking and nightlife

Don't dally when pondering dinner: most of Perpignan's **restaurant** shutters seem to roll down at 10pm sharp, though several **brasseries** stay open till midnight, including the popular *Arago* and *Café Vienne* in the palm-shaded place Arago – this and avenue Général-de-Gaulle have the greatest concentration of places to eat.

Perpignan is not great for **nightlife**, but it does have plenty of **cafés**. Start on place de la Loge – call in at *Brasserie de la Loge* or *Grand Café de la Bourse* – and place de Verdun, where the *Grand Café de la Poste*, shaded by huge plane trees, is the best. *Café la Paix* in place Arago is another popular choice, but best of all is the huge, airy *Palmarium*, on the opposite side overlooking the River Basse, a low-key, self-service place, where you can linger for hours over a coffee. All of these serve reasonably priced *menus* at mealtimes.

Most of Perpignan's **clubs** are on the fringes of town, but in the centre you can dance at *Napoli*, 3 bis pl Catalogne (Wed–Sat 11pm–3am; €8), and *L'Uba*, 5 bd Mercader (Wed–Sat 11pm–3am; closed mid-July to mid-Aug; €10). *La Baratina* is a large disco at 5 bis pl de la Sardane, which caters for all ages (Tues–Sun 11pm–3am; free–€10). In July and August the town comes alive on Thursday nights with a **street festival** featuring markets and music.

Restaurants

L'August'Inn 37–39 rue des Augustins ☎04.68.35.11.29, ⓦwww.augustinn.fr. A new restaurant owned by the young chef Eric Planes, whose aim is to serve dynamic, inventive cuisine drawn from a range of influences, at reasonable prices. Lunch *menus* from a ridiculous €12, dinner at €33 – reservations are strongly recommended. The menus change weekly – check the website for the latest.

Casa Sansa 2 rue Fabriques-Nadal ☎04.68.34.21.84. This city's best Catalan cuisine is served up in this comfortable establishment, founded in 1846, in one of the old town's most beautiful streets. Expect to pay about €40 per person. Wheelchair-accessible. Closed Sun.

Le Chap' 18 bd Jean Bourrat ☎04.68.35.14.14. The sophisticated *Park Hôtel* restaurant features an excellent Mediterranean *gastronomique carte* at altogether reasonable prices. *Menus* €28 at lunch, and €30 dinner. Closed Sun.

Le Divil 9 rue Fabriques d'En Nabot ☎04.68.34.57.73. An excellent old-town choice, this comfortable, low-key dining room features a diverse *carte* of Roussillonnais specialities, tending heavily towards beef, although the scallop dishes are an excellent "surf" option. Lunch is available weekdays for €13, while dinner *menus* include a bistro option (€18) or a full dinner for €35.

Le Mas Vermeil 1700 chemin de la Roseraie ☎04.68.66.95.66. A bit of a trek (4km) out from the centre, but well worth it to dine and drink in this beautifully renovated Catalan-style farmhouse. Prices are reasonable: *menus* €20 at lunch and starting from €28 at dinner, with a variety of fish and meat main dishes. There is also a less formal *bistro* room.

Nature et Gastronomie 37 quai Vauban ☎04.68.59.0038. Perpignan's stop for organic food – which includes a restaurant, tearoom and grocery – offers tasty organic meat and fish dishes, such as scallops with ginger and pepper, or lamb flank in thyme flower. The desserts are excellent, whether the pastries or artisanal ice creams. Open for lunch Tues–Sat, with *menus* from €13.50.

La Route de Tanger 1 rue du Four St-Jean ☎04.68.51.07.57. Welcoming Moroccan restaurant serving traditional tagines and couscous, as well as more adventurous fusion recipes. *Menu* €15. Closed Sun & Mon lunch.

Le Sud 12 rue Bausil ☎04.68.34.55.71. Eclectic and delicious Mediterranean cuisine served up in the heart of Perpignan's Romany quarter. Check ahead as the restaurant hosts many exhibitions and events. *Menus* begin at €25. Open for dinner Tues–Sun; closed Jan–March.

Tarteline 10 rue la Petite Monnaie. Good stop for delicious homemade quiches and tarts, to eat in or take away. Open lunchtime only Mon–Fri (except hols). *Menu* for €10 (also children's *menu*).

Le Tire Bouchon 20 av Général-de-Gaulle ☎04.68.34.31.91. A small family-run brasserie, the best of those around the station. *Menu* at €13, although an à la carte meal for two can easily run to more than €50. Closed all Sun, Mon & Wed eve.

Listings

Car rental Besides Avis, at 13 bd du Conflent
(℡ 04.68.34.26.71), most companies are along av
Général-de-Gaulle, including Budget at no. 9
(℡ 04.68.56.95.95); Europcar at no. 28
(℡ 04.68.34.65.03); Leclerc at no. 27
(℡ 04.68.34.77.74); and Sixt at no. 48
(℡ 04.68.35.62.84). Europcar, Budget and Avis also
have offices at the airport.

Cinemas Rive Gauche, 29 quai Vauban
(℡ 04.68.51.13.84) and Cinéma Castillet (see
p.292), 1 bd Wilson (℡ 08.92.68.01.29;
ⓦ cine-movida.com), both show some VO
(undubbed) films.

Hospital Centre Hospitalier, av du Languedoc
(℡ 04.68.61.66.33), on the north side of the city,
reached via av Maréchal-Joffre.

Pharmacy Grande Pharmacie de la Loge, 4 pl de
la Loge.

Police Av de Grande Bretagne ℡ 04.68.35.70.00,
and allée Marc-Pierre ℡ 04.68.66.30.70.

Rugby Perpignan's Rugby à XV team, USAP, has
long held a place in France's First Division, and
has won the championship four times. Call
℡ 04.68.61.18.18, or go to ⓦ www.usap.fr.

Swimming Champs de Mars, rue Paul-Valéry
(Mon & Sat 12.15–1.30pm, Tues, Thurs & Fri
6.30–8pm; covered; €3).

Around Perpignan

Heading north from Perpignan towards Narbonne along the N9, the main attraction is the enormous stronghold of **Salses-le-Château**, built to dominate the strategic strip of land between the Étang de Leucate and the uplands of the Corbières. East of Perpignan is its beach resort, **Canet-la-Plage**, with a good if rather windswept beach, while the village of **Cabestany**, to the southeast, has a museum dedicated to the eponymous medieval master-sculptor.

Salses-le-Château

Fifteen kilometres from Perpignan is the fortress of **SALSES-LE-CHÂTEAU** (daily: June–Sept 9.30am–7pm; Oct–May 10am–12.15pm & 2–5pm; €7), constructed by the Spanish in the fifteenth century to guard the northern border of Roussillon from French attack. It's a curious structure – set low within a deep moat, like a cannon-age fortress, but with the basic design and overall squareness of a medieval castle, it represents an intermediary stage in the evolution from early to modern fort. Salses withstood four sieges before it was taken by the French in 1642; with the shift of the frontier south to the mountains, the fortress was first abandoned and then later used as a prison until it was declared a monument in 1886. In the village, which lies to the east of the castle, the **Musée Catalan d'Histoire** (hours vary – check with the tourist office in Perpignan; free) has a small collection of arms as well as archeological relics dating from the Roman period, when the Via Domitia passed through town.

The narrow strip of sand which hedges in the **Étang de Leucate** to the northeast of Salses is buried under a holiday conurbation, but **windsurfers** may be attracted to this part of the coast for the relentless winds which pelt the lagoon. The northern end of the *étang* has parking along the spit and is the best place to get in the water.

Salses is a fairly easy **bike** ride (wind permitting) from Perpignan; alternatively, **trains** arrive at the gare SNCF, just west of the fortress, while **buses** stop at the place de la République, where you will find a small **tourist office** (July & Aug daily 9am–7pm; Sept–June Mon–Fri 9am–6pm, Sat 10am–5pm; ℡ 04.68.38.66.13). The only accommodation is the **chambre d'hôtes** *La Salsepareille* (℡ 04.68.38.61.70, ⓦ www.salsepareille.com; English spoken; ❸) in a century-old house in the village centre, which serves solid, local meals (€23). Otherwise, there's the **campsite** *International* on RN9 (℡ 04.68.38.60.72, ⓦ www.camping-roussillon.com). The only good **restaurant** is the twelfth-century farmhouse and bakery *Auberge de Vespeille*, on route d'Opoule (☎04.68.64.19.51; Sat & Sun only in spring and autumn, Sun only in winter), with an open-hearthed fire in its rustic dining room. Alternatively, stock up on supplies at the Wednesday-morning **market**.

Canet-la-Plage

Perpignan's own beach resort, **CANET-LA-PLAGE**, is 12km to the east (bus #1 from Perpignan; departures every 20min), with everything you'd expect from a beach town: sun, fun, bars and music. The only sight here is the **aquarium** (daily: July & Aug 10am–8pm; Sept–June 10am–noon & 2–6pm; €6), home to over three thousand species, including shark, piranha and coral. The town's **tourist office** (July & Aug daily 9am–7pm; Sept–May Mon–Sat 9am–12.30pm & 2–6pm, Sun 10am–noon & 2–5pm; ☎04.68.86.72.00, ⓦwww.ot-canet.fr) is in the central Espace Mediterranée. **Hotels** tend to be over-priced in high season; the one that stands out is the luxurious *Le Mas de la Plage et des Pins* (☎04.68.80.32.63, ⓦwww .lemasdelaplageetdespins.com; ❼) at 34 av du Roussillon, a beautifully renovated farmhouse set among a stand of centenary pines. There are several **campsites**, including the four-star *Ma Prairie* (April–Sept; ☎04.68.73.26.17, ⓦwww .maprairie.com) in avenue des Coteaux, which also rents out tents. Among the wide range of **restaurants**, an excellent option is *Le Don Quichotte* at 22 av de Catalogne (☎04.68.80.35.17; closed Mon & Tues), with chef Gilbert Gris's *gastronomique menus* from €17 (weekday lunch) to €43 (three-course dinner). The local **market** is held in town on Wednesdays and at the beach on Tuesdays and Sundays.

Cabestany

Fans of medieval art and sculpture will want to make a pilgrimage to **CABESTANY**, 5km southeast of Perpignan, where the eleventh- to fourteenth-century church of **Notre-Dame-des-Anges** is home to a remarkably vividly carved **tympanum**, the discovery of which in 1930 led to the identification of the Master of Cabestany (see box below). You can see further examples of his sculpture at the museum and resource centre, the **Musée Maître de Cabestany**, in the church of Ste-Marie in the village centre (Tues–Sun 10am–12.30pm & 2–6/6.30pm; €3).

The Master of Cabestany

The actual name of the **Master of Cabestany** has long been forgotten, but the work of this genius of masonry comprises one of Languedoc's most important medieval legacies. The twelfth-century itinerant **sculptor**, whose speciality was human figures in high relief, worked as far afield as Tuscany and Catalonia, but the greatest concentration of his works can be found in a wide band of territory stretching from Castelnaudary to the sea. Doorways, cloisters, tombs and tympanums – over 120 works found so far – all bear the distinctive mark of his vivid style. His large-handed, bulbous-eyed portraits are set apart not so much by their realism, but by the obvious brilliance with which they were executed, which seems to endow the mute stone figures with a life and soul of their own. The most dramatic example of his work can be found at **St-Hilaire** (see p.107), while others survive at Cabestany (above), Lagrasse (see p.264), Rieux-Minervois (see p.268), Passa (p.312), St-Papoul (p.88) and Le Boulou (see p.312). Several works have been identified just over the border in Catalonia, including at the magnificent monastery of San Pere de Rodes (only 25min by car from Le Boulou), and one piece now resides in the Cloisters collection of the Metropolitan Museum of Art in New York. A **museum** and resource centre dedicated to this redis-covered master and to the history of Romanesque sculpture has been opened in Cabestany, outside Perpignan (see above).

The Fenouillèdes

Stretching out to the northwest of Perpignan, the **Fenouillèdes** is the range of scrubby limestone hills that marked the inland border between France and Spain until the Treaty of the Pyrenees gave Roussillon to France in 1659. It is a rich area to discover, with highlights including the caves at **Tautavel**, where some of Europe's earliest hominids have been discovered, and several Cathar castles, the most famous being **Quéribus** and **Peyrepertuse**. Further west, you can explore the dramatic **Gorges de Galamus** and continue to another Cathar stronghold at **Puilaurens**. The main artery through the Fenouillèdes is the D117, running westward from Perpignan to Quillan (see p.111); all the sights can be accessed from various points along this road, whether you're driving or reliant on the bus. If you have time to take the hills in by foot, however, head out on the **Sentier Cathare**, which leads west into the pays de Sault (see p.112), or the **Tour du Fenouillèdes**, a seven-day circuit that links the main sights of the region (for information on this see the tourist office in Perpignan, or visit their website – see p.290).

Tautavel

In 1971, archeologists working at the Caune de l'Arago, a cave near the village of **TAUTAVEL**, 20km northwest of Perpignan on the edge of the Fenouillèdes, discovered the front part of a skull of *Homo erectus* – an evolutionary midpoint between the African *Homo habilis* and modern *Homo sapiens* – dating back to half a million years ago, a period from which scarcely any other human remains have been found in Europe. The reconstructed skull, with its enormous cranial ridge and low eye sockets, is displayed in Tautavel's **Centre Européen de la Préhistoire** (daily: April–June & Sept 10am–12.30pm & 2–6.30pm; July & Aug 10am–7pm; Oct–March 10am–12.30pm & 2–5pm; €8), the centrepiece of a small but extremely moving exhibition which includes stone tools, animal bones and casts from the floor of the cave. The **cave** itself (April–June visits by arrangement with the museum) is situated in a low hill on the opposite side of the Verdouble valley. All the finds – some 250,000 objects – have been removed, but it's exciting to stand where primordial hunters dwelt half a million years ago.

Quéribus

The Cathar stronghold of **QUÉRIBUS**, the easternmost of "mother" Carcassonne's five "sons", is a short detour off the D117, from the turn-off at Maury, 10km beyond Estagel. If you don't have transport of your own, take the Perpignan–Quillan bus to Maury, from where it's a steep two-hour uphill walk. Visible on its turret of bare rock long before you reach it, the **castle** is much bigger than it looks, since much of the **interior** (daily: Feb & March 10am–5.30/6pm; April–June & Sept 9.30am–7pm; July & Aug 9am–8pm; Oct 10am–6.30pm; Nov & Dec 10am–5pm; €5) is below ground level. A single stairway links all the various structures, including the so-called **salle du palmier** in the polygonal keep, where the vaulted ceiling is supported by a graceful pillar sprouting a canopy of intersecting ribs.

Quéribus was constructed at the end of the tenth century, and belonged successively to the count-kings of Barcelona and Aragón and the counts of Fenouillèdes. After the fall of Montségur in 1244 it became the refuge of some of the last surviving Cathars (see *The Land of Cathars* colour section), an affront that King Louis IX decided to erase. His opportunity came in 1255, when the local lord who sponsored the Cathars, Chabert de Barbaira, was captured by royal forces and forced to cede this and other castles as his ransom. But, unlike at Montségur, the Cathar garrison here had time to escape, probably south across the mountains.

The closest amenities to Quéribus are 3km west, in **CUCUGNAN**, which has crumbling vestiges of its own castle and vineyards all around. It also has a **tourist office** (July & Aug daily 9am–7pm; April–June, Sept & Oct Mon–Sat 10am–noon & 2–5pm; Nov–March Mon–Fri 9am–noon & 2–4pm; ℡04.68.45.69.40). The best place to **stay** is the *Auberge du Vigneron* (℡04.68.45.03.00, Ⓦwww.auberge -vigneron.com; ❸), in the centre of the village, and which also has a good **restaurant** (closed Sun eve & Mon; €20–30).

Peyrepertuse

Four kilometres northwest of Cucugnan, another of the five "sons" of Carcassonne, **PEYREPERTUSE**, is the largest and one of the best preserved of the **Cathar castles** (daily: early Jan, Feb, Nov & Dec 10am–5pm; March & Oct 10am–6.30pm; April–June & Sept 9am–7.30pm; July & Aug 9am–8.30pm; €5). Its age and history are nearly identical to those of Quéribus, with Paris assuming definitive control here by treaty with Catalonia-Aragón in 1258. It's a ten-minute drive along the D14 from Cucugnan, or you can approach the *château* on **foot** via the Sentier Cathare. The setting of the castle, draped the length of a jagged ridge with sheer drops at most points, is its most impressive feature. No single architectural feature among various cisterns, chapels and towers claims attention, but from the highest chamber, the **Chapelle San Jordi**, there are sweeping views east to the Mediterranean and Perpignan, with Quéribus perched on its rock stalk in between.

Near Peyrepertuse, the village of **DUILHAC** coils picturesquely at the eastern foot of the castle ridge. Here you'll find a shop and bakery, plus the comfortable, stone-clad *Auberge la Source* (mid-Feb to mid-Dec; ℡04.68.45.02.17, Ⓕ04.68.45.02.17; ❷), on the northerly through-road, with a restaurant (*menu* from €10.50; closed Tues off-season) and rooms. Better **accommodation**, however, can be found in **Rouffiac des Corbières**, 3km north, where the *Auberge de Peyrepertuse* on the main through-road (mid-Jan to mid-Dec; ℡&Ⓕ04.68.45.40.40; ❷) has excellent en-suite rooms and serves hearty food (€16; closed Wed). There's also a **campsite**.

▲ Peyrepertuse

The Gorges de Galamus and Puilaurens

From Rouffiac, the D14 winds westwards to the **Gorges de Galamus**, a short but impressive limestone *défilé* worn through the ridge by the River La Boulzane, although most visitors enter the gorge at its downstream end, 3km out of St-Paul-de-Fenouillet. At this end there's a free car park and the start of a path to the exquisitely sited **Ermitage de St-Antoine**, about halfway down the gorge's east flank (10am–6pm) – a huge, sanctified grotto thrusting deep into the cliff, from where a steep path, culminating in a rock ladder, drops down to pools below. The river is deep enough for swimming, and the gorge is also a popular **rafting** venue: contact Sud Rafting, 16km west of St-Paul at the crossroads near Axat (℡04.68.20.53.73, ℮esudrafting@libertysurf.fr), which also offers canyoning through Galamus, as well as rafting and hydrospeed trips through the Aude gorges.

    ST-PAUL-DE-FENOUILLET itself has little to offer aside from its role as staging point for **buses** west, and a jumping-off point for exploring the Galamus Gorges: you can get detailed information at the **tourist office** (℡04.68.59.07.57, ⓦwww.st-paul66.com) on boulevard d'Agly. The best **hotel** is the funky *Le Châtelet*, on the main road (℡04.68.59.01.20, ⓦwww.chatelethotel.com; ❹), whose amenities include a pool and a spacious garden. The **campsite** is in avenue 16 Août, along the riverbank, south of the main road (open year-round; ℡04.68.59.09.09, ⓦcamping-agly.com). You may also want to stock up on local produce at the weekly **market** (Wed & Sat) in place du Foyer Rural.

    Some 18km west of St-Paul along the D117, at tiny **Lapradelle** you'll find the turn-off for the **castle** at **PUILAURENS** (Feb, April & Oct to mid-Nov daily 10am–5pm; March Sat, Sun & hols 10am–5pm; May daily 10am–6pm; June & Sept daily 10am–7pm; July & Aug daily 9am–8pm; €4), another of Carcassonne's "sons", perched majestically on a 700m-high ridge. Built originally by the Visigoths, Puilaurens was enlarged not long before its captured lord, the Cathar Chabert de Barbaira, turned it over to Crusader forces as a condition of his release. You enter from the west, via a stepped maze of *chicanes* (staggered low walls); much of the interior is dilapidated, but make sure you catch the **view** east over pined hills from outside the southeastern gate, and the point on the **western donjon** complex where you're allowed briefly on the curtain wall to take in the vista in the opposite direction.

    You'll find homey **rooms** and solid local fare back in Lapradelle at the *Hôtel du Viaduc* (℡04.68.20.53.01; ❸).

The Fenouillèdes railway

The best and most relaxed way to appreciate the rugged landscape of the Fenouillèdes is the **Train du Pays Cathare et du Fenouillèdes**, a narrow-gauge rail line refurbished as a tourist route. Starting from the station at **Rivesaltes**, 7km north of Perpignan, it climbs along the vine-clad route of the Agly river before turning up the valley of La Boulzane. Climbing through forests of fir, it arrives at **St-Paul-de-Fenouillet** (see above) and threads the **Gorges de Galamus**, before stopping at Caudies-des-Fenouillèdes. From here it continues to **Lapradelle** (from where a stiff three-kilometre walk leads up to the castle of **Puilaurens**) before the final seven-kilometre leg takes it to the end of the line, at Axat, near Quillan (see map on p.96).

    The train, which was inaugurated in 1904, runs irregularly from May to October, with daily departures in July and August. The full return fare is €18.50 per adult and €12 for under-14s, and the journey takes around 2 hours 30 minutes each way. See ⓦwww.tpcf.fr for **information** on departures and reservations (also ℡04.68.59.99.02).

The lower Têt valley

From Perpignan, the Têt valley (also known as the Conflent), provides a fast if initially not very scenic route southwest into the Pyrenees. The **lower Têt valley** is that stretch running up to the peak of Canigou, and its most interesting parts are found some 30km west of Perpignan, where **Ille-sur-Têt** provides a jumping-off point for the spectacular rock formations of **Les Orgues** to the north and, just west, the narrow Boulés gorge climbs south to the region of Les Aspres, within whose wooded isolation you'll find the magnificent Romanesque **priory of Serrabone**. Further west along the valley, you'll come to **Prades**, a good access point for the Canigou mountain and, skirting the north side of the famous massif, you reach **Villefranche-de-Conflent**, which marks the transition to the upper valley, covered on p.307. Both regular trains and buses run along this part of the valley.

Upstream towards Prades

Heading out of Perpignan along the N116, a detour from the river's course at St-Féliu will take you 6km south to **THUIR**, although if you are driving or cycling you can reach it more directly by taking the D612. The town is known chiefly as the main producer of the red aperitif wine called Byrrh (pronounced "beer"), and you can visit the **winery** at 6 bd Violet (April–June, Sept & Oct daily 9–11.45am & 2.30–5.45pm; July & Aug daily 10–11.45am & 2–6.45pm; Nov–March Tues–Sun 10.45am–3.30pm; €2) and taste the sweet ferment that is aged in a cathedral-like gallery designed by Gustave Eiffel.

From Thuir you can head directly to Ille-sur-Têt along the D615 or go via **CASTELNOU**, 4km west. Capping a hilltop, this lovely stone village is strong on medieval ambience, and has a well-preserved gate and walls, as well as a tenth-century **castle** (daily: late June to late Sept 10am–7pm; Oct to mid-June 11am–5/6pm; €5), with good views and a **restaurant** (noon–2pm & 7–10pm, closed Wed off-season; roughly €15). The best day to come is Tuesday, when a local **market** breathes extra life into the village (June–Sept). If you're interested in buying the castle, at time of writing it's on the market for a cool €2.5 million.

Back on the river, 12km beyond Castelnou, **ILLE-SUR-TÊT** has an attractive medieval quarter of narrow alleys, within which a well-run **Centre d'Art Sacré** (April to mid-June, Oct & Nov Wed–Sun 2–6pm; mid-June to Sept Mon–Fri 10am–noon & 2–7pm, Sat & Sun 2–7pm; €3.50) is housed in the seventeenth-century **Hospice d'Illà** – the local headquarters of the medieval Hospitaller Knights – and hosts temporary exhibitions of local religious art. More remarkable are the clay cliffs just across the River Têt, a kilometre or so on the road north towards Sournia, and which the elements have eroded into extraordinary figures known as **Les Orgues**, so called because of their resemblance to organ pipes. Rising dramatically up from a deep tributary of the Têt, they can be explored by a series of **footpaths** laid out within the gorge (daily: Feb–March & Oct 10am–noon & 2–5.30pm; April–June & Sept 10am–6.30pm; July & Aug daily 9.30am–8pm; €3.50).

The priory of Serrabone

The most compelling stop en route to Prades involves a detour south from Bouleternère, 5km after Ille-sur-Têt, up a perilous eight-kilometre track to Roussillon's celebrated **priory of Serrabone** (daily 10am–6pm; €4). The location of the simple church, set as it is on a high hilltop, against a precipitous and wooded drop, is impressive; in the grounds around the priory, a botanical garden has been set up to showcase the region's diverse flora. The building's modest facade conceals a strange cloistered gallery, which looks out on the hills, and leads inside to the church's equally curious interior. Here, the almost windowless nave is dominated by an exquisitely decorated tribune of rose marble – an unusual "indoor" cloister, reminiscent of some Spanish Mozarabic churches and perhaps a faint echo of Córdoba's great mosque. Excavated columns found here suggest that much of the original priory – founded in the twelfth century – was as elaborate as the tribune. From the foot of the hill on which the priory sits, the road continues 5km south to the village of Boulés d'Amont. From here a harrowing nine-kilometre drive brings you to the **chapel of La Trinité**, just before the Col Xatard (752m). Superb ironwork adorns the outside of the door, and inside there's a *Christ en Majesté* – a Gothic sculpture in which a regally robed Christ reposes impassively on the Cross.

Practicalities

Ille's **gare SNCF** is a five-minute walk south of the town centre, which is where you'll find the town's **tourist office** in square de la Poste (July & Aug Mon–Sat 9am–noon & 2–6.30pm, Sun 9am–noon; Sept–June Mon–Fri 9am–noon & 2–6pm, Sat 9am–noon; ⓣ04.68.84.02.62, ⓦwww.ille-sur-tet.com). Accommodation in the area is limited to **chambres d'hôtes**, such as the palatial *Les Buis*, 37 rue Carnot in Ille (ⓣ04.68.84.27.67, ⓦwww.lesbuis.com; English spoken; ❺); the atmospheric and comfortable *Peu del Causse*, at 6 Carrer del Canigó in Thuir (ⓣ04.68.53.42.47, ⓦwww.peudelcausse.com; ❹); and the deluxe *Casa del Arte*, set in a renovated eleventh-century farmhouse, also in Thuir (ⓣ04.68.53.44.78, ⓦwww.maison-hotes-casadelarte.com; English spoken; ❻). The **restaurant** *Entre-Mers* (closed Tues & Wed eve & Sat lunch) on 19 pl de la République, in Ille, offers a diverse *carte* (*menus* from €15) with an emphasis on local seafood and Alsatian dishes, the best place in Languedoc for an authentic *baeckeoffe* (but not in summer!). In Thuir *La Casa DaLie* (closed Wed; ⓣ04.68.53.03.92, ⓦwww.casa-dalie.fr) offers excellent Catalan cuisine served in a dining room decorated in homage to the great Surrealist (*menus* from €25).

Prades and around

Midway along the Têt valley, **PRADES** is by far its biggest town. Distinctively pink with its marble masonry and pavements, it is the birthplace of Thomas Merton, the twentieth-century Catholic mystic who eventually settled in a Trappist monastery in Kentucky. It is best known, however, for hosting the annual summer **music festival** (see p.289) founded in 1950 by the Catalan cellist **Pablo Casals** (or Pau Casals in Catalan). In exile from Franco's Spain, Casals spent the second half of his life here, composing such works as the oratorio *The Crib* and the popular *Song of the Birds*. The one-roomed **Musée Pablo Casals** (Mon–Fri 9am–noon & 2–5/6pm; free), in the same building as the tourist office (see opposite), commemorates the virtuoso, who died in 1973, two years before Franco. In the main place de la République you'll find the **church of St-Pierre**, which contains a huge and sumptuous seventeenth-century retable, a masterpiece by the Catalan sculptor Joseph Sunyer. Prades is in fact conspicuously Catalan in feel, hosting a summertime Catalan university course (ten days in August; ⓦwww.ucestiu.com) and having established the first Catalan-language primary school in France. On Tuesday and Saturday mornings there's an excellent produce **market** in the square and surrounding streets.

Much of the music festival takes place at the restored ninth-century Benedictine monastery of **St-Michel-de-Cuxà** (Mon–Sat 9.30–11.50am & 2–5/6pm, Sun 2–5/6pm; €4), whose single, ponderous square tower suddenly appears above a copse of poplars 3km south of the town, on the orchard-lined road to Taurinya.

St-Michel reached its peak in the eleventh century and then went into slow decline: closed and abandoned in 1790, much of its stone was pillaged during the Revolution, some of it eventually finding its way – like many other Romanesque fragments from the region – to the Cloisters Museum in New York. Today the highlights of a visit include a subterranean crypt consisting of a circular chapel dating back to the monastery's foundation, and the remains of the broad cloister, whose columns are capped by fine twelfth-century details.

Practicalities

The **gare SNCF** is at the southern edge of Prades, about ten minutes' walk from the centre; **buses** set you down on avenue Général de Gaulle (RN116), the main road through the centre of town. The **tourist office** (mid-June to mid-Sept Mon–Sat 9am–noon & 2–6pm, Sun 10am–noon; mid-Sept to mid-June Mon–Fri 9am–noon & 2–6pm, plus Sat 9am–noon in early June & early Sept; ℡04.68.05.41.02, Ⓦwww.prades-tourisme.com) is at 4 rue Victor-Hugo, with the **music festival office** next door (℡04.68.96.33.07, Ⓦwww.prades-festival -casals.com): it's a mine of information on walking trails, biking trails and climbing the Pic du Canigou. You can **rent bikes** at Cycles Flament, 8 rue Arago.

For good-value **accommodation**, you can't beat the faded elegance of the white-painted, simply furnished *Hostalrich* at 156 av Général de Gaulle (℡04.68.96.05.38, ❷), run by a family who were friends of Casals. More luxurious accommodation is available close by in Molitg-les-Bains, including the excellent *Château de Riell* (April–Oct; ℡04.68.05.04.40, Ⓦwww.chateauderiell .com; ❽), set in a picture-perfect castle, and with a highly rated (and highly priced) restaurant. The beautifully sited municipal **campsite** (April–Sept; ℡04.68.96.29.83, Ⓦwww.leconflent.net) in the valley, just east of the centre of Prades off chemin du Gaz, also has chalets for rent.

Villefranche-de-Conflent and around

Beyond Prades, the Têt valley narrows dramatically, becoming a gorge 6km further on, where the high walls of **VILLEFRANCHE-DE-CONFLENT** almost block the way. As there's almost no construction outside the walls, externally at least the town looks much as it did three hundred years ago: an elongated, two-street place squeezed between the palisade just to the south and the river. Within the ramparts, the most evocative area is along the bank of the Têt, by the thirteenth-century **church of St Pierre**; the best view is from the far side, from where the weathered red-tiled roofs and the tower of the twelfth-century **church of St-Jacques** peer over the ramparts.

Villefranche dates from 1092, when Guillaume Raymond, Count of Cerdagne, granted the charter for the town, meant as a strategic bulwark against the counts of Roussillon. Some remnants from that period still stand, notably the **Tour d'en Solenell** on the little square known as the **Placette**. In 1654 Villefranche – then controlled by Spain – was besieged by Louis XIV's troops, and fell after eight days' fighting. After the Treaty of the Pyrenees confirmed their annexation of Roussillon, the French rebuilt the Spanish fortifications according to plans drawn up by Vauban.

As you walk the immense and maze-like **ramparts** (daily: late Jan to May & Oct–Dec 10am–12.30pm & 2–5/6pm; July & Aug 10am–8pm; June & Sept 10am–7pm; €5), their vulnerability to attack from the surrounding heights is obvious – a defensive weakness that Vauban remedied by adding various bastions and building the upper fort now known as **Fort Libéria** (daily: July & Aug 9am–8pm; Sept–June 10am–5/6pm; €5.50), rising high above the main town on the steep northern bank of the Têt. The castle has seen more service as a prison than as a fortress; its interns have included a group of seventeenth-century noblewomen of the court of Versailles, locked up in isolation and silence for over thirty years, on allegations of witchcraft and poisoning. You can reach the fort by hiking up the winding dirt road that starts just outside the eastern gates; alternatively, the fort provides transport in a jeep (€8, entry included), either from outside the Porte de France or at the insipid new **museum** opposite the ticket office for the ramparts.

The caves
The most celebrated incident in Villefranche's history was the 1674 revolt against French rule, which culminated in the betrayal of the rebellion's leader, Charles de Llar, and his co-conspirators by Llar's own daughter, Inès. His hiding place was the **Cova Bastéra** (daily: April–June 10am–6pm; July & Aug 10am–7.30pm; Sept–Nov 10am–5.30pm; €8), a cave which he could enter and exit from within the walls of the town – today the entrance is just west of the town walls on the N116. Incorporated into Villefranche's defences during the time of Vauban, the cave has a decidedly Dungeons-and-Dragons feel – atmospheric, but not spectacular. If you plan on visiting it, consider buying a combined ticket (€12), also good for the spectacular **Grottes des Grandes Canalettes** (same hours; 1hr guided tour; €8, or €12 including 7pm *son et lumière*), located across the highway from Villefranche. Entry is via a 160-metre passageway, hollowed out by water over the past four hundred million years; the water dripping down the sides is now directed over moulds to create limestone images for sale at the shop. Beyond a door you then enter a succession of huge chambers crammed with stalactites, stalagmites, pillars and tiny, feathery formations.

Practicalities
Mainline trains from Perpignan terminate in Villefranche, at the **gare SNCF** (℡04.68.96.56.62), 400m north of the town; for onward *Train Jaune* services (see box, p.307), simply change platforms. **Jeep excursions** up the Canigou depart from outside the *gare* (to book, call M. Bouzan on ℡04.68.05.62.28). The **tourist office** at the entrance to the town (Feb–Dec Tues–Thurs, Sat & Sun 10am–noon & 2–5pm; ℡04.68.96.22.96, ⓦwww.villefranchedeconflent.com) sells local hiking and biking guides (€5–10). The only **hotels** are south of the old town: the magnificent old **B&B** ⚘ *Auberge du Cèdre* (℡&ⓕ04.68.96.05.05; ❸) just east of the old walls, near the *gare*, which serves abundant home-cooked meals for guests; and the lovely *Terminus* (℡04.68.05.27.03; ❸) in the old station itself. The **campsite**, *Mas de Lastourg* (April–Nov; ℡04.68.05.35.25, ⓦwww.camping -lastourg.com), is just off the main highway. **Market** day is Saturday, with vendors gathered around the place de l'Église. Villefranche's best **restaurant** is *La Senyera* (closed Wed & Tues & Thurs eve), at 81 rue St-Jean, featuring grilled meats and superb *terroir* stand-bys including snail and duck dishes.

The Pic du Canigou and around

Rising to a height of 2785m between the Tech and Conflent valleys, the **Pic du Canigou** (*Canigó* in Catalan) is the great landmark of Catalonia, dominating the whole of the Roussillon lowlands. Situated well inside French territory, the mountain became a symbol for Catalonia's lost independence in the course of the nineteenth-century literary renaissance, and came to signify Catalan cultural unity, endorsed today by the small flags and other patriotic paraphernalia festooned from its summit cross. Before modern geographic surveys had covered the whole of the Pyrenees, the Canigou was thought erroneously to be the range's highest peak – it does, however, overshadow the rest of the **Canigou massif**, wedged between the two rivers. The massif has been protected as a nature reserve and the peak (when not clouded) affords breathtaking views; if you're intent on reaching the summit, you must **hike**, and the most direct route is from the **Chalet des Cortalets** (2150m) on the peak's northeastern slopes – you can get to this by vehicle or on foot. **Vernet-les-Bains** on its northwestern slopes is the place from which to get to the key sight around Canigou – the **monastery of St-Martin-du-Canigou**, easily accessible by car. Before setting out towards the summit, be sure to check the weather conditions. In general, the best time of year to hike up is the autumn, when there is no snow on the summit (as in late spring); summer is not the best of times to make the ascent, as the heat can be uncomfortable and humidity reduces visibility from the top.

To the summit via the Chalet des Cortalets

Most hikers tackle le Canigou from the *Chalet des Cortalets*, a busy **refuge** a couple of hours from the summit. You can get to the chalet from either the east or the north. The easternmost route is the quiet and impressively steep (but not difficult) approach from **Valmanya**, which you can drive or **hike** to (along the GR36) from Vinça, some 20km to the north. From the village, a narrow road climbs a further 5km west, before petering out – you must then use the GR36 to complete the remaining 8km to the chalet. Approaching from the north, there is a jeep track to the refuge from near **Prades**. A scenic but busy alternative, this route provides the gentlest ascent to the chalet and is the one used by **jeep-taxis** (roughly €30 per person) from Prades; try Corbières Grand Raid (☎04.68.05.24.24). If you're **driving**, take the D35 out of the south side of Prades to Villerach (8km; signposted as "Clara-Villerach"), from where an unpaved *route forestière* dirt track rises to the chalet – an hour's drive. This is a superb approach, often running close to the River Llech, each turn revealing a new arrangement of rock, water, sky and forest. An ordinary car can easily get as far as the ruined hut at Prat Cabrera (1650m), an hour's walk from the *Chalet des Cortalets*, and – with extra care and ideal conditions – all the way to Cortalets itself.

A maquisard hideout in the last war, and consequently heavily shelled by occupation forces, the restored **Chalet des Cortalets** (June–Oct; ☎04.68.05.63.57) is run by the Club Alpin Français. There are double rooms (❷) as well as dorm beds (€22), while **meals** in the bar-restaurant cost about €15. Be warned that the main lodge can get overcrowded, and the tracks bring up jeeps full of revellers (as opposed to walkers) at weekends to picnic at the tables around the little **lake**, ten minutes' walk west of the refuge.

The summit

The well-marked **hike to the summit** goes past the larger lake, with its fine view up into the summit cirque, then climbs south along the ridge connecting with the **Pic Joffre**, which often teems with lizards at sunset. It takes about ninety minutes and provides only a slight sense of exposure as you reach the wrought-iron summit cross and *table d'orientation*. Even though it's the process of getting to the top that makes Le Canigou so memorable – rather than the experience of standing on the peak – the views encompassing everything from Andorra to the sea are wonderful.

At midsummer (technically June 21 but in Catalonia observed on the eve of June 23–24, the Festa de Sant Joan), the refuge and the peak are a frenzy of activity as seemingly half the population of Catalonia congregates for merrymaking and the kindling of the traditional bonfire that is then relayed to light numerous others in Catalan villages on both sides of the frontier. Even at other times there is often a patriotic Catalan or two prepared to camp for the night beside the peak's highest cairn.

Vernet-les-Bains and St-Martin-du-Canigou

The biggest village on the Canigou's slopes and the major stop en route to the famous abbey of St-Martin is the pleasant if slightly stuffy spa-town of **VERNET-LES-BAINS**, whose easiest approach is via the D116 for 10km south from Villefranche. English visitors such as Rudyard Kipling made the place fashionable during the last century and a waterfall, 3km out of town on a well-marked track, is even called the **Cascade des Anglaises**. Along with the thermal paraphernalia of plunge-pools and institutional adjoining therapy wings – first installed in 1377 – a range of more contemporary pastimes is now offered (mountain biking, canyoning, hydrospeed and caving), though the baths are still the focus of activity. Often overlooked, the old quarter's warren of alleys is capped by the ninth-century but much-restored double church of **Notre Dame del Puig/St-Saturnin**, which incorporates remaining bits of a castle.

From Vernet-les-Bains, a paved road and a footpath lead 2.5km south to **Casteil**, an appealing, quiet hamlet, close to the **monastery of St-Martin-du-Canigou**, a ubiquitous sight on local book covers, postcards and posters. Access to the monastery is only by a thirty-minute climb up the continuation of the footpath, or by jeep transport from Casteil along a steep, narrow road. Inaccessibility helps protect the place from becoming over-commercialized – as does its continuing use by an active religious community. Built from tan stone and roofed with grey slates, the monastery ranks as one of the most gorgeous monuments in the eastern Pyrenees, and the surrounding woods of sweet chestnut, beech and aspen form an unbeatable backdrop to the pinnacle of rock on which it stands. Founded in 1001 by Count Guifred de Cerdagne, it was severely damaged by an earthquake in the fifteenth century and thoroughly pillaged after abandonment in 1782. Restored through the twentieth century, the glory of the place resides in its **cloister capitals**, reassembled in unity by a bishop of Perpignan. The monastery is now occupied by an unusual mixed order of monks and nuns, called the "Beatitudes", with a sprinkling of lay workers. Ordinarily, visitors are allowed only on **guided tours** (hourly departures: Feb–May & Oct–Dec Mon–Sat 10–11am & 2–4pm, Sun 10am, 12.30pm & 2–4pm; June–Sept Mon–Sat 10am–noon & 2–5pm, Sun 10am, 12.30pm & 2–5pm; €5).

A good follow-up to the monastery is the **Église de Sainte-Marie** (June–Sept 10am–noon/1pm & 2–5/6pm) in Corneilla, halfway between Vernet and Villefranche. This eleventh-century church is a pristine example of Pyrenees Romanesque; there are no frescoes, but the altar is flanked by two polychrome carved Virgins.

Practicalities

Vernet's **tourist office** is quite central, at 2 rue de la Chapelle (June–Sept Mon–Fri 9am–noon & 2–6.30pm, Sat 9am–noon & 3–6pm, Sun 10am–12.30pm; Oct–May Mon–Fri 9am–noon & 2–6pm; ℡04.68.05.55.35, ⓦwww.ot-vernet-les-bains.fr), close to where the buses stop. **Jeep-taxis** to the monastery and up Canigou (roughly €30 per person) can be arranged through Garage Villacèque (℡04.68.05.51.14).

An excellent choice of **hotel** is the classic-style *Princess*, in rue des Lavandiers (mid-March to Nov; ℡04.68.05.56.22, ⓦwww.hotel-princess.com; ❹), which does good-value half-pensions and has excellent rates on family-sized rooms. An even better option, however, is the cosy 🍴 *Le Molière*, a couple of kilometres out of Vernet in Casteil (☎04.68.05.50.97, ⓦwww.lemoliere.com; ❸), whose restaurant serves fine country cooking. There are also plenty of **campsites**: the nearest is *Les Cerisiers* (April–Nov; ☎04.68.05.66.38, ⓦwww.camping-les -cerisiers-vernetlesbains.com).

Aside from Casteil's delightful *Molière* **restaurant** in an apple orchard (€17–25), there's the elegant *Le Cortal* (closed Mon & Oct–Nov), up in Vernet's old quarter behind the church at rue du Château, where you can easily spend around €40 a head. On Mondays, Thursdays and Saturdays Vernet's place de la République is home to a bustling morning **market**.

The upper Têt and the Capcir

The lower Têt valley finishes at Villefranche-de-Conflent, above which the shaggy flanks of the **upper Têt** (Conflent) close dramatically around the narrow-gauge *Train Jaune* rail line and N116, which forge their separate ways along the river up to **Mont-Louis**, at the top of the Têt. En route, interspersed with abandoned villages colonized by hippies and New Age travellers, are a number of small hamlets, on the valley floor or perched just above, which make serviceable bases for excursions into the hills. Of these, the hot springs and the splendour of the nearby **Carança gorge** make **Thuès-entre-Valls** one of the most accessible and rewarding. North of Mont-Louis, a sedimentary plateau called the **Capcir** spreads towards the gorges of the upper Aude. Bare and extremely flat, dominated in the centre by the large artificial lakes of Matemale and Puyvalador, it is cradled by densely wooded slopes that sweep up to Pic Madrès and the Carlit massif, with

---

The Train Jaune

The best way to move into the uplands of the Parc Régional Naturel des Pyrénées Catalanes is on the **Train Jaune**, once an essential local service, but now more of a fun ride – in summer some carriages are open-air. Built in the early twentieth century, the railway climbs for 63km from **Villefranche** (427m) up to **Latour-de-Carol** (1231m), where it connects with the Transpyrenean railway (Toulouse–Barcelona). Tourism saved the scenic narrow-gauge line from closure early in the 1970s, but its future remains uncertain. As it is, return tickets are valid for only 24 hours, with **fares** double those of French mainline services; for example, Villefranche to **Mont-Louis** and back (the most popular stretch) costs €17.80 (€8.90 one way).

From late May through to September there are five to eight **departures** a day in each direction; between 7.30am and 6.30pm from Villefranche and between 9am and 5.30pm from Latour-de-Carol. The descent takes just over two hours and the ascent an extra thirty minutes; there are connections with the Villefranche–Perpignan line within ten to twenty five minutes of each arrival and departure. Since most of the line is single track, there are often delays caused by long halts at Mont-Louis or Font-Romeu to allow the uphill train to pass. The train is scheduled to stop only at certain stations, and if you want to alight at one of the smaller, unstaffed stations (designated *arrêts facultatifs* on carriage placards) you have to notify the driver in advance. Similarly, to get on at such stations, you have to flag the train down. Beware when walking near the line, as the electrified "third rail" which provides power for the train is exposed and is a potential safety hazard.

For **information** on timetables and prices call ☎08.92.35.35.35 or check ⓦwww .trainstouristiques-ter.com.

only the pistes of the **ski resorts** Les Angles, Formiguères and Puyvalador inter-rupting the trees. One of the harshest winter climates in southern France also makes this excellent **cross-country skiing** terrain. The Capcir woodlands, with their sprinkling of *gîtes* and hotels, provide ample opportunities for **hiking** during warmer months, well within the capabilities of a novice walker; for information on the area's more challenging trails or longer circuits like the four-day **Le Tour du Capcir**, which winds around the plateau, contact local tourist offices (see p.310). In July and August, and during the ski season, all the main Capcir villages and resorts are served by a **taxi-bus**, which departs from the Mont-Louis/La Cabanasse train station.

In 2004, the three upland regions of the Haut Conflent, Capcir and Carlit were incorporated into the **Parc Régional Naturel des Pyrénées Catalanes**, covering almost 1400 square kilometres including 64 communes and villages and their 21,000 inhabitants. The aim of the park is to protect and preserve the fragile habitat and indigenous traditions of the region, and to provide services for visitors. The park's **administrative office** is at 1 rue Dagobert, 66210 Mont-Louis (℡04.68.04.97.60, ⓦwww.pyrenees-catalanes.fr).

The Carança gorge area

Less than an hour from Villefranche the *Train Jaune* stops at **Thuès-Carança**, from where a clearly signposted path leads just west of the village of **Thuès-entre-Valls** to the entrance to the spectacular **Gorges de Carança**. The gorge, as the signs at the entrance advise, is to be visited at your own risk. After a short walk from the car park the path divides: the lefthand path (signposted for Roc Madrieu) climbs steeply up the wooded side of the valley, while the righthand path (over a small bridge) follows the more spectacular corniche route; the two paths converge at the Pont des Singes, a suspension bridge. The first ninety minutes of corniche walkway are the most amazing, poised over sheer four-hundred-metre drops – not for the vertigo-prone. Next is a series of nerve-racking catwalks, ladders and wobbly, metal suspension bridges, these last not advisable for heavily laden walkers.

As you would expect, there is little by way of services in this rugged and under-populated stretch, but you'll find enough accommodation to make an overnight visit possible. At Nyer, 7km down the line, there's a **campsite**, *La Catalane* (℡04.68.97.07.63), but far more enticing is Thuès-entre-Valls' delightful **gîte-campsite** next to the church, *Mas de Bordes* (℡04.68.97.05.00, ⓕ04.68.97.11.51), with self-catering suites (❸). This restored farm is part of a substantial property that includes its own outdoor hot springs, a remote log cabin and a meadow for pitching tents. The place is always packed in July and August, when you must book ahead, but it's worth trying to fit it into your plans for a night or two. Good *table d'hôte* suppers are provided for overnight guests for about €13, *vin compris*. Information on local excursions can be obtained from the local Maison de la Réserve in Nyer (℡04.68.97.05.56, ⓔreserve.nyer@libertysurf.fr). The **nature reserve** itself (open year-round; free) consists of over 22 square kilometres of mountain wilderness between 700m and 2663m in altitude, and is home to rare and varied Pyrenean flora and fauna, including the Pyrenees lily, bearded vulture and royal eagle, as well as wildcats.

Mont-Louis

At 1600m, the garrison town of **MONT-LOUIS** is the highest on the Têt, only 14km southeast of the river's source, the Lac des Bouillouses. Known as the gateway to the Cerdagne, Mont-Louis is the quintessential work of Louis XIV's military engineer Vauban, and its massive moat-ringed **ramparts** (always open;

free), built between 1679 and 1682, represent a glorious but failed effort to close off the Spanish frontier. Though promoted as a resort, Mont-Louis is still essentially a military town (now a commando training centre), and apart from the walls, its only other attraction is the world's first **solar oven** (*four solaire*), built in 1949 and now open for one-hour **guided tours** (daily: mid-June to mid-Sept 10am–6pm; mid-Sept to mid-June 10am–5/6pm; €6); the huge mirror for the *four* stands in the moat, just to the left of the main gate, the Porte de France.

The town's **tourist office** is in rue du Marché (July & Aug daily 9.30am–6pm; Sept–June Mon–Sat 9am–12.30pm & 2–6pm; ☏04.68.04.21.97, Ⓦ www.mont-louis.net). Unfortunately, there are no recommendable hotels in town; the closest **campsite**, *Pla de Barres* (mid-June to mid-Sept; no reservations), lies 3km west along the road towards Lac des Bouillouses. Mont-Louis's **market** days are Tuesday and Thursday.

The Capcir ski resorts

All the **Capcir ski resorts** (Ⓦ www.capcir-pyrenees.com) lie on, or just off, the D118 road, served by taxi-bus from the Mont-Louis/La Cabanasse train station. Nearest to Mont-Louis, **LES ANGLES** (Ⓦ www.lesangles.com) is the area's largest and a favourite with snowboarders: it has 50km of pistes – half of them red, with the top run at 2325m. Chalets predominate rather than high-rises, but the old village has still been almost completely swamped. Six kilometres further north, **FORMIGUÈRES** (Ⓦ www.formigueres.com) is far more attractive, with its shops (some selling outdoor gear), cafés and crêperies giving it the feel of a provincial town. Its **church of Ste-Marie** features an unusual triangular facade culminating in the belfry; inside is an excellent seventeenth-century *majestat*, or "Christ in Majesty", typical of the Catalan regions. The pistes here total just 20km, with no really tough runs, but a good-value seasonal pass is available at the local tourist office (see p.310). Moreover, standing at the heart of 100km of marked trails, Formiguères is the perfect place for **cross-country skiing**; this sort of skiing requires no lessons – experience teaches you how to avoid falling over – and equipment rental can cost less than half downhill piste rates. The ski station at **PUYVALADOR** (Ⓦ www.puyvalador.com), at the north end of the Capcir plateau, is 5km west of its namesake reservoir and village (which has no amenities).

There are only 25km of pistes, but with a top station at 2380m it has breathtaking views, and is known for its excellent off-piste skiing. In summer the Formiguères and Puyvalador **télésièges** provide access to the Lac Bouillouses nature reserve (early July to Aug; €5).

Practicalities

There are **tourist offices** (both daily: June & Sept 9am–12.30pm & 4–6.30pm; July & Aug 9am–1.30pm & 2.30–7pm; Oct–May 8.30am–1pm & 3.30–7pm) at Les Angles (℡04.68.04.32.76, Ⓦwww.les-angles.com) and at Formiguères (℡04.68.04.47.35, Ⓦwww.formigueres.net). The Bureau Montagne in Les Angles (℡04.68.04.34.30, Ⓦwww.guide-montagne-pyrenees.com) can provide **guides** and equipment for summertime activities, such as horse riding, mountain biking and canyoning.

In Formiguères the best **hotel** is the *Picheyre*, 2 pl de l'Église (℡04.68.04.40.07, Ⓦwww.picheyre.com; ❹), whose restaurant serves up hearty mountain fare in an elegant, but not overly formal, dining room (from €25). In Angles you can choose between five hotels, including the slightly pricey *Llaret*, 12 av de Balcère (Jan–March, July & Aug; ℡04.68.30.90.90, Ⓦwww.hotel-llaret.com; English spoken; ❺). **Market** days are Saturday in Formiguères and Tuesday in Les Angles.

The Cerdagne

The French **Cerdagne** is half of the ancient Catalan county of La Cerdanya, chopped in two by the seventeenth-century Treaty of the Pyrenees. It is the highest point of the Sègre watershed which descends south to Catalan Lleida, and the sunniest area in the French Pyrenees, the ripe colours of summer grain and hay on its treeless, rolling hills reinforcing this impression. Curiously, the Cerdagne consists of the hamlets and countryside surrounding the sizeable Spanish enclave of Llívia – the result of a technicality in 1659's Treaty of the Pyrenees. To its northeast, the ski-centre of **Font-Romeu** is the biggest town in the region. To the south, **Saillagouse**, **Err** and **Bourg-Madame** ring the island of Spanish territory and can be traced west to **Latour-de-Carol**, which marks the terminus and frontier-crossing of the railway which ascends the Ariège valley from Toulouse; north of Latour is the excellent ski-station of **Porté-Puymorens**. As with the upper Conflent valley, the *Train Jaune* provides the best access to the entire area.

Font-Romeu and around

Sprawling at the foot of Roc de la Calme, in the southeast corner of the Carlit massif, **FONT-ROMEU** (Ⓦwww.font-romeu.fr), together with the nearby **Pyrénées 2000** (Ⓦwww.pyrenees2000.com), is one of the best-known ski areas in the Pyrenees. Its reputation, though, is somewhat unjustified, given that its top station is a mere 2200m, with a maximum vertical descent of just 400m, and there are few really challenging pistes. It does, however, have some good cross-country skiing – more than 110km of marked trails. In summer you can also get up to the **Lac Bouillouses nature reserve** by *télésiège* (early July to late Aug; €6) or via *navette* (July & Aug; €5), which departs every fifteen minutes from Pla du Barrès in Font-Romeu.

Aside from the nightlife, the town is known for its famous **Virgin statue**, a source of devotion and the origin of Font-Romeu's name, meaning "pilgrim's spring" in Catalan. The legend tells of a cowherd uncovering a buried figure of the Virgin – a recurring motif throughout upland Catalonia – having been led to the spot by a bull. The statue is now housed in the **Ermitage**, a short stroll from the main town, off avenue Emmanuel Brousse (early July to early Sept daily 10am–noon & 3–6pm; free), much altered since its fourteenth-century construction. On September 8 the Virgin is taken down the hill to the hamlet of **ODEILLO**, just south of Font-Romeu, returning on Trinity Sunday the following year.

Practicalities

The *Train Jaune* **station** is at **Via**, from where it's a fairly steep two-kilometre walk north to Font-Romeu, passing Odeillo about halfway. **Accommodation** in Font-Romeu tends to be expensive, but with eighteen thousand beds you should be able to find something. For a list of holiday apartments ask at the **tourist office** (daily 8.30am–7pm; ☎04.68.30.68.30, ⑲www.font-romeu.fr) near the top of avenue Emmanuel Brousse. The best **hotel** deal is *L'Oustalet*, in rue des Violettes (☎04.68.30.11.32, ⑲www.hotelloustalet.com; ❹), with an outdoor swimming pool, children's playground and other amenities. *La Chaumière*, at 96 av Emmanuel Brousse (☎04.68.30.04.40; closed Sun & Mon, part June & July), is one of the town's best **restaurants**, serving up solid mountain fare, with *menus* from €18. **Market** day is Wednesday.

West to Porté-Puymorens

Beyond Odeillo, the *Train Jaune* winds its way across the wide open plain to the south side of the Cerdagne, to depopulated **SAILLAGOUSE** (1320m), also along the N116, and a base for the glorious twelve-kilometre round-trip **hike** through the **Gorges du Sègre**. The next *Train Jaune* stop is on the north edge of **ERR**, a tiny village at the foot of heavily wooded Puigmal – and another place with a "found Virgin" legend. The twelfth-century effigy is housed in the **Chapelle de la Vierge**, considerably enlarged in the eighteenth century. Separated from it by the cemetery is the church of **St-Genis**; the cloister which was once attached to the church is now in the Philadephia Museum of Art. Skirting the Spanish enclave of Llívia, the *Train Jaune* reaches the frontier at **BOURG-MADAME**. Once a major bazaar, today it's visibly depressed and fading. It is the best place, however, to buy souvenirs such as earthenware. From Bourg-Madame, the *Train Jaune* continues for fifteen minutes to the end of the line, the Gare Internationale of

> ### Trekking and climbing on the Carlit massif
>
> Both spectacular and easy to access, the **Carlit massif** is a popular trekking location. Three major walking routes which range in difficulty from moderate to extreme – the **HRP**, the north–south **GR7** and the trans-Pyrenean **GR10** – as well as marked secondary trails, cross the massif, while parts of the GR7 and GR10 comprise sections of the less demanding **Tour du Carlit**, aimed at hikers of medium experience. The ascent of **Pic Carlit** (2921m) itself is within the capabilities of any reasonably fit person, especially from Lac des Bouillouses, accessible either by car or foot, on its eastern slopes (13km up the very narrow but paved D60 road).
>
> There's plenty of **accommodation** and **food** at the Bouillouses reservoir. The CAF-run *Refuge des Bouillouses* (June–Oct & Dec–April; ☎04.68.04.93.88, ©bouillousesrefuge @orange.fr; obligatory half-board ❹), stands east of the dam wall at just under 2000m. Nearby is the smallish, privately managed *Auberge du Carlit* (☎04.68.04.22.23, ⑲aubergeducarlit.free.fr) which has rooms (❷) as well as half-board (❺), and a *gîte* (dorm beds €13.50). Just above the west end of the dam at 2050m looms the gigantic *Refuge les Bones Hores* (Easter–Oct; ☎04.68.04.24.22, ⑲www.boneshores.com; obligatory half-board ❸), popular with families.

LATOUR-DE-CAROL/ENVEITG, the interchange for trains south towards Barcelona and north towards Toulouse. Finally, north of Latour-de-Carol on the N20 or by train, on the western slopes of the Carlit massif, the ski station above the village of **PORTÉ-PUYMORENS** (ⓦ www.porte-puymorens.net) is probably the best the French Catalan Pyrenees has to offer. The seventeen runs here are fairly evenly distributed among all difficulties, with the highest points at a respectable 2400m and 2500m. There are also 25km of trails for *ski de fond*, a snowboarders' "board park" and a whole gamut of non-ski leisure facilities (including horse riding, bike trails and fitness). In summer the resort opens for hikers and walkers, providing a base for day-trips into the peaks.

Practicalities

Saillagouse's *Train Jaune* station is actually across the river, about a fifteen-minute walk from the town's *mairie*, where you'll find a small **tourist office** (July & Aug Mon–Sat 10am–1pm & 3–7pm; ☎04.68.04.55.35, ⓔ mairie-saillagouse@orange .fr). You can stay at the *Hôtel Planes* on place de Cerdagne (☎04.68.04.72.08, ⓦ www.planotel.fr; ❹), whose atmospheric fireside dining room serves up elaborate *gastronomique* fare (chef Jean Luc Planes will match a wine to each of the four courses of the *menu plaisir* for €39). There are several **campsites**, of which the three-star *Le Cerdan* (Nov–Sept; ☎04.68.04.70.46, ⓦ www.lecerdan.com) has the best facilities. Local produce can be found at Saillagouse's **market** (Tues & Fri) and at Bourg-Madame's on Saturdays.

The Tech valley and the Albères

Running more or less parallel to the Têt valley, but roughly 30km further south, the **Tech valley** (or Vallespir) is the southernmost in France, endowed with exceptional sunshine (300 days a year) and relatively low rainfall which nurtures a flora that includes oranges, cacti and bougainvillea – as well as dense forest on the higher, wetter slopes. Heading up the valley will take you through the Spanish ex pat art centre, **Céret**, and on to **Arles-sur-Tech**, the gateway to the exciting **Gorges de la Fou**. Further upstream, the upper Tech is dominated by **Prats-de-Molló**, where the main road departs from the river to reach the Spanish frontier. The northern face of the Pyrenees, rising out of the sea at the rugged Côte Vermeille and bordered by the Tech to the north, is known as the **Albères**. Here, a myriad of paths – a traditional route of shepherds, refugees and smugglers – cross the frontier into Spain, marked officially by the village of **Le Perthus**. Access into both regions from Perpignan by car or bus is via **Le Boulou**, where the N9 splits to head straight south for Le Perthus, and west to shadow the Tech valley as the D115.

Le Boulou and around

The cork capital of France, **LE BOULOU**, 20km south of Perpignan, is a fairly nondescript little spa town, although it is worth stopping at the **Église Ste-Marie**, the doorway of which features a fine frieze by the "Master of Cabestany" (see box, p.297). There is also a small **history museum**, the Espace des Arts (Tues–Sun 9am–noon & 2–6pm; free), with more works by the master. Die-hard fans should drive or cycle 14km north to the outskirts of **Passa**, where the cloister, **Monastir del Camp Prieuré** (Fri–Wed tours at 10am & 11am & 3, 4, 5 & 6pm; €4), features more of the anonymous sculptor's work. To further tempt, the monastery is now a wine *domaine*, where you can taste local vintages. Le Boulou's **tourist office** (July & Aug Mon–Sat 9am–12.30pm & 2–6.30pm; Sept–June Mon–Fri 9am–12.30pm

& 2–6pm, Sat 9am–12.30pm; ☎04.68.87.50.95, ⓦwww.ot-leboulou.fr) is in the central place de la Mairie. The best **accommodation** option is the elegantly rustic 🛌 *Le Relais des Chartreuses* (Feb to mid-Nov; ☎04.68.83.15.88, ⓦwww.relais-des -chartreuses.fr; ❹), set in an old Catalan *masia* (farmhouse), at 106 av d'En Carbouner in Le Boulou. You can enjoy fantastic veal and lamb dishes at the **restaurant** *Le Cédrat* (☎04.68.83.01.20) on the route de Perthus (*menus* from €19).

Heading east from Le Boulou will take you past a number of other Romanesque monuments (see box, p.319), or head a few minutes south, where the Tech cuts by on its way to the sea, to visit the remarkable **chapel of St-Martin-de-Fenollar** (mid-June to mid-Sept daily 10.30am–noon & 3.30–7pm; mid-Sept to mid-June Mon & Wed–Sun 2–5pm; €3) in **MAUREILLAS-LAS-ILLAS**, an ancient village of stone-clad houses. Its twelfth-century frescoes are the best Romanesque wall paintings in Roussillon, and their clarity and simplicity of line may well have influenced Picasso, who sometimes stayed in nearby Céret.

Le Perthus

Nine kilometres south of Maureillas, **LE PERTHUS** was marked in history on the night of February 5, 1939, when a column of twenty thousand Spanish Republicans arrived at the border post to seek sanctuary in France. Nowadays consumer armies descend here every day, disgorging from coaches to spend their money on foodstuffs, booze and perfume, or to cross the border to fill up their tanks in Spain. The main landmark hereabouts is **Fort de Bellegarde** (June–Sept 10.30am–6.30pm; €3), which looms on a peak above the town. Built in the sixteenth century and later reinforced by Vauban, it comprises two rows of dilapidated buildings and the deepest well in Europe (63m) within an enclosure of mighty walls, and gives superb views south into Spain and north across Roussillon. In Roman times the Via Domitia crossed the Albères 2km to the west at the **Col de Panissars**, accessible by the narrow road which continues past Fort de Bellegarde, and is probably the way that Hannibal came in 218 BC. When Pompey returned to Rome fresh from putting down a rebellion in Spain a century and a half later, he ordered a triumphal monument to be built at the col, and the excavated base of this edifice is now visible through a cordon of barbed wire.

For **accommodation**, there's *Chez Grand-Mère*, at the summit of the main road (☎04.68.83.60.96; ❸), or the municipal **campsite** *Les Oliviers* (mid-Jan to mid-Dec; ☎04.68.83.12.86), east of the town centre. The best option for a meal is to hop across the border to Spain, where any of La Jonquera's many bustling **roadside eateries** will lay out an all-you-can-eat buffet or a hefty four-course meal in the €8–12 range. If you do nip into Spain, taking the toll *autoroute* (less than €3) will avoid the excruciatingly long delays through bottle-necked Le Perthus.

Céret

Just 10km or so upstream along the Tech from Le Boulou lies the cherry capital of southern France, **CÉRET**, a friendly and bustling place with a shady old town of narrow and winding streets, still dominated by its much-built-into medieval fortifications. The best time to visit is during any of the town's famous **festivals** (see box, p.289), which have a markedly Catalan and Spanish flavour, including *sardanas* and *corridas* held in the arena to the north of town – but you'll have to plan ahead, as accommodation sells out well in advance. At the entrance to the town, the single-arched **Pont du Diable** was said to have been built by the Devil in 1321 in return for the soul of the first Cérétan to cross. The engineer who made the bargain duly sent a cat over first, but the trick backfired as none of the locals would then risk the Devil's vengeance by using the bridge themselves. Like Prades on the Têt, Céret was a place of refuge for escapees from Franco's fascist regime, with many artists passing through or staying here. At that point, the town was already a creative colony, having been a temporary home to luminaries such as Pablo Picasso, Marc Chagall and a clutch of Catalan and French artists, including Pierre Brune, who in 1950 opened the **Musée d'Art Moderne** at 8 bd Maréchal Joffre (July to mid-Sept daily 10am–7pm; mid-Sept to June Wed–Mon 10am–6pm; €8). This museum's small but varied collection includes works by the Fauvists, Cubists and Surrealists, as well as pieces by recent artists such as Tàpies, but the highlight is a series of painted bowls with bull motifs by Picasso. Keep an eye out also for the **war memorial** by Aristide Maillol in the old town and the **monument** to the composer Déodat de Séverac by the Catalan sculptor Manolo in avenue Clémenceau. If you head north 100m from the town centre on avenue d'Espagne, you'll come upon **Le Capelleta** (Sat 10.30am–12.30pm & 3.30–7pm), a tiny church with a well-executed Romanesque lintel over the entrance, which houses temporary art exhibitions.

Practicalities

The **tourist office** (July & Aug Mon–Sat 9am–12.30pm & 2–7pm; Sept–May Mon–Fri 10am–noon & 2–5pm, Sat 10am–noon; ℡04.68.87.00.53, Ⓦwww .ot-ceret.fr) is at the top of avenue Clémenceau, on the corner of boulevard Maréchal Joffre. The most central **accommodation** is at the charming one-star ⚲ *Vidal*, housed in the old bishop's palace, off place Soutine (℡04.68.87.00.85; ❷). A more upscale option is A *Le Mas Trilles* at Le Pont de Reynes, 2km outside Céret (℡04.68.87.38.37, Ⓦwww.le-mas-trilles.com; ❽), set in a seventeenth-century *mas* overlooking the Tech. Of the local **campsites**, the best is *Les Cerisiers* (Feb–Dec; ℡04.68.87.00.08, Ⓦpagesperso-orange.fr/camping.cerisiers), just a ten-minute walk from the town centre.

As for **eating**, try the bistro-crêperie, *Le Pied dans le Plat* (closed Sun; from €14), or adjacent pizzeria, both on place des Neuf-Jets, with outdoor seating. Another reliable choice is the atmospheric *Bisbe* (℡04.68.87.00.85), set in the old bishop's palace at 4 pl Soutine, serving up Catalan-style cooking in a funky dining-room (from €13). Social life at the *Grand Café* in boulevard Maréchal Joffre is not what it was when the "bande Picasso" hung out there, but it's still a good place to sit outside with a glass of wine and a plate of frites. Saturdays see a morning farmers' **market** along the old walls, the street stalls groaning with local produce.

Arles-sur-Tech and around

Continuing upstream from Céret, the next town which merits a visit is **ARLES-SUR-TECH**, renowned for having preserved the curious folk traditions of the eastern Pyrenees – try to make it for one of the several festivals that are celebrated throughout the year (see box, p.289). The heart of the town is formed by its compact medieval quarter, centred on the eleventh-century **abbey-church of Ste-Marie** (July & Aug Mon–Sat 9am–7pm, Sun 2–5pm; Sept–June Mon–Sat 9am–noon & 2–6pm, Sun 2–5pm; Nov–March closed Sun; €3.50). Before passing through the main door built into its impressive facade, check out the grilled-off marble block just to the left. This is the *sainte tombe*, a fourth-century sarcophagus, revered for the pure water which miraculously issues from it, and which plays a key part in the town's ancient religious rituals. Look out also for the curious *simiots*, half-human, half-monkey creatures carved on the church. The interior has a number of good **chapels**, as well as an elegant thirteenth-century **cloister**.

From Arles, you can access the nearby **Gorges de la Fou** (℡04.68.39.16.21; April–Nov daily 10am–6pm weather permitting; €6.60), one of the great – if touristy – spectacles of the eastern Pyrenees. Follow the signposted turning off the main highway west of Arles or ascend the trail leading off the D115, 3km west of

The Pyrenees: bear facts

Local peoples' fascination with **bears** goes back to the very dawn of our species. Cave paintings depict them, while excavations at Chauvet cave (near Nîmes) suggest that bears and hominids shared living space 32,000 years ago. For early societies around the world bears were feared and respected as embodiments of the power of nature and of virility – a force to be reckoned with and a rival to be hunted down. Until modern times, when they were hunted almost to extinction, bears continued to roam the wooded slopes of the Pyrenees, preying on game and herds, and inspiring awe among village-dwellers.

From the 1980s **conservationists** struggled to save the species, but in vain. The remaining three indigenous bears have now been shot by poachers: the last – "Canelle" – was found dead in 2004. Even before then, the French and Spanish governments had initiated a programme to reintroduce the species, releasing Slovenian and Croatian bears in the high valleys along the frontier. But there are few protected habitats on the French side of the *cordillera*, and shepherds oppose the programme, claiming that it puts their herds in danger, despite generous (and often-abused) compensation payments. On top of this, a Hunting and Fishing Party runs in local elections advocating the right to kill the animals.

Today, ursine totems and costumes are standard features of folk festivals in the mountains, and the closest you're likely to come to seeing a bear is at the **fêtes de l'ours**, or "bear festivals", celebrated in villages such as St-Laurent-de-Cerdans. The ancient festivals mark the date when hungry bears emerged from hibernation. Traditionally, village youths would go out to capture a live animal to prove their masculinity, but gradually this was transformed into a symbolic hunt, in which libidinous gangs of youths pursued a villager dressed in a bear costume (for a vivid re-creation see 1983's film *The Return of Martin Guerre*).

town. You need at least an hour to cover the 1500m of metal walkway to the end and back, squeezing between 200m-high walls, so close together that they have trapped falling rocks. In places, water erosion has made the walls as smooth as plaster, and the force of the torrent during storms in 1988 swept part of the walk away – when storms threaten, the route is closed.

South of the main road a tortuous side-road ascends through forests of sweet chestnut to the village of **ST-LAURENT-DE-CERDANS**, an important junction on the World War II refugee route to Spain. Here the local history museum, **Musée des Arts et Traditions Populaires** (June–Sept daily 9/10am–noon & 2/3–6pm; July & Aug daily 10am–noon & 2–7pm; Oct–May Mon–Fri 9am–noon & 2–6pm; €2), preserves rural arts such as the manufacture of espadrilles, the traditional esparto woven shoes favoured by refugee guides (*passeurs*). If at all possible, visit the town in early February for the colourful Fête de l'Ours (see box above). The **market** is held on Saturday. Further on at tiny **COUSTOUGES**, the spine of the Albères rises northeastwards to the highest point of the chain at **Roc de France** (1450m).

Practicalities

Buses stop in Arles a short walk from the **tourist office** (July & Aug Mon–Sat 9am–7pm, Sun 2–5pm; Sept–June Mon–Sat 9am–noon & 2–6pm, Sun 2–5pm; Nov–March closed Sun; ☎04.68.39.11.99, ⊛www.ville-arles-sur-tech.fr), in rue Barjou at the top of the town, which has suggestions for walks and trails around Arles, and also stocks a list of *chambres d'hôtes*. The place to **stay** is the comfortable two-star *Les Glycines*, 7 rue du Jeu-de-Paume (☎04.68.39.10.09, ⓔhotelglycines @orange.fr; ❸), which also has the town's best **restaurant**, with a shaded terrace and Catalan specialities (*menus* from €18). There are several **campsites**, including the scenic *Riuferrer* (℡04.68.39.11.06), on the west side of town, near the mouth of the Freixe stream.

Prats-de-Molló

From Arles, the road climbs 19km to the medieval city of **PRATS-DE-MOLLÓ**, and its sister town of **La Preste**, famous as a spa since 1302. The present road follows the path of a former railway (the station houses can be seen along the way), since the old road, along with houses and bridges, was washed away in the disastrous floods of October 1940. In the seventeenth century, when the Treaty of the Pyrenees subjected this area to the outrageous tax policies of Louis XIV, Prats-de-Molló and a number of other towns and villages revolted against the French Crown.

Fort Lagarde (April–June & Sept–Nov Tues–Sun 2–6pm; July & Aug daily 10.30am–1pm; €3.50), which dominates the town from above, was built in 1680 under the direction of Vauban, as much to subdue the local population as to keep the Spanish at bay; the town walls, raised on fourteenth-century foundations, are another Vauban relic from this period. The fort has been beautifully restored, and the superb views all around from the ramparts compensate for the twenty-five minutes it takes to climb up. An extra attraction here is the **Visite-Spectacle** on summer afternoons, when horsemen dressed as cavaliers re-create eighteenth-century cavalry training, with trick riding, sword fights and the firing of muskets and cannons.

With Canigou at its back and the River Tech in front, picturesque Prats-de-Molló has now become a tourist attraction but is still surprisingly unspoilt – particularly the old *ville haute* within the city wall, with its steep, cobbled streets and ancient fortified church. In summer, the pedestrianized streets buzz with activity; the rest of the year the hotels are locked up, and the locals pass the time playing *boules* under the plane trees of El Foiral, the huge square outside the walls, where markets and fairs have been held since 1308.

Practicalities

The **tourist office** in place du Foiral (July & Aug daily 9am–12.30pm & 1.30–6.30pm; April–June, Sept & Oct Mon–Sat 9am–noon & 2–6pm; Jan–March, Nov & Dec closed Sat; ℡04.68.39.70.83, ⓦwww.pratsdemollolapreste.com) has a wealth of information, including maps and advice for walking in the Haut-Vallespir. There is a good selection of **hotels** here. At the upper end of the scale is the *Grand Hôtel Thermale* (℡04.68.87.55.02, ⓦwww.laprestelesbains.com; ❻), a *château*-like old-fashioned spa with excellent amenities at a very reasonable price. Also good-value is the family-oriented *Le Relais*, 3 pl Joseph Trinxeria (℡04.68.39.71.30, ⓦwww.hostellerie-le-relais.com; ❷), which also serves decent meals. A better choice of **restaurant**, however, is *Costabonne* at 6 pl du Foiral (℡04.68.39.70.24), renowned for its home-made foie gras (*menus* from €13.50). There are plenty of local **campsites**, too, including *St Martin* in avenue de Vallespir (Feb–Dec; ℡04.68.39.77.40, ⓔcamping .st.martin@orange.fr). Stock up on supplies at the local **market**, held Wednesday and Friday mornings.

The Côte Vermeille

When the nineteenth-century Fauvists discovered the **Côte Vermeille**, which extends southeast from Argelès-sur-Mer to the Spanish border, they found natural inspiration for their revolutionary use of colour: the sunsets (from which the coast earned its name) are a gentle red, the sea is turquoise and, as Matisse wrote, "no sky is more blue than that at Collioure". **Elne**, inland, once Roussillon's main town, is the gateway to the coast, and proceeding south you'll pass the broad sandy beaches of **Argelès**, before reaching the characteristically rocky coves of **Collioure**, **Banyuls** and **Cerbère**. The beauty of this stretch of coastline has inevitably been exploited, but cut up along the trails into the hills at the back of the resorts and you'll often be on your own. Public transport along the coast is good, with a regular train and bus service connecting all the major points of call.

Elne

Standing on a hill just 6km from the sea, the first stop on the coastal transport line is **ELNE**, an ancient fortified town that was once the capital of Roussillon. Despite the heavy beach-bound traffic whizzing past on the main road, the old town, inside the sixteenth-century ramparts, is eerily quiet after dark. Its one great attraction is the former **cathedral of Ste-Eulalie** (daily: April–Sept 9.30am–5.45/6.45pm; Oct 9.30am–12.15pm & 2–5.45pm; Nov–March 9.30am–11.45pm & 2–4.45pm; €5), the seat of Roussillon's bishops until their transfer to Perpignan in 1602. The **cloister**, built from Céret marble, is the highlight: one intact side of twelfth-century Romanesque pillars and capitals, immaculately carved with motifs such as foliage, lions, goats and biblical figures, is complemented on the other sides by fourteenth-century Gothic work. Opposite the cathedral, at 3 rue Balaguer, is the **Musée Terrus** (same times and ticket as the cathedral), dedicated to the landscape painter Etienne Terrus (1857–1922), a contemporary of the Fauvists and friend of sculptor Aristide Maillol (whose bust of Terrus stands on the Plateau des Garaffes, nearby).

Practicalities

The **gare SNCF** (☎04.68.22.06.15), on the main line from Perpignan to the Côte Vermeille, lies about ten minutes' walk west of the old town; **buses** stop at the parking area in the centre, near the cathedral. The **tourist office** is in place Sant Jordi (June & Sept Mon–Fri 9.30am–noon & 2–5pm, Sat 9.30am–noon; July & Aug Mon–Fri 9.30am–noon & 2–6pm, Sat 9.30am–noon; Oct–May Mon–Fri 9.30am–noon &

▲ Cathedral carvings, Elne

2–5pm; ☎04.68.22.05.07, ⓦwww.ot-elne.fr), in the old town. Of the **hotels**, the rather pricey *Cara Sol*, in boulevard Illibéris on the edge of the old town (☎04.68.22.10.42, ⓦwww.hotelcarasol.com; ❺), has great views from the front rooms over the Tech valley, the Albères and Canigou. The cosy B&B, 🍴 *Aux Remp' Arts* (☎04.68.22.31.95, ⓦwww.remparts.fr; ❹) at 3 pl Colonel Roger is a great deal, with comfortable rooms and studios, and an excellent **restaurant** featuring imaginative dishes and good service (from €15; closed Tues lunch & Wed). There are three **campsites**, the best of which is *Le Florida* (April–Oct; ☎04.68.37.80.88, ⓦwww .campingleflorida.com) on route Latour Bas Elne. The local **market** is held on the place de la République (Mon, Wed & Fri).

Saint-Cyprien

Five kilometres northeast of Elne lies the sleepy old village of **SAINT-CYPRIEN**, clumped around a tiny square, the place de la République, where you'll find **Les Collections de Saint-Cyprien** (July & Aug daily 10am–noon & 2–6/7pm; Sept–June Wed–Mon same hours; €6). Its tiny permanent collection contains a few pieces of interest, notably Dalí's sculpture *Venus de Milo with Drawers*, but it also hosts excellent and often provocative temporary exhibitions of contemporary and modern art. Five kilometres east of the village is the beach town of **Saint-Cyprien-Plage** and the Dantesque holiday development of Saint-Cyprien-Sud. Beyond the densely built-up developments which surround Saint-Cyprien-Plage, there's a **beach** with abundant amenities, and that is quieter and more suitable for families than nearby Argelès.

Saint-Cyprien-Plage's **tourist office** is on quai Rimbaud (July & Aug daily 9am–8pm; Sept–June Mon–Sat 9am–noon & 2–6pm, Sun 10.30am–noon & 3–7pm; ☎04.68.21.01.33, ⓦwww.saint-cyprien.com). There's no shortage of **accommodation** at the beach, including the functional *Mar i Sol*, 8 rue Auguste-Rodin (☎04.68.37.31.00, ⓦwww.hotelmarisol.com; ❹), and the four-star *Île de la Lagune* on boulevard de l'Almadine (☎04.68.21.01.02, ⓦwww.hotel-ile-lagune .com; ❾), with a highly recommended **restaurant**, *L'Almadine* (€50 and up).

Argelès-sur-Mer and around

Poised on the northern edge of the Côte Vermeille, **ARGELÈS-SUR-MER** has the last wide, sandy beach on the coast. At the end of the Spanish Civil War

The Death of a Poet

As Francisco **Franco**'s fascist forces tightened the noose on Catalonia in early 1939, Republican refugees, both soldiers and civilians, poured over the French border. Far from being welcomed they were herded into **concentration camps** that sprang up through Languedoc-Roussillon and along the Pyrenees, including those at Argelès, Agde, Vernet and Rivesaltes. Republican soldiers, suspected of being Communists (illegal in France), were immediately disarmed and detained, and many were sent to the special "punishment" camp set up in Collioure castle, where up to five hundred men were subject to **forced labour**. In the other camps, some of which had capacities of ten thousand, malnutrition and disease were rampant. Among the civilians who crossed in February 1939 was **Antonio Machado**, one of the leading figures of Spain's "Generation of '98" cultural movement. The 64-year-old poet and playwright, widely famous for his literary output and his characterization of "the two Spains" locked in conflict, would not survive. Exhausted, only four days after his arrival and internment he died and was buried in the Collioure cemetery, and thus became, alongside Lorca, a cultural martyr of the Spanish Civil War and a symbol of the blind destructiveness of such struggles.

Romanesque in the Albères

The northern slopes of the Pyrenees and the plains that spill out below them were heavily populated in the Middle Ages, a fact attested to by the numerous churches and monasteries which were built here a millennium ago. This was not the wealthiest area, and these humble foundations cannot compete with the grandeur of Toulouse or the North of France, but the very fact that they were relatively isolated and poor means that many of their original features, which would have been remodelled and effaced elsewhere, have been left intact. **Romanesque churches** here are typically compact and squat, with few windows and single-naved chapels capped by primitive barrel-vaulting. The surviving artwork from this period is chiefly in sculpture and painting. Sculptors, the most famous being the "Master of Cabestany" (see box, p.297), devoted their attention to capitals and corbels, which they shaped into complex vegetal and geometric patterns or carved into biblical scenes peopled by bulbous-featured human figures. Rarer, and more striking, are the magnificent frescoes which once fully covered the interiors of many of these buildings.

In addition to the better-known sites, such as Elne (see p.317) and St-Martin-de-Fenollar (see p.313), several other churches can be taken in on a circuit of the area. West from Argelès, you'll pass the N114, after which a minor road leads 3km to **St-André** (non-suicidal cyclists should avoid the busy D618), whose old abbey-church houses the **Musée Transfrontalier d'Art Roman** (mid-June to mid-Sept Tues–Sun 10am–noon & 2.30–7pm; mid-Sept to mid-Nov & mid-March to mid-June Tues–Sat 10am–noon & 3–6pm; €2). A further 5km takes you to **St-Génis**, once home to an ancient Benedictine abbey; although most of it has disappeared, the remaining two-metre lintel over the doorway of the **church**, dating from 1020, is one of the earliest examples of Romanesque sculpture in France. When it's open (daily: June–Sept 10am–noon & 2/3–6/7pm; Oct–May 9.30am–noon & 2–5pm; €2) you can visit its thirteenth-century Romanesque **cloister**, with striking marble designs and excellent sculptures. From here the D11 leads 3.5km south to Laroque-des-Albères, then west to Villelongue-dels-Monts, where a steep and winding road, intermittently signposted to the "Église" leads up to the former Augustine convent and pilgrims' hostel of **Santa Maria Vilar** (daily 2.30pm & 6pm; 1hr guided tour €4). Originally founded in 1089, the present church dates from 1149, although sections, like the impressive Carolingian hall, are older. The main attractions here are the beautiful eleventh- and twelfth-century **fresco murals**, featuring both geometric and human motifs. Santa Maria is also home to a well-reputed Festival Lyrique, featuring Gregorian Chant and troubadours (☏04.68.89.64.61; July & Aug Sat 9pm; €16).

thousands of refugees lived in camps here, their numbers including the Republican poet Antonio Machado, who failed to survive the first harsh winter of his arrival (see box opposite). Nowadays, more than any other resort on this section of coast, this is a mass-tourist town, wooing its visitors with holiday essentials like mini-golf, gambling tables and beauty contests.

The town itself is divided in two: the old **Argelès-Ville**, a little inland, and the new **Argelès-Plage**, which receives an annual inundation of up to 300,000 French, Belgian, Dutch and English visitors. Plage Nord and Plage des Pins are **beaches** of the smooth, sandy and potentially windblown variety, whereas **Le Racou** – the first bay of the Côte Vermeille – is more intimate and offers a taste of mountain coastline. Either way, Argelès-Plage is a centre for noisy, ebullient, youthful hedonism, a landscape of neon lights and fast food with a background of loud music and the rattle of scooters.

Practicalities

The **gare SNCF** is a few minutes' walk west of the centre of Argelès-Ville, while **buses** stop opposite the Hôtel de Ville. An hourly bus service (€2) runs in summer between the station, the old town and Plage-Nord. There is a summer-only **tourist office** in the old town by the Hôtel de Ville on allée Ferdinand-Buisson (July & Aug Mon–Sat 9am–12.30pm & 3–6.30pm); the main office is on place de l'Europe in Argelès-Plage (July & Aug daily 8.30am–8pm; Sept–June Mon–Fri 9am–noon & 2–6pm, Sat 9am–noon; ☎04.68.81.15.85, ⓦ www.argeles-sur-mer .com), on the corner of avenue des Platanes and avenue des Mimosas. Several places, including Vélocation on the beachside avenue du Tech (☎04.68.81.61.61), rent out **bikes** and **motorbikes**.

Accommodation can be difficult to find in midsummer, especially for a short stay. The best choice in the old town is ⚘ *Auberge du Roua* (☎04.68.95.85.85, ⓦ www.aubergeduroua.com; ❻), a beautifully renovated *masia* on chemin du Roua, while for those on a budget, an excellent deal is the small, resort-style *Acapella* at 1 chemin de Néguebous (☎04.68.95.89.45, ⓦ www.hotel-acapella.fr; ❸), with many amenities, including a pool; apartments are also available. There are more than fifty **campsites** in the neighbourhood: the three-star *Beauséjour* near Centre Plage (May–Sept; ☎04.68.81.10.63, ⓦ www.camping-lebeausejour.com) has good beach access. The best **restaurants** in town are *La Tramontaine* (☎04.68.81.11.11) at 17 rue de la Marende, featuring Catalan-Languedocian seafood cuisine (*menus* from €23; closed Mon off-season), and the dining room of the *Lido* (☎04.68.81.10.32), 50 bd de la Mer, which has *menus* from €23, and a poolside buffet on Wednesdays and Sundays. If you are touring around the local Romanesque churches (see box, p.319), head for chef Bart Thoelen's *Les Palmiers* (closed all Mon & Sat lunch; ☎04.68.89.73.61) in Laroque-des-Albères and sit down to a hearty suckling pig or fresh and local fish dishes (depending on the season). *Menus* start at €22 for lunch, double that in the evening.

Collioure

Eleven kilometres down the coast from Argelès-sur-Mer, **COLLIOURE**, a true Côte Vermeille town, which to a certain extent still banks on its maritime and artistic past, sits nestled in a picturesque cove. Established as a trading port by the Phoenicians and ancient Greeks, Collioure was later occupied by Romans, Visigoths and Arabs. Altogether, the place has been the focus of nearly a dozen territorial squabbles, including four invasions by the French and two by the Spanish. The sixteenth-century **Fort St Elme** overlooking the town from the south (now privately owned), and the seventeenth-century **Fort Miradou** to the north (still used by the military), are reminders of this turbulent past. In the early 1900s, invaders of a different sort came; the group of painters – including Matisse and Derain – known as the **Fauvists** (*les Fauvistes*) made Collioure their summer base. Some of their original work adorns the bar at *Les Templiers* (see opposite); you can also follow the "Chemin du Fauvisme" around the town, a trail of twenty repro-ductions of paintings by Matisse and Derain placed on the sites where they were painted (a map is available from the tourist office; regular guided tours €6). Housed in the beautiful Villa Pams on the edge of the town on route de Port-Vendres, Collioure's **Musée d'Art Moderne** (daily 10am–noon & 2–6pm, Sept–June closed Tues; €6), has a small permanent collection which includes Picasso's poster *Hommage à Antonio Machado*, commemorating the Spanish Republican poet and martyr, who is buried in the town (see box, p.318). It also hosts temporary exhibitions by artists associated with the region.

The artistic tradition of Collioure survives today, albeit with less distinction; the forest of easels that occupies the promenade in summer produces mainly tourist souvenirs, but there are also a few serious commercial galleries. Many of these are in the old quarter of the town, the **Mouré**, whose steep, narrow streets are lined by pastel-tinted houses and assorted shops and cafés. Lateen-rigged fishing boats might be moored in the **harbour** itself, or drawn up on the palm-lined beach; those no longer used by fishermen are now beautifully restored and sailed as pleasure vessels by their new owners. The **château-royal** (daily: June–Sept 10am–5.15pm; Oct–May 9am–4.15pm; €3), the imposing fortress which dominates the harbour, was founded by the Templars in the twelfth century, rebuilt and used as a sometime residence by the kings of Mallorca and Aragón two hundred years later, and modernized by Vauban after the Treaty of the Pyrenees. There's little, however, to see inside. On the other hand, the two **beaches** which bookend the castle are worth the time, although they become hopelessly crowded in summer months. One is sandy and the other stony, so you can take your pick, or head up to the **nude beach** just around the cape at the town's north end.

At the opposite end of the harbour, the **church of Notre-Dame-des-Anges** was erected in the seventeenth century, replacing the ancient Sainte-Marie, razed on the orders of Vauban. The distinctive round bell tower – once doubling as the lighthouse – onto which it was grafted has been damaged many times by storm and war: the base dates from the thirteenth century, the middle from the fourteenth to seventeenth centuries, and the bell chamber from the nineteenth. It's worth taking a look inside (8am–noon & 2–5.30pm) to see the magnificent gilt retable, carved and painted in three tiers by Joseph Sunyer.

Practicalities

Collioure's **gare SNCF** is less than ten minutes' walk west of the centre, along avenue Aristide Maillol; **buses** stop at the central car park, off avenue Général de Gaulle. **Parking** on the street is almost impossible: head, instead, for the large and reasonably priced car park on the hill that rises over the sea behind the castle. The very helpful **tourist office** is just behind the harbour on place du 18 Juin (July & Aug Mon–Sat 9am–8pm, Sun 10am–6pm; Sept–June Mon–Sat 9am–noon & 2–6/7pm; ℡04.68.82.15.47, Ⓦwww.collioure.com) and there is also a seasonal information kiosk (July–Sept Mon–Sat 9am–5pm) in the small tower by the beach on the other side of the castle.

The quieter Plage Boutigue, southeast of the harbour, has some desirable sea-view **hotels**, the best of which is ⚐ *Triton*, 1 rue Jean-Bart (℡04.68.98.39.39, Ⓦwww.hotel-triton collioure.com; ❺). The most unusual accommodation is *Hostellerie des Templiers*, 12 quai de l'Amirauté (℡04.68.98.31.10, Ⓦwww.hotel -templiers.com; ❺; reservations essential), in which the individually decorated rooms, staircases and dining rooms are filled with original artworks; try to get a room in the main building, rather than in the less attractive annexes. For something quieter, but pricier, there's the very stylish *La Casa Païral*, in impasse des Palmiers (mid-Feb to Dec; ℡04.68.82.05.81, Ⓦwww.hotel-casa-pairal.com; ❼) with amenities including wi-fi, cable TV and a private garden. The best **campsite** here is *La Girelle* (℡04.68.81.25.56, Ⓔcampinglagirelle@orange.fr), north of town in the sheltered bay known as L'Ouille.

No single **restaurant** stands out in terms of food, but the most atmospheric is *Les Templiers* in rue Camille Pelletan, a dark café-bar well known to the Fauvists, and now filled with drawings and paintings donated by Matisse, Maillol, Picasso and Dufy, among many other artists. While in town, try to sample the famous salted anchovies, a local stand-by and an important component in Roussillonais cookery. **Markets** (Wed & Sun morning) are held in place du Maréchal Leclerc. X Trem Bike (℡04.68.82.59.77) at 7 av Général de Gaulle rents **bikes** and **scooters** by the day or week.

Port-Vendres

The next settlement southeast, **PORT-VENDRES** (the Roman Portus Veneris: "Port of Venus"), a five-minute ride from Collioure, is marred by the busy main road, but for a genuine, unsophisticated fishing port, this is your best (indeed only) choice on the Côte Vermeille – though you probably won't want to stay longer than it takes to have a look around the port and tuck into a fish lunch. A huge fish-processing factory dominates one side of the harbour, while sardine- and tuna-fishing boats are moored under the Maillol-designed war memorial opposite, with nets and other paraphernalia piled along the harbour wall. Salt has taken its toll on Maillol's work, and the uncharacteristically draped figures have lost limbs, noses and various other features. Four kilometres south of town is one of the region's newest and most original attractions: the **Site de Paulilles** (Sat & Sun 9.30am–6pm; free), an industrial tourism site, centered on a nineteenth-century dynamite factory (founded by Nobel) that is being allowed to revert to nature. In addition, it includes nature trails, and a workshop that restores traditional fishing boats, and has become in its first year of operation the most visited tourist site in Languedoc-Roussillon.

There is a regular Saturday **market** in Port-Vendres, as well as a Thursday-morning "Peasants' market" (mid-June to mid-Sept), but it's worth stopping in for lunch or dinner at the numerous quayside fish **restaurants** on any day of the week. The best of these is Philippe Bessière's *Côte Vermeille* (closed Sun & Mon off-season; ℡ 04.68.82.05.71) which has *menus* from €29 (*vin compris*).

Banyuls-sur-Mer to the Spanish border

As the road crosses the Col du Père Carnère and drops down towards the Plage des Elmes, the once-elegant wine town of **BANYULS-SUR-MER**, 6km south of Port-Vendres, comes into view, with dry-stone walls and orderly rows of vines stretching into the hills behind it. Banyuls is famous for its dessert wine, which the French tend to drink as an aperitif; if you fancy a tipple, take a 45-minute **guided tour** of one of the larger cellars, such as the Cellier des Templiers in route du Mas-Reig (April to early Nov daily 10am–7.30pm; early Nov to March Mon–Sat 10am–1pm & 2.30–6.30pm; €3).

You shouldn't leave Banyuls without visiting the **Laboratoire Arago**, a large white building overlooking the port. Run by the marine biology and land ecology department of the Sorbonne, its **aquarium** (daily: July & Aug 9am–1pm & 2–9pm; Sept–June 9am–noon & 2–6.30pm; €4.60) comprises over forty tanks of fascinating and rare local specimens, including seahorses, bright red starfish and wicked-looking eels, and is supplemented by a comprehensive display of local birds. The coastal waters of this area, rich in marine life due to the Pyrenees' steep underwater descent, were the first *réserve marine* to be declared in France, indeed throughout the Mediterranean. If you have the necessary qualifications you can **dive** within the reserve area by contacting Plongez Rederis Club, at the port (℡ 04.68.88.31.66, Ⓦ www.rederis.com).

Striking out of town, the four-kilometre **hike** from Banyuls to **Maillol's tomb** and house makes a pleasant excursion up into the vine-clad Albères. Sculptor **Aristide Maillol** (1861–1944) was a Banyuls native famous for his fleshy nude sculptures. He is buried at his farm, La Baillaurie, now restored as the **Musée Maillol** (May–Sept daily 10am–noon & 4–7pm; Oct–April Wed–Mon 10am–noon; €3.50), which contains his personal art collection, featuring works by Duchamp, Bonnard and Picasso. The artist's tomb is topped by his *La Pensée*. To get here, walk the length of avenue Général de Gaulle, until you pass under a bridge. Shortly afterwards, where the road curves around to the right, take the left-hand road, following the line of a river: signs from here point to the "Musée et Tombeau de Maillol". The round trip takes about two and a half hours.

Practicalities

The **gare SNCF** is at the very western edge of town, while **buses** stop on the coastal boulevard. The **tourist office** is on the seafront, opposite the *mairie* (July & Aug daily 8.30am–8pm; Sept–June Mon–Sat 9am–noon & 2–5/6pm; ⊤04.68.88.31.58, ⑩www.banyuls-sur-mer.com). ⚓ *El Llagut*, 18 av du Fontaulé (⊤04.68.88.00.81, ⑩www.al-fanal.com; ❹ with breakfast; closed Nov & Dec), is a reasonably priced **hotel** on the seafront near the port, where many of the rooms have a balcony and sea view. Another good option is the comfortable and well-equipped *Les Elmes* (⊤04.68.88.03.12, ⑩www.hotel-des-elmes.com; ❻) perched on the cliffs at the north end of town, with a private beach. There's **camping** at the muncipal site, *La Pinede*, on route des Crêtes (April to mid-Nov; ⊤04.68.88.32.13, ⒠camping.banyuls@orange.fr).

Banyuls has a good choice of **restaurants** specializing in fresh seafood. The most expensive, with starched tablecloths and live lobster tanks, are lined up opposite the seafront, but there are also several less pricey choices: the best of these is *Les Canadells*, just off the main boulevard at 4 av Général de Gaulle, with delicious *menus* (from €14 at lunch, €18 at dinner; closed Sun eve & Mon Oct–March) and specializing in *zarzuela* (Spanish fish stew) and other fishy dishes. For something more formal, go to *La Littorine* in *Les Elmes* hotel, where you can savour roast lobster, fire-grilled bass, or squid in its own ink (expect to spend around €40). The local morning **market** is held year-round on Sundays and Thursdays.

Cerbère

The Côte Vermeille comes to an end at **CERBÈRE**. The harbour is quite pretty and the mountain backdrop impressive, but the beach is negligible. Depending on the service, train passengers have to change either here or on the Spanish side of the border, at the much nicer **Port Bou**, where the rail line changes track size. In Cerbère, you can **stay** and **eat** at *La Dorade* on the harbour (⊤04.68.88.41.93, ⑩www.hotel-ladorade.com; ❸) or **camp** at the muncipal *Camping Cap Peyrefite*, on the beach of the same name (⊤04.68.88.41.17).

Travel details

Trains

The main railway line runs along the coast via Perpignan. SNCF buses may run in lieu of trains on these lines; services are reduced on Sundays and holidays. The *Train Jaune* (see p.307) also runs a service up the Tech valley to Latour-de-Carol/Enveitg (linking with the Ariège valley rail line to Toulouse), and the *Train du Pays Cathare et du Fenouillèdes* (p.300) serves the Fenouillèdes to Axat.

Perpignan* to:
Cerbère, via Elne, Argelès, Collioure and Banyuls-sur-Mer (hourly; 40min).
Latour-de-Carol, via Ille-sur-Têt, Prades and Villefranche-de-Conflent/Vernet (several daily; 3–4hrs).

Nîmes*, via Rivesaltes, Salses, Narbonne*, Béziers* (connections to Bédarieux), Agde, Sète and Montpellier* (several hourly; 2hr 10min–2hr 45min).
Paris* (many daily; 5hr+).
Toulouse*, via Rivesaltes, Salses, Narbonne*, Carcassonne* (connection to Quillan) and Castelnaudary (several hourly; 2hr 30min–3hr 45min).
Villefranche-de-Conflent/Vernet, via Ille-sur-Têt and Prades (several daily; 45min).
Rivesaltes (*Train du Pays Cathare et du Fenouillèdes*) to: Axat, via St-Paul-de-Fenouillet and Lapradelle/Puilaurens (seasonal, several daily; 2hr 15min).
Villefranche-de-Conflent/Vernet (*Train Jaune*) to: Font Romeu/Odeillo/Via, via Nyers, Thuès,

Mont-Louis and Bolquère/Eyne (several daily; 1hr 26min).

Latour-de-Carol/Enveitg, via Nyers, Thuès, Mont-Louis, Bolquère/Eyne, Font Romeu/Odeillo/Via, Saillagouse, Err and Bourg-Madame (several daily; 2hr 30min–3hr).

Buses

Many lines have no or reduced service on Saturdays, Sundays and holidays, and in summer months. Main bus lines follow the coast or run up the Fenouillèdes, Tech and Conflent valleys. The Roussillon Interplages shuttle runs frequently from Port-Bacarès to Collioure and back (July & Aug only), connecting the beach towns between. See ⓦ www.cg66.fr for a route map and full schedules.
Argelès to: Céret (daily; 1hr 15min); Le Boulou (daily; 1hr); St-Génis (weekly; 50min).

Arles-sur-Tech to: Coustouges (daily; 35min); St-Laurent-de-Cerdans (daily; 30min).

Latour-de-Carol/Enveitg to: Font-Romeu (several weekly; 25min); Formiguères (several weekly; 1hr 30min); Mont-Louis (several weekly; 55min); Puyvalador (several weekly; 1hr 35min).

Mont-Louis to: Font-Romeu (daily; 15min); Latour-de-Carol/Enveitg (daily; 1hr).

Perpignan to: Argelès (several daily; 35min); Arles-sur-Tech (several daily; 1hr); Banyuls-sur-Mer (several daily; 1hr 15min); Cabestany (many daily; 10min); Cerbère (daily; 1hr 35min); Céret (daily; 45min); Collioure (several daily; 45min); Elne (many daily; 20–45min); Font-Romeu (daily; 2hr 30min); Ille-sur-Tet (hourly; 15–35min); Latour-de-Carol/Enveitg (daily; 3hr); Le Boulou (several daily; 25–30min); Le Perthus (daily; 50min); Narbonne (daily; 2hr 30min); Passa (daily; 45min); Prades (several daily; 1hr); Prats-de-Molló (daily; 1hr 55min); Rivesaltes (hourly; 20min); Quillan (daily; 1hr 30min); St-Cyprien (several daily; 15min); St-Génis (several daily; 35min–1hr); St-Paul-le-Fenouillet (several daily; 50min); Salses (several daily; 15min–1hr 5min); Thuir (several daily; 25min); Vernet (several daily; 1hr 25min); Villefranche-de-Conflent (many daily; 1hr 20min); Vinca (many daily; 55min).

Prades to: Bourg-Madame (daily; 1hr 55min); Casteil (daily; 20min); Mont-Louis (several daily; 55min); Thuès (daily; 40min); Vernet-les-Bains (several daily; 25min); Villefranche (several daily; 15min); Vinca (weekly; 15min).

Rivesaltes to: Tautavel (daily; 30min).

St-Paul-le-Fenouillet to: Axat (daily; 30min); Quillan (daily; 45min).

Villefranche-de-Conflent to: Casteil (daily; 15min).

Contexts

Contexts

History

The two areas of Occitan Languedoc and Catalan Roussillon, in addition to their own cultural particularities, have strong historical differences. Languedoc was traditionally ruled by a native aristocracy, while Roussillon fell into the ambit of Catalonia, fated to become part of modern Spain. Even before they were integrated into the nation-state of France, though, their geographical proximity meant there were parallels and connections; each enjoyed its "golden age" in the Middle Ages, which may account for the nostalgia with which the inhabitants regard the period, and their shared borders saw considerable movement and contact.

Prehistory

The earliest traces of the human occupation of Languedoc and Roussillon date from the early **Paleolithic era** (Stone Age): the cranial remains of the slight but upright *Homo erectus*, discovered in the 1970s at Tautavel, near Perpignan, date back nearly half a million years. These early ancestors, who do not appear to have harnessed fire, hunted with the aid of simple stone weapons and tools and lived off the abundant (and dangerous) fauna of the region, which included wolves, hippos, rhinos, wild sheep and goats and the ferocious cave bear, whose claw marks are still visible on cave walls in the region (for example at Limousis, in the Montagne Noire). As the evolutionary tree branched off, taller and smarter **Neanderthal** humans appeared, dominating the local scene during the mid-Paleolithic era (approximately 150,000–35,000 BC). With a better tool-making capability than *Homo erectus*, the Neanderthals were able to pursue the mammoths and elephants of the Languedocian plain, and the remains of burial places scattered about the Pyrenean foothills dating from this time point to the beginnings of culture and religion.

It was not until the late Palaeolithic era that **modern humans** (*Homo sapiens*) came to monopolize the area, thriving especially in the Magdalenian period, some 14,000 years ago, which followed the last retreat of the glaciers. The earliest **cave paintings** of the Ariège valley (at Niaux and Mas d'Azil) date from this period and show the preoccupation of this early people with the hunt. In addition to cave art, they fashioned the small corpulent "Venus" statuettes, which are generally considered to relate to fertility rites.

With the invention of the harpoon, the development of fishing began to draw people towards the coasts of modern Roussillon. Nevertheless, the mid-altitude caves remained the favoured habitat into the Mesolothic and Neolithic (middle and new Stone Age) periods, which lasted here until about 1500 BC. Several important innovations occurred in the Neolithic era: **agriculture** and **animal husbandry** came into being in the fifth millennium BC, as did the use of grain-storage facilities. **Mining** and smelting were developed for the crude utilization of metals, such as copper, and better management of fire also permitted the manufacture of ceramics. Technical improvements encouraged specialization and this, in turn, trade, which seems to have first arisen among the lowland settlements of the Narbonnais plain. It was also in the last millennium of the Stone Age that the **dolmens** (megalithic henges) and **tumuli** (burial mounds) which dot the mid-level Pyrenees and Haut Languedoc appeared.

The Bronze Age

The Bronze Age in Languedoc and Roussillon was an era of great movement and change. Around 800 BC, the **Celts** arrived and began displacing the indigenous peoples, and an area roughly analogous with modern Languedoc – stretching from Nîmes in the east past Toulouse in the west – came under the hegemony of the Volcae, one of several large Celtic tribal groups who dominated the South of France. Meanwhile, **Phoenicians** and **Greeks** began to arrive on the region's shores. They set up outposts (such as Maguelone and Port-Vendres) and began to trade with natives, who lived for the most part in fortified hill-top towns now known as **oppida** (plural of the Latin *oppidum*, or "town"), such as the settlement of Ensérune. As archeological finds have confirmed, the native tribes were not uncivilized "barbarians" as Romans were later wont to claim, but participants in complex, technologically capable societies linked to extensive trade networks. Their rich culture is evinced by the objects that have survived them: skilfully worked bronze weapons and jewellery. Although perhaps not comparable with contemporary civilizations of the eastern Mediterranean, they had their own diversified agricultural and craft-based economies and stratified social structures. Their one weakness was that they were not oriented towards the sea and so needed intermediaries such as the Phoenicians to reach foreign markets.

The Romans

In the fourth century BC, the **Romans** embarked on a series of campaigns of conquest which brought the whole Iberian peninsula and the bulk of Greek possessions under its power and set it against the **Carthaginians**, heirs of Phoenicia in the western Mediterranean. The Romans were the ultimate victors, and the futile rumble of **Hannibal**'s elephants across the length of Languedoc in 218 BC presaged the beginning of a long colonial period in southern France. A few decades later the **Via Domitia**, the Rome–Cadiz superhighway, was built along the Languedoc coast, facilitating Roman military and economic expansion, and the Roman city of Narbo was founded. By about 70 BC all of what is now France south of Lyon and Toulouse constituted Narbonensian Gaul. With the completion of the conquest by **Julius Caesar** and his successor, the Emperor **Augustus**, the zone was elevated to the rank of an imperial province, and subdivided (in 27 BC), so that Narbonne became the capital of the lands from the Rhône to the Pyrenees.

Enjoying the benefits of Pax Romana, the region enjoyed an easy prosperity under the first emperors. Trade flourished (wine was a big export item) and there were major settlements at Baeterra (Béziers) and Nemausus (Nîmes). Nîmes became the region's most important city in the mid-second-century under Antoninus Pius – an emperor who lavished favours on his home town. During this period, Roman organizational infrastructure and slave labour permitted the elaboration of architectural projects of a scale and complexity that would not be duplicated for fifteen hundred years. This is particularly true in the case of public civic architecture, such as Nîmes' huge amphitheatre, **Les Arènes**, the nearby aqueduct, the **Pont du Gard**, and the **bridges** at Sommières and Ambrussum. Religious buildings, the finest surviving example of which is Nîmes' **Maison Carrée**, were based on Greek styles – temples usually consisting of a *cella* or inner sanctum (the abode of the god), ringed by a colonnade of columns which were topped by decorative capitals. Less grandiose remains of civic and residential structures can be found at Loupian and Ensérune, along the length of the Via Domitia. The cities and settlements of Roman Languedoc-Roussillon have yielded a wealth of intricate mosaics and Roman-style civic and religious statuary.

But there were rocky times ahead for the empire, as the expansion on which its prosperity had depended slowed. Domestic economic crises were compounded by the growing threat of neighbouring powers: Persia in the east, and "barbarians" in North Africa and northwest Europe. While the frontiers under attack by **Franks** and **Goths** were far from Languedoc, the disruption of the empire's stability had economic repercussions which reached Gallia-Narbonensis. The growing dissatisfaction and malaise in the empire encouraged a certain trend towards new religions such as the Mithras cult and **Christianity**, which spread rapidly through urban Languedoc. The latter was seen as a threat to the imperial order and a series of emperors set about trying to quash it. The fiercest persecutions, which saw Christians submitted to all manner of brutal public tortures and executions, were carried out under Valerian and Diocletian between 257 and 311 – many of the area's martyred saints date from this era.

When **Constantine the Great** became sole emperor in 324, he proclaimed Christianity a tolerated religion and it quickly took hold in the towns and cities of Languedoc. With the capital of the empire now in far-off Constantinople, the bishops, who were appointed in each Roman town after 391, helped hold together the decaying fabric of administration. In the new, contracting Christianized empire, Nîmes and Narbonne waned, as Roman cities in Provence, such as Arles, came to the forefront. But great changes were afoot, and as central power declined, people left the cities, taking refuge in smaller fortified towns and villas, and frequently trading off their liberty for the protection of a powerful patron. Imperial policy in the east was to deflect the waves of semi-nomadic steppe peoples westward, a tactic which saved the core of the empire, but brought about its disappearance in the west.

After the Romans

In the fifth century wave after wave of these small but aggressive invading bands passed through Languedoc and Roussillon: first the Suevi, then the Vandals and finally the **Visigoths**. It was the last of these who set up a durable kingdom, which in its greatest extent covered the southwest of France and most of Iberia. Their first capital was **Tolosa** – modern Toulouse – and they initially ruled, in name, as Roman imperial governors. At this time, however, a rival group, the **Franks**, had coalesced in the Low Countries and, led by King Clovis (482–511), drove southwards, incorporating Toulouse into their Kingdom of Aquitaine. Most of Languedoc and Roussillon, however, known then as **Septimania** (either after its seven great cities: Narbonne, Agde, Béziers, Maguelone, Lodève, Nîmes and Uzès, or after the Roman Seventh Legion which was garrisoned in the area), remained under the Visigoths.

The weak and conflictive Visigothic kingdom was dealt a deathblow by **Muslim armies**, which arrived in Iberia around 711. Wiping out the Spanish Visigothic nobility in a single battle, they quickly conquered most of modern Spain and Portugal, and small raiding parties crossed the Pyrenees, taking Toulouse and Septimania in the 720s. The most northern of these groups was turned back near Poitiers by Charles Martel in 732. Numerically too few to hang onto such an extensive area, the Muslims occupied the towns, exacting tribute and using them as raiding bases. In the years that followed the battle of Poitiers, the Muslims were turned out of Toulouse, Carcassonne and eventually their coastal enclaves as one by one these fell to the Franks; it was to prevent their return that Martel destroyed the town of Maguelone (see p.230). This long campaign was carried out under the leadership of **Pepin the Short**, the first Carolingian king (751–68), and it was his successor, **Charlemagne** (Charles the Great), who pushed the Muslims back over the Pyrenees. Languedoc was absorbed into the **Frankish Empire** and Roussillon became part of the semi-autonomous frontier region known as the **Spanish Marches**. After the decline of Roman power in the west, the empire continued in the east, but despite the fact that Constantinople was now its capital, its rulers continued to bear the title "Emperor of Rome". During Charlemagne's era, it so happened that it was a woman, Irene, who was in power in Constantinople; seeing an opportunity to enhance his prestige – given that no one actually held the title of "Emperor" – Charlemagne journeyed to Rome and had the pope crown him as "Holy Roman Emperor" in 800. Thus, his dominions, which covered almost all of western Europe, came to be known as the **Holy Roman Empire**, and the papacy, which up till then had been little more than an ordinary bishopric, gained justification for its later claims to be the power which could (or not) crown emperors.

The counts and feudalism

Despite his centralizing policies, Charlemagne followed Germanic custom, separating his kingdom among his heirs, and Languedoc fell into the **Kingdom of the Western Franks**, more or less contiguous with modern France. When its second king, Louis the Stammerer, died heirless in 879, the kingdom rapidly disintegrated, leaving power in the hands of local **counts**, although nominally Charlemagne's other descendants held the highest authority. Among the local nobility, one family, the **"Raymonds"** or "dynasty of St-Gilles", eventually came to dominate. They had ruled Toulouse since 840, thanks to a grant by Pepin II, and by the late 900s they were to all intents and purposes independent rulers. As such, they began to expand, absorbing neighbouring territories, such as Albi, or co-opting other, lesser noble lines, such as the **Trencavels** of Carcassonne, as vassals. **Raymond IV** ruled a realm which stretched from Toulouse to the banks of the Rhône; it was he who adopted the surname of "St-Gilles", in honour of his favourite possession. Meanwhile, the most powerful lord of the Spanish March, **Guifré el Pelós** ("Wilfred the Hairy"), Count of the Cerdagne, Girona and Barcelona, was granted independence from the empire. Roussillon, then dominated by Elne, came under his power; it is at this point that Languedoc's and Roussillon's histories as separate regions begin, and over the course of the centuries that followed their paths would be linked, but not united again until Louis XIV's formal annexation of Roussillon in the 1600s.

In these early medieval centuries, what little industry and urban life existed under the Romans all but disappeared. Western Europe became overwhelmingly agrarian, developing an economy of near subsistence in which the noble class siphoned off the meagre surplus and provided military protection to the masses. Local magnates depended on military strength to maintain their power and protect their subjects, obtaining warriors by granting lands in exchange for loyalty, and **feudal** structures developed. Religion, too, was a largely private and local affair: noble lords built churches and monasteries and put them under the charge of their friends and relatives, who lived comfortably off the income from these posts. The common folk continued to depend as much on traditional pre-Christian beliefs and magic – just as well, since most local priests knew no more than a smattering of Church Latin and were not particularly exemplary in their moral life. Learned culture, too, all but vanished with the disappearance of towns, and was maintained only by the monks who lived in isolated and introspective communities – fortresses of faith, hidden in isolated valleys and on remote mountainsides.

Twelfth-century revival

In the twelfth century the picture began to change rapidly. A shift away from subsistence, possibly as the result of climatic change and aided by improvements in agricultural technology, allowed the population to grow, while under the counts the region began to enjoy a stability which stimulated **trade** and **industry**. People started to move around Europe looking for better opportunities; towns expanded, shaking Toulouse and the cities of Septimania back to life. The agrarian social structures which had developed in the previous period were not suitable for town life, and the counts, anxious to promote economic growth, recognized that by extending liberties and privileges to the townsfolk, their own position could be improved. Oligarchic **town councils**, such as the **Capitolo** in Toulouse, were formed, sharing in or taking over urban administration and further stimulating growth.

Changes were afoot in the Church as well: the papacy was in the process of becoming a geopolitical power, initiating a level of bureaucracy and organization which would give it control of the resources and policies of local churches – traditionally the turf of the nobles. Some efforts were made to improve the priesthood, too, to ensure that priests were educated and lived, at least in appearance, morally upright lives. On the popular level, **pilgrimage** played an important role, carrying ordinary believers across Europe, to Rome or Santiago de Compostela; along the way they visited local churches such as that at St-Gilles and came into contact with a wider Christian world. A wave of reformation also swept over the **monasteries**, where the degenerate and locally independent Benedictines were replaced by new, pious and strict orders, most importantly the Cistercians, who were controlled by a strong central organization.

With all of this new wealth, secular and religious culture began to revive. Great churches were raised in the towns, and old cathedrals were replaced by new, more grandiose and elaborate structures. The courts of the counts' palaces became the focus of a new culture as well, one which sought refinement in the **courtly traditions** of elaborate manners, rich clothes and imported luxuries. The most visible manifestation of this new culture was the tradition of courtly love and the **troubadours**. These singing poets – the first of whom is said to have been Guilhem de Peitieu, count of Poitiers and father of Eleanor of Aquitaine, Queen of France and, later, England – composed odes of yearning, unrequited love to anonymous "dark ladies", and satirical barbs aimed at local nobles. Their language of choice was not Latin, which had previously been the only voice of culture, but the local vernaculars, Occitan and Catalan. It was also in this era that the rites and rituals associated with feudalism, such as heraldry and the tournament, began to be formalized – precisely when the feudal world began to decline.

However, with this period of revival came a greater demand for fulfilment, directed at the Church from just about every corner. The newly wealthy and increasingly literate craftsmen, the **burghers**, who had no role to play in the warrior-aristocratic culture of the court, wanted a level of political power and social prestige which reflected their economic standing and, better educated than before, began to look for more satisfying theological answers than the still feudal-oriented Church could provide. Town life generated new social problems, particularly among the urban poor, which the Church – effectively a social welfare organization in the countryside – was not equipped to address. The peasants, too, were dissatisfied; although increasingly interested in Christianity, a shortage of priests meant they were frustrated by a lack of pastoral care. In short, the Church was seen as **corrupt** by everyone but the nobility, a situation aggravated by the taxes which people were forced to pay to support it. In addition, Latin, once widely spoken, was the only accepted sacred language – preserving the mystery of the Church, but now acting to cut off the faith and Scripture from the common folk.

Although their religious consciousness was high – local nobles, such as the Crusader Raymond of St-Gilles, distinguished themselves by reclaiming the Holy Land from the Muslim "infidels" – the upper classes in Languedoc began to find themselves turning against the Church too, but for a different reason. The nobility considered it their natural privilege to control local institutions, including bishoprics, parishes and monasteries and, unconcerned by the theological preferences of their subjects as long as they continued to pay their taxes, resented papal expansionism as a threat to their own power.

In the meantime, neighbouring Roussillon, though it went through most of the same social and economic processes as Languedoc, followed a distinctive political and religious course. In the centuries following Guifré el Pelós, his descendants, the **counts of Barcelona**, had been struggling to gain supremacy over their various rival counts in Catalonia, who did not want to recognize them as overlords. They were aided in this campaign in 1142 when Ramon Berenguer IV married the princess of Aragón, obtaining the title of King of Aragón for his heirs. Thus Barcelona became the capital of a multinational monarchy and its rulers, the count-kings, were to govern one of the great powers of the medieval Mediterranean. Linked by ties of marriage to noble houses in Languedoc and further east in Provence, they angled for political expansion, and for a time their holdings included Montpellier and various parts east of the Rhône. Indeed, the counts of Toulouse became their vassals – although this was merely a formality, amounting more to a pact of mutual assistance than a recognition of the count-kings' authority.

Catharism and the Albigensian Crusades

In the climate of dissatisfaction with the Church, popular **heresies** began to spring up, led by men who preached to the people in their own language and led lives of austerity and poverty, in emulation of the Apostles and in contrast to the wealthy and aloof Catholic clergy. The Church tried at first to quash the problem with force, but then, co-opting the impulses which drove the heretics, licensed two new groups, the Dominican and Franciscan preaching friars who – in contrast to the isolated monks – were to minister and preach among the common people. But the damage had already been done, and the most successful of the new heresies, **Catharism** (see *The Land of the Cathars* colour section), had become firmly entrenched. This doctrine was a variant on ancient Middle Eastern beliefs combined with Christianity, a dualistic creed which portrayed the material world as evil and the spiritual world as good. It resonated among the common folk (who appreciated its populism) and nobles (who wanted to set themselves apart from the influence of Rome and its northern French political allies), and a shadow counter-Church began to organize itself, holding its first Council at St-Félix-de-Lauragais in 1167. In most of the major towns of Languedoc, and the countryside around Toulouse and south of the Aude, this new Church gained a strong presence. Here, the nobility, including the counts of Toulouse, the Trencavels of Carcassonne and a whole array of minor barons, remained Catholic themselves, but gave free reign to Cathar preachers to spread their religious message. As Roussillon did not develop an urban society as quickly as Languedoc and the count-kings had a more favourable political attitude to the papacy, Catharism was discouraged from gaining a strong hold here. Preachers and refugees did arrive in Catalan lands, but they could not live openly in their faith, for fear of persecution.

By the end of the 1100s the Catholic Church had become a powerful corporation, and it was not about to brook the loss of Languedoc to the heretic Cathars – or **Albigensians**, as they are commonly known. When persuasion failed to convert the heretics or influence the Cathar-protecting lords of Languedoc, and excommunication had little effect, the papacy turned to military force. Although it hardly had a formal army, the papacy could count on the support of powerful multinational monastic organizations such as the Cistercian Order, whose headquarters, Cîteaux, was in northern France, and which was dominated by noble families from the north. These same families, which had been united under the Capetian kings of France, began to look hungrily at the extensive but fragmented lands of the counts to the south. Papal efforts to bring the Cathars back into the fold began as early as 1150, and in 1204 **Raymond VI** of Toulouse was excommunicated for refusing to persecute his Cathar subjects. However, the Albigensians and their lords would not cave in – the papal legate Pierre de Castelnau was murdered at a parley in 1208 – and **Pope Innocent III** called a Crusade, providing the northern nobles with the ideological justification to wage war on Languedoc. They were joined by knights from across Christendom, drawn by the allure of religious redemption and loot.

The campaign was led initially by **Arnaud Amaury**, abbot of Cîteaux, whose campaigns carried him rapidly across the littoral from Nîmes, which gave up without a fight, to Béziers. Here, faced by the refusal of the town's Catholics to give up their Cathar neighbours, he ordered the wholesale slaughter of the town's occupants; some twenty thousand are said to have perished.

At about this time, the ageing Crusader **Simon de Montfort** set his sights on the Cathar lands and, taking up leadership of military operations, embarked on a campaign marked by its terror and efficiency. Carcassonne was taken, and with it **Count Raymond VI**; thereafter Cathar towns and fortresses were besieged one by one, including Lastours, Minerve, Hautpoul, Lavaur, Termes and Puivert. Almost without exception they fell or surrendered, and the unfortunate defenders were executed or mutilated and sent on as blunt warning to the next victims; the only survivors were those on the inaccessible southern border: Quérigut, Peyrepertuse and Montségur.

After a brief exile in England, **Raymond VII** returned to lead a counter attack, calling on the aid of various allies, including his liege-lord **Pere the Catholic**, Count-King of Catalonia-Aragón. Fresh from a decisive victory against Spanish Muslims at Las Navas de Tolosa, Pere went into the field at Muret (14km south of Toulouse) in 1213, but was singled out and killed by de Montfort's men, dealing a grievous blow to Raymond's forces.

It took five more years of fighting to turn the tide against the northern forces, who were deprived of their leader de Montfort (who had assumed the title of Count of Toulouse), when his head was smashed in by a missile outside the walls of Toulouse. His son Arnaud attempted to carry on the campaign, but could not sustain his position and returned to his lands in the north, carrying with him his father's dead body and broken dreams. After this long-drawn-out battle, Raymond had no choice but to make **peace** with the papacy in order to recover his lands, reaffirming his Catholicism and recovering his scarred and battered territories. These he began immediately to fortify, founding strategic strongholds such as Cordes-sur-Ciel.

However, despite Raymond's concessions and preparations, **Occitan independence** was not to last. By the mid-1220s the French king, **Louis VIII**, swelled by victories over the English Crown, turned his own sights south, proclaiming a fresh Crusade against the Occitan Cathars, who continued to live discreetly in Raymond's lands, or openly under the defiant and unconquered barons of the south. This time the exhausted forces of the counts and local nobility could not respond, and after a brief campaign much of Languedoc came under the direct power of the king of France. Louis VIII's aggressive policy was followed up by his heir, Louis IX (later St Louis), who came to the throne in 1226 and finished off the job. With the counts out of the way, the papacy sent in the **Inquisition**, led by the Dominican Order. Their job was to investigate and root out heretics, employing torture if necessary, and urging them to recant before turning them over to the king's forces to execute. Needless to say, they were not popular among the local citizenry, and there was some relief when a band of renegade Cathars sallied out of their stronghold at Montségur in 1242 to **massacre** a band of Inquisitors at Avignonet-Lauragais. The royal reaction was immediate: an army of six thousand was assembled and laid siege to the fortress in 1243. Eight months later, when it fell, the garrison of two hundred was burnt alive. Subsequent mopping-up operations finished with the surrenders of Puilaurens and Quéribus in 1256. Catharism had disappeared as a political force and, confined to secrecy and isolation, was hunted into extinction over the next century.

But royal policy was not wholly destructive in Languedoc, as its aim was not to lay waste to the region but to extinguish possible sources of rebellion and resistance. From the time of de Montfort's death, the kings had worked to re habilitate the area, particularly through the founding of royal **bastides**, such as Revel and Réalmont. These planned and usually fortified towns were set up by royal charter. Ruled by a council, they answered directly to the king rather than to an intermediary noble, and were given privileges such as the right to hold a market. Thus, they strengthened the royal position and, with their liberties and self-determination, helped to boost the economy.

On the fringes of Languedoc, mountainous **Foix**, like Toulouse, had been an independent county since about the time of the Carolingian disintegration. Over the following centuries, it remained isolated, even more than Roussillon, from the modernizing trends which were shaping Languedoc. That said, the counts of Foix were sworn enemies of the French Crown and allied themselves with the Raymonds during the Albigensian Crusade; in the campaigns that followed, the county managed to escape more or less unscathed, and when the French Crown threatened in the 1270s, the ruling house eluded their control by forging a marriage alliance with the neighbouring kingdom of Béarn.

Except for the loss in battle of Count-King Pere, **Roussillon**, too, all but escaped the effects of the Albigensian Crusades. The death of Pere, and the period of uncertainty that followed, when his 5-year-old son, Jaume, was made king, entailed the end of any Catalan-Aragonese pretensions in Provence, so the French Crown had a long breathing period in which to consolidate its power there. Roussillon, however, remained for the moment firmly in the Catalan-Aragonese ambit, and its nobility was drawn towards the campaigns of conquest which the count-kings carried out against their Muslim neighbours (Valencia, Mallorca and Menorca), and Sardinia and Sicily. When **Jaume the Conqueror** died after a 63-year reign, he divided his kingdom between his elder son Pere (who received the mainland holdings south of the Pyrenees) and Jaume, who became **king of Mallorca** and count of Roussillon and Montpellier. Perpignan served as his mainland capital. The kings of Mallorca allied with the French against their Barcelona-based rivals, and in the 1280s Roussillon served as the springboard for the French invasion of Catalonia, launched in retribution for Catalan seizure of French-ruled Sicily.

The Hundred Years' War

Under **Philip le Bel** (1285–1314), France became a superpower. The astute king managed his treasury well, disbanded and appropriated the funds of the wealthy Knights Templar and brought the papacy under his ominous protection in Avignon.

But royal domination of Languedoc brought only short-lived peace and prosperity to the region. Philip's male line had failed, and Edward III of England, Philip's grandson through his daughter, claimed the throne. Edward's family, the Plantagenets, were French in origin, and the language and culture of their court were northern French, but the prospect of Edward taking the throne was highly undesirable to a large section of the French nobility, who stood to see themselves marginalized by such a turn of events. So they invoked (or, rather, invented) the "ancient" French Salic Law, which forbade succession to the throne through the female line, and resisted the English claim. These were the circumstances that provoked the series of conflicts which came to be known as the **Hundred Years' War** – essentially a struggle between two French royal houses.

England took the early advantage, defeating the French at Crécy in 1346 and capturing the French king shortly afterwards. Meanwhile, the king's son, Edward, Prince of Wales (known as the **Black Prince**), was unleashed on Aquitaine and ravaged the Aude valley. These military campaigns coincided with a series of disasters, including **crop failures**, the arrival of the **Black Death** and the Jacquerie peasant uprising. In 1360, a **truce** was called and part of western Languedoc remained under English control until nine years later, when **Charles V** began a campaign which all but expelled the English from France.

Unfortunately, Charles' successor, **Charles VI**, was considered mentally unfit to rule, and a struggle ensued between the dukes of Burgundy and Orléans, who had been entrusted with the care of the realm. The English intervened on the side of the Burgundians, against the Duke of Orléans and his Armagnac allies, and began to reconquer the country. After a series of defeats, including Agincourt in 1415, all seemed lost for the French Crown. It was then that the peasant girl **Joan of Arc** appeared on the scene, and helped to turn the tide against the invaders, claiming divine guidance and rallying the French forces in a campaign to push the English off the mainland. Five years later, **Charles VII** entered Toulouse in triumph; a French king was once again master of Languedoc, and although the reconquest of the former royal territories dragged out over the length of the fifteenth century, France emerged from the struggle as a unified, powerful national kingdom.

In this protracted period of **crisis**, the people of Languedoc coped as best they could. Population decreased, agriculture suffered and traditional industries, such as leather-working, which accounted for the prosperity of the Tarn region, were almost extinguished. However, in the mid-fifteenth century it was discovered that a local plant, **woad**, could be made to yield a fine blue dye, *pastel*, a high-priced luxury commodity much in demand by the fabric industry of the day, thus provoking an economic renaissance which lasted for over a century. Toulouse, still ruled over by a council of burghers, took the lead in this industry. Fortunes were made, fine palaces were raised, and the city's famous university was founded, turning Toulouse into a centre of culture. On the Occitan coast, Montpellier (which had been bought by the French Crown in 1349) was also driven by the growing textile industry and set up its own prestigious university.

As had happened with the Albigensian Crusade, Catalonia was not involved directly in the Hundred Years' War, but it did have to contend with France's relentless efforts to chip away at its holdings north of the Pyrenees, Cerdanya and Rosilló (the **Cerdagne** and **Roussillon**), and through the fourteenth and fifteenth centuries, they were shifted back and forth between the two powers. In 1462, when **Louis XI** mounted a military campaign against Roussillon – seizing it in response to the Catalan-Aragonese capture of French-dominated Naples – Catalonia was on the verge of a major realignment. The marriage of Ferran (Ferdinand) of Aragón and Isabel of Castile in 1469 laid the foundations for the creation of the Kingdom of Spain, and the ultimate submission of Catalonia and its dependencies to Madrid; it thus became a secondary concern, and Roussillon was set further on the periphery.

The rise of Protestantism and the Wars of Religion

Despite the peace which came with re-establishment of a strong monarchy in France under **François I** (1515–47), there was much dissatisfaction in Languedoc and Roussillon. This resentment took two forms: that towards the Church on the part of the people, and that towards the Crown and the northern nobility on the part of local lords and magnates. As had happened in the Cathar period, the interests of these two groups coincided, and even more so after 1483, when the Crown gained direct control over the Church in France. So social and political discontent was once again voiced on religious terms – this time the revolutionary movement was **Protestantism**.

The new faith first arrived in Haut Languedoc close on the heels of **Martin Luther**'s defiance of Church authority in 1519. However, French Protestantism, or the **Huguenot** movement (named after an obscure Swiss political event), tended to follow the teachings of **John Calvin** (Jean Cauvin), which had a clearer political message. Calvin had studied theology at the conservative University of Paris and had been swept up in the wave of reforming theology which very quickly provoked a clampdown by the religious and royal authorities. He fled into exile in Geneva, which became a hotbed for the Protestant creed that he formulated. His beliefs focused on the omnipotence of God and predestination, denying hierarchies and earthly elites and concentrating on hard work and pastoralism – a recipe for success among the artisanal classes – and it spread like wildfire in Paris and through Occitania.

By 1559, **Calvinism** was established as a religion and organization in France, and had the support of some of the kingdom's greatest noble houses, despite the persecution which had been carried out by François I's son Henri II. When Henri died (in an accident allegedly presaged by Nostradamus), the succession of two weak child-kings gave the rival **noble factions** led by the Protestant Bourbons and the

Catholic Guises the opportunity to battle for control of the realm. Forty years of bloody and relentless civil war followed, of which the most notorious episode is the **St Bartholemew's Day massacre** of 1572, in which the Protestant elite, who had come to Paris for a royal wedding, were ambushed. A nationwide campaign against Protestants ensued, during which some 20,000 were killed. The violence was not all one-sided, however: the Calvinists committed atrocities as well, among them the murder of Nîmes' Catholic clergy in the **Michelade massacre** (1567).

The wars were finally concluded by the victory of Henri, King of Béarn (or Navarre, and a successor of Gaston Fébus of Foix), the leader of the Protestant faction. It was, however, politically impossible for him to become king as a Huguenot, so having decided that "Paris is worth a Mass", he converted and was crowned as **Henri IV** of France in 1593. Thanks to his accession, Foix was incorporated into the French realm. Six years later, he proclaimed the **Edict of Nantes**, which granted political and religious freedom to the Hugenots and the right to maintain certain fortified strongholds.

Although most of Languedoc had been ruled by the Catholic Guises, its population was strongly Protestant. Castres became a "protected zone" for Huguenots, and home to one of the four **courts** empowered to mediate legal disputes between Catholics and Protestants. In Nîmes, some three quarters of the population converted to Calvinism, while Montpellier was home to the Protestant Theological Institute. In the east, most of the towns – mainly herding and textile centres – were firmly Huguenot but, despite regional imbalances, the new pluralistic French society seemed to function well.

The Age of Absolutism

The liberal vision of Henri IV was not to last, however. When he was assassinated by a Catholic reactionary, his year-old son **Louis XIII** came to the throne under the strict control of his staunchly Catholic mother, Marie de Medici. In 1624, that supreme Machiavellian **Cardinal Richelieu** managed to wrest control from the queen. Richelieu made it his mission to establish France as an absolutist Catholic state, and for almost two decades he was the sole power behind the Crown. He immediately set about stripping the towns and cities of their defensive walls (to prevent revolt) and then began reducing Protestant strongholds. He also adopted an aggressive foreign policy, attacking France's neighbours and taking Roussillon. But his heavy-handedness provoked reaction at home. In 1622, the Protestant Duke of Rohan raised a **revolt** in the Cévennes (just north of Hérault) and although after seven years of fighting he was forced to make a settlement with Richelieu which stripped the Huguenots of political power, he maintained their freedom to worship.

Heavily Protestant Languedoc was not pacified, however, and shortly thereafter its royal governor, **Henri de Montmorency**, raised a revolt against Richelieu which spanned the region from Nîmes to Toulouse. He was no match for the cardinal, who defeated him in battle at Castelnaudary in 1632 and led him off to be beheaded on the place du Capitole in Toulouse. The vindictive Richelieu then exacted revenge on Henri's heirs by transferring the title of First Duchy of France from the house of Montmorency to the loyally Catholic dukes of Uzès.

In 1643, the "Sun King" and supreme absolutist **Louis XIV** came to the throne. Continuing the centralizing policies initiated by Richelieu, he hamstrung the French nobility by obliging them to take up residence at his palace in Versailles and to participate in its expensive and regimented court life. His megalomaniac tendencies ("I am the state") led him to embark on a series of costly and ultimately disastrous military adventures, the successful episodes of which are recorded on the Roman-style monuments, such as the equestrian statue and triumphal arch of Montpellier, which he erected to commemorate his grandeur. He waged **war** in Flanders, Germany and Spain, managing to secure the permanent annexation of the Cerdagne and Roussillon with the **Treaty of the Pyrenees** in 1659.

The able management of his successive prime ministers, Mazarin and Colbert, managed to preserve the kingdom from financial ruin, and it was Colbert who gave the green light to Riquet's visionary project of linking the Atlantic and Mediterranean by canal. The main channel of the **Canal du Midi**, which stretched from Toulouse to Agde, was opened in 1666, sparking an economic recovery in the region, which had languished in depression since the wane in demand for the local *pastel* dye (thanks to the discovery of cheaper alternatives in the Indies); the canal allowed locally grown grain to be shipped to distant markets. But on the whole, Louis' reign was not a happy one for Languedoc and Roussillon. In 1674, the **Catalans** rose up against French rule, which they found even more oppressive than that of the Spanish Habsburgs, against whom they had risen a generation earlier. The **uprising** was brutally crushed, and its leaders imprisoned and executed in Perpignan.

A decade later, Louis moved against the Protestants by issuing a **Revocation of the Edict of Nantes** (1685), which deprived the Huguenots of their rights and outlawed their religion. Half a million Protestants chose to flee the country, including many merchants and textile workers, dealing a grievous blow to the industry on which the prosperity of eastern Languedoc depended. Those who remained were subjected to **oppression**; they were spied on and hounded, forced to carry on their services in secret and brook the humiliation of having soldiers billeted in their homes. Intransigent Protestants were imprisoned, among them Marie Durand, locked up for over thirty years in a tower in Aigues-Mortes. Some feigned conversion, some were deported to the colonies, and others fled to the "desert" – the wild and isolated hills of the Cévennes. It was here that they rose again in protest, in what is known as the **Camisard revolt**. The spark came in July 1702 when the parish priest of Chayla arrested and detained a small group of fugitive Protestants. A group of villagers stormed the castle to free them and in the course of the struggle the priest was killed. Knowing that retribution would be swift and cruel, Protestants across the Cévennes (mostly refugees from Languedoc proper) began a guerrilla war which pitted their forces, numbering between three and five thousand, against some thirty thousand royal troops. The shirts they wore as a sign of recognition earned them the popular name of Camisards (from *chemise*, French for "shirt"). Battles raged across the region, with one of the greatest confrontations taking place at **St-Hippolyte**. The guerrillas and civilian population took refuge where they could, hiding in the remote hills or in caverns, like the Grotte des Demoiselles, south of Ganges.

In the course of the struggle two leaders emerged: the aristocratic **Jean Cavalier**, and the commoner **Roland**. Unable to conclude the struggle militarily, the French commander Villars began to negotiate with Cavalier at Nîmes, offering him the rank of colonel, command of a Protestant legion which would fight for the French abroad, and a hefty annual salary in exchange for submission. Cavalier accepted, greatly undermining the uprising. The former leader left France and served the English, eventually being named governor of Jersey. Roland continued the struggle, but later the same year was killed in battle, bringing an end to the revolt.

In the century or so before the Camisards episode, Languedoc had been tamed into discontented submission by France, ruled by the princes of Conti, members of the ruling Bourbon family, since the defeat of Montmorency. Pézenas, which had been the region's capital since the 1450s, became a paler southern Versailles, especially in the 1650s when **Armand de Bourbon** lavished his patronage on the town, playing host for a time to the playwright Molière and his company.

The absorption of Roussillon, while it aggrandized France, struck a blow against the towns of the Aude valley, which up until then had enjoyed a trade-based prosperity thanks to their position on the Spanish frontier. As part of Madrid's empire, in which Church institutions like the Inquisition kept a very tight lid on any potential sources of dissent or heterodoxy, Protestantism was basically unknown in Roussillon during its efflorescence, and by the time of the region's annexation, it was virtually a spent force.

The Revolution

Languedoc and Roussillon were not the only areas which chafed against the Sun King's absolutism. As the **economic crisis** deepened, taxes were driven up, forcing the masses of the kingdom, the *sans-culottes* ("trouserless"), into an ever more desperate state of poverty. A series of bad harvests compounded the problem, and indebted smallholders had their lands repossessed and were reduced to penury and near-servitude. In order to gather the revenue which was necessary to maintain the court, fund expensive military adventures and service the spiralling national debt, the ruling class resorted to **tax-farming**. Speculators paid the Crown a set sum upfront and were then free to extract as much as they could from the area under their control. This excluded most of the nobility, many of whom enjoyed hereditary exemptions, and the largest single land-holder, the Church, which paid no royal taxes and continued to collect its own. At the same time, the Crown's growing obsession with control bred a fear of rebellion, which became self-fulfilling. Law was completely subverted to royal authority, and suspected troublemakers were imprisoned indefinitely without charges, by writ of the feared letters of cachet, or orders of detention.

These **dictatorial** tendencies worsened over the course of the eighteenth century, as Louis XIV's successors continued his absolutist style of ruling and his disastrous policy of foreign intervention. **Louis XV** (1715–74) carried France into the Polish and Austrian Wars of Succession and the Seven Years' War, as a result of which the kingdom lost all of its colonies. Ironically, the king also encouraged the extraordinary literary and philosophical blossoming, in which Voltaire and Rousseau figured, among others, and which laid the ideological foundations for the Revolution that was shortly to follow.

Poor grain harvests continued after Louis XV's death in 1774, provoking riots and unrest. Royal finance ministers attempted to institute reforms, but to little avail. In Languedoc, the new king Louis XVI's conciliatory policies were chiefly noted in the form of the **Edict of Toleration** (1787), which was aimed at diffusing the rebelliousness of the Protestants by restoring their rights and liberties. The situation was such that the king was forced in 1789 to summon the Estates General (the equivalent of parliament) for the first time in nearly two centuries. The newly constituted Third Estate, made up of commoners, who for the first time joined the nobility and clergy in government, called for the formation of a National Assembly.

When in the months that followed the country rose in **revolution**, Languedoc and Roussillon were solidly Jacobin (revolutionary). Even Montpellier, at that time a wealthy bastion of Catholicism and cotton lords, could not resist. In 1791, the French Republic was declared and as southern troop levies marched towards the capital, a young medical student from Montpellier composed the "War Song of the Army of the Rhine", better known as **La Marseillaise**, which was adopted eventually as the national anthem. The Revolution was a focus for the discontentment of diverse groups in the south: the Protestants, the poor, the Occitans and the local magnates, all of whom had a bone to pick with Paris or the monarchy. But although the monarchy fell, Paris persevered, emerging as the capital of a sharply centralized and thoroughly French state.

The short and bloody revolutionary experiment was centred in Paris, and Languedoc felt its influence chiefly in the administrative novelties which were introduced, the most durable of which was the division of the region (as with the rest of the country) into administrative **départements**. The rationalist (and centralist) policies of the new government ensured a break with historical traditions in defining these areas. They were based on geography, for the most part on the major river valleys. Roussillon became the culturally neutral Pyrénées-Orientales.

The Napoleonic era and the nineteenth-century republics

The rise of revolutionary France did not, however, bring about a change in foreign policy, which remained aggressive. The **armies** of the Republic, among whose leaders figured a young **Napoleon Bonaparte**, lashed out against their neighbours on all sides. Back at home, power had devolved to a five-member **Directory**, whose heavy-handed governance was met with growing resentment by the populace. When Bonaparte returned from his defeat by the British in Egypt, he set a coup d'état in motion, which saw him elevated initially, in 1799, to First Consul, and subsequently, to **Emperor**. His campaign of European domination brought him up against practically every other power in Europe and, after initial successes in Germany and Spain, his campaign in Russia brought about the decimation of his Grand Army and his ultimate ruin.

Although most of the Napoleonic Wars took place on foreign soil, Languedoc was to feel the sting of the emperor's defeat. **Wellington**'s British expeditionary force, which had been sent to aid Spain and Portugal, pushed its way across the peninsula and dealt the French a severe defeat at Toulouse in 1814.

For the next forty years France and Languedoc returned to monarchy, with the reigns first of the Bourbon **Louis XVIII** (1814–24) and **Charles X** (1824–30), and then **Louis-Philippe** (1830–48) of the house of Orléans. The Bourbons, who had obviously learnt nothing from previous experience, immediately embarked on a heavy-handed Catholic-oriented policy, and were brought down by popular revolution in 1830. The throne was then taken by Louis-Philippe, the candidate of the middle-class elite, a commercial nobility no less despised than their aristocratic forebears. He was unseated in the **revolution of 1848**, European socialism's *annus mirabilis*, which saw uprisings in capitals across the continent. But the Second Republic quickly gave way to the **Second Empire**, when Bonaparte's crafty nephew gained the throne as **Napoleon III** in 1852. Protests followed his seizure of power, such as the one in Béziers, where troops opened fire on a crowd of republican demonstrators led by the town mayor. As a tactician, Napoleon III proved as unsuccessful as his namesake, first embroiling the country in the bitter Crimean War, and then in 1870 provoking the ignominious **Franco-Prussian War**, which saw his own capture and the subsequent German siege of Paris.

Although Roussillon continued to drift in agrarian poverty, Languedoc weathered all these events with some measure of good fortune. While the bulk of the population suffered in poverty, the **textile industry**, based on wool and cotton and later on silk, boomed. The herds of the uplands of the Cévennes and Haut Languedoc were the chief source of raw material, and the fast-flowing rivers provided the energy to run the newly mechanized factories. All along the fringe of the mountains, towns which had up to then been insignificant villages – Castres, Mazamet, Ganges, St-Hippolyte – enjoyed unprecedented good fortune. As coal was discovered, new industries, such as **mining** and **glass-making** (at Albi and Carmaux), sprang up, and when the railways arrived in the middle of the century, the towns along their route benefited additionally from better access to distribution networks. Of course, this good fortune tended to remain in the hands of a relative few – the factory owners and merchants – and this fact contributed to the popularity of egalitarian and **socialist ideologies** among the masses of the region.

The era of the **Third Republic**, which followed France's defeat at the hands of the Prussians, was one of introspection, not least because of the massive war indemnities which the state was forced to pay. Socialists were scapegoated, and there were mass executions at the hands of the new reactionary regime: in excess of twenty thousand were killed in Paris alone. Nor was all well in Languedoc and Roussillon, as outside the industrial areas the people of the countryside still eked out only the most meagre of livings. Many left, frequently for Paris, compounding the capital's social and economic problems. The new, modern **wine industry** which had developed along the littoral provided a seasonal source of income for many, and stimulated related industries, such as bottle-, cork- and barrel-making, but in 1875 the vineyards were decimated by phylloxera. This was followed by a second epidemic which attacked mulberry trees, the silkworm's staple food, precipitating a crisis in the silk industry.

A marked tendency towards the Left continued to colour local politics, partially fuelled by resentment towards remote and indifferent Paris. These political trends were personified in **Jean Jaurès**. Born in Castres, he was drawn to Paris as a brilliant student but later returned to his home region of Tarn. Here he entered politics and embarked on a series of labour-oriented campaigns, helping to organize miners' unions, and setting up co-operative, worker-run factories. He joined other liberals in defending **Alfred Dreyfus**, a Jewish army officer wrongly convicted of espionage in 1898, and founded the communist newspaper *L'Humanité* in 1904 and a new socialist party in 1905. Speaking out against the anti-German nationalist hysteria that gripped the country in the years leading up to World War I, he paid with his life, assassinated by a nationalist in 1914.

However, popular politics in Languedoc and Roussillon were not divided strictly across ideological lines, as the cross-class solidarity of the **wine revolts** would show. As the wine industry recovered in the last years of the nineteenth century from the blow dealt by disease, it received further setbacks. A series of abundant harvests drove down the price of grapes, and the combination of competition from cheap Algerian vintages and a law permitting sugar to be added during fermenta-tion (reducing the amount of grape pulp required) decreased demand. Wages plummeted and unemployment rose. Led by the innkeeper, Marcellin Albert, half a million protesters turned out in Montpellier in 1907, and similar numbers rose up in other wine towns, like Béziers and Narbonne. People across the class spectrum depended on the wine industry, so the uprising had the character of a regional revolt. The interior minister, Georges Clémenceau, responded by sending in the troops, but the locally levied 17th Infantry Regiment sympathized with their countrymen and mutinied. They were packed off to Tunisia in short order, and troops from the north were sent in to quell the "Midi madness". In the confrontations between army and civilians, shots were fired and there were some casualties, but the episode served to instigate the creation of a regional wine board to manage prices and quality and to bring stability to the industry.

The two world wars

In 1914, the diplomatic strain between Europe's uniformly conservative powers finally snapped, and the **assassination** of the Austrian Archduke Ferdinand at the hands of a Serbian nationalist in Sarajevo led to a diplomatic chain reaction which brought about **World War I**. The French were particularly anxious for revenge for their recent defeat at the hands of Prussia, which had deprived them of the Rhenish provinces of Alsace and Lorraine. After an initial German advance, both sides settled in for a long-drawn-out campaign of near-static trench warfare, along a 400km front stretching roughly from the Swiss border to Ostend, which was to last four years.

On the "Western Front" France (with allies Britain and eventually the US) and Germany ground away at each other in the first modern mechanized war; over its course the front shifted almost imperceptibly, but an exhausted Germany surrendered in 1918. France paid a high price for its eventual victory – almost one and a half million dead. Although none of the fighting took place in Languedoc and Roussillon, the **cenotaphs** which mark the centre of every hamlet and village bear dramatic testimony to the price they paid in the struggle.

Languedoc and Roussillon limped through the 1920s and 1930s, suffering along with the rest of Europe in the postwar **flu epidemic** (which claimed more lives than the war) and the **Great Depression**. Weak postwar democracies arose in Italy and Germany and were quickly replaced by dictatorial fascist regimes, and a prelude of the struggle to come took place in Spain, where General Franco's attempted coup set in motion a civil war in 1936. The bitter struggle, from which France – along with the rest of the Allies – remained aloof and uncommitted, lasted until 1939. As fascist troops took over Catalonia and the Basque country, tens of thousands of **refugees** poured over the border, the Catalans arriving initially in Roussillon.

A few months later, German soldiers stormed over the Polish border, initiating **World War II**. The following year they circumvented France's defensive white elephant, the Maginot line, and arrived in Paris in June. For the first time in seven hundred years Languedoc and Roussillon found themselves independent of Paris as they were incorporated into the puppet **Vichy Republic**, which enjoyed a fictitious independence under the World War I hero turned traitor, **Henri Pétain**. He collaborated with the **Nazis**, facilitating the repression of their opponents, the deportation of "undesirable elements" and the wholesale transportation of southern French citizens to labour camps and factories in Germany.

In 1942, the Germans decided to dispense with even the illusion of autonomy in the South and brought the whole region under their direct control. Repression was intensified, but the local guerrilla **resistance**, the **Maquis**, benefited from a stiffened resolve on the part of the populace. Across France as a whole there were about as many active collaborators with Nazi rule as resisters, but Resistance activity in Languedoc and Roussillon was considerable, the efforts of local companies like the famed Maquis Bir Hakeim of Haut Languedoc, or of individuals like Jean Mance of Béziers, who founded the National Committee for Resistance, proving a significant element in the war. In their mountain redoubts in the Pyrenees and Cévennes and in the hills of Haut Languedoc, they withstood German air attacks and pacification missions, while the civilian population suffered direct reprisals for their collusion with the rebels. In the Cerdagne and Roussillon, clandestine *passeurs*, motivated by either ideals or profit (or a combination of the two), helped to slip people and contraband back and forth over the frontier with neutral Spain.

From 1943 on, the disasters of the Russian campaign focused German manpower in the east, and with the **allied invasions** of Italy in 1943 and Normandy in 1944, the undergunned Maquis finally had a chance, and began to mount an open military campaign. The first towns which they managed to recover were mere mountain hamlets, like Mourèze, near Clermont-l'Hérault, but when the Germans sent a column of three thousand troops to retake the upper Hérault, they were fended off after a fierce day-long battle with the local Resistance. Memorial plaques which pepper the streets of Toulouse and other major towns recall the Maquis who fell in the widespread **street-fighting** of 1944. By the end of that year, France had been liberated.

Recent history

In the postwar **Fourth Republic** France endeavoured to recover from the damage wrought by four years of occupation and two invasions. Europe's colonial age was coming to an end and for France this signalled nationalist revolts in Indochina and Algeria. In Languedoc and Roussillon, the wine industry recovered and mining continued, but with the advent of cheaper synthetic fibres, the textile industry all but disappeared. **Poverty** and **depopulation** continued and served to channel political consciousness ever more to the Left.

Former general and self-proclaimed liberator of France **Charles de Gaulle's** conservative **Fifth Republic**, which came in 1958 on the heels of France's entry into the new European Common Market, gradually became something of a dictatorship. In the South, certain progressive economic policies were embarked upon, including the construction of **reservoirs** and **hydroelectric facilities** and the articulation of a region-wide irrigation plan.

Meanwhile in **Algeria**, native unrest led to open rebellion, and when de Gaulle reacted by announcing the abandonment of the **colony**, the *pieds-noirs* (so-called by the natives for their custom of wearing shoes) – the French population who had ruled it since 1830 – felt betrayed and carried out a brief armed resistance. With the **Accord of Évian** (1962), they agreed to be settled, along with the **harkis**, their native Algerian allies, in Languedoc. The influx of this population – a largely educated and skilled workforce – gave new life to the cities of the coast (notably Montpellier, Narbonne and Perpignan), although the welcome which the *harkis* received was hardly warm. Forty years later, they continue to protest the official neglect to which they have been subject.

The **Student Revolution** of 1968 presaged the departure of de Gaulle, who resigned in 1969 after a failed attempt to widen his already broad powers by popular referendum. The unrest of that summer also heralded an era of openly **left-wing politics** in Languedoc and Roussillon. In the elections of the years that followed, Languedoc voted massively in favour of the socialists and communists, encouraged by the areas' traditional economic marginalism and an antipathy to the conservative north.

The nation, however, remained under **conservative rule** through the presidencies of Georges Pompidou (1969–74) and Valéry Giscard d'Estaing (1974–81). In this era of baby boom and general prosperity, the infrastructure of Languedoc and Roussillon was improved by the construction of *autoroutes* and the improvement of roads. The **tourist industry** also received stimulus through the revitalization of the abandoned Canal du Midi and the creation of regional parks, such as that of Haut Languedoc. The area still retains a shadow of its former textile industry, but manufacturing has been dominated in the west by the high-profile **aviation industry**, based in Toulouse. The city had been a pioneer of flight since before the days of St-Exupéry, and served as a hub for Africa and South America between the wars. It was here that the Concorde was first tested, and the European joint-venture Airbus Industries was founded.

Despite these recent successes, the region remains underpopulated and relatively poor, and *départements* such as Aude, Ariège and significant parts of Hérault are now actively stimulating tourism as a way of bringing investment and employment. Whether as a result of these efforts, or as a consequence of overcrowding and rising prices in traditional Anglo destinations like the Dordogne, British travellers and property investors have moved into Languedoc and Roussillon, both as a holiday destination and as somewhere to set up home.

As the French population ages, waves of northern retirees are heading south to the affordable property and agreeable climes of Languedoc and Roussillon – a trend which is seen with a jaundiced eye by many natives, who perceive in it a modern reprise of the invasions of the past. Some also see the massive influx of North African immigrants from France's former colonies and protectorates as an invasion, and this has served to divert part of the traditional extreme Left vote, paradoxically, to the **extreme Right**. The 1995 municipal elections gave a surprisingly high return to the parties of the far Right, dominated then by Jean-Marie Le Pen's racist **Front National**. It is not without irony that Roussillon's "Perpignan la Catalane" should be ruled by an extremist French mayor. At the *région* level, the Right scored well in the 1998 elections; the UDF–FDR coalition's (President Chirac's power base) 22 seats added to the FN's thirteen made for a narrow majority over the 31 seats won by the socialists and resurgent communists.

As parties geared up for the 2002 elections, it appeared that the region would return to its traditional socialist orientation, with the FN splintered and the **Chirac government** discredited by an influence-peddling **scandal** involving government contracts which seemed to point at the president's office. Few were prepared for what was to come. The first electoral round was met with record voter apathy and abstention, particularly among socialist voters. This knocked out Jospin's party from the race and catapulted Le Pen into second position. In a typical irony of politics, leftist voters came out for the second round and voted in Chirac, seen as the lesser of two evils.

The social negligence born out of the elitism of Chirac's right and of the French political class in general was dramatically demonstrated in November 2005, when the death of two youths of North African descent while being pursued by police in a Paris ghetto ignited nationwide riots. Government arrogance fuelled the indignant desperation of France's marginalized Maghrebian youth – assimilated but unaccepted by the national mainstream. Then-President of the Hauts-de-Seine *département*, **Nicholas Sarkozy**, disdainfully dismissed the rioters as *racaille* ("scum"), adding further fuel to the fire. The *banlieues* of Paris erupted, and as the evening news broadcast images of burning cars and clashes with police, unrest spread across the country and to Languedoc, most notably to Toulouse. By early 2006 tensions had calmed and attention focussed increasingly on the upcoming presidential elections. In the April 2007 election, right-of-centre Nicholas Sarkozy succeeded in trouncing the internally fractured socialists, and neutralizing the far-Right racist parties by leaning in their direction on certain issues. In Languedoc and Roussillon, the affluent coastal areas tended to support the conservative candidate, while the struggling interior was largely socialist. This trend was reflected by the election in 2008 of a socialist to the *mairie* of Toulouse (the first in a half-century). The other municipal elections reflected little change, with Perpignan and Nîmes remaining to the right and Montpellier to the left.

Unlike some of France's other regions, such as Corsica, Alsace, the Pays Basque and Brittany, the issues of a distinctive **language** and **identity** do not seem to have made their way into the political dialogue of either Languedoc or Roussillon. For all the resentment these regions may feel towards Paris, and despite the survival or revival of their native tongues, there is no doubt among the people of the region that their future lies within France. It is perhaps this confidence that led a member of the governing UMP to amend Article 1 of the French Constitution to recognize "regional languages" as "part of the cultural heritage" – the first such concession in the history of France.

Books

Most of the books listed below are in print and in paperback – those that are out of print (o/p) should be easy to track down either in second-hand bookshops or through Amazon's used and secondhand book service (🅦 www.amazon.com). Note that while we recommend all the books listed below, we do have our favourites and these have been marked with a 🎄 symbol.

History

General

CONTEXTS | Books

🎄 **Alfred Cobban** *A History of Modern France* (3 volumes: 1715–99, 1799–1871 and 1871–1962). Complete and very readable account of the main political, social and economic strands in French history, from the death of Louis XIV to mid-de Gaulle.

Colin Jones *The Cambridge Illustrated History of France* (o/p). A political and social history of France from prehistoric times to the mid-1990s, concentrating on issues of regionalism, gender, race and class. Good illustrations and a friendly, non-academic writing style.

The Middle Ages

🎄 **Natalie Zemon Davis** *The Return of Martin Guerre*. A vivid account of peasant life in the sixteenth century Pyrenean village of Artigat. The return of a long-lost villager sparks a sensational and gripping courtroom drama.

🎄 **Emmanuel Le Roy Ladurie** *Montaillou*. Village gossip of who's sleeping with whom, tales of trips to Spain and details of work, all extracted by the Inquisition from Cathar peasants of the eastern Pyrenees in the fourteenth century.

Stephen O'Shea *The Perfect Heresy*. Lively but partisan, nonacademic account of the history of the Cathar Church and faith, and the Catholic campaign mounted to wipe it out.

Linda M. Paterson *The World of the Troubadours: Medieval Occitan Society,*

c.1100–1300. Scholarly but clear survey of medieval Occitan culture and society.

Mark Pegg *The Corruption of Angels: The Great Inquisition of 1245–1246*. An intimate look at the lives of peasants, townsmen and nobles of the Lauragais seen through the eyes of the Cathar-hunting Inquisition.

Jonathan Sumption *The Albigensian Crusade*. Concise but eloquent portrayal of the Albigensian Crusades from the beginnings of the Cathar movement through to the fall of Montségur.

René Weiss *The Yellow Cross: The Story of the Last Cathars, 1290–1329*. Lively historical detective work built on the same sources as Montaillou. An energetic, engaging read, not overly academic in tone.

The Wars of Religion

Joseph and Francis Bergin *The Rise of Richelieu.* An interesting look at Richelieu's rise to power, presenting the cardinal as a complex Machiavellian figure, who was not without his convictions.

Mack Holt *The French Wars of Religion, 1562–1629.* A recent survey of the whole period of the Wars of Religion.

Felix Platter *Beloved Son Felix* (o/p). Fascinating diary of a young Swiss man who sets out to study medicine in sixteenth-century Montpellier.

Eighteenth and nineteenth centuries

Anthony Crubaugh *Balancing the Scales of Justice: Local Courts and Rural Society in Southwest France, 1750–1800.* Engaging new academic study of local court documents, revealing the subtleties of peasant life in Languedoc in the era of the Revolution.

Norman Hampson *A Social History of the French Revolution.* An analysis that concentrates on the personalities involved, with particular emphasis on the *sans-culottes*.

Christopher Hibbert *The Days of the French Revolution.* Well-paced and entertaining narrative treatment by a master historian.

J.M. Thompson *The French Revolution.* A detailed and passionate account, first published in 1943, but still the classic depiction in English.

Twentieth century

H.R. Kedward *In Search of the Maquis: Rural Resistance in South France 1942–1944.* Dry, but full of fascinating details about the brave struggles of the countless ordinary people across France who fought to drive the Germans from their country.

Barbara Tuchman *The Proud Tower.* A portrait of England, France, the US, Germany and Russia in the years 1890–1914. It includes a superb chapter on the extraordinary passions and enmities aroused by the Dreyfus Affair, and on the socialist movement in the run-up to World War I, centring on the life of Jean Jaurès.

Paul Webster *Pétain's Crime: The Full Story of French Collaboration in the Holocaust.* The alarming story of the Vichy regime's collaboration with the Holocaust, and the bravery of those, especially the communist resistance, who attempted to prevent it.

Alexander Worth *France 1940–1955* (o/p). Emotionally engaged portrayal of the taboo Occupation period in French history, followed by the Cold War and colonial struggle, years in which the same political tensions and heart-searching were at play.

Society and politics

Jose Bové *The World is Not for Sale: Farmers Against Junkfood*. A manifesto by the US-raised self-proclaimed saviour of French ecology and cuisine.

Bernard Henri-Lévy *Adventures on the Freedom Road: The French Intellectuals in the 20th Century*. Clever and complex essays by the contemporary philosopher-celebrity, mercilessly analyzing the response of great French thinkers to the key events of the century. Easy to dip into, surprisingly readable and very provocative.

Ian Ousby *Occupation: The Ordeal of France 1940–1945*. Nonacademic book which reflects the recent trend to deflate the myth of massive resistance to the Nazis. Examines the development of the Resistance and the counterweight of collaboration.

David Thomson *Democracy in France Since 1870*. An inquiry into why a country with such a strong socialist tradition should have had so many reactionary governments.

Art and architecture

John Berger *The Success and Failure of Picasso*. Although most strongly associated with Provence, Picasso was also influenced by and influenced Roussillonais artists. Perhaps the best one-volume study of Picasso in English.

Kenneth J. Conant *Carolingian and Romanesque Architecture, 800–1200*. Good European study with a focus on Cluny and the St-Jacques pilgrim route, which includes strong coverage of the sections through Languedoc.

Julia Bloch Frey *Toulouse-Lautrec: A Life*. An intimate look at the life of the painter, with emphasis on his friends, family, and artistic contemporaries.

Walter F. Friedlaender *David to Delacroix* (o/p). Respected survey of French art from the late seventeenth to late nineteenth centuries, from Neoclassicism through to Romanticism, and including figures who were influential in Languedoc and Roussillon.

John Golding *Cubism: A History and an Analysis 1907–1914* (o/p). Excellent work on the formative stages of Cubism, particularly relevant for a journey to Céret.

Sarah Whitfield *Fauvism*. A survey of the movement, accompanied by colour plates, emphasizing the major figure of Matisse, but with good material on Maillol and lesser-known artists.

Regional literature

Anonymous *Aucassin et Nicolette*. Dating from the fourteenth century, perhaps the first European musical play. Recounts the impossible love between a prince of Beaucaire and a former Muslim slave-girl in Tarascon.

Michael Baigent, et al. *Holy Blood, Holy Grail*. Learn what happened to the Holy Grail, how Jesus didn't die on the cross, how the Knights Templars are a force to be reckoned with and how Rennes-le-Château is the key.

Alessandro Barrico *Silk*. Sensual love story set in the aftermath of the silk crisis of nineteenth-century Languedoc.

Sophie Burnham *The Treasure of Montségur: A Novel of Cathars*. A thirteenth-century bodice-ripper in which Cathar Jeanne recounts her sex-tinged heretical past to a Catholic lover.

Julius Caesar *The Gallic War*. A highly subjective but majestically written account of the Roman experience in France.

Charmaine Craig *The Good Men: A Novel of Heresy*. Another bodice-ripping tale of heretical lust and unrequited love set in fourteenth-century Montaillou.

Alphonse Daudet *In the Land of Pain*. Memoirs and notes which chart the nineteenth-century Beaucaire author's descent into the latter, fatal stages of syphilis.

Lawrence Durrell *Spirit of Place: Letters and Essays on Travel*. A collection of letters to friends and contemporaries, including T.S. Eliot, written during Durrell's retirement in Sommières.

André Gide *If It Die…An Autobiography*. Gide's spiritual autobiography, sensual and introspective, including his time spent in Uzès.

Arthur Guirdham *Cathars & Reincarnation*. In this non fiction study an English schoolgirl is allegedly hypnotically induced to recall her past life as a Cathar.

Christopher Hope *Signs of the Heart: Love and Death in Languedoc*. Award-winning South African-born novelist writes about his life in Languedoc – a playground for effetely complacent if ill-at-ease ex pats.

Patrick Moon *Virgile's Vineyard: A Year in the Languedoc Wine Country*. In this light memoir Patrick Moon struggles to rehabilitate the dilapidated farm and vineyard he has inherited in Languedoc, accomplishing it with the help of a young local wine-maker. In the sequel, *Arrazat's Aubergines: Inside a Languedoc Kitchen*, he takes on the cuisine.

Angela Murrils & Peter Matthews *Hot Sun, Cool Shadow: Savouring the Food, History and Mystery of the Languedoc*. A food writer and illustrator travel Languedoc in search of wine, fine local cuisine, interesting characters and the surroundings that inspired so many artists.

Zoé Oldenbourg *Destiny of Fire*. Historical novel set in the age of the Albigensian Crusade, written by a respected French historian.

Gaston Phébus *The Hunting Book of Gaston Phébus*. Beautifully illuminated facsimile edition of a 1405 manuscript of the Count of Foix's hunting manual.

Antoine de Saint-Exupéry *Night Flight*. The Toulousain aviator and author of *The Little Prince* recounts in novel format the dangers and exhilaration of flying the southern Atlantic route in the 1920s and 30s.

Janet Shirley *Song of the Cathar Wars*. Translation of two contemporary accounts of the Cathar wars of 1204–1218, written by a Crusade supporter and an Occitan sympathizer.

Gustaf Sobin *Luminous Debris: Reflecting on Vestige in Provence and Languedoc*. Sixteen essays stroll poetically through the distant past of Southern France.

Helen Stevenson *Instructions for Visitors: Life and Love in a French Town*. In her memoir this novelist, freshly divorced and searching for a new life, sets up in rural Languedoc, and finds love (or at least sex) – but not without complications.

Robert Louis Stevenson *Travels With a Donkey in the Cévennes*. Traveller, spy and author, Robert Louis Stevenson tours Camisard country in the mid-nineteenth century, reflecting on the land and people of upland Languedoc.

Paul Thorpe *The Standing Pool*. In this suspense novel two Cambridge academics take their young child on sabbatical for a year to Languedoc. The house they have rented seems

idyllic, but soon sinister elements begin to appear…

Paul Valéry *Selected Writings*. A good introduction for English-speakers to the thoughts and writing of the Sètois Symbolist.

Travel books and guides

Jenny Baker *Simple French Cuisine: From Provence and Languedoc*. Comprehensive guide to southern French cooking with easy-to-follow recipes arranged thematically.

Sabine Baring-Gould *In Troubadour-Land: A Ramble in Provence and Languedoc*. A very British, late nineteenth-century aristocratic ramble through the French south, offering an interesting perspective of the region under the Third Republic.

James Bromwich *The Roman Remains of Southern France*. The only comprehensive guide on the subject – detailed, well illustrated and approachable. In addition to accounts of the famous sites, it will lead you off the map to little-known discoveries.

Glynn Christian *Edible France*. A guide to food rather than restaurants, concentrating on regional produce, local specialities, markets and the best shops for buying goodies to bring back home.

Cicerone Walking Guides. Neat, durable guides, with detailed route descriptions. Titles include *Cycling the Canal du Midi*; *Walking in the Languedoc*; *The Way of St James*; *The GR10*; *Coast to Coast through the French Pyrénées*; and *Walks and Climbs in the Pyrénées*.

Henry Cleere *Southern France*. Written by a true expert, this

gives detailed information and background on 34 archeological sites, famous and obscure.

Nina Epton *The Valley of Pyrene* (o/p). Lively 1950s-era memoir of a tour through Ariège, peppered with entertaining anecdotes.

Barbara J. Euser *Floating Through France: Life Between Locks on the Canal du Midi*. A collection of poems and essays inspired by the Canal du Midi; perfect reading as you float along.

David Everett *Buying and Restoring Old Property in France*. Recently updated, this is the classic reference book for *émigrés* and home-buyers.

Footpaths of Europe *Walking the Pyrénées* (o/p). Route guide covering the system of GR footpaths, illustrated with 1:50,000 colour survey maps. It is an English version of the Pyrenees *Topoguide des Sentiers de Grande Randonnée* (see opposite and p.30).

Peter Gorley *The Wines of Languedoc-Roussillon*. Lively, fact-packed guide to wines and *domaines*, with complete information on visiting times, recommended vintages and tips for the aspiring *oenologue*.

David Hampshire *Living and Working in France*. Now in its seventh edition, this comprehensive book offers everything for the long-term traveller or resident, from house purchasing to signing on.

Dick Hilbers *The Nature Guide to the Camargue, La Crau and Les Alpilles*. Part of the Crossbill series, published by a non profit organization that promotes conservation, this travel book (and field guide) takes you way off the beaten track and into the lagoons and marshes of the Camargue.

Rion Klawinski *Chasing the Heretics: A Modern Journey through Languedoc*. A traveller's account of the Cathar heresy and the Albigensian Crusade, arranged in a guidebook format. A good handbook for those who want to make a Cathar-themed trip.

Kev Reynolds *Walks and Climbs in the Pyrénées*. The classic English guide for walking in the Pyrenees.

Paul Stranq *Languedoc-Roussillon: The Wines and the Winemakers*. Richly detailed and well-illustrated survey of the *domaines*, vintners and vintages of southwest France.

John Sturrock *The French Pyrénées* (o/p). Well-written travelogue emphasizing the history of the French side of the range. Covers the mountains from coast to coast, with significant sections on Ariège and Roussillon.

Topoguide Series. Books featuring detailed maps and hiking instructions (in French, but not hard to follow for anyone with a working knowledge of the language). A volume is published for each *région* (50 routes) and *département* (30 routes) covered in this Guide. Widely available in French bookshops and tourist offices.

Henri de Toulouse-Lautrec *The Art of Cuisine*. Culinary masterpieces from the diminutive artistic genius.

Film

La Dérive (Paula Delsol, 1964). Quintessential *nouvelle vague* tale of rebellion involving a wistful guitar-playing lead and a series of complex love triangles. Superbly filmed, however, and a window onto the beachside lifestyle of Palavas in the 1960s.

I Forgot to Tell You *J'ai oublié de te dire* (Laurent Vinas-Raymond, 2009). Marie, a young girl with no money and little hope, leaves the north of France for the countryside near Perpignan. Here she meets Jaume (Omar Sharif), an old man who was once a Tour champion and is an accomplished painter.

Lacombe, Lucien (Louis Malle, 1974). The third in Malle's coming-of-age of trilogy is set in occupied southwest France, where the brutish young Lucien discovers the alluring power of collaboration with the enemy and reveals the tensions and dangers of Languedoc during the German occupation. Nominated for Best Picture Oscar and won a BAFTA in the same category.

The Secret of the Grain *La graine et le mulet* (Abdel Kechiche, 2007). In Sète, an ageing North African dockworker dreams of escaping drudgery and starting a restaurant in this subtle and tender family drama. The film won 18 awards, including a César for Best Picture (2008).

The Return of Martin Guerre *Le retour de Martin Guerre* (Daniel Vigne, 1982). Award-winning film that vividly recreates the world of the Pyrenees of the *ancien régime*. When Martin Guerre (Gérard Depardieu) returns to his wife after years away he is welcomed; however, when he begins to demand his wife's rights to the family wealth, suspicions arise.

Silk (François Girard, 2007). The film adaptation of Alessandro Barrico's novel of the same name, featuring Michael Pitt and Keira Knightley, is richly evocative of Languedoc in the late nineteenth century.

Vendémiaire (Louis Feuillade, 1918). The first film shot in Languedoc.

Filmed on location in Aigues-Mortes, this silent movie evokes the peasant nationalism of the early twentieth century, through the experiences of a wounded soldier who has returned from the Great War.

Language

Language

Occitan and Catalan

B y the time the Roman Empire in the west disintegrated, Latin had become the language of daily speech in nearly all of what is now France. Over the course of the following centuries, spoken Latin began to evolve into local variants and eventually into new Romance languages, from Spanish to Romanian. In the south of France (and in part of modern Italy) Occitan (pronounced ok-si-tán) or the Langue d'Oc developed – so called for its word for "yes", which set it apart from the northern French Langue d'Oïl ("oui"). Occitan itself had discrete regional variants, chief among them Provençal in the east (including Nîmes), Limousin in the north, Gascon in the west (including Ariège and the Vall d'Aran in Spain) and Languedocien, from the Corbières to the Camargue. In northeast Spain and across the present-day border into southern France emerged the Catalan language, which bears similarities to both Occitan and Castilian Spanish. Ironically, the name Catalan derives from the same root as the name of its chief rival language, Castilian, both terms referring to the castles which covered the landscapes of each region.

Occitan language and culture

Around the turn of the first millennium, a distinct Occitan literary language emerged, thanks to the wealth of the southern counts and their patronage of **troubadours**. These poets composed and performed works which were sung accompanied by music, for which they were also known as *trovadors* or *jongleurs* ("players" [of instruments]). The themes of their works varied from popular or religiously toned epics, like the *Chanson de Roland*, to portrayals of courtly love, considered to be the most elegant of subjects. Across these could be found recurring motifs, including righteous battle (for example, against the infidel), unrequited love and, above all, the glorification of good manners, sophistication and virtues, such as knightly loyalty or pious chastity. The poetry of courtly love was not erotic in nature; the idea was that the poet should be recognized as honourable by the noble woman (or man) who was the object of the work. The genre was so idealized that the great troubadour Jaufré Rudel claimed to have fallen in love with the countess of Tripoli without having ever laid eyes on her. Troubadours were not merely court entertainers – many were noblemen themselves, and the first is said to have been the powerful duke, William IX of Aquitaine, father of Eleanor of Aquitaine, later Queen of England. But the bulk of them were not wealthy, and they practised their art as a way of ingratiating themselves with a noble house, and entering its service, much as a knight would.

The Albigensian Crusades of the thirteenth century brought about the end of many of the native ruling families in Languedoc and led to an influx of northern nobles. Naturally, these were French in cultural orientation rather than Occitan, and the literature declined as sources of patronage dried up and it waned as an administrative language. Occitan literature persevered in prose, which emphasized secular and narrative themes. The decline of the language was met with some alarm, and in 1323 a group of poets from Toulouse determined to save the poetic tradition of the troubadours by instituting the **jocs florals** ("floral games") – a sort of poetic Olympics in which winners were awarded gilded flowers. The tradition has continued since that time, held annually on May 3, although in 1694, Louis XIV Frenchified it and established in Toulouse a society called the Académie des Jeux Floraux, which administers the games to this day. Thanks to the Jocs Florals, Occitan survived as a literary language for a time, but with the increasing centralization of the realm, devolved once again into an unwritten language of common speech. In 1539, on the eve of the Wars of Religion, François I declared at Villers-Cotterêts that French – the dialect of the **Langue d'Oïl** which was spoken in the area around Paris – was to be the only language of administration in his realms.

As the language of education and administration, French thus displaced Occitan, which was – and sometimes still is – referred to insultingly by Francophones as *patois* ("the dialect"). It was not until the mid-nineteenth century that it was revived in literature, in an intellectual environment which saw people across Europe establish or re-establish literatures for their own languages. The major figure in the new Occitan literature was **Frédéric Mistral**, the venerated Provençal poet and cultural messiah. Born in 1830, Mistral spent a lifetime working to revive and modernize Provençal Occitan as a written and spoken language, producing countless works of literature and grammar, and campaigning in favour of Occitan folk practices, such as *tauromachie*. His efforts were recognized on an international level when he received a Nobel Prize in 1904. Meanwhile, philologists strove to standardize the language, which had degenerated into countless local variants as a result of its subjugation to French.

Nevertheless, reform was slow. Although it may have been the common language of the villages and fields through the middle of the twentieth century, the relentlessly centralist policies of the state and the greater diffusion of French-language education and literacy conspired against Occitan's revival. In Toulouse, the **Escola Occitana** (1919) and the **Institut d'Études Occitanes** (1945) were founded to promote and modernize the language, but it was not until 1951 that it was permitted to teach Occitan in schools, and only in 1969 that educational authorities officially ranked it as a language.

Ironically, the only area which has Occitan as an official and dominant language is Spain's **Vall d'Aran**, a tiny valley high in the Pyrenees to the southwest of Toulouse. **Aranese**, as the seven thousand or so inhabitants call the language, is in fact the Gascon dialect of the Langue d'Oc. In Languedoc proper, efforts continue to revive the language, but since the 1920s the number of speakers has decreased from ten million to two million – an optimistic estimate which sets the proportion of Occitan speakers as fourteen percent of the whole of Languedoc. (By contrast, in Corsica some fifty percent of the populace speaks native Corse.) Nevertheless, the language is experiencing something of a revival both across southern France and in northwest Italy, where there was a major Occitan festival in 2006. In addition, there are Occitan-language newspapers (such as the weekly *La Setmana*), radio stations (*Ràdio País*) and television broadcasts, and bilingual public schools have been established in Albi, Toulouse, Monestiès and St-Sulpice. Most importantly, in 2006, Occitan (and Catalan in Roussillon) became mandatory subjects in the region's schools, in a programme undertaken by the Montpellier Academy. As a visitor, you're unlikely to encounter Occitan either spoken or written, apart from the Occitan street signs which are frequently set alongside their French counterparts.

Although readership and audiences are limited, authors such as **Max Roqueta**, **Bernat Maciet** and **Marcèla Delpastre** have begun to publish novels in Occitan, theatre companies tour performing original and traditional works, and musical groups of the 1980s and 90s, like the **Fabulous Troubadours**, created the modern Occitan musical style called **nòva cançon**, which blends traditional melodies and instruments with modern styles, and still has a hardcore following today. A recent edition to the regional music scene is **Lo Còr de la Plana**, who blend polyphonic singing in Occitan with hand-claps and percussion, with an energy and intensity uncharacteristic of *a capella* groups. For the most part, however, Occitan musicians have adopted other genres, from jazz, blues and folk, to rap and punk fusions (here known as *ragga-aïoli*), and of course regional and linguistic identity do not necessarily coincide – Toulouse's **Zebda**, a strongly regional-minded group whose mix of politics and music is reminiscent of America's Rage Against the Machine, sings exclusively in French.

Although Languedoc is rich with customs and traditions that set it apart from the rest of France, such as water-jousting and *tauromachie*, it is thoroughly subsumed in the French identity. There is no independence movement here such as exists in Corsica, the Basque Country or Brittany, and regional identity is vague, focusing with romantic nostalgia on episodes of northern French oppression such as the Albigensian Crusades and the Wars of Religion. Bernat Lubat, a renowned Occitan jazz musician, expresses an opinion on the subject of regional independence which is representative of the overwhelming majority of the area's inhabitants: "The desire for independence seems to me neither interesting, nor realistic, nor even poetic."

Catalan language and culture

Most of the world's six to ten million Catalan speakers live in Spain, in a band of territory stretching south from the Pyrenees to Valencia, and in the Balearic Islands (though proponents of Valencian, Mallorquin and Menorquin hold these to be distinct languages). The 120,000 Catalan speakers of France live in the *département* of Pyrénées-Orientales, which incorporates the Catalan cultural regions of **La Cerdanya** and **Rosselló**, and has its capital at Perpignan (Perpinyà in Catalan). Here, they represent 34 percent of the population, although only half of that figure claims a high proficiency level.

The **Cerdagne** and **Roussillon**, traditionally part of the realms of the Counts of Barcelona, were long disputed in border wars waged with the French. The French Crown took permanent control of the territory in the 1620s under Richelieu, but the land was not formally ceded by Spain until the Treaty of the Pyrenees (1649), negotiated by Louis XIV. Curiously, a fine reading of the text of the treaty allowed Spain to maintain control of the town of Llívia, a few kilometres inside the French border, which has remained a Spanish enclave, to this day.

Catalan, like Occitan, was a language of troubadours of the Middle Ages, and had a healthy tradition of narrative literature before Spanish or English. One of the most famous early Catalan works is the autobiographical *Llibre del fets* (Book of Deeds), written in the thirteenth century by the great count-king, **Jaume I the Conqueror**, son of Pere the Catholic, who was killed by Simon de Montfort at

Muret. Throughout the Middle Ages, Catalan culture flourished thanks to the powerful maritime dominion of Barcelona. The count-king Joan I the Hunter (1387–96) instituted a Catalan version of the **Jocs Florals**, in imitation of the Occitan contest. Winners were given a real, rather than a golden flower – an early reflection perhaps of the famous Catalan frugality. But as happened to Occitan, the domination of powerful "foreign" administration – in this case, the Hapsburgs of Madrid – contributed to the marginalization of the language, and literary usage declined after the fifteenth century. This process was exacerbated in Roussillon by the French takeover in the seventeenth century. Like Occitan, Catalan was proscribed from official use, and denigrated to the status of a peasant *patois*.

The wave of regional and national consciousness which swept through Europe in the mid-nineteenth century washed over Catalonia, in northeast Spain, as well. Here the linguistic renaissance was spearheaded by the philologist **Pompeu Fabra i Poch**, who set about standardizing the Catalan grammar, and writers, such as the poet **Manuel Milà i Fontanals**. In 1859, the Catalan Jocs Florals were revived. With the victory of strongly Castile-centric Franco in the Spanish Civil War, a stream of Catalan refugees spilled over the border into France, giving the native language and culture an additional boost in Roussillon and the Cerdagne. Catalan was proscribed under the fascist dictatorship in Spain, but the postwar period in France signalled a liberalization of language laws and the admission of Catalan to the state school curriculum, with mandatory instruction beginning in autumn 2006.

Today, however, while there is a lively literary, television and cinema culture in Catalonia proper, in Roussillon it is almost nonexistent. Some Catalan folkloric customs have survived the centuries of French domination, though, and still contribute to the defined flavour of Roussillon. Among these are the distinctive **Christmas customs** (see box, p.293), and the penitents' processions of **Setmana Santa** (Holy Week). A recent addition is the **sardana**, brought to Roussillon by the refugees of 1939, and a symbol of Catalan nationalism. It is a popular dance, in which participants, frequently wearing the traditional woven *espardinya* shoes, form a circle linking hands and do a slow hopping dance to the minor strains of an eleven-piece *coblá* (orchestra). Each dancer places some object (frequently a handbag) in the centre, which is said to symbolize sharing; and the dance is undemanding enough that young and old alike can participate.

The sizeable independence movement in Spanish Catalonia advocates the unification of all of the *Països Catalans*, including Roussillon and the Cerdagne, as a separate state. Indeed, the most potent symbol of Catalan identity, towering **Mont Canigou** (*El Canigó* in Catalan), sits in French territory, between Prades and the border. An imposing mountain casting its shadow over all of Roussillon, it had long been venerated by the region's inhabitants when a monastery was founded on its slopes by the grandson of Guifré the Hairy in 1001. Over the centuries its symbolism intensified, and for Catalans it became their sacred mountain, celebrated in literature such as Jacint Verdaguer's epic *Canigó* of the late nineteenth century. To this day it is the site of a yearly midsummer torchlit pilgrimage to celebrate the *día de Sant Joan* (St John's Day) on the eve of June 24. The traditional pagan solstice holiday, celebrated here, as in many societies, by

Studying Catalan

Naturally, the best place to **study Catalan** is in Catalonia proper, but if you are determined to do so in Roussillon, your best option is to take a course at **Prades'** Catalan summer university (℡ 04.68.96.10.84 and (34)933.172.411, ⓦ www.ucestiu.com).

raising a great fire, stands as a Catalan "national" holiday, celebrated in both Spanish and French Catalonia. But aside from annoying graffiti on buildings and road signs, there is little evidence of nationalist fervour on the French side of the border. Although Catalan speakers of Roussillon, and even many non-speakers, delight in the distinctiveness which the region's diluted Catalan identity gives them, they tend to recall the revolts against the French merely for their sense of rose-tinted nostalgia. The region is culturally very much closer to Paris than Barcelona – convincing confirmation of its predominantly French sensibility can be found in the election in 1995 of the extreme right-wing mayor of Perpignan, Jean-Paul Alduy of the Nouvelle UDF, who not only remains in power today, but was also made senator in 2001.

French

Although Occitan is still spoken among some older rural folk and by recent students of the language, it serves little purpose for visitors. Catalan, while more current, is nevertheless a second language throughout Roussillon and the Cerdagne. As a foreigner speaking French, you will be understood by all and you will not offend anyone's regional sensibilities.

French can be a deceptively familiar language because of the number of words and structures it shares with English. Despite this, it's far from easy, though the bare essentials are not difficult to learn and can make all the difference. Even just saying "Bonjour Madame/Monsieur" and then gesticulating will usually get you a smile and helpful service. People working in tourist offices, hotels and so on, almost always speak English and tend to use it when you're struggling to speak French – be grateful, not insulted.

Of the **phrasebooks** and **dictionaries** available, the *Rough Guide French Dictionary Phrasebook* is a handy and comprehensive companion, with both English–French and French–English sections, along with cultural tips for tricky situations and a menu reader. There's also the *French and English Slang Dictionary* (Harrap/Prentice Hall) and *Dictionary of Modern Colloquial French* (Routledge) – both volumes are a bit large to carry, but they are the key to all you'll ever want to know about the French vernacular.

French pronunciation

One easy rule to remember is that consonants at the ends of words are usually silent. *Pas plus tard* (not later) is thus pronounced "pa-plu-tarr". But when the following word begins with a vowel, you run the two together: *pas après* (not after) becomes "pazaprey".

Vowels are the hardest sounds to get right. Roughly:

a	as in hat		i	as in machine
e	as in get		o	as in hot
é	between get and gate		o, au	as in over
è	between get and gut		ou	as in food
eu	like the **u** in hurt		u	as in a pursed-lip version of use

More awkward are the combinations *in/im*, *en/em*, *an/am*, *on/om*, *un/um* at the ends of words, or followed by consonants other than *n* or *m*. Again, roughly:

in/im	like the **an** in **an**xious		on/om	like the **don** in **Don**caster said
an/am,	like the **don** in **Don**caster when			by someone with a heavy cold
en/em	said with a nasal accent		un/um	like the **u** in **u**nderstand

Consonants are much as in English, except that: *ch* is always "sh"; *c* is "s" if followed by *e* or *i*, or if it has a cedilla beneath it (ç); *h* is silent; *th* is the same as "t", *ll* is like the "y" in yes; *w* is "v"; and *r* is growled (or rolled).

French words and phrases

Basic vocabulary

French nouns are divided into masculine and feminine. This causes difficulties with adjectives, whose endings have to change to suit the gender of the nouns they qualify. If you know some grammar, you will know what to do. If not, stick to the masculine form, which is the simplest – it's what we have done in this glossary.

today	aujourd'hui	that one	celà
yesterday	hier	open	ouvert
tomorrow	demain	closed	fermé
in the morning	le matin	big	grand
in the afternoon	l'après-midi	small	petit
in the evening	le soir	more	plus
now	maintenant	less	moins
later	plus tard	a little	un peu
at one o'clock	à une heure	a lot	beaucoup
at three o'clock	à trois heures	cheap	bon marché
at ten-thirty	à dix heures et demie	expensive	cher
at midday	à midi	good	bon
man	un homme	bad	mauvais
woman	une femme	hot	chaud
here	ici	cold	froid
there	là	with	avec
this one	ceci		

Numbers

1	un	21	vingt-et-un
2	deux	22	vingt-deux
3	trois	30	trente
4	quatre	40	quarante
5	cinq	50	cinquante
6	six	60	soixante
7	sept	70	soixante-dix
8	huit	75	soixante-quinze
9	neuf	80	quatre-vingts
10	dix	90	quatre-vingt-dix
11	onze	95	quatre-vingt-quinze
12	douze	100	cent
13	treize	101	cent un
14	quatorze	200	deux cents
15	quinze	300	trois cents
16	seize	500	cinq cents
17	dix-sept	1000	mille
18	dix-huit	2000	deux mille
19	dix-neuf	5000	cinq mille
20	vingt	1,000,000	un million

Days and dates

January	janvier	Sunday	dimanche
February	février	Monday	lundi
March	mars	Tuesday	mardi
April	avril	Wednesday	mercredi
May	mai	Thursday	jeudi
June	juin	Friday	vendredi
July	juillet	Saturday	samedi
August	août	August 1	le premier août
September	septembre	March 2	le deux mars
October	octobre	July 14	le quatorze juillet
November	novembre	November 23 2002	le vingt-trois novembre deux mille deux
December	décembre		

Talking to people

When addressing people, you should always use *Monsieur* for a man, *Madame* for a woman, *Mademoiselle* for a young woman or girl. Plain *bonjour* by itself is not enough. This isn't as formal as it seems, and it has its uses when you've forgotten someone's name or want to attract someone's attention.

Excuse me	Pardon	OK/agreed	d'accord
Do you speak English?	Parlez-vous anglais?	please	s'il vous plaît
		thank you	merci
How do you say it in French?	Comment ça se dit en français?	hello	bonjour
		goodbye	au revoir
Comment vous appelez-vous?	What's your name?	good morning/ afternoon	bonjour
My name is…	Je m'appelle…	good evening	bonsoir
I'm English	Je suis anglais[e]	good night	bonne nuit
Irish	irlandaise[e]	How are you?	Comment allez-vous?/ Ça va?
Scottish	écossais[e]		
Welsh	gallois[e]	Fine, thanks	Très bien, merci
American	américain[e]	I don't know	Je ne sais pas
Australian	australien[ne]	Let's go	Allons-y
Canadian	canadien[ne]	See you tomorrow	À demain
a New Zealander	néo-zélandais[e]	See you soon	À bientôt
yes	oui	Sorry	Pardon/Je m'excuse
no	non	Leave me alone	Fichez-moi la paix! (aggressive)
I understand	Je comprends		
I don't understand	Je ne comprends pas	Please help me	Aidez-moi, s'il vous plaît
Can you speak slower?	S'il vous plaît, parlez moins vite		

Finding the way

bus	autobus/bus/car	bus stop	arrêt
bus station	gare routière	car	voiture

train/taxi/ferry	train/taxi/ferry	Where are you going?	Vous allez où?
boat	bâteau	I'm going to...	Je vais à...
plane	avion	I want to get off at...	Je voudrais
train station	gare (SNCF)		descendre à...
platform	quai	the road to...	la route pour...
What time does it leave?	Il part à quelle heure?	near	près/pas loin
		far	loin
What time does it arrive?	Il arrive à quelle heure?	left	à gauche
		right	à droite
a ticket to...	un billet pour...	straight on	tout droit
single ticket	aller simple	on the other side of	à l'autre côté de
return ticket	aller-retour	on the corner of	à l'angle de
validate your ticket	compostez votre billet	next to	à côté de
valid for	valable pour	behind	derrière
ticket office	vente de billets	in front of	devant
how many kilometers?	combien de kilomètres?	before	avant
		after	après
how many hours?	combien d'heures?	under	sous
hitchhiking	autostop	to cross	traverser
on foot	à pied	bridge	pont

Questions and requests

The simplest way of asking a question or making requests is to start with *s'il vous plaît* (please), then name the thing you want in an interrogative tone of voice. For example:

Where is there a bakery?	S'il vous plaît, la boulangerie?	Question words:	
		where?	où?
Which way is it to the Maison Carrée?	S'il vous plaît, la route pour la Maison Carrée?	how?	comment?
		how many/ how much?	combien?
Can we have a room for two?	S'il vous plaît, une chambre pour deux?	when?	quand?
		why?	pourquoi?
Can I have a kilo of oranges?	S'il vous plaît, un kilo d'oranges?	at what time?	à quelle heure?
		what is/which is?	quel est?

Accommodation

a room for one/two people	une chambre pour une/deux personnes	a room on the courtyard	une chambre sur la cour
a double bed	un lit double	a room over the street	une chambre sur la rue
a room with a shower	une chambre avec douche	first floor	premier étage
a room with a bath	une chambre avec salle de bain	second floor	deuxième étage
		with a view	avec vue
for one/two/ three nights	pour une/deux/trois nuits	key	clé
		to iron	repasser
Can I see it?	Je peux la voir?	do laundry	faire la lessive

sheets	draps	breakfast	le petit déjeuner
blankets	couvertures	I don't want...	Je ne veux pas de
quiet	calme	breakfast	petit déjeuner
noisy	bruyant	Can we camp here?	On peut camper ici?
hot water	eau chaude	campsite	un camping/terrain de
cold water	eau froide		camping
Is breakfast	Est-ce que le petit	tent	tente
included?	déjeuner est compris?	tent space	emplacement
I would like...	Je voudrais prendre	youth hostel	auberge de jeunesse

Cars

service station	garage	put air in the tyres	gonfler les pneus
service	service	battery	batterie
to park the car	garer la voiture	the battery is dead	la batterie est morte
car park	un parking	plugs	bougies
no parking	défense de stationer/	to break down	tomber en panne
	stationnement interdit	gas can	bidon
petrol station	poste d'essence	insurance	assurance
fuel	essence	green card	carte verte
(to) fill it up	faire le plein	traffic lights	feux
oil	huile	red light	feu rouge
air line	ligne à air	green light	feu vert

Cycling

to adjust	régler	inner tube	chambre à air
axle	axe	loose	déserré
ball-bearing	roulement à billes	to lower	baisser
battery	pile	mudguard	garde-boue
bent	tordu	pannier	pannier
bicycle	vélo	pedal	pédale
bottom bracket	logement du	pump	pompe
	pédalier	puncture	crevaison
brake cable	cable	rack	porte-bagages
brakes	freins	to raise	remonter
broken	cassé	to repair	réparer
bulb	ampoule	saddle	selle
chain	chaîne	to screw	visser/serrer
cotter pin	clavette	spanner	clef
to deflate	dégonfler	spoke	rayon
gear mechanism	dérailleur	to straighten	redresser
frame	cadre	stuck	coincé
gears	vitesses	tight	serré
grease	graisse	toe clips	cale-pieds
handlebars	guidon	tyre	pneu
to inflate	gonfler	wheel	roue

Health matters

doctor	médecin	stomach ache	mal à l'estomac
I don't feel well	Je ne me sens pas bien	period	règles
medicines	médicaments	pain	douleur
prescription	ordonnance	it hurts	ça fait mal
I feel sick	Je suis malade	chemist	pharmacie
I have a headache	J'ai mal à la tête	hospital	hôpital

Other needs

bakery	boulangerie	bank	banque
food shop	alimentation	money	argent
supermarket	supermarché	toilets	toilettes
to eat	manger	police	police
to drink	boire	telephone	téléphone
camping gas	camping gaz	cinema	cinéma
tobacconist	tabac	theatre	théâtre
stamps	timbres	to reserve/book	réserver

Menu reader

Basic food terms

l'addition	bill/check	lait	milk
beurre	butter	moutarde	mustard
bouteille	bottle	œuf	egg
chauffé	heated	pain	bread
couteau	knife	poivre	pepper
cru	raw	salé	salted/spicy
cuillère	spoon	sel	salt
cuit	cooked	sucre	sugar
emballé	wrapped	sucré	sweet
à emporter	takeaway	table	table
fourchette	fork	verre	glass
fumé	smoked	vinaigre	vinegar
huile	oil		

Snacks

Un sandwich/une baguette	a sandwich	au pâté (de campagne)	with pâté (country-style)
au jambon	with ham	croque-monsieur	grilled cheese and ham sandwich
au fromage	with cheese		
au saucisson	with sausage	croque-madame	grilled cheese and bacon, sausage, chicken or egg sandwich
à l'ail	with garlic		
au poivre	with pepper		

pain bagnat	bread roll with egg, olives, salad, tuna, anchovies and olive oil
panini	toasted Italian sandwich
tartine	buttered bread or open sandwich
œufs	eggs
au plat	fried

à la coque	boiled
durs	hard-boiled
brouillés	scrambled
omelette	omelette
nature	plain
aux fines herbes	with herbs
au fromage	with cheese

Pasta (*pâtes*), pancakes (*crêpes*) and flans (*tartes*)

nouilles	noodles
pâtes fraîches	fresh pasta
pâte	pasta or pastry
raviolis	pasta parcels of meat or chard – a Provençal, not Italian invention
crêpe au sucre/ aux œufs	pancake with sugar/eggs
galette	buckwheat pancake

socca	thin chickpea flour pancake
panisse	thick chickpea flour pancake
pissaladière	tart of fried onions with anchovies and black olives
tarte flambée	thin pizza-like pastry topped with onion, cream and bacon or other combinations

Soups (*soupes*)

baudroie	fish soup with vegetables, garlic and herbs
bisque	shellfish soup
bouillabaisse	soup/stew with chunks of assorted fish
bouillon	broth or stock
bourride	thick fish soup
consommé	clear soup
garbure	potato, cabbage and meat soup

pistou	parmesan, basil and garlic paste, added to soup
potée auvergnate	cabbage and meat soup
potage	thick vegetable soup
rouille	red pepper, garlic and saffron mayonnaise served with fish soup
soupe à l'oignon	onion soup with rich cheese topping
velouté	thick soup, usually fish or poultry

Starters (*hors d'œuvres*)

assiette anglaise	plate of cold meats
crudités	raw vegetables with dressings

hors d'œuvres	combination of the items listed left
hors d'œuvres variés	plus smoked or marinated fish

Fish (*poisson*), seafood (*fruits de mer*) and shellfish (*crustacés or coquillages*)

aiglefin	small haddock or fresh cod	praires	small clams
anchois	anchovies	raie	skate
anguilles	eels	rouget	red mullet
barbue	brill	saumon	salmon
baudroie	monkfish or anglerfish	sole	sole
bigorneau	periwinkle	thon	tuna
brème	bream	truite	trout
bulot	whelk	turbot	turbot
cabillaud	cod	violet	sea squirt
calmar	squid		
carrelet	plaice		

Fish dishes and terms

claire	type of oyster
colin	hake
congre	conger eel
coques	cockles
coquilles St-Jacques	scallops
crabe	crab
crevettes grises	shrimp
crevettes roses	prawns
daurade	sea bream
éperlan	smelt or whitebait
escargots	snails
favou(ille)	tiny crab
flétan	halibut
friture	assorted fried fish
gambas	king prawns
hareng	herring
homard	lobster
huîtres	oysters
langouste	spiny lobster
langoustines	saltwater crayfish (scampi)
limande	lemon sole
lotte de mer	monkfish
loup de mer	sea bass
maquereau	mackerel
merlan	whiting
moules (marinières)	mussels (with shallots in white wine sauce)
oursin	sea urchin
palourdes	clams
poissons de roche	fish from shore-line rocks

aïoli	garlic mayonnaise served with salt cod and other fish
anchoïade	anchovy paste or sauce
arête	fish bone
assiette du pêcheur	assorted fish
beignet	fritter
darne	fillet or steak
la douzaine	a dozen
frit	fried
friture	deep-fried small fish
fumé	smoked
fumet	fish stock
gigot de mer	large fish baked whole
grillé	grilled
hollandaise	butter and vinegar sauce
à la meunière	in a butter, lemon and parsley sauce
mousse/mousseline	mousse
pané	breaded
poutargue	mullet roe paste
raïto	red wine, olive, caper, garlic and shallot sauce
quenelles	light dumplings
thermidor	lobster grilled in its shell with cream sauce

Meat (*viande*) and poultry (*volaille*)

agneau (de pré-salé) — lamb (grazed on salt marshes)

andouille, andouillette — tripe sausage

bifteck — steak

bœuf — beef

boudin blanc — sausage of white meats

boudin noir — black pudding

caille — quail

canard — duck

caneton — duckling

contrefilet — sirloin roast

coquelet — cockerel

dinde, dindon — turkey

entrecôte — rib steak

faux filet — sirloin steak

foie — liver

foie gras — (duck/goose) liver

gigot (d'agneau) — leg (of lamb)

grenouilles (cuisses de) — frogs (legs)

langue — tongue

lapin, lapereau — rabbit, young rabbit

lard, lardons — bacon, diced bacon

lièvre — hare

merguez — spicy, red sausage

mouton — mutton

museau de veau — calf's muzzle

oie — goose

onglet — cut of beef

os — bone

poitrine — breast

porc — pork

poulet — chicken

poussin — baby chicken

ris — sweetbreads

rognons — kidneys

rognons blancs — testicles

sanglier — wild boar

steak — steak

tête de veau — calf's head (in jelly)

tournedos — thick slices of fillet

tripes — tripe

tripoux — mutton tripe

veau — veal

venaison — venison

aïado — roast shoulder of lamb stuffed with garlic and other ingredients

aile — wing

au feu de bois — cooked over wood fire

au four — baked

baeckoffe — Alsatian hotpot of pork, mutton and beef baked with potato layers

blanquette, daube, estouffade, hochepôt, navarin, agoût — types of stew

blanquette de veau — veal in cream and mushroom sauce

bœuf bourguignon — beef stew with Burgundy, onions and mushrooms

canard à l'orange — roast duck with an orange and wine sauce

canard pâté de périgourdin — roast duck with prunes, foie gras and truffles

carré — best end of neck, chop or cutlet

cassoulet — casserole of beans and meat

choucroute — pickled cabbage with peppercorns, sausages, bacon and salami

civet — game stew

confit — meat preserve

côte — chop, cutlet or rib

cou — neck

coq au vin — chicken cooked until it falls off the bone, with wine, onions and mushrooms

cuisse — thigh or leg

épaule — shoulder

en croûte — in pastry

farci — stuffed

gigot (d'agneau) — leg (of lamb)

grillade	grilled meat
garni	with vegetables
gésier	gizzard
grillé	grilled
hâchis	chopped meat or mince hamburger
magret de canard	duck breast
marmite	casserole
médaillon	round piece
mijoté	stewed
pavé	thick slice
pieds et paques	mutton or pork tripe and trotters
poêlé	pan-fried
poulet de Bresse	chicken from Bresse – the best
râble	saddle
rôti	roast
sauté	lightly cooked in butter
steak au poivre	steak in a black peppercorn sauce
steak tartare	raw chopped beef, topped with a raw egg yolk
tagine	North African casserole
tournedos rossini	beef fillet with foie gras and truffles
viennoise	fried in egg and breadcrumbs

Terms for steaks

bleu	almost raw
saignant	rare
à point	medium
bien cuit	well done
très bien cuit	very well done
brochette	kebab

Garnishes and sauces

américaine	white wine, cognac and tomato
arlésienne	with tomatoes, onions, aubergines, potatoes and rice
au porto	in port
auvergnat	with cabbage, sausage and bacon
béarnaise	sauce of egg yolks, white wine, shallots and vinegar
beurre blanc	sauce of white wine and shallots, with butter
bonne femme	with mushrooms, bacon, potatoes and onions
bordelaise	in a red wine, shallot and bone-marrow sauce
boulangère	baked with potatoes and onions
bourgeoise	with carrots, onions, bacon, celery and braised lettuce
chasseur	white wine, mushrooms and shallots
châtelaine	with artichoke hearts and chestnut purée
diable	strong mustard seasoning
forestière	with bacon and mushrooms
fricassée	rich, creamy sauce
mornay	cheese sauce
pays d'auge	cream and cider
périgourdine	with foie gras and possibly truffles
piquante	gherkins or capers, vinegar and shallots
provençale	tomatoes, garlic, olive oil and herbs
savoyarde	with gruyère cheese
véronique	grapes, wine and cream

Vegetables (*légumes*), herbs (*herbes*) and spices (*épices*)

ail	garlic
anis	aniseed
artichaut	artichoke
asperge	asparagus
avocat	avocado
basilic	basil
betterave	beetroot
blette/bette	Swiss chard
cannelle	cinnamon
câpre	caper
cardon	cardoon, closely related to artichoke
carotte	carrot
céleri	celery
champignon, cèpe, chanterelle	types of mushrooms
chou (rouge)	(red) cabbage
choufleur	cauliflower
concombre	cucumber
cornichon	gherkin
échalotes	shallots
endive	chicory
épinard	spinach
estragon	tarragon
fenouil	fennel
férigoule	thyme (in Provençal)
fèves	broad beans
flageolets	white beans
gingembre	ginger
haricots (verts, rouges, beurres)	beans (French/string, kidney, butter)
laurier	bay leaf
lentilles	lentils
maïs	corn
menthe	mint
moutarde	mustard
oignon	onion
panais	parsnip
pélandron	type of string bean
persil	parsley
petits pois	peas
piment	pimento
pois chiche	chick peas
pois mange-tout	mangetout

pignons	pine nuts
poireau	leek
poivron (vert, rouge)	sweet pepper (green, red)
pommes de terre	potatoes
primeurs	spring vegetables
radis	radish
riz	rice
safran	saffron
salade verte	green salad
sarrasin	buckwheat
tomate	tomato
truffes	truffles

Vegetable dishes and terms

alicot	puréed potato with cheese
allumettes	very thin chips
à l'anglaise	boiled
beignet	fritter
biologique	organic
duxelles	fried mushrooms and shallots with cream
farci	stuffed
feuille	leaf
fines herbes	mixture of tarragon, parsley and chives
gratiné	browned with cheese or butter
à la grecque	cooked in oil and lemon
jardinière	with mixed diced vegetables
mousseline	mashed potato with cream and eggs
à la parisienne	sautéed in butter (potatoes); with white wine sauce and shallots
parmentier	with potatoes
petits farcis	stuffed tomatoes, aubergines, courgettes and peppers
pimenté	peppery hot

piquant	spicy	**sauté**	lightly fried in butter
pistou	ground basil, olive oil, garlic and parmesan	**à la vapeur**	steamed
râpée	grated or shredded	**en verdure**	garnished with green vegetables

Fruit (*fruit*) and nuts (*noix*)

abricot	apricot
noix de acajou	cashew nut
amande	almond
ananas	pineapple
banane	banana
brugnon, nectarine	nectarine
cacahouète	peanut
cassis	blackcurrant
cerise	cherry
citron	lemon
citron vert	lime
datte	date
figue	fig
fraise (des bois)	strawberry (wild)
framboise	raspberry
fruit de la passion	passion fruit
grenade	pomegranate
groseille	redcurrant
mangue	mango
marron	chestnut
melon	melon
mirabelle	small yellow plum
myrtille	bilberry
noisette	hazelnut
noix	nuts
orange	orange
pamplemousse	grapefruit
pastèque	watermelon
pêche	peach
pistache	pistachio
poire	pear
pomme	apple
prune	plum
pruneau	prune
raisin	grape
reine-claude	greengage

Fruit dishes and terms

agrumes	citrus fruits
beignet	fritter
compôte	stewed fruit
coulis	sauce of puréed fruit
crème de marrons	chestnut purée
flambé	set aflame in alcohol
fougasse	bread flavoured with orange-flower water or almonds (can be savoury)
frappé	iced

Desserts (*desserts* or *entremets*) and pastries (*pâtisserie*)

bombe	moulded ice-cream dessert
brioche	sweet, high-yeast breakfast roll
calisson	almond sweet
charlotte	custard and fruit in lining of almond fingers
chichi	doughnut shaped in a stick
clafoutis	heavy custard and fruit tart
crème Chantilly	vanilla-flavoured and sweetened whipped cream
crème fraîche	sour cream
crème pâtissière	thick, eggy pastry-filling
crêpe suzette	thin pancake with orange juice and liqueur
fromage blanc	cream cheese
gaufre	waffle
glace	ice cream

Île flottante/ œufs à la neige	soft meringues floating on custard
macaron	macaroon
madeleine	small sponge cake
marrons Mont Blanc	chestnut purée and cream on a rum-soaked sponge cake
mousse au chocolat	chocolate mousse
omelette norvégienne	baked Alaska
palmier	caramelized puff pastry
parfait	frozen mousse, sometimes ice cream
petit-suisse	a smooth mixture of cream and curds
petits fours	bite-sized cakes/ pastries
poires belle hélène	pears and ice cream in chocolate sauce
tarte tatin	upside-down apple tart
tarte tropézienne	sponge cake filled with custard cream topped with nuts
tiramisu	mascarpone cheese, chocolate and cream
yaourt, yogourt	yoghurt

Dessert dishes and terms

barquette	small boat-shaped flan
bavarois	refers to the mould, could be a mousse or custard
coupe	a serving of ice cream
crêpe	pancake
gênoise	rich sponge cake
pâte	pastry or dough
sablé	shortbread biscuit
savarin	a filled, ring-shaped cake
tarte	tart
tartelette	small tart

Glossary

French terms

abbey abbey

auberge de jeunesse youth hostel

basilique basilica

bassin reservoir

bastide planned, usually fortified town of the thirteenth century, typically laid out on a grid in a square or octagonal area

boîte nightclub/discotheque

cabane shepherd's hut

canton district

causse limestone plateau, typically with deep crevices and near-vertical stratification

chambre d'hôtes bed and breakfast

château fort, castle, mansion or country house

circulade ancient hamlet, laid out in concentric circles

cirque deep, steep-walled basin on a mountain, usually comprising the upper end of a river valley

cité citadel: the fortified section (usually the oldest and highest part) of a town

cloche belltower

col pass

colombier dovecote

découverte open-pit mine

défilé narrow gorge, canyon

département administrative area, similar to an English county, within a region

domaine estate

donjon castle keep

écluse canal lock

église church

enceinte area falling within the walls of a castle or town, or the defensive enclosure itself

étang coastal lagoon, normally salt-water and connected to the sea

évêché palace or property pertaining to a bishop, or archbishop (*archevêché*)

faubourg extramural suburb, usually referring to late medieval town extensions built outside the walls of the original encelnte

fête festival

gardian cowboy of the Camargue

gare station

gare routière bus station

gastronomique elaborate and imaginative gourmet cuisine

grotte cave

halles market building

horloge clock

hôtel de ville town or city hall

hôtel particulier private mansion or palace

joute joust; water-jousting

mairie office of the mayor: town hall

manade Camarguais cattle or horse ranch

maquis World War II Resistance fighter

masia traditional Catalan farmhouse

monastère monastery

musée museum

navette shuttle service

pays country, land

pic peak

place square

point bridge

pont du diable arched medieval bridge

pont vieux old bridge

porte gateway

préfecture main office, headquarters

prise de l'eau dam

région administrative region

son et lumière sound and light show

source spring

terroir literally meaning "soil", refers to traditional peasant cooking, using local ingredients

TGV Train de Grande Vitesse, high-speed train

thermes hot-springs or spa

tour tower

usine factory, workshop

ville basse lower town

Artistic, architectural and archeological terms

ambulatory passage round the outer edge of a church's choir

apse semicircular termination at the east end of a church

Art Deco geometrical style of art and architecture popular in the 1920s and 30s

Art Nouveau Ornamental style of art and architecture which developed in the late nineteenth century, emphasizing decorative detail and avoiding straight, clean lines

artesonado Spanish-style cabinet-work ceiling

Baroque High Renaissance period of art and architecture, distinguished by extreme ornateness, exuberance and complex spatial arrangement of interiors

bas-relief stone carving with a shallow three-dimensional aspect ("high relief" sculpture has very pronounced depth)

Carolingian dynasty founded by Pepin the Short; mid-eighth to early tenth centuries, named after its finest king, Charles the Great (Charlemagne); also refers to art, sculpture, etc of the time

caryatid sculpted female figure used as a column

chapterhouse room in a monastery or church where the clergy met daily to discuss business and administrative affairs

chevet east end of a church

Classical architectural style incorporating Greek and Roman elements (such as pillars, domes, and colonnades), at its height in France in the seventeenth century and revived in the nineteenth century as Neoclassicism

clerestory upper storey of a church, incorporating windows

crenellation battlements along the top edge of a wall or tower.

Cubism early twentieth-century art movement which used overlapping planes and geometric shapes in defiance of pictorial perception

curtain wall straight upright medieval defensive wall

dolmen Neolithic stone formation, frequently consisting of a henge

faïence porcelain and glazed earthenware decoration

Fauvism artistic school of early twentieth-century France, characterized by vivid colour

fin-de-siècle referring to the turn of the twentieth century

folly overly ostentatious rural dwellings of seventeenth- to nineteenth-century aristocracy

fresco wall painting – durable through application to wet plaster

frieze sculpted decorative band, typically along the upper or lower limit of a wall, and usually in low relief

Gothic architectural style of the thirteenth to sixteenth centuries, characterized by pointed arches, rib vaulting, flying buttresses, broad windowed surfaces and a general emphasis on verticality

Impressionism late nineteenth-century French style of painting which emphasized the perception of objects through the effect of light, rather than shape

majesté Romanesque and early Gothic sculptures of Christ on the Cross (*majestat* in Catalan)

Merovingian Dynasty ruling France and parts of Germany from the sixth to mid-eighth centuries; also refers to art, etc of the period

moulin a mill

Mozarabic Arab- and North African-influenced art and architectural style from Spain, brought to France around 900–1100 by Christians

narthex entrance hall of a church

nave main body of a church

nymphaeum Roman or Greek shrine to a nymph, typically located at a fountainhead or spring

oppidum pre-Roman hill-top settlement

opus mixtum Roman building technique consisting of interspersed layers of stone and brick

Orientalism study of Eastern and, particularly, Middle Eastern peoples from a Western and usually imperialistic and heavily romanticized perspective, from the late seventeenth to nineteenth centuries

pantocrator depiction of Jesus as "Lord of all Creation"

polychrome painted in colour

refectory dining room of a monastery

relief the three-dimensional quality of a sculpture; its depth

Renaissance artistic/architectural movement developed in fifteenth-century Italy and imported to France in the sixteenth century

retable altarpiece

Romanesque Early medieval architectural style distinguished by squat, rounded forms and naive sculpture

rood screen barrier set in some churches between the area of the altar and choir and the rest of the nave (where the main congregation gathers)

sarcophagus Latin for "coffin," referring to carved stone tombs

stucco plaster used to embellish ceilings, etc

Surrealism early twentieth-century art movement whose apparently irrational juxtaposition of contrasting images expressed subconscious thoughts

tauromachie bullfighting on

transept transverse arms of a church

tribune apse containing a bishop's throne; a gallery or raised area in a church

trompe l'oeil decorative technique popular in the Baroque period, wherein a two-dimensional painting gives the impression of being a three-dimensional object

tumulus Neolithic burial mound, frequently concealing a dolmen

tympanum a sculpted panel above a church door

vault an arched ceiling or roof

voussoir sculpted wedge-shaped stones in the arch over a church door

- **Read** Rough Guides' trusted travel info
- **Access** exclusive articles from Rough Guides authors
- **Update** yourself on new books, maps, CDs and other products
- **Enter** our competitions and win travel prizes
- **Share** ideas, journals, photos & travel advice with other users
- **Earn** points every time you contribute to the Rough Guide community and get rewards

BROADEN YOUR HORIZONS

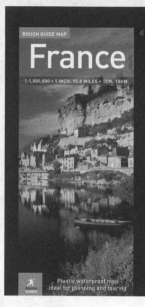

Small print and Index

A Rough Guide to Rough Guides

Published in 1982, the first Rough Guide – to Greece – was a student scheme that became a publishing phenomenon. Mark Ellingham, a recent graduate in English from Bristol University, had been travelling in Greece the previous summer and couldn't find the right guidebook. With a small group of friends he wrote his own guide, combining a highly contemporary, journalistic style with a thoroughly practical approach to travellers' needs.

The immediate success of the book spawned a series that rapidly covered dozens of destinations. And, in addition to impecunious backpackers, Rough Guides soon acquired a much broader and older readership that relished the guides' wit and inquisitiveness as much as their enthusiastic, critical approach and value-for-money ethos.

These days, Rough Guides include recommendations from shoestring to luxury and cover more than 200 destinations around the globe, including almost every country in the Americas and Europe, more than half of Africa and most of Asia and Australasia. Our ever-growing team of authors and photographers is spread all over the world, particularly in Europe, the US and Australia.

In the early 1990s, Rough Guides branched out of travel, with the publication of Rough Guides to World Music, Classical Music and the Internet. All three have become benchmark titles in their fields, spearheading the publication of a wide range of books under the Rough Guide name.

Including the travel series, Rough Guides now number more than 350 titles, covering: phrasebooks, waterproof maps, music guides from Opera to Heavy Metal, reference works as diverse as Conspiracy Theories and Shakespeare, and popular culture books from iPods to Poker. Rough Guides also produce a series of more than 120 World Music CDs in partnership with World Music Network.

Visit www.roughguides.com to see our latest publications.

Rough Guide credits

Text editor: Melissa Graham
Layout: Ajay Verma
Cartography: Maxine Repath
Picture editor: Harriet Mills
Production: Rebecca Short
Proofreader: Diane Margolis
Cover design: Dan May, Chloë Roberts
Photographer: Jean-Christophe Godet
Editorial: London Andy Turner, Keith Drew,
Edward Aves, Alice Park, Lucy White, Jo Kirby,
James Smart, Natasha Foges, Róisín Cameron,
James Rice, Lara Kavanagh, Emma Traynor,
Emma Gibbs, Kathryn Lane, Monica Woods,
Mani Ramaswamy, Harry Wilson, Lucy Cowie,
Alison Roberts, Joe Staines, Matthew Milton,
Tracy Hopkins, Ruth Tidball; Delhi Madhavi
Singh, Lubna Shaheen, Jalpreen Kaur Chhatwal
Design & Pictures: London Scott Stickland, Dan
May, Diana Jarvis, Mark Thomas, Nicole Newman,
Sarah Cummins, Emily Taylor; Delhi Umesh
Aggarwal, Jessica Subramanian, Ankur Guha,
Pradeep Thapliyal, Sachin Tanwar, Anita Singh,
Nikhil Agarwal, Sachin Gupta

Production: Liz Cherry
Cartography: London Ed Wright, Katie Lloyd-
Jones; Delhi Rajesh Chhibber, Ashutosh Bharti,
Rajesh Mishra, Animesh Pathak, Jasbir Sandhu,
Karobi Gogoi, Alakananda Roy, Swati Handoo,
Deshpal Dabas
Online: London Faye Hellon, Jeanette Angell,
Fergus Day, Justine Bright, Clare Bryson, Aine
Fearon, Adrian Low, Ezgi Celebi; Delhi Amit
Verma, Rahul Kumar, Narender Kumar, Ravi
Yadav, Debojit Borah, Rakesh Kumar, Ganesh
Sharma, Shisir Basumatari
Marketing & Publicity: London Liz Statham,
Jess Carter, Vivienne Watton, Anna Paynton,
Rachel Sprackett, Laura Vipond; New York Katy
Ball, Judi Powers; Delhi Ragini Govind
Digital Travel Publisher: Peter Buckley
Reference Director: Andrew Lockett
Operations Assistant: Becky Doyle
Operations Manager: Helen Atkinson
Publishing Director (Travel): Clare Currie
Commercial Manager: Gino Magnotta
Managing Director: John Duhigg

SMALL PRINT

Publishing information

This fourth edition published September 2010 by
Rough Guides Ltd,
80 Strand, London WC2R 0RL
11 Local Shopping Centre,
Panchsheel Park,
New Delhi 110017, India

Distributed by the Penguin Group
Penguin Books Ltd,
80 Strand, London WC2R 0RL
Penguin Group (USA)
345 Hudson Street, NY 10014, USA
Penguin Group (Australia)
250 Camberwell Road, Camberwell,
Victoria 3124, Australia
Penguin Group (Canada)
195 Harry Walker Parkway N, Newmarket, ON,
L3Y 7B3 Canada
Penguin Group (NZ)
67 Apollo Drive, Mairangi Bay, Auckland 1310,
New Zealand
Cover concept by Peter Dyer.

Typeset in Bembo and Helvetica to an original
design by Henry Iles.
Printed in Singapore
© Brian Catlos 2010
Maps © Rough Guides

No part of this book may be reproduced in any
form without permission from the publisher except
for the quotation of brief passages in reviews.
392pp includes index
A catalogue record for this book is available from
the British Library
ISBN: 978-1-84836-532-2
The publishers and authors have done their best
to ensure the accuracy and currency of all the
information in **The Rough Guide to Languedoc
& Roussillon**, however, they can accept no
responsibility for any loss, injury, or inconvenience
sustained by any traveller as a result of
information or advice contained in the guide.

5   7   9   8   6   4

Help us update

We've gone to a lot of effort to ensure that
the fourth edition of **The Rough Guide to
Languedoc & Roussillon** is accurate and
up-to-date. However, things change – places
get "discovered", opening hours are notoriously
fickle, restaurants and rooms raise prices or lower
standards. If you feel we've got it wrong or left
something out, we'd like to know, and if you can
remember the address, the price, the hours, the
phone number, so much the better.

Please send your comments with the subject
line "**Rough Guide Languedoc & Roussillon
Update**" to ©mail@roughguides.com. We'll credit
all contributions and send a copy of the next
edition (or any other Rough Guide if you prefer)
for the very best emails.

Have your questions answered and tell others
about your trip at ®www.roughguides.com

Acknowledgements

The author would like to thank the following people for their support and assistance: Hélène Aznar, Melissa Graham (excellent editor!), the *Languedoc Sun*, Hervé Rieu (director of OT Haut-Couserans) and Núria Silleras-Fernández.

Readers' letters

Thanks to all the readers who have taken the time to write in with comments and suggestions (and apologies if we've inadvertently omitted or misspelt anyone's name):

Denise Aitkin, Bernard Beard, Josephine Beker, Padraic de Bhaldraithe, Emma Bridge, Ruth Cullingford, Patrice Dixon, Jeff Fletcher, Paul Fletcher, Sarah Franks, Nell Hegarty, Peter and Sue Jacques, Gabor and Beryl Otvos, Sally Pabst, Chris Ritchie, Peter Serres, Keith Stansfield and Steve Topley.

SMALL PRINT

Photo credits

All photos © Rough Guides except the following:

Introduction
p.1 Petite Camargue horseman © Hemis.fr/
Superstock
p.2 Carcassonne and vineyard © Johanna Huber/
SIME/4Corners Images
p.6 Uzès market, place aux Herbes © David
Noton Photography/Alamy
p.7 Collioure fishing boat © Michael Busselle/
Robert Harding
p.9 Street party, Sète © Bruno de Hogues/Getty
Images

Things not to miss
01 Cordes-sur-Ciel © David Noton Photography/
Alamy
02 Mouré quarter, Collioure © Nicolas Rung/
Authors Images/Tips Images
03 Oysters and prawns on market stall © Andrew
Holligan/DK Images
05 Poster advertising La Goulue at the Moulin
Rouge, Paris (colour litho), by Henri de
Toulouse-Lautrec © Private Collection/
Stapleton Collection/Bridgeman Art Library
06 Train Jaune on the Séjourné viaduct © Mark
Zylber/Alamy
07 Vernet-les-Bains and Mount Canigou © John
Frumm/Hemis/Axiom Photographic
08 French bullfighter, Mehdi Savalli, during the
Pentecost Feria in Nîmes © Patrick Frilet/
Hemis/Photolibrary
09 Water-jousting, Sète © Bruno De Hogues/
Getty Images
10 Montségur © Gonzalo Azumendi/Superstock
11 Petite Camargue *gardians* and horses ©
Hemis.fr/Superstock
13 La Grotte de Niaux © Jean-Marc Charles/
Superstock
14 Transhumance, Pyrenees © Andia/Alamy
15 Carcassonne at sunset © Konstantin Kalishko/
istockphoto.com

The Land of the Cathars colour section
View from Quéribus © Javier Sobrino/Superstock
Château de Quéribus at sunset © Travelpix Ltd/
Getty Images
Madeleine church, Béziers © Andia/Alamy
*Expulsion of the Albigensians from Carcassone in
1209* (c.1300–c.1400). Artist: Unknown © The
British Library/Imagstate/Tips Images
Minerve © Mark Zylber/Alamy
Lastours © Cris Haigh/Alamy
The Burning of the Books or *St Dominic and the
Albigensians* by Pedro Berruguete (c.1450-
1504) © Gianni Dagli Orti/Museo del Prado
Madrid/The Art Archive/Alamy
Montségur summit © Doug Pearson/AWL Images
Ltd

Food and wine colour section
Grape harvest in Fitou © Hemis/Alamy
Etienne Rousselot's cassoulet at the *Hostellerie
Etienne*, Castelnaudary © Hemis/Alamy
Honey for sale, Narbonne © Photononstop/
Superstock
Anchovies, Collioure © Michael Melford/National
Geographic Creative/Getty Images
Cheese stall, Pézenas market © Peter Huggins/
Alamy
Wine barrels, Abbaye de Valmagne © Bon
Appetit/Alamy
Gaillac vineyard autumn harvest © Hemis/Alamy
Fitou grapes © Hemis/Superstock

Black and whites
p.124 St-Lizier view with snowcapped Pyrenees
© Max Alexander/DK Images
p. 208 Aigues-Mortes © L'Office de tourisme
d'Aigues-Mortes www.ot-aiguesmortes.fr

Index

Map entries are in colour.

INDEX

385

INDEX

Map symbols

maps are listed in the full index using coloured text

– – –	Chapter boundary		🏛	Monument
– – – ∙	International boundary		♜	Tower
– – ∙∙	Regional boundary		♟	Fortress
⌇⌇⌇⌇	Steps		♥	Museum
═══	Motorway		⌂	Abbey
═══	Road		🜊	Monastery
▰▰▰	Pedestrianized street		⚲	Church (regional maps)
━━	Railway		ⓣ	Tram stop
━■━	ATM Railway		Ⓜ	Metro station
– – –	Footpath		✈	Airport
– –	Ferry route		★	Bus stop
──	River		⊠─⊠	Gate
◆	Point of interest		@	Internet café
▲	Mountain peak		🅿	Parking
⌖	Mountain range		⊞	Hospital
♙	Mountain refuge		ⓘ	Tourist office
⊃⊂	Mountain pass		⊠	Post office
〜	Gorge/cliff face		🎿	Skiing
⌒	Cave		▰	Building
⋀⋀	Spring		┿	Church (town maps)
∴	Ruins		▒	Park/forest
☰	Lighthouse		⌐┤	Cemetery
⊙	Statue		▨	Saltpan
♜	Castle		░	Beach

So now we've told you about the things not to miss, the best places to stay, the top restaurants, the liveliest bars and the most spectacular sights, it only seems fair to tell you about the best travel insurance around

WorldNomads.com

keep travelling safely